THE CRUCIAL YEARS: 1939–1941

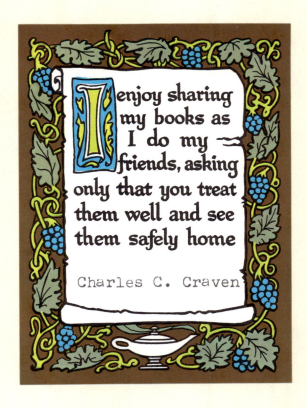

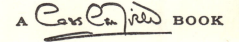

Hanson W. Baldwin

THE
CRUCIAL
YEARS
1939-1941

The World at War

HARPER & ROW, PUBLISHERS
New York Evanston San Francisco
London

Acknowledgment is gratefully made for permission to reprint the following:

Excerpts from volumes of *The Second World War* by Winston Churchill:
The Gathering Storm: Copyright 1948 by Houghton Mifflin Company.
Their Finest Hour: Copyright 1949 by Houghton Mifflin Company.
The Grand Alliance: Copyright 1950 by Houghton Mifflin Company.

Lines from "Tommy" by Rudyard Kipling, from *Rudyard Kipling's Verse*, Inclusive Edition. Doubleday & Company.

Maps on pages 22, 69, 84, 103, 158, 218, 238, 272, and 394, and endpapers are by Jean Paul Tremblay.

Maps on pages 117, 134, 142, 286, 335, and 386 are from *The Encyclopedia of Military History* by R. Ernest Dupuy and Trevor N. Dupuy. Harper & Row, Publishers, Inc. Copyright © 1970 by R. Ernest Dupuy and Trevor N. Dupuy.

The map on page 412 is from *The War in Maps. An Atlas of the New York Times Maps* by Francis Brown and Lucas Manditch. Copyright © 1946, 1973 by Oxford University Press, Inc. Reprinted by permission.

Portions of this work originally appeared in the *New York Times*.

THE CRUCIAL YEARS: 1939–1941. Copyright © 1976 by Hanson W. Baldwin. All rights reserved. Printed in the United States of America. No part of this book may be used or reproduced in any manner whatsoever without written permission except in the case of brief quotations embodied in critical articles and reviews. For information address Harper & Row, Publishers, Inc., 10 East 53rd Street, New York, N.Y. 10022. Published simultaneously in Canada by Fitzhenry & Whiteside Limited, Toronto.

CONTENTS

I. THE SWORD IS DRAWN

1. The Road to War — 14
2. The Beginnings: 1939 — 64

II. THE YEAR OF PERIL: 1940

3. War in the North—Scandinavia — 89
4. *Blitzkrieg* in the West — 113
5. The Death of the Third Republic — 141
6. The Battle of Britain — 153
7. The War at Sea — 168
8. Keystone of Empire — 178
9. The Italian Invasion of Greece — 187
10. The Blitz — 192

III. MARCH OF CONQUEST: 1941

11. "Victory Through Air Power" — 201
12. The Battle of the Atlantic — 206
13. East and West of Suez — 226
14. The Western Desert — 242
15. The Cockpit of the Mediterranean — 266
16. *Blitzkrieg* in the Balkans — 282

IV. THE GLOBAL WAR: 1941

17. Russia—The "Unknown War" — 322
18. Pearl Harbor — 373
19. The War in the Pacific — 392

20.	Asia for the Asiatics	422
21.	The Aftermath of Pearl Harbor	449

RETROSPECT 463

Acknowledgment 470

Notes and Sources 471

Index 501

Maps

The China Campaign	22
The Polish Campaign, September 1–28, 1939	69
The Winter War—Finland, November, 1939–March, 1940	84
Conquest in the North—Denmark and Norway, April–June, 1940	103
Campaign in the West—First Phase	117
Campaign in the West—Situation May 21, 1940	134
The Battle of France	142
The Battle of Britain, August–September, 1940	158
The War at Sea	218
The Desert Campaigns and East Africa	238
Cockpit of the Mediterranean	272
The Invasion of Yugoslavia and Greece	286
German Summer Offensive of 1941	335
Pearl Harbor	386
Japan Strikes in the Pacific, December, 1941	394
War in the Philippines	412

Illustrations

following page 240

The Wehrmacht in the suburbs of Warsaw, September 1939 (U.S. Army, captured German photograph)
Troop ship *Orama* sinking during evacuation of Narvik, Norway, June 8, 1940
German troops advancing through a Flanders village, May 29, 1940
German infantry attacking in a Belgian village, May 1940
Poilus flushed from a French village, June 1940
Paris beneath the Nazi heel, June 1940
A Lockheed Hudson flies above the boats assembled off Dunkirk, May–June 1940 (British Commonwealth Photograph, Crown Copyright Reserved)
A bombed building falls, London, 1940 (City of London Police)
German firemen at the bombed Anhalter Railroad Station, Berlin, 1940
Soviet peasants dig entrenchments in the summer of 1941
Ruin and devastation in Russia
Young Communists hung by the Nazis
Soviet sappers cut through defensive German wire
Australians burying Italian dead near Jarabub, Cyrenaica, November 1941
British Bren gun carriers enter Palmyra, July 1941

following page 288

Atlantic convoy: U.S. aircraft carrier *Ranger*, November 1941 (Navy Department)
Convoy duty, fall 1941 (Navy Department)
A torpedoed British tanker flames and dies (Navy Department)
Japanese planes over Pearl Harbor, December 7, 1941 (U.S. Navy, captured Japanese photograph)
USS *Arizona* explodes, Pearl Harbor (U.S. Navy, courtesy of Tom Maloney)
Destroyer *Shaw* explodes, Pearl Harbor (U.S. Navy, courtesy of Tom Maloney)
Wreckage of destroyers *Cassin* and *Downes*, Pearl Harbor (U.S. Navy, courtesy of Tom Maloney)
Cavite Navy Yard, Philippine Islands, December 10, 1941 (U.S. Army)
Wreckage of submarine *Sealion*, Cavite Navy Yard, December 17, 1941

General Masaharu Homma lands at Lingayen Gulf, Philippines, December 24, 1941 (Navy Department, courtesy of Dr. Diosdado M. Yap, editor-publisher, *Bataan Magazine*, Washington, D.C.)

The conquerors move toward Bataan (Navy Department, courtesy of Dr. Diosdado M. Yap, editor-publisher, *Bataan Magazine*, Washington, D.C.)

Death of the *Prince of Wales* off Malaya, December 10, 1941

What is the past, after all, but a vast sheet of darkness in which a few moments, pricked, apparently at random, shine?

JOHN UPDIKE, *The Astronomer*

I

THE SWORD IS DRAWN

I

The Road to War

On the night of February 27, 1933, smoke and flames gutting the Reichstag building in Berlin marked the Wagnerian end of the short-lived German democracy.

The mysterious Reichstag fire, actually set by a small group of Nazi Brown Shirts but ignited by a half-crazy dupe, the Dutch Communist Marinus van der Lubbe, served to consolidate and strengthen the grip of Nazi totalitarianism upon Germany. Adolf Hitler had just become Chancellor of a coalition government, in alliance with the right wing of German politics. The carefully planned conflagration in the Reichstag, heralded as a Communist revolutionary conspiracy, was actually part of a Nazi blueprint for dictatorship—a major step on the road to ruin, a Greater Reich completely subjugated to the will of one man, and a world engulfed in the greatest war in the history of mankind.

"On the evening of Friday, February 24, 1939, a short, disheveled man with grizzled hair upon his head and a worried frown upon his face took a walk along the East River in New York, accompanied by his wife, Florence, and a small brown dachshund named Einstein. It was a walk which neither the man nor his wife would ever forget."[1]

That afternoon Bill Laurence, science reporter for the *New York Times*, had heard two internationally known physicists—Enrico Fermi, a refugee from Mussolini's Italy, and Niels Bohr of Denmark —confirm, at a meeting at Columbia University, the first experimental fission of the atom. Laurence had imagined the sequential dangers to mankind, the possibility of an explosive chain reaction of the little-known element, uranium #235, and he was pouring out his soul to his wife.

Laurence brooded and waited. Not until May 5, 1940, just before the German legions poured into France and after Berlin physicists had started an extensive uranium research program, did the *New York Times*, in a front-page story written by Laurence, announce the isolation of a highly explosive element, uranium #235—1 pound of which was equivalent in power to 15,000 tons of TNT.[2]

World War II did not merely introduce a new era in the history of mankind; it represented the end of a millennium, the beginning of a time of unprecedented mass peril. Men had tried in the past, with considerable success, to destroy their fellows, but through all the ravages of Alexander and Genghis Khan, during the Thirty Years' War and the Spanish Inquisition, in World War I, in the Napoleonic conquests, and in the Crusades there had always been some happy valley untouched by conflict or terror; whole countries and continents had remained immune. World War II's fighting touched farther shores, reached more infinite horizons, than ever before; even more important, the weapons it introduced—jet aircraft, long-range missiles, nuclear warheads—canceled terrain barriers, soared above oceans, conferring upon man for the first time in his history the capability of ravaging the remote and the tranquil and of destroying himself or his civilization.

World War I was, for the American people, the last crusade. It was a war uncluttered and uncomplicated, which suited the American self-image of morality and righteousness; it was simply a war of the good guys against the bad guys. In a psychological sense the United States was a youthful stalwart, bright with the hope of tomorrow.

World War II—a far greater conflict fraught with immeasurable consequences to the nation's future—was fought under different banners. Until Pearl Harbor, the United States was a nation divided and ambivalent, frustrated by the bitter history of the twenties and thirties, favoring Britain but opposed to entry in the struggle.[3] To a people still in the throes of a deep depression, with the wounds of the Civil War in Spain and the Japanese aggression against China still unhealed, the words of George Washington about the avoidance of foreign wars had great appeal. The Japanese surprise attack on Pearl Harbor gave the United States no option; America went to war united in all its immense mature strength, yet with somewhat less of the high expectations and shining purpose of yesteryear.

And not until all of Europe and part of Asia had been swept by conquest.

The Absolutism of Left and Right

As always in past wars, man and his unbridled passions caused World War II. The political systems he had built, the economic structures he had created, the technology he had evolved, and the values he lived by were the imperatives of conflict. Pestilence, famine, and strife rode across Europe in the wake of World War I. The collapse of ancient empires—the czardom of Russia, the Central European patchwork of Croats and Slavs, Magyars and Germans; the weariness of great peoples—bled white by the immense slaughters of four years of trench warfare—combined to form an unstable historical mixture slow in reaction but explosive in content.

Woodrow Wilson's professorial idealism proved long in form but short in substance. The United States retreated after World War I into neo-isolationism and repudiated the Princeton teacher in the White House; it abandoned the League of Nations and sought safety in unilateral disarmament and in arms pacts signed with nations whose interests and ambitions were in basic opposition to American goals. Washington took refuge in the so-called rule of law and forgot that "scraps of paper"[4] had no meaning when absolutism strode across history. International treaties became the refuge of scoundrels, or of well-meaning but hapless men whose names, like those of so many statesmen once hailed as great, were destined for the dustbin of the past. In retrospect, these agreements, so loudly hailed at the time as the salvation of man and the linchpin of a stable warless world, represent a sad chronology of failure. The Washington Naval Disarmament Conference of 1921 (attended by the United States, Britain, France, Japan, and Italy) attempted to limit and to stabilize naval armaments. It was supplemented by the London Naval Treaty of 1930 and the Locarno Pact (1925), and the non-aggression supplement (1926) to the German-Russian Rapallo agreements, which collectively "guaranteed" peace in Europe; by the Kellogg-Briand Pact[5] (1928, ratified by the Senate in 1929), which sought to outlaw war; and by the futile Geneva Disarmament Conference of 1932–34, which offered no sanctions save the ultimate they were intended to prevent—war itself.

The very idealism which permeated the Wilsonian era helped to contribute, ironically, to the world's growing malaise. In Europe the Versailles Treaty (1919), which formalized the end of World War I, created, in the interest of the "self-determination" of peoples, new nations, or enclaves with disparate ethnic groupings. In Yugoslavia, an unnatural marriage between Serbs and Croats was consummated; Czechoslovakia was created, with the political cancer cells of the Sudeten Germans deep in her body politic; Poland was reborn for the fourth time in 150 years, with new frontiers and part of East Prussia in her fief; a new political hybrid, born out of compromise and expediency—the so-called Free City of Danzig, and the long appendix of the "Polish Corridor" that led to it—were carved out of the former imperial Germany; and Germany was stripped of Alsace-Lorraine (seized from France after the Franco-Prussian War of 1870–71).

The glowing coals of revisionism and revenge thus created were banked for a time after World War I; but later they were stoked and fed by demagogues and dictators, and helped to lead to World War II.

Indeed, so great had been the ravages of World War I, so deep the festering wounds left by "peace," that little time was needed for Europe and the world to settle into opposing ideologies, contrasting and adversary political systems, cynicism rather than idealism.

The absolutism of the left represented by communism was the first of the postwar dictatorial systems to establish hegemony over a great power. It was not done without convulsions; the short-lived Kerenski government in Russia (1917), which succeeded the last of the Czars, was overthrown by a small Bolshevik minority. The result was further death and devastation—more than two years of civil war —Reds against Whites, with inept Allied intervention at Archangel and in Siberia; the threat of Bolshevism in defeated Germany (December 1918 to February 1919); the short-lived Béla Kun Communist government in Hungary (March–August 1919); and the recession of the Red tide, turned back by Józef Pilsudski at the gates of Warsaw (August 1920). In 1922, the Union of Soviet Socialist Republics was formed, the first permanent Communist government on earth.

Gradually, in the name of the people but at the expense of the people, the struggle for power in Russia was settled; and in 1924, Joseph Stalin, a Georgian peasant, assumed the mantle of the dead Lenin, and started to consolidate his power as the dictator of the largest country in the world. It was not long before his grip squeezed the lifeblood from all who opposed him; in 1928, forced collectivization of individually owned farms began, and ultimately more than 5 million kulaks and peasants were liquidated.[6] Darkness closed down over Russia, and through the years, Joseph Stalin, the benevolent-appearing "Uncle Joe" of World War II, became an absolute tyrant, unrivaled by the Czar.

In Italy, it was an absolutism of the right that prospered—a dictatorship given to gestures and posturings that were peculiarly Latin. In 1922, Benito Mussolini and his Black Shirts came to power in

Rome, and gradually assumed the privileges and prerogatives of the ancient Caesars. Gabriele d'Annunzio, lyrical political troubador, romantic lover, poet of nationalism, helped to pave the way for fascism by stirring the multitude with his seizure of the disputed city of Fiume, at the head of the Adriatic, in 1919. Fascism itself, founded by Mussolini, was a strange blend of nonsense and realism, of symbolism, tradition, and emotion postulating a superficially benevolent "corporate state," which "made the trains run on time," but which differed little from the absolutism of the left in its end effects. Fascism gradually suppressed the unorthodox, put down political opposition, made King Victor Emmanuel of Italy a figurehead, and established a police-state dictatorship—much less efficient, somewhat lighter in its touch, less dangerous to the world because less powerful, but no less a dictatorship than the regimes in Russia and Germany.

And, like most dictatorships, Mussolini's was ambitious. Il Duce (The Leader) wanted nothing less than to restore the ancient glories of Rome. Early on in the Fascist regime, the symbolism was made explicit: the bundle of *fasces* (sticks or faggots) familiar from the days of imperial glory, and a dramatic large-scale map on the ruined walls of the Colosseum showing the geographic extent of the ancient Roman Empire and its boundaries, present and future. Slowly the boundaries began to expand.

A twenty-year friendship treaty with Ethiopia became in time an excuse for conquest. On October 3, 1935—portent of things to come —Italy invaded Ethiopia in massive attack without a declaration of war. While the League of Nations debated, faltered, and attempted in a footless exercise to support principle with compromise, Mussolini completed his first conquest.[7]

Addis Ababa, the capital, was captured on May 5, 1936; Haile Selassie became an exile, and on May 9, a faceless Italian king became "Emperor of Ethiopia." Ethiopia had been added to Somaliland and Eritrea and Libya in the Italian colonial diadem. The diadem was shortly to become a crown of thorns; the title of emperor a brief and bombastic one. But Mussolini and the nation he controlled lived in ancient dreams, impressed with their own power. The pattern of aggression without punishment was confirmed, and power was on the march.

In Germany, the shadows of the future were early seen. One of the world's most ancient cabalistic symbols—the swastika—had made its appearance soon after World War I; and in 1923, the Austrian

World War I corporal and house painter Adolf Hitler, with General Erich Ludendorff beside him, attempted the famous Beer Hall "Putsch" in Munich. It met with ludicrous, indeed ignominious defeat. But Hitler—in jail—became a hero-martyr to many Germans and wrote a book destined to shake the world, that strange blend of fact and fantasy, idealistic aspirations, naïve assumptions, and megalomaniac ambitions entitled *Mein Kampf*.

Mein Kampf ultimately sold millions of copies in German-speaking lands, where people hungered for the past glories of order and discipline, power, and economic stability. After a period of disorder and street fighting between Communists and National Socialists, the Nazi Party, aided by its uniformed toughs, the Brown Shirts, became a political force in Germany in 1933, won the last free election with 44 percent of the total vote, and took Germany out of the League of Nations. Again, a dictatorship of the right had emerged, its effects but little different for the dissident and the unconvinced than in Russia or Italy. Trade unions were suppressed, political opposition liquidated; a rule of terror by Brown Shirt gangs replaced a rule of law; the first of millions of Jews were beaten or murdered, and again the long, long night of absolutism settled over a nation.

The examples of political indulgence Europe set were catching. All over the world nations divided into dictatorships of right or left, each differing in detail, in background, atmosphere, personalities, but all equally disastrous in their effects upon freedom and the human spirit. In vast areas of the earth, Man in the late 1920's and 1930's seemed of little consequence; it was the state and its glories, the power of the ruler, not the ruled, that mattered.

In 1936, just after a leftist coalition government with Communist participation had taken power, Spain—once almost master of the world and repository of its treasures, now only an appendage of Europe—became a battleground of these rival ideologies in a civil war whose seeds were sown with the deposition of Alfonso XIII in 1931 and the establishment of a republic. Like the German experiment in democracy, the republic was short-lived; its demise hastened by attempts to reduce the great gap between rich and poor, to loosen somewhat the ironclad grip of the Roman Catholic Church on the land of the Inquisition and Torquemada, and by attempts by radicals and Communists, rightists and reactionaries, to seize power in Catalonia and Asturias, Barcelona and Seville. The inevitable conflict burgeoned in a succession of crises. A general named Francisco Franco ferried troops across the Strait of Gibraltar in German transport aircraft, and led a revolt against the republic. For two and a half years the bloody contest ravaged the sere hills and plateaus of Spain and tore raw wounds in the sunlit cities and towns— Barcelona, Madrid, San Sebastián.

The war rapidly became a precursor of things to come, a death struggle between two absolutist ideologies. This was not merely a *Spanish* civil war; both right and left quickly understood its deeper significance. Fascist Italy and Nazi Germany contributed men, money, planes, and weapons to Franco's cause; Russia sent planes, advisers, tanks, and artillery to the Popular Front government; the Communists recruited volunteers around the world (enlisted in "International" battalions and brigades),[8] solicited funds, contributed weapons, and maintained a worldwide drumbeat of propaganda.

But the dying was not quick. Madrid was besieged and fought over for twenty-eight months; two Italian divisions were routed at Guadalajara and Brihuega (March 1937); the town of Guernica achieved a kind of somber immortality on April 26, 1937, when German Luftwaffe pilots, flying for Franco, bombed it promiscuously and wantonly; the Basques were crushed, ships of both sides sunk or damaged by plane or submarine, thousands tortured or executed. But gradually, torn by internecine conflicts, the so-called Loyalists weakened; Franco extended his grip to city after city, town after town. The struggle finally ended in the first months of 1939, its slow death throes veiled (in retrospect) by what history held in store—the start, that same year, of World War II.[9]

The Spanish Civil War, fought with that peculiar ferocity that was to characterize much of World War II, cost something like 600,000 combatant and civilian dead—most killed in action, many executed, others dead in air raids, and including an estimated 200,000 dead from starvation or disease.[10] It had been a testing ground for many of the weapons of World War II: tanks, dive bombers, air transport, area and terror bombing, guerrilla warfare.

But most of all, it was an opening chapter to that ultimate confrontation between right and left that was to be settled in a far larger arena than the cockpit of Spain.

In the Orient, the political alternatives offered little choice for those men who would be truly free. Japan, crowded in rocky and inhospitable islands, nurtured in the spiritual code of the *Bushido*, bred on the mysticism of an obsolescent absolutism—the divine right of kings, the Sun-God Emperor—her Army trained with Prussian rigidity, veered more and more to the right. Military fanatics, inviolable in their self-righteous egoism, launched plot after plot, conspired and assassinated. Thought-control squads and snooping police were a precursor of 1984,[11] and the government became "civilian" and "democratic" in name only.

In 1931, as the long, global economic depression set in, Japanese troops conquered Manchuria, wrenching it from the debilitated body of China, and established a puppet state called Manchukuo.

The Japanese militarists who planned and executed the Manchurian operations of September, 1931, will probably be regarded by history as the first active aggressors of World War II. There is a direct and significant interconnection between their actions and those others, in Ethiopia, the Rhineland, Spain, China, Austria, Czechoslovakia, and Albania which culminated in general war in Europe. . . . [The Pacific phase of World War II] was merely the logical result of the events which began in Manchuria.[12]

Eighteen months of diplomatic crisis followed. But Secretary of State Henry L. Stimson and the United States stood virtually alone in support of a hard line; the League of Nations, to which the United States did not belong, satisfied itself with a commission of inquiry, and Britain and other large powers backed away.

The deed was done; aggression was rewarded, and more was to come. The Japanese landed 70,000 men at Shanghai in 1932, and after a month of fighting forced the Chinese to abandon an economic boycott instituted after the Manchurian aggression. Repeated incidents and continuous infiltration by Japan in and around China's northern provinces led in 1937 to a clash between Chiang Kai-shek's Kuomintang troops and the Japanese near the Marco Polo Bridge close to Peking. The so-called China Incident ensued, a large-scale Japanese invasion of China which led to and merged with the global conflict that was to follow.

Many Japanese felt themselves destined for dominance in the Far East . . . and in the world; the militarists' arrogance and lust for conquest knew no bounds. Tokyo envisaged a "Greater East Asia Co-Prosperity Sphere" under Japanese hegemony, its members bound by economic interests, its emotional rallying cry of "Asia for the Asiatics" based on anticolonialism and anti-Westernism.

Yet despite the quick capture of Peking by the Japanese in July 1937, the fall of Chiang Kai-shek's provisional capital, Nanking, later the same year, and the flooding and unchecked tide of Japanese aggression over much of China, the definitive solution always eluded

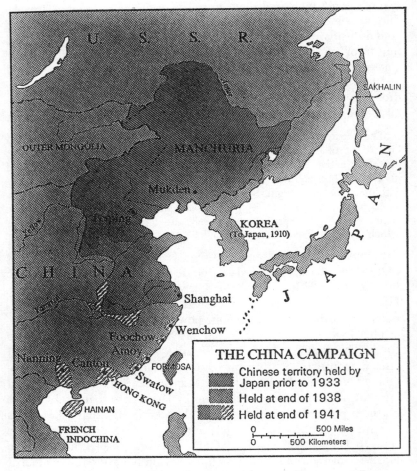

Japan. The ruthlessness and rapacity of the Japanese—155,000 to 200,000 civilians slaughtered in an orgy of rape, looting, and killing after the fall of Nanking; and the deliberate bombing of U.S. and British gunboats anchored in the Yangtze near Nanking (the famous *Panay* Incident)[13]—outraged world opinion and fortified Chinese hatred and opposition. And a few lonely Chinese victories, most of them Fabian or Pyrrhic in their ultimate results, immensely encouraged the Chinese, desperate for self-esteem. They sustained a tenacious defense of Shanghai in 1937. They won local victories at P'inghsinkuan in 1937 (the defeat of a Japanese division by a division of the Chinese Communist Eighth Route Army) and at

Taierhchwang and Chengchow in 1938; and they mired a Japanese advance by breaching the Yellow River dikes.

But the same ideological dichotomy that had drawn a line across half a world marred the Chinese defense. Chiang Kai-shek and his Kuomintang Party had turned a conglomerate of warring satrapies into a loose kind of coalition by dint of cajolery, force, "silver bullets" (bribes), and power politics. Yet unification was far from complete. In the hills and barren reaches of northwestern China, Mao Tse-tung and Chu Teh, supported by several hundred thousand followers, had sought refuge after a five-year civil war had driven their Communist followers from the lusher south. There, after "The Long March" of 1934-35, the defeated Communists bided their time, hoarded their strength, tightened their discipline, and waited in the wings of history.

In the East as in the West, absolutisms stood face to face.

While the dictatorships chose sides, made war, or launched aggressions, and the tide of tyranny—right or left—spread across the world, those great nations where men lived by different ideas and breathed freer air stood more or less aloof. They remained fascinated onlookers but immersed primarily in their own problems. They were not immune to the cleavage of right and left; the cross-currents of communism and fascism swirled and eddied in the politics of the entire world—perhaps most of all, among the great powers, in France, her past a chasm between the Communes and Bonapartism, her present scarred by passionate political prejudices and selfish vested interests. The United States, from the "two chickens in every pot, two cars in every garage" laissez-faire of the 1920's, had swung suddenly to bank failures and depression. And then, in the 1930's, to the nasal, radio-spellbinding "fireside chats" of Franklin Delano Roosevelt, who, in his New Deal, proceeded to redistribute the wealth, strengthen labor unions, make the federal government each man's keeper, and, in the process, create classes in a hitherto largely non-class-conscious society. The social and political revolution in the United States was preceded by one in Britain, where the socialization program of the Labour Party, accelerated by thousands of unemployed, was ultimately to lead to Sir Malcolm Beveridge's "cradle-to-the-grave" welfare state.

But for all these bonfires that would ultimately merge in the great conflagration of World War II, there was common tinder: human want, the Great Depression of the thirties, and—in Germany—the preface of an unrestrained, disastrous inflation.

The Collapse of the Economy

Ever since man created money, its control has been the subject of debate and interpretation. With the evolution of ever-more complex societies and the growth of international competition, the "laws" of economics have consistently defied exact formulation, or, when formulated, have been perverted by political, psychological, or other considerations.

The German economy in the early years of the republic (1921–23) underwent the most uncontrolled and disastrous inflation in modern history. World War I and the German defeat, the loss of overseas colonies and the waste of resources, had weakened the mark, although not very badly (it declined in value from about 4 to 6 marks to the dollar). But postwar Germany was torn by troubles, attempted putschs, assassinations, reparations for war damage in goods and services (coal and timber, particularly), and the specter of greater payments to come; and the mark, without political or economic stability, steadily declined. In January 1923, France and Belgium occupied the Ruhr, the heart of German industrial power, a move which had been prevented by Woodrow Wilson in 1919. The resident Germans—some 8 million of them—reacted with passive resistance; most of them refused to work to provide French reparations, and the German government turned inflation into galloping inflation by printing paper money to meet their needs. The situation in the Ruhr was not the sole cause of the wild inflation, which stemmed initially from a mark debilitated by defeat. There was—and has been—no similar depreciation in any other nation; Allende's Chile and the worthlessness of Confederate money after the defeat of the South in the American Civil War offer only remote, and different, parallels.

But the result was to contribute greatly to Hitler's later rise. By July 1922, the mark had fallen from 6 to a dollar after the Armistice of 1918 to 500 to a dollar. By early 1923, it took 20,000 marks to match a dollar. From then on, the sky was the limit. Prices for goods and services changed by the month, by the week, by the day, and then by the hour as the average citizen tried to keep pace with the diminishing value of his currency. A man might order soup at one price and before it was served find that the price had doubled. People carried suitcases full of worthless notes to pay for a loaf of bread; as they stood in line to buy it, the money they had dwindled in value so that, in the end, they could buy only a slice instead of a loaf. In late 1923 the mark had dropped to 4 trillion, 200 million to the dollar. It was worthless, and many of the wealthier German families and virtually all of the middle class—that middle-of-the-road element essential to social and political stability in any modern industrialized society—had been wiped out. The result was a lasting bitterness which provided a ready receptivity for doctrines of extremism. Upon the ruins of this broken middle class, Hitler built his power.

There was scant economic breathing space, for the somber period of a world depression—again unparalleled in its extent, duration, and severity in modern history—began in 1929. In Wall Street, as the stock market crashed on October 19, 1929, and sagged further and further despite support from J. P. Morgan and Co., and other bankers, men who had been wealthy the night before leaped out of windows, penniless and hopeless. Factories closed, banks shut, small businesses went bankrupt by the thousands, and unemployment spread across the land. All sorts of pump-priming schemes were tried. A whole alphabet of new agencies burgeoned in Washington: the CCC (Civilian Conservation Corps—unemployed youths supported and paid by the federal government in return for forestry and other work), the WPA (Works Progress Administration—public works, roads, etc., paid for by the federal government); and a new President, who was to be elected and elected again for an unprecedented four terms, proclaimed boldly that "the only thing we have to fear is fear itself."

But there was no surcease. The long lines of men seeking work grew and grew; in Washington a "bonus army" of World War I veterans tried to pressure the government for federal bonuses, and was ultimately dispersed in July 1932 by strong but not ruthless action by Army troops and police led by General Douglas MacArthur, then Army Chief of Staff, acting under President Hoover's orders. It was a time of mobility; the freight trains were full of "hoboes"—some few the castoffs of society, but many men seeking any work anywhere. Shantytowns of scrap lumber and tin grew in Riverside Park, and on Manhattan street corners jobless white-collar executives who had been earning $10,000 to $20,000 a year sold apples or pencils.

The United States abandoned the gold standard, and the origins of cheap money—an inflation still uncured today—commenced. The $20 gold piece, that staple of Christmas presents and graduation gifts for more than three decades, became a coin collector's curio.

The bad time spread across the world. International trade declined; tariff barriers increased, leading in the United States to the Smoot-Hawley Act of 1930. In England the industrial cities languished; coal miners on "the dole" (government welfare subsistence) lived in hopeless lassitude. Germany suffered; France, too; nor were the Orient, Africa, and South America immune. As in all wars, economic distortions and distress were a root cause of World War II.

Hitler's rise to power at first exacerbated these problems. But gradually unemployment eased in Germany. The confiscation of Jewish property provided capital and the elimination of Jews from the economic bloodstream provided jobs. Public works and *Autobahns* were started, and a rigidly controlled economy regulated employment, prices, profits. Under the "financial wizard" Dr. Hjalmar Schacht, some ruthless and complex financial legerdemain (involving cartels, barter deals, currency manipulations, preferential tariffs, and other discriminatory practices), led to considerable German economic expansion in markets and trade in Eastern Europe, Latin America, and to some extent in the Middle East. Germany, preparing for war, practiced a stark *autarky:* an attempt at economic self-sufficiency, including the use of substitutes like buna or synthetic rubber for imported raw materials. The result, an amazing economic recovery, strengthened Hitler's rule internally and led to closer ties between Germany and her natural allies (usually at the latter's expense), and to additional friction between Germany and the European democracies.

The New Technology

An arms race, originally primarily naval in character, was another cause of conflict, and, as so often in history, the attempt to control it merely sharpened suspicion, intensified rivalries.

The Washington Naval Disarmament Conference of 1921-22 had established a 5-5-3 ratio between the great powers, using capital ships (battleships and battle cruisers) as the yardstick. The United States and the British Empire were to be roughly co-equal in strength, Japan second to these powers, and France and Italy approximately equal fourths.

The United States took the treaty seriously, even scrapping ships already launched or building; but it found, by 1930, when the London Naval Disarmament Conference met, that it had used restraint in vain. At London the battleship provisions of the Washington Conference were extended to cruisers, destroyers, and other combat ships—but at a price. The American ratio had remained at 5; the British had risen to 5.2; and the Japanese to 3.25. In 1937, as soon as the naval treaties (denounced by Japan in 1934) had expired, Tokyo laid down two battleships, *Yamato* and *Musashi*, "the largest and most heavily armored warships in the world, with a standard displacement of 63,700 tons, an overall length of 866 feet and an 18.1 inch main battery."[14]

In 1922, the United States had built up 1.1 million tons of combat naval shipping; Britain, 1.4 million; and Japan, 547,000 tons. By 1941, the Japanese tonnage had almost doubled; the United States had added only 37,000 tons; and Britain 218,000.[15] It was unilateral disarmament at its worst.

The treaties also perpetuated the status quo of most naval bases and facilities in the Pacific (excluding Japan, Hawaii, and some distant British bases like Singapore). Thus the United States retained the political and moral responsibility for the defense of Guam and the Philippines but was denied the right to provide the military defenses to carry out those responsibilities.

Yet the Japanese had developed in the so-called Mandated Islands (the Marshalls, the Marianas, and the Carolines) a spiderweb of naval and air facilities which stretched directly athwart the transpacific routes to Asia and its offshore islands. Japanese naval ambitions, the startling rise of Japanese seapower, and Tokyo's drive for hegemony in the Western Pacific were direct causes of World War II.

Yet the habit was catching; and the arms race was certainly not confined to the Pacific. Under Hitler, German rearmament, in violation of the Versailles Treaty, led in 1935 to the reinstitution of conscription, and a slow but definite increase in the growth of German naval and, especially, airpower. In a futile attempt to eliminate the naval aspects of competition that in an earlier era had been one of the causes of World War I, Britain agreed to an Anglo-German Naval Treaty (1935) which, in theory, limited the Reich to 35 percent of British tonnage but allowed Germany parity in submarines.

As always in the past, however, quantitative restraints stimulated technological competition. The German designers, who had been limited until 1935 by the Versailles naval restrictions to ships no larger than 10,000 tons, evolved designs for "pocket battleships"—the *Deutschland* and the *Graf Spee*—with much greater firepower than any ship of similar tonnage (10,000 tons) in the world. Meanwhile German submarine experts were busy evolving the designs of World War II.

The advent of the new technology was also a destabilizing factor. Gradually, almost imperceptibly, the industrial revolution was merging into the technological revolution. The development of the internal combustion engine; of radio, radar, and electronics; of mechanized farming; and of assembly-line techniques was beginning to change the life patterns and mores of the old social systems. Agrarian economies were being replaced by urbanized, industrial complexes; the automobile—especially in America—was wrenching men from their roots and creating a volatile, mobile society, and bus, truck, plane first complemented, then competed with, railroad and ship. The new technology promised great blessings and greater horrors; its military applications—though few then comprehended their potential—were revolutionizing the art of war. Ambitious would-be conquerors, beguiled by the new capabilities of modern arms and by the theories of men like Giulio Douhet, an Italian airman, Major General J. F. C. Fuller, and Captain B. H. Liddell Hart,[16] foresaw the possibility of *Blitzkrieg*, or lightning war.

The new technology, moreover, extended the voice of the demagogue, facilitated the centralization of power, and exacerbated friction and conflict. The crises of yesterday in far-off corners of the world, which were often resolved before the news reached the capitals of the great powers, now were flashed to Washington and Tokyo, to London, Paris, and Berlin, to arrive with the morning coffee. Propaganda—the war of words—commanded the airwaves of the world, and in nearly every country the power of the leaders, who dominated communications, increased, overshadowing in the public mind Parliament and the people.

In such a climate, the old values and ancient beliefs were discarded by some, doubted by many; the loyalties men lived by were strained to the breaking point. Psychologically, the world climate of the thirties was a spawning ground for extremism.

In the United States, men out of work were naturally receptive to the shibboleths of the left; hundreds of thousands flirted with communism, attracted by the doctrine of communal living and a Socialist society; thousands joined the party. In New York's Union Square Communist rallies sometimes ended in riot as the mob provoked and fought "Whalen's Cossacks," the New York police force under Grover C. Whalen, then police commissioner.

In Germany, after pitched battles between left and right, the Nazi bully boys triumphed; in Japan, the Sun-God Emperor and the semimystical, complex hierarchy of the Establishment set the nation on a more and more nationalistic and aggressive course.

In most countries the brotherhood of man was put on the back burner; there were race riots and lynchings. The Japanese exclusion acts (official U.S. immigration policies approved by Congress between 1921 and 1924, which completely excluded Japanese and other Orientals) aroused resentment in Japan.

The democracies were experiencing disillusionment with the past, doubt about the present, and a general loss of faith. The aura of the World War I "crusade for democracy" had faded. In Washington the Senate's Nye Committee, with Alger Hiss as a counsel, held much-publicized hearings on the "merchants of death," the arms manufacturers and salesmen who were vilified as one of the root causes of World War I. The first great crusade had left a bitter taste, and the Nye Committee hearings helped to lead to the passage between 1935 and 1937 of unprecedented legislation, the so-called neutrality acts, which were supposed to keep the United States out of war. The pacifists, led in many instances by churchmen, campaigned against arms of any kind. In the English-speaking countries, many asked: "Who wants to die for Danzig?" and some young students supported the so-called Oxford motion: "Never again to die for King and Country."

In France, socialism fought with capitalism, and clericalism with both. The once-great arms plants suffered from obsolescence and the general letdown that followed World War I; and the act of nationalizing large segments of the industry, coupled with bureaucratic fumbling, reduced production to a trickle as well as adversely affecting quality. Léon Blum's "Popular Front" government in 1936 used demagoguery and slogans, "Bread, Peace and Liberty," but tried and failed to reform the moribund French economy. The result was greater political fragmentation and reduced production at the very moment when Germany was arming to the teeth.

It was a time of inner searching and outer exhibitionism, the time in America of prohibition, gang murders, and gun battles in the street, of flagpole sitters, roller derbys, and the dance marathon.

Never, perhaps, in history had democracies been so ill-prepared for war psychologically as in the 1930's, and certainly never was the absolutist and autocratic mentality so determined to settle for anything less than complete conquest.

This, then, was the background, these some of the causes of World War II: a raddled global economy; a world divided by clashing political ideologies; economic and arms competition; a public opinion confused and groping, hesitant when it should have been bold, aggressive when it should have been restrained.

But most of all the fundamental cause of World War II was as ancient as man: the desire of individuals for greater and greater power, of nations for conquest and empire.

The Cast

The characters upon whom the spotlights played during the six years of World War II and its preface were as varied in capabilities, attributes, and characteristics as a painter's pigments; but they had at least one quality in common—all of them liked the reins of power and knew how to manipulate them.

Each of the leaders of World War II was inexorably a product of his peoples and his times; each identified himself with the sweep of history and the future of his country; each possessed, in his own way, the power of self-dramatization.

Adolf Hitler, who preached the Nietzschean doctrine of a German superman, was a perverted genius, ruthless and malevolent, intuitive, charming, and humorless; he was a natural mimic, with an acute sense of political timing; a man of unbridled ambition, "sheer vindictiveness," and one who could play upon his people's passions like a fiddler on his strings. This leader, who "believed neither in God nor in conscience ('a Jewish invention, a blemish like circumcision') . . ." appeared to some as "a Siegfried come to reawaken Germany to greatness for whom morality, suffering and the 'litany of private virtues' were irrelevant."[17]

Except for his eyes, Hitler's physical appearance was commonplace, unimpressive, plebeian—even, with the "smudge" of mustache and the forelock of hair over his forehead, slightly funny. The man's eyes betrayed his inner passions, contradictions, and force; but "speech was the essential medium of his power . . . [he] talked incessantly . . . whipping himself and his audience into anger or exaltation by the sound of his voice." He could "bewitch" an audience with the "occult arts of the African medicine-man or the Asiatic Shaman . . . the sensitivity of a medium and the magnetism of a hypnotist. . . ." He was a mixture of "calculation and fanaticism . . . charismatic [but] astute and cynical . . . a man without religion, without philosophy, without principles [who] . . . balked at nothing."[18]

Hitler's magnetism in the eyes of the German people was an almost uncanny force, impossible to explain in rational terms yet essential to an understanding of why a great nation followed this political Pied Piper to destruction. He was, to many Germans, demi-God;

women who touched him in a crowd would not wash their hands for days. His looks were against him—almost clownlike, ideal for caricature and the comedians of the night clubs; yet he held an entire people in thrall.

Mussolini, with his great jaw, tight lips, and Caesarean profile, looked the part he played far more than did Hitler. He shared, with Hitler, intense egotism and self-confidence and the orator's ability to sway a crowd. He had been in power for seventeen years when World War II started; he was fifty-seven and to him Hitler, at fifty, was something of a political parvenu, who had copied some of the trappings of Italian fascism. Yet Hitler had a greater inner fire, and above all could depend upon a much stronger and more easily disciplined people, for the Germans were far less wedded than the laissez-faire Latins to the dangerous concept of freedom. Mussolini was fleshy, sensuous, arrogant; unlike Hitler, he had well-developed carnal appetites. He sired a large family and kept at least three mistresses. He had few firm beliefs except in himself—although he paid casual obeisance to a superhuman deity.

He had no illusions about his power; he knew it was based not only on respect and love but on fear, and he had a kind of contempt for those he stirred with phrases. He once told Emil Ludwig: "Even a dictator can be loved, provided that the mob has a healthy fear of him, too. The mob loves strong men. The mob is a female."[19]

Mussolini was a strong man in his milieu and in his era of history, but his dreams of a new Rome could not be realized by his peoples; the easygoing Italians—individually brave and daring—had none of the organized efficiency, the military skills of the Germans, and they were but a weak blade as tool of empire. Mussolini himself lacked finesse, judgment, and timing; his dictatorial powers, long wielded, corrupted him and his Fascist state, as absolute power always does. And when Hitler, the usurper of the grandeur of fascism, achieved his first conquests, Mussolini's jealousy and his desire to match the Germanic triumphs took precedence over his wisdom.

Joseph Stalin, né Iosif Vissarionovich Djugashvili, oldest of the dictators (he was sixty when World War II started), was a cobbler's son. As a boy, he was sent to a Greek Orthodox monastery in Tiflis, Georgia, but early became an apostate and conspiratorial revolutionary, who utilized many pseudonyms—"Sosso," "Kobo," "David Ivanovich," and finally "Stalin," man of steel.

He had lived the life of the underground for seventeen years in the days of the czars, repeatedly exiled to Siberia, and sentenced to prison. Yet his rise after Lenin's death in 1924 was swift, its principal ingredients a skillful adjustment of Lenin's mantle, merciless ruthlessness, and a marked aptitude for the deadly machinations which marked the road to power in perhaps the darkest epoch of Russian history.

Stalin appeared benevolent, but he was unencumbered by loyalties to any save himself; his hooded or "shadowed" eyes betrayed his rapacity. Like all the gauche, egalitarian, and suspicious Bolsheviks, he was gruff, rough, discourteous. But he had, if he wished, infinite patience and could assume a veneer of charming propriety; he could wait while impatient rivals hung themselves or became enmeshed in a carefully spun web. Like the other great dictators, he too was armored in egoism; but his implacable strength, his subtle ability to maneuver human beings (both of which were applied to a peasant people oppressed by hundreds of years of history), conferred upon him in the end more absolutism than Mussolini or Hitler ever enjoyed. He had organizing ability and he understood, at least in broad terms, the art of strategy and the science of tactics. Above all, he was the arch-conspirator. He knew how to cling to personal power, and the mistakes he made—though they cost Russia dearly—nearly always strengthened his own grip.

It was both the strength and the weakness of Soviet communism that it brooked no dissent, no opposition to the party line. Black was white if Stalin made it so; the facts of science, of history, were rewritten repeatedly to accord with the latest nuances of dialectical materialism.

In the Orient, dictatorships were woven of a different cloth; the only common denominator with the West was man's yearning for power.

The Japanese leaders who planned Pearl Harbor and took the nation into aggressive war came from a stock fostered by many centuries of feudalism, Byzantine conspiracy, subterfuge, and deceit. Hirohito the "Sun-God" (in Japan, Tenno or Tenno Heika ["Son of Heaven"]), upon whom his people never dared to look, was one of the last of the absolute monarchs. So confirmed was he in his unchallenged position that he appeared to rule from the wings, and, with Prince Konoye, Marquis Kido, and others, pulled the strings when he chose of many of the puppets who occupied center stage. Hirohito was thirty-eight in 1939 when World War II began. Although pictured as a nearsighted dabbler in the biological sciences and a man who was captive of his advisers, his real power was great if not supreme, and he exercised it with the help of a complex hierarchy of royal relatives, military leaders, and Zaibatsu politicians—sometimes with restraint, but always with an eye to the dynasty's future.

His peculiar authority, rooted in mythology, was nurtured further by the ambivalence of the Japanese people, a cultured, poetic, and at times gentle race—considerate hosts, loyal employees—but collectively volatile, sadistic, and rapacious; disciplined and obedient to authority, convinced always of Japan's destiny to rule.

To Americans, the Chinese leaders, like those of Japan, appeared baffling, largely because of the great gulf between the value systems of East and West. Chiang Kai-shek was an exceptional warlord—strong, ruthless, ambitious—who could be urbane, cultured, and stubborn. Like the Japanese, he thought not only in terms of battles won and lost but of more distant goals, consolidating his personal power. He was helped greatly in his initial relationship with Americans by his beautiful wife, one of the famous Soong sisters. Madame Chiang (Soong Mei-ling), like her husband ambitious and conniving, was a graduate of Wellesley and spoke perfect English.

Chiang's rule of China, that vast land riven by generations of dissent, was less than complete. In the far northwest, a rotund leader who had drunk long at the springs of Marx and Lenin dreamed of a peasant revolution and a dictatorship of the proletariat, trained his Communist Eighth Route Army, and bided his time. In hard ruthlessness and single-minded obsession Mao Tse-tung matched the dictator in the Kremlin.

It is difficult, if not impossible, to compare men like these with the leaders of the Western democracies, whose entire life style, though devoted to the acquisition of political power, paid at least overt obeisance to the will of the people. Men like Winston Churchill and Franklin Delano Roosevelt, inculcated in a Christian philosophy, educated in the classics, knew far more about the world around them than Hitler and Mussolini or the despotic rulers of Russia and Asia. But their power was far more limited; they had generally to convince and persuade rather than command. To the dictatorships, human life was of little consequence; to the Anglo-Saxons, a supreme factor in any equation of conflict was always the cost in blood.

In feeling, tradition, outlook, Winston Churchill was one of the great Victorians. But he towered above them all. His magnificent command of the English language, his ferocious energy and questing mind, and his receptivity to new ideas rallied the last of English courage and turned a defensive war—a struggle for survival—into a crusade against evil. He was a master of aphorisms and rounded, rolling syllables; of Sir Stafford Cripps, an austere vegetarian who eschewed many of the good things of life, Churchill once said: "There, but for the Grace of God . . . goes God."

He had a wry humor: "Although always prepared for martyrdom, I preferred that it should be postponed." His mother, Jennie Jerome, was an American, yet he demonstrated a fierce loyalty to the Crown and the British Empire. He was never ashamed of its imperial power; he once said (though history had the last word) that he had not become the King's first minister to preside over the dissolution of the British Empire. "He had a passion for detail. . . . In the midst of war and grand strategy . . . he had time to note the pleasures of the flesh in Marrakech in Morocco, and the plumbing in Yalta."[20]

Churchill had been more or less in the political wilderness since World War I and the failure at Gallipoli when he was First Lord of the Admiralty; his prescience in the 1930's in detecting the unrelenting ruthlessness of Hitler's ambitions and urging British rearmament was ignored, even ridiculed. He was considered a Jeremiah, a Cassandra; as late as 1937, visiting American correspondents were advised in London "not to bother to make an appointment with Churchill; he was a maverick or a crackpot."[21] Yet, despite criticism and political isolation, he hewed to the line.

He could be, and often was, politically ruthless; some of his Labour Party opponents hated him and unfairly equated their struggle against him as one of good against evil. He did have, it is true, some of the pirate in him, and he paid obeisance to the vanished glories of the imperial past.

Just as Franklin D. Roosevelt is hated still by many of his generation in the United States, a minority of Englishmen still harbor venomous thoughts about Churchill. Most of these "flowers of evil" memories have flourished in the rank soil of political and social prejudice and have been nourished by myths that have little or no truth. But Churchill was, as Ronald Lewin has written in *Churchill as Warlord*, a "man of excess . . . in emotion . . . in egocentricity, in physical and mental energy . . . in his single-minded concentration on selected objectives."

Nevertheless, he was a man for the moment. Churchill, perhaps more than any other figure of the Western world, invoked the spirit of indomitability and led Britain out of the abyss of defeat.

The life style of the man who came to supreme power at sixty-six and whose destiny it would be to turn the course of World War II was unique. His "siren suit," and two fingers raised in the V-for-Victory sign, became symbols of courage. He ignored most of the rules of good health; a great cigar was nearly always clenched between his lips; he was moon-faced and chubby; he drank quantities of brandy and his working habits exhausted and exasperated younger men; he napped in the afternoon and worked most of the night. But he thought big; he was never daunted; and he had the power to inspire men.

Franklin Delano Roosevelt, who was in his second term as President of the United States when World War II started, and who was elected to an unprecedented third term before the Japanese attack on Pearl Harbor, was, like Churchill, an aristocrat, of independent means. Born in 1882, he early showed a political bent. He was an Assistant Secretary of the Navy in World War I in the presidency of Woodrow Wilson and an unsuccessful Vice Presidential candidate (with James M. Cox heading the Democratic ticket) in the 1920 campaign. Then, suddenly, his career seemed broken, his active life ended by poliomyelitis, which paralyzed him from the waist down. His illness and his struggle to master his disability probably fashioned his character even more than his early career. He emerged from the shadows to nominate "Al" Smith ("The Happy Warrior") for the presidency in 1924, walking slowly to the podium with heavy steel braces on his legs.

Despite braces, heavy canes, and willing arms to lean upon, FDR was practically immobile—save in the swimming pool—for the rest of his life; but he was far from static in his dreams of a "New Deal" and in his ambitious plans. Like many cripples whose resolute determination has triumphed over their physical weakness, he became more and more self-confident—indeed stubborn. His ego was greatly magnified, and his optimism seemed unbounded. FDR's great abilities, particularly marked in the political field; his understanding of the common man; his mastery of the new art of radio (his "fireside chats," always starting "My Friends," won him millions of votes); his intuition, charm, vindictiveness (he once presented a bitterly critical opposition columnist with a mock Iron Cross);[22] his ruthlessness and his skillful manipulation of men kept him in the driver's seat of American political power for twelve years. As a wartime leader he would display great weaknesses, veering from overboldness to overcaution, and following the tides of public opinion like a will o' the wisp. His blind spots were pronounced, particularly about the world around him and some of his wartime peers (notably Stalin). Frances Perkins, his Secretary of Labor, called him "the most complicated human being I ever knew." And Henry Morgenthau, Jr., his Secretary of the Treasury, wrote that: "Roosevelt is an extrordinarily difficult person to describe . . . weary as well as buoyant, frivolous as well as grave, evasive as well as frank . . . a man of bewildering complexity of moods and motives."

The contradictory adjectives that history has linked with FDR are legion. Robert Sherwood said of him:

> Although he was progressive enough and liberal enough to be condemned as a "Traitor to his class," and "That Red in the White House," he was in truth a profoundly old-fashioned person with an incurable nostalgia for the very 'horse and buggy' era on which he publicly heaped so much scorn.[23]

Roosevelt was beloved and hated; admired more beyond the seas than in his own country, he was perhaps more complex than any of the other great leaders of World War II.

The men who helped to direct the destinies of other powers caught up in the maelstrom of global conflict—France, Belgium, Yugoslavia, The Netherlands, and the smaller countries of Europe and the Orient—were, for the most part, steersmen of history but not navigators. They did not set the course; essentially they were, like Reynaud and Gamelin in France, relics of history or chips on the wave of the future. Some of them, like Pétain, were men with immense reputations who had outlived their times. But here and there in the murk of mediocrity there shone a name as yet undiscerned, such as that of Charles de Gaulle of France.

Build-up in the West

The United States was incomparably the strongest power of the fifty-eight nations that participated in World War II.[24]

But the 16,112,566 men and women who were to wear U.S. uniforms throughout the war were only a fraction of those who served in combat or support. Before the shooting stopped, about 70 to 80 million armed men of many nations and all continents—28 to 30 million on the German-Italian-Japanese side, the rest Allied or associated powers—had been mobilized. Hundreds of millions of others, women and children as well as men, shouldered no guns, wore no uniforms, but suffered nevertheless in the front lines of Total War—the bombed, the dispossessed, the slave laborers, the refugees.

The United States, with immense but latent power at the start of World War II, had a minuscule Army, and a Navy just beginning to remedy the weaknesses of the years of euphoria.

In 1939, the United States Army—a volunteer professional Army with no draft to support it—totaled about 220,000 men (including the Army Air Corps, then a part of the Army), scattered all over the United States, the Caribbean, the Panama Canal Zone, Hawaii, and the Philippines. There were only five divisions—including a horsed cavalry division—in the United States, and these were below strength. Tanks, which were to play so large a role in the *Blitzkrieg* victories to come, were represented by the Army's only armored unit: one mechanized cavalry brigade, which, ironically, completed a "march" to the New York World's Fair at Flushing Meadows—the so-called World of Tomorrow—just as war started. The 110 clanking tanks and armored cars of the 7th Mechanized Brigade made a powerful impression, but the seeming strength was minute when projected against the battles to come.

The National Guard, with some twenty-two incomplete divisions, added potential power, but it was ill-trained, badly equipped—in some instances led by political officers and manned by undisciplined recruits who enjoyed horseplay and thought nothing, at summer camp, of creeping into the officers' tents at night and stuffing their boots with raw eggs.

But there were compensatory strengths in addition to the buffer of space provided by the oceans and the margin of time that was to be granted by the British Fleet and the Royal Air Force. The noncoms were professionals; most were competent. The officers' corps of the U.S. Army, most of them West Pointers, was the backbone of the service. It included some deadwood, which still thought in terms of the Indian wars. But most officers—men like George Patton, Dwight Eisenhower, Omar Bradley, George Marshall, "P." Wood, Douglas MacArthur—studied their profession, worked at it, lived and loved it. Primarily as a legacy of World War I, they had been provided one of the best officer schooling systems in the world, with Leavenworth (the staff school) and the Army War College at the apex of the pyramid. Some of the tactical concepts were obsolescent; Leavenworth was still teaching linear defense in the late thirties. Yet there was an eager urge to experiment with armored and mechanized forces, a new triangular division, or improved artillery techniques. A mobilization plan for both manpower and industry and raw materials had grown, with the help of Bernard Baruch and other key civilians, out of the lessons of the first war; it was essentially sound in concept and philosophy.

Like the Army, the U.S. Navy had both strengths and weaknesses at the start of World War II. Its principal deficiency was size, the inadequacy of its strength to meet a two-ocean commitment to the Atlantic and the Pacific. (Japan, at the time of Pearl Harbor, maintained a Navy stronger than the combined U.S. and British *Pacific* fleets.) Despite the lessons of the first war, the U.S. Navy was woefully unprepared to meet the undersea menace. The battleship was still generally regarded as the capital ship of navies, and in 1939, there were only five U.S. carriers in commission—the *grandes dames* of naval aviation *Saratoga* and *Lexington,* and the *Ranger, Yorktown,* and *Enterprise.* Cruiser strength was grossly inadequate for the convoying, scouting, patrolling, and gunfire support missions the Navy was to face.

Yet the seeds of most of the revolutionary tactics and techniques that distinguished the sea phase of World War II had been sown, and carefully nurtured, by the hard core of Annapolis professionals. Silent, apolitical sun-downers like "Ernie" King, irascible disciplinarians, often stiff and uneasy except on the quarterdeck, these men nevertheless pursued doggedly and devotedly the tenets of their craft.

The Naval Academy at Annapolis had single-mindedly stuck to its purpose of producing truly professional naval officers; and the Naval War College at Newport, building on the great heritage of Luce and Mahan, had developed basic tactical and strategic concepts that would be the guideposts to victory in World War II:

It was . . . at the Naval War College [Admiral Richard G. Colbert, USN, said in a speech to the Graduating Class in Newport on June 30, 1973] that the Pacific island campaigns of World War II were fought in the '30's, leading to [Admiral] Chester Nimitz's classic acknowledgment of debt to the college. Nothing he found in World War II Pacific campaigns surprised him, he said, save the *kamikaze.* . . .

College war games showed and documented the need for the Panama Canal. . . .

Naval strategists [at Newport] working with Marine Corps tacticians at Quantico revolutionized U.S. amphibious doctrine in the 1930's. . . .

The basic task organizations that our Navy adopted just before World War II [Task Unit, Task Group, Task Force] were developed [at Newport]. . . .

Standard operation orders and the operation plan format were developed. . . .

Carrier task force organization and tactical doctrine were first tested in theory . . . at the Naval War College. . . .

Dive-bombing and torpedo plane attacks were routine in the fleet exercises of the thirties (Pearl Harbor was successfully attacked by planes from the *Saratoga* in 1938, three years before the Japanese attack). Amphibious landings had been practiced as early as 1924 and developed by the Navy and Marines during the 1930's. A fleet train of tankers and other auxiliaries had been established—precursor of the great service forces which gave the U.S. Navy far greater mobility and sea endurance during World War II than any prior fleet in any prior period. Antiaircraft protection was grossly inadequate, and some ship designs and torpedo developments deficient; but radar had been born and was in operational development; new high-pressure, high-temperature steam installations were in use for ship steam plants; and by the time the United States entered the war, the design of what were to be the backbone of the wartime Navy—the *Essex*-class aircraft carriers, the *Fletcher* destroyers, and the *Cleveland* and *Baltimore*-class cruisers—had been completed. The moribund shipbuilding industry of the 1920's had been gradually revived by the Vinson-Trammel Act of 1934, and the "Two-Ocean Navy" shipbuilding program that eventually amplified it.

The U.S. Marine Corps, "soldiers of the sea" specially trained for assault upon land positions from ships, numbered only 19,406 in 1939, but they were a magnificent body of men, with high esprit and devotion.

At the outbreak of war in 1939, the U.S. Navy numbered only about 110,000 men and some 9,000 officers; its future strength was still in gestation—on shipbuilding ways, in folios of blueprints, in mobilization plans. Again time, the two years between the invasion of Poland in 1939 and Pearl Harbor in 1941, was a gift of the gods; the theory would become practice, the blueprints hardware.[25]

Military aviation in the United States was divided, as it was in Japan, between Army and Navy. The prescient but undisciplined "Billy" Mitchell, who had made a reputation in World War I in command of U.S. Army aviation in France, stirred up a hornet's nest in Washington in the 1920's by his zeal for airpower. Airpower zealots focused public attention on air potential; their hyperbole and cantankerous, often undisciplined methods caused constant friction within the services and between Army and Navy. But the feuds, in retrospect, did more good than harm.

The Navy's control of ship-based aviation was ultimately confirmed—though not conclusively until war came. The "Battleship Admirals" were forced to give place, if grudgingly, to the increasingly evident power of the plane. In the Army Air Corps, a parallel development led to the establishment of a General Headquarters Air Force under General Frank M. Andrews, to develop "independent" missions of airpower, and later (in June 1941 and March 1942) to the organization of quasi-independent U.S. Army Air Forces, commanded by General "Hap" (H. H.) Arnold. True, the airpower enthusiasts had drunk over-freely from the theories of the Italian airman Giulio Douhet, as well as from Lord Trenchard, father of the Royal Air Force in Britain, and "Billy" Mitchell in the United States.

To the Army Air enthusiasts of that era, the bomber was supreme, war could be won by aircraft alone, and it was perfectly possible to drop a "bomb in a pickle barrel" from 20,000 feet. No matter that an obscure lieutenant colonel named Claire L. Chennault vigorously opposed these theories at the Army Air Corps Tactical School in Alabama (Chennault believed that fighters had first to win the "air battle" by establishing local air superiority); no matter that events were later to disprove most of the "Bomber Generals'" prewar claims. Airpower had caught the popular imagination; the fear of urban bombardment was immense. The B-17 Flying Fortress—then the best four-engined bomber in the world—had been in service since 1937, and the B-24 bombers went into production in 1941.[26] Each was to play a great role in the air battles of World War II.

Yet, in 1939, the Army Air Forces numbered only 2,546 planes of all types, and the U.S. Navy added another 900 so-called first-line combat aircraft.[27]

Hidden by secrecy under the code name "Magic," the United States had developed a major military asset: a cryptologic establishment "preeminent" in the field of codes and ciphers. In one decade Washington had become considerably more sophisticated than it was in 1929, when Henry L. Stimson, Secretary of State to President Herbert Hoover, closed the State Department's "Black Chamber," a cryptanalysis section, with the observation that "Gentlemen do not read each other's mail." By World War II, Mr. Stimson (like the country) had changed. As Secretary of War, he was privy to "Magic," and the code-breaking activities of the Army Signal Corps, under a shy genius—"the greatest cryptologist," William Frederick Friedman—and of the Navy's communications intelligence organization, fathered by Laurence F. Safford. The invaluable warning this provided of Japanese plans and operations was to become an important U.S. advantage, particularly in the Pacific.[28]

But undoubtedly the major assets of the United States were its unequaled industrial-economic strength, its technological advancement, and the innovative improvisation and organizing ability of its people.

The faint beginnings of a unified planning system for Army and Navy had been forged between the wars; and many of the doctrines and contingency plans, though faulty in detail, were generally sound in outline.

Before World War II it was accepted as a kind of military axiom in most of the war offices of Europe and the West that the French Army was "the best in the world." It had emerged from World War I, despite the mutinies and the bloodletting, with an enhanced reputation; its great figures—"Poppa" Joffre, Pétain (the hero of Verdun), Gamelin, Weygand, and others—loomed majestically on the military landscape. The Army often looked bad; the soldiers slouched. Bored and indifferent about their duties, they failed to salute; there seemed none of the *élan*, the vigor, that characterized the goose-stepping Prussians, the energetic Japanese, the optimistic Americans, or the solid English "Tommies." But the experts provided swift reassurance to the skeptics and doubters: "The French *poilu* always looks sloppy; the Army is far better than it looks."

In 1937 General Maurice Gamelin, then Chief of Staff, was completely confident about his country's military strength. "My soul," he said, "is at peace." The remark—one of the most fatuous misjudgments of the time—was a product of national complacency, social schism, and the poverty of French military leadership at the top levels. The senior French generals were old; they had, as Saul K. Padover has put it, "fine nineteenth-century minds"; and "theirs was a strategy of passivity, dominated by *'le fétichisme de la ligne Maginot.'* "[29]

The French Army of 1939 was the product of a nation torn by dissension, by that same ideological rift between right and left that fractured the political structure of Europe, but widened to a chasm in the case of France by nostalgic dreams of Napoleonic glories and a deep fear of communism. Doctrine, strategy, tactics, all were confused or obsolescent; lip service was still paid to the *offensive à l'outrance* which had cost France so terribly in World War I, but the psychology and spirit were defensive and the linear concept of defense was still taught in the age of the plane and the tank. A "Great Wall" of France, the Maginot Line (named for the French War Minister who sponsored it), had been built in the 1930's in the form of huge underground fortresses and heavily protected gun emplacements, connected by fortified firing points and cleared zones of fire, along the German border from Switzerland to Belgium. The fortifications were intended to protect the newly regained provinces of Alsace and Lorraine, and were extended past Luxembourg—but not across Belgium. The "Line" was immobile, static, and linear, but technically formidable and hailed as "impregnable." Its chief weaknesses were that it could be outflanked rather than directly assaulted, and that it revealed a national state of mind.[30]

Tactical concepts were similarly static in prewar France. French tanks and artillery were well designed and numerous but armored forces were tied largely to the infantry; tanks were parceled out and not concentrated; there was only limited support for the tactical ideas of Charles de Gaulle, who advocated the use of tanks en masse in deep penetrations and wide envelopments and with massed firepower.

The Army mustered the equivalent of about 37 to 40 divisions in metropolitan France—some 600,000 to 650,000 men—plus another half million reserves mobilizable in two months, and millions more at staggered periods. The colonial Army added a numerically impressive reserve strength. The total French manpower under arms was to reach at peak strength about 5 million men.

The French Navy, at the outset of war, was formidable in heavy ships, comprising eight battleships, about eighteen cruisers, and one carrier—a total of more than half a million tons of combat shipping. It numbered about 118,000 seamen, active and reserve.

The French Air Force, which had probably suffered more heavily in the between-the-wars period than any of the French services from neglect, technical and tactical backwardness, and the politicization and socialization of the French armed services and their supporting arsenals, numbered somewhere between 2,700 to 3,300 so-called first-line "modern" aircraft, with other older planes in reserve. Its 64,000 men included many dedicated and skilled pilots, such as Antoine de Saint-Exupéry (a reservist). But the aircraft production rate was small; none of the designs was distinguished; and the organizational and command systems—and the doctrine that animated them—contributed to dispersion of effort.[31]

Italy as a military power exhibited major weaknesses, of which perhaps the greatest were organizational and administrative inefficiency and senile generalship. Her Army was numerically impressive. Her Navy, with six battleships built or building, some twenty-two heavy and light cruisers, and a large flotilla of destroyers and light craft, was strategically placed to dominate the Mediterranean, which Mussolini boasted was *Mare Nostrum*. An independent Air Force was well trained in high-level bombing but had virtually no experience in dive-bombing, low-level attack techniques, or the difficult art of air support for ground and naval forces.

* * *

The British Empire of 1939 was, in physical and industrial strength, a shadow of its Victorian prime. The British pound no longer dominated the world's money markets. The loosening of the imperial ties that bound the far-flung dominions to the mother country was already evident, despite the pageantry and power that London could muster upon occasions of imperial pride. On paper, the Royal Navy was equal to any. But the loss of control of its air arm from 1918 until 1937 to the Royal Air Force had handicapped it greatly; despite seven aircraft carriers in commission, plus six authorized, it was far behind the U.S. and Japanese navies in the application of airpower to the peculiar problems of sea warfare.

Moreover, the Royal Navy had no control whatsoever in 1939 over land-based maritime aircraft. The agreement of 1937 restored to the Navy only ship-based aircraft. Thus the important long-range ship patrol, antisubmarine, and antimine planes, operating from land bases, were not even under the Navy's operational control at the start of war but were part of the RAF's Maritime Command, which in the prewar build-up had been low on the list of priorities. Other weaknesses in the British Fleet were technical as well as organizational. Naval radar applications were not given high priority until 1939; very limited progress had been made in the detection of underwater submarines; and the British antisubmarine forces were grossly inadequate in number and design to meet the menace of the modern submarine.

Yet there was an aura of derring-do about the British Navy; men like Andrew Cunningham and Lord Louis Mountbatten carried on the Nelsonian tradition, and seagoing know-how was often superlative. Britain had "fed her sea for a thousand years," and even at a low point in history the British Navy was a powerful symbol of imperial power.

The volunteer professional Army, its horizons largely bounded by colonial wars, was small (about 175,000 regulars, some six to seven divisions—exclusive of the Indian Army, and the armies of Canada, Australia, and the Dominions). It included its share of Colonel Blimps, inherited from the stable, secure Victorian past, but also had its free spirits and freethinkers: young generals like Alexander and the ascetic Montgomery, and as theorists former officers like Fuller and Liddell Hart. It clung to the old but was not unreceptive to the new (its 25-pounder howitzer was one of the fine artillery pieces of the war).

From relatively humble beginnings, the British armed forces were to grow at peak strength to 4,683,000 men and women in uniform in June 1945 (exclusive of Commonwealth forces).

The numerically small Royal Air Force was deeply influenced by Douhet and Lord Trenchard; its belief in its own omnipotence—which would cost the British dear—was personified by Air Marshal "Bomber" Harris, a ruthless advocate of night-saturation bombing as a means to victory. But the RAF, despite weaknesses, was one of the most high-spirited, and for aerial fighting one of the best-trained, air forces in the world; it had developed two fighters—the Hawker Hurricane and, particularly, the Vickers Supermarine Spitfire—which were perhaps the finest interceptors of that day. And the white cliffs of England were guarded in 1939 by a radar "fence," the first air warning and control system of its kind in the world.

Radar (a U.S. Navy acronym for *ra*dio *d*etection *a*nd *r*anging) was in development or initial operation in the United States, France, and Germany, as well as England, by the start of war; but the only warning and locating stations (twenty in all along the east and southeast coasts) were in England. The detection of aircraft by electromagnetic rays was a key development, which ranked in some ways with the development of nuclear energy. The basis of its development dated back to 1886 and the work of Heinrich Hertz, but the operational development of World War II radar started in the United States in the 1920's and was continued almost simultaneously during the 1930's by other scientists working in Europe. The U.S. Navy had installed an experimental set aboard an old destroyer as early as 1937. By wartime, a number of U.S. men-of-war were equipped with crude, limited, but operational radar useful either against planes or ships.

In Britain, Robert Alexander Watson-Watt was the principal architect of the new detection and location system, and by early 1935 he had proved its potentialities sufficiently to convince Air Chief Marshal Sir Hugh Dowding, who became Commander-in-Chief of the Royal Air Force Fighter Command in mid-1936. Dowding, after a demonstration by Watson-Watt, "took steps," in the words of the British official history, *The Defense of the United Kingdom*, "whose consequences were perhaps as decisive for his country as any event recorded in British history." He recommended accelerated funding and development, and by 1939 the British had installed the "first operational radar system anywhere in the world"—a fact which would tip the balance in the harsh days to come.

In some other technical innovations the British were ahead of the state of the art. The cryptographers of His Majesty's Secret Intelligence Service, with the aid of reconstructed German Enigma cipher machines supplied by Polish agents, and Polish and French cryptographers were trying to break German codes well before the start of war. These first machines were augmented later by a machine, with its vital keys, retrieved from a German aircraft shot down in the early days off Norway, then by another Enigma captured from a German Army signals unit in France and by still a third one salvaged from a captured German U-boat. With the help of hundreds of intercepted messages, the British at Bletchley Park (headquarters of the wartime S.I.S.) deciphered throughout the war many top-level German operational and administrative messages. This highly important flow of data—some of it frequently forecasting German plans and future operations—was code-named "Ultra." It complemented and paralleled the U.S. "Magic" and led to a number of military coups, though none so dramatic as those in the Pacific.

The Germans, for their part, broke the British Admiralty code and read Admiralty and other British messages during part of the war; and other combatants, including the Russians, achieved periodic breakthroughs in the business of reading each other's mail. All of these battles in the electronic analytical war were important—some highly important—but none alone was decisive.

Britain's superior technology and the advanced "state-of-the-art" in some key developments such as radar, sonar, and cryptology were to compensate, in moments of high peril, for certain grave weaknesses of the armed services.

Build-up in the East

The Japanese armed forces were divided between Army and Navy, bred under different military traditions, but with the same basic philosophy. Each controlled its own airpower; each service had its own plans and ambitions—never fully reconciled; short of the Emperor there was no really unified command. Japan was a poor nation, completely dependent upon external sources of oil, then food-deficient and rice-importing, with a meager 7–8 million tons of steel production annually (as compared to the United States, with 65 million).

Yet she had elements of great military strength. Her position in the Western Pacific was remote, relatively unassailable, protected by a network of islands; in this area her Navy was supreme. Unlike the democracies, she had had long experience of war, with almost continuous fighting in China and the mainland since the Manchurian Incident of 1931–32, as well as the large-scale "test" battles of Nomonhan and Changkufeng and the raids along Russia's Siberian frontier (1936–39). Both in China and against Russia Japan had suffered some major reverses, but the "loss of face" led only to lust for revenge and conquest. And Japan's masses were willing; one of the island kingdom's major assets was the fantastic energy and ingenuity and the fanatic, disciplined devotion of its people, taught to die rather than surrender, believing implicitly in the ultimate triumph of the Sun-God Emperor. No matter if they fight only with broomsticks, it is hard to defeat in war a people with such a spirit.

In 1939, the Japanese armed forces numbered about 1.3 million, most of them in the Army, including about forty to forty-five regular and reserve divisions, manned by well-trained conscripts with a leaven of long-term skilled professionals. The Manchukuo (Manchurian) Army, including Manchurian and Mongolian mercenaries, numbered the equivalent of eight to ten divisions; there were two divisions in Korea, thousands of men engaged in the unfinished China Incident, and others stationed in the home islands or garrisons elsewhere in the Pacific.

The Japanese Navy—150,000 to 200,000 strong—was a highly trained, competent force, bred in the proud traditions of Tsushima, where Admiral Heihichiro Togo in the Russo-Japanese War annihilated a Russian fleet. By war's start, Tokyo had outbuilt the United States in carrier strength; the Japanese had ten in commission, compared to the U.S. seven. The Rising Sun also flew over ten battleships (with others building) and a large fleet of light and heavy cruisers, destroyers, and seaplane tenders. The naval air arm numbered more than 2,000 land-based and carrier-based aircraft; Army aviation added another 1,000 to 1,500 planes. Of these about 2,700 planes and 6,000 pilots, most of them with more flying hours and longer training than their American counterparts and with combat experience in China, were in operational units.

Japan possessed a vast trained reserve of military manpower, and at peak strength during World War II her military forces would grow to about 6.1 million men.

A great body of mythology about Japanese characteristics and abilities had accumulated in American and to a lesser extent British thinking. The war would quickly disabuse the Allies of these antic notions.[32] The Japanese sent into combat thoroughly trained, excellently equipped forces. Some of their leaders, like Admiral Isoroku Yamamoto, commander of the Japanese Combined Fleet, were extremely capable. The Army was skilled in jungle and night fighting, inured to hardship and privation, capable of long, exhausting marches. The Navy's carrier-based fighter, the Mitsubishi Zero, was one of the great combat planes of World War II, far more maneuverable and more effective in combat in the early stages of the war than the American aircraft that opposed it. The Japanese cruisers were faster—though more lightly armored—than U.S. ships; their destroyers were more heavily armed. Optical instruments were excellent, and the Japanese "Long Lance" torpedo (a 24-inch monster with a 1,210-pound warhead) was faster, more powerful, had a greater range and far greater reliability than any comparable American torpedo. The Japanese Navy—although initially without radar—specialized in night torpedo attacks and night gunnery, and these skills were to cost the United States heavily. But the Japanese Navy's submarine doctrine was deficient, and its convoying and antisubmarine warfare capabilities completely inadequate to meet the needs of an insular empire dependent upon overseas sources of food and raw materials.

In addition to the major weakness of an economic-industrial base completely inadequate to challenge the United States, and their insular inability to sustain a long war, the Japanese suffered from serious—indeed, fatal—deficiencies. Primarily because of their feudalistic Emperor system, they demonstrated a myopic underestimation of their enemies. Their intelligence system was completely outclassed, and their propensity for reporting defeats as victories was an inherent frailty of their absolutist ideology. The Japanese astigmatism would continue, unlike a similar U.S. prewar malady, through most of the conflict.

The armed forces of the Soviet Union were much of an unknown; few rated them highly. In sheer numbers they were formidable, and their defensive capabilities were immensely enhanced by the vast, roadless spaces of Russia and her severe climate. But the Soviet divisions engaged in the Winter War against Finland were inept and fumbling and suffered, as in World War I, enormous casualties. The huge malevolent purges of 1937–38 had resulted in the execution, imprisonment, or exile of thousands of Red Army officers, including most senior and experienced generals (Marshal M. N. Tukhachevski, Deputy Commissar for Defense; Marshal Vasili K. Bluecher, commander in the Far East; the two senior naval commanders; every army corps commander; and most division commanders).[33] The recsult had been devastating; the midnight knock on the door by the secret police had far more than decimated the officer ranks of the Army; it gave the political commissars control of the Red Army at the start of World War II, with consequent tactical paralysis.

Like many of the armies of that day, the Red Army of World War II was essentially one of foot soldiers; it was, indeed, an "armed horde"—with some crack units, many excellent tanks, but with most of the units utilizing horsed transport or civilian labor, living off the land, driving cattle before them, killing, raping, and pillaging as they advanced.

In sheer numbers of armed men, tanks, and guns, the Soviet armed forces were, or became, the largest in the world. At peak strength in World War II, the Russian services would number some 12.5 million; probably at least 20 to 30 million men wore the uniform at one time or another. In peacetime the Army counted close to 2 million, organized in more than one hundred incomplete divisions backed up by at least another hundred cadre divisions. Most of these were infantry, but there were many horsed cavalry divisions. Mobilization, keyed to regional army districts, was slow, and transport and logistic support grossly inadequate, but manpower was almost unlimited and fully expendable. As in Japan, where to die in battle was glorious, casualties placed no restraint on commanders or tactics. The Soviet artillery was excellent and probably more numerous than in any other Army; the self-propelled 76.2 mm., the SU-85, and the SU-100, as well as the towed pieces, enjoyed both range and accuracy. Other outstanding weapons in design or production in 1939 were the Soviet T-34 tank (about 34 tons in weight, mounting a 76.2 or 85 mm. gun, and capable of a speed of 33 miles an hour), which came into service in quantity in 1940; the Katyusha rocket and rocket launcher; and the heavy but extremely serviceable and reliable automatic weapons and small arms. In general, Soviet ordnance design was austere, crude, and with few "creature comforts," but sound and effective. The major Soviet weaknesses initially were lack of antiaircraft, of logistic support, of leadership, discipline, training, and morale and tactical concepts. Most of the large numbers of tanks and self-propelled guns—perhaps as many as 20,000 at the start —were parceled out in small packets to infantry or other units and were not initially used in mass.

The Soviet Navy, long neglected, and supported by a shipbuilding industry which held the world's record for slowness of construction, was in no way a deep-sea force and had no real seagoing tradition. Its role was in fact envisaged as a flanking unit of the land forces; it was supposed to protect the coasts of the Narrow Seas—the Arctic, the Baltic, the Black Sea—from enemy amphibious assault. Its virtually land-locked and obsolete battleships and cruisers and few destroyers were of minor importance. The only fractionally significant elements of strength were its dedicated, well-trained naval infantry (for land fighting); its submarine fleet—primarily coastal types, but the largest in the world with more than 200 ships; and its numerous minesweepers, minelayers, and shallow-water coastal units.

The Soviet air forces in 1939 were probably the largest in the world, but their strength was quantitative, not qualitative. Total aircraft may have numbered as many as 6,000 planes, but these were divided between air defense, Army support, the Navy, and long-range bomber forces. A few of the Army support planes—particularly the Ilyushin (Il-2) Stormovik, which did not come into service in quantity until the middle of the war—were good antitank, close-support craft. The Yak-3 was a crude but maneuverable low-altitude fighter. But long-range bombing know-how was primitive, the navigation techniques so obsolete and training so inadequate that Soviet bombing pilots frequently failed to find their targets. Air defense was initially completely ineffective, and at the start of the war Soviet airpower was definitely second-rate.

Behind the massed numbers was an unsuspected mass-production capability in the factories of Soviet Russia and a quick adaptability to change which was to alter the course of the war. Yet, in 1939, the Red armed forces were a fear-ridden, dispirited mass, infiltrated by the secret police, their tactical concepts, organization, doctrine, and strategy dominated by Communist Party ideology. It was an Army crippled by Joseph Stalin and his aides, who, like all revolutionaries for a century and a half, feared the threat of "Bonapartism."

Compared to the Russian colossus, Poland, which had maintained her precarious freedom between two potential enemies since World War I, was a pygmy. As a nation, despite her almost wholly agrarian character, residual feudalism, and dictatorial-paternalistic government, Poland was more modern than Russia; leavened by French influence, she was more Western. The country had not been crippled between the wars by the collectivization of land, the outlawing of religion, or the great purges of communism; the backbone of the Polish armed forces was the tough and hardy Polish peasant, who often owned, tilled, or "sharecropped" his own plots of ground, worshiped God, and owed an inherent devotion to Poland's proud past. Yet as a military nation Poland was not only hopelessly outclassed by her giant neighbors, but also fielded obsolescent forces. And in modern war, courage and devotion—although indispensable ingredients to a nation's martial greatness—are never enough.

Poland's ground forces were primarily foot soldiers, with horsed transport and horsed cavalry. The horsemen were magnificent; to have seen Pilsudski's "Own Regiment," with lances and sabers and pennons flying, with machine guns firing from troikas (four-wheeled carts drawn by three galloping horses), was to have witnessed a martial pageant at once superb and unbelievable. But it was not modern war. The Regular Army numbered about 280,000 to 300,000 men, organized in about 30 below-strength infantry divisions, an incomplete mechanized cavalry brigade, and masses of horsed cavalry. It could be fleshed out to more than 1 million. It had a few tanks, some coastal and frontier fortifications, and a fortified town in Brest-Litovsk. The Navy was negligible, and the Air Force had, like the French, some very well-trained and daring pilots and about 800 to 1,000 planes of all types—none of them really comparable to the world's best.[34]

The other smaller powers of Europe were dwarfed by the armed forces of the larger states. Yugoslavia, with her mountainous terrain, had a long tradition of guerrilla warfare; Greece, aided by geography, fielded some fifteen divisions with obsolete equipment but stout fighting heart; Rumania, with her corseted and perfumed officer corps, corrupted by King Carol, offered manpower and little else; Bulgaria and Hungary had some tough fighting men. Except for the Finns, Scandinavia, which had long lived in peace, had few defenses; and Belgium and The Netherlands, with some 12 to 15 divisions (at full strength) between them, and 600 to 800 planes, were minor factors in the equation of military power.

German Rearmament

Looming over Europe and the world of 1939 was the Third Reich of Adolf Hitler that was intended to last a thousand years. As a prepared military power Germany was by far the most modern, and the strongest in the world. In just twenty-one years since the 1918 defeat and the subsequent restrictions of the Treaty of Versailles, Germany had developed armed forces much better trained, better organized, and with a tactical doctrine superior to any in the world. The treaty restrictions which had limited the German Army during the days of the Weimar Republic and until Hitler's renunciation in 1935 to an Army of 100,000 long-term professionals had been a blessing in disguise. Under the leadership of Colonel General Hans von Seeckt, and with the connivance of thousands of Germans, the numerous specific restrictions of the Versailles Treaty—which supposedly prohibited German land, sea, and air rearmament, curtailed military research and development, and outlawed military aviation and the "state within a state" (the German General Staff)—were flouted, ignored, or circumvented. In the early days, German-Russian cooperation permitted German research and development, tactical experiment, and aviation development in Russia. The 100,000 long-term professionals became, in time, the most highly trained soldiers on earth, all of them cadres for a vastly expanded German officer and non-com corps. Thus, when Germany resumed conscription in 1935, the knowledge was already in existence, the cadre ready for quick expansion.

At the start of the war, the German Army was homogenous in race, in language, and, above all, in basic ideology and concepts—an immense help to any military force. Its discipline and organization, both traditional characteristics of the Germanic mentality, were outstanding. There is no doubt it had been stirred by the Hitlerian oratory and by Hitler's successes. The mutterings of scattered discontent in the officer corps did not reflect the mass, and the German officer corps, in any case, with its elastic concepts of "honor" and its pledge of fealty to *Der Fuehrer*, had bred few men of moral courage. *Élan* was high; the average German tended to accept the legend of the "stab-in-the-back" in 1918—the surrender of an undefeated Army by a civilian regime, shaken by Red-inspired mutinies and civic disorders. Hitler's determination to make Germany the supreme power in Europe, and the world, undoubtedly had the psychological support of a majority of the German people, who were never ones, in any case, to revolt against authority, and who had been badly shaken by the economic problems of the twenties and thirties, the Communist bid for power, and the fighting in the streets.

By 1939, there were about 800,000 men—more than 50 divisions—in the regular German Army, with more than 1 million men in reserve. This was the nucleus of armed forces that were to increase, at peak strength, to more than 10 million. There were some major deficiencies in the German Army of 1939, including a shortage of trained communication personnel and other specialists. Contrary to public impression, most of the German Army of that day depended upon horsed transport, supplemented by railroads and requisitioned civilian-owned and government trucks, for supply. But there were six Panzer (tank) and four light divisions, nucleus of the great Panzer armies that were to sweep across Europe.

At the outset the German tanks were mobile and dependable, but not particularly impressive in technology. Most of them were too light and inadequately armed. The most powerful was the 26-ton Mark IV, with a short-barreled 75 mm. gun; the lightest, a 6-ton "tankette" of limited range and utility, armed with two machine guns, none of them superior to French designs. But Heinz Guderian, exponent of armored forces, had won Hitler's ear; and, unlike the tank forces of other nations, the Germans had grouped their armor in large units, capable of massing rapidly against any objective and exploiting success swiftly. The German generals' study of the next war—not the last one—had convinced some of them, too, that massive close air support of ground armies, particularly in mobile warfare, was essential to victory. The Luftwaffe had accordingly developed the Junkers (Ju-87) Stuka dive bomber, and the Messerschmitt (Bf 109) fighter (both tested in the Spanish Civil War) into the finest planes of their type in the world. The German Air Force had trained and worked in close cooperation with the tank units of the German Army, and long before the opening shots of World War II, *Blitzkrieg* or lightning war was in tactical gestation in the Reich.

By September 1939, the Luftwaffe numbered about 4,300 first-line aircraft and the German aircraft industry was producing some 700 planes a month, with a capability of more than double that number. There were weaknesses. Although some air leaders of the Reich agreed with the theories of Douhet about independent or strategic "victory through air power," the German Air Force of 1939 was primarily a tactical air force—trained, equipped, and organized to cooperate with surface forces. It had no four-engine bombers, and its two-engine medium bombers, though effective aircraft, had limited range-load capabilities.

The German Navy, despite great technical competence and in some instances a considerable qualitative superiority, was ill-prepared for a war against some of the world's greatest seapowers.

. . . the Fuehrer had slight appreciation of the significance of sea power and only faint glimmerings of naval strategy. He was *landsinnig* (land-minded), obsessed with a geopolitical theory very similar to that of the *blocus continental* through which Napoleon had hoped to strangle England.[35]

Major effort had been focused in the prewar years on strengthening the Army and its supporting air forces, and though the Navy had been expanded considerably and had built or was building some of the most advanced individual capital ships in the world, they were few in number. There were no aircraft carriers in commission; there was no naval air arm as such (Luftwaffe units were attached); and there were fifty-seven submarines in service but only forty-six U-boats operationally ready for combat,[36] of which about half were limited, by cruising radius, to North Sea or coastal operations. It was not a Navy that could protect German maritime commerce, nor could it challenge its enemies in open battle.

As a supplement to German rearmament, Hitler had ordered the start in 1937 of construction of the West Wall or "Siegfried Line"— a defensive system of carefully camouflaged concrete-and-steel bunkers, tank traps, and obstacles along the French frontier. As history speeded to crisis, acceleration of the project (originally initiated on a twelve-year timetable) was ordered, and the wall was being extended to cover, not only the French, but the Luxembourg, Belgian, and part of the Dutch frontiers. The Organization Todt, a massive German paramilitary construction service named for its head, had partially completed these works in September 1939. At war's start the West Wall was strong. Hitler described it as "impenetrable," and thought it had changed the political map of Europe. But it was unfinished and at the last hastily armed.

The German industrial and economic capacity was strong; it provided the basic sinews for large-scale war, although in 1939 it was not organized or directed to a production capability adequate to replace massive ammunition, gasoline, aircraft, and other war expenditures.

The doctrine of *Blitzkrieg*, therefore, although well adapted to the concept of a rapid, single-front victory, was in no way adequate to meet the ravening demands of a many-front, long-drawn-out war of attrition.

Hitler expected the former: quick victory. Neither he nor Germany was ready for full-scale war in 1939; the German armament program had set 1942 or 1943 as the year of readiness.

Hitler got war, which his blood-and-iron philosophy of power had always anticipated; but he did not get the war he wanted. And the West got a war it didn't want, in large part because Western weakness and Western appeasement encouraged Nazi recklessness.

The Era of Appeasement

The golden age of appeasement flowered from 1935 to 1938.

The march to war hurried to a quickstep after Hitler had denounced the military restrictions of the Treaty of Versailles in 1935, and established conscription.

France, her nightmare fears of German militarism reawakened, forged a defensive alliance with Communist Russia, strengthening her posture against external foes and weakening her defense against internal enemies by widening the chasm with her right-wing dissidents, who feared communism more than Nazism.

The crises followed in rapid tempo.

In March 1936, German troops goosestepped, to cheers, back into the demilitarized Rhineland for the first time since 1918, and Hitler simultaneously denounced the Locarno Pact of 1925, which had been hailed as stabilizing Europe. The other signatories, France, England, Belgium, and Czechoslovakia, talked, fulminated, but did nothing. Italy held aloof. In October 1936, a semiformal Rome-Berlin "Axis" was started; Germany recognized Italy's conquest of Ethiopia, and Mussolini, in effect, recognized Hitler's special interest in Austria.

Just one month later, the Axis was extended; Germany and Japan signed an Anti-Comintern Pact (joined by Italy a year later when Rome simultaneously withdrew from the League of Nations). The totalitarian alliance was formed: Tokyo-Rome-Berlin.

In the same month of November 1937 when the Tokyo-Rome-Berlin Axis was born, Hitler—unknown to the world—formalized his blueprint for aggression. In a top-secret meeting in the Reich Chancellery in the Wilhelmstrasse, Berlin, with his military chiefs and his Foreign Minister, he again emphasized Germany's need for *Lebensraum* (living room) in the East; specified France and England as the "hate-inspired" countries that stood in Germany's way; and elaborated his plans for war. The first goals of conquest were Austria and Czechoslovakia, which must be overcome, he said, with lightning speed (*blitzartig schnell*) to prevent effective intervention. The time for conquest: 1938 to, at the latest, 1943–45; Germany "had nothing to gain from a prolonged period of peace."[37]

There followed an almost frantic attempt by the West to shore up with "scraps of paper" (non-aggression pacts, treaties of friendship, and "guarantees") the balance of power in Europe. New pacts proliferated; few had any meaning. All the great powers meddled in the Balkans, jockeying for position. Far from guaranteeing peace, this "pactomania," as John W. Wheeler-Bennett describes it, provided small markers on the road to war since the agreements promised security without the means and above all the will to provide it.[38]

Austria, a German-speaking country long the object of *Anschluss* (union), and riddled by Nazi plots and coups, was the first overt victim. Austria had been a semi-Fascist state, even before Chancellor Engelbert Dollfuss was allowed to die slowly in a pool of his own blood after being shot in the throat by Nazi extremists in an attempted putsch in Vienna in July 1934. By March 1938, Austria was ripe for the plucking. Nazi toughs rioted in the streets; bombings were commonplace; Arthur von Seyss-Inquart, an Austrian Nazi, "the first of the quislings," was in charge of the police and internal security, and the pressure on Chancellor Kurt von Schuschnigg, "a man of impeccable Old World Austrian manners," had been tightening for months. He resigned with Nazi mobs in the streets shouting: "Sieg Heil! Sieg Heil! Hang Schuschnigg!" and the last words of his moving speech were: "God protect Austria!"[39]

On March 11 and 12, 1938, German troops marched into Austria. Mussolini, who had formerly opposed German ambitions in Austria, stood pat. "I will never forget him for this," Hitler said with joy. The West did nothing and Austria became part of the Third Reich.

No matter that the new and expanding German Army experienced supply problems, mechanical difficulties, tank breakdowns on its short, unopposed march of triumph. The deed was done; German troops now stood on the borders of Italy, close to the Danubian plain.

There was no breathing space.

From March to September, Hitler and his mouthpieces sounded the tocsin of hate and fear. Democratic and progressive Czechoslovakia was to be the next victim, a country that had peculiar appeal to the West, because sprung full-blown from the brow of Woodrow Wilson, and led since World War I by statesmen—Tomás G. Masaryk, Eduard Beneš, and Jan Masaryk—respected or venerated in the free chancelleries of the world.

A major crisis in May was narrowly bridged as Czechoslovakia ordered partial mobilization, Britain and France seemingly backed Prague, and Hitler apparently showed restraint. But the Western firmness was more apparent than real and Hitler's timetable for "Case Green," the destruction of Czechoslovakia, had not been changed; 1938 had now become a firm date. On May 30, unknown to the West, *Der Fuehrer* signed a military directive which stated: "It is my unalterable decision to smash Czechoslovakia by military action in the near future."[40]

The boundaries of Czechoslovakia included the so-called Sudetenland, along its German frontiers, and a German-speaking minority of some 3,250,000 people. Many of these, swayed by Nazi propaganda and antagonized by some discriminatory Prague policies, acted as Hitler's "Fifth Column." With an orator's skill, and a fine sense of timing, Hitler played upon all the strings that stir the passions of men, and by the time the harvests were ending in Europe the continent faced the greatest crisis since the "lamps went out" in August 1914.

The Munich crisis of September 1938 has come to be known in history as a synonym for appeasement, with Prime Minister Neville Chamberlain of Great Britain cast as the principal villain. But it is more accurately characterized as the inevitable and traumatic result of years of obtuse, wrongheaded policies in the West, of colossal misjudgments in London and Paris of Hitler and his supporters, of parsimonious neglect of the apparatus of military power, and of the completely wrongheaded "do-goodism" of well-meaning liberal pacifists. Chamberlain was a tired, well-meaning, somewhat fatuous old man of sixty-nine, honest but marked by a "rigidity" of mind, vain and limited, egocentric and obstinate. But he represented the British people of 1938. The threat of war with all its horrors was Hitler's greatest propaganda weapon; he urged it to the full, to dragoon, to frighten, to subvert. At nearly any cost—save freedom—Britain wanted to avoid war. Chamberlain had few cards; he had inherited the complacent military weakness passed on to him by his predecessors, Ramsay MacDonald and Stanley Baldwin; he had only started serious rearmament, and then slowly, in 1937, although feeble efforts to modernize the RAF had been initiated by his predecessors.

And the Britain of 1937–38 was torn by the same ideological differences that swept the world. Sir Oswald Mosley and his British Fascist Party had temporarily attracted even so erudite a man as Harold Nicolson, and maintained a capacity for small-scale disorder disproportionate to its size. But it had little political influence, and had been of far less importance in the shaping of British thought and the formulation of British policy than the intellectuals and well-born, who (as in France) feared communism more than fascism. The so-called Cliveden set (named for the home of Lord Astor, then owner of *The Times* of London), who as political scientists were intellectual dilettantes, helped to pave the way to Munich. There were a few, like Unity Mitford, sister-in-law of Mosley, who were emotionally unbalanced by Hitler's hypnotic attraction. There were anti-Semites and pro-Fascists; there were some who felt a guilt complex about the restrictive terms of the Versailles Treaty; there were German- and French-haters; and there were those—sincere but misguided—who advocated peace at any price. Confronted with major crisis, this British Establishment behaved, in the prewar years, as Laurence Lafore has put it, "like plumbers fussing with the Johnstown flood." But for the most part, they were, as A. L. Rowse says, "essentially middle-class, not aristocrats."

They did not have the hereditary sense of the security of the state, unlike Churchill, Eden, the Cecils. Nor did they have the toughness of the 18th Century aristocracy. They came at the end of the ascendancy of the Victorian middle-class, deeply affected as that was by high-mindedness and humbug. They all talked, in one form or another, the language of disingenuousness and cant. . . . This, and the essential pettiness of the National Government, all flocking together to keep Labour out, was deeply corrupting, both to them and to the nation. It meant that they failed to see what was true until too late, when it was simply a question of survival.[41]

Furthermore, although this was not known until years after World War II, Chamberlain went to Munich with the solemn and unanimous appraisal of his military chiefs that Britain must, at any cost, avoid war for at least a year. She was too weak, in 1938, to oppose the Nazi ground legions and, above all, the Luftwaffe.

The Chiefs of Staff were "categorical . . . the country was not ready for war . . . no measures of force . . . could now stop Germany from inflicting a crushing defeat on Czechoslovakia. . . . Any involvement . . . at this stage could well lead to an ultimate defeat [of Britain]. . . . No matter what the cost, war must be averted until the rearmament program began to bear substantial fruit."[42]

Lieutenant Commander P. K. Kemp, R.N., head of the historical section of the British Admiralty, who first revealed the existence of the Chiefs of Staff judgment in his book *Key to Victory*, correctly comments that this document placed Chamberlain "in a position from which there was no escape; national prestige, national honour, the obloquy of future generations, none of these could weigh against his overriding duty to his country, to gain time."[43]

And so Chamberlain, hectored and chivvied, "with an abiding horror of war," and bearing the inescapable burden of national weakness —the "representative of a power grown weak and lethargic from the fruits of victory"—encountered "the master of a people which had arisen lean, virile and vengeful from the ashes of defeat."[44]

The result, after a series of three historic meetings, was inevitable though shameful. Prague, rather than Berlin, received what amounted to an ultimatum—from its own allies—a plan concocted in the West to avert war. It represented complete capitulation by the West, and for Czechoslovakia, "threatened, traduced, betrayed," it was the end. Prime Minister Daladier and Foreign Minister Bonnet of France had thrown into the wastebasket of history another "scrap of paper," the French-Czechoslovak mutual-assistance treaty. Britain, ally of France, had encouraged and even suborned the dishonorable reversal. Russia, also tied by treaty to Czechoslovakia, professed willingness—though with some conditions—to come to Prague's aid; but the Czechs did not know whether to fear Soviet friendship more than German enmity. In any case, the Russian treaty was operative only if France fought, and there was no common Russian-Czechoslovak frontier. This meant that Russian troops if they were to reach Czechoslovakia would have to cross Poland or Rumania, and these countries quickly let it be known that permission would be refused.

At Munich, on September 29-30, 1938, Hitler and Mussolini, Chamberlain and Daladier agreed to the transfer of Czechoslovakia's predominantly Sudeten territories to Germany and to the immediate German military occupation of these areas. There were other provisions that seemed to ameliorate the Czechs' unhappy lot, but they were window dressing. Jan Masaryk, then the Czech ambassador in London, had put it well to Chamberlain and Lord Halifax (British Foreign Minister) when he heard the terms: "If you have sacrificed my nation to preserve the peace of the world, I shall be the first to applaud you. But if not, gentlemen; God help your souls!"[45]

The surrender at Munich was popular in the West. The British Fleet, mobilized for crisis in September 1938, dispersed; the antiaircraft guns left Hyde Park and the Tuileries; collectively, the West breathed a sigh of relief. Daladier, back from Munich, was cheered at Le Bourget. At 10 Downing Street in London the crowd sang "For He's a Jolly Good Fellow" to the smiling Prime Minister, with his umbrella, who approved the infamous pact of Munich with perhaps the most mistakenly fatuous remark of modern history: ". . . peace with honour. I believe it is peace for our time."[46]

Munich was the end of appeasement, a landmark on the road to war. It was another scrap of paper. On October 5, under pressure from Berlin and in fear of his life, President Beneš resigned and fled to exile in England. Poland and Hungary, as well as Germany—with Hitler's encouragement—tore great bites of territory from the stillquivering body of the Czechoslovakian state. And on March 15, 1939, Hitler entered Prague in triumph. Czechoslovakia was completely dismembered, most of it to be annexed or "protected" by the German Reich.

As Sir Nevile Henderson, British ambassador to Berlin, wrote later in his final report (September 20, 1939): "On the 15th March, by the ruthless suppression of the freedom of the Czechs . . . Hitler hoisted the skull and crossbones of the pirate . . . and appeared under his true colours as an unprincipled menace to European peace and liberty."

For England, Munich meant time gained, that one element for which there is no substitute in war.

Between Munich and September 1939—in the space of one year—Britain introduced conscription, started to bring up to full strength and then to double the twelve divisions of the Territorial Army (the British equivalent of the U.S. National Guard or reserves), put all twenty of her radar stations in operation, completed or started aircraft "shadow factories," doubling output, and increased the strength of the Royal Air Force Fighter Command by ten squadrons. At the time of Munich German aircraft production averaged 436 monthly (for 1938), but was generally thought by the West to be considerably higher (a victory for German propaganda and bluster). But France was completing only fifty planes monthly, and the British not many more. In 1938 there were only 93 eight-gun Hurricanes (the newest fighter) among the 759 planes, most of them obsolete, available to meet the threat of some 1,200 German bombers. By war's start, the Hurricane and the even newer and faster Spitfire had replaced a large portion of the obsolescent fighters. In September 1939, the RAF could dispose of 1,476 aircraft (as compared to the Luftwaffe's 4,300), but British plane production had risen to between 700 and 800 aircraft monthly, approximately equal to Germany's. The slow-moving British moved at last after Munich.

The surrender and betrayal, with the rapid disillusionment that was to follow, had awakened many Western peoples to the true nature of Hitler's ambitions and the worthlessness of his word, had alerted them to their danger, and had hardened the resolve of many politicians. The armaments factories of the West went to three shifts. But for this, the price had been high; gone now, disarmed and demobilized, were the thirty-five Czech divisions; the formidable fortifications—the "Little Maginot Line" (built with French advice) along the German frontier; and the natural defensive line of the Sudeten mountains. The "bastion of Bohemia" was in German hands, the swastika dominant in Central Europe, the French position almost fatally weakened, and Russia, alone and isolated, suspicious of the West. In Germany, Hitler's success further paralyzed the long-moribund German resistance movement. In particular, it disarmed the underground opposition of the officer corps, headed by Generals Ludwig Beck, Chief of the General Staff until August 18, 1938, and Werner von Fritsch, who had feared Hitlerian failure more than Hitler himself.

The internal opposition to Hitler in Germany, led chiefly by men who were more opportunistic than principled, had been gradually isolated and fractionalized long before Munich. Hitler had used the black-uniformed military Schutzstaffel (SS), along with the Gestapo and tacit if not active Army approval, to smash Ernst Röhm and the brown-shirted bully boys of the Sturmabteilung (SA) who had helped to bring him to power. The blood purge of June 30, 1934, had destroyed one unscrupulous group of scoundrels. But the Army, by condoning mass murder, had sacrificed its moral position, and had built up a paramilitary rival in Himmler's death's-head troops, the SS. On August 2, 1934, Field Marshal Paul von Hindenburg—the "wooden Titan," Germanic hero of World War I, and twice President of the German Reich—died. Hitler assumed the title of both Fuehrer and Reichschancellor. He immediately bound the officer corps of the German Army, that organization which had been "a state within a state," to him by a personal oath of fealty:

I swear before God to give my unconditional obedience to Adolf Hitler, Fuehrer of the Reich and of the German People, Supreme Commander of the Wehrmacht, and I pledge my word as a brave soldier to observe this oath always, even at peril of my life. . . .

From then until World War II was irretrievably lost and Germany destroyed, the ebb and flow of military opposition to Hitler was anticlimactic. In early 1938 Hitler had consolidated his power over the military when Field Marshal Werner von Blomberg, the War Minister, had married a woman with a checkered past— Fräulein Erna Gruhn (Hitler and Göring were in attendance). The resultant scandal sullied the strong concepts of "honor" of the officer corps and led to the resignation of Blomberg; the dismissal of Fritsch, Commander-in-Chief of the Army, on trumped-up homosexual charges; and the assumption of the office of War Minister and "immediate command over the whole armed forces" by Hitler. The Oberkommando Wehrmacht (OKW) was established, with Field Marshal Wilhelm Keitel, a lackey in uniform, as Chief of Staff of the High Command. Then came Munich, with Hitler's "intuition" and timing once again confirmed by bloodless conquest. The rug was pulled from beneath the reluctant feet of military conspirators who loved not honor more but defeat less.

Hitler's power position, externally and internally, was tremendously strengthened by Munich, and he moved now toward Armageddon.

On March 23, 1939, Hitler in a *coup de main* entered Memel in Lithuania (one of the three Baltic republics), a city that had been Lithuanian since the Versailles Treaty. More "liberated" Germans were added to the Reich. England and France, which had "guaranteed" Memel's integrity in the Treaty of Versailles, still did nothing. But for most of the world, particularly the British, the blinders were off; it was to be the last of Hitler's bloodless triumphs.

The continued persecution of the Jews and of hapless minorities that were in the German grip, and above all *Kristalnacht*, the "Night of the Broken Glass" of November 9/10, 1938, had revolted free world opinion. A nationwide pogrom, carefully arranged and organized by the Nazi Party, ostensibly in answer to the assassination by a German Jewish refugee of a German Embassy official in Paris, burned most of the synagogues in Germany and thousands of Jewish businesses, and resulted in the death, injury, or imprisonment of numbers of Jews. The Jews were progressively eliminated from German economic life, and thence from life itself. The pogrom resulted in the recall of the U.S. ambassador to Berlin and a similar recall of the German ambassador to Washington; thereafter, the embassies were under *chargés d'affaires*, and United States and free world public opinion hardened against Hitler.

But it was the final rape of Czechoslovakia in March 1939 that forced a basic change in British, and to a lesser extent French, policy. Chamberlain felt the political heat of indignant opinion within his own party and from an aroused electorate. Now the Nazi pressure upon the Poles was not taken lightly. About two weeks after Hitler entered Prague, the die was cast. Chamberlain pledged "to lend the Polish government" all support in Britain's power, and France, he said, stood "in the same position in this matter."

Within seven months the world had come full cycle. In September 1938, Czechoslovakia to the British was that "faraway" country, torn by quarrels between "people of whom we know nothing." In late March 1939, a nation even farther away, with a culture, political system, and society even more alien to Western concepts, became, to the British and French, a *casus belli*.

The months that followed offered an alarmed world cyclical periods of hope, but Hitler was not to be deterred. In April, Mussolini's casual legions started the conquest of primitive Albania, and, unknown to the outside world, Hitler on April 3 issued "Plan *Weiss*" to the German armed forces, directing completion of preparations for the conquest of Poland by September 1.

Frantically now, the British who had stood aloof, and the French who had signed a treaty with Moscow but at Munich declined to invoke it, tried to enlist the Russians in a common cause against Hitler. Stalin would have none of it. He had been excluded from Munich, and the betrayal had reinforced the Communist suspicions of the West. The Russians played a schizophrenic diplomatic game; they talked with British, French, and Germans. But in early May the handwriting on the wall of history began to be legible; Maxim Litvinov, the Russian-Jewish Foreign Minister who had tried to align the U.S.S.R. with the West and had urged collective security, was dismissed, to be succeeded by Vyacheslav Molotov.

Throughout the summer of 1939 the gathering clouds of war obscured the future's horizons. A strident, staccato drumbeat of propaganda, threats, and bombast emanated from Berlin; demands for German "rights" in the Polish Corridor and in the Free City of Danzig were accompanied by street demonstrations, agitation, the infiltration of a German *Freikorps* into Danzig, and increasing German military mobilization and concentration. In the West frenzied preparations were under way for the war that most men did not want but few any longer thought could be averted.

On August 12, Count Galeazzo Ciano, Italian Foreign Minister and son-in-law of Mussolini, noted in his diary on a trip to Germany that: "Hitler is . . . implacable in his decision. . . . He has decided to strike and strike he will . . . the great war must be fought while he and the Duce are still young."[47]

And on August 22, with German naval vessels already leaving port for the high seas, Hitler forecast the shape of the war he was to wage in a rambling, frenetic monologue to his service chiefs at Obersalzberg: "Be steeled against all signs of compassion! . . . Be hard. . . . Be without mercy. The citizens of Western Europe must quiver in horror."[48]

One day later three German Army Groups, already on the frontiers, assumed operational command of the largest armies mobilized since World War I.

And that same night (August 23/24) in the Kremlin came the thunderclap that shook the world. With many toasts in vodka, Stalin and the Nazi Foreign Minister Ribbentrop, after weeks of negotiation, signed a non-aggression pact containing a secret protocol which gave Russia a free hand in Finland, Estonia, Latvia; in Poland east of the Narev, Vistula, and San rivers; and in Rumanian Bessarabia. Later, in a secret modification on September 28, 1939, Lithuania was added. Poland was doomed; the West had been checkmated by one of the most cynical and short-lasting marriages of convenience of any time between arch-enemies of right and left.

On the last day of peace, August 31, 1939, a German underground group, masked as a "choral society," donned the black uniforms of the Nazi SS (Elite Guard) in the Free City of Danzig. That same night near Gleiwitz in German Silesia, close to the Polish border, Alfred Helmut Naujocks, member of the Nazi SS, led a fake "Polish" raid against a German radio station, seized it, and broadcast a fiery and provocative speech in Polish before "fleeing" toward the Polish frontier, leaving a bullet-ridden body on the station's doorstep. The body, that of one of Naujocks's men, added verisimilitude to the faked "raid." Gleiwitz was one of several staged incidents along the Polish frontier arranged by the Nazis to buttress Hitler's claims of Polish "provocations" and to provide for the squeamish or confused historical "justification" for German aggression. But the camouflage was thin. German troops were already on the march, Nazi bombers en route to Polish airfields, when the frantic phrases stuttered from the Gleiwitz transmitter.

As the last day of the old world ended, sandbags were piled against the House of Commons in London, and the evacuation of 3 million children, women, invalids, and aged started from London and other English cities tense under the specter of heavy bombing. France mobilized. Germany had more than 2.6 million men in uniform, 1.5 million poised against Poland, 1 million in the West.

At 4:40 A.M. on September 1, the bombs fell on Polish airfields, and the old German battleship *Schleswig-Holstein*, on a "friendly" visit to Danzig Harbor, shelled the Polish fortress of Westerplatte, opening a crescendo of the guns that would not end for six long years.

In Rome on September 1 at 3:00 P.M. Il Duce, waiting to see the way the straws would fall, announced Italy's "non-intervention."

In Paris, as the German legions moved steadily into Poland and the Poles died in unequal combat, the French Cabinet, still split by ancient animosities and modern fears, debated throughout September 2 a belated offer by Mussolini to "mediate."

But it was far too late. At 11:00 A.M. (British summer time) on Sunday, September 3, the British government announced that a "state of war" existed between Britain and Germany. France joined at 5:00 P.M.

And that night in the sad and halting voice of a man who had schooled himself to overcome the tremor of his tongue and his inner anxieties, King George VI of Britain, last monarch of the Greater British Empire, reluctant King who had received the scepter from an abdicated monarch, spoke to his people:

"For the second time in the lives of most of us, we are at war. . . ."

2

The Beginnings: 1939

The last four months of 1939 marked the end, forever, of the old world. The semifeudalistic societies of Eastern Europe, inherited from the kings and emperors of yesterday, responded for the last time to the tocsin of mobilization; the armies marched to death. Polish horsemen shattered their lances against the steel of German tanks; bombs fell upon the ancient baroque architecture of Warsaw and in a month of *Blitzkrieg* Poland was conquered—and dismembered—for the fourth time in her unhappy history. In the West great armies of Germans and of Frenchmen, with a small British Expeditionary Force, crouched behind their fortifications, probed and patrolled, but fought no battles; the term "phony war" was born. As in every conflict, the men who sailed the seas were among the first to press the grapes of wrath. German U-boats sent great ships of England to their doom; the Port of London was almost closed by a new type of mine; and deep in the South Atlantic, near the River Plate, ships flying the White Ensign and the Swastika dueled to the death. Soviet Russia—exacting her pound of flesh from the secret protocol of the German-Russian Non-Aggression Treaty—occupied eastern Poland, forced the Baltic countries to cede base sites and military enclaves, and sent an invading army blundering in bloody combat through deep snow and subzero cold to a "Winter War" against the recalcitrant Finns.

The Polish Campaign

The doughty Poles had fighting heart—but little else. Caught in a geographic vise between great powers, a natural land-bridge from east to west, outflanked by German East Prussia to the north and German-dominated Slovakia to the south, Poland was ill-favored by nature for defense. She had no natural defensive terrain barriers, save a few of the passes through the Carpathians, the Pripyat Marshes in the east, and, when in spate, the great Polish rivers. Across the wide roadless plains "General Mud" was the chief obstacle. But in September 1939, at the end of a hot dry summer, dust proved but a petty obstacle.

The Poles went to war in a hopeless political position. Their leaders, like the led, were a stubborn and overconfident people with a split personality; they hated, feared, and respected the Germans, their best trading partners; they hated and despised the Russians, their largest neighbor. Marshal Edward Rydz-Śmigly, Inspector General of the Armed Forces, had once summarized these ambivalent attitudes aptly: "With the Germans we risk losing our freedom. With the Russians we shall lose our soul."

From the Munich crisis through the troubled year of 1939, Poland had equivocated. Warsaw had sacrificed sympathy in the West by slicing Teschen and other ethnic enclaves from dying Czechoslovakia, and the Polish leaders seemed to live in a fool's paradise, despite the steadily increasing tempo of Nazi propaganda. The Russian-German Non-Aggression Pact sealed Poland's ultimate doom; even so, the Polish resistance might well have been more effective had the strategy been more realistic and the nation's full strength mobilized. But M-Day was not ordered until August 30, a bare thirty-six hours before the whirlwind struck; and the Polish plan of defense was an impossible one: a discontinuous, cordon defense of the indefensible—the entire 1,750 miles of frontier with Germany. Warsaw tried to defend everything and, in the event, lost everything.

The Polish Regular Army numbered less than 300,000 men, organized in 30 infantry divisions, a large amount of horsed cavalry, and an incomplete mechanized cavalry unit. It depended chiefly on horse-drawn transport, plus requisitioned civilian vehicles, and, like its mobilization procedures (thirty to sixty days for full mobilization), it was slow-moving—almost static. There were more than 1.5 million reservists, but when the Germans attacked, the maximum Polish strength was perhaps 800,000 to 1 million men (some 27 to 30 divisions or their equivalent), of whom hundreds of thousands were still en route to their units, many still in civilian clothes. The Polish forces were concentrated chiefly in small armies or geographic groupings: the Narev Group (from Lomzà to Lithuania along the East Prussian border); the Modlin Army; the Pomorze Army in the Corridor; the Poznań Army; the Lódź Army; the Cracow Army; the Carpathian Army in the south; and a special Navy-commanded coastal defense zone covering the maritime approaches to Danzig, Gdynia, the Hel Peninsula, and the Corridor, with reserve concentration areas to back up these armies throughout the country—the strongest near Warsaw. Some discontinuous field, and concrete-and-steel fortifications, were sited on the Hel Peninsula and around various Polish towns; and perhaps 500 to 700 combat aircraft, many obsolescent, supported the ground units.[49]

Against the static stubbornness of the Polish military past, the Germans posed the imaginative mobility of the Germanic military future. Their campaign plan was based on quick victory—a gigantic Cannae or battle of annihilation—envisaging a double inner and outer envelopment of Polish Army units west of the Vistula River, then of Warsaw in an inner encirclement, and then a vast outer pincer movement crossing around Brest-Litovsk, Bialystok, and the Bug River. The strongest German forces were concentrated as Army Group South under General Karl Gerd von Rundstedt, which comprised the Fourteenth, Tenth, and Eighth Armies, a total of thirty-four divisions, deployed from north of Breslau to the Dunajec River in Slovakia. The Poznań bulge into Germany, in the center, was lightly held by frontier guard units. Army Group North under General Fedor von Bock comprised two armies of about twenty-one divisions: the Fourth, based on Pomerania, and the Third on East Prussia. The ground forces were supported by two air fleets—1,600 planes, and a strong naval force in Danzig Bay—a total of more than 1.5 million men.

It was, from the first, unequal jousting. Despite the protracted death roll of the Nazi propaganda drums, the Germans achieved tactical surprise. The citizens of Danzig awoke on September 1 to find black-uniformed SS troops patrolling the streets of the city and the Swastika flying above City Hall. At twelve principal Polish airfields and at some seventy-five dirt strips and smaller fields, bombs fell in the early morning hours, and hangars, fuel, maintenance facilities, and aircraft went up in smoke.

The tanks rumbled, the caissons creaked, raising great clouds of dust across the bone-dry Polish plains, and the first of Europe's "army in tears"—thousands of women and children and old men, driving cattle before them—crowded the few roads, hampering Polish mobilization. From the first it was, for Warsaw, chaos. Communications were cut, impossible orders given; a coherent, centrally controlled defense quickly degenerated into isolated battles of confused men fighting blindly against attacks from all directions. Only against the coastal defenses near Danzig were the initial German attacks repulsed, and it was but brief glory.

The German campaign was based upon speed. Some 3,000 tanks, grouped chiefly in 6 of the new Panzer (armored) divisions, 4 light divisions (motorized infantry and tanks), and 4 motorized divisions, rumbled across the heat-hardened Polish plains, forded the sluggish rivers, bypassed strong points, sliced deep into Polish command and supply areas, and whistled up the fear-inspiring Stukas, which dived like falcons at their prey. The German infantry moved behind them mopping up, eliminating points of resistance, crushing by sheer firepower and weight of numbers the fortified areas and heavy concentrations which the tanks could not reduce.

The Poles fought stoutly but not well. There were sporadic checks to conquest, tenacious defense. The martial strains of Poland's national anthem sounded everywhere:

> . . . as long as we live,
> Poland shall not perish.

But those who sang it had not long to live.

The small Polish Air Force, outnumbered four to one, outclassed in all but courage, fought a valiant but hopeless fight. A total of 160 to more than 200 German aircraft was claimed by the Poles during the campaign, but by the second day of war only 20 Polish aircraft of the fighter brigade could take to the air. The mass German air attacks on the main bases at Warsaw, Grudziadz, Toruń, Łódź, Czestochowa, Radom, Katowice, and Cracow, and on auxiliary bases, resulted in rapid decimation of the Poles. Many aircraft were destroyed on the ground and in air combat. On numerous strips undamaged Polish planes, dispersed and camouflaged, lay immobile—eagles without wings—earth-bound by the incessant German bombings of maintenance, fuel, and supply facilities.[50]

By September 3, the ill-fated Polish Corridor had been completely eliminated, the magnificent horsemen of the Pomorze Cavalry Brigade—saddle leather creaking—having died in droves charging German tanks. The Third and Fourth Armies of Army Group North were linked. By the second day of war Czestochowa had fallen; and on the sixth ancient Cracow, with its magnificent university, its French culture, its medieval buildings—a cradle of Poland's greatness—was in German hands. On September 5, as Tenth Army units from Army Group South turned north toward Warsaw in a wide enveloping movement, General Franz Halder noted in his diary: "Enemy as good as beaten."

* * *

The campaign was a recurrent succession of brief stands, fierce fighting by bewildered Poles, continuous outflanking movements, and retreat or encirclement.

The Polish High Command tried to group its battered and scattered armies into three groups, one north of the Vistula, another from Warsaw to the junction of the Vistula and the San, and the third in the south. It was already too late. The German tanks drove boldly deep into the heart of Poland, disregarding the old concept of a linear advance—flanks exposed to counterattack—but always moving. In cities, towns, and junctions, the Nazis were occasionally helped by the activities of Fifth Columnists (traitors in civilian clothes) and German spies and saboteurs, whose activities were tremendously magnified by the panic of defeat.

By September 8, the 4th Panzer Division reached Warsaw's suburbs; the next day a few German tanks penetrated briefly into the city's streets, and the merciless siege and bombardment of a city crowded with refugees started. Other tanks swept south of the city in a wider envelopment further to the east. By September 10, the Wehrmacht was already concerned with plans for the administration of the conquered Polish territories. Polish units, skeletonized, red-eyed from fatigue, some without ammunition, tried desperately to evade the Luftwaffe. They retreated steadily but aimlessly, fought and ambushed and died.

The 11th Polish Infantry Division near Przemyśl by September 13 numbered only about 2,000 men:

> The German aeroplanes raided us at frequent intervals. There was no shelter anywhere: nothing but the accursed plain. . . . After one of the raids we counted 35 dead horses, and a few days later the divisional artillery lost 87 horses in a single raid. Such a march was not like the march of an army; it was more like the flight of some Biblical people, driven onward by the wrath of Heaven, and dissolving in the wilderness.[51]

By mid-September, the Polish campaign had become a series of disconnected battles of encirclement and annihilation. The fortified cities of Warsaw and Modlin were surrounded and dying under bombardment; a *Kessel* (or "pocket," a German term later to become familiar in the lexicography of World War II) of the remnants of some 12 to 13 Polish divisions near Kutno was bombed and shelled into collapse (with 40,000 prisoners and thousands dead). Brest-Litovsk was entered, and its old fortress reduced by September 17; Tenth Army units were fighting in the "acres of ruins" that had been

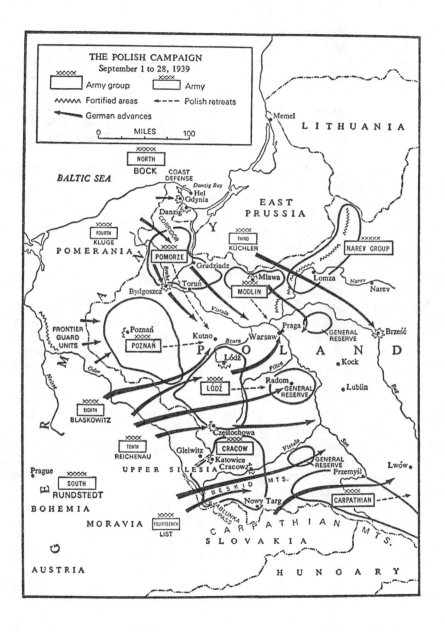

Lublin by the same day. Radom and another great pocket of Poles had been overrun (60,000 prisoners), and far to the south Lwów—last site of the Polish government and High Command which had been transferred from beleaguered Warsaw—was surrounded, and Przemyśl captured.

On September 17, in a surprise blow to all but Hitler, Stalin, and their entourage, thirty-five Red Army divisions and nine tank brigades invaded Poland from the east. It was a *coup de grâce* to a nation already vanquished. The Russians marched against minor Polish resistance, for the Polish Army had been concentrated in the west against Germany, and there were elements of only two infantry divisions and two cavalry brigades to meet the Soviet advance to the Bug and San rivers. Moscow's jackal-like snatch surprised even some of the German troops; there were sporadic shooting incidents between the suspicious soldiery of Poland's two traditional enemies as the Russian and German armies stood face to face.

The anticlimactic agony which followed stirred the world. Marshal Rydz-Śmigly, the Polish President Ignacy Mościcki, and other government leaders fled on September 18 to uneasy sanctuary in Rumania, accompanied by a considerable number of Polish pilots and Air Force ground personnel ordered to France and England to continue the fight. Small units and stragglers holed up in swamps and forest, or fled across the frontiers, and the Oberkommando Wehrmacht commenced to shift forces to the Western Front. Lwów surrendered on September 21. The ordeal of encircled Warsaw—exposed to the full deliberate fury of Nazi *Schrecklichkeit* or terror bombing—continued until September 27. Much of the city was in ruins, the dead unburied, sewers destroyed, the streets dark at noon with smoke and fire and dust, the famished people tearing still-quivering flesh from the bones of dying horses, 16,000 untended wounded lying in bomb-pocked, flame-gutted hospitals. Yet, until the sudden deathly silence at the end, when General Juliuscz Rommel, former commander of the Łódź Army, senior officer in Warsaw, surrendered 140,000 Polish troops, the Warsaw radio broadcast pitiful appeals for aid, followed always by an electronic signature—the first sweet, plaintive notes of Chopin's "Polonaise."

Modlin, with its forts, held out for two more days, then General Wiktor Thomme on September 29 surrendered 24,000 troops—one-sixth of them wounded—to the German Third and Eighth Armies. The Hel Peninsula on the Baltic Sea, heavily fortified, endured for a month shellfire from the guns of the ancient *Schleswig-Holstein* and the bombs of the Stukas before it surrendered with 5,000 men on

October 1. The final organized resistance ended at Kock, when 17,000 surrounded Poles laid down their arms to the Tenth German Army. The rest was "duck-shooting," sniper fire, sporadic brushes with groups of armed Poles who hid out in the deep forests or the swamps.

Poland was but memory. Yet the campaign had clearly forecast what was to come. The swiftness of the victory astounded the world. The tactics of *Blitzkrieg* were peculiarly German, influenced in their evolution by the theoretical writings of a French officer, Charles de Gaulle, by the British Major General J. F. C. Fuller, and by Captain B. H. Liddell Hart. Heinz Guderian and a few other tank enthusiasts had developed the concept of deep penetration and had had the boldness to execute it; the exposed flanks "covered" only from the air, the constant mobility, the whistling Stukas, the surprise attacks, the unrelenting air and artillery bombardments of cities, the use of traitors and saboteurs and deliberate terror tactics—"surrender or die"—were added ingredients.

German spearheads had fought their way across Poland from 200 to 400 miles in two to three weeks, using the tank en masse as an arm of assault, penetration, and exploitation. Western faith in static positions and fixed fortifications was shaken. With some slight exaggeration and great fanfare, the Germans called the victory *Der Feldzug der Achtzehn Tage*, "The Campaign of the Eighteen Days," and showed, with considerable effect around the world, a film of the triumph. The stubborn courage of the Poles cost Berlin a total of almost 46,000 casualties, about 10,500 dead. But the cost was disproportionate: about 100,000 Poles killed or driven across the frontiers or deep into swamps and forests; 700,000 others captured, along with thousands of guns and mortars and tons of ammunition; all except 5 of the light units of the Polish Navy (which escaped to Britain) captured or sunk, and an Air Force wiped out; 22 million people—slave laborers and factory workers—bowed beneath the crooked swastika.

The campaign revealed weaknesses in the German Army, which the Germans were quick to recognize and remedy; but it also demonstrated—to the surprise of the West—the qualities of "initiative and flexibility" which many Westerners had been unwilling to associate with the coercive regimentation of Hitler. And it clearly forecast the horrors to come. As early as September 10, General Halder had noted in his diary: "SS artillery of the Armd. Corps herded Jews into a church and massacred them. . . ."

On October 26, 1939, Dr. Hans Frank, a fervent Nazi upon whom

Hitler could depend "to put his racial theories as expressed in *Mein Kampf* into practice," took charge of a newly created party-oriented Government-General of Poland, despite Army opposition. The appointment was made to ensure the "ruthless destruction of the Polish nation."[52]

Frank was the first of the notorious Gauleiters, and he was to sow a whirlwind of horror in Poland; under him, "Nazi barbarism reached an incredible depth."[53] In retrospect, the transfer of conquered Poland from Army to party leaders presaged the ultimate end—still years removed—of Germany's bid for total conquest. For the merciless tortures of the SS and the Gestapo; the elimination of Jews, the intelligentsia, and all potential leaders; and the treatment of conquered peoples as ethnic slaves were to lead ultimately to Hitler's undoing.

In Poland Hitler had found war, but not the short war he wanted; to his surprise, French and English armies waited in the West.

The Western Front

Hitler, with arrogant contempt for his enemies, had not really believed until shortly before war started that Britain and France would fight. Nevertheless, he had concentrated in the West a newly mobilized Army Group C, with General Ritter von Leeb commanding. It was initially weak, only twelve regular divisions and some twenty-one reserve divisions supported by two reduced-strength air fleets. But a quick victory in Poland would enable rapid reinforcement of the West, and both Hitler and his military advisers believed that Leeb's troops, crouched behind the unfinished Siegfried Line (West Wall), could fight delaying actions until Poland was conquered.

The German calculations proved correct; in the event, the Nazis need not have feared attack for none came. The French mobilization was slow—some authorities have even described it as "lethargic."

General Maurice Gamelin, the French (and Allied) Commander-in-Chief, paid little more than lip service to his promise to mount a diversionary attack to aid Poland. It was a feeble gesture. A few French troops—elements of some nine divisions from the Fourth and Fifth Armies—moved across the German frontier near Saarbrücken on a 16-mile front to a depth of about 5 miles. They ventured past abandoned villages against light German resistance to within artillery range of some of the positions of the Siegfried Line. There they halted. Understandably, neither the Poles nor the Germans were impressed. Just two weeks later, the French troops began to retire again to the vicinity of the Maginot Line. By October 24 the invading forces had withdrawn on orders, under light German follow-up attack, to their original positions. The Germans lost about 198 killed in October regaining a few inconsequential square miles of border territory. The French had lost their troubled soul; their morale, already bad, was weakened; and "many were the spreaders of doubt and dissension."

The British Expeditionary Force, convoyed to France without loss, protected by minefield barriers across the Channel, was not fully deployed until September 27, when Poland was dead. Viscount Gort, the British general commanding the BEF (four divisions of two corps, totaling more than 152,000 men), was placed under the French Commander-in-Chief, "Northeast Theater of Operations." He deployed his troops along the Belgian frontier between the French Seventh Army on the seaward flank and the French First Army to the east. The French, confident in the strength of the Maginot Line, called up thousands of reservists and started to build up their ground strength in the West to an ultimate total of about 1.7 million men, nine armies of about ninety divisions.

It would seem enough for the blow that might have eased Poland's anguish. But the Germans were mobilized and ready when war came; the Allies on the contrary were far from ready and their build-up came far too slowly.

It was a question of too little and too late—the saddest words of any war. Thus, in the fall and winter of 1939-40 the war in the West came to be known as the "Phony War," or the *"Sitzkrieg"* (Sitting-down War) and, in France, as the *"Drôle de guerre."* From the Luxembourg border to Switzerland there were reciprocal patrols, brief forays and probes; from the Luxembourg border to the Channel supply bases were organized, field fortifications and tank traps built, while both sides built up their strength—and waited.

The War at Sea

As always, the Germans drew first blood, even though at war's start the Kriegsmarine was clearly inadequate for maritime warfare.

". . . In one sense," Admiral Karl Doenitz (in command of German submarines as a commodore at the start of the conflict) later said, ". . . the war . . . was lost before it began because . . . Germany was never prepared for a naval war against England. . . ."

Until the last Hitler had not really expected war against Britain and France before 1942 at the earliest, and even after the quick conquest of Poland he anticipated that a peace could be arranged. His Navy numbered only two modern capital ships—the battle cruisers *Scharnhorst* and *Gneisenau* (with two powerful battleships, *Bismarck* and *Tirpitz*, nearing completion)—as compared to Britain's fifteen; there were no aircraft carriers, while Britain had seven. About fifty-seven U-boats flew the Swastika of the Third Reich, of which only about forty-six were ready for sea. (There were more, but they were training vessels or out of commission.) Most of these boats were small, with a cruising radius limited to the North Sea and British coastal waters.

The odds against the German Fleet were further lengthened by a French increment to the British strength. France had only one aircraft carrier but two new powerful battle cruisers—*Dunkerque* and *Strasbourg*—seven older capital ships and two nearing completion, plus a large number of cruisers and destroyers.[54]

There were other major weaknesses. The Kriegsmarine had been low on Hitler's list of priorities. There was no naval air arm as such, few long-range reconnaissance and patrol aircraft, and cooperation between the Luftwaffe and the Navy was grudging and inadequate. But nearly all of the German ships were modern. Many of the British vessels dated back to World War I.

In September 1939, thirty-nine U-boats were at stations on the high seas; the pocket battleships *Graf Spee* and *Deutschland*, with their supply ships, had disappeared from German ports into the wilderness of waters; and Grand Admiral Erich Raeder, Commander-in-Chief of the Navy, ordered the traditional tactics of the inferior seapower—the *guerre de course* (guerrilla warfare) or attacks upon enemy commerce and shipping. Aided by minebelts and the Luftwaffe, the Navy had enough strength to fend off a close blockade of the German coast; and, in any case, the Third Reich, thanks to *autarky*, the development of synthetic substitutes, and stockpiling, was no longer as vulnerable to sea strangulation as the Kaiser's Germany had been. Her most important import, high-quality iron ore from northern Sweden's Luleå mines (imported also by Britain), was relatively invulnerable to enemy attack; it moved through the landlocked Baltic, or through Norwegian coastal waters.

On the first day of war, September 3, Britain declared a blockade of Germany, but it was a futile gesture. The Admiralty had suffered for years from the effects of pacifism and lack of funds, and only a few remembered the words of J. S. Corbett, the English naval historian:

Of late years the world has become so deeply impressed with the efficacy of sea power that we are inclined to forget how impotent it is of itself to decide a war against great continental states, how tedious is the pressure of naval action unless it be nicely coordinated with military and diplomatic pressure.[55]

Nor could England know that her blockade of Germany would soon become a hopeless attempt to engirdle a continent.

More important than the British declaration of blockade was the simultaneous return of Winston Churchill to the seat of power. Prime Minister Chamberlain, who had only a year before boasted of "peace in our time," recalled Churchill from the political wilderness on the opening day of war. On the evening of September 3, with the great Victorian back once again in his familiar seat in the Admiralty (left in disgrace in 1916 after the failure of the Gallipoli campaign), a signal went out to all ships that wore the White Ensign: "Winston is back."

Just twelve hours after Britain went to war, on September 4, the liner *Athenia*, outward-bound from Liverpool to Montreal with 1,400 passengers, was sunk without warning in the cold seas west of the Hebrides by U-30 under Lieutenant Commander Fritz-Ludwig Lemp. One hundred and twelve, including 28 Americans, died. The attack was contrary to Hitler's commands. German submarine warfare started with U-boat captains under strict orders to make no surprise attacks on merchant ships unless they were armed or escorted by naval vessels. Ludwig Lemp pleaded that *Athenia* was running darkened and on zigzag courses to avoid torpedoes; in any case the self-imposed restrictions of both sides would not last long.

Britain armed her merchant vessels and gave them orders to ram enemy submarines. And Hitler, convinced at length that Britain was in the war to stay, moved progressively toward a total blockade of the "tight little isles," which became virtually unlimited in November, then completely so by August 1940. To Britain, which "stood or fell by her imports" (68 million tons in 1938), a successful enemy blockade meant nothing less than slow strangulation.[56]

The blows fell in quick succession:

September 17—His Majesty's Aircraft Carrier *Courageous*, two destroyers in escort, sank at dusk off the western approaches with 519 dead, victim of a spread of torpedoes from U-29; Lieutenant Commander Otto Schuhart.

October 14—Lieutenant Commander Günther Prien, U-47, braved the lion in his den. His vessel penetrated an unfinished maze of blockships, negotiated tide rips, shoals, and twisting channels, and under flickering northern lights in a moonless night sank His Majesty's battleship *Royal Oak* at anchor in Scapa Flow, the heart of British seapower. Twenty-four officers, 809 men, went down with their ship.

Mid-November—Two out of three of the deep-water channels into the Thames and the Port of London were closed by enemy mines. Germany, from the war's start, had scored "tactical and technical surprise" by her extensive use of influence or magnetic mines, familiar in principle since World War I but, as used by the Germans, with many innovations. Initial mining successes using both contact and magnetic mines claimed as victims a new cruiser, *Belfast*, her back broken in the Firth of Forth, November 21; the battleship *Nelson*, seriously damaged in approaches to Loch Ewe, December 4; and twenty-seven merchant ships, one destroyer sunk, and many other ships damaged by mines in this single month. British unpreparedness had paved the way: ". . . the entire British minesweeping force [was] . . . designed only to deal with moored contact mines."

For a time the German magnetic mine (laid by surface ships, submarines, and then planes), which sank in checkered patterns in shoal water to the ocean floor, threatened Britain with starvation. But on November 23, "the period of groping for knowledge in the dark" ended when a metal cylinder about 8 feet long and 2 feet in diameter, with 650 pounds of high explosive, was recovered from Shoeburyness mudflats. "It was dissected at great personal risk by Lt.-Cmdr. J. G. D. Ouvry . . . [who] . . . discovered that the German mine was fired by a change in magnetism . . . and that it required the passage of a ship built in the northern hemisphere, which would therefore have its north magnetic pole downwards. . . ."[57] Now an antidote could be developed. Special minesweepers were built, and steel ships were girdled with electrified cables—de-Gaussing apparatus—to neutralize the vessels' magnetism. Nevertheless by the end of a gloomy December, British coastal shipping had been disrupted, some 263,000 tons of merchant ships had been sunk by mines, and the U-boats had claimed an additional 421,000 tons of Allied vessels.

It was not all gain for Hitler. Extensive British minefields were laid both off the British and the German coasts and in the North Sea. Mining and countermining continued, and British submarines, mines, and surface ships all claimed victims: the light cruisers *Leipsig* and *Nürnberg*, damaged in Heligoland Bight by a British submarine, *Salmon* (Lieutenant Commander E. O. B. Bickford) on December 13; nine U-boats sunk in 1939, one of them, U-29, in a futile attack on aircraft carrier *Ark Royal* (September 14), when its torpedoes ran true but detonated prematurely.

Blockade and counterblockade, thrust and riposte. For Britain, the struggle represented a mortal duel.

A duel with paradoxical elements. Geography and the facts of naval power had conferred tremendous advantages upon the Allies in the wide oceans which both linked and divided the far-flung global empires of Britain and of France. The Allies enjoyed a maritime network of refueling facilities and naval bases scattered all over the Seven Seas; Hitler's Germany—unlike the Kaiser's—had no overseas colonies. Thus the sea-keeping ability of the German raiders was limited by their fuel and stores capacity. It could be extended, although with difficulty, only by vulnerable supply ships, or by secret caches maintained—hopefully—by "benevolent Neutrals."

The advent of land-based patrol aircraft, with extended range and antisubmarine instruments, had increased the vulnerability of German raiders in the wide seas far from Europe, and particularly of surface ships.

But, while Britain was far better able to protect her empire and to control the far seas against Germany than she had been in World War I, she was less able to protect herself. The aircraft—as the great cities of England were to discover—had bridged the Narrow Seas, and plane, mine, and modern technology had tremendously complicated the task of protecting shipping around the British Isles. The British military organization, like the German, complicated still more the task of defense. The Royal Navy was no longer the sole buckler of England; the Fighter Command of the Royal Air Force must guard the sky approaches and the RAF's Coastal Command operated all land-based antisubmarine and shipping patrol planes. The closest kind of coordination and cooperation—significant by its absence at the start of war—was required to make the system work. On an average day, some 2,500 seagoing and coastal vessels, flying the Red Duster, were at sea carrying the lifeblood of England.

The British maritime task, therefore, was dictated as always by geography, technology, and the enemy. Defense of the home base, toward which all the ships at sea funneled as through a bottleneck, was the primary task; therefore the Home Fleet, based at Scapa Flow and other Scottish ports, in the Humber, and at Portland, was by far the strongest. The Mediterranean—particularly its narrow approaches, Gibraltar and the Red Sea–Suez—was second priority; the British assumed responsibility for the eastern half; the strong French Fleet for the western. Based at various foreign stations around the world were strong forces of cruisers, destroyers, and patrol and minecraft, augmented by ships of the Dominion navies, by a few French destroyers and submarines in the South Atlantic and the Far East, and by a strong French force—the formidable battle cruisers *Dunkerque* and *Strasbourg*, an aircraft carrier, and thirteen cruisers and destroyers at Brest.

The Germans, on the other hand, concentrated their efforts in the northern part of the North Sea and on oceanic warfare against merchant shipping.

It was deep in Southern latitudes that World War II's first dramatic clash, gun against gun, between tall ships of the old enemies occurred.

Well before war started two of Germany's three pocket battleships, the *Graf Spee* and *Deutschland*, followed by supply ships *Altmark* and *Westerwald*, had steamed out into the Atlantic unknown to the British Admiralty.

The *Deutschland* took up station in the North Atlantic, shrouded in fog and wild weather; the *Graf Spee* steamed, unobserved, south of the Equator. The oceans were their hunting ground, and rich pickings loomed. The pocket battleships, with six 11-inch guns, outgunned all the world's cruisers, and their powerful diesel engines gave them speeds of about 26 knots—faster than most ships that were strong enough to destroy them. Unlike World War I's surface raiders, they were equipped with reconnaissance aircraft.

The raiders commenced stalking their victims on Hitler's orders in late September. *Graf Spee*'s first kill was the British steamship *Clement*, which sank off the coast of Brazil on September 30; her radioed "RRRR" (enemy warship) and her crew, rescued by another vessel, gave word that a raider was at large. The hunt was on. But the waste of waters was wide indeed, and to course the wilderness of the high seas takes time and patience and cunning.

On October 5, far to the east, *Graf Spee* captured SS *Newton Beech*, and had claimed three more victims—sunk or captured—on the Cape of Good Hope trade routes before the middle of October. She rendezvoused with supply ship *Altmark* in mid-Atlantic for refueling and transfer of merchant prisoners; back again—in the South Atlantic and around the Cape in Mozambique Channel—to chivvying and tearing at the arteries of empire. Then back to the Atlantic to refuel again; more victims claimed and a course laid for plentiful hunting grounds of merchant shipping: the approaches to the broad estuary of the River Plate, leading to the rich ports of Montevideo and Buenos Aires. *Graf Spee* had sunk nine ships in about two months of hunting.

But now her luck ran out. A hitherto obscure British commodore, Sir Henry Harwood, flying his broad pendant in light cruiser *Ajax*, added his name to the roll call of fame by anticipating the actions of Captain Hans Langdorff, skipper of *Graf Spee*. Aided by Admiralty intelligence appraisals, Harwood believed that the German raider would be tempted by the rich pickings off the Plate, and he disposed his three ships accordingly. His hunch paid off; *Graf Spee* steamed into trouble off the Uruguayan coast at 0552, early in the morning of December 13, as the commodore had estimated.

The Germans sighted the British vessels first but wrongly identified them as a cruiser and two destroyers. *Spee* opened fire first—at 0617—three minutes after the British ships had sighted her. Recognition was slow but stunning.

"My God," said the skipper of *Achilles*, "it's a pocket battleship."

By rights Harwood should have been outmatched. He commanded only two light cruisers, *Ajax* and New Zealand's *Achilles*, each with eight 6-inch guns, and heavy cruiser *Exeter*, six 8-inch guns, as compared to *Graf Spee*'s six 11-inch monsters and eight 5.9-inchers. *Graf Spee*'s total weight of broadside was heavier than that of all the British cruisers combined, and she had a great range advantage. But the "Limeys" had a faster pair of heels (a 6-knot edge) and a faster rate of fire. And even slight damage to *Graf Spee* would mean the end of her marauding; with no base available and the laws of neutrality enforced, the damage could not be fully repaired except in German ports. The British, therefore, were ready to risk all to win all.

Harwood's battle plan divided his force: the light cruisers harrying one flank of the German, *Exeter* on the other quarter. *Graf Spee* concentrated first on *Exeter*; she was soon a shambles, scuppers literally running blood, bridge out of action, steering shifted aft, forward turret wrecked and its Marine gun crew virtually wiped out, bridge upper works and sides pockmarked and holed with shell fragments, fires everywhere, a heavy list to starboard. Yet for forty-five minutes the skipper, blood streaming from a face wound, conned his ruined ship from after control with a boat's compass, passing his orders to engines and after steering wheel by word-of-mouth through a chain of ten sailors. One man with both legs shot off epitomized *Exeter* when he "said on inquiry" that he was "not doing too badly under somewhat adverse circumstances." The pounding was too much; the heavy cruiser's speed gradually slowed. The entire main battery, save for one 8-inch gun served by hand, was silent, and by 0730 *Exeter* limped out of action.

Yet *Ajax* and *Achilles*, like terriers, were harrying the mastiff. Their 6-inchers stung the enemy; *Spee* shifted her fire. *Achilles* took a blow on the midriff, and at 0725 an 11-inch shell destroyed both of *Ajax*'s after turrets. A few minutes later her topmast was shot away. Harwood knew he had damaged the enemy, but he was hurt and *Spee*'s fire had not slackened. At 0740 he turned away out of range, but with his light cruisers still snapping at the heels of the enemy.

Graf Spee was more damaged than Harwood knew. Langsdorff, himself slightly wounded, took her up the Plate into neutral waters at Montevideo to try to effect repairs and to bury his dead. It was her last port. *Spee* was structurally sound and all guns were still operating, even though she was pocked on sides and bow with holes from three 8-inch and about seventeen 6-inch shell hits and splinters from near-misses. But her most serious damage was a hole in her bow above water and a hit in the control tower. She counted thirty-six dead, fifty-nine wounded.

Despite German pleas, Uruguayan authorities insisted that *Graf Spee* leave port within ninety-six hours or be interned. Langsdorff was given *carte blanche* by Berlin. His decision was a hard one; complete repairs within the time limit were impossible. His galley was wrecked, he could serve no hot food, and he did not think temporary repairs made by the ship's company were adequate to make the ship seaworthy. Off the Plate on the horizon loomed the top hamper of battle-scarred *Ajax* and *Achilles*, joined on December 14 by heavy cruiser *Cumberland*, which had steamed hard from the Falkland Islands to replace *Exeter*. And clever British psychological warfare apparently persuaded Langsdorff that an aircraft carrier, the battle cruiser *Renown*, and other more powerful warships were also nearby.

In the evening dusk of December 17, just before the deadline, *Spee* weighed anchor for the last time. The three British ships off the coast cleared for action, but in shoal water, at 1956, *Graf Spee* died— her back broken, her stout plates shattered—her "main-mast collapsed like a stalk of corn before a scythe," blown up by her own crew.

Langsdorff saw to his men, attended the funeral for his dead, and amidst a forest of stiff-armed Nazi salutes raised his hand to his cap brim in the salute of the old Imperial German Navy. He followed his ship in death on December 20—a bullet wound in his head.

The British toll: *Exeter*, sixty-one dead, twenty-three wounded; *Ajax* and *Achilles*, eleven dead, several wounded.[58]

In the North Atlantic *Deutschland* had even sparser pickings than *Graf Spee*. The raider, with engine trouble, had been recalled to Germany, slipping through the British blockade aided by mists and darkness in early November. Her toll: only two ships, one of them an American freighter *City of Flint* (a seizure which brewed up a teapot tempest in Washington).

In late November, it had seemed that bigger things were in the making in the storm-roiled seas of the Iceland-Faeroes gap. Germany's two most powerful ships, the battle cruisers *Scharnhorst* and *Gneisenau* (nine 11-inch guns; 31 knots speed, 32,000 tons), made a high-speed sortie into open waters near Iceland in attempts to dislocate shipping movements. At dusk on November 23, almost midway between the Faeroes and Iceland, *Scharnhorst* sank with ease His Majesty's Ship *Rawalpindi*, an armed auxiliary cruiser with four 6-inch guns (formerly a merchant liner), in a brief fourteen-minute action. The battered liner, literally blown apart, went down with her flag flying, and with most of her crew (twenty-one were picked up by *Scharnhorst*). She scored one hit. The two battle cruisers, aided by a wild gale and low visibility, eluded frantic British search and returned safely to Wilhelmshaven on November 27.

The "Winter War"

With a reverberation felt round the world, bombs from Soviet aircraft fell on Finnish Helsinki and Viipuri on November 30, heralding a new and confusing war. There was no declaration. Moscow, once again, callously vitiated a non-aggression pact. But there had been warning; the Finns were mobilized and ready. The collapse of Poland and the Soviet threats to Estonia, Latvia, and Lithuania were accompanied and followed, as early as October, by Russian pressure upon Finland. Moscow demanded cession of several Finnish islands in the Gulf of Finland, the lease of a naval base on the Finnish mainland to Russia, the cession of a wide strip of the Karelian Isthmus—approach route and land-bridge from Helsinki to Leningrad—in order to push the Leningrad defenses 38 kilometers further to the west, and other concessions. The Finns negotiated, but Stalin soon tipped his hand. He was anxious about the security of the ancient capital of Leningrad and the sea approaches through the Gulf. "To be sure," he told the Finns on October 14, "we have good relations with Germany, but everything in this world can change."[59]

The Finns, a stout people, proud and independent, would have none of it even though Baron Carl Gustaf von Mannerheim, "father" of their country, urged concessions, knowing that Finnish valor could impose delay but not defeat.

The Russian attack was massive but ill-prepared. Unlike the flat plains of Poland, Finland was armored by nature, a land consisting entirely of natural obstacles. Mannerheim had mobilized some 300,000 to 400,000 men, many of them behind a cleverly sited and well-camouflaged but discontinuous line of fortifications (chiefly machine-gun bunkers) commanding the 70-mile-wide neck of the Karelian Isthmus between the Gulf and Lake Ladoga.[60] Lightly armed troops, equipped with skis and snowshoes and well trained for fighting in lake regions and dense forests, patrolled the vast, sparsely populated wilderness north of Lake Ladoga to the strategic port of Petsamo, a Finnish enclave between Norway and Russian Murmansk on the Arctic Ocean.

Moscow apparently anticipated that the terror bombing of Finnish cities, a naval bombardment of Hangö and other ports, activities by Finnish Communists, and a great show of force would call what the Kremlin seemingly interpreted as a Finnish bluff. Some half a million Russians, ultimately increased to more than 1 million (including all supporting forces), had been ranged on the Finnish frontiers.

These were organized into four armies, roughly equivalent to the Western Army corps in size: the Seventh on the Karelian Isthmus in the south; the Eighth, north of Lake Ladoga; the Ninth in the Kandalaksha sector; and the Fourteenth along the Arctic coast. A fifth Army was ultimately added and the ground forces were supported by about 3,000 planes and 1,500 tanks.

The Russians apparently anticipated only token resistance. There were numerous bands, ready for triumphal marches, and propaganda units. Moscow established a puppet Finnish Communist government on the frontier and counted upon a Communist version of Fifth Column techniques, or internal uprisings.

They had a rude awakening, softened only by some minor initial successes. Soviet forces seized some of the Gulf of Finland islands, evacuated by the Finns, pushed deep through the forests and increasing cold toward Suomussalmi and the only rail line linking Finland and Sweden around the Gulf of Bothnia, and captured ice-free Petsamo in the north and the nearby undefended Finnish nickel mine at Salmijarvi.

But the bands did not play. The few Finnish Communist Fifth Columnists were quickly jailed, and on the Karelian Isthmus troops of the Leningrad military district marched to their deaths. The first Soviet attacks on the Mannerheim positions were disastrous. ". . . In the initial fighting in December . . . the Russians would advance in close formation, singing, and even hand in hand, against the Finnish minefields, apparently indifferent to the explosions and the accurate fire of the defenders. . . ." One attacking wave after another was "mown down to the last man by a few well-placed automatic weapons. . . . The fatalistic submission which characterized the infantry was astonishing. . . ."[61]

In Karelia, the main communications "avenue" into Finland, the Russians seized a few lightly defended miles of frontier territory; but they battered in vain against the Mannerheim Line, the few penetrations swiftly sealed off and regained by Finnish counterattacks. And in retreat they left behind windrows of dead, and writhing wounded soon to die.

Further north in the forests, the initial Soviet successes turned to grisly nightmares as the Finns—harassing and retreating—chivvied and finally cut the Soviet lines of communications through the dense birchwood forests and the deepening snow. The *Bielaja Smert* or "White Death" (the Finnish Commandos on skis with white camouflage uniforms) were everywhere, invisible yet omnipresent, using their small unit *motti* and *sissi* tactics of harassing the enemy, severing his supply lines, and cutting him up into small encirclements. North of Lake Ladoga, the Finns, toward year's end, sent the Russians reeling back in disorderly retreat toward the captured Finnish rail town of Suojarvi. Then—aided by snow and biting cold as well as time and distance—they lured, cut off, and ultimately surrounded at the village of Suomussalmi the 163rd Russian Division, recently transferred without winter uniforms from the Ukraine's broad plains to the bitter cold of the dark Finnish forests.

The Russians lay in the snow in 40-below-zero temperatures, froze, and died; campfires meant sure death from lurking Finnish snipers. The Finns knew all the tricks of winter woodsmen: "They lay underground as comfortable as any hibernating animal, in dugouts lined with skins and roofed with birch logs . . . [each] with a Finnish

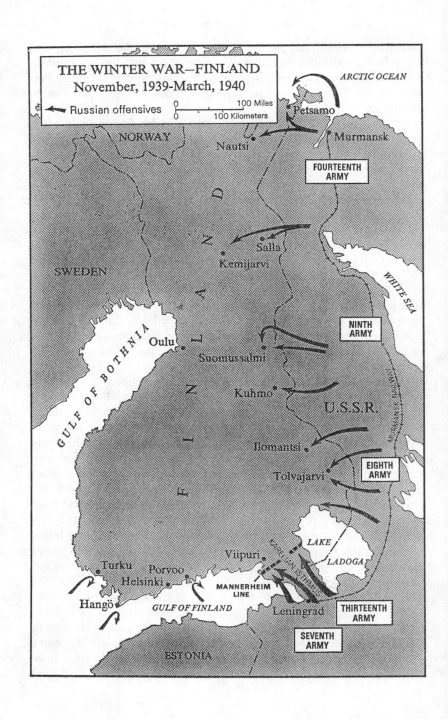

stove, designed to burn wood without a spark or a trace of smoke."

It was still and silent death: "Under the blazing stars the trees were motionless. The whole world was as lifeless as the moon and as cold as its unsunned side."[62]

The 163rd Russian Division, enfeebled, and encircled by the Finnish Commandos and frontier guards, was brought to final bay by the Finnish 9th Division. The Russians, instead of cutting their own losses, sent another division—the 44th Motorized—reeling across the frontier to its doom in a region of few roads and deep snowdrifts. It got to within 5 miles of the beleaguered 163rd at Suomussalmi; then, bogged down, was in turn cut off and surrounded. On Christmas Eve, while baubles hung in the Finnish dugouts deep beneath the snow, the Soviet troops with frozen trigger fingers, frost-blackened toes, and cold-marbled noses tried vainly to cut their way out of the white death trap. By the end of December, as the Finnish 9th Division attacked the encircled Russians, the 163rd Division had been annihilated. The 44th Motorized had not long to live. Meanwhile at Tolvajarvi, on December 12, two Finnish regiments almost completely destroyed the Russian 139th Division, and, using their "bundle of sticks" or *motti* tactics, repulsed with heavy losses the Soviet 75th Division.

Suomussalmi, Tolvajarvi, and other battles in the snow created a profound and misleading impression in the West. Photographs of the scenes of the white death—Russian cadavers rigid in the snow, an arm above the implacable blanket of white caught in the violent contortion of death, the very blood of dying frozen in red stains—provoked both scorn at the Soviet ineptitude which had sent so many men to their deaths and sympathy for Finland's 4 million people fighting off a Goliath of 200 million.

The Soviet attack upon Finland, which had ground to a stalemate at the end of 1939, confused and complicated the issues and policies of war as well as political sympathies. The Finns had long been regarded as part of Western Europe's culture, even an *avant garde* of that culture, as indeed they regarded themselves, and they were greatly admired as a people in England, France, and the United States. Finland's few emigrants had won her many friends, and Mannerheim was a name known and respected in the West as well as in Finland.

The Soviet attack, preceded by the cynical Russian participation in the partitioning of Poland and the Kremlin's moves into the Baltic countries, had tremendously angered the democracies.

On December 14, Russia was expelled from the League of Nations in the last major gesture and perhaps the most fitting of the League's futile history. But it was gesture only. By year's end there was talk of aid—money, men, munitions—to "gallant Finland," and large segments of public opinion regarded both Stalin's Russia and Hitler's Germany as common enemies.

The Western Hemisphere, led by the United States, reacted to the guns of Europe with an unprecedented proclamation: the establishment of a "Neutrality Zone" about 300 miles in width around the Western Hemisphere (minus Canada and European colonies). This was clearly in contravention of the doctrine of "Freedom of the Seas" which the United States had always supported. But it was only the first move in "the bizarre history of American neutrality," and it was followed on November 4, 1939, by repeal of the arms embargo provisions of the neutrality acts, and provision for what became known as "Cash and Carry"—the first step in the establishment of the huge industrial capacity of the United States as the "arsenal of democracy."

The war, as 1939 came to a close, was still a European war. True, great ships had foundered on the high seas far from Europe's coasts, and the restrictions of trade, economic warfare, preemptive buying of strategic materials, and all the supporting phalanx of policies that comprise modern war had been felt around the world. But only European countries had been directly affected; one—Poland—had died; three—the Baltic states—were dying; and on the Western Front from the Alps to the sea, the armies lay quiescent. Even in Finland, the ill-matched antagonists were catching their breaths, regrouping. In the calm before the storm history was waiting.

II

THE YEAR OF PERIL
1940

The year's beginning gave little hint of the convulsions soon to come. In the West's capitals the New Year brought frustration, impatience, uncertain groping—but none of the horrors so long anticipated. Both the popular press and many of the "experts" had dramatized and magnified the foreboding predictions of the Italian general, Giulio Douhet. When the war opened, London expected devastating air bombardments with a toll of more than half a million dead. It did not happen. Yet between 1,250,000 and 2 million women and children—many from big city slums—had been evacuated from England's great cities to the countryside. And now, as the "phony war" continued on the Western Front, the irritations and dangers of the blackout, the separation of families, the frictions of evacuation, and the relaxation of nerves that had been stretched to bowstring tension led to national letdown and carping criticism.

King George VI, never a man to "shrink from duty," expressed the mood of his people in a broadcast to his threatened empire on Christmas Day, 1939:

A new year is at hand. We cannot tell what it will bring. . . . I said to the man who stood at the Gate of Year, "Give me a light that I may tread safely into the unknown." And he replied, "Go out into the darkness, and put your hand into the Hand of God."[1]

In Berlin, too, the war seemed unreal, its chief manifestations "cold, and a coal shortage."

William L. Shirer, the American correspondent, noted in his diary "more drunkenness on the Kurfürstendamn last night (New Year's Eve) than I've ever seen in Berlin." But the attempt at an alcoholic nirvana was accompanied by a comfortable dogmatism about Germany's power. "I haven't met a German yet who isn't absolutely certain [of victory]."[2]

The behind-the-looking-glass atmosphere would not last long. Already men were killing one another. The "phony war" ended swiftly and the tide of conflict rose abruptly to the flood.

The gallant Finns were forced to sue for peace; Denmark and Norway felt the blast of *Blitzkrieg;* Belgium and The Netherlands were overrun; France died. Winston Churchill took the helm of power in Britain and rallied his beleaguered countrymen in the darkest days of empire to "fight on the beaches . . . to fight in the streets"; Fighter Command of the Royal Air Force—the few to whom the many owed so much—won a decisive battle in the skies. Italy entered the war and the Tripartite Axis, Rome-Berlin-Tokyo, was confirmed; Mussolini, hungry for glory, jealous of the conquests of Hitler, invaded Greece, sent his troops into British Somaliland, and across the Libyan frontier into Egypt. An English general named Wavell, in quick riposte, routed the hapless Italians in a desert offensive, and at sea, the Italian Fleet was decimated by guns, bombs, and torpedoes in duels with the British off Calabria, near Crete, and at Taranto. Russia, girding for what was to come and emboldened by Hitler's preoccupation with the West, completed her seizure of Lithuania, Latvia, Estonia, and part of Rumania; while Carol, Rumania's playboy King, abdicated under Nazi pressure to live out a futile life with his red-haired mistress Magda Lupescu in nostalgic grandiloquence near Lisbon. In Asia the dark clouds gathered as Japan occupied parts of French Indochina, and Washington embargoed the export of all steel and scrap shipments to Tokyo.

The United States, divided in bitter debate, moved, crablike, toward war. Franklin Delano Roosevelt was elected, despite charges of dictatorship, to an unprecedented third term, defeating a personable man named Wendell Willkie.

The year 1940 would be one of spreading fury.

3

War in the North—Scandinavia

Finland—"The Winter War"

In the cold forests and deep snows of the northland, the static war of the Western Front seemed far away—even surrealistic—to those who in Finland suffered, fought, and perished. The Winter War was grim, bitter, and unrelenting: a war against nature and against man. In December, Finnish familiarity with the environment and terrain, the acclimatization of their troops to deep snows and extreme cold, their superior equipment and far better mobility and tactics plus skillful leadership and undaunted courage, had resulted in victory after victory. Again, in January, the hapless Russian *moujiks* froze and died.

Near Suomussalmi, the Finnish 9th Division completed from January 1 to 8 the destruction of the 44th Motorized Division, which had bogged down in deep snow. The Finns cut the division into small units, encircled each, and aided by a relentless winter (colder than for many years) annihilated it. Something like 28,000 Russians were killed in December and January in the Suomussalmi fighting or froze to death; some 1,300 frostbitten prisoners were taken, along with tanks, artillery, small arms, and divisional equipment. The Finns lost about 900 killed, almost 2,000 wounded. Weeks later, visiting journalists saw the carnage:

Lying where they had fallen . . . kneeling, or even standing upright, their arms raised to the skies, were the bodies of frozen Russian soldiers. From the moment when they met their death time and decay had been annihilated for them by the force of bitter cold. Their faces . . . were not quite natural, the blood was too blue beneath the skin; but otherwise their expressions seemed to register still the final emotion which died with them so many days ago.[3]

For Moscow, January 1940 was a month of reassessment, regrouping, and resupply. Blooded and surprised, the Russian colossus drew back, reorganized his command, revised his strategy, brought up his reserves.

Marshal Kliment E. Voroshilov, who had been, since 1925, People's Commissar of Defense, a military incompetent, was nominally the overall Commander-in-Chief. But Marshal S. K. Timoshenko (like Voroshilov, an "old Bolshevik" and trusted Stalin subordinate) wielded the sledgehammer as "Front" Commander, and after the Finnish War Voroshilov was shunted aside. Another Soviet Army— the Thirteenth—was echeloned into line on the Karelian Isthmus (key to the heart of Finland), next to the battered Seventh Army. The ancillary offensives through the forest and lakes north of Lake Ladoga were largely abandoned; masses of artillery were concentrated instead on the isthmus, and the Communists prepared to bull their way through the Mannerheim Line by sheer mass and power.

The offensive opened on February 1, with at least thirty Russian divisions in line across the isthmus, driving hard against eight to ten

Finnish divisions. In contrast to the December attacks, the Soviet troops were now supported by tremendous artillery barrages and air bombardment. In one twenty-four-hour period an observer estimated that the Russians pounded the Finnish positions with some 300,000 shells; concrete pillboxes were blown up; dugouts became rubble. The attacks were incessant and unending—sometimes four or five a day. Hordes of Slavic manpower pushed ever westward, then ebbed eastward, broken by Finnish fire, leaving behind them along the high-water mark of their advance the bloody bodies stacked across the snow.

The main thrust point of the Soviet drive was the Summa sector, and here, at last, the sheer weight and ruthlessness of numbers began to tell. Until February 11, the Finns hurled back, with mounting slaughter, attack after attack. But between the 11th and the 13th the unending battering snapped a link in the Mannerheim Line; at Summa, the Russians made a breakthrough.

The Mannerheim Line was sited to cover the most defensible part of the peninsula; back of it there was easier going. The Finns were tired. Some of them, groggy from the ceaseless bombardment, were walking automatons. Mannerheim had committed most of his reserves; there was little left. And the Russians had now concentrated some forty-five divisions against Finland's nine.

The breakthrough at Summa forced a fighting withdrawal of the entire southwestern flank of the Finnish defenses. By early March, the retreating Finns had bent back their isthmus front to the vicinity of the important port city of Viipuri (Viborg), on the Gulf of Finland. Between March 1 and 4, elements of several Soviet divisions had outflanked the fortified land positions by crossing the thick ice of Viipuri Bay, and the Hammer and Sickle was now firmly planted on the main road to Helsinki in the nexus of Finland's heartland communications. It was the end, and the realistic Finns knew it.

A pragmatic people, they had taken soundings as early as January in the tricky diplomatic waters of Europe to determine the prospects of a negotiated peace. Germany had been the intermediary, but the results were negative. The time was not propitious. The Russian defeats in December 1939 and January 1940 had put Moscow's prestige on the line. Military balance must be redressed.

But at the same time Western sympathy, and what London and Paris interpreted as Western self-interest, became a factor. In England Winston Churchill as First Lord of the Admiralty expressed the British opinion:

Finland alone—in danger of death, superb, sublime Finland—shows what free men can do. . . . Nothing could be sadder than that this splendid northern race should at the end be destroyed and in the face of incredible odds should fall into a slavery worse than death. . . .[4]

In Washington, the U.S. Congress provided $30 million for non-military aid. The strong swing of public opinion coincided with *realpolitik*. The dependence of Germany upon the Swedish sources of high-grade iron ore near Luleå was the basic military rationale for the Allied plans for aid. An expeditionary force sent to Finland, via the railroad that linked Norwegian Narvik to Luleå, could help the Finns in their gallant fight against the Russians, and at the same time seize the mines and railroad and deny the Swedish iron ore to Germany, thus tightening the blockade.

From December 1939 into March of 1940, Paris and London made fanciful and somewhat grandiose plans for an expeditionary force variously projected as 6,000 to 57,000 men as the tide of public sympathy for Finland rolled to the flood. But they were paper plans; Sweden adamantly, and Norway somewhat less so, announced their opposition to any military landing by any foreign power on their shores. Both countries permitted limited aid to transit their soil, and Sweden sold large quantities of arms and ammunition to Finland. Foreign volunteer battalions were openly recruited in London, Sweden, and the United States; but, in the event, only two reinforced battalions of Swedish volunteers and one company of Finnish-Americans reached Finland shortly before the end.

After the Karelian breakthrough, the Western plans became larger, the promised deadlines were advanced, and the Russian conditions for peace grew tougher. At this moment in history, Finland occupied the catbird's seat. The war seemed to pivot around her. The two great authoritarian dictatorships—Russia and Germany—were regarded as uneasy allies, but allies just the same; the West thought the forging of a common front against both was imperative to their ultimate purpose (in retrospect, who now can view this as mistaken?). The Winter War had confused the issues, making it difficult to determine the true enemy.[5]

But the Finns are tough, physically and morally. They faced their moment of truth—a moment upon which the future history of Europe might hinge. They assessed the unpreparedness of the West, the strong neutralist sentiment in the United States, and the fearful caution of Sweden and Norway. The issue was clarified in Helsinki; if Finland was to live, there must be peace—at the Russian price.

It was a heavy price, a harsh peace, that the Finns signed in Moscow on the evening of March 12, 1940. Finland lost the Karelian Isthmus—land-bridge and key to their country, as well as Viipuri, the important Gulf city, many industrial areas, islands and bases on the Gulf of Finland, Petsamo in the north, and areas north of Lake Ladoga. Some 10 percent of the Finnish population lost their homes, and Finland lay almost defenseless.

Yet her image was bright throughout the world. Courage in adversity breeds respect. In the Winter War, the Finns lost some 25,000 killed and missing; 43,000 wounded. The dead lie now in serried ranks in the mournful beauty of a war memorial cemetery near Helsinki, ranged in marbled tiers around a cenotaph and the grave of Baron Carl Gustaf von Mannerheim, a great captain of his time. The Winter War was, and will long remain, a Finnish hour of glory:

> . . . how can man die better
> Than facing fearful odds
> For the ashes of his fathers
> And the temples of his gods?[6]

The Communist Russian image, by contrast, had been tarnished not only morally but physically. The Russians suffered an estimated 200,000 casualties (killed, wounded, missing). A Soviet general is said to have remarked: "We have won enough ground to bury our dead."[7]

The Red Army had emerged triumphant but inept. The Soviet political miscalculation, logistical problems, strategic mistakes and tactical blunders, sophomoric leadership, and the ruthlessness of the cannon-fodder attacks and air raids against cities and civilians, generally denied it respect. Berlin, London, Washington, and Paris drew conclusions—conclusions that were in fact too sweeping. The Russian colossus was discounted. Its great leaders of World War II had not yet surfaced, its capability to learn by its mistakes was not yet fully understood. And, above all, the Russian soldier was too much disparaged.

One war had ended, yet the killing had scarcely begun.

Denmark and Norway

The geographical position of Denmark and Norway in any war between the great powers of Europe was strategic and therefore precarious. They dominated the approaches to the Baltic. They flanked the peninsula of Europe. They were cornerstones in the edifice of blockade and blockade-running. Denmark fronted the North Sea, key alike to German ports and British harbors. The deep Norwegian fjords, which gave squarely upon the Norwegian Sea and the Atlantic, offered inviting bases for submarines and surface raiders. Both countries provided air bases. From Narvik in the north, for a thousand miles to the Skagerrak, Norwegian territorial waters provided what Churchill called a "covered way"—the Indreled, or Inner Leads between the indented coasts and offshore islands. German ships, running the British blockade, could set their course for the Far Northern latitudes—region of mists and storms and low visibility—make landfall in the Inner Leads, and get home free. Around the Lofoten Islands and the North Cape curled the arduous sea routes to Murmansk and Russia's Arctic ports. And the Norwegian port of Narvik and the Inner Leads provided a sea highway for a commodity precious to Germany—iron ore. Germany had imported something like 22 million tons of iron ore in the last prewar year of 1938. The British estimated their blockade had cut off some 9 million. But at least another 9–11 million tons of high-grade ore were being shipped from the Swedish Kiruna-Gällivare mines. In the summer some of this transited the Swedish port of Luleå, and thence by ship through the Baltic, while some was shipped by railroad to Narvik and thence through the Leads to German ports. In winter when the Gulf of Bothnia was frozen and Luleå locked by ice, all of it was dependent on the Norwegian route.

Even more important than the iron ore were the economic consequences of the domination of Scandinavia by either side. Denmark was a great trading partner of England's; Norway, a major maritime nation.

To both sides Denmark and Norway were important; hence, from the outset, their neutrality was threatened. In the case of Norway, in particular, there was an internal cause for alarm. Vidkun Quisling, who would go down in history as the man whose name was synonymous with traitor, commanded a small but noisy following of Norwegian Nazis, and he got Adolf Hitler's ear. His followers did not have strength enough to usurp power, but they had power enough to rock the boat.

International law being what it is—a loose collection of generalisms, severely hedged and limited by custom, precedent, or vague agreement, and, in the event, often mangled by the politics of power—it was inevitable that sooner or later the Inner Leads would become part of the theater of war. Both sides wanted to use Norway's neutral waters to their advantage; to both sides, necessity knew no law.

The German supply ship *Altmark*, which had been paired with the pocket battleship *Graf Spee*, eluded the British blockade and reached the sheltered Leads off Trondheim on February 14. Out of sight battened down in her holds were 299 British merchant seamen, prisoners taken from the vessels sunk by the *Graf Spee*. *Altmark* was sighted by aircraft of Coastal Command on the 16th. Captain Philip L. Vian, R.N., flying his pendant in destroyer *Cossack*, established on Admiralty orders another precedent for the textbooks. On the night of February 16, he took *Cossack* into Jösing Fjord, defied and threatened Norwegian torpedo boats whose skippers had objected to this violation of Norwegian neutrality, then laid his ship alongside *Altmark* and boarded by force. Six Germans were killed, six wounded; one British seaman was shot. The prisoners in the holds answered the boarding party's shouts, "The Navy's here," with great cheers. A feat of doubtful legality, it was hailed in Britain.

More was quickly to follow.

Churchill had pressed for mining the Leads since war was declared. At length in April 1940 the fields were laid in three separate areas squarely in the shipping lanes in what were euphemistically termed "neutral" waters. The minelayers were covered by a British naval force, and British troops were embarked and ready to occupy Norwegian ports if German reactions indicated retaliation. As the long Northern winter slowly surrendered to the spring of 1940, contingency planning on both sides had envisaged surprise coups, the Allies in order to bring aid to Finland and to control the iron-ore traffic and the "covered passage" of the Leads; the Germans to protect that traffic and preserve the security of the passage. With the accession of Paul Reynaud to power in France on March 21, the planning for aggressive Allied action in Scandinavia accelerated.

Reynaud was dynamic, convincing; he had a mind that was "alert, lively, brilliant," and in the murk and mire of prewar French politics he had been right many times. But as history was to show, he was a man with defects of character; most severe of all, faced with hard alternatives he could not make up his mind.

Premier Reynaud, upon whom the fate of France chiefly rested in the final months of the Third Republic, had lived for years with Mme Hélène des Portes, a former friend of his wife . . . and when M. and Mme Paul Reynaud were invited to dine at the American Embassy, there always was a question which lady would attend. At one dinner both arrived, proving a neat protocol problem. Mme des Portes was an exceptionally determined Frenchwoman, and her frenzied political activity and her doubts about the war were the gossip of Paris. Even after war broke out, she persistently urged Reynaud and his ministers to negotiate peace with Hitler's Germany. . . .[8]

Finland's surrender in March eliminated one of the Allied Scandinavian motivations; the strategic significance of Scandinavia however still loomed large. In the event it was the Germans who moved first and swiftest in an audacious campaign that again surprised the world, although it was not without warning.

The British minelaying expedition on April 8 had been preceded by clear signs of German naval activity in the Baltic ports and Heligoland Bight; a warning had even come from Copenhagen on April 4 of an impending Nazi attack on Norway. But the British Admiralty guessed wrong; Berlin's boldness was then novel to the world. Except for convoy covering forces, most of the British Fleet—saving *Renown* and fourteen destroyers protecting the minelayers—was in port at Scapa Flow on April 7 when large German convoys, heavily escorted, started moving northward up the Norwegian coast. That night the fleet put to sea and shaped a course far to the north to cut off German raiders, but too far seaward to intercept the German invasion convoys. "There was thus," the British official history comments, "a complete failure to realise the significance of the available intelligence—let alone to translate it into vigorous and early counteraction."

In Germany, as in England, the German Navy was the first to perceive and then to emphasize the strategic importance of Scandinavia. From suggestions in the first month of war called to Hitler's attention by Grand Admiral Erich Raeder on October 10, 1939, grew the plans for "Operation *Weser*," the Nazi occupation of Denmark and Norway. For a few months the Fuehrer's preoccupation with a projected campaign in the West obscured *Weserübung*, but on February 19, infuriated by the *Altmark* incident, Hitler told General Alfred Jodl, Chief of the Operations Staff of the German armed forces, to "equip ships. Put units in readiness." On March 1, he issued a formal directive for conquest, stressing the importance of surprise.

And surprise it was—despite the intelligence warnings. The successful conquest of Norway was dependent primarily upon shipping, and the German Navy and the Merchant Marine had to transport the bulk of the invasion forces to Norway's principal ports—some of them 1,000 miles from German harbors—in the face of vastly superior British seapower. The Luftwaffe would fly cover over the Skagerrak and within range of its bases, but in the decisive first phase—the seizure of ports and the establishment of airheads—Norway was primarily a naval show, the only one during the war which was fundamentally dependent upon the German Navy.

"*Weser*" was built around simultaneous assaults upon Denmark and the Danish islands by land and sea, and upon Oslo, the Norwegian capital; Kristiansand, commanding the Skagerrak; Stavanger; Bergen; and Trondheim and Narvik by sea, supplemented within range by airborne transport. Two divisions and one motorized brigade were assigned to the Danish conquest. General Nikolaus von Falkenhorst, his initial force of approximately 150,000 soldiers protected and transported by virtually the entire German Navy, 800 combat aircraft, and 20 transport planes of the Luftwaffe, commanded the troops assigned to Norway. The objective was to beat the British to the punch.

The Danish Army consisted simply of palace soldiers, picturesque to tourists but useless on the battlefield; the Norwegian forces, although of tougher fiber, numbered less than 15,000 regulars, poorly armed.

In the murk of the Northern dawn at about 7 A.M. on April 8, a British destroyer, *Glowworm* (Lieutenant Commander G. Broadmead Roope commanding), was groping northward in heavy seas west-nor'west of Trondheim, following the track of battle cruiser *Renown* toward Vest Fjord off Narvik. *Renown* and her destroyer escorts were covering the British minelayers blocking the Leads. *Glowworm* had fallen out of formation to search for a man overboard. Suddenly, she blundered on a German destroyer, part of the covering expedition for the Narvik landings. It was wild weather and only two salvos from *Glowworm*'s 4.7-inchers were fired before the enemy destroyer disappeared in sea blur. But before the ratings had been stood down to the mess decks for breakfast, a second German destroyer—*Bernd von Arnim*—was sighted.

"The wild rolling of the ship, the seas tumbling along the decks and the spray flying up to blur telescopes and binoculars made shooting difficult. . . .[The German] plunged and rolled so wildly that her superstructure was damaged and she narrowly escaped capsizing. . . ."[9]

Heavy cruiser *Hipper*, part of the Narvik covering force, and mounting 8-inch guns, answered *Bernd von Arnim*'s call for help. *Hipper* loomed suddenly out of the clutter of mist and dark and tumbling waters at point-blank range. *Glowworm*'s skipper got off a contact report as *Hipper*'s shells sieved the destroyer's light plating. Then, at bay, *Glowworm* launched torpedoes—none hit—made smoke, and finally turned to ram. Her bow, crumpled like tin plate, struck *Hipper* just abaft her starboard hawse hole and raked and ground down the cruiser's hull, wrenching away about 130 feet of armor belt and the cruiser's starboard torpedo tubes. *Glowworm* was finished. Burning furiously, she wallowed in heavy seas until at about 9:00 A.M. she blew up. Thirty-eight of her crew were picked up by the Germans; Roope, her skipper, reached *Hipper*'s side in the icy water, clutched vainly at a rope, was swept away and drowned; he lives in British tradition with a posthumous Victoria Cross.

The chance contact should have been a clue to Nazi intentions. But it was muffed. And slow communications and faulty interpretation flawed another chance. In the Skagerrak at noon on April 8, Polish submarine *Orzel*, which had escaped from her country's débacle, stopped and sank German transport *Rio de Janeiro* after crew and passengers had taken to the boats. Norwegian sailors picking up the survivors discovered German soldiers in uniform, who boasted they had been en route to Bergen with guns and transport. Reuters, the news agency, reported the event. The Norwegian government did nothing; the British Admiralty and the British Fleet were still preoccupied with the fear that heavy German naval forces might be preparing a breakout into the Atlantic. History's opportunities rarely knock twice.

In the faint light of a stormy dawn on the 9th, at the time when German assault transports were making their landfall at assigned ports, the blind groping again resulted in a brief chance contact—this time north of the Arctic Circle off the Lofoten Islands dominating the entrance to the Vest Fjord and Narvik. British battle cruiser *Renown*, with six 15-inch guns, one destroyer in company, stumbled amid gigantic seas upon German battle cruisers *Scharnhorst* and *Gneisenau* (each with nine 11-inch guns), part of the Narvik covering force. So huge was the seaway, so wild the wind, that the leviathans had slowed to quarter speeds. Even so, when *Renown* opened fire at 19,000 yards, she fired "at a bobbing cork." All the more remarkable, then, that both sides scored hits. *Renown* took two heavy shells—no vital damage; *Gneisenau* lost her foretop and fire control equipment, took a splinter through the fore turret, and a third hit in her AA battery. Vice Admiral Günther Lütjens, the German commander, took his ships bow-on into the towering seas at 28 knots—green water battening aboard with every plunge, wracking the ships' frames, threatening to wrench the forward turrets from their barbettes. *Renown*, slowing, then speeding up as the sea dictated, fell behind, sighted the Germans again—a brief flurry—and by 6:15 A.M. *Scharnhorst* and *Gneisenau* had disappeared in the wild waters of the Arctic.

The chances were forever gone; in the meantime, the German invaders had made their landings.

The landings were covered and preceded on the night of April 8 by a heavy Nazi bombing of Scapa Flow, which produced more sound and fury than damage (the fleet was at sea), and on April 9, another *Blitzkrieg* started. Danes pedaling to work on their bicycles in Copenhagen encountered what they at first thought were movie extras—a column of German soldiers marching toward the Royal Palace. The palace guard fired a few shots; the Germans answered. King Christian ordered the shooting stopped and Denmark capitulated to a virtually bloodless conquest.

The situation in Norway was not much different. Once ashore, the Germans knew that at best the Norwegians could impose delay, ensure harassment, but had no hope of victory. Speed was the essential. They must secure the principal ports and command all the main airfields and communication routes before the British could react. And speed and surprise were achieved despite the fact that, in Raeder's words, the "operation [was] contrary to all the principles . . . of naval warfare."

The initial assault forces were all small—nowhere more than 2,000 men—and they were transported primarily in warships or hidden below decks in merchant vessels, ore carriers, or coal ships. Quisling and his Fifth Columnists helped a little, particularly in Oslo and Narvik. But "if there had not been a single quisling in Norway the country would still have been overwhelmed . . . it would have taken longer—but not much longer."[10]

Stares of bewilderment and amazement greeted the small Nazi assault forces, which were quickly reinforced by air and sea. Parachutists dropped from the sky, and transport planes landed with reckless haste in an unending runway parade at Oslo and Stavanger. Within some twelve hours, on April 9, every major airfield in Norway and all of the principal ports were under German control, in one of the most audacious, stunning, and successful operations of the war. By sky and sea, the vanguard of the assault troops from some three divisions (163rd, 69th, 3rd Mountain) was being rapidly reinforced and supplied; soon it had been augmented by men and matériel from four more divisions (the 181st, 196th, the 214th, and the 2nd Mountain)—later reinforced by other units.

Nevertheless, the German Navy suffered its most grievous losses of the war.

In Oslo Fjord, first blood was shed on the night of April 8, when the German convoy was challenged at the entrance by a lone Norwegian patrol boat in a brave but futile gesture. The Norwegian spread an alarm to which Oslo paid scant attention, then died—with its captain—under German machine-gun fire. Part way up the fjord two Norwegian forts, designed to guard a minefield which had never been laid, were taken from the rear by German landing parties; Horten, the naval base, was surrendered, with minor resistance, at 7:30 A.M. on the 9th after threat of remorseless bombing from the air.

But Oscarborg saved Norwegian honor and imposed delay upon the German seaborne attack on Oslo. This old fort, built during the Crimean War, sported three 280 mm. Krupp-model 1905 guns and some torpedo tubes, which commanded the narrowest neck of the channel, 10 miles from Oslo. *Blücher*, the newest German cruiser (8-inch guns) was fired, torpedoed, and sunk with a loss of about 1,000 men, including most of the staff of the commanding general of the Oslo assault. *Lützow* (formerly *Deutschland*) was damaged (the next day she was torpedoed and badly damaged off Denmark by a British submarine). The German ships hastily moved out of range, debarking their troops on the east side of the fjord to push toward Oslo by land. Oscarborg was reduced by gunfire and air bombardment but for twenty-four hours it had checked the seaborne assault.

In the final reckoning this made only one difference. At 8:00 A.M. Fornebu Airfield at Oslo had been assaulted by airborne troops; Norwegian AA guns shot down three German aircraft and damaged five. There was a mix-up; the transports landed before the paratroopers, but the Germans compensated by boldness and speed; they put their heavily loaded planes down on the runway almost wingtip to wingtip and nose to tail, regardless of damage. Kjeller Military Airfield nearby was taken almost without opposition, and the airheads gained were built up rapidly during the day. Nor was real opposition possible. Nineteen Curtiss Pursuit planes, the only relatively modern fighters in the country, lay in crates shipped from America, still unassembled.

By noon some six companies reinforced—about 1,500 men—had been landed, and the capital of Norway—population 300,000 people—had surrendered as an "open," or non-combat, city. The delay sufficed to give the bewildered Norwegian government time to order evacuation of Oslo by some key government agencies, and King Haakon VII escaped, ultimately to London, to become another monarch in exile.

Kristiansand and its satellite objectives, Egersund and Arendal, fell quickly; heavy fog and Norwegian guns imposed but slight delay. The only triumph reaped from burgeoning disaster was the sinking on the evening of the 9th by British submarine *Truant* of lighter cruiser *Karlsruhe*, which—her escort duties completed—was standing out of Kristiansand. Stavanger also fell in hours, first to German parachutists, then to follow-up seaborne forces, which lost to a Norwegian torpedo boat one "coal-boat," loaded to the gunwales with war equipment. With Stavanger went Sola, the best and most strategically located airfield in Norway, and with it, too, went most of the Allied hopes of successful resistance to the German blitz.

Bergen and Trondheim, the second and third largest of Norway's cities, both fortified, also fell in confusion and surprise with scant resistance. Cruiser *Königsberg* was damaged at Bergen by shore batteries; holed up in port, hurt and with engine trouble, she was sunk the next day, April 10, by British naval aircraft, flying from extreme range from their base in the Orkneys. "The first major ship of either side to be destroyed by attacks from the air," it was a portent. A German destroyer was beached at Trondheim and resistance at the city's airfield proved irrelevant, as the resourceful Germans "immediately improvised an airstrip on the ice for their transport planes. . . ."

Far to the north, strategic Narvik also fell quickly. German destroyers forced the Vest Fjord and steamed into harbor, where they torpedoed two old 4,000-ton Norwegian coastal defense ships (with 300 men lost). German troops ashore marched into the town's market square in driving snow at 5:00 A.M. They bore signs in Norwegian: "Be calm. Take things easily. We come to help you against the English."

The Narvik seizure—strategically important because it was the railhead for Sweden's iron ore—was helped, though only slightly, by the defection of a Norwegian apostate officer, a follower of Quisling. It was nevertheless audacious and bold. Narvik is some 600 airline miles north of Oslo; there were no reliable land communications between the port and the rest of Norway. It was too remote from German bases for air transport, and the assault force of some 2,000 men, under Major General (later, promoted to general) Eduard Dietl, was isolated save by sea.

* * *

The world was astounded—the Allies confused, Norway stunned. In some twelve hours, despite vastly superior British seapower, the Hitler blitz techniques had conquered two more countries.

Public reaction in Britain, France, and the United States was bitter, and the wounded British lion laid about what should have been its domain of waters with fierce reaction.

Narvik was first. Captain B. A. W. Warburton-Lee in flotilla leader *Hardy*, followed by *Hunter* and *Havoc*, with *Hotspur* and *Hostile* patrolling the sea approaches, groped his way in appalling weather at dawn high water on April 10 into Narvik Harbor. Five larger and more modern German destroyers were still in port, two refueling from one tanker. Warburton-Lee, following the audacious precepts of Nelson's great friend and flag captain for whom his flagship was named, achieved complete surprise. The little British ships fired fifteen torpedoes and laid about them with their 4.7-inch guns; the heavier Germans (1,800 tons, five 5-inch guns) were stunned, believing they were being attacked by aircraft. The German flotilla leader *Wilhelm Heidekamp* was badly damaged, and later capsized; her commodore was killed. The back of another German, *Anton Schmidt*, was broken; she sank in halves. The three other enemy ships (*Lüdermann, Künna, Raedel*) were badly knocked about. *Hotspur*, called in from her patrol station, sank two merchant ships. Then all five "Limeys" had another crack at the crowded harbor and four more German merchant ships went down.

It was still only 6:00 A.M.; the clouds of smoke and fire rose high above the snowscape. But, withdrawing down Ofotfjord, the British flotilla was bottled between the five other German destroyers, which (along with the five in Narvik Harbor) had comprised the German escort force.

Warburton-Lee ordered: "Keep on engaging enemy!"

It was his final command. The heavier German guns soon took their toll. A shell burst swept *Hardy*'s bridge; steam lines were severed; on fire forward, she was beached in a smoking, fiery pall. The survivors and wounded, numbed by icy water, struggled ashore; Warburton-Lee died on the beach, posthumous V.C. *Hunter* and *Hotspur* were hit and collided; *Hunter* sank; *Hotspur*, riddled by seven 5-inchers, was nursed out of action by her two remaining sisters. The Germans, wounded and short of fuel and ammunition, broke off the battle; the British, hurt but triumphant, withdrew from the fjord, sinking on the way the German ammunition ship *Rauenfels*.

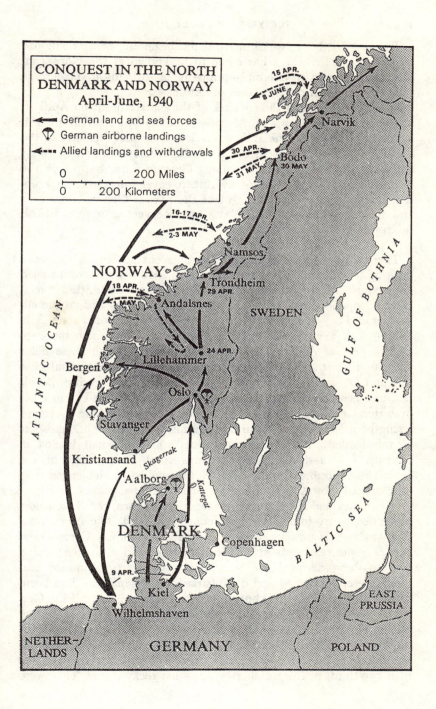

The first battle of Narvik marked the beginning of a two-month sea-air-land melee which has come to be known as the Norwegian campaign. It was an attempt—primarily by Britain—to rake some coals of triumph from the ashes of defeat.

What had begun in the icy dark of the Narvik fjords on April 10 was finished three days later. Abortive bombing by aircraft from British carrier *Furious* on the 12th was followed on the afternoon of the 13th by a bold attack by British battleship *Warspite* (15-inch guns) and nine destroyers on the remaining German ships, trapped in the Ofotfjord and Narvik Harbor by British naval forces off the Lofotens, gathering for the kill. Eight of the newest German destroyers and one submarine were sunk[11] at a cost of severe damage to British destroyers *Eskimo* and *Cossack*.

There followed in Norway and its adjacent sea and air space a bruising series of land, sea, and air battles, with the antagonists each desperately strengthening and building up their committed forces. Despite superior British naval strength, the Germans had all the advantages. They controlled the largest field in Norway at Sola (Stavanger), 325 miles from British bases in Scotland; also the large Danish field at Aallborg, and Fornebu at Oslo. From these fields German aircraft achieved air superiority over south and central Norway and Denmark, dominated the Skagerrak and the eastern North Sea, and even challenged the dominance of the British Home Fleet in waters it once had sailed supreme. Relentlessly, the Germans strengthened their Norwegian bridgeheads. Day and night, transport aircraft loaded with men, ammunition, and equipment landed in Norway. Day and night, supply ships crept under cover of the Luftwaffe to southern and central Norwegian ports, challenged only intermittently by Allied submarines and occasional planes.

What they had failed to win by superiority at sea, the British now proceeded to try to achieve by inferiority on land. The Allied reaction was swift, if unwise. A sizable Allied Expeditionary Force—some 14,000 troops, elements of a British division and a French Alpine division—long destined for Scandinavia had been assembled and briefed, even embarked and disembarked. Its original aim had been, first, to aid the Finns and control Sweden's iron ore; then, if the Germans reacted to the mining of the Leads, to beat Berlin to the punch. Far larger forces—two more French Alpine divisions, units of the Foreign Legion, Poles and British regulars and territorials, totaling almost 60,000 men—were also earmarked for Norway, but less than two-thirds of this number ever saw her rocky shores. They were too late. The Germans in the first week poured 24,000 troops into Norway and the Allies were outnumbered and outgunned from the start.

Piecemeal but rapidly, the Allied force was transported to three widely separated landings on the Norwegian coast: at Narvik (April 15), Namsos, north of Trondheim (April 17); and Åndalsnes, southwest of Trondheim (April 17–18). The objectives were to seize the northern part of Norway and the iron-ore railroad; to capture Trondheim with a kind of pincer movement before the Germans could link it with their Oslo beachhead; to help the brave but scattered resistance of the Norwegians at Elverum and Hamar; and to block the German land drive via rail and road through Valdres, the Gudbrandsdal and Romsdal valleys from Oslo to the north.

Aided by volunteers, the Norwegians, despite surprise and confusion, had succeeded in a kind of scratch mobilization; and here and there, some units (particularly the Norwegian 2nd and 4th divisions) had imposed delay, achieved ambushes, and surprised the small German forces. But it was an improvised resistance, as were the Allied landings.

Major General Sir Adrian Carton de Wiart, one-armed, one-eyed hero of World War I, was commander of all the operations around Namsos. But the line of command was in fact blurred. There was difficulty with the Norwegians, and, in the event, not only Carton de Wiart, but Major General B. C. T. Paget, commanding the forces at Åndalsnes (who was directly under the War Office), and many lesser commanders found themselves operating autonomously and piecemeal. From the beginning the scene was chaotic. The docks and ports were completely inadequate; the mixed forces—Royal Marines armed only with rifles; sailors; French Alpine troops and British regulars and reservists—were heterogeneous, and Major General Paget, south of Trondheim, trying to halt the German push up the vital valleys, never received artillery, tanks, or medical support and had only sporadic communication with his units.

There were some successes. The British advanced rapidly against virtually no opposition to Dombas and, with the Norwegians, mopped up a scattered small force of about 200 German parachutists —many of them injured by their low-altitude jumps.

But spring was coming to Norway. The snow was melting. The Allied logistics were impossible; and the long nights of the Arctic summer were starting, with endless hours of prime hunting time by the German Luftwaffe. The small docks at the tiny ports where Allied troops were disembarking were demolished; the little towns themselves became rubble heaps. A desperate plan to force the fjord of Trondheim was abandoned when it became clear that the Royal Navy would have to run the gantlet, not only of German shore batteries but of the Luftwaffe.

The wildly improvised planning made it clear "that there was scarcely anyone [on the Allied side] who visualized the whole picture or possessed a clear conception of practicable objectives."[12]

The fighting on the ground in central Norway was a campaign in retrograde for the Allied forces; many of the forward units—untrained and unequipped for combat in the snow, with no entrenching tools and no heavy weapons support—were decimated in small actions. The back-pedaling British fought, held briefly, then were outflanked and overwhelmed.

Leland Stowe, in a dispatch to the *Chicago Daily News*, reported that the vanguard of the British force, trying to check the Germans, totaled fewer than 1,500 men:

They were dumped into Norway's deep snows and quagmires of April slush without a single antiaircraft gun, without one squadron of supporting airplanes, without a single piece of field artillery. . . . [British officers said], "We have simply been massacred. . . . It is the planes. . . . We were completely at the mercy of the Jerries. Their bombers flew low over us at five hundred feet. They scattered us. We were up to our hips in snow. . . ."[13]

By April 26–27, it was quite clear that the Norwegian campaign was doomed; evacuation of Allied forces from central Norway was ordered as soon as possible. Instead of counterattack and conquest, it became a question of evacuation and *sauve qui peut*. By 2:00 A.M. on May 2, what was left of the Allied force that had landed at Åndalsnes was embarked from the smoldering wreckage of the town and other nearby areas. The next night, as—in De Wiart's words— "the translucent twilight over the hills around the harbor became brighter [and] full daylight was fast approaching," the last of the Allied rearguard was embarked at Namsos.

British and French personnel casualties during the abortive Allied attempt to seize Trondheim and hold central Norway had been relatively light (though a few individual units lost heavily). Some 5,084 were evacuated from the Åndalsnes area, and almost 6,000 from Namsos. The Allied forces left behind most of their heavy equipment; British destroyer *Afridi* (subsequently sunk by the Luftwaffe as she steamed homeward) shelled and fired, as she retired, Allied trucks abandoned on the quay at Namsos. And still, throughout the long day of evacuation as the tired survivors jammed the decks, the Allied evacuation fleet, steaming toward England through the Norwegian Sea, was harried and torn by German aircraft; ships were damaged and French destroyer *Bison*, afire and helpless, was sunk.

As T. K. Derry, the official British historian, has written: ". . . The failure of the two expeditions south and north of Trondheim" was due to the "virtually unchallenged supremacy of the enemy in the air, which rendered our bases, their sea approaches, and the lines of communication . . . quite untenable."[14]

The story of Narvik, isolated by land except for tortuous snowblocked trails and precipitous cross-country terrain, and beyond immediate effective range of the Luftwaffe, differed in degree but not in results. Only the dying was slower.

A mere 2,000 German troops—including Austrian ski troops—had been landed there under Major General Eduard Dietl, and in the second battle of Narvik on April 10, their supporting naval forces and supply ships had been sunk. The British dominated the sea approaches; initially there was no German air cover; Dietl's men were widely dispersed to cover the fjords and some of them had pushed up the rail line against minor Norwegian resistance to the Swedish frontier, which they reached on April 16. Some 200 Norwegian troops who had escaped from Narvik when the Germans landed formed the nucleus of a slowly growing Norwegian 6th Division, which was being mobilized some 50 miles north of Narvik. In any war college textbook, the situation would have appeared grim for the Germans, apparently cut off from support and faced with increasing enemy strength. But war seldom goes according to the book.

The British missed their golden moment on April 10. For a short time, as the flaming German destroyers exploded and sank under British guns in the harbor, German troops evacuated the town of Narvik—some of them trudging laboriously toward Sweden up the Björnfell, "zigzagging . . . up the steep slope—their dark rows [standing] out against the snow wall like curving snakes."

That night Thedor Broch, the young Mayor of Narvik, and his constituents were singing "Tipperary" in the town hall, anticipating imminent British landings.

Not until April 15 in fact did the first British troops land in the Narvik area, near Salangen, 30 airline miles from Narvik itself. Long before then, Dietl had his men in hand; panic was gone, and the town and harbor were strongly garrisoned. Once again the Allies were too late.

Initially, the instructions issued from the War Office and the Admiralty were at odds. The Army commander, Major General P. J. Mackesy, was cautious (he must, indeed, emerge in history as one of the most cautious commanders of the war). The naval commander, with the resounding cognomen of Admiral of the Fleet Lord Cork and Orrery, was bold. Not until too late was Lord Cork named "top dog" and even then his authority was greatly restricted. The German position was strengthened with the addition of another mountain battery, flown in by Ju-82's, which landed on the frozen ice of Hartvigvatn near Narvik. And on April 19 as the Allied forces moved with agonizing slowness from their original landings across the ice-flecked fjords and snow-covered hills toward Narvik 30 to 40 miles away, the weather coated the German positions in a protective armor of ice and cold and snow. The howling blizzard would last until April 26.

As General Mackesy, resisting the pleas for boldness of both the Navy and his French second-in-command, General M. E. Bethouart, moved his forces at tortoise pace across miles of jagged, snow-covered ridges in a wide enveloping movement toward Narvik, the Allies landed some 3,500 men halfway between Narvik and Namsos to delay the German northward advance. From Mosjoen to Mo to Bodö, where the road network ended, the slowly retreating Allied forces—bolstered by the skillful tactics of the so-called Independent Companies (genesis of the later Commandos)—fought successful delaying actions throughout the month of May against German ground troops, at first inferior in numbers, then strengthened to a slight superiority.

At Narvik, spring thaw followed spring blizzard, and with clear skies and consolidated positions to the south, the Luftwaffe came to prey. Then Dietl was reinforced. On May 13, with the Allies still far from Narvik, Lieutenant General C. J. E. Auchinleck landed near Narvik to become General Officer Commanding of the Northwest Expeditionary Force—the first of this general's ill-fated commands. It was already almost a month too late, and the German blitz against the Low Countries, which had been launched on May 10, made Narvik an expensive and pointless sideshow. Auchinleck surveyed the situation and requested more forces, saying he could not be responsible for "the safety of his force" unless he received major reinforcements. On the night of May 24/25 he was ordered to evacuate northern Norway. But it was not yet the end.

Auchinleck, determined to exact some measure of retribution from disaster and as a means of covering his retirement, closed the Allied pincers on Narvik. And on May 27–28, as a preliminary to evacuation, Allied troops fought their way into the town supported by a heavy bombardment by three cruisers and five destroyers. It was, for Narvik, a kind of *coup de grâce*: "House after house . . . was hit and took fire. Soon the burning houses formed a continuous wall of flame along the shore."

But the Germans did not quit. Mile by fighting mile, they stubbornly resisted the Allied advance along the rail line toward Sweden; Dietl, with some 6,000 troops and his back to the snow wall on the Björnefell 3 miles from the Swedish frontier, was still a tough opponent. And there was no time; the world of the West was in the balance. London, fighting for its life, managed the evacuation of some 25,000 Allied troops from northwest Norway between June 3 and June 8. The belated capture of Narvik was hollow glory. The Germans never surrendered, and the Swastika soon flew again over the battered town.

Allied personnel casualties in the land fighting, in the Narvik and associated operations, were relatively small in a war in which more men died than in any conflict in history. About 13,100 British were evacuated; 11,700 French and Poles; some Norwegians. The British lost 506 men—most of them in the delaying actions from Mosjoen to Bodö—a grand total of 1,869 British killed on land during all Norwegian operations. The French and Polish casualties for the entire Norwegian campaign numbered 530; the Norwegians themselves lost an estimated 1,335 dead in all operations, plus thousands of others wounded or captured, including many civilians or quasi-civilians. The German total—the highest in the Norwegian campaign—numbered 2,921 killed and wounded, and 2,375 missing, including those lost at sea.

At the end, as at the beginning, the hounds of fate dogged the British. *Scharnhorst, Gneisenau, Hipper*, and four destroyers, under orders to bring relief to Dietl by attacking Allied bases at Harstad and near Narvik, blundered on the British evacuation convoys on June 8. A tanker and trawler and troop ship *Orama*, carrying German prisoners of war, were sunk. Aircraft carrier *Glorious*, her decks crowded and hampered by Gladiators and Hurricanes evacuated from the improvised Allied field near Narvik, was steaming homeward escorted only by two destroyers. The German battle cruisers opened fire at 14 miles; in two hours, *Glorious*—sieved, out of control, a flaming torch—sank in the cold waters long before the slow Northern sunset. The two "small boys," *Ardent* and *Acasta*, tried to screen her with smoke and hold off the ravening enemy with torpedoes; *Ardent* was torn apart and capsized. *Acasta* had more luck.

She ducked in and out of the smoke and put a torpedo into *Scharnhorst* which flooded two engine rooms, reduced her speed, put the after turret out of commission, and killed forty-eight men. *Acasta* died game—riddled, wrecked, most of her crew killed or wounded. Her sole survivor in the icy water saw the skipper leaning over the bridge take a cigarette from his case and light it as his ship died under him. ". . . He waved 'Goodbye and goodluck'—the end of a gallant man."[15]

But *Acasta* may have saved the rest of the British convoy, including *Devonshire* 100 miles to the west, with a royal passenger, the King of Norway and his government-in-exile, aboard. The German task force shaped course immediately for Trondheim to put damaged *Scharnhorst* out of danger. (Ironically, *Gneisenau*, her sister, was torpedoed and damaged by British submarine *Clyde* as she steamed out of Trondheim on June 29.)

The Allied survivors of the Norwegian campaign straggled home to safety and a nation in shock.

Hitler's dominion now reached to the North Cape, and Norway—land of the Vikings—faced the long dark night of conquest.

By mid-June—despite far more major operations in France—Germany had transported to Norway by sea "108,000 troops, 16,000 horses, 20,000 vehicles, and 110,000 tons of stores and equipment, with a loss of only 2,400 men and 21 ships (112,000 tons)," out of a total transport and supply fleet of 270 ships and 100 trawlers—1,200,000 tons.[16]

The German naval losses were heavy: 3 cruisers; 10 destroyers; 4 submarines; 11 other vessels, plus many major and minor units damaged and in shipyard for months to come. The losses were to affect adversely German naval capabilities in future operations. The British and French lost one carrier, two cruisers, eight destroyers, and numerous smaller ships, as well as many major and minor ships damaged and out of action at a time of crisis and survival when they were most needed. Allied losses would have been far heavier if the German U-boat torpedoes had not failed to function; the magnetic detonators often misfired. And the Luftwaffe, although a decisive arm in the Norwegian campaign, found that high-altitude bombing was usually grossly inaccurate against moving ships. Nonetheless, heavy cruiser *Suffolk* was badly damaged by air attack, and light cruiser *Curlew* and some destroyers were sunk.

It was clear that the wings of the air overshadowed the sea; a new equation had been introduced into war. No longer could the British surface fleet alone ensure the dominion of the seas; airpower ravaged, harried, wearied, and struck the fear of God into the hearts and souls of surface combatants.

"The Norwegian campaign was a defeat of British sea power. . . . The Germans did what they wished to do at sea, the British failed to stop them or achieve their own objectives."[17]

There was some strategic consolation for both sides even if, for the Allies, it was sparse. The damage to the docks and ore-loading operations at Narvik, most of it—ironically—accomplished by effective German sabotage when they were forced out of the town at the end of May, took almost six months to repair; and even in 1941 only a fraction of the prewar total was shipped from Narvik. Indeed, never again until war's end was Narvik to assume its prewar importance in the ore trade.

Against this must be set confirmation of German control over the Baltic and its entrances and, indeed, over all the Swedish ore trade; the complete denial to Britain of the heavy timber and ore exports from Norway; a strategic position in Northern Europe par excellence; and the enforced withdrawal of British naval patrols from the Shetlands-Norway passage to the more distant and more difficult Iceland-Faeroes gap. Germany would never suffer vital shortages of iron ore throughout the war.[18]

But Norway yielded even more significant results politically. In Britain a change in leadership took place which, viewed from the perspective of thirty years, can only be judged as decisive: Winston Churchill came to supreme power.

On April 4, just five days before the Nazi invasion of Denmark and Norway, Prime Minister Chamberlain had twitted Hitler in a public speech about the German inactivity on the Western Front. ". . . One thing is certain," he said; "he missed the bus."

On May 7, the words came back to haunt him. Denmark and Norway had been conquered; the Norwegian campaign had revealed to the British people the divided councils, poor command and management, sloppy planning, indecision, and unpreparedness of the British. Norway, which Englishmen had thought was easily protected by the British Fleet, had been a psychological catastrophe. Seapower—the shield of empire—had proved fallible. The opposition to Chamberlain reached a crescendo in the House of Commons when, in an attack upon the government, Leopold Amery, Conservative Party rebel and old friend of Chamberlain, quoted the ringing words of Cromwell in another generation: "You have sat too long here for any good you have been doing. Depart, I say, and let us have done with you. In the name of God, go!"

The debate dragged on in anger, impatience, and frustration for three more days. Churchill, as First Lord of the Admiralty, was in an anomalous position. He owed loyalty—and his rescue from political limbo—to Chamberlain. He was as responsible as any minister, indeed more than most, for the Norwegian campaign. And as Lord Halifax, the Foreign Secretary, had noted in his diary of May 3: ". . . on Winston certainly rests the main responsibility for the abandonment of the naval attack on Trondheim."

Norway, and particularly the hesitant planning to force the fjord to Trondheim with the guns of the fleet, bore much resemblance to the situation at Gallipoli in 1916 which had exiled Churchill from public office. His detractors, and even his friends, recalled his shortcomings. He was a dabbler in strategy; his mind gave off sparks but, too many said, with the coruscating wastefulness of a Guy Fawkes Day rocket. He had been a man of all parties, and the traditional British mistrust of brilliance and imagination was a liability for Churchill in the political crisis that now faced his country.

Chamberlain survived a vote of censure—barely. Then on May 10, the long-quiescent Western Front burst into flame as The Netherlands and Belgium were invaded. Chamberlain tried futilely to form a national coalition government, with Labour Party participation, then went to the King. His suggestion of Churchill as his successor was a near thing. Until almost the last, Halifax was preferred; the King, in fact, "suggested Halifax."[19]

But Churchill was finally summoned to the Palace at 6:00 P.M.

"I want to ask you to form a Government," the King said.

Thus, then, on the night of the tenth of May, at the outset of this mighty battle, I acquired the chief power in the State, which henceforth I wielded in ever-growing measure for five years and three months of world war. . . .

I felt as if I were walking with Destiny, and that all my past life had been but a preparation for this hour and this trial. . . .

I was sure I should not fail . . . I slept soundly and had no need for cheering dreams.[20]

The sense of unity often imposed by imminent danger, and the psychological lift of the spirit incidental to a national coalition government headed by a man who more than any other could make the pulse of the nation surge, were Churchill's most immediate contributions to the hour of peril. But gradually he put into effect machinery for the higher direction of the war, which he had had to try to improvise without the powers to impose it during the Norwegian campaign. The War Cabinet and its Defense Committee, the development of the British Joint Chiefs of Staff organization, and the system of coordinated commands that were to be created around the world were among Churchill's contributions to victory. He became Minister of Defense as well as Prime Minister.

But most of all, it was the image of the man himself—his indomitability and defiance in the face of overwhelming odds. Never had it been needed more, for England was in greater danger than in any era since the days of William of Orange.

4

Blitzkrieg in the West

The Shaping of "Plan Gelb"

On the Western Front, Allied leaders—all of them veterans of the Great War—recalled the opening German gambit of 1914, the Schlieffen Plan to "make the right wing strong." That strategy of another war had almost succeeded; the German armies, wheeling wide through Belgium, had nearly enveloped French and British forces and only just missed capturing Paris. The Battle of the Marne, twenty-six years earlier, had residual traumatic effects on Allied planning in World War II—handicapped also until the event by the determined neutrality of The Netherlands and Belgium, and the refusal of both countries to permit any comprehensive joint military planning with France and Britain.

Nevertheless, until after January 1940 there was some reason to believe that history might repeat itself.

There had been, it is true, early suggestions in Germany that what was good enough for Count Alfred von Schlieffen (until 1912 the German Army's Chief of Staff) was not good enough for Adolf Hitler. Soon after the Polish campaign ended—as early as mid-October 1939—Hitler had told his generals of his "irrevocable decision" to attack in the West, and during planning discussions had tentatively suggested the possibility of an attack through the forested Ardennes toward Sedan, a penetration of the Allied line at the hinge, and a roll-up of all Allied forces caught between the breakthrough and the sea. But it was only a suggestion, and the development of the ultimate German plans would be shaped by many varied factors.

Not the least of the factors in the development of "Plan *Gelb*" (Yellow) was the apathy, the worry, and the tacit opposition of some of the German generals, notably General Walther von Brauchitsch, Commander-in-Chief of the Army. The undercurrent of military opposition to Hitler, led in a Hamlet-like fashion by Colonel General Ludwig Beck, who had resigned as Chief of the General Staff at the time of the Munich crisis in 1938, simmered throughout the war but never erupted until it was too late. The opposition expressed itself in objections and temporizing during the fall and winter of 1939, in plan after plan, revision after revision, postponement after postponement. Most of the postponements were due to bad weather. Hitler had originally fixed the date for the *Schlact* (blow) in the West as November 12; there were, ultimately, some twenty-nine delays or chronological revisions. The "manifest disapproval" of some of the higher German commanders—none of it very forceful—and the foot-dragging which resulted in incomplete plans led to some of the postponements; but Hitler on November 23 brusquely refused the tender by Brauchitsch of his resignation as Army Commander and in a conference in the Reichschancellery in Berlin insisted on a Western offensive while reasserting his own dominant position as *Der Fuehrer*.

His authority was unexpectedly assisted by the Venlo Incident of October and November 1939, which coincided (by accident or Hitlerian design) with a bomb explosion at a Nazi rally in the Munich Beer Hall on November 8, just after Hitler had spoken and left. Seven of the old-line Nazis were killed, sixty-three injured; Hitler was furious. Then three men acting on the direct orders of Heinrich Himmler—Walter Schellenberg, chief of the foreign branch of the Nazi intelligence service; a German secret agent, "F479," who had been covertly working in Holland; and the same SS leader, Alfred Naujocks, who had led the fake "Polish" raid on the German Gleiwitz radio station prior to Hitler's Polish invasion—lured two British secret agents to the Dutch-German frontier at Venlo and, with the help of carloads of armed men, kidnaped them. Himmler, parroting Hitler, blamed the Beer Hall bomb explosion on the British secret service. The incident gave Hitler a pretext to consolidate his power over his doubtful generals.

The two British agents, Captain S. Payne Best and Major R. H. Stevens, had been acting with the direct approval of the British government. Through German agent "F479," they were attempting to contact Germans who, they thought, represented an anti-Hitler military conspiracy in Germany. Together with a Dutch intelligence officer who was mortally wounded in the exchange of gunfire that accompanied the kidnaping, Best and Stevens had come to Venlo on November 9, 1939—the day after the Beer Hall explosion—and were promptly hustled across the frontier, taken to Berlin, and made Exhibit A in Hitler's case against England.

The Venlo Incident had three direct or tangential effects: it was used to suborn further the German opposition to Hitler, to consolidate his power with the people, and to turn German wrath against England; it influenced the timing of the campaign in the West; and it helped to reveal to the Nazis some of the covert organization of the British and Dutch secret service, thus handicapping British espionage in Germany at a crucial time, and serving later as a pretext for the Nazi invasion of The Netherlands. Miraculously, Best and Stevens survived Gestapo interrogations and spent the war in Nazi prisons and concentration camps, a fact which later caused raised eyebrows among the cognoscenti of the undercover world. Georg Elser, a German Communist who lived in Munich and was the admitted architect of the Beer Hall bomb plot, but who—some now think—was an SS patsy, was not so fortunate. He was never tried; he spent the war in concentration camps and died at the end, murdered by the Gestapo or killed by Allied bombs.

Despite Venlo, the right wing of the German armies was still strong in Nazi planning as the year 1940 opened. Until fate again intervened . . .

After almost weekly postponements of the German attack through the fall and early winter, Hitler had again set D-Day for January 17. Major Helmut Reinberger, however, moved briefly onto the stage of history on January 10 to force another postponement. Contrary to orders, Reinberger, a Luftwaffe staff officer, took with him in a German plane many of the plans for the Nazi attack in the West. The plane lost its way and landed in Belgium. Reinberger twice tried to destroy the incriminating evidence, but the partially burned documents were retrieved by the Belgians and the data passed on to the British and French.

Then the Scandinavian campaign and bad weather intervened; by spring, the German attack plans had been completely changed.

Instead of a modified version of the *Schlieffen* (Swinging Gate) Plan of 1914, "*Sichelschnitt*" (Scythe Cut) took its place. "*Sichelschnitt*" came to fruition in February, arising primarily out of Hitler's original suggestion and the concept of Fritz Erich von Manstein, one of the most brilliant of the German generals but then a lower-ranking one. The main weight of the attack was shifted from extreme right flank to center; the *Schwerpunkt* was to penetrate Allied lines between Liège and Sedan, with rapid exploitation by armored forces to the West, north of the Somme River to the sea, a roll-up and encirclement of all Allied forces north and west of the penetration, and a fast conquest of The Netherlands and Belgium and northwestern France to deny the Allies the use of Channel ports and airfields.

On May 10, 1940, the German armies in the West comprised about 118 infantry divisions, 10 armored divisions, a horsed cavalry division, and 6 motorized divisions—some 2.5 million men.[21] Forty-five of these were in general reserve. Rundstedt's Army Group A (with four armies), which was to penetrate the Ardennes and drive against Allied forces from Liège to Luxembourg, with its main effort at Sedan, was assigned forty-four divisions—including three of the motorized divisions and seven of the ten armored divisions. To the north Army Group B, commanded by Bock, with about thirty divisions, including three armored and two motorized organized in two armies, was responsible for the conquest of Holland and northern Belgium north of Liège-Namur. Opposite the strong Maginot Line defenses from the Moselle to Switzerland, Army Group C (commanded by Colonel General Ritter von Leeb), aided by the West Wall, was assigned only nineteen divisions and a static defensive role. There were about 2,700 tanks available to the German ground forces, most of them concentrated in Army Group A. The ground forces were to be supported by two Luftflotten of the German Air Force—some 3,200 to 3,300 planes. As in Poland, speed, surprise, and rapid penetration of enemy rear areas by armored vehicles, with command of the air ensuring heavy air support for the ground forces, were the tactical rules of engagement. Apparently reflecting some of the ideas of Manstein, then his Chief of Staff, Rundstedt had emphasized as early as October 1939 that the objective of "Operation *Gelb*" should be not merely an advance to the Somme, but the annihilation of all enemy forces north of the river.

On May 10, when the blow fell, the Allied (French and English) forces in the West numbered about 2 million men, organized into three Army Groups covering the French frontier from the Strait of Dover to Switzerland. The Third Army Group (General A. M. B. Besson) of one army—chiefly fortress troops—occupied the strong defenses behind the Rhine River; and the Second Army Group (General A. G. Prételat) was organized in three armies—mostly static fortress units—manning the Maginot Line from Montmédy to Épinal.

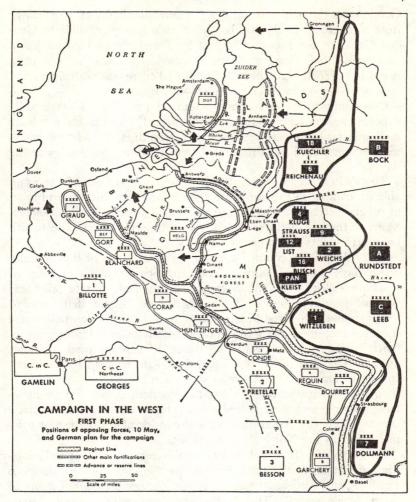

CAMPAIGN IN THE WEST
FIRST PHASE
Positions of opposing forces, 10 May, and German plan for the campaign

The left wing—the First Army Group (General Gaston H. Billotte) —from Montmédy to the sea, numbered, including the British Expeditionary Force, some five armies. General Henri H. Giraud's Seventh Army held the extreme western flank, debouching on the sea between Dunkirk and Ostend; the BEF, with ten divisions, was next in line between the Lys and Escaut rivers; then came the French First Army (J. G. M. Blanchard); the Ninth Army (André G. Corap); and the Second Army (C. L. C. Huntziger).

The command relationship was remote and involved. General A. J.

Georges was the field commander (Commander-in-Chief, Northeast) from Switzerland to the sea, but he in turn was responsible to General Gamelin, the French Chief of Staff and nominal Allied Commander-in-Chief. However, Gamelin could coordinate but not command the French Navy and Air Force, and there was no truly unified command—either national or Allied—in France.

Communications—and hence command and control—were sadly deficient and not keyed to a mobile war. There was far too little radio and far too much dependence on land lines, a syndrome which was perhaps a product of the static French military psychology of the day.

The French Air Force numbered about 1,300 to 1,400 planes available for combat in the northeast (plus a large but uncertain number of others scattered across France, deadlined for repairs or obsolete). Many of the so-called front-line planes were obsolescent. The British based 416 planes in France.

The Allied forces counted about 2,700 tanks, some of them considerably more powerful in armor and armament (but not in range or maneuverability) than the German Panzers. But, despite prior suggestions from the junior officer Charles de Gaulle that armored forces should be massed in large units, most of the Allied tanks were scattered piecemeal along the front in battalions or brigades or as infantry support. There were only three French armored divisions, newly formed and widely separated, three light mechanized divisions, and an incomplete British armored division.[22]

In addition to the forces along the Western Front, France maintained reserve and skeletonized units (chiefly mountain and fortress troops) along the Italian frontier and considerable numbers of colonial forces in her North African colonies.

King Leopold III of Belgium ostensibly commanded, at full mobilization, an army of about 650,000 men—more than 22 divisions (with support forces and fortress troops, 900,000 men), but many of them never served. The Netherlands command, under Queen Wilhelmina and General Henri G. Winkelman, similarly was never fully fleshed out; at full strength it was supposed to total 400,000 men—nine divisions. The Low Countries each had elaborate though individual plans for defense, involving some heavy fortifications, waterlines, canals, and extensive flooding. But the Dutch and Belgian planning was unilateral, not coordinated; until the last the small countries tried to cling rigidly to their neutrality, hoping—all past history to the contrary—that Hitler meant what he said when he repeatedly proclaimed that he would respect it.

The Allied strategy, in contrast to the German, was defensive; they still thought in terms of the trench stalemate of World War I and, despite the *Blitzkrieg* in Poland, believed that any offensive could ultimately be blunted while eventual slow strangulation by blockade would defeat Germany. But even in the implementation of this strategy, there was a confusion of purpose. The huge and elaborate fortifications of the Maginot Line proper ended at Montmédy near the Luxembourg-French-Belgian border. But a so-called Little Maginot Line—considerably less impressive yet still strong—had been built to the bulge in the Belgian frontier at Givet; and after 1936, when Belgium abandoned her alliance with France and reverted to a hopeless neutrality, the French extended the Little Maginot Line to the sea. The flat terrain, the high-water table, and other difficulties slowed the work, and also limited the strength of the defenses, although during the winter of 1939 both French and British had supplemented this section of defenses along the Belgian frontier with field fortifications.

Both armies were trained for, and expected, more or less static fighting. But on May 10, when the Germans attacked, the entire left wing of the Allied forces abandoned the Little Maginot Line fortifications along the Belgian border and moved northward into Belgium and southern Holland toward the Meuse, the Dyle River Line, and Breda (between Antwerp and Rotterdam). Their move was exactly what the Germans wanted.

Yet no one—not even Hitler—anticipated the full dimensions of the victory to come.

In part the success of *"Gelb"* was the result not so much of the new tactics the Nazis had introduced, nor of careful planning, excellent training, and superb battlefield effectiveness, as of the obliging nature of the Anglo-French strategic plans. From their winter positions on the French-Belgian frontier, the entire left or western wing of the Allied forces swung north, pivoting like a gate into the Low Countries when the Germans attacked. Rundstedt struck at the hinge and the gate fell, splintered.

The Conquest of Holland

D-Day was May 10, H-hour 0545. Before dawn from German fields all along the Western Front, the Stukas and the fighters rose to strike. From Luxembourg to north of the Zuider Zee, the Wehrmacht smashed across the frontiers of three countries. Through the forested roads and winding trails of the Belgian Ardennes, the

Panzers rumbled—spearheaded by the 19th Armored Corps (1st, 2nd, and 10th Panzer divisions) of General Heinz Guderian, "father" of the Wehrmacht's armored force, whose motto was: *"Nicht kleckern, klotzen!"* (Don't disperse, concentrate!)

There had been warnings; the French military attaché in Bern had even predicted the date correctly ("between May 8th and 10th") and that "the main effort will be made on Sedan." But the warnings went unheeded. The French, still divided though at war, were living behind the looking glass; their generals basked in the complacency of past glories: ". . . the wireless played *Monica* or *J'attendrai*, and thoughts turned sadly to last year's summer holidays. . . ."[23]

While the great armored mass of the German main effort, screened by the heavy forests of the Ardennes and the deep valleys of Luxembourg, rumbled toward the vital Allied hinge position between Sedan and Namur, General Georg von Küchler's Eighteenth Army (from Bock's Army Group B) on the extreme northern flank smashed rapidly into Holland. German parachutists, appearing to the amazed Dutch like men from Mars, dropped around The Hague, and near Moerdijk, Dordrecht, and Rotterdam, seizing airheads at various airfields well behind the Dutch defensive positions, some of them inside the "Fortress of Holland." The new tactic of vertical envelopment, made possible by the plane, thus neutralized surface obstacles, and the parachutists were aided, particularly near Rotterdam, by a Fifth Column of resident Germans and Dutch Nazis. The parachutists seized intact the great bridges south of Rotterdam and held them, as the 9th Panzer Division broke through the light Dutch frontier positions, skirted or penetrated the Peel Marshes and, despite obstacles and some flooded terrain, roared toward the sea with little opposition. The breakthrough at Sedan was still three days away on May 10; the swift German advance into Holland and northern Belgium was part of the Nazi plan—a lure to entice the Anglo-French forces northward into the trap.

The Allies took the bait; the whole left wing swung creakingly northward into the Low Countries. Giraud's French Seventh Army on the seaward flank even pushed its advanced elements briefly into the Breda region of southern Holland, but not for long. For in The Netherlands, it was no contest. The Dutch, their years of martial greatness centuries past, were completely outclassed in matériel, training, tactics, and techniques. They never recovered from the shock and ruthlessness of the initial blows. Heavy air attacks decimated, then eliminated, the few Dutch aircraft; bombs, dropping in The Hague and near other cities, contributed to the chaos; waterways and harbors were mined from the air; and the German legions brushed aside light resistance in an inexorable advance.

Here and there Dutch troops achieved transient victories and now forgotten glories; they counterattacked at Katwijk, Valkenburg, Ockenburg, and Ypenburg, and recaptured the airfields briefly. But the Nazis were at the gates of the inner temple; they had quickly reached the Rhine estuary, and in two days the Dutch were beleaguered, cut off from aid by land from their allies.

In succession, the Germans broke through the first Dutch defensive position based on the Maas and the Yssel rivers north to the Zuider Zee, and then through the Gelb Valley-Peel Marshes defenses toward the heart of the country: the great cities of Amsterdam, The Hague, and Rotterdam, filled with the wealth of the Dutch burghers and the ancient art of the old masters.

At Doorn the deposed Kaiser, Wilhelm II, who had lost an earlier war, still lived in exile. The new generation of conquerors paused briefly in pursuit of the retreating Dutch to pay him simple homage —a guard of honor. But Hitler brooked no rivalry from old monarchs; the guard was soon withdrawn.

By the second and third days of the offensive, advancing German tanks and infantry had reinforced some of the key airheads around the Rhine estuary and the misnamed "Fortress of Holland" was breached on its southern flank.

The German Luftwaffe ruled—an absolute monarch—in the skies and swooped to destroy anything Dutch that moved in daylight hours.

On the morning of May 14, the Dutch still held the dike across the Zuider Zee to the province of Friesland in the north (overrun by the Germans), and in the east their Fortress Holland line from Muiden on the Zee to Corinchem was virtually intact. But they had no reserves; their towns and cities were burning; and the Germans were in the southern environs of Rotterdam in force, with a bridgehead across the river. At this point, Hitler's *Schrecklichkeit* policy again surfaced. The German radio demanded surrender or Holland's great cities would be destroyed from the air, and simultaneously the OKW ordered the use of the Luftwaffe to end quickly all Dutch resistance. After negotiations for the surrender of Rotterdam had started, the ultimatum was graphically illustrated. Most of old Rotterdam flamed and died under German bombs on the early afternoon of the 14th, with some 800 dead civilians torn and mutilated in the pyre of rubble.[24] General Winkelman, the Dutch Commander-in-Chief, broadcast his readiness to surrender. At 11:45 A.M.

on May 15 the capitulation document was signed and another country, conquered in five days, came under the spreading power of the swastika.

By the callous conquest of a small nation whose neutrality Hitler had long insisted he respected, the Nazis had won some strategic assets; The Netherlands, under Germany's domination, denied airfields and great ports to the British, provided advanced bases for bombers and radar sites for early warning of enemy attacks. And, from a military point of view, at small cost. The German Eighteenth Army, which overran The Netherlands, scarcely outnumbered the nine divisions and assorted brigades and regiments of the Dutch defenders. The German casualties (except among the 4,500 *Fallschirmjaeger* or paratroops engaged) were light; the Nazi domination of the skies was a major factor in the small costs and the quick victory; so, too, was the tremendous German superiority in firepower (particularly artillery) and mobility. The airborne troops—two regiments of paratroopers under General Kurt Student, and four regiments of infantry landed behind Dutch lines by German Junkers transports at captured airfields and by seaplanes on the Rhine estuary—played a disproportionate role in the quick victory. Nor were the Dutch casualties initially heavy. Dutch official figures tot up only 5,200 military personnel killed throughout the war in Europe, many of them in the five days' war. But May 10–15, 1940, was, for the phlegmatic Dutch, only the beginning of suffering for those who stayed under the Nazi yoke.

And that, save for those Dutchmen overseas (concentrated most heavily in the Dutch East Indies—Indonesia), included most of them. Queen Wilhelmina, the royal family, and most of her government escaped to Britain aboard British men-of-war after an abortive early attempt by the German invaders to seize them. The Dutch gold reserves and diamond stocks were transported across the Channel to safety, and Dutch and British demolition parties destroyed oil reserves at Amsterdam, Flushing, Rotterdam, and The Hook. But it was small consolation for another country lost.

The Collapse of Belgium

The conquest of Holland was only a minor part of the German design in the West; most of the Eighteenth Army now quickly pivoted toward the south to become the right flank of the German drive through Belgium and northern France.

As Holland was rapidly overrun, the German main effort was

focused much farther south. Reichenau's Sixth Army (in Bock's Army Group B) struck hard, driving through the "Dutch appendix" of Maestricht early on May 10 at the hinge of the forward Belgian defense line—Liège, and its defenses—and against Fort Eben Emael, where the Albert Canal swung west from the Meuse River. Tactics new to modern warfare, and the thoroughness of the Germans in training and rehearsal, paid quick battlefield dividends. Half the Belgian Air Force was destroyed on the ground in the initial surprise attacks. As in southern Holland, troops of a special combat battalion ("Bau-Lehr" Battalion), speaking Dutch, dressed in Dutch military police uniforms, and aided by Dutch Nazis who followed a Dutch "Fuehrer"—Anton Mussert—tried to seize key bridges across the Meuse and other waterways. They were aided by glider-borne assault units, small but heavily armed, which neutralized prepared bridge demolitions before the defenders could detonate them, and captured intact some of the main highway crossings over the Albert Canal, leading south into the heart of Belgium.

Eben Emael itself, with an assigned garrison of some 1,200 Belgian troops, two 120 mm. and thirty 60 mm. and 75 mm. artillery pieces, plus numerous machine guns and automatic weapons, was considered a modern fort—its defenders protected by gun cupolas or casemates and armored with concrete and steel.

But, in Milton's words:

> What boots it at one gate to make defense,
> And at another to let in the foe?

Nine German gliders of the Koch Storm Detachment, carrying eighty-five men, landed, without warning, at first light in a ground mist on top of the casemates and roof of the great fort. Flame throwers were used at the gunports, and shaped or "hollow" charges (which focus the explosive force of projectiles into powerful cone-like jets of flaming gas) penetrated the steel of the casemates and machine-gun positions, blinded the defenders, and spread flame and smoke within. The German attackers, reinforced by paratroops and engineer troops and protected from Belgian counterattack by screaming Stukas, quickly forced their way into the smoke-filled galleries. In less than an hour, the fort was beleaguered and virtually useless. German ground units reached the airborne contingents on the morning of May 11. At about noon Fort Eben Emael—a key to the Meuse-Albert Canal Line—surrendered, with twenty-three dead and several score wounded, to an assault group that had lost six killed and nineteen wounded. The key bridges and the captured fort, defenses that had been expected to delay the Germans for "at least a week," had been overwhelmed in about thirty hours.[25]

The Meuse-Albert Canal Line was breached, the Belgian advanced positions no longer tenable; by the evening of the 11th the Belgian troops were retiring—harried by air attacks, still more or less intact but exhausted, without artillery or tank support—to the so-called Dyle River Line. Above them in the skies, what was left of the Belgian Air Force died heroically but futilely in forlorn attempts to bomb the German-held bridges across the Meuse and the Canal. Behind the Belgians, from Givet to the sea, French and British troops were moving north into Belgium. As long ago as November 1939, despite the opposition of General Georges (commanding the northeast theater of operations), the French and British governments had decided, in case the Germans violated Belgian neutrality, to swing their left flank forward to the Dyle River Line and to defend a front in Belgium from Antwerp to Louvain to Namur and Givet. The Allied gate swung slowly; it had been expected to take about five days, perhaps more, for some thirty-three Allied divisions to close along the Dyle and to reinforce, strengthen, and extend the line to be held by the Belgians. In the event, the Allies, by forced marches, reached the Dyle in three to four days but with too little too late; the Germans got there first.[26] And the Allied armies, whose plans, until war came, had been coordinated with those of the Belgians only through military attachés, expected to find completed fortifications awaiting them; in fact these were, at best, scratchy or unfinished.

As the great battles opened both sides invoked the martial ardor of their peoples:

. . . The watchwords for France and all her allies are: courage, energy, confidence.

As Marshal Pétain said twenty-four years ago: *"Nous les aurons."*

GAMELIN

. . . Soldiers of the Western Front, your hour has come. The battle that is beginning . . . will decide the fate of the German nation for the next thousand years. Do your duty! The blessings of the German people go with you.

HITLER

But words without action represent rhetoric; Hitler's grandiloquence was buttressed by sheer power.

By the night of the 12th of May, after three days of fighting, seven German Panzer divisions—the *Schwerpunkt,* or main effort of the entire Nazi plan—had brushed aside the Chasseurs Alpins and light French and Belgian horsed cavalry units in the Ardennes and had closed up to the Meuse River. The 13th was the day of decision. From Houx to Sedan, the Meuse was crossed; one of the first bridgeheads was established by the 7th Panzer Division, commanded by a then unknown German general named Erwin Rommel, who was to skyrocket to fame as perhaps the greatest armored tactician of World War II. It was at Sedan, once before a locus of disaster, that the heaviest blow fell. The Germans struck with fury through the Stenay Gap, a natural terrain gateway at the hinge of the Allied line, where Corap's Ninth Army joined Huntziger's Second Army. Again, the Stukas played the cacophonic prelude; the nerve-chilling "diabolical" noise of the dive bombers and the crash of bombs preceded the rumbling tanks. General Rundstedt, commanding Army Group A, watched as Guderian's Panzer corps established a long deep bridgehead across the Meuse on either side of Sedan. It was perhaps the weakest point in the French Western Front; the best of the French divisions had moved north into Belgium, and the Sedan area was held by the overextended French 55th and 71st divisions—most of them elderly reservists with little training, and with about half their complement of antitank guns. They had no protection against the roaring dive bombers; there was scarcely a French plane in the skies above them. The 55th collapsed under the German pounding by late afternoon of the 13th. General Guderian crossed the Meuse in a boat and committed his tanks. "Sickle Cut" had worked as planned.

In the words of the British official history, "the German breakthrough on the Meuse determined the whole course of the campaign. . . ."[27]

In the days to come thousands of refugees fled the chaos of defeat only to find it still with them. The clogged roads littered with burned-out trucks, disabled tanks, peasant families on foot, in carts, or in buses, formed ribbons of sluggish humanity, harried by the vulture-like Stukas.

To meet the crisis on the ground, the outnumbered squadrons of France and the Royal Air Force put all they had into a gallant but puny effort against the German-held bridges along the Meuse and across the Albert Canal. They imposed slight delay, no more, and by the night of May 14, 45 of 109 RAF Battle and Blenheim bombers which had attacked the enemy in the Sedan area had been lost.

The freshet of the German breakthrough quickly swelled into a roaring torrent, as the Panzers widened the breach. The left flank of Huntziger's Second Army collapsed; Corap's Ninth Army, directly in the vortex, virtually vanished. Its diary on the morning of the 15th tersely summarized disaster: "No information—communications cut —liaison unworkable—back areas blocked with convoys and wrecked columns—petrol trains in flames—wholesale chaos . . ."[28]

The German Panzers, with the Stukas overhead, turned northwest toward Boulogne, the Channel ports, and the sea. On the night of May 15 General Gamelin, who so short a time before the war had said: "My soul is at peace," was "overwhelmed by the reports reaching him from all sectors of the front." He called M. Daladier, the Minister of National Defense.

In his office in the rue Saint-Dominique in Paris, Daladier heard the incredible news. He shouted into the phone: "No! What you are saying cannot be true! . . ."

He had just heard that a German armored column had reached an area between Rethel and Laon, with virtually nothing in its path; that nearly all French reserves were already committed, and only a single corps stood between the Nazis and Paris.

William Bullitt, the American ambassador, heard Daladier say: "So it means the destruction of the French Army?"

"Yes, it means the destruction of the French Army."[29]

The frantic, pleading messages of foreboding flashed across the seas from Paris to London (for more air support); from London to Washington (for all kinds of aid); London to Paris; Belgium to London. . . . And Paul Reynaud, Premier of France, sent for an old Marshal of France—Pétain of Verdun fame, now ambassador to Madrid.

By the morning of May 16, the Allied left wing that had advanced so bravely into Belgium just six days before was ordered to abandon the Dyle Line, and to commence withdrawal—the first stage to the Escaut—to start on the night of the 16th. The Allied commanders in the closing trap knew they were in trouble, but they did not yet understand they had no place to go. For King Leopold III of Belgium, Commander-in-Chief of the Belgian armed forces, the order to abandon the Dyle Line was bitter indeed; it meant the loss of Belgium's principal cities, including its capital. Yet he complied.

Everywhere were the refugees—the handcarts, the piled possessions, the straggling French *poilus*—dirty and defeated, often unarmed and beaten. Everywhere were the Stukas and the German fighters—pitiless, relentless—and always close behind the fleeing mob roared the terrible clamor of the tanks.

Hans Habe, who served in the French Army in a regiment of foreign volunteers, sums up in his classic *A Thousand Shall Fall* the demoralization and disintegration of the French:

More and more cars full of fleeing officers passed us, and every last one of them was piled high with bottles, packing-cases, food. . . . Desertion was taken for granted: officers left their companies, companies left their regiments; regiments dwindled to vanishing-point. . . .

The soldiers stole whatever came to their hands. . . . Thousands of soldiers hobbled along the highway, and out of their pockets hung bottles, women's shoes, neckties, ribbons, toys. A negro soldier was carrying three or four women's corsets. The ribbons hung down and twisted round his legs. Baby carriages rolled along, bearing champagne, cognac, shirts, clocks, umbrellas, coffee-mills. . . .

The witches' sabbath increased in horror and absurdity. . . . Several big cheese stores had been completely plundered . . . the Port de Salut, Roblechons, Roqueforts lay on the road by the hundreds. . . . For several minutes our car drove through cheese. The wheels sank into the soft yellow mass. . . . The best things that the best men of France, the peasants of this peasant country, had created by the sweat of their brow, were thrown on the road and trampled on. Champagne, the product of hundreds of years of diligence and skill, flowed in the ditches. . . .[30]

Here and there brave men stood and died to try to stem the flood; in a sharp night action at Avesnes, heavy French tanks blocked the route of Rommel's Panzers for a few hours, until—the charred hulks smoldering and the town reeking of burnt human meat—the spearhead of aggression moved on.

Gaps opened in and behind the German Panzer units as they drove headlong toward the sea. The French 4th Armored Division (one of four in the French Army and the only one employed in an armored mass as a unit) exploited some of these gaps between May 16 and 19 in thrusts from the south against the German flank. At Laon and near Péronne, the attacks made some progress under the driving leadership of a newly promoted French general, Charles de Gaulle. But the division, newly formed, was incomplete and tanks were too few; the counterattacks quickly ran out of steam. This short sharp roweling of the German southern flank probably accentuated Hitler's jitters; General Halder, the Army Chief of Staff, noted in his diary on May 18:

The Fuehrer unaccountably keeps worrying about the south flank. He rages and screams that we are on the best way to ruin the whole campaign and that we are leading up to a defeat. . . .

In fact, the Germans were amazed at their success. The High Command mistrusted it, and even Rundstedt, whose Army Group A was the architect of the breakthrough, was cautious and fearful of an Allied push from south of the Somme or against the Verdun-Sedan pivot.

Indecision at the top was translated into a brief "stop" order for Guderian's rampaging Panzers, but the Panzer leader and his fellow field commanders understood the signs of the enemy's dissolution far better than their superiors, and after brief but bitter argument the drive to the sea continued.

In those days from mid-May onward illusion dominated reality in the Allied command system. The French and British never caught up with events; heads rolled, commanders were changed, frantic orders were issued and countermanded.

Alarmed, Churchill flew to Paris to rally his Allies; on the evening of May 16, the famous French journalist Pertinax recorded:

The French Premier [Reynaud] and the Minister for National Defense [Daladier] were both seated, facing each other in the study of the Place du Palais-Bourbon apartment. Daladier was all hunched up, burdened with the weight of poignant sorrow; Reynaud held his head erect. He was silent and looked like some broken mechanical toy. The British Prime Minister paced up and down the room, urging them on: "Don't be discouraged. Did you ever suppose that we should be able to win without first suffering the worst possible reverses?"[31]

Giraud, hastily shifted from command of the Allied left flank (Seventh French Army) to the vortex of the whirlwind, to relieve Corap of command of the shattered Ninth Army, was captured. The remnants of his army simply dissolved (May 17) in long lines of prisoners, retreating units, and streams of stragglers. Pétain, recalled from Madrid, became Deputy Premier under Paul Reynaud; General Maxime Weygand, recalled from the Middle East, relieved Gamelin in the hot seat on May 19.

The French High Command "failed to realize the tempo of . . . battle dictated by the enemy. Every maneuver, conceived on too short-term a basis, was already outstripped by events at the very moment of its translation into orders."[32]

That day, May 19, the Germans reached the sea at Abbeville, and German infantry, lagging behind the armor, were commencing to build up the German southern flank along the Aisne and the Somme. About half of the Allied armies were encircled in northern France and Flanders.

As always in catastrophe, rumor magnified the German power; the dry rot of defeat sapped what had been called "the finest Army in the world," and the terror of the Panzers and the Stukas—this new form of warfare—infected a whole people. Retreat became rout.

In Britain, old men and boys, armed with shotguns, ancient rifles, and clubs, were formed into Home Guard units; in Paris, the Quai d'Orsay and other ministries had commenced to burn their papers, and tons of documents were tipped out of the windows into a bonfire in the courtyard.

As early as May 19, after a consultation with Billotte, commanding the Allied First Army Group, Lord Gort raised the possibility in a message to the British War Office of an enforced evacuation of the BEF from the Channel ports.

The German armor, with units facing south across the Somme, sent spearheads swinging north along the Channel coast toward Boulogne, Calais, and a place destined to become a byword in the history of World War II—Dunkirk.

On the night of the 20th, Churchill tartly answered a suggestion by President Roosevelt that the British Fleet should find shelter in American ports in the event of England's defeat:

. . . our intention is, whatever happens, to fight on to the end in this island . . . in no conceivable circumstances will we consent to surrender. . . . If members of the present Administration were finished and others came in to parley amid the ruins, you must not be blind to the fact that the sole remaining bargaining counter with Germany would be the Fleet, and if this country was left by the United States to its fate, no one would have the right to blame those then responsible if they made the best terms they could for the surviving inhabitants. . . .[33]

On May 21 a mixed force of British infantry and tanks, with little artillery support, bolstered the defenses of Arras and counterattacked southward into the northern flank of the 20-mile-wide German corridor that stretched from Sedan to the sea. A coordinated French attack by two divisions of the French First Army south toward Cambrai was planned but was delayed until the 22nd. A hoped-for simultaneous attack of Allied forces northward from the Somme River line never developed. The result was predictable, though for a time Rommel's 7th Panzer Division had some severe fighting, and took heavy losses until the British attack was stopped by artillery. Billotte, commander of the beleaguered and encircled Allied forces, was killed in an automobile accident; chaos and confusion were compounded, and the Allies had shot their bolt.

There were more plans for counterattacks and many bold declamations, but they were all, as Telford Taylor notes, "fantasy."

Arras was surrendered on May 23, the German corridor to the sea widened to 50 miles as the Germans squeezed the Allied pocket, and the surrounded Allied divisions—pounded by land and from the air— were fighting for their lives, their backs to the sea. From May 22 to 25, Boulogne and Calais were invested and captured in stiff fighting. Boulogne was held by a ragtail, bobtail "army" of French and Belgian recruits in training, 1,500 British of the Auxiliary Military Pioneer Corps, small units cut off in the encirclement, stragglers stiffened at the last moment by reinforcements from England of two battalions of the Guards Brigade. It was a forlorn stand, though a gallant one; British destroyers crammed with troops (one overloaded with 1,400 men) evacuated most of the soldiers, at the last "firing over open sights at enemy tanks, guns and machine guns only a few hundred yards away."

Calais, hastily reinforced from England, in part with Territorial (militia) troops, some of them armed "only with pistols," fought to the death. For "the sake of Allied solidarity" and to win time for the hard-pressed BEF to the north, evacuation was eschewed for the Calais troops, and it was not until late on the 26th—the old city choked with debris, fires raging unfought, and dust and smoke a pall over the Citadel—that the Germans cut up and isolated the defenders and cleaned out the last pockets of resistance. For the soldiers of Calais (dead, wounded, or prisoners for the long years of war) there was a *summa cum laude* of history, and a footnote reference that there, and at Boulogne, the defenders had tied down two of Guderian's three armored divisions, while the BEF and the French First Army hurriedly formed defense lines around Dunkirk.

As the Germans drove north along the seacoast, the French First Army, backed by the BEF, refused its flank and tried to build up a hastily improvised defensive front along the northern shoulder of the German corridor to the sea. The new front—in the rear of the troops in Belgium—forced the thinning out and extension of the Belgian defenses along the Escaut (Scheldt), and then a retreat to the Lys. As the British faced south and tried to free troops for a counterattack, the Belgians took over the entire 60-mile front to the French frontier. It was a task beyond their strength, and their situation became increasingly desperate as the pocket around the encircled Allies squeezed tighter and tighter.

Some of the Liège forts—now far in the rear of the front—were still holding out, invested and bypassed, tiny Belgian islands in a rising German sea. The northern Belgian flank was now threatened from Walcheren Island; the Belgians were cut off from their principal supply dumps and limited to a few inadequate ports; the roads were clogged with refugees fleeing from the Germans; and perhaps 2 to 3 million people were crammed into a few hundred square miles under merciless harassment from the skies.

King Leopold had repeatedly warned his allies in person, by messages (some of which were never received), and through Admiral of the Fleet Sir Roger Keyes, special liaison officer of the British War Cabinet with the King, that Belgian resistance could not last much longer. On May 25, Leopold in an order of the day urged his troops to "fight on with all our strength and with supreme energy," and promised "whatever happens, my fate will be yours." The next day, while British forces were starting their withdrawal toward Dunkirk, the French mission in Belgium was warned that "the Army has nearly reached the limits of its endurance," yet the Belgians fought on—in one area from Roulers to Ypres behind an improvised tank barrier of 2,000 railroad cars piled end to end.

On May 27, with British, French, and Belgian units decimated and mixed in confusion in the shrinking pocket, the Belgian front along the Lys from Zeebrugge to Ypres was flanked and ruptured—then shredded by violent German attacks. Only now, on the morning of the 27th, was Leopold informed of the British decision to evacuate. Gort was telegraphed a warning of impending Belgian collapse. French liaison officers were told that "Belgian resistance is at its last extremity; our front is about to break like a worn bowstring." The condition of the Army, the congestion of the roads, the dominance of German airpower made a retreat to the Yser impossible; the last reserves had been committed, and the plain truth was that the Belgian Army was no longer fully responsive to command.

The Allied commanders in the pocket knew of the imminent collapse; on the morning of the 27th Gort and French commanders, planning the last desperate fallback to Dunkirk, omitted the Belgians from their calculations, as their situation was "obscure."

At 5:00 P.M. Leopold, after informing both the French and British liaison missions, sent an emissary to the headquarters of the Eighteenth German Army asking for an armistice. At 11:00 P.M. on May 27, the King, told that Hitler demanded "unconditional surrender," accepted the unequivocal terms, and along much of the Belgian front firing ceased at 4:00 A.M. on the 28th. The Belgian Army, which had attempted to call to the colors some 900,000 men just eighteen days before, became prisoners of war; Leopold, true to his word, stayed with his people, and went into a kind of protective house arrest, at German order, in the Château of Laeken.

Immediately a storm of fury, contempt, and vituperation was heaped upon the royal captive's head by Premier Reynaud and others in the French government, by London, and even by Belgian ministers who were in Paris. On the afternoon of the 28th, Reynaud told the French people by radio that Leopold had committed a "deed without precedent in history"; he had abandoned his allies and laid down his arms without warning. Churchill suspended judgment for a week, then told Parliament that Leopold had surrendered "suddenly, without prior consultation, with the least possible notice, without the advice of his ministers, and upon his own personal act." Lloyd George, the Welshman of World War I fame, who was never known for understatement, declared that "you can rummage in vain through the black annals of the most reprobate kings of the earth to find a blacker and more squalid example of perfidy and poltroonery than that perpetrated by the King of the Belgians."

What made all this calumny more believable at the time was similar criticism, though less harshly phrased, by the Belgian Prime Minister, M. Hubert Pierlot, who was in Paris, and by other Belgians in exile. Though Leopold was Commander-in-Chief of the Belgian armed services, the Cabinet-in-exile which had fled to Paris questioned his right to surrender as "unconstitutional and illegal." Leopold, a prisoner at Laeken, was dubbed the "traitor king"—a crooked cross to bear, indeed, for the son of the revered King Albert of World War I, whose courage and princely bearing made him one of the hero figures of that earlier epoch.

The criticism of the time was plainly unjustified. The historical record—particularly the papers of Admiral of the Fleet Sir Roger Keyes—shows that until the last, Leopold was faithful to his allies and that the Belgian Army fought to the limit of its capabilities. Repeatedly Keyes, Gort, the French, and the British were warned of the impending collapse, and the Belgian surrender did not take place until the King had made many efforts—some of them unsuccessful because of confusion and destroyed communications—to inform London and Paris as well as the Allied commanders in the pocket.

The fury of the attacks upon Leopold was in part the product of general catastrophe and of the normal human search for scapegoats; in part the result of the Reynaud government's specific attempt to shift the blame for débacle to other shoulders than their own. It was also due to political differences in Belgium, to the personality of Leopold, and in part to the controversial decision by the King to remain with his people rather than to flee, like other monarchs and conquered governments, to join the regimes in exile in England.

There were undoubtedly those in France and Britain who could not forget that Leopold, after the death of his father King Albert, had abrogated in 1936 the defensive alliances with France and England made by Albert after World War I and had chosen a policy of strict neutrality.

The old schism in Belgium between Flemings and Walloons, a product of political, religious, economic, and language differences, persisted in 1940, as it does today. The King's decision to remain in his conquered land—which made him, some charged, Hitler's "stooge"—rather than to escape to England helped to increase these differences. Churchill pointed out that the Belgian Cabinet maintained the trappings of constitutional rule in London and believed the King's presence in conquered Belgium during the war "divided" the nation.[34]

Leopold never emerged from the shadow of May 27, 1940, nor did his presence in Belgium save her from the heavy hand of German conquest. Louvain and its priceless library of close to 1 million volumes, burned in World War I, rebuilt with American aid, was again destroyed. Thousands of Belgians died in Nazi concentration camps or work gangs. Leopold survived the war only to abdicate in 1951 after some 57 percent of the Belgian people had voted to recall him from his refuge in Switzerland, where he had moved when freed at war's end from German internment. The opposition of the Socialist and Liberal minority and the Walloons and antimonarchists, and the unpopularity among many of Leopold and particularly of his second wife, a commoner, were so vociferous that the King without a country turned over the scepter and the crown to Baudouin, son of his first marriage.

The end for Leopold III, who did his duty as he saw it and paid the reckoning, was thus delayed for weary months and years; but for the Belgian Army the eighteen-day war had ended, and their nation was conquered.

The Miracle of Dunkirk

To what was left of three French armies and the British Expeditionary Force in the pocket, the collapse of the Belgians was *coup de grâce* to an already mortally wounded corpus. The shoulders of the 50-mile-wide German corridor to the sea were solidly buttressed along the Somme by German infantry; all attempts to slice through

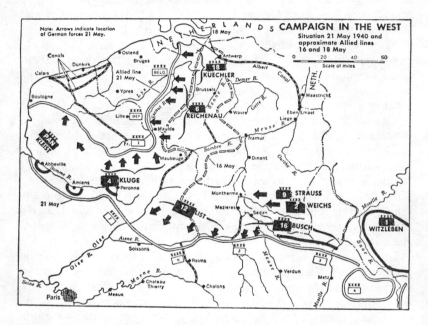

it had been beaten back and the coils of encirclement were constricting.

By May 21, Gort had become convinced that evacuation was virtually the only course left open to him. By the 26th, *before the Belgian surrender*, London agreed. After a meeting between Reynaud and Churchill in London, Gort was instructed by the War Office: "No course open to you but to fall back upon the coast."

Plans had been in the making for a week, and almost 28,000 Englishmen—"useless mouths"—had already been sea-lifted from the Channel ports by the evening of May 26, when Admiral Sir Bertram Ramsay was ordered by the Admiralty to commence "Operation Dynamo," the code name for what has come to be known in English history as the "miracle of Dunkirk."

It was a miracle which had already been given a major helping hand by Hitler himself. On May 24, with German Panzers 10 to 20 miles from Dunkirk—much closer than the bulk of the BEF—Hitler approved the issuance of a stop order by Rundstedt to his armored forces.

Only one British battalion was covering some 20 miles of front along the Aa Canal-River. Bridges were unblown and complete disaster seemed in the making. Yet the Panzers halted in their tracks. This—not the later evacuation—was, for the British, the real and inexplicable "miracle of Dunkirk."

The halt order was and remains enigmatic, incomprehensible, one of the great controversies of World War II. With what General Keitel described as "the greatest encirclement battle in history" starting and the "annihilation of all the British, French and Belgian forces still fighting in Flanders" impending, why did Hitler halt his spearheads at a crucial moment?

Since the surprising success of the German breakthrough on the Meuse and the armored push to the sea, both Hitler and Rundstedt, commanding Army Group A, had been concerned about the southern flank of the German corridor along the Aisne and the Somme. Both men greatly overestimated the recuperative powers of what was left of the French Army south of the Somme; both feared counterattacks, and at this moment when the gods favored the bold, caution appeared to triumph. The British counterattack at Arras on May 21 had mauled a few German units and alarmed Hitler and the High Command. Tank losses in the German armored spearheads had been fairly heavy (an estimated 50 percent in some units); the troops were tired; and the Panzers were reaching the mucky fields of Flanders, crisscrossed with canals and drainage ditches, flooded by inundations, where tanks could easily be mired down.

Rundstedt, one of the more cautious and overrated German generals of World War II, approved and tentatively initiated the armored stop order, although Hitler bore ultimate responsibility.

The Panzer divisions which had led the charge across France must be withdrawn from battle, Hitler ordered, regrouped and reorganized for the second phase—the push south from the Somme. The reduction of the Allied pockets in Flanders would be left to the infantry and to the German Air Force.

This crucial decision, a great mistake of World War II, was possibly influenced by political as well as tactical considerations. Hermann Göring, the second man in the National Socialist hierarchy, who had Hitler's ear and was head of an air force that was peculiarly the creation of the Nazi Party, claimed for the German Air Force (GAF) the pride of *coup de grâce* for the encircled Allies. Boastfully he proclaimed in the exaggerated phrases used by many airpower enthusiasts of World War II that the Luftwaffe would "settle Dunkirk's hash with planes alone," and he warned Hitler that if the GAF were not allowed to exterminate the Allied forces, he (Göring) —a prominent Nazi—would lose prestige to those always troublesome Army generals. Hitler himself, who fluctuated throughout the war between violent denunciations of Britain and admiration of British achievements, indicated that his eventual aim (according to Liddell Hart) "was to make peace with Britain on a basis that she would regard as compatible with her honor to accept."[35] Hitler's subsequent actions did little to bolster this assertion, but *Der Fuehrer's* ambivalence, his violent gyrations between grandiose concepts and daring execution, angry outbursts and panicky caution, seemingly influenced the standstill order of May 24.

For two crucial days, from May 24 through May 26,[36] the clanking tracks of the Panzers were silent while all that stood between the German van and Dunkirk were hastily improvised scratch forces raked together from rear area units.

When the tanks started moving again, on the afternoon of May 26, it was too late; the BEF, still fighting hard, had begun with the help of their French Allies to draw up a sketchy perimeter defense around Dunkirk, and the evacuation started.

What followed was high drama, bitter tragedy and triumph, miracle indeed. For none involved, the British included, had believed large-scale evacuation was possible; London had hoped to rescue perhaps 45,000 men, a fraction of the BEF.

From the Narrow Seas and the Cinque ports around England, Flag Officer, Dover, Vice Admiral B. H. Ramsay gathered up flat-bottomed Dutch *schuyts* and sloops, corvettes and *chasseurs*, yachts and barges, hoppers and lighters, trawlers and drifters, destroyers and gunboats, lifeboats and motor boats and launches—cockleshells and spit kits, greyhounds and plodders—and sent them, first singly, then in twos and threes, then in convoys of dozens and hundreds, across the roiled waters of the Strait to Dunkirk. Drake's Drum beat once again throughout England in moment of alarum.

The Royal Navy organized Operation Dynamo, and by far the greatest number of those rescued from death or captivity were saved by the larger ships it mobilized: 56 destroyers and torpedo boats; 45

personnel carriers, channel or coastal passenger ferries; 268 minesweepers, trawlers, and drifters.

But from Harwich and Margate, from the Wash to North Foreland, past the Goodwin Sands to Dover and Folkestone, and from the little ports on the south coast of England the small craft came—the yachts and motor boats, lifeboats and wherries—a heterogeneous armada, some as small as 16 feet, bearing names that spoke of past history and present domesticity, names prosaic and names romantic: *Wings of the Morning; Willie and Alice; Windsong; Palmerston; Princess Maud; Mata Hari; Nelson; Our Lizzie; Pearl; Silver Queen; Bonny Heather; White Orchid; Mare Nostrum.*

Off burning Dunkirk and its torn and littered beaches from May 26 to June 4, it was an English *Mare Nostrum*—though not without the ever-present sacrifice of men and blood and ships that the gods of the sea demand.

With the Belgian collapse, an immediate threat from Nieuport to the northern flank of the Allies was temporarily met by a patchwork of Franco-British forces. Two corps of the French First Army, bits and pieces of the Seventh, and all of the remaining units of the BEF were in rapid retreat by May 28 to the 22-mile perimeter around Dunkirk. But no general French evacuation orders had been issued, and at least two corps, five to seven French divisions, plus straggling remnants of others, were cut off by Rommel's rampaging Panzers in a great sack around Lille, with no hope of breakout.

The Dunkirk defenses were improvised and hasty. British and French were in name-calling disagreement; communications were cut, there was little or no coordination, no unified command. Nevertheless, Admiral Jean Abrial, French naval commander of the Channel ports garrison, had done much with little in a few days, and Ramsay from his command gallery cut into the white chalk cliffs of Dover sent Captain W. G. Tennant, R.N., to Dunkirk to organize, at that end, the British part of the evacuation. French First Army and naval troops held 5 to 6 miles of the southern loop around Dunkirk as far as Mardick; other French troops were straggling or fighting their way seaward outside these lines; and the British stood along the Dunkirk-Bergues-Furnes Canal and up the coast toward La Panne. The whole area was amphibious, much of it flooded by inundations, drainage canals, and ditches—poor country for tanks; only the roads and a few dry patches emerged from mud and water. The perimeter extended about 22 miles along the sea; it was 6 miles deep at its widest point, narrowing to a mile or two on the flanks. Behind the retiring troops, with the German coils tightening about them, were the seaward gates—the only egress from an inferno of bombs and shells. The town of Dunkirk was a shambles of blazing ruins, the inner basins littered with wrecks—its docks destroyed, unusable—the outer harbor, deep water, protected by two long moles or breakwaters, and to the north to La Panne 10 miles of sandy, shelving beaches—the gradient far too gradual, the water too shoal for all save small boats. Behind the beaches was a narrow strip of dunes. And always overhead the Luftwaffe, the Stukas and the fighters, bombing the ships, strafing the beaches . . . and the thunder of the guns.

Such was the setting for the last days of the BEF in Flanders; there were not many who thought to live and fight another day.

Then, amidst chaos and defeat, came another forlorn effort mounted to win time, to create diversion. . . . What was left of De Gaulle's 4th Armored Division (about 100 tanks), plus other hastily concentrated French units, mounted a three-day assault, May 28–31, on the large German bridgehead south of the Somme at Abbeville. It made initial progress, stove in some of the German front, and drove deep salients into the southern face of the bridgehead. But inadequate force, the attrition of exhaustion, and skilled, tough German defenses wore down the attackers; gradually the French attack petered out and died. . . .

In the Dunkirk bridgehead chaos unlimited slowly yielded to chaos confused but organized. The roads were clogged and forever bombed; at the perimeter defenses, lengthy altercations between Allies were frequent as British troops compelled retreating French to abandon their vehicles and heavy equipment before entering the beachhead. Pyres of smoke from demolitions and burning equipment and the pall from battered Dunkirk trailed along the dunes. The scream of diving planes, the staccato bursts of strafing, and the whine of falling bombs punctuated disaster. And in the harbor the recriminations of defeat and confused orders led to blows between Allies. French *poilus* who boarded British evacuation vessels were at first thrown off bodily by British sailors. Each blamed the other; both blamed the Belgians.

German bombs destroyed Dunkirk's water supply; with thousands of wounded thirsting for water, Ramsay had to send water barges to the ravaged port. The heterogeneous armada of big ships and small, of spit kits and greyhounds, ran the gantlet day and night of German bombs and strafing, of artillery fire along the French coast, of mines and torpedoes and E-boats. Many were sunk, many, many more were wounded, but they kept coming.

The moles of Dunkirk's outer harbor saved thousands; destroyers and ferries tied up to them and took aboard hundreds of men—French and British alike—until their freeboard disappeared and they heeled dangerously. Almost 18,000 men came back to England on May 28; on the 29th, as *Mona's Queen* and *Wakeful* and *Grafton* and *Drifter* and *Nautilus* died and the sky battles flared above them, the count of evacuees rose to more than 47,000.

From the beaches as well as the moles, long queues of men, hunched in British stoicism—some of them standing neck-deep in the sea—waited for small boats to ferry them to deep water and the doubtful safety of the big ships and the cross-Channel gantlet.

. . . The queues stood there, fixed and almost as regular as if ruled. No bunching, no pushing . . .

Dunkirk front was now a lurid study in red and black flames, smoke, and the night itself all mingling together to compose a frightful panorama of death and destruction. Red and black all the time, except for an occasional flash of white low in the sky miles away to the left and right where big shells from coastal defense guns at Calais and Nieuport were being hurled into the town.

Down on the beach you immediately felt yourself surrounded by a deadly evil atmosphere. A horrible stench of blood and mutilated flesh pervaded the place. There was no escape from it. Not a breath of air was blowing to dissipate the appalling odour that arose from the dead bodies that had been lying on the sand, in some cases for several days. We might have been walking through a slaughter-house on a hot day. The darkness, which hid some of the sights of horror from our eyes, seemed to thicken this dreadful stench. It created the impression that death was hovering around, very near at hand. . . .

"Water . . . Water . . ." groaned a voice from the ground just in front of us.

It was a wounded infantryman. He had been hit so badly that there was no hope for him. Our water-bottles had long been empty, but by carefully draining them all into one we managed to collect a mouthful or two. A sergeant knelt down beside the dying man and held the bottle to his lips. Then we proceeded on our way, leaving the bottle with the last few drains in it near the poor fellow's hand . . .[37]

From May 26 to June 4, the big ships and the small, joined now by ships flying the French Tricolor, braved the fiery gantlet across the Channel to the dying port of Dunkirk and its corpse-littered beaches. Lord Gort was ordered out; Sir Alan Brooke and then, later, General Harold Alexander held the British rearguard; then they too, and all living British soldiers, were picked up from the moles and the sand, as the French held off the ravaging enemy for a few more hours.

In these nine days a total of about 338,226 men[38] were lifted across the Channel, some 225,000 British, the rest French and Belgian. The British made of Dunkirk a moral triumph, and, indeed, it was a drama that stirred the world; as always in adversity the best of the English character shone out of the murk of defeat. But it was no victory; wars are not won by evacuations.

The men who reached England were no longer an army save in spirit. Shaken, some shattered, many wounded, they were disorganized, decimated, disarmed—nearly all of their equipment left behind in Flanders. Twenty-two tanks of some 704 sent to France were returned to England; little artillery came back; many small arms, even uniforms, were lost. And the costs of the lifesaving operation were huge: six British and three French destroyers were sunk, nineteen other British destroyers damaged; eight of forty-five passenger ferry ships that participated were sunk, nine others badly damaged. A total of 235 of the approximately 848 Allied ships and vessels and boats that took part were lost, and at least forty-five others damaged. The Royal Air Force, outnumbered and flying in skies far from its bases, lost 106 fighters (the Germans only 58 around Dunkirk, another 75 in other areas) during Operation Dynamo. Both the Luftwaffe and the RAF failed; both demonstrated—simultaneously— the capabilities and limitations of airpower. Despite Göring's boast, the Luftwaffe could not prevent the evacuation; on the other hand, the RAF could not protect it.[39] Dunkirk was the Royal Navy's triumph—the "miracle" was fashioned by the small ships and the large.

But no claims of a moral victory could disguise the sweeping character of the German triumph.

On June 4, with the flames of Dunkirk visible from the Dover Cliffs, Churchill spoke to Parliament to rally his people for the worst that was still to come:

. . . we shall not flag or fail. We shall go on to the end, we shall fight in France, we shall fight on the seas and oceans, we shall fight . . . in the air, we shall defend our island . . . we shall fight on the beaches, we shall fight on the landing-grounds, we shall fight in the fields and in the streets, we shall fight in the hills; we shall never surrender, and even if . . . this island . . . were subjugated and starving, then our Empire beyond the seas, armed and guarded by the British Fleet, would carry on the struggle, until, in God's good time, the New World, with all its power and might, steps forth to the rescue and the liberation of the Old.

The drumbeat phrases were heard around the world, and Britons everywhere girded up their loins. A vast ocean away, the New World —still inward-looking—was aroused, stirred, and perturbed.

5

The Death of the Third Republic

On June 5, the Nazi legions struck south across the Somme.

Some 140 German divisions, many of them fresh, faced the equivalent of about 64 Allied divisions most of which were mauled, battered, half-strength or second-line, with inadequate equipment, indifferent morale, and often poor leadership. Thirteen were static divisions, manning fortifications of the Maginot Line; three were partially horsed cavalry; the so-called armored divisions were decimated and exhausted; many of the infantry divisions used horse-drawn artillery and supply, and were colonial troops or were still being formed. So desperate was dying France that the French soldiers who were evacuated from Dunkirk to England were hastily transported back to France, and dumped between Caen and the Seine to be engulfed piecemeal in conquest, "units from seventeen different divisions . . . hopelessly intermingled," unarmed, half-clad.[40]

The British still had 140,000 troops south of the Somme after Dunkirk, most of them manning depots, supply and communication lines, and all the rear area facilities that had been established—prior to catastrophe—in anticipation of building up in France a far larger expeditionary force. But few of these were fighting units. What was left of the British 1st Armored Division—in reality a light mechanized division, with limited potential—was still in combat, with a small composite force raked up from disparate units, the improvised Beauman "Division" and the 51st Highland Division. The kilted Scotsmen, including the Black Watch and other famous regiments, had won military immortality in World War I as "the ladies from Hell," but reputations meant nothing to the German Panzers.

The Last Days

Despite Allied attempts during the Flanders fighting to eliminate them, the Germans had successfully held three large bridgeheads south of the Somme, at Abbeville, Amiens, and Péronne. Now, on June 5, two German Panzer divisions punched from each of the bridgeheads into the greatly overextended and thinly held Allied lines. Bock's Army Group B, on the western (seaward) flank (from the Channel to east of Soissons), struck first. It was followed on June 9 by the major attack by Rundstedt's Army Group A (from Soissons to Montmédy), with eight armored divisions; and on June 14, by a minor holding attack against the French Maginot Line and Rhine defenses by Leeb's Army Group C. The plan was simple: to break through the thin defenses, surround and destroy piecemeal, roll back the flanks—one against the sea, the other against the Swiss frontier— with the fortifications of the Maginot Line outflanked and taken from the rear.

Against this juggernaut, the French deployed five so-called armies from the Channel to the Meuse: the Tenth (Altmayer) on the seaward flank; the Seventh (Frère) and Sixth (Touchon) in front of

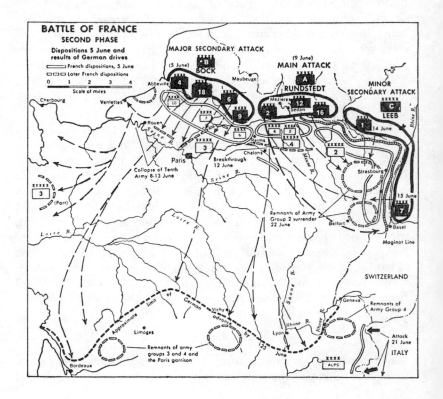

Paris; and the Fourth (Requin) and Second (Freydenberg) joining the Maginot Line defenses.

". . . with inadequate forces and in a mood of inevitable defeat . . . the French High Command waited for the opening of the final battle. . . ."[41]

From the first, it was hopeless; some divisions were attempting to hold fronts as long as 20 miles in broken country. To try to compensate for the disparity in numbers and mobility, the French and British at first attempted to fortify villages and hold strong points.

To no avail; the Panzers simply bypassed the strong points, roared into rear areas, and the following infantry washed—like the rising tide—over the cinders of resistance.

Of many of these men and units, it can only be recorded that they died. They won no combat immortality and scant breathing space.

It was high summer, and the days were long and blazing hot. . . . Dive-bombers roared down on their positions and they were shelled, mortared and machine-gunned. . . . The Highlanders fought, as Highlanders do—and as their casualties bear witness. The 7th. Argyll and Sutherland lost (in one day, June 5) 23 officers and nearly 500 other ranks, killed, wounded and missing; and the whole division was cruelly mauled.[42]

By the night of June 6, Marshal Pétain, Deputy Prime Minister under Reynaud, who had alluded that morning to the possible need to negotiate with the Germans, was telling General Spears, the British liaison officer in Paris: ". . . c'est sans espoir."

The same involved command relationships, inadequate communications, the same time lag in intelligence of enemy movements and in decisionmaking characterized, on the Allied side, the final battle for France as had marked the Battle of Flanders. Deep German penetrations completely disrupted the already fragile French defenses, and rivers of refugees, in spate upon the roads, impeded couriers, supplies, all movement.

Attempts to plug the gaps were futile:

The 17th. Infantry Division (10th Army) was being brought up in lorries to reenforce the front; but owing to an error in the transmission of orders the vehicles were unloaded too far north. Suddenly the German armor was upon the lines of lorries that covered the road, twenty men to a lorry. Chaos. Panic. The riflemen hurriedly got into line, soldiers were running in all directions, the battered, overturned lorries were in flames. No deployment was possible. Infantry and artillery alike scattered and faded into the countryside. Half the infantry and nearly all the artillery fell into German hands. . . .[43]

By June 10, the Germans were in Rouen, and spearheads were sweeping toward the coast behind the left flank of the British and French positions, with most of the 51st Highland Division and thousands of French trapped between the Panzers and the sea. Paris was being outflanked from the west, and the main German effort was yet to be felt.

As the men of the sea once again stood in to shore to succor the men of the land, the jackals gathered; Italy, hungry for spoils, entered the war. In Rome, Mussolini on the afternoon of June 10 strutted to the balcony of the Palazzo Venezia, while below him thousands roared for glory. Scowling, his dark jowls working, Il Duce shouted:

Fighters of the land, the sea and the air, Blackshirts of the Legions and the Revolution, men and women of Italy, the Empire and the Kingdom of Albania; Listen!

The hour marked out by destiny is sounding in the sky of our country: the hour of irrevocable decisions.

The declaration of war has already been notified to the ambassadors of Great Britain and France. . . .[44]

That night, in a speech in Charlottesville, Virginia, President Roosevelt encircled in black the first of many "days of infamy": "On this 10th of June, 1940, the hand that held the dagger has struck it into the back of his neighbor. . . ."

Reynaud and his government left Paris that evening, as thousands of fellow citizens had done before them. The French radio announced the evacuation and signed off with its futile clarion: "*Aux armes, Citoyens!*"

De Gaulle, now an Undersecretary for Defense to Reynaud—raised too late to a position of limited power—left with the Prime Minister at midnight, bound for Orléans:

Cars buffeted each other amid the oaths of tyro drivers. The villages were already "fortified," retiring into their shells like towns in the Middle Ages. In front of the anti-tank wall, linked with ancient carts and broken-down cars, drivers and passengers were asked for their papers. A stationary line of fugitives stretched far into the distance. . . .[45]

Along the coast between the Somme and the Seine, some 60,000 encircled men—the remnants of more than five divisions—died slowly between the 10th and 12th. About a third escaped by sea, through Le Havre or other ports; some went to England, some were moved further southward on the French coast—hopefully to fight again. But fog and *Blitzkrieg* trapped most of the Highland Division, its glories of World War I to be shadowed now by long years of somber captivity.

Disaster inspired dissension; the Allies squabbled, as the Germans moved. Churchill once again flew to France on June 11, but settled nothing; he spent the night in the Château du Muguet (near Tours) and wrote a characteristic footnote to history in the conference room of the château the next morning:

. . . An apparition which . . . resembled an angry Japanese genie, in long, flowing red silk kimona, over similar but white garments, girdled with a white belt of like material, stood there, sparse hair on end, and said with every sign of anger: "Uh Ay ma bain?" [It was Churchill, who found that the château's facilities left much to be desired]. . . . But as usual he made his meaning perfectly clear even in French, and his needs were attended to. . . .[46]

East of Paris Rundstedt's legions hammered over the old battlefields of World War I and crossed the Marne—rampart then, sandcastle now—at Châlons and Château-Thierry, driving ever southward.

The End of Glory

In these last days of the Third Republic, three persistent motifs dominated the dirge of defeat. One was French: the recurrent demand for more planes, more aid from Britain, and "clouds" of aircraft from the United States. Two were British, one shared to a lesser degree by Washington: repeated attempts by the British to persuade Reynaud and the French government to flee to North Africa or elsewhere to legitimatize a government-in-exile outside metropolitan France and to rally the empire against the Germans; and urgent efforts to secure the French Fleet against a German takeover. With disintegration, national aims diverged; each government thought first in terms of its own priorities.

Despite Churchill's fiery apostrophes, an undefended Paris was declared an "open city" on June 13, and the next day—June 14—Le Havre fell; the French government fled still further south from Tours to Bordeaux, and in the early morning Parisians wept as units of Küchler's Eighteenth Army marched in triumph along the Champs-Élysées, route of vanished glories.

Everywhere except on the Italian front it was over, save the recriminations and the tears. On June 17, German troops crossed the

Loire, and Panzer units, curving eastward, approached Besançon near the French Alps.

The French defense, collapsing at all points, was further weakened by a government decision to declare all towns of more than 20,000 people "open cities," thus forgoing their defense.

Three French armies, manning the Maginot Line and the Rhine defenses and now facing a frontal attack by Leeb's Army Group C, had waited too long to retreat; hundreds of thousands of them were trapped. German units captured some of the outer works and filtered between the great fortress casemates. Part of the French gold reserve was transported, via cruiser, to Dakar.

In Bordeaux as the Third Republic lay dying, the decadence of disaster was limned against the *haute cuisine* of France, "the lunches and dinners at the Chapon Fin; the excellent food and splendid wines [were] sampled in an atmosphere of death and destruction. . . ."[47]

On June 16, Churchill played his last card in a desperate effort to keep France officially fighting. He sent Reynaud an offer of union: "France and Britain shall no longer be two nations, but one Franco-British Union."

Reynaud, the politician for peacetime but not for crisis, nevertheless sought to keep France in the war. Not so his ever-present mistress, the Comtesse Hélène des Portes. Major General Sir Edward Spears, the omniscient observer, who was Churchill's personal liaison officer with the French government, saw her read the text of the suggested proclamation of union, as a secretary started to type it, with a mixture of "rage and amazement."

Messages from Reynaud and a "former Naval Person" (Churchill) poured into Washington; Roosevelt was warned that only American entry into the war could save France, that Hitler's acquisition of the French Fleet would endanger the United States. Roosevelt replied with sympathy but noted that only Congress could declare war, and that neither Congress nor the American people were prepared to fight. Churchill and Reynaud, French and British generals, talked of forming and holding a Breton "redoubt."

General Sir Alan Brooke, who had distinguished himself at Dunkirk, had been placed in command of all British forces in France, and the 52nd Division and elements of the 1st Canadian Division had been sent to France. By June 14, Brooke had convinced Churchill that the British must leave. British, French, and Polish troops streamed to Cherbourg, Brest, St. Malo, St. Nazaire—just ahead of the enemy tanks—and were lifted to England.

The night of June 16 wrote, for France, the end of glory. A Cabinet crisis had developed. As early as March 28 the French and British governments had formally agreed to fight to the finish together. Neither would make a separate peace. Reynaud used the British offer of common citizenship as his final card to keep France officially in the war. But the majority of the ministers, moved in part by the ancient Anglo-French suspicions and jealousies, viewed with frosty disdain Churchill's offer of union, and favored an armistice. Weygand and Pétain ridiculed the idea of continued British resistance without France; "in three weeks" (some French generals had predicted) "England will have her neck wrung like a chicken." Reynaud resigned. Pétain took his place and immediately initiated armistice discussions.

Pétain, a hero of yesteryear, was now eighty-four. He was conscious of his reputation, which—in a France bred on a great past—surrounded him like an aura. To some Englishmen he appeared, in the words of Lord Lloyd, Secretary for the Colonies, "vain . . . and ga-ga." But De Gaulle, much later, was to describe him best—this hero who had outlived his time:

> . . . The whole career of that exceptional man had been one long effort of repression. Too proud for intrigue, too forceful for mediocrity, too ambitious to be a time-server, he nourished in his solitude a passion for domination, which had long been hardened by his consciousness of his own value, the setbacks he had encountered, and the contempt he had for others. Military glory had already lavished on him its bitter caresses. But it had not satisfied him, since it had not loved him alone. And here suddenly in the extreme winter of his life, events were offering to his gifts and pride the opportunity—so long awaited!—to expand without limits; on one condition however: that he should accept disaster as his elevation's scutcheon and should adorn it with his glory . . . under the outer shell the years had gnawed his character. Age was delivering him over to the maneuvers of people who were clever at covering themselves with his majestic lassitude. Old age is a shipwreck. That we might be spared nothing, the old age of Marshal Pétain was to identify itself with the shipwreck of France. . . .[48]

Disaster and crisis also harshly illuminated the limitations of Weygand, "by nature a brilliant second" but not a supreme commander:

> . . . if the qualities demanded for staff service and those required by command are in no way contradictory, they should not be confused. To take action on one's own responsibility, to want no mark upon it but one's own, to face destiny alone—the harsh, exclusive passion charac-

teristic of a chief—for these Weygand had neither the inclination nor the preparation. . . . he had not, in all his career, ever exercised command. . . .[49]

Weygand had been called in too late to retrieve the situation and had long been convinced that defeat was inevitable. Like so many French generals, obsessed with *honneur;* like the French Army, which in entirely different context resembled the German military's "state within a state," Weygand was preoccupied with his troops. The government, which had started the war, must end it; the Army would not face the ordeal of a *military* surrender.

Pétain shared this feeling, and so the French sued for peace.

Hitler took his time about it. On June 18, he met in Munich with Mussolini.

In London, Charles de Gaulle, an austere figure with a flaming passion who believed France was not France without *La gloire,* broadcast to Frenchmen everywhere a call for continued resistance.

The lines were drawn, and in Bordeaux, as the bickering continued in the new Pétain government among those who wished to flee to Africa and those—Pétain, the chief—who wished to stay in France, the shadow of the ambitious, enigmatic, fascistic man who was to become the eminence grise of the Vichy regime—Pierre Laval—loomed over the council tables.

On June 21, the Armistice terms were given to General Huntziger, who met Hitler in the railway car near Compiègne where Germany had admitted defeat in 1917. A German band played *"Deutschland über Alles."* But it was not until June 25 that the shooting was to stop, and Mussolini tried, in the interval, to cash in on his cheap investment of glory. He started some thirty-two Italian divisions moving across the passes of the Alpes Maritimes and along the Riviera coast into southern France. The French, with German Panzers roaring down the Rhône Valley behind them (the Germans reached Lyons on June 19 and were moving east toward Grenoble on the 23rd), had the equivalent of only six second-class, depleted divisions —many of them static fortress troops—to oppose the new enemy. They had, however, the advantage of strong fortifications, and very difficult terrain plus bad weather. The Legions of Mussolini were not the Legions of the Caesars; only near Menton did the Italians make feeble gains. France garnered bitter solace by stopping in its tracks the three-pronged Italian assault.

On June 25, the firing died.

It was armistice, not peace, and the terms were harsh. Most of the

French Army were prisoners of war; they were to remain so until war's end. Most of France, including Paris and the Atlantic coast, was to be occupied by the Germans; the French government would function within permissive limits as defined by the victors in about two-fifths of France (including the Mediterranean coast); German anti-Hitler political refugees were to be surrendered to the Gestapo; and French men-of-war were to be demobilized or disarmed, under Armistice Commission supervision. A separate Italian Armistice—upon which Hitler insisted—saved the Roman face but was written in terms of military realities. There were to be some demilitarized zones but no Italian occupation; the spoils of war had eluded Mussolini.

On June 28, the deposed Premier, Paul Reynaud, distracted by defeat and his responsibilities to history, was driving with his paramour, Madame des Portes, to Le Grès. The car swerved from the road and struck a plane tree. Madame des Portes died instantly; Reynaud was almost scalped.

In far-off Indochina the Rising Sun of Japan demanded—and received—the cession of some French authority. It was the first step in the dismemberment of empire.

And the Pétain government set up shop in a town once noted for its water—Vichy—but forever since a synonym for a puppet state, collaboration, and shame.

"Operation Catapult"

But the tragedy was not yet played out.

The Armistice terms—written and unwritten—which dealt with the French Fleet, were, in the British view, suspicious and equivocal, particularly a clause which stated that the "French Fleet . . . shall be . . . demobilized and disarmed under German or Italian control." No matter that various members of the French government had assured both British and U.S. representatives that the fleet would never be allowed to fall into German hands;[50] that the French ships were the only major bargaining chip Vichy possessed; that the Navy was the basis of the ambitious Admiral Darlan's political power and that without it he was nothing; no matter that, in any case, all of the major ships had fled the French Atlantic ports before the Panzers overran them and were beyond reach of the Germans in British ports, in Alexandria, Egypt, or in North Africa. . . .

On June 28 Churchill ordered the Admiralty to prepare "Operation Catapult," and despite the openly expressed horror of many

British naval officers, on July 3 the blow fell. In Plymouth, Portsmouth, Falmouth, and Sheerness, armed British troops "in carpet slippers" stole aboard 2 French battleships, 2 cruisers and about 200 destroyers, sloops, submarines, minesweepers, and patrol craft, surprised or clubbed the deck watch, and overcame the sleeping officers and men. Only in the giant submarine *Surcouf* was there real resistance: three British, one Frenchman killed, two British wounded. In Alexandria, one French battleship, four cruisers, three destroyers, and a submarine were anchored, surrounded by a far superior British Fleet. The French ships, under British ultimatum, were ultimately immobilized, then neutralized.

But at the Algerian naval base of Mers-el-Kebir, at Oran, men who were allies yesterday became bitter enemies that July day. Under orders, despite his personal objections, Vice Admiral Sir James Somerville opened fire upon *Dunkerque* and *Strasbourg*, two of the most modern French capital ships, as well as on two older battleships and a clutch of cruisers, destroyers, and other vessels. The British Fleet (a battle cruiser, two battleships, an aircraft carrier, two cruisers, and eleven destroyers) was far superior to Admiral Marcel Gensoul's squadron, but even so the results were disproportionate. After a futile day-long parley and constant proddings from London, the reluctant Somerville opened fire at 5:54 P.M. on a day that is still regarded by many Frenchmen as "stained with infamy."

The holocaust was swift. The French ships were moored or at anchor or with steam low; they were "sitting ducks." Battleship *Brétagne* blew up; *Provence* got under way but was soon a flaming pyre and ran aground; *Dunkerque*, attacked again the next day by air, was badly damaged and out of action; the stern of the destroyer *Mogador* was blown off. Some 1,297 French seamen died; the British were untouched. Of the major units only *Strasbourg*, boldly conned, escaped through a British-laid minefield to Toulon, where she was joined later by the seaplane tender *Commandant Teste* and some cruisers, destroyers, and smaller units from Oran and Algiers. The next day, July 4, the new battleship *Richelieu*, attacked at Dakar by torpedo planes from the British carrier *Hermes*, was damaged and immobilized for a year.

The British purpose—to avoid at all costs loss of their supremacy at sea—had been accomplished at an inordinate price.

In retrospect, the British attack, deplored and resisted until the last moment as "appalling" by most of the British senior officers concerned, was erroneous because unnecessary. After the event, London learned what a British naval intermediary had been told at the last moment by Admiral Gensoul, that on June 24 Admiral Darlan had ordered all French ships to resist any attempt by the Axis Armistice Commission to seize them—either by scuttling or by flight to the United States. But this would not have been enough for Churchill or the British War Cabinet, who regarded Darlan as something of a German puppet, and who insisted upon neutralization of the French Fleet, that is, immediate scuttling or actual seizure by British crews.

The British attack upon an old ally had profound psychological and political effects. The suspicion, jealousy, and mistrust of Britain and of British motives—always latent in many Frenchmen, and acute since the frictions of Dunkirk and the cataclysmic Battle of France—were enormously nourished. The position of De Gaulle was complicated and greatly weakened; the birth pangs of the Free French movement became a long travail. Vichy was strengthened, and particularly the ambitious rightist Pierre Laval. Everywhere Frenchmen were divided; their country had two enemies: Germany —and Britain. Oran and Mers-el-Kebir delayed for many, many months the harnessing of the energies of freedom-loving Frenchmen in the cause of liberty which should have been the common *oriflamme* of the West.

Yet in Britain and to a lesser extent in the United States, the British actions were condoned. More important—and perhaps a key to Churchill's decision—was the ruthless determination to fight on that these actions indicated. Cordell Hull, U.S. Secretary of State at the time, wrote later in his memoirs (after a discussion with Churchill): "Since many people throughout the world believed that Britain was about to surrender, he [Churchill] wanted by this action to show that she still meant to fight."[51]

And Churchill himself recorded in *Their Finest Hour*: "After Oran, it became clear to all countries that the British government and nation were resolved to fight on to the last."

Vichy Ignominy

In France, Pierre Laval, "shrewdest, most forceful personality in Vichy . . . ruthlessly ambitious politician," was becoming the dominant figure in a regime convinced that "perfidious Albion" would soon be conquered. Laval's intense egoism and complete lack of principle had convinced him he could ride the coattails of disaster to second place in the New Europe he foresaw of Germany supreme. His first act, abetted by Pétain and French rightists, was to demolish the constitutional guarantees of the French past, and to introduce into the Assembly a new Constitutional Law, which made of truncated France an authoritarian dictatorship with Pétain as "chief of state." Opposition was dangerous, but some valiant souls—many of them later tried and imprisoned for their courage—opposed; even more abstained.

The enigmatic Reynaud, his head swathed in bandages, was one of those "excused" from voting—an easy way out between fear and conscience. Over the last important act of his political life, he temporized and compromised. But with his women, fate had decided for him. His mistress dead, Madame Reynaud was supreme. Robert Murphy, who was American chargé d'affaires in Vichy, saw her triumph on July 10 when the Constituent Assembly ratified tyranny:

I was lunching with the former Minister of Aviation, Guy la Chambre, and his wife, and at a nearby table sat M. and Mme. Paul Reynaud, he swathed in bandages after his close call with death on the highway. . . . Everyone was sombre and dispirited—except Mme Reynaud, who came over to our table and recounted to Mme La Chambre the pungent details of the highway accident which took the life of her husband's mistress. As she rose to rejoin M. Reynaud, she exclaimed with some emotion, "Now, chérie, for my revenge!"[52]

It was an ignominious curtain in history for a man who faltered instead of leading. In the famous phrase of Pertinax, Reynaud must be counted among the "gravediggers of France."

In six weeks France, supposedly the world's greatest land power, had been conquered by lightning war. From the North Cape to the Pyrenees the Swastika reigned, and from the Pripyat Marshes and the Carpathians to the muddy estuaries of the great western rivers there was no power to oppose Hitler.

The physical statistics of conquest were disproportionate. The Germans lost about 27,000 men killed, another 18,000 missing, and more than 111,000 wounded—a total casualty list of about 156,000. The entire British Expeditionary Force had suffered 68,000 casualties and had been cut up, captured, and thrown out of Europe; months of reorganization and replacement would be required. The French tabulated—until the wholesale surrenders started and record-keeping bogged down—123,600 men killed, missing, captured, 200,000 wounded. Ultimately between 1.5 and 2 million French soldiers were corralled in POW camps or pens; their entire Army—minus the colonial forces overseas—had been routed, dismembered, or captured; the nation itself lost. The political and psychological effects of the defeat were profound. A shock wave went round the world, and Hitler had acquired an aura of invincibility.

Across the Narrow Seas—for so many centuries ramparts to imvasion, but spanned now by the plane—Britain stood alone.

6

The Battle of Britain

An Era of Deadly Peril

On June 18 Churchill told the House of Commons that "the Battle of Britain is about to begin. . . ."

Upon this battle depends the survival of Christian civilization. Upon it depends our own British life, and the long continuity of our institutions and our Empire. The whole fury and might of the enemy must very soon be turned on us. Hitler knows that he will have to break us in this island or lose the war. If we can stand up to him, all Europe may be free and the life of the world may move forward into broad, sunlit uplands. But if we fail, then the whole world, including the United States, including all that we have known and cared for, will sink into the abyss of a new Dark Age, made more sinister, and perhaps more protracted, by the lights of perverted science. Let us therefore brace ourselves to our duties, and so bear ourselves that, if the British Empire and its Commonwealth last for a thousand years, men will say "This was their finest hour."[53]

For the first time since Napoleon, Britain girded for invasion. General Sir Edmund Ironside, now Commander-in-Chief of the Home Armies, having been succeeded as Chief of the Imperial General Staff by General Sir John Dill on May 27, had few resources. Dunkirk and the Battle of France had been a débacle; not a single British division—there were twenty-seven, including Canadians, Australians, and New Zealanders—had its full complement of men and weapons. The units were static; as Ironside said: "The Army had not been trained to take the offensive; to create an offensive spirit suddenly, with no mobility, no armour and no training was impossible."[54]

A system of fixed defenses—roadblocks, tank traps, pillboxes, and entrenchments—was hurriedly thrown up behind the most likely landing areas. Troops and civilian contractors worked day and night; their frantic work started long before the shooting in France ended as London foresaw the inevitable. It was inexpert energy; many roadblocks were so constructed they could be easily flanked; some pillboxes were sited facing the wrong way. Nevertheless, the defenses grew; and mobile reserve units gradually were created to back up the local strong points and mount counterattacks. Coast guards and watchers—many of them drawn from the Home Guard—lined the cliffs and beaches behind minefields, barbed wire, and heavy guns; airfields were protected, after a fashion, by riflemen, Bren guns mounted in trucks, and airmen hastily trained as soldiers. Almost half the population of the East Anglian and Kentish coastal towns (more than 200,000 people) was evacuated inland; those who remained were warned that in case of invasion they must stay in place—no matter what the cost—to avoid a repetition of the clogged and saturated roads of France, inundated by refugees, virtually unusable by the military. Even petrol pumps near the sea were partially drained of their supplies or marked for demolition; piping was laid to spread oil upon the ocean and turn great patches of it into a sea of flame.[55] Britain was in deadly earnest.

Yet, despite the antipathy of Americans for "foreign wars," Britain did not stand quite alone. The United States was slowly but surely becoming the "arsenal of democracy." At the same time, the fall of France spurred a tremendous expansion of the U.S. armed forces, including the induction, beginning in September 1940, of National Guard units into federal service, and the start of construction of a "two-ocean Navy," to be capable of meeting any combination of enemies in Atlantic or Pacific. President Roosevelt's "short-of-war" policy, an "a-neutral" stance deliberately stacked to aid the Allies, had led first to the transfer to Britain of many "surplus" arms—including half a million Enfield rifles, more than 100 million rounds of .30-caliber ammunition, 500 75 mm. field guns, 500 3-inch mortars with ammunition, 35,000 machine guns, and automatic rifles and other equipment. This matériel started to flow into Britain in the early summer of crisis; the small torrent of unending aid eventually grew into a great river of supplies of all kinds which literally enabled British survival.

A key item in Britain's aid requests, first specified by Churchill on May 15 soon after he became Prime Minister, was destroyers. The Prime Minister asked for the loan of fifty or so old four-piper destroyers, of World War I design, and his initial request was repeatedly and urgently renewed as heavy destroyer losses in the Scandinavian and French campaigns, the demands of antisubmarine warfare, and the strain of Italian entry into the conflict spread the available British ships thin. The threat of invasion led to an agreement in principle on July 24 between Britain and the United States, formalized by signature on September 2, to provide fifty U.S. destroyers to the British Fleet in exchange for sites for U.S. bases in the Bahamas, Jamaica, Antigua, St. Lucia, Trinidad, and British Guiana. The British threw in "for free" base rights for the United States in Argentina, Newfoundland, and Bermuda, and, in the event, the United States delivered not only the fifty promised destroyers but also ten Coast Guard cutters, the last by April 10, 1941. Washington had stretched the definition of "neutrality" to its limit, yet the measures taken in the summer and fall of 1940 not only prepared the United States for active war more than a year later but fitted the dichotomous yearnings of the American people. Public sentiment supported the Allies by a considerable majority but was also overwhelmingly opposed to participating in actual shooting war. The measures approved in Washington clearly indicated that the government of the most powerful industrial nation on earth understood the potential danger to the United States of the sweeping Hitler victories.[56]

After the fall of France, there was a brief slowdown. *Blitzkrieg* cannot continue incessantly, and, in fact, Hitler had not decided what to do next. There were no developed strategic plans in Berlin to follow the end of the French campaign; the size and speed of that victory had surprised the Germans as well as the world. And the hesitant, ambivalent attitude of Hitler and his Army and Navy leaders toward England—the Air Force was more bumptiously confident— contributed to delay.

It is true that as early as November 15, 1939, Admiral Raeder had directed the Seekriegsleitung or Naval Operations Office to study the "possibility of troop landings in England."[57] But this was a kind of "mad" idea, as Raeder later said, and nothing was crystallized.

On May 21, Raeder again discussed the possibility of invasion, this time with Hitler, and all the services had given cursory thought to the problem.

But it was not until July 2 that Supreme Headquarters issued its first directive, which included the prophetic words: ". . . a landing in England is possible, providing that (1) air superiority can be attained. . . ."[58]

On July 16, Hitler ordered the preparations of plans for a "landing operation . . . if necessary" against England. But at the same time his thoughts were already turning toward Russia, and he was preparing for his so-called peace speech in the Reichstag on July 19. He and most of his generals were convinced that England was finished. His mixed attitude toward England—a sneaking admiration of the British and their empire, combined with resentment at their world hegemony and their influence on the continent—found full expression in these July days. Planning for an attack had started. Yet Hitler nourished hopes that England would "see it my way," and yield to a fait accompli: the conquest of Western Europe and the end of fighting. In his speech in the Kroll Opera House in Berlin on July 19 he paid brief obeisance to peace while bitterly attacking Churchill and extolling the conquests and glories of the Third Reich: "In this hour I feel duty bound before my conscience once again to direct an appeal to reason even in England. . . . I see no ground that should force the continuation of this struggle. . . ."[59]

It was—perhaps deliberately—a feeble gesture; Hitler may have already made up his mind that Britain would never agree to Nazi hegemony on the continent. It was in any case the final "peace" gesture, peace on Hitler's terms. There was no sign of compliance from London, and by the last week of July, thirteen German divisions began to concentrate near the Channel coast. All over Germany the words of an old German naval drinking song of World War I (set to new melody) sounded in concert halls, parks, and over the radio:

> Denn wir fahren, denn wir fahren,
> Denn wir fahren gegen Engelland . . .

"Operation Lion" (twisting the Lion's tail), subsequently renamed "Sea Lion," meshed into gear. The meticulous matching of requirements against resources, the estimated strengths of the enemy, the comparative statistics of power, the availability of transport, all were compiled and tabulated. By July 31, a tentative invasion date was set for September 15, and transports, barges, tugs, trawlers, and small craft were concentrating in the Channel ports and near the Strait of Dover. By September 1,700,000 tons of transport shipping, almost 2,000 barges and ferries, and more than 400 tugs, plus many miscellaneous craft, had been assembled, and assault troops had made mock amphibious training landings along the French coast. It was true there was bickering among the German armed services; the Navy, in particular, was doubtful of success.

The final compromise plan, after long debate about broad or narrow frontal attack, envisaged assault landings by 50,000 men in two hours on a 60- to 70-mile discontinuous front along the south coast of England from near Brighton to near Folkestone. About 10,000 men of the 7th Parachute Division were to land from the air near Hythe; the rest were to be seaborne. In all, some 125,000 men were to storm ashore in the first day, increasing to 23 divisions, principally from the Sixteenth and Ninth German Armies in the first six to eight weeks. Nor did the planning stop there. In Holland and Norway, as well as in France, large units made obvious preparations—as part of a cover and deception plan for the real landings—for feints against other parts of England, Scotland, and even Southern Ireland.

The Nazi projects were not merely paper plans. Preparations for the occupation, government, and utilization of a conquered England were worked out in the usual meticulous Teutonic detail; British citizens to be arrested and sent to concentration camps were listed, in some cases by name, and signs were prepared to be tacked to the doors of requisitioned property.

It was, for England, an era of deadly peril; as Churchill later acknowledged, for many weeks in that summer of 1940, 150,000 German troops landed in England could have wrought havoc.

Yet the *Herrenvolk* could not walk on water. The Royal Navy and the Royal Air Force guarded the sea and air ramparts, and Hitler himself saw the operation as an "exceptionally bold and daring undertaking." He itemized four major prerequisites for success: Luftwaffe air superiority over the Strait of Dover and the landing beaches (a fundamental requirement); successful employment of long-range guns mounted on the French coast opposite Dover; barrier minefields, to help the guns interdict the British Navy from disrupting the transport lanes; and good weather.

It was the first of these—the struggle for air superiority—that was to achieve high drama in those long summer days as the ground soldiers waited and the invasion fleet assembled.

The odds seemed uneven. Three German air fleets were concentrated for the battle: Luftflotte 2 (Field Marshal Albert Kesselring commanding), based in Holland, Belgium, and northeast France; Luftflotte 3 (Field Marshal Hugo Sperrle commanding), based in France; and Luftflotte 5 (Colonel General Hans-Jürgen Stumpff commanding), based in Norway and Denmark. These fleets had about 3,350 assigned aircraft, but only about 75 percent were fully serviceable and Luftflotte 5, in Norway and Denmark, was too far from decisive English targets to play more than a minor role in the Battle of Britain. About 900 to 1,000 single-engined Messerschmitt 109's and a few twin-engined Me-110 fighters were used in the battle, with about 1,000 bombers—Heinkel 111's, Dornier 17's, and Junkers

88's augmented by about 300 Junkers 87's (the famous Stuka dive bombers).

Air Chief Marshal Sir Hugh Dowding, a dour, offish, and prickly man but a real professional, Air Officer Commanding the RAF Fighter Command, had 704 serviceable aircraft on August 11, 620 of them eight-gunned Hurricanes and the newer Spitfires; 289 planes in reserve. British aircraft factories, under the spur of the French defeat and the acidulous Lord Beaverbrook, newly appointed Minister of Aircraft Production, had turned out 1,665 planes in July, and almost 500 of them were fighters (as compared to only 157 fighters in January 1940). There were serious weaknesses; the great losses in Scandinavia, France, and the Low Countries had decimated the pilots list; the thin red line of fighter pilots had been augmented by Canadians, Poles, Czechs—still there were not enough.

Britain had in position as the battle opened only about one-quarter of the antiaircraft guns she needed. Searchlights and parachute and cable devices, propelled skyward by rockets, were part of the defense. Tethered barrage balloons—not enough for the targets they were assigned to protect—were streamed around aircraft factories and important sites to imperil low-level attacks. But by far the most important element in the British scheme of defense, later described as "possibly the best investment ever made by a British government,"[60] was the radar chain. This was not complete at the time the battle opened; it did not protect all of Britain but was sited to defend London and the areas of England closest to the continent. Radar, then in its infancy, provided early warning of air attack; if properly operated and if the blips on the radar screens were accurately analyzed and evaluated, they gave "Stuffy" Dowding the capability of concentrating his fighters against the major German bomber attacks. Radar was a key element in the battle. "If the oracle spoke clearly and was understood," the RAF might win; "if it failed them or they mistook its message, then defeat was almost certain."[61]

The Germans knew the chain existed, and planned to deal with it, but they did not adequately value its effectiveness. A strange anomaly, since the Luftwaffe had electronic tricks of its own; medium-frequency radio beacons guided the German bombers (as navigational aides) to their targets. The *Knickebein* directional beams—a code word standing for "googly" or "bent-leg"—even provided a rather accurate fix at night or in bad weather over British targets. A physicist assigned to Air Ministry intelligence, Dr. R. V. Jones, working with scrappy clues recovered from the wreckage of German bombers, played a hunch, proved the feasibility and actual existence of the directional beams, and devised means of spoofing, or bending (neutralizing) them. The Battle of Britain was the first skirmish in what has become, in a quarter century, an unending "silent war" of electronics versus ECM, or electronic countermeasures.

There was no complete hiatus between the Battle of France and the Battle of Britain, although the German raids of June and July, gradually mounting in intensity, were sporadic. In July the major objectives of the GAF were British ports and coastal convoys from Plymouth to the Strait of Dover. But only 30,000 tons of shipping were sunk by aircraft, and the ports of England—the coronary arteries through which flowed the lifeblood of nourishment from overseas—continued, despite the crump of bombs, to work the clock around. The GAF effort was still too small and too dispersed; its only result, to increase the strain upon Fighter Command.

The Bombs of August

The *Adlerangriff*, or "Eagle Attack," envisaged by Hermann Göring as a knockout blow against Fighter Command, was timed to start four to six weeks before the amphibious invasion.

The preliminary phase—attacks directed primarily against ports and convoys—started, most British historians calculate, about July 10; the main battle opened, by various reckonings, between August 8 and August 13, which the Germans called "Eagle Day."

In the opening phase of the battle, the primary German objectives were airfields, aircraft factories, and radar stations, with ports and Channel convoys as secondary targets. Most of the attacks were in daylight; night bombing was still in its infancy.

RAF Fighter Command's No. 11 Group, headquartered at Uxbridge, defended England's "heartland"—London and the counties of Essex, Kent, Sussex, Hampshire, and Dorset. Early on August 8, the radar screen showed sixty blips or "bogies" (unidentified aircraft) approaching the Isle of Wight. Hurricanes and Spits rose like a swarm of hornets; the fighters vectored by ground control to intercept. The blips were identified as "bandits" or enemy, and soon the cry of "Tallyho" sounded across the airwaves as a few young men of England dived against the Stukas and the Ju-88's.

A convoy was the German objective; in morning and afternoon as the skies buzzed with the angry hum of straining engines and vibrating props, contrails scarred the clouds, and comet smoke and brief blazing pyre inscribed requiem for vanquished pilots. It started badly for England, with six ships sunk, six damaged. The convoy scattered

—ships skittering across the ocean in all directions to escape the fury from the skies.

On the 11th and 12th Stukas and Heinkels, covered by Me-109's, struck Portland, Weymouth, Portsmouth, and coastal convoys, and, in major strength, bombed airfields and radar stations.

On the 12th the Germans scored again. The radar stations—their 360-foot steel masts towering high on crags and headlands—were conspicuous visual targets; the station at Ventnor on the Isle of Wight was clobbered (not to be replaced until August 23 by a substitute at Bembridge).

It had been a costly preliminary, with heavy shipping losses for Britain; 100 German aircraft had been shot down or crashed, 73 RAF fighters.

On August 13, "Eagle Day,"[62] 1,400 German aircraft flew against England in the largest attack of air warfare. The radar stations picked them up across the Channel, as the German swarms climbed skyward over Amiens, Dieppe, Cherbourg, and the No. 11 Group of Spits, Hurricanes, and old two-seater Defiants scrambled to meet them. Southampton was pocked with bombs, and from Margate to Southend the stuttering yammer of guns echoed across the skies. It was, for England, a "boiling summer's day"; the English airmen flew in shirt sleeves, "absolutely soaked in sweat." Pilot Officer D. M. Crook of 609 Squadron, in a Spitfire, was vectored into some 200 German aircraft over the Isle of Wight. He dived "straight down into the middle" of a scrum of GAF fighters, blazed away with his eight guns, narrowly escaped collision, pulled out in a long shuddering blackout of "terrific speed," watched a flaming Messerschmitt splash into the sea, and got back to Middle Wallop to drink a pint of iced Pimm's that evening.

Twelve British airfields and stations were attacked that day. Seven were lightly damaged, two more heavily. The cost to the attackers was forty-five German bombers; to the defenders, thirteen fighters.

The Germans thought it a good beginning; General Halder noted in his diary: "Results very good. . . . Eight major air bases have been virtually destroyed."

That night there came a more ominous development. Bombing Gruppe 100, specially trained in night operations, damaged an important Spitfire aircraft factory at Castle Bromwich, starting a campaign of nighttime terror from the skies that was to continue for years to come.

August 15 was a day of combat unprecedented in air warfare. Almost 1,800 German planes attacked Britain—500 bombers, 1,300 fighters; from Norway to France, the GAF struck with full available power against the stubborn British.

Against Scotland and the northeast coast, the results were limited. No. 13 Group in the north scored heavily; the twin-engined Me-110's —the only German fighters with range enough to fly across the North Sea from Scandinavian bases—were "very unhappy," pitted against "Spits" and "Hurries." The Heinkels destroyed twenty-four houses in Sunderland, roughed up an airfield at Driffield, where the British lost ten planes on the ground, and detonated an ammo dump —but the cost was prohibitive; bombers without Me-109 coverage were too vulnerable. General Stumpff of Luftflotte 5 henceforth canceled daylight attacks and reverted to night bombing.

In southeastern England, where 100 plane raids struck north of the Thames and 200 to 300 Nazis roamed over Hampshire and Dorset, the damage was more serious. Two aircraft factories were hit, some airfields damaged. But the British indubitably won the day's battle in the skies; they claimed 182 enemy planes, and 53 probables, against losses of 34. Like nearly all statistics of air battle, the claims were greatly inflated. The Germans actually lost 75 aircraft, far less than the British claim, but nevertheless a staggering one-day kill and the largest single toll of any one day in the Battle of Britain.

Göring, feeding his prize stallions at his country estate, was well pleased. Until further notice he directed that the principal target objective should continue to be the RAF, but—the first of several mistakes—he discounted the effectiveness of the attacks on radar sites and underestimated the damage so far done to them.

On August 16, 400 bombers, covered by 1,300 fighters—a tribute to the toughness of the British defense—scored heavily; 2 Ju-88's diving out of the low overcast destroyed 46 British aircraft in their hangars at Brize Norton, and damaged other fields.

On the 18th the Germans again drew blood: hangars blasted at Kenley, an important sector station of No. 11 Group, four Hurricanes destroyed on the ground, runways cratered, communications damaged, and hits which marred the effectiveness of six radar stations. But the Germans lost seventy-one aircraft—second-highest single-day toll of the battle—and the famous Stukas were decimated and most of them withdrawn from the battle.

Until August 24, there was relative respite; heavy cloud banks over England blinded the great flying fleets. The period from August 24 to September 6 was, in retrospect, the decisive phase of the Battle of Britain. Both sides had been heavily shaken. Since the first week in

August, the Germans had lost somewhat less than 400 aircraft; the British thought they had shot down almost twice that many. Fighter Command had lost 213 planes, and the bombed factories had not fully replaced them; Dowding had started to eat into his reserves. More important, the shortage of pilots had been accentuated; 154 British pilots had been killed or wounded, only 63 new ones trained.

The onslaught of late August and early September when 1,000 plane raids racked England daily was, as Göring then saw, "the decisive period of the air war against England." The fundamental objective was Fighter Command's No. 11 Group, guardian of the British heartland—its inner ring of airfields around London, communications, repair and supply depots, and sector commands. The reasoning was sound: paralyze the air defense of southeastern England and local air superiority—in the area selected for invasion—would be won. Kenley, Biggin Hill, Hornchurch, North Weald, Northolt, Manston were attacked again and again; runways were dotted with bomb craters, buildings were wrecked, and delayed-action bombs hampered clean-up. Two factories were damaged, one of them the source of half of England's supply of Hurricanes; the pilot strain and pilot shortage grew acute, and on August 31 Fighter Command suffered its heaviest losses of the battle: thirty-nine planes downed (the Germans lost forty-one), fourteen pilots killed.

It was at this crucial juncture that the British goaded Hitler into a great mistake. On August 25/26, one night after London had been hit by a few stray bombs from German aircraft lost in the dark, the night bombers of the RAF raided Berlin. The raids, like other offensive sorties by British aircraft over Germany since May, were minor—pinpricks, not wounds—but the psychological effect upon the German people and most of all upon *Der Fuehrer* was enormous. Night after night during the closing days of August and the first days of September, the night bombers of Britain wheeled in the bursting flak and searchlights' glare above Berlin and other objectives.

It was a blow to Hitler's pride, acknowledged in a raging speech on September 4: "The British drop their bombs indiscriminately. . . . If they attack our cities, we will rub out [raze] their cities from the map. . . ."[63]

On September 7, the Luftwaffe suddenly changed its principal bombing targets from the hard-pressed No. 11 Group to London. There was a technical excuse; the Germans thought they had worn down the RAF more than they had done. The GAF intelligence estimated Fighter Command had only 350 fighters left; actually, there were about 650. And daylight bombers over London would force the remnants of Fighter Command to mortal and decisive combat in the skies.

In the afternoon 400 bombers, 600 fighters—cruising in stepped-up formation from 12,000 to 30,000 feet, "like the escalator at Piccadilly Circus"—struck Woolwich and the docks at West Ham; by nightfall the line of the Thames had become a sea of flames.

Night brought no relief; 250 German bombers maintained from 8:00 P.M. to 4:00 A.M. a "slow agonizing procession" over the capital. The night defenses were primitive; only one bomber was lost.

"Invasion Imminent"

Photo reconnaissance had shown that the moment of truth was drawing near; the invasion ports across the Channel were clogged with barges, motor boats, ferries, shipping.

That night—September 7—at 8:07 P.M. the code words "Cromwell —Invasion Imminent" flashed across England; in some sectors Home Guard commanders rang churchbells to muster their men, believing the invasion had started. But while the men and women of England stood guard on headlands and chalk cliffs and mined beaches, Hitler, with ambivalent ambitions and one eye turned to the East, was still pondering. On September 3—unknown to the British—he had set a tentative D-Day of September 21, with the final decision reserved until September 10–11.

The Western world watched in horrified fascination as London burned and history waited. Many observers agreed with Colonel Charles Lindbergh that the German geographical, numerical, strategic, and technical advantages were enormous and that Britain fought a losing fight. Day and night the bombing continued; the smoke and flames formed a beacon and aiming point visible miles away. The East End, the docks, the railway stations were hit. By the morning of September 9, fires were raging unchecked; streets were blocked with debris; the dead lay unburied and unfound in the wreckage of many homes. Yet, on the 10th, Hitler—still uneasy—postponed the final decision until September 14. On the 11th, the 12th, the 13th, the raids continued; many of the daylight raids were broken up or turned back short of major objectives, but at night the antiaircraft barrage was a weak defense. The heart of London suffered; Downing Street, Trafalgar Square, Buckingham Palace were hit.

The British were not passive, however. British long-range artillery in the Dover cliffs, mosquito craft of the British Navy, and the bombers of Bomber Command harassed the invasion ports, and on September 12, the headquarters of Naval Group West reported to Berlin:

> Interruptions caused by the enemy's air force, long-range artillery and light naval forces have . . . assumed major significance. Ostend, Dunkirk, Calais and Boulogne cannot be used as night anchorages . . . because of the danger of . . . bombing and shelling. Units of the British fleet are now able to operate almost unmolested in the Channel . . . further delays are expected in the assembly of the invasion fleet.[64]

On September 14, Hitler still temporized. He postponed invasion, saying, "The necessary degree of air supremacy has not yet been attained."

September 15 has been well described as "the fiercest, most confused and most widespread struggle" of the Battle of Britain; about 1,000 planes (five fighters escorting every bomber) were vectored against London. The earphones sounded the sightings:

"Tallyho! Bandits! Twelve o'clock high!"

"*Achtung—Schpitfeuer!*"

At night, against a full moon, 181 bombers set new fires, blocked railway stations, killed hundreds of civilians.

Britain was shaken—but fighting still; the Germans, on September 15, lost sixty aircraft.

That night and the next and the next and the next Bomber Command was out in force; by September 21, an estimated 12.5 percent of the transports and invasion barges assembled by the Nazis in the Channel ports had been sunk or damaged.

On September 17, Hitler faced the facts. He still kept an eye on October, but: "The enemy air force is . . . by no means defeated. . . . The weather situation . . . does not permit us to expect a period of calm. . . . The Fuehrer, therefore, decides to postpone 'Sea Lion' indefinitely. . . ."

Although the British did not know it until September 23, when their reconnaissance aircraft reported a marked reduction of invasion shipping in the Channel ports, it was a decisive victory of World War II.

On October 4, Churchill cabled Roosevelt: "The gent has taken off his clothes and put on his bathing suit, but the water is getting colder and there is an autumn nip in the air. . . ."

On October 12, the German armed forces were officially told that "Sea Lion" would be "postponed" until the spring of 1941. The Germans maintained deception and cover forces, simulating attacks on

Britain through the winter and into the spring. But by then, new horizons and other conquests loomed. England had been saved.

A temporary salvation, it was in a military sense negative triumph. Britain had survived acute peril, but other perils confronted her, and on those dark horizons of the fall of 1940, there was no discernible way that Hitler's hold on the continent of Europe could be challenged.

The Battle of Britain demonstrated the capabilities and the limitations of airpower. It corrected—for the discerning—many of the prewar misconceptions, but also led to oversimplified and tragic exaggerations of its capabilities. Both the British and the Germans had grossly overestimated the effects of bombing upon industrial production and civilian morale; and both had grossly underestimated the air strength required to achieve important results. The concept of Douhet that aerial fleets could—without aid from surface forces—win great wars had been enthusiastically but not critically accepted by far too many airmen, and the "bomb-in-the-pickle-barrel" propaganda (to advertise bombing accuracy) had, in fact, been translated into area attacks by both sides against urban areas and civilians. The bomber had been hailed as supreme, but it was the fighter that won the battle.

The German Air Force was essentially a tactical air force with no four-engined or long-range heavy bombers, and no fighters of adequate range and maneuverability to protect its bombers over targets in Scotland and northeast England. The British, on the other hand, had developed heavy night bombers, and, at the same time, had produced highly maneuverable, heavily gunned fighter interceptors.

Both sides greatly exaggerated at the time the losses of the other. The RAF claimed—and believed its own claims—that from July 10, start of the "warm-up," through October 31, they had shot down 2,698 Nazi planes. The actual German loss was 1,733 (221 destroyed by antiaircraft fire). The Germans claimed the destruction of 3,058 British aircraft—and apparently believed most of their claims; they actually shot down 915.

The lack of enthusiasm of many German military leaders for "Sea Lion," and particularly Hitler's own ambivalence, was a major reason for failure; as Major General J. F. C. Fuller wrote, "Sea Lion was often contemplated but never planned." The German admirals had great respect for the "do or die" capabilities of the British Navy; they believed—correctly—that in the crunch of an actual attempted invasion the British Fleet would be risked, even in the Narrow Seas, to the last ship to prevent it. The Strait of Dover was a major psychological as well as a geographical barrier.

Even so, "Sea Lion" could probably have succeeded if the Germans had concentrated their airpower against No. 11 Group and southeast England. From first to last a localized and temporary air superiority over southeastern England was the basic requirement. The GAF came close to achieving this when it focused its efforts against airfields, factories, and radar sites, and low-level attacks, to escape radar detection, could have blinded Fighter Command. Group Captain J. E. Johnson, in *Wing Leader*, later wrote:

. . . the Luftwaffe could have won air domination over southern England within two weeks and would have then been ready for the next phase of their campaign—the isolation of the battlefield. . . . Then, opposed only by a British Army still handicapped by the loss of much equipment at Dunquerque [sic] and by a Royal Navy fighting at a great disadvantage in the narrow confines of a Channel dominated by the Luftwaffe, the German airborne troops might easily have seized a suitable piece of Kent in which to establish and build up an invasion force. . . .[65]

Perhaps the most mournful word in history is "if." The Germans might have won, might have successfully invaded and conquered England in 1940, if they had tried. Their own mistakes, their own uncertainties, as well as the skill and courage of the British, kept them from the test.

Stung by the British bomber raids on Berlin and other German objectives, Hitler and Göring switched objectives in the midst of the campaign. From that day forward, war in the air has centered upon the mutual attempts of both sides to destroy the enemy's will and capability to resist by heavier and heavier area-bombing attacks on industries, cities, transportation targets, and the humble dwellings of civilian populations. The bombing in the Battle of Britain set a pattern for what was to culminate at Hiroshima.

Yet, despite all the factors that contributed so materially to British victory, there can be no gainsaying the triumph of the Few. It was a near thing, the Battle of Britain, won by a "narrow margin." A handful of the young men of Britain and the empire and "Stuffy" Dowding, the keeper of the gates, fashioned the margin. The immortal tribute of Winston Churchill to Fighter Command: "Never in the field of human conflict was so much owed by so many to so few" (August 20, 1940), is an enduring monument to the best qualities of the British race.

7

The War at Sea

Mare Nostrum—*The Mediterranean*

The Italian entry into the war and the collapse of France immediately imperiled the British lifeline through the Mediterranean to Egypt and the Suez Canal, the keystone of empire.

Mussolini had proudly dubbed the Mediterranean "*Mare Nostrum*" (Our Sea), and his fleet, backed up by Italian land-based aircraft, and with bases in North Africa, Sicily, Italy, and Pantelleria (a tiny island at the chokepoint of maritime routes in the Central Mediterranean), had some major advantages.

Unlike the British Navy, which had to guard maritime trade routes in many oceans and a far-flung empire, the Italians concentrated their major strength in the Mediterranean, with some submarines and light forces south of the Suez Canal in the Red Sea based on Italian Somaliland's port of Massaua.

Mussolini, just before Italy entered the war, had ordered an offensive naval policy, but Admiral Domenico Cavagnari, Chief of the Italian Naval Staff, believed that Italian naval strategy must be defensive—its principal tasks the safeguarding of the Adriatic and Tyrrhenian seas and of maritime routes to Libya and the Dodecanese. By agreement with the Germans, the Italians would seek to engage and pin down in the Mediterranean as many enemy forces as possible; they would participate in the Atlantic submarine war south of the latitude of Lisbon, and might send raiders and submarines into the Indian Ocean.

Technically, the Italian Navy compelled some admiration; the ships were fast and well gunned if too lightly armored, and Italians had pioneered the development of midget submarines and "human" torpedoes. In June 1940, two of Italy's four old battleships had been modernized, and two new additional ships—the sleek, 30-knot, 35,000-ton *Vittorio Veneto* and *Littorio*, each armed with nine 15-inch guns—were to join the fleet in August. Two other new battleships and many cruisers, destroyers, and small craft were on the building ways but far from commissioning. The renaissance of the Italian Navy had not been completed by the outbreak of war and there were some grave weaknesses: no radar; inadequate antisubmarine warfare capabilities; major shortages of fuel oil; deficiencies in doctrine and training for torpedo attacks and night actions.

But the most serious of the Italian weaknesses was the Navy's complete dependence upon the Regia Aeronautica, the Italian Air Force, for air support; there were no carriers, and even air reconnaissance was assigned to, not operated by, the Navy. Leadership at the top levels was not comparable, with rare exceptions, to the professionalism and experience of the British. Morale was a moot point. The Italians thought it high (the Navy certainly was in better fettle than any of Mussolini's armed services), and there could be no question about the individual bravery of many Italian officers and men. The British were inclined to deprecate the fighting spirit of the Italians, but their more serious weakness was their inability to function effectively for long periods as a fighting team. They could and did rise to high moments, but they could not sustain them. Nevertheless, the statistics of Mediterranean warfare show that the Italian Navy, aided, of course, by their favorable central geographic position and their rimming land bases, gave as good as they received in the fierce actions in the Narrow Seas that began in June 1940.

Their principal British nautical protagonist was based at Alexandria, Egypt, under the British Commander-in-Chief, Mediterranean, Admiral Sir Andrew Cunningham, a tough and aggressive admiral cut in some ways in the Nelsonian pattern. Under Cunningham's command at start of war were battleships *Warspite*, *Barham*, and *Malaya*, a small aircraft carrier, seven cruisers, and about thirty destroyers and escort vessels plus submarines and miscellaneous craft. Later reinforcements added considerable strength. Force H at Gibraltar was commanded by Vice Admiral Sir James Somerville, who was something of an eccentric and often took his cat and canary with him to action stations on the flag bridge. Originally assembled to neutralize the French Fleet at Oran and to guard the Atlantic against surface raiders, Force H, with varying composition, was also employed to reinforce Cunningham, or to ram through convoys to Malta at frequent intervals during the war, and to guard the Western Mediterranean—an added British responsibility after the French defeat.

Like all British forces everywhere, Cunningham's had some very serious weaknesses as the first shells were fired. The British at Alexandria were trying to make bricks with very little straw. They lacked reconnaissance aircraft, 8-inch gun cruisers, destroyers, and AA guns. They were handicapped by poor gunnery and inadequate range (modernized *Warspite* was at first "the only ship in the fleet" which could shoot effectively at ranges comparable to the Italian battleships'). There were some major ammunition shortages: only 800 rounds of 6-inch shells in the Canal Zone, about 50 percent of normal supply. The inadequacy of the Alexandria base, its remoteness from the sources of supply, the poor docking facilities, continuous air raids, and the dependence upon Egyptian workmen "who would not work on the day of an air-raid or the day after," made maintenance of the old British ships difficult. "The *Malaya* was untrustworthy . . . because of 'condenseritis.' The *Ramilies*'s boilers were dying on us, as had the *Royal Sovereign*'s. The 8-inch cruiser *Kent* also suffered from chronic condenser trouble. . . ."[66]

Malta—A Key to Victory

The Italian advantage of position and the danger of air and submarine attacks in the narrow strait between Sicily and Cape Bon (Tunisia) forced the rerouting of British commercial shipping and most military convoys around the Cape of Good Hope, which added three weeks' transit time to the logistical supply route to Egypt. Occasional convoys through the Mediterranean and from Gibraltar to the key British base at Malta ran the gantlet of air-sea attack, usually with some—and sometimes heavy—loss. The tiny rock-bound island of Malta, 60 miles south of Sicily's eastern coast, long a British naval base, gradually became, under Italian (and later German) airpower, untenable as a repair base or operating base for heavy ships. But its important geographical position, quickly recognized by the Royal Navy and the RAF (and by the Italian Navy) although never fully appreciated either by the Axis powers or the British Army,[67] was the only counter Britain had to the Axis geographical advantages in the Central Mediterranean. Malta, used as an air base and a base for submarines and light naval craft, could harry and imperil the Italian (and Axis) north-south lines of sea communication to North Africa, just as Sicily, Sardinia, Pantelleria, and bases in Libya could harry and imperil British east-west maritime routes. It was a case of check and countercheck in the Central Mediterranean. Indeed, much of the subsequent history of World War II in this theater revolved around the mutual efforts of both sides to interrupt the logistical arteries of the other.

In this campaign, Malta—in retrospect—played a key role; Commander Bragadin, Italian Navy, has written that "Malta proved to be without a doubt the principal factor in the Allied victory in the Mediterranean."[68]

The little island had only one radar set, forty-two antiaircraft guns, twenty-four searchlights, and three old Gloucester Sea Gladiator Fleet Air Arm fighters dubbed "Faith, Hope, and Charity" (flown by RAF pilots) for defense when Italy entered the war. The fury of the bombs was quickly felt. Malta was hit first on June 11, and throughout June there were some thirty-six attacks by day and night which killed about seventy civilians—the first of thousands during World War II. It was the Battle of Britain in miniature, and at the end, the Maltese felt Londoners could tell them nothing about air raids; indeed, the George Cross was awarded to the island fortress, in April 1942.

The initial Italian attacks on Malta, aimed at docks and airfields, were generally inaccurate, but they caused enough damage to force the temporary abandonment of the island as a submarine base. In any case, both British and Italian submarines were experiencing major difficulties and suffering high losses in the opening months of war.

The Italians had 105 submarines, almost twice the number with which Germany started the war. Britain, originally, had only ten in "The Med," reinforced soon by old submarines transferred from the China station. No less than forty-six Italian submarines—almost as many as the total number of U-boats Germany had at the start of World War II—were sent out on patrol in the Mediterranean in early June. Yet they "accomplished very little . . . suffered heavy losses," many were damaged, and a total of nine were destroyed or missing, including four which had tried to operate in the Red Sea. (One, the *Gallilea*, was captured by the British.)

Torricelli died gallantly in unequal fight off Massaua. She was crawling along the surface, damaged, on June 23 when she was sighted and engaged by three small British destroyers and two gunboats. Before the submarine was hit and scuttled she had put *Shoreham* out of action, and destroyer *Khartoum*, ravaged by raging fires from a hit by *Torricelli's* 100 mm. shells, exploded and sank. The British gunnery in this and other early actions was extremely poor, as it had been in some phases of the Battle of Jutland a quarter century earlier.

British submarines fared little better than their enemy; by August, five had been lost in the Mediterranean, and Cunningham wrote to the First Sea Lord: "it is not a question of sending them where they will be useful, but where they will be safe."[69]

On June 28, the old Italian destroyer *Espero*—in convoy with other destroyers, loaded with deckloads of ammunition and equipment for the Italian Army in Libya—was sighted by a British reconnaissance aircraft, and ultimately sunk, after two hours of poor marksmanship, by British cruisers in the afterglow of sunset.

It was the first of several brawling, bruising surface clashes in the Mediterranean during the summer of 1940, some of them chance encounters, some the product of air sightings. Both sides felt "blinded." Their air reconnaissance was inadequate; the Italian Navy bitterly complained about what they felt was a lack of airborne eyes; on the other hand, Admiral Cunningham said his ships could not move anywhere without detection. The truth was that airborne reconnaissance, primitive though it was in those opening days of slug fest, was already altering profoundly the tactics of naval war in narrow seas. No ship anywhere in "The Med" was safely beyond range of aircraft "reccy" and this introduced a new factor in the war at sea. Yet chance and coincidence still played a part . . .

On July 9 both fleets brushed in futile battle off Calabria. Each was escorting convoys, the Italians to North Africa, the British from Malta to Alexandria. Despite attacks by planes from aircraft carrier *Eagle* and long-range gun duels, the action was mostly flame and thunder. Italian battleship *Cesare* and cruiser *Bolzano* were damaged—both by shell fire; British cruiser *Neptune* was damaged. Each convoy reached its destination unscathed, neither fleet seriously hurt; the Italians, with superior speed, broke off the action.

The British, disappointed, were more impressed by far with the Regia Aeronautica than the Italian Navy was. Long before the surface duel—and long after it, until the British Fleet returned to Alexandria—Her Majesty's ships were bombed again and again by Italian planes based on the Dodecanese Islands and other airfields. Cruiser *Gloucester*'s bridge was hit; her captain died; she was henceforth steered and fought from after control. Battleship *Warspite* and her escorting destroyers were attacked thirty-four times in four days; once on July 12, en route Alexandria, twenty-four bombs geysered the sea along port side of *Warspite*, a dozen off the starboard bow—all within 200 yards. Australian cruiser *Sydney* disappeared in "towering pillars of spray as high as church steeples."

Although little damage was done to the Royal Navy, the unending attacks chafed and grated; it was ceaseless torture from the skies, and the men of the British Navy came to have hearty respect for the men-of-war above them. Admiral Cunningham considered the Italian high-level bombing in formation, from 12,000 feet or so, initially, until the Italians were worn down by attrition, "the best I have ever seen, far better than the Germans."[70] Ships are notoriously difficult targets for high-level attack; if Rome had developed the dive-bombing and torpedo techniques later used so effectively in the Pacific War, the early days of the war in the Mediterranean might well have told a different tale.

But the British had their revenge; on July 19, cruiser *Sydney*, with five destroyers, encountered two enemy light cruisers near Crete; *Bartolomeo Colleoni* was sunk in a running fight.

It was hit-and-run, quick skirmish, and sudden flight from June through fall in the Mediterranean. Both sides passed convoys; Hurricanes, flown off old carrier *Argus*, reinforced beleaguered Malta in early August and again less successfully in November (eight out of twelve aircraft ran out of fuel and were lost at sea). Cunningham was reinforced by more battleships and cruisers and a modern carrier, the *Illustrious*; at long last, in the shortening days of autumn, the Royal Navy baited the Italian Fleet in its lair.

"Taranto Night"

On November 11 (twenty-two years from the day when that earlier Great War ended), twenty-one old Swordfish aircraft—lumbering and slow but dependable—rose from the decks of the British carrier, *Illustrious*, 170 miles from the magnificent Italian harbor of Taranto on the heel of the peninsula. Takeoff was shortly before 9:00 P.M. Eleven planes were armed with torpedoes with magnetic detonators; the rest carried flares and bombs. U.S.-built Glen Martin reconnaissance aircraft based on Malta had overflown Taranto and supplied Cunningham with photographs and details of the well-defended harbor, where the Italian battle fleet lay protected by nets and barrage balloons. It was the first major attack from the air upon a surface fleet; it underlined the growing importance of the aircraft carrier, and it demonstrated graphically the new capabilities and the new hazards that airpower had contributed to seapower.

"Taranto Night," as the Italians called it, resulted in a major British victory with minuscule loss.

The attacks, in two waves, started about 11:00 P.M. and continued into the early morning of November 12. Taranto was quickly illuminated like a sound-and-light fantasy, as the Italians pumped 14,000 rounds of antiaircraft fire into the night skies. Flares, limning the silhouetted battleships, dimmed a three-quarter moon, and the crump and flash of bomb explosions distracted the defenders. Torpedoes did the damage. There were two bomb hits on a cruiser and destroyer; neither bomb exploded. But the torpedoes—launched from 30 feet altitude by the Swordfish, after a long shallow dive from 4,000 feet—passed under the protective nets, and the magnetic exploders detonated five torpedoes under the keels of the anchored Italian battleships; several others failed to explode. The toll: the old battleship *Cavour*, heavily damaged and beached, never to live again (dragged into dock but still unrepaired at war's end); the new *Littorio*, carefully moved after Italian divers had found an unexploded torpedo in the mud under her keel, out of action for four to five months; and the *Duilio*, also out of action for half a year. Two British aircraft had been shot down. The lesson should have been obvious, but Pearl Harbor was still to come.

About 1:15 A.M. on November 12, the British added to their laurels by intercepting an Italian convoy of four merchant ships and two escorts off Valona. All four ships were sunk, and an old destroyer escort badly damaged.

Admiral Cunningham later commented that:

Taranto, and the night of November 11–12, 1940 should be remembered forever as having shown once and for all that in the Fleet Air arm, the Navy has its most devastating weapon. In a total flying time of about six and a half hours—carrier to carrier—twenty aircraft [one had aborted] had inflicted more damage upon the Italian fleet than was inflicted upon the German High Sea Fleet in the daylight action at the Battle of Jutland.[71]

November 27 brought anticlimax off Cape Spartivento (Sardinia) when the main fleets brushed at arm's length, as the British passed a convoy through the Mediterranean from Gibraltar to Alexandria (with Somerville's Force H in the principal role). A feckless, long-range gun fight at high speed, with no damage to either side, was followed by air attacks by aircraft from British carrier *Ark Royal* against *Vittorio Veneto* and Italian battleships. Admiral Angelo Campioni wisely broke off the action—nothing but thunder of the guns, shell spouts, and the white wakes of wasted torpedoes.

The year ended in the Mediterranean with both sides hurt. But not mortally; Italy had lost almost 167,000 tons of merchant ships by December 31, yet neither side had seriously interrupted the maritime supply lines of the other. Malta was more secure than at the start of war, and for Italy, the slow but steady toll from bombs and mines and shells and torpedoes was the beginning of the death of a thousand cuts.

U-Boats in the Atlantic—The "Happy Time"

In the cold northern waters and grim seas of the Atlantic the pace was brisker and the toll relentless. Around the coasts of England the Germans tightened their strangulation grip. Mines and bombs, U-boats and E-boats, and—on the high seas—surface raiders were the instruments of destruction: no ship was ever safe, even in harbor. Eighty German minelaying aircraft dropped their eggs in or near English waters every night; on the night of December 12/13, fifty mines were laid in the Thames estuary alone—some of them with a four-and-a-half-day delay mechanism to foil the sweepers. In each of the dark months of October, November, and December, twenty-four ships died, backs broken or hulls stove in, from mines alone; and during all of 1940 more than half a million tons of merchant shipping were sunk by mines. Frantically, the British reacted; their fleet of little sweepers—wooden minesweepers, converted fishing trawlers, whale-catchers, drifters—increased from 400 to more than 700 vessels in 1940, and all over the world shipyards were turning out more of the doughty little craft to British account.

To the trawlers and the small craft who daily carried on with their deadly fishing for the hidden mines, sweeping was one of the war's most hazardous jobs. The detonators were always variable, sometimes set for long delay so that repeated sweeps did not reveal the hidden danger. Often, very often, the sweepers died to save the big ships. Day after day in that long winter the magnetic mine contributed its awful toll, ships and men torn apart into almost unidentifiable remains:

. . . There were sacks. Heavy, half-frozen sacks. Red, and even in spite of the frost, dripping a little with that same red. Wherever possible, remains from mined trawlers were identified, taken on stretchers to the Mortuary and given burial, according to their several Faiths. Sometimes it was not possible to identify the remains. . . .[72]

German air attacks near the British coasts exacted a lesser toll, and the RAF Fighter Command flew protective cover. But further at sea —beyond effective radar and ground control range—the German attacks, coupled with U-boat warfare, were increasingly dangerous. On October 26, the Canadian Pacific liner *Empress of Britain* (42,348 tons) was bombed and fired 70 miles northwest of Donegal Bay, Ireland; in tow, two days later, she was torpedoed and sunk by submarine U-32. Her loss, like that of so many other ships in the western approaches, was a direct result of the Irish Republic's "neutralist" stance and its refusal to grant Britain air or naval base facilities.[73]

In October alone, U-boat sinkings (the largest to date in the war) were sixty-three ships of 352,407 tons, most of them within 250 miles of "Bloody Foreland"—the northwest coast of Ireland.

The British defensive efforts were handicapped not only by shortages of ships, planes, and trained men, but also by divided council. The Coastal Command of the RAF was responsible for land-based maritime reconnaissance and was—or should have been—a vital factor in the protection of shipping. But at this stage of the war it was not well equipped for its role, and there was no command relationship with the Royal Navy; sea and air efforts were "coordinated," in other words, there was divided responsibility and dispersion of effort. Not until December 4, when Churchill ordered the Admiralty to assume operational control of Coastal Command (an order gradually implemented in the next few months after the necessary communications and command posts had been established), was this defect remedied. Like so many democracies responsive to competing pressure groups within and without government, the British learned the hard way.

The period from July through October 1940 was what the Germans themselves called "the happy time" for U-boat warfare. Antisubmarine measures were still weak and inadequate; many ships were sailing independently, and the convoy system (which extended only partway across the Atlantic) was not yet adequately organized. The German Navy now had access to coastal harbors from the North Cape of Norway to the Spanish frontier, and Brest, Lorient, and La Pallice in France had already become U-boat bases. Later in the year the submarine commanders started to operate against convoys in groups—the genesis of the "wolfpack" tactics. On August 17, Hitler had declared a total blockade of the British Isles and shipping under any flag was warned it would be sunk at sight if it approached the enemy coast. The effectiveness of the U-boats was tremendously increased when the Focke-Wulf, four-engined Kondor (F.W. 200), a long-range reconnaissance plane, started operations in August. This aircraft, developed from a German commercial airliner, was able to overfly all the western approaches and, in addition to providing aerial eyes for the U-boats, it had a bombing capability. These were the days of the German U-boat "aces"; one of them, Otto Kretschmer, in U-99, sank the British armed merchant cruisers *Laurentic* and *Patroclus* on November 3.

By the end of 1940, twenty-two German U-boats had been sunk;

the number in operational status had actually been halved from war's beginning to twenty-two. But a slow-starting German construction program was more than catching up with losses. And, in 1940, almost 4 million tons—1,059 ships—of British, Allied, and neutral merchant shipping had been sunk, some 2,186,158 tons of it by submarines.

German auxiliary surface raiders had put to sea in 1940 bound for the far reaches of the oceans; of these, *Atlantis, Orion,* and *Thor* (each with six 5.9-inch guns and four torpedo tubes) preyed successfully for many months in 1940 and 1941 upon British shipping in the Central and South Atlantic and Indian and Pacific oceans. One of them, *Komet,* aided by Soviet icebreakers, steamed through the floe ice and past the barren Soviet capelands of Siberia by the difficult Northeast Passage into the Bering Sea and the Pacific.

In October, pocket battleship *Admiral Scheer* (six 11-inch guns) steamed into northern latitudes, rounded Iceland, passed through the Denmark Strait, evaded detection, and broke out into the North Atlantic. She announced her presence with grim statistics. On November 5, aided by her scouting planes, she intercepted a Halifax convoy escorted only by converted merchant cruiser *Jervis Bay,* former liner, hastily armed with four old 6-inch guns. The thirty-seven ships in the convoy scattered like chickens fleeing a hawk, and found dispersed sanctuary in the gathering darkness of the North Atlantic. *Jervis Bay,* commanded by Captain E. S. F. Fegen, R.N., steamed toward *Scheer* at high speed, sent out a position report of the German raider to the Admiralty, and tried to engage and distract the enemy. *Scheer* opened fire at 18,000 yards—far beyond the range of *Jervis Bay*—and the merchant cruiser was quickly sieved. As the day died she sank aflame, taking with her Captain Fegen (posthumous V.C.) and 200 officers and men. But *Jervis Bay* had saved her convoy; *Scheer,* undamaged, sank only five of the thirty-seven ships. Then she got away scot-free to roam the North and South Atlantic and the Indian Ocean and return safely to home base on April 1, 1941, with 100,000 tons of shipping sunk.

The *Admiral Hipper,* 8-inch gun cruiser, followed *Scheer* to sea in late November, but her pickings were poor. She fell in on Christmas Day, 1940, with a heavily escorted British troop ship convoy bound for the Middle East, and found she had blundered into a hornet's nest. British cruiser *Berwick*—one of three with the convoy—was damaged, but scored a hit on *Hipper;* the German put into Brest on December 27 for repairs, the first major German ship to use the French Biscay ports.

At year's end, the war at sea was a toss-up. Britain had lost heavily. Her imports had fallen drastically and the noose of sea blockade was slowly tightening. But German commerce had been largely swept from the high seas, and the blockaders were in turn blockaded, even though (unlike the British Isles) with a continent to draw on.

8

Keystone of Empire

Winston Churchill, the old Victorian, was later to state that he was "not the King's First Minister [in order] to preside over the dissolution of the British Empire." Egypt and the Suez Canal were considered the keystone of Empire, not only as a route to India and the East, but as the focus of British spheres of influence and positions in Kenya, the Sudan, and Somaliland, and in Palestine, Jordan, Aden, and Iraq. A strategic and political *point d'appui*, Egypt was also a center of British economic influence in the rich and increasingly vital oil lands around the Persian Gulf.

The French collapse immediately altered the military picture in the area. The Italian position in Libya—its supply lines once threatened by the superior Anglo-French Navy and subject to squeeze between British Egypt and French Tunisia and Algeria—was enormously strengthened as the French North African colonies paid an uneasy but definite obeisance to Vichy. In French Syria, the largest Allied army in the region also opted for Pétain.

The way was seemingly open for the Italian conquest of weakly held British possessions.

Churchill knew, in that summer of defeat of 1940, that Lieutenant General Sir Archibald Wavell, General Officer Commanding-in-Chief in the Middle East, was far outnumbered and outgunned by the Italians. At home there was the grim prospect of invasion, and abroad, on the seas and on land and in the air, too little everywhere against too much. The old, old problems that democracies defending the status quo always face when warring with autocracies, eager for conquest, confronted Britain in that summer of crisis.

Yet Churchill never wavered. There was a consistency of strategic thought on his part where the Middle East and North Africa were concerned which represented an understanding of the immense stakes—political, strategic, economic—involved in the area. Time and again Churchill took grave risks to reinforce the Middle East, even when Britain was spread thin at home. Michael Howard, the British historian and analyst, has called the Middle East "a center of gravity of British forces . . . second only to the United Kingdom itself."

As combat operations started, the British in Africa suffered from the same frustrations and divisions that hampered the application of military power at home. There was no unified command then—or later—in the Middle East. Wavell commanded the land forces; Admiral Cunningham the Mediterranean Fleet, or that segment of it east of Malta; and Air Chief Marshal Sir Arthur Longmore was Air Officer Commanding-in-Chief. "No member of the triumvirate was supreme; none was even *primus inter pares*."[74] There was no unified staff, not even a single combined headquarters, and the areas covered by land, sea, and air commands did not coincide. To add to the confusion, Cunningham, the naval commander, had no direct control over the Red Sea–Gulf of Aden–Persian Gulf area (which *was* part of Wavell's fief). The Navy's East Indies station included all waters south and east of Suez.

(This situation was not modified until July 1941, when a resident "Minister of State" was sent to the Middle East to represent the British War Cabinet and to provide political guidance to the separate Commanders-in-Chief, a typically British compromise.)

The Middle East land and air components suffered from even graver weaknesses than the Navy.

When Italy declared war, Wavell had only 36,000 men in Egypt: an understrength 7th Armored Division, destined to become known to fame as the "Desert Rats"; the 4th Indian Division, minus a brigade; a brigade group of the New Zealand Division; and a number of independent battalions and supporting forces. There were some 27,500 troops in Palestine (including an understrength horsed cavalry division and two Australian brigades) but only a few of them were fully trained and equipped, and they were earmarked, in any case, for Palestine and possible operations in Iraq, where German agents were already active. In the Sudan, with a frontier of 1,200 miles, there were three British battalions and a native defense force of about 9,000 men. About 8,500 troops defended Kenya, and there were some 1,500 indigenous levies in British Somaliland near the important "Horn" of Africa, and a garrison of two Indian battalions in Aden. In Africa in 1940 the "thin red line of Empire" was indeed thin.

In adjacent French Somaliland, General Paul L. Le Gentilhomme, the French commander, maintained an anti-Vichy, pro-British attitude. But his forces were too small to be effective, and in mid-July he was forced to seek refuge in Aden.

The British strength in the air was particularly weak. There was a total of something over 200 aircraft in Egypt and Palestine, all of them old, some obsolescent, including 96 Blenheim bombers and 75 Gladiator fighters. In Aden, Kenya, and the Sudan, there were another 170 to 200 assorted aircraft, all again old.

The Italians had far greater numerical strength—particularly in land forces. In Libya and the Dodecanese Islands, the Italian aircraft numbered 140 bombers, 101 fighters, and 72 other types, and there were 213 additional planes in East Africa. The principal Italian bomber, the S 79, carried a heavier bombload and had a longer range than the Blenheim Mark I, which was the wheelhorse of the British bomber fleet in the area. The fighters were more evenly matched; the Italian CR 42 had "a slightly better performance" than the Gladiator, but British maintenance and supply and British pilots were far superior to their enemy.

On land, the Italian superiority in numbers was enormously discrepant. In Libya, there were nine regular army divisions, three Black Shirt (Fascist) divisions—smaller in size—and two Libyan native divisions, plus a great many supporting troops, all organized in two armies: the Fifth and the Tenth. The total was more than 200,000 armed men, under the command of a cautious but ruthless leader, Marshal Rodolfo Graziani, who in June succeeded Marshal Italo Balbo, killed in an airplane accident. In conquered Ethiopia, Eritrea, and Italian Somaliland, Amedeo Umberto, Duke of Aosta, commanded an additional 371,000 troops (including air and naval units), about 112,000 of them white, the rest natives. Most of these men had been trained and organized as internal security and military police forces.

These enormous totals seemed to ensure Italian victory, but in North Africa God was not on the side of the big battalions. The British had no complete divisions, and there were severe shortages in artillery and ammunition; nevertheless the Italian equipment was generally old, and—except for the politically fervid Black Shirt units, and a few small units with exceptional leaders—morale was low.

Wavell, who bore the heavy burden of meeting this armed horde, was a quiet military intellectual, a "stalwart and a clear-sighted . . . soldier,"[75] who wrote considered philosophical essays about war and leadership. Rommel, who had made his mark in the Battle of France and who was to win undying fame in North Africa, considered Wavell the only one of the British generals "who showed a touch of genius."[76] This was probably overpraise, and, in any case, Wavell in World War II was fated to preside over forlorn hopes. But he did possess one, at least, of the attributes of military greatness: he understood the simplicity of strategy. Just before Italy entered the war, Wavell had distilled the essence of victory in a paper emphasizing the importance of the Middle East:

1. Oil, shipping, air power, sea power are the keys to this war, and they are interdependent.
Air power and naval power cannot function without oil.
Oil, except very limited quantities, cannot be brought to its destination without shipping.
Shipping requires the protection of naval power and air power.
2. We have access to practically all the world's supply of oil.
We have most of the shipping.
We have naval power.
We have potentially the greatest air power, when fully developed.
Therefore we are bound to win the war.[77]

East Africa

The sheer weight of Italian numbers won peripheral victories in the summer of 1940. Between July 4 and 7, Italian forces from Ethiopia pushed aside some light British covering units and captured the frontier posts of Karora, Kurmuk, Gallabat, and Kassala in the British Sudan. The effects—except in the case of Kassala, an important road junction not too far from Khartoum and the Nile—were of more prestigious than military importance. Power breeds respect, or at least caution, and the power of the British Raj in the Sudan was obviously—in the native mind—less invincible than had been thought. The result was to plague the British: recidivism of some tribes to banditry.

From August 3 to 19, the Italians overran British Somaliland and took the port of Berbera across from Aden. The outmatched British forces, a potpourri of four races (Major General A. R. Godwin-Austen commanding) incongruously equipped with camels and two Bofors antitank guns, fought valorously but vainly in the thorn bushes and stony wadis before evacuating under order.

In Kenya, the frontier post of Moyale, covering desert tracks inland, was taken by the Italians on July 13; but it was a hollow triumph—the British were biding their time. From August on, with the South Africans as sinews of the effort, a supply line was built up over earthen tracks all the way from a railhead at Broken Hill in northern Rhodesia to Nairobi. By year's end, "some 9,000 vehicles . . . many driven by inexperienced Africans" had made the 1,500-mile trip "over sand, stones, cotton soil, desert and bush, up steep grades and over passes."[78] This largely unsung accomplishment —one of the great supply epics of the war—was to fuel, later, the British conquest of Ethiopia.

The Western Desert

But Egypt and her Western Desert were the principal stage of the major African campaigns.

For years to come the battlefield would be sand and wilderness. In strong contrast to the thickly populated regions of Europe, the Western Desert—except for a few small coastal towns between Alexandria and Tripoli—was inhabited only by "gazelle, hares . . . horned vipers . . . desert rats . . . scorpions . . . spiders . . . snails"— and a few Bedouin tribesmen, wrapped in camel-hair cloaks and rugs, the women draped with "massive ear-rings and ropes of coins."

It was a "beige-colored" battlefield, a "slightly undulating landscape . . . stringy greyish clumps of scrub . . . hard bare sand . . . great ridges of stone. . . . Always . . . dust—dust as fine as snuff or flour which can seep through closed lips and eyelids, through any clothing, which gets into food and bedding and gun barrels and aeroplane engines," above all, an empty desert, "uncannily, almost frighteningly empty."[79]

Across this vast empty space ran one main east-west coastal road commanded by guns from the sea and bombs from above; inland was desert immensity, where there were few landmarks and navigation was by the stars. Here, the "land battleship" (the tank) was to come into its supreme kingdom; here, the tactics of land war were to resemble closely the tactics of the sea. Here, as at sea, there was "nothing for the support of armies; every article required for life and war had to be carried there."

Upon this strange battlefield, where sandstorms and flies and thirst were part of life, the major battles ebbed and flowed along the coastal strip. Of varying width, bordered inland by the Libyan Plateau, this strip was marked by a rugged escarpment of about 500 feet, most of it impassable except at a few points to vehicles. Here men broiled in summer sun and froze in winter darkness; here they lost their way and died of thirst, with shimmering mirages of beautiful lakes their last conscious thoughts.[80]

The war in the Western Desert had a unique quality. It became, in a sense, a personal tourney. The armies and the divisions were personified—to a greater extent than elsewhere—by their leaders; in other theaters the war was too immense, too impersonal, for any save a very few to make their mark. In the desert, reputations bloomed or died quickly; each contestant knew the names—and nicknames—of the others' leaders: "Butcher" Graziani; General Annibale Bergonzoli (whose name sounded, to the British Tommy, like a cheese) was called "Electric Whiskers," because of his wiry unkempt beard. From a kind of contemptuous sympathy for the hapless Italians, the British attitude in the desert turned to grudging but admiring respect for the German Afrika Korps which ultimately reinforced the Italians, and in turn, the Afrika Korps came to understand and appreciate the dogged tenacity—when properly led—of the British soldier. The other side's outstanding leaders even won the hearty admiration of their foes; in great measure Rommel was to owe his fame to the admiration of the British for his tactical skill, front-line leadership, and "correct" attitude toward combat. Rommel himself was later to describe the African conflict as *"Krieg ohne Hass"* (War without Hate), thus epitomizing a factor found on no other World War II battlefield: a residual medieval quality of chivalry.[81]

First blood went to the offensive-minded British, who, under the field command of a fighting Irishman, General Richard O'Connor (with recent combat distinction from operations against the Pathan tribesmen on the Northwest Frontier and Arab guerrillas in Palestine), undertook small-scale actions against Italian frontier posts. British patrols captured some seventy prisoners on June 11; the hapless Italians were not even aware that war had been declared. On June 14, Fort Capuzzo and Fort Maddalena on the Cyrenaican frontier were taken by elements of the 7th Armored Division; on the 15th, a British ambush on the coastal road—well inside Libya—between Bardia and Tobruk, killed and captured more than one hundred Italians, including a general officer who was the Tenth Army's engineer. Another small-scale action on the same day on a desert track behind the Italian frontier positions confirmed the initial British advantages.

The Italian reaction to these setbacks was slow but definite. They reinforced the frontier in force, reoccupied Fort Capuzzo, and Graziani commenced a slow build-up, urged on by Mussolini's incessant proddings. They were helped in their invasion preparations by the anti-British attitude of King Farouk and some leading Egyptians, who were hedging their bets with the Axis powers in case of a British defeat. Although in essence a British protectorate, Egypt had never declared war, and there were still thousands of resident Italians, some of them agents and spies for their homeland.

Nevertheless, the shape of things to come was clearly telegraphed by the summer's statistics; between June 11 and September 9, there had been about 3,500 Italian casualties, 150 British.

The Italians commenced prefatory air attacks on September 9, and within a few days the long-expected Graziani offensive opened. Five divisions, with two others in reserve, and a tank group crossed the Egyptian frontier. The axis of advance was the coastal road. On September 13 and 14, the Italians and their native Libyan levies took Sollum as British covering forces delayed and then fell back, and Halfaya Pass, a bottleneck near the frontier, was seized. The 1st Black Shirt Division captured Sidi Barrâni on the coast on September 15; the light British covering forces skirmished and withdrew, and, with the Navy, harassed the enemy's communications.

It was the high tide of Italian effort in Egypt, a far cry, indeed, from the glowing prospects held out by Mussolini to Hitler (in a letter on July 17) of the capture of Alexandria and the conquest of the Delta.

With Sidi Barrâni, some 50 miles inside the Egyptian frontier, under the Italian flag, the Italians halted and began to establish a series of fortified camps. They also improved the road and water supply from the frontier to their forward positions—a job which they performed with distinction. General O'Connor's Western Desert Force had planned a heavy counterattack from the beginning, and now, based on Mersa Matrûh (some 75 miles east of Sidi Barrâni where the Egyptian railroad system petered out in the desert), the British built up their forces and bided their time. Compared to the Italians, who were dependent upon a tenuous and inadequate coastal road for supply, the British, with railroads, roads, and ships, had a marked logistical advantage. In October and November patrols probed the Italian positions and fortified areas, and a plan was formed. The British, though slightly reinforced by the end of November (principally with the heavy I, or "Matilda," tank), were still far outnumbered, with two divisions—the 7th Armored and the 4th Indian—as the core of their power. But Wavell was correctly convinced that in all save numbers he enjoyed marked superiority.

The Italian invasion of Greece on October 28, and the transfer there from Egypt of some RAF squadrons and their supporting elements threatened "Operation Compass," the British counterattack. But the Air Officer Commanding-in-Chief robbed Peter to pay Paul —a familiar gambit in the opening years of war—and risked the transfer of squadrons from Aden and the Sudan, and from the air defense of Alexandria.

The British blow fell—a rapier, not a bludgeon—on December 9, under a dull sky and with a *khamisen* wind (sandstorm) commencing to blow over the desert. During November, O'Connor's patrols had found and developed a gap in the Italian system of fortified camps south of Sidi Barrâni, as well as weaknesses in the defenses of the individual forts. Elements of the 4th Indian Division probed between the forts at Nibeiwa and Rabia, assaulted Nibeiwa—achieving complete tactical surprise—and overran it in less than five hours. An Italian general was killed and 2,000 prisoners taken; the British casualties were 8 officers and 48 men.

Simultaneous holding attacks, supported by naval bombardments, against Maktila and Sidi Barrâni fixed the Italian defenders. On December 9 and 10, the British proceeded to roll up, in succession, one after another of the fortified desert camps south of Sidi Barrâni. By December 10, British armored cars were operating across the coastal road near Bucbuq, far in the rear of the Italian advance positions, and entire Italian divisions—the survivors, despite instances of gallantry and effectiveness, fighting in hopeless confusion—were cut off. By the evening of December 12, after only three days of fighting, the sole Italians still fighting in Egypt were small forces near the frontier at Sollum and Sidi Omar. Sidi Omar fell on December 16, and Graziani withdrew from Sollum, Fort Capuzzo, and other frontier posts to Bardia in Cyrenaica. In three days the British had captured 38,300 Italian and Libyan prisoners, had destroyed or routed a good part of the Tenth Army, and had seized 237 guns, 73 tanks, and more than 1,000 vehicles. The cost: 624 men killed, wounded, and missing.

The lessons were clear; the Italians, who had no armored divisions in North Africa, were at a sad disadvantage in an arena where the tank was king; but they failed fundamentally in the two areas that mattered: the competence of their commanders and the will to fight. The British keystone position in the Middle East obviously had nothing to fear from the Italians.

The British pressed their advantage, building up supply depots along the coastal road and overcoming the water shortage by transporting 12,000 gallons by road from Mersa Matrûh and by coastal water tankers to Sollum. By the end of the year, the 6th Australian Division, which had replaced the 4th Indian, was investing Bardia, defended by 45,000 men (equivalent of four small divisions) and some 400 guns.

It was a nice Christmas present for a hard-pressed empire, but the seesaw pendulum of desert war had only just begun.

Elsewhere in areas of the African continent far from the sands of Egypt, the jockeying for position incidental to the collapse of France led to tangential operations in Dakar, French Senegal, and in the international port of Tangier across the strait from Gibraltar.

In confused and confusing naval operations between September 7 and 25, the British and General de Gaulle's scanty Free French forces undertook to win the important port of Dakar, on the strategic bulge of Africa, from Vichy—their first offensive operation. But "Operation Menace" was another fiasco that hurt De Gaulle's cause and cost the British both casualties and prestige. An attempt to take the Dakar Airfield failed completely, and De Gaulle's overtures to the Governor were rebuffed. Communications between the British Admiral J. H. D. Cunningham (not to be confused with the Mediterranean Cunningham) and De Gaulle's troop transports failed; a minor landing was easily repulsed. The French shore batteries and the guns of the damaged French battleship *Richelieu,* moored in port, aided by two cruisers and by submarines, gave the British more damage than they dished out. Battleship *Resolution* and cruiser *Cumberland* were seriously hurt by shells or torpedo and two destroyers were hit. The fiasco—due to a combination of inadequacies in the command structure, hasty planning, poor judgment in London, and insufficient intelligence—resulted in "total failure." Indeed, the attack was not only premature psychologically and politically, but strategically unnecessary.

And on November 4, the Spaniards, motivated perhaps in part by ideological affinity with the Axis powers, perhaps in part by the British forays against French African colonies, seized strategic Tangier on the southern flank of the Strait of Gibraltar.

9
The Italian Invasion of Greece

The dreams of ancient glory which motivated the subconscious of the Italian Fascists led, on October 28, to an Italian invasion of Greece—one of the most ill-fated expeditions in history. There had been many incidents and ample forewarning. On August 15, the old Greek cruiser *Helle* had been torpedoed and sunk without warning by an Italian submarine.[82] Mussolini was fretful and resentful of the conquests and achievements of Hitler; his own entry into the war had earned him nothing. And now, in the fall of 1940, *Der Fuehrer's* schemes, focused on Britain during the summer, were turning eastward.

Rumania was a keystone in the struggle for power in Southeastern Europe. Russia had annexed Rumanian Bessarabia and northern Bucovina in June, during the French campaign; later, in August and September, Moscow, catering to the Bulgarian Slavs and to the Hungarians, put pressure on Bucharest to cede part of Transylvania to Hungary and part of Dobrudja to Bulgaria. Berlin and Rome, attempting—each for its own purpose—to check the Soviet bid for influence and allies in the Balkans, forced compliance under the guise of mediation. The cession of Rumanian territory, particularly to Hungary, an ancient and hated rival, completed the already simmering political upheaval in Rumania. King Carol, attempting impossible compromise, established a coalition government of military leaders and fascistic Iron Guards, who promptly deposed him. Carol fled the country and history on September 6; his son Michael I was a sad boyish figurehead, and General Ion Antonescu, supported by his bully-boy Iron Guardists, became "Conducator"—a grandiose synonym for dictator.[83] Hitler had his eye on the Rumanian oil wells, and in October he sent a strong German military mission to Bucharest while the Luftwaffe undertook the defense of the Ploesti oil region. Rumania was now solidly in the German camp, and Mussolini was uneasy; the Balkans—particularly Yugoslavia and Greece—were considered by Rome to be part of the Italian sphere of influence.

Mussolini had occupied Albania and deposed the feudal monarch, King Zog, in 1939 as part of the expansionist aggressions that led to World War II; now he used as pretext the Albanian claims to border territories in Greece.

On October 19, after many hesitations and indecisive reversals, he wrote Hitler that he intended to attack Greece. A meeting between the two dictators was arranged in Florence for October 28, and here Mussolini presented *Der Fuehrer* with a fait accompli. Italian troops had crossed the Greek frontier that morning in what was anticipated as a quick and easy victory; the Italians believed there would be little resistance and even a Greek uprising.

Never was forecast so erroneous. Inexplicably, on the eve of war, part of the Italian Army, actually in the ferment of reorganization, was demobilized. Nine divisions already in Albania were expected to occupy coastal Epirus in ten to fifteen days; later, the Italians, reinforced to some twenty divisions, planned to capture Salonika and all of Greece and Crete. General Count Sebastiano, Visconti Prasca (like many of the Italian generals, a rank-conscious political incompetent), commanded the Italian forces: "hollow Legions," as Mario Cervi's definitive book[84] has called them—troops without winter uniforms, poorly trained, poorly led, above all poorly supported. Between Prasca and the General Staff there was major friction; many of the senior Italian generals were opposed, though equivocally, to the invasion.

The 140,000 men of the Italian forces (six divisions plus one in reserve), who were ordered by the Duce to "attack with the greatest determination and violence," were organized into two army corps, one in Macedonia and one in Epirus, on either side of the Pindus mountain range.

Two other Italian divisions guarded the Yugoslav frontier in the north. The rest, augmented by Albanian levies, launched a four-pronged attack along a 150-mile mountainous front from the Yugoslav frontier to the Adriatic Sea just as the wind and rain and snow of winter started. The Italians had some light tanks, a regiment of motorized artillery, many mortars, some good mountain troops, and about 400 aircraft, and they had, on paper, more mobile and better armed forces.

General Ioannis Metaxas, the Greek dictator, dressed in a nightshirt and a flowered dressing gown, had received a three-hour ultimatum from Rome at 3:00 A.M. on October 28. Initially, he could count on about three and a half divisions under arms. And he was uneasy about Bulgaria. So far, Sofia had politely rejected Mussolini's blandishments and refused to participate in the assault against Greece, but the Bulgar-Greek enmity was enduring. General Alexandros Papagos, Greek Commander-in-Chief, listed an ultimate force of about fifteen to eighteen divisions at full mobilization, but only a part of these could be deployed against the Italians. They were poorly armed, with virtually no antiaircraft or antitank weapons, and poorly trained; supported by about 120–150 obsolescent aircraft. But initially along the Albanian frontier the Italians enjoyed only a slight numerical advantage; the Greeks were armored by their terrain and by the fortitude of their spirit; they were fighting for their country and their morale was high.

At first the Italian forces, despite torrential rains and supply problems, made fairly rapid gains. A column on the coastal road reached the Kalamas River 8 to 10 miles inside the Greek frontier and established a small bridgehead across it. Its objective was Janina, nodal point of a small road network through the Pindus Mountains, which, if captured, might yield access to the Plain of Thessaly and cause the collapse of the Greek northwestern front. In the center, the Julia Division, with many tough Alpini, carried five days' rations and four days' fodder for its mules. Its orders were to skirt the flanks of Mount Smolikas (8640 feet) and take Metsovon on the edge of the Thessalonian plain. In the north, near the Yugoslav border, the objectives were secondary; from the Moravec Plateau two columns were to move toward Florina and Kastoria.

From the beginning, it was tragic military farce.

The Greeks, under orders to utilize an elastic defense, gave up a few miles of rugged ground as they mobilized and strengthened their forces. The mud was on their side; flooded rivers, in spate from torrential rains, were too swollen at most crossings for bridging; the Italian bridging equipment, in any case, was not equal to the task. The Italian air superiority was nullified by weather. Men and vehicles toiled through calf-deep mud, or froze on barren mountainsides 4,000 to 5,000 feet above the sea. The Greeks used their mountain artillery and few mortars with precision, and their hardy foot soldiers cut in and around and behind the invaders, severing supply lines. By November 1, the Greeks counterattacked in western Macedonia, and, in the center, the Julia Division was stalled, with the enemy behind it as well as around it.

The Greek forces, strengthened initially by troops withdrawn from the Bulgarian frontier, routed the best of the Italian Albanian levies: the 1,000-man Tomor Battalion, which fell apart under Greek counterattack. In Rome on November 1, Marshal Badoglio, who had been Chief of Staff of the Italian Army since 1925, with Mussolini's approval ordered the first two of many additional divisions to Albania.

It did no good. By November 7, Italian troops were stalled along the coastal road on the raging Kalamas River. The Julia Division in the center—its men with "long beards, reddened, deep-set eyes, scratched hands; their grey-green uniforms . . . covered with a thick crust of mud . . . their black helmet feathers . . . frayed,"[85] started to pull back from its most advanced positions about 12 miles short of the Metsovon Pass into Thessaly. In western Macedonia, the Greeks were established on the strategic Moravec Plateau in Albania and were driving toward the communication hub of Koritsa—an offensive which threatened to turn the entire Italian position.

Frantic reinforcement and reorganization of the Italian forces in Albania, ordered by Il Duce on November 6, started; on November 9, the fatuous Prasca was replaced by the equally fatuous General Ubaldo Soddu; and on November 11, Prasca ("who was both culpable and a victim," as Cervi describes him) was retired from the Italian Army.

His successor, Soddu, did not long exercise command; at the year's end he, too, was replaced, as Greece and Albania became a graveyard of Italian hopes and reputations. But lower-ranking victims were not enough. Mussolini, discomfited and angry, sought senior scapegoats. Marshal Pietro Badoglio, who had been an amorphous Chief of the General Staff of the Italian Army for fifteen years, was ousted on December 4. Badoglio was old and indecisive, a weak man; but he took the rap for Count Galeazzo Ciano, Mussolini's son-in-law and Foreign Minister (who had urged the invasion of Greece), and for Mussolini himself. In retirement, Badoglio brooded and bided his time. His successor, Marshal Ugo Cavallero, was much of a kind; he was to take on the unusual dual role of Chief of Staff and field commander in Albania.

The Italian Supreme Command existed in name only; it was, as Cervi puts it, "a building rather than a body." Mussolini was de facto Commander-in-Chief and strategic planner, but with no unified staff to help him. The rest, like so many Italian military trappings, was eyewash.

Neither Rome nor new generals could change the basic equation of combat. Most of the Italians had little yen for combat and they were ill served by their leadership and support; the troops starved and froze. By November 18, the Greeks, on the warpath now, had captured Erseke; on the 22nd, the strategically important town of Koritsa; and by December 9, Pogradec, far inside Albania. All along the front, the closing months of 1940 saw the Italian Army shredded, weary, in retreat; the wounded lay festering and gangrenous in inadequate hospitals; the dead lay where they fell. On the Adriatic front the Greeks moved from the Kalamas in their own territory to capture Porto Edda in Albania on December 6 and Himera on December 23. By the year's end much of Albania was in Greek hands, and Mussolini's bid for bargaining power and prestige had completely backfired.

And to Hitler's irritation, the Italian assault had "invited" the British into Greece.

On November 3, the first Royal Air Force contingents—advance guard of an ill-fated host—landed in mainland Greece. The British had commenced to shift contingents to the Greek island of Crete on October 29, two days after Mussolini's invasion started.

The Balkans, despite Hitler's wishes, had become a theater of war. Just one day later, on November 4, he ordered planning for a Greek invasion.

Until the British intervention, Hitler had hoped to dominate and stabilize his southern flank by political and economic power. His Mediterranean strategy had envisaged strangulation of Britain at both ends of the great sea. He had attempted to persuade Francisco Franco, the Spanish dictator, to participate in an attack upon British Gibraltar, but Franco preserved his benevolent neutrality. At the eastern end of the Mediterranean, Hitler hoped to deny the British bases in the Balkans, to oust them from the Middle East, and—later—to seize Egypt by a land drive from Libya. Now, Mussolini's blundering had put British bombers within easy range of Ploesti, in 1940 an important source of German oil.

So Mussolini, instead of achieving an Italian sphere of influence in the Balkans, merely ensured a greater German interest. German pressure forced Hungary and Rumania—neither very loth—to join the Axis in late November 1940. And in the last two months of 1940 four RAF squadrons—bombers and protective fighters—were operating regularly against Valona, Durazzo, and other Italian ports and supply lines in Albania. The Greek fields they used at Eleusis, Tatoi, and elsewhere were protected by a small composite British ground force of engineers, antiaircraft, signal, and other units—all commanded by Air Commodore J. H. D'Albiac. It was the beginning, for the British, of a much larger commitment they could ill afford, but Winston Churchill understood the political, moral, and psychological importance to the course of the war of the British Alliance with Greece.

10

The Blitz

For Britain, just commencing to stand down from the summer invasion alert, the last months of the year were perhaps the darkest of the war. In this winter of 1940-41, termed by Constantine FitzGibbon "The Winter of the Bombs," London and other historic cities were targets night after night as the German blitz through the air followed the Battle of Britain.

To most Englishmen the far-off victories and remote defeats had far less reality than the unending local trial by fire. Civilians had become soldiers; and the cities—both British and German—were the front line, subject, as in the Middle Ages, to sack and ruin.

The blitz represented a new page in the story of the war, an attempt, on an ever-ascending scale, to develop all-out "strategic warfare." The plane as an instrument of air battle meant that an attack could actually be carried through space (over seas, rivers, and mountains) deep into an enemy's heartland. Enthusiastic airmen, many believing their own propaganda, others reaching out for power, studied the theories of Douhet and "Billy" Mitchell, Alexander de Seversky and Lord Trenchard, noted the psychological results of the German Zeppelin, Gotha, and Giant raids on British cities in World War I, and advanced a new strategic concept, to which they stubbornly adhered through all the years of World War II. The way to win modern wars, it was held, was to leap above the surface forces and strike directly at the enemy's capability and will to resist. At first, this doctrine was dressed up in euphemisms; the objectives were important communications junctures or chokepoints, power plants and war-vital industries. But it was clear, given the bombing accuracies—or rather inaccuracies—of those days, that strategic attack from the air added up to area devastation.

In the heavily industrialized and thickly settled countries of Europe, attacks on such "military" targets meant inevitably the bombing of towns and cities, of homes and civilians, of women and children as well as men. And in time, as each side took off the gloves, as each side's enthusiasts urged "just a little more" and rage substituted for reason, the city and the civilian became the frank and open object of "strategic" air attack. (Indeed, "Bomber" Harris, of the RAF Bomber Command, was later to support vigorously a policy of bombing German workers and their homes in order to reduce German war production.) No one man was responsible for this; the airmen and the military leaders of both sides were supported by the politicians and heads of state—Churchill, Roosevelt, and Hitler.

And so what started in late 1940, as the fires blossomed in London, continued unending throughout World War II; cities and men in thousands died beneath the bombs, and ancient urban treasures dissolved in ravage all over Europe.

In 1940, the GAF had a tremendous advantage in the geographic situation of its bases and in numbers. But the Germans had built an air force primarily to support their ground armies; they had no four-engined bombers and, unlike the British, had not specifically prepared for independent strategic air operations. They had used bombers against both Warsaw and Rotterdam, but in both instances these attacks were ancillary to ground victories already won, and they were sporadic, not continuous. British and Germans equally had shown some restraint in bombing in the opening months of war. In the first month, British bombers had attacked German naval bases at Brunsbüttel and Wilhelmshaven, Sylt and Heligoland, and elsewhere. And, about May 10–11, two days after some German bombs had fallen near Canterbury (apparently by accident), the British started a small-scale systematic attack, intensified as far as possible during the Battle of France, on communications and industries in Germany itself. The Germans attacked a legitimate military target, the Home Fleet's base at Scapa Flow in the Orkneys on March 16, 1940; the British retaliated with raids against a German base on the island of Sylt.

The Battle of Britain, starting as an attempt to choke off Britain's seaborne supplies and to blind and then destroy Fighter Command, culminated in September in the area attacks against London, and in the tit-for-tat (though much smaller) raids against Berlin. The attacks on London, commencing in the last phase of the Battle of Britain in September, opened the new phase in aerial warfare. The German bombers had suffered heavily in the day attacks in the Battle of Britain. On the other hand, their somewhat experimental night attacks against the Merseyside docks around Liverpool and Birkenhead on August 28 to 31—though highly inaccurate, except on the last night of August, when the commercial center of Liverpool was burned by 160 fires—had cost them only 7 bombers, about 1 percent of the total number of sorties (a sortie is one aircraft, one mission). The Germans learned their lesson.

The daylight bomber attacks on England continued intermittently, in dwindling scale, but from September on, the main German effort in the independent bombing campaign was covered by darkness. Every night from early September to the middle of November, an average of about 160 German bombers (augmented from October by a handful of Italian planes) dropped about 8,300 tons of high explosive and thousands of incendiary canisters on London alone.

The city was hard-hit; docks and railways were heavily damaged; on one night, October 15, when 400 bombers were over London, all traffic was stopped at five of London's busiest railway stations and at four others choked to a third of its normal volume. A main sewer burst by bomb blast, flooding a subway tunnel; water mains burst; 400 civilians died, 900 were injured; 900 fires were started. Unexploded bombs, and delayed-action "land-mines"—huge naval mines more powerful than any bombs, dropped by parachute—endangered civil defense and caused great sections of London, including St. Paul's Cathedral, to be roped off while bomb disposal units braved the exquisite dangers of de-fusing. The UXB's (Unexploded Bombs) were chiefly delayed-action machines, but some were duds; all had to be treated gingerly. At one time in late November, there were some 3,000 of these time machines lying about in rubble and dirt in the London area alone, each of which caused evacuation of nearby houses, diversion of traffic, and snarls in daily living.

The UXB disposal detachments "seemed different from . . . ordinary men. . . . They were gaunt, they were haggard, their faces had a bluish look, with bright gleaming eyes and exceptional compression of the lips. . . ."

One UXB squad consisted of three people, "the Earl of Suffolk, his lady private secretary, and his rather aged chauffeur. They called themselves, 'the Holy Trinity' . . . their prowess . . . got around among all who knew. Thirty-four unexploded bombs did they tackle with urbane and smiling efficiency. But the thirty-fifth claimed its forfeit. . . ."[86]

The damage to London from land mines, bombs, and incendiaries was "serious"—particularly to the dock area—"but not crippling."

But the rage from the skies reached out for other cities: Liverpool and Manchester, Birmingham, and a name forever written in the memory of those times, Coventry.

From mid-November on, the Germans—surprised at the failure of London to collapse—struck out far and wide over England against British industries and communications. And Coventry, with its famed cathedral and its aircraft industry, was the target of a devastating raid on November 14. Churchill and the RAF had some hours prewarning of the attack. Various "Ultra" messages, designating Coventry as the target with operational details of the planned attack, were intercepted and deciphered—some forty-eight hours before the raid, some in midafternoon of the 14th. It was too late for an orderly evacuation, a measure which might, in any case, have alerted the Germans to the "Ultra" secret. About 450 bombers—directed to cripple the city's aircraft industry and supporting services—set, within an hour of the raid's start, "a sea of fire visible for many miles."[87] It was bright moonlight; the guiding radio beams were not necessary, and, in any case, after the first few raiders, the pillar of fire served as beacon during the long night to the unending German squadrons. Coventry, "outwardly stricken almost beyond repair . . . the center of the city a smoking ruin . . . had suffered a fearful blow; but its wounds were far from mortal." British antiaircraft guns brought down only one bomber; the night fighters had no luck.

All over the British Isles those months of winter meant terror from the skies. Cardiff and the south coast ports were hit, Bristol, Swansea, Plymouth, the Clydeside, and even Belfast in Northern Ireland resounded to the bombs.

Germany did not escape scot-free. British airmen frankly favored wide-ranging retaliatory raids against German cities, but their means did not match their ambitions. RAF Bomber Command then disposed of only about 200 to 300 effective operational aircraft (in contrast to 700–800 available to the Germans for night operations). Nevertheless, in a series of what amounted to area attacks directed primarily against the morale of the German people, and the German synthetic oil production facilities, the night skies over Berlin, Essen, Munich, Hamburg, and Cologne were loud with the sound of aircraft engines, and the glare of searchlights and red trails of tracers crisscrossed the clouds. The attacks were pinpricks—but disturbing; they exposed the hollowness of Germany's claims to invulnerability, seeming to show, as the advocates of strategic air warfare had always claimed, that "the bomber always gets through." In December, as the short days of winter closed in and the skies of northern Europe were blanketed with clouds, Bomber Command's efforts weakened; in all that month there were 1,385 British bomber sorties. Many of these never found their targets, and of the bombers dispatched thirty-seven were missing, twenty-three crashed.

As the year died, there was no doubt that English cities were suffering. And London, throughout the war the principal focus of

Nazi *Schrecklichkeit*, seemed to be dying with the year. The merciless German attacks were unending.

This trial by dark was a tacit acknowledgment of some of the tactical fallacies of the war's beginning. The Battle of Britain had shown that, in daytime, the fighter—properly deployed—could inflict unacceptable losses on the bomber. Starting with the German mass attacks on Liverpool and then London in late August and early September 1940, the strategic air campaign was waged by the British and the Germans chiefly at night. Despite radar, darkness blinded the defenders, aided the attackers; the hours of darkness were the bombers' kingdom, particularly on clear moonlit nights—"the bombers' moon"—when visibility was enough to aid accurate navigation but not sufficient to facilitate interception.

Yet like the constant ebb and flow of the sea upon the shore, the battle was never clear-cut; sometimes the day raids peaked in intensity; always defense and offense parried and thrust in ceaseless flux.

Fighter Command trained pilots in night operations, began to use airborne radar, installed night-landing devices on some of its airfields, and throughout the winter sent aloft increasing numbers of twin-engined Blenheims, Beaufighters, Defiants, and—ultimately—single-engined Hurricanes to be vectored to interception or to patrol bomber approaches. Yet it was really the skill, the eyesight, and the luck of the individual pilot that mattered in the darkness; radar could do so much, but the vital visual interception to get within gun range was the pilot's job. From sound locators, huge listening "ears," the defense progressed to a new GCI (or Ground-Controlled Interception —radar), which—paired with searchlights—could help the pilots to intercept.

Even so, the night bombers had it mostly their own way in 1940, with antiaircraft guns and barrage balloons as their principal concern. The AA guns of those days depended chiefly upon sound locators to direct their fire; there were only a few imperfect radar gun-laying sets. Much of the firing was, in the words of General Sir Frederick A. Pile, commanding antiaircraft, "largely wild and uncontrolled shooting," with a "prodigious" expenditure of ammunition and almost as much danger to the public from falling shards of AA shells as from bombs. In September and October 13,000 civilians had been killed, 20,000 injured in London; yet the enemy from September 7 to November 13 lost only 81 planes to the defenders of the night skies—54 shot down by AA fire, 8 by fighters, 4 destroyed by balloon cables, the others from unknown causes.[88]

Fog, ice, rain, and snow—the inclement winter weather of Northern Europe—gave the British Isles some respite for half of December; for fifteen nights the skies were quiet, the raids minor. On the other 16 days there were eleven heavy raids, with London again the focus, and five fairly heavy ones. Christmas passed in the blacked-out city, but the year was not yet done; on December 29, London burned in the last raid of 1940. The raid was not the heaviest of the year. Only 136 bombers roared across the night, as the searchlights wheeled and darted and the AA shells exploded; but the results were devastating. Incendiaries set 1,500 fires, most of them in the heart of the City around St. Paul's Cathedral. The oil-bombs used at the start of war had been succeeded by thermite incendiaries—tiny spitting objects, some with antipersonnel explosive devices—which were carried in the thousands by German bombers. On December 29, some 613 canisters of incendiaries were sown about the City; the streets were "illuminated by a hundred sizzling blueish-white flames," which made a curious "plop-plopping sound as they fell on roads and pavements."[89]

In the City of London, the commercial and ancient architectural heart, "fearful damage was done by fires which quickly became uncontrollable." Ancient churches, the Guildhall, County Hall, the Tower of London, and nine hospitals were damaged in that one evening.[90] The devastated area, edged by the damaged but still miraculously standing masterpiece of Christopher Wren, the Cathedral of St. Paul, was the largest in all of Britain.

In this battle against the will of men, the front-line fighters in the streets and rubble of the city were a "fourth service" of the Crown. Thousands of men and women in what was renamed the Civil Defense Service were organized under Herbert Morrison, Minister of Home Security, in various air-raid precaution activities. Some 1,400 fire brigades were integrated into a single National Fire Service, supplemented by a great swarm of volunteer and drafted personnel as roof-watchers. Others were trained to dig the living from the rubble of destruction.

But it was the civilians, particularly the poor in the crowded slums of London, who chiefly felt the stress and trial of will. Thousands of them night after night slept in basements, under tables in their homes, in backyard "Anderson" shelters and brick or trench shelters in the streets; and thousands sought the deeper security of the London Underground.

They died and they suffered; they lost their homes and their possessions, their pets and their children. But they endured with largely unbroken will.

Before the war, the government's medical advisers "had anticipated several million cases of acute neurosis or hysteria. . . . Mass neurosis was . . . expected" from the trauma of bombing.

In fact, "quite the contrary occurred . . . the number of persons with neurotic illnesses or mental disorders attending clinics and hospitals actually declined. There was no increase in insanity: there were fewer suicides: drunkenness declined by over 50 per cent: there was less disorderly behavior. . . ."[91]

"In frequent peril, deprived of many familiar comforts, often short of sleep and sometimes of hot food and water, compelled . . . to find their way with feeble torches through a gloom relieved at times by the glare of fires, the flash of bombs and guns or the pale gleam of an unwelcome moon, dwellers in London endured much during the long nights of the deepening winter. Yet the public temper . . . remained firm. . . . For millions of Londoners the night offensive of 1940" brought home the "need for individual self-sacrifice" and national teamwork, and steeled them "for the long years of slogging war that lay ahead."[92]

London could cope, even with the greatest conflagration in its modern history.

Across the Atlantic, the Americans, moved by the broadcasts of Edward R. Murrow, watched in fascinated horror and pride of blood as Churchill and a stammering King rallied their people.

During 1940, the war had spread across the Mediterranean deep into Africa; the political map of Europe was altered. And on December 18, 1940, after months of indecisive planning, Hitler issued in great secrecy Fuehrer Directive No. 21—"Operation Barbarossa"—for the invasion of the Soviet Union. On December 29, while London burned, Roosevelt, in one of his famous fireside chats, declared:

If Britain goes down the Axis powers will control the Continents of Europe, Asia, Africa, Australasia and the high seas and they will be in a position to bring enormous military and naval resources against this hemisphere. It is not exaggeration to say that all of us in all the Americas would be living at the point of a gun—a gun loaded with explosive bullets, economic as well as military.

The "phony war" had long since ended; 1940 had forever changed the world. And Total War was just beginning.

III

MARCH OF CONQUEST
1941

In 1941 *Blitzkrieg* slowed to attrition. The European War gathered, festered, and burst into a global struggle on all the continents and all the seas.

The tide of war surged back and forth in the Western Desert, and Haile Selassie returned at last to his ancient kingdom behind a victorious British Army.

Yugoslavia and Greece succumbed and all of the Balkans lay beneath the Swastika. For the first time in history, soldiers moved through the air to conquer an island.

The bombing blitz continued. At sea, the merchant seamen died—in flaming oil, in stormy seas, in icy waters, or with cracked lips and empty stomachs adrift in lost lifeboats. The great navies clashed; *Bismarck*—proudly named and stoutly built—was sunk after a dramatic sea chase, and off Cape Matapan in the Mediterranean, the Italian Navy lost heavily in one of the great sea battles of the war.

Churchill and Roosevelt met in secret conference in Newfoundland waters and agreed upon the impeccable principles of the "Four Freedoms," and the Atlantic Charter.[1] Rudolf Hess, one of Hitler's principal aides, flew solo, undetected by either German or British radar, from Germany to Scotland in order, he said, to intercede in the interests of Anglo-German peace.[2]

New names blazed like comets with brief or dying fame across the pages of history. The star of Wavell declined, that of Rommel rose, and men spoke of an American general named Marshall and of "Ernie" King.

11
"Victory Through Air Power"

The harsh winter weather of the British Isles—great layerings of clouds, rain, and icing conditions—and the wear and tear on the Luftwaffe of the heavy and continuous fighting of 1940 limited the German air attacks in January and February of 1941. London and the western ports suffered; gradually, approaching convoys, ports, and shipping facilities again became the principal focus of the Nazi bombardiers.

It was, for the British capital, modest surcease. The sirens still howled intermittently, the blackout continued, the fires still flared.

And in March, with better weather and a bombers' moon, London, Glasgow, Plymouth, Hull, Liverpool, Portsmouth, Bristol, and Birmingham were all attacked.

With the help of improved navigational beams, the Germans attempted sporadic "precision" bombing of a few British aircraft factories, usually with the same dismal results that had characterized most of the efforts of the "bomb-in-the-pickle-barrel" enthusiasts.

The British air defenses made, as the official history saw it, "modest but appreciable progress"[3] in the first months of the year. So-called airborne minefields, or explosives dropped in the paths of German bombers, were failures, and ground and airborne searchlights played a minor role. But balloon cables and antiaircraft guns—crewed, in part, by women—brought down a major share of the ninety Nazi bombers lost in all raids in the first three months of 1941. Passive defenses, radio countermeasures and decoy fires to simulate incendiaries and lure German bombers to false targets, were of some effectiveness. But the most important development was again in the field of electronics: the increasing capability of GCI (Ground-Controlled Interception) to vector twin-engined night fighters to the vicinity of raiding bombers, and the use of airborne radar to guide the interceptors to within gun range.

It was a dramatic development, which altered the conquest of the night. The twin-engined Beaufighters and other aircraft (usually with a pilot and radar operator to each plane) patrolled in a fixed area of sky near a radar beacon, and were then directed toward the enemy raiders as blips on the cathode tubes of the AI (Airborne Intercept) were monitored by the radar operator.

"Hullo, Two Four. There's a customer for you just coming into the shop."

We had to move quickly. . . . It was another Heinkel. We were below a thick ceiling of cloud . . . and John went right in to eighty yards and gave it one short burst. There was a shower of debris . . . and the big Heinkel rolled over to the right into an absolutely vertical dive. As I pressed my face against the perspex of the dome I gave John a running commentary of what was happening.

"It's going straight down on the right . . . it's still going straight down . . . it's gone in!"

It had all happened with a horrible swiftness, and the Heinkel was splattered over the ground like hot clinkers thrown from a boilerman's shovel.[4]

Most night interceptions were neither as simple nor as rapid as the one described in April 1941. Despite the magic eye of radar, patrolling the night skies was still a chancy business, and more often than not the long patrol was futile, the intercept lost. German losses were light.

In April 1941, Hitler's *"Drang nach Osten"* (Push to the East) started to divert German air strength from the assault upon England. Some 150 German bombers were shifted to support of the Nazi campaign in the Balkans; and by late June, with the opening of the attack upon Russia, two-thirds of the Luftwaffe's operational strength was concentrated in the East, with less than 300 bombers—about half of them serviceable—based in the West to carry on attacks against Britain and its convoy bottlenecks. Throughout the rest of the war, the air attacks upon Britain were to continue with varied intensity, but never again was the Luftwaffe as such able to marshal so great an armada as during "the Winter of the Bombs."

It was ironic that the night raids started to diminish in intensity about the time Air Marshal W. S. Douglas, who had succeeded "Stuffy" Dowding as Chief of the RAF Fighter Command on November 25, had mustered (by May 15) some fifteen night fighter squadrons of the twenty he wanted. Night interception was still haphazard and yielded few certain kills; on the other hand, eight months of night bombing by the Luftwaffe had failed to "halt the machinery of production and distribution . . . or to break the national will to fight."[5]

But the Luftwaffe's *l'envoi* to Britain did not come until April and May, when London suffered under the heaviest attacks yet delivered on any English town. Belfast and its important Harland and Wolff Shipyard was also heavily blasted, and on May 16 Birmingham bowed beneath the bombs and flamed from thermite incendiaries. In the last great raid on London on May 10, as Rudolf Hess, Deputy Fuehrer, dropped by parachute into Scotland after his mysterious solo flight from Germany, 507 planes dropped 711 tons of bombs and almost 2,400 incendiary canisters—in retaliation, the Nazis said, for the much smaller RAF bombing of Berlin and other German cities.

From April through the summer and into the fall of 1941, ships and shipping suffered around the British Isles as the Germans—the focus of their effort shifted to Russia—tried with submarines and planes to blockade Britain. During the last six months of the year, 70 percent of Fighter Command's defensive sorties were flown in shipping protection missions. The Luftwaffe lost about 147 bombers in this period, some of them to Britain's defenders of the night skies—heavy losses indeed, requiring continuous replacements for the small elements of the Luftwaffe that still remained in the West.

During 1941 the greatly increased use of incendiaries, the slow but perceptible progress in the effectiveness of air defense, the painfully apparent inability of the bombers to find (much less to destroy) precision targets, the shift of the main weight of the attack to night bombing, and—above all—the substitution, for strategic purpose, of vengeance raids led inevitably, on both sides, to more and more promiscuous terror attacks on urban areas and peoples. The sack and rapine of cities—unacceptable in warfare since the Middle Ages—became commonplace on both sides, and men papered over their moral repugnancy and ethical distaste with the excuse of exigent justification. Civilization, in the dark ages of World War II, was skin-deep; soon, on the wings of the wind, men frankly tried to burn and batter in the name of victory.

The misconceptions and mistakes, the distortions and euphemisms which passed, in those days, for "air strategy" were well illustrated in 1941 by the wildly exaggerated forecasts and evanescent claims of the British Air Staff, and the sporadic policies of Bomber Command of the Royal Air Force.

There were something less than 500 aircraft and crews (most of them twin-engined Vickers Wellingtons, or Handley Page Hampdens) available in most of 1941.[6] The great four-engined Lancaster, which was to bear the brunt of the air war against Germany in the last years of the conflict, did not appear in operating squadrons, and then only in small numbers, until 1942.

Yet, with so small a force, men in high places in the British Establishment, including Air Chief Marshal Sir Charles Portal, Chief of

Air Staff, and the British Chiefs of Staff, believed they could cause a "quick death clinch." This was to be accomplished within four months by the destruction of seventeen principal synthetic oil plants in Germany. Oil was the fundamental target; German morale (i.e., cities and people), more brittle they thought than the British, was to be a secondary target. Such a task, it was felt by many of the air enthusiasts (with the other chiefs trailing along), was well within Bomber Command's capabilities. The dogmatism of these fatuous appreciations was, however, viewed with skepticism by Winston Churchill, a military pragmatist.

The truth, of course, was that in 1941 British airmen, influenced particularly by Lord Trenchard and by the dramatization of the Douhet thesis prior to the war, believed their own propaganda. It was strategic wishful thinking of the worst sort, as unproven and untried theories were tested once again in the night skies over Germany.

The oil campaign—given the force and techniques then available—was doomed to failure before it started, but it was also influenced by Churchill, who was one of the more ferocious advocates of "an-eye-for-an-eye" area bombing, and by the periodic diversion of a considerable part of Bomber Command's strength to attacks on shipping. In particular, the command turned to deal with U-boats at sea and under construction, the factories that produced Focke-Wulf long-range maritime reconnaissance aircraft, and to intermittent attacks against *Hipper, Scharnhorst,* and *Gneisenau* sheltering in the harbor of Brest.

The lack of concentration and the dispersion of effort, common to both sides in the early years of the air war, played a part in the first failure of the oil campaign. Perhaps even more important was the influence of bad weather, and ineluctable evidence—gathered by British photographic reconnaissance aircraft—that the anticipated bombing results could not be realized. What is now called "post-strike reconnaissance" was new in World War II, and it was not until late 1940 and 1941 that the British found from past bombing photographs that their vaunted bombing accuracies were in complete error. Many navigators, wandering in the grim, cloud-wracked night skies of Northern Europe, never found their assigned targets—even when the target was an entire city. There were no "smart" guided bombs in those days, and most of the gravity weapons usually burst hundreds or thousands of yards, even miles, from target. (In January 1941, CEP—Circular Error Probable—was estimated at 300 yards on moonlight nights; later estimates indicated it was actually closer to 1,000 yards.)[7]

And so the Royal Air Force bombing campaign against Germany in 1941, marked by euphoria, was quickly deflated by fact, and by diversion of effort to help loosen the strangling noose of blockade. Gradually through the summer and fall, Bomber Command shifted from attempts to strike precision targets to general attacks on railroads and inland transportation targets, and finally to area targets. The ultimate result, the assault upon cities, which largely governed British bombing policies throughout the rest of the war, was forced upon Bomber Command simply because they discovered they could hit nothing else.[8] There was no other means by which Britain could strike against the Reich except through the air.

The Air Staff asked for 4,000 bombers, and promised German destruction in six months, given this force. Churchill, wiser by far than his air advisers, was all for morale and area bombing, but noted that "it is very disputable whether bombing by itself will be a decisive factor . . . all that we have learnt . . . shows that its effects, both physical and moral, are greatly exaggerated."

Finally, in the closing months of 1941, realism took over. The high efficiency of German antiaircraft defenses, and improving Nazi night fighters took a heavy toll. In the first 18 nights of August, for instance, 107 British bombers were lost; and 37 bombers out of a total force of 400 on the night of November 7.

In mid-November, with some British bombers diverted to the Middle East theater, the order went out to conserve Bomber Command's strength, to husband its efforts, and to retrain and prepare for a heavier offensive in the months to come. And at the turn of the year a man who was to become known as "Bomber" Harris—Air Marshal Sir Arthur Travers Harris—took over the reins of Bomber Command. He was an advocate of "Total War" against Germany, and a man who, like an American general later to be known to fame, believed he could bomb the enemy "back into the stone age."

The British bombing offensive of 1941, which dropped 41,000 tons of bombs on Germany, caused negligible damage and forced relatively little diversion of German military effort. Production of planes, ships, and munitions increased—as it was to do in the years to come —despite the British raids. Morale did not break. The British lost, in 1941, 914 aircraft of Bomber Command in night and day raids; the day raids for each protagonist proved to be crippling. But on both sides the civilians were the chief sufferers, blasted, burned, or crushed, victims of the new ferocity in war.

Victims, too, not only of the ruthlessness of twentieth-century war but of fatuously mistaken judgments. In Germany, the past failures of the Luftwaffe to live up to the predictions of the airpower enthusiasts had done little to tone down the extravagant ebullience of Hermann Göring. In Britain, Churchill's heavy dependence upon his personal scientific adviser Frederick A. Lindemann—Lord Cherwell—whose estimate of bombing damage in area raids was to prove highly exaggerated, reinforced men's natural inclination toward savagery. Not that Lindemann and his estimates of how to win a war did not have opponents. Sir Henry Tizard, who had been a foremost proponent of the radar chain which had saved Britain in 1940, thought Lindemann's estimates of anticipated damage were much too high. He said so in no uncertain terms, but the confrontation between the two most influential scientists in Britain could have but one outcome. Lindemann had Churchill's ear and personal confidence; Tizard fell from grace. Only after the fact would he be proved far more correct than his victorious opponent.

The bombing campaigns of World War II, which gradually developed on both sides into unrestricted attacks upon cities and civilians, were to lead inevitably to the holocausts of Hamburg, Dresden, and Tokyo, and to the trauma of two cities of which few Occidentals had ever heard—Hiroshima and Nagasaki.

These campaigns were not merely the end products of malevolence and hatred. One of Churchill's primary preoccupations (one might almost say obsessions) throughout the war was the avoidance of mass British casualties. The national hemorrhage of World War I, and its cost to British greatness, weighed heavily on English minds and inevitably affected strategic thinking. Churchill's addiction to peripheral operations around the coastline of Europe rather than to frontal assault and strategic bombing was in part the product of the British past. Not only to London but to the air enthusiasts in Berlin and Washington, "Victory Through Air Power" seemed a cheap way to win.

12

The Battle of the Atlantic

From the beginning of the war, the Battle of the Atlantic was a struggle, on the part of Britain, for survival; on the part of Germany, it meant a bid for the final victory over hated Albion denied her by

British air- and seapower. It was a war of attrition, of endurance, which no one could win quickly. In 1941 the struggle took on ever-increasing scope and fury in a vast campaign of mines, bombs, and torpedoes, of submarines, aircraft, E-boats, or small fast craft operating in the Narrow Seas, and surface ships of every type flying every flag. Each side attacked the other's shipping; both sides used every known tactic and trick of war to exercise control of the seas.

German blockade runners and captured prizes slipped now and again through the British net, with cargoes of scarce rubber, manganese, jute, and tea, even though synthetics were beginning to fill the gaps for the natural raw materials which the Reich had so much needed in prewar days.

For Germany, able to draw upon the resources of a continent, the losses of her shipping were an embarrassment; to Britain they represented a jugular peril.

The Western Approaches

The struggle extended across vast latitudes and longitudes of ocean, from the ice-choked Arctic through the howling forties, from the Bay of Biscay and the Strait of Gibraltar to the coasts of North America, and through the trade winds of the tropics deep in the South Atlantic.

But the principal, and by far the most important, stage was the North Atlantic and the western approaches to the British Isles; and the chief antagonists were German U-boats, British surface ships, and, increasingly, British maritime aircraft.

In January 1941, German U-boats ready for sea operations numbered only twenty-two—the lowest figure of the entire war. The losses of the prior year, and the inevitable lag in gearing the Reich's shipyards and training schools to mass production, had reduced the ready strength of the U-boat fleet. True, those submarines on patrol had become, with their crews, tough, experienced veterans, but even the best of the U-boat skippers had scant success in the wild gales of a North Atlantic winter. The submarines of that day were not true submersibles like the nuclear-powered giants of today. Their submerged speeds and endurance—dependent upon electric batteries which required frequent recharging on the surface—were very limited, and the U-boats spent most of their time on the surface; indeed, to reach proper attack positions against convoys they usually had to run, conning tower awash, powered by their diesel engines.

In the smothering fury of the winter storms attack was frequently impossible; U-boat watch officers were lashed by steel belts to their tiny bridges to save them from the ravening sea, and the struggle often was not against their fellow men but for survival.

The sea boiled and foamed and leaped continually under the lash of gales that chased one another across the Atlantic from west to east. U-230 struggled through gurgling whirlpools, up and down mountainous seas; she was pitched into the air by one towering wave and caught by another and buried under tons of water. . . . The cruel winds whipped across the wild surface at speeds up to 150 miles an hour . . . the wind punished us with driving snow, sleet, hail and frozen spray. It beat against our rubber diver's suits, cut our faces like a razor and threatened to tear away our eye masks. . . . Below, inside the bobbing steel cockleshell, the boat's violent up-and-down motion drove us to the floorplates and hurled us straight up and threw us around like puppets. . . .

Even in the milder months of spring and summer, the North Atlantic was rarely still, and going to sea in a U-boat was a test of fortitude:

The motion of the boat was a perpetual swinging, swaying, rocking, rolling and listing. Inside, the humidity was intolerable. Moisture condensing on the cold steel hull, ran in streaks into the bilges. Food turned rotten and had to be thrown overboard. Bread became soggy and mildewy. Paper dissolved. Our clothes were clammy and never dried and whatever we touched was wet and slimy. For days we had no proper navigational fix. We could not shoot a single star nor did we see the sun or the moon. Only the daily trim dive brought relief from rocking and spray. Down in the quiet depth we finished the work we otherwise could not perform, had a meal without losing it on the deck plates or in the bilges. . . .[9]

January and February were poor pickings for the U-boats as winter ravaged the western ocean, and British aircraft ranged farther and farther seaward from the coastal littoral.

Sinkings were up in March but this, too, was a grim month for the Germans. Five of their submarines were sunk—about one-fifth of their available operational U-boats. More important, three of the five were commanded by the Third Reich's top U-boat aces: Günther Prien of Scapa Flow fame in U-47; Otto Kretschmer in U-99, who was picked out of the sea and captured along with most of his crew; and Joachim Schepke in U-100. Their fame was fleeting, their achievements brief; their end—and the manner of it—marked the finale of the era of individual U-boat exploits. From then on, coordinated attack, the wolfpacks and the planes, would count for most.

The sinkings increased sharply in spring and early summer, and the Germans had some long-term advantages going for them. They were using the French Biscay ports, a shorter route to the Atlantic, for submarine bases; the German U-boat command shifted to Lorient, France. From the North Cape to the Spanish frontier, U-boats could find shelter in Nazi-dominated ports. Submarine production was up; the number of operational U-boats constantly increased in 1941—from twenty-two in January to ninety-one a year later. Types were being standardized and equipment improved; ultimately the type VII-C U-boat became the backbone of Germany's undersea fleet. During the war a total of some 567 of this class alone was built and commissioned. They were simple but highly maneuverable and effective U-boats displacing 769 tons surfaced, capable of deep (for that day) submergence to between 300 and 600 feet, armed with twelve to fourteen torpedoes, two small AA guns, and manned by forty-four men. They had a cruising range of about 9,000 miles surfaced, at 10 knots, but only 130 miles submerged, at 2 knots.

These tiny fighting craft, with none of the creature comforts associated with the giant submarines of today, wrought havoc in the North Atlantic. Increasingly, until Hitler turned to the East, they were aided in their *spurlos versenkt* policy by far-ranging aircraft of the Luftwaffe, and by the new long-range Focke-Wulf maritime reconnaissance planes.

Wings Above the Sea

In Germany, as in Britain, little attention had been paid to the absolute necessity of air-sea cooperation. Like the Coastal Command of the RAF, the Luftwaffe was inexperienced in, and unequipped for, maritime operations, and even more than the RAF, the Luftwaffe—in one sense a political instrument for Göring's ambitions—held jealously to every scrap of its power. (One of the Ten Commandments of the airpower enthusiasts of that day was that *all* aircraft should be under a single, central command; in the case of Germany, Göring.)

Admiral Doenitz understood the vital importance to the U-boat campaign of aerial reconnaissance, but he had lost all the prewar arguments with Göring and had been unable—until he pulled a *tour de force* in December 1940—to secure any kind of real cooperation from the Luftwaffe. Then, while Göring was away from the halls of power on a hunting trip, Doenitz was able to persuade General Jodl, who in turn persuaded Hitler, that the Kondors based at Bordeaux should be assigned to Doenitz's U-boat campaign. Göring was furious, but the Kondors ultimately remained—like the Coastal Command of the RAF—under the Navy's operational control. Yet in many ways it was too late. The range of the Kondors was inadequate, the crews ill-trained, navigation over water faulty. Their work improved as the war continued, but the smooth cooperation between surface ships, submarines, and air which was—and is—the essence of modern seapower was never achieved, and the maritime aircraft of the German Navy never reached their full potential, fortunately for the British.

On the other hand, the transfer of operational control of the RAF's Coastal Command to the British Navy contributed materially to the margin of victory in the hard-fought war against the U-boats. The new implement of warfare, the airplane, properly employed was now, as imminent events were to prove, the major weapon in the exercise of sea control. The theorists of "pure" air war had obscured the vital importance of the airplane to land armies and naval forces. But slowly in 1941, as Fighter Command extended its protective patrols over coastal and nearby convoys and Coastal Command reached ever farther seaward, the influence of airpower upon seapower became apparent to both sides.

April was a bad month, the worst of the year for the Allies; almost 700,000 tons of British, Allied, and neutral shipping—195 ships—were lost in all war theaters, most in the North Atlantic. Submarines claimed almost 250,000 tons, German aircraft 324,000.

Admiral Harold R. Stark, U.S. Chief of Naval Operations, wrote early in April before the full toll of the month's sinkings was known that "the situation is obviously critical in the Atlantic." He continued in much the vein of his predecessor in an earlier war, Admiral W. S. Sims:

"In my opinion, it is hopeless except as we take strong measures to save it. The effect on the British of sinkings with regard both to the food supply and essential material to carry on the war is getting progressively worse."[10]

The submarine toll increased sharply in May and June as the Luftwaffe sinkings dropped off. During early summer and part of the fall, there was a sharp reduction in ship losses as the delicate balance between offense and defense shifted and British air defense of the western approaches became more effective. But by December, total losses from E-boats, raiders, mines, aircraft, and submarines were up again to the year's second high—583,000 tons—and the toll for the year from all causes was almost 1,300 merchant vessels—4,328,000 tons.

By the end of the year, thirty-five German and eighteen Italian submarines had been sunk, a marked upward trend from the forty-two destroyed in 1940. The great majority were sunk by British and Allied surface ships, but the plane, as a hunter-killer, was coming into its own.

The toll was high but not high enough. Throughout the year the convoy system, constantly better organized and better protected, was the British answer to the deep-sea threat.

Some 3,434 British merchant ships and almost 1,000 Allied merchantmen had been armed in some fashion by the spring of 1941, chiefly with antisubmarine and antiaircraft guns; some few had rocket projectors, cables, and kites to deter low-altitude aircraft attack. The defensive armament was usually of more psychological than physical significance; it contributed to the morale of the merchant seamen and, en masse, added to the strength of a convoy.

Great armadas of ships of approximately equal speeds made up in Halifax and Sydney, or in British west coast ports, plodded back and forth across the North Atlantic, routed by the Admiralty on evasion courses to escape known concentrations of German submarines. They were protected by destroyers, corvettes, and often (against the threat of surface raiders) by cruisers, a battleship, or an armed merchant cruiser. Sunderland and Catalina flying boats, and Wellingtons, Whitleys, and Hudsons—long-range maritime aircraft (an increasing number of them manufactured in America)—flew seaward from the British Isles, from British-occupied Iceland, and from Canada as far as their range permitted. Other convoys formed in Freetown (Sierra Leone) on the bulge of Africa, or in Gibraltar, for the north-south runs.

The protective aircraft played an increasingly important role; U-452 was sunk in August by a Catalina and a small trawler, and U-570, which surfaced directly beneath the bomb bay of a low-flying Hudson, surrendered—probably the first submarine "captured" by a plane—was towed to Iceland, and ultimately became His Majesty's Ship *Graph*.

After January 1941, listening devices and radar sets on escort vessels were fitted into the aircraft of Coastal Command. These supplemented the DF (Direction Finding) sets, and, sometimes with the help of decrypted "Ultra" messages, enabled the Admiralty to plot U-boat positions in a submarine tracking room in London.

In turn Admiral Doenitz met the concentrated protection of shipping which was the objective of the convoy system by organizing his operational U-boats in "wolfpack" attacks, which the British had not anticipated and were in no way equipped to meet, and by distributing his boats over numbered grid-squares of the ocean, where convoy courses were laid. Increasingly as the Focke-Wulf Kondors and U-boat crews gained experience, sighting intelligence reports—radioed from far at sea—would flow back to the German U-boat "situations room" in Lorient, where the submarine staff would evaluate them and direct a mid-Atlantic battle. The growing sophistication of offense and defense more or less forced such a system upon the Germans; it yielded, for many months, great results, but it had the disadvantage—a lethal one later in the war—of revealing by the telltale radio messages to base, and by the beacon signals sent out to guide the wolfpack to the kill, the German U-boat dispositions.

The scarcity of escort vessels had led the British to spread their forces very thin. In the early months of 1941, escort vessels based in Canada turned back before convoys reached mid-ocean; those based in Iceland or Britain did not pick up the convoy until it passed the point of no return. There is no teacher like experience. This practice ended in late May when Convoy H.X. 126 lost nine ships to a wolfpack attack by nine U-boats. From then on, continuous surface escort—no matter how small and inadequate—was provided each convoy across the Atlantic. A sizable increase in destroyers, escorts, corvettes, and trawlers—the product, primarily, of straining British-Canadian shipyards—helped, though marginally, to fill the gap.

But full ocean coverage by air was still not possible. In 1941, the limited range of land-based planes, flying from bases in the British Isles, Iceland, and Canada, Gibraltar and Africa, left a 300-mile-wide "air gap" in mid-ocean where convoys could be protected by surface ships alone. German U-boat commanders, harried when closer to land by aircraft which had quickly proven their value in antisubmarine operations, exploited the mid-ocean "dead space."

The convoy battles were vicious, unending, and so many variables affected the outcome that now the defense, then the attack, won victories. In June, south of Greenland, H.X. 133, originally escorted by only four men-of-war, was harried by a pack of ten U-boats. But the British managed to concentrate thirteen escorts in the battle; seven merchant ships were sunk. U-556 and U-661 never returned to port.

In September, a bad month, merchant ships died like flies in the waters of the Atlantic. Two slow convoys south of Greenland lost twenty vessels and one escort at a cost to the Germans of two U-boats; farther south, convoys homeward bound from Freetown and Gibraltar lost, respectively, seven out of eleven, and nine out of twenty-five merchantmen, and the U-boats got away scot free.

The Unneutral Neutral

A new factor, the power of the former colony across the seas, increasingly influenced the course of the Atlantic war in 1941.

The United States Navy, on orders, moved from "neutrality patrols" and "short-of-war measures" to a state of undeclared war. Increasing cooperation between Washington and London in 1940, involving close, high-level, military-liaison "preliminary" staff conversations in September 1940, and the "destroyers-for-bases" deal, progressed in early 1941 to detailed secret staff conversations in Washington and to more and more active participation by the United States in the sea war against Germany. The staff conversations resulted in a so-called ABC-1 Staff Agreement between the United States and Britain, of March 27, 1941, predicated on the basic strategic conception that Hitler and Germany were the major enemies. They also led, ultimately, to the modification and development of the "Rainbow" war plans, based upon the assumption of a war between the United States and all the Axis powers, and thence to the development of the ABCD (or alphabet) plans—the assumption of war in the Pacific between Japan and America, Britain, China, and the Dutch. Stemming from these agreements grew the clearly defined task of the United States Navy: the "protection of shipping of the Associated Powers" (U.S.-Britain, *et al.*), particularly in the northwestern approaches to the United Kingdom.

Practically speaking, this meant the gradual but inevitable involvement of the United States in convoy operations in the North Atlantic.

In retrospect, it is easy to see that the so-called short-of-war measures taken by Washington in rapid succession in 1940–41 might ultimately have involved the United States in all-out war against Germany and Italy whether or not there had ever been a Pearl Harbor. Our thinly disguised "neutrality"—though it appealed to millions of Americans—became more and more, as 1941 moved toward that fatal December, an unrestricted war at sea, with the United States an active participant.

The sinkings of a "neutral" passenger ship with the exotic name of *ZamZam* and of the SS *Robin Moor* added to the tension in

Washington. *ZamZam* was of Egyptian registry, and Egypt, then under King Farouk, maintained the hauteur of neutrality, although it was occupied by British troops and was the principal British base in the Middle East. Some 150 passengers aboard *ZamZam* carried U.S. passports and were traveling, in accordance with the somewhat unrealistic provisions of the Neutrality Act, aboard an ostensibly neutral ship. Nevertheless, it was sunk by German surface raider *Atlantis* (no passengers were lost). The *Robin Moor* was considered to be an even more flagrant dereliction on the part of the Germans since she flew the American flag, carried no war matériel, and was bound for South Africa, far from the focus of war.

But these incidents were of less importance on the road to war than U.S. actions.

Casco Bay, Maine, was developed as a U.S. destroyer base, and U.S. Marines raised the American flag over a desolate village called Argentia, in Newfoundland, in mid-February, as the U.S. Navy prepared to take an active part in convoy protection across the North Atlantic. Admiral Ernest J. King became Commander-in-Chief of the newly designated Atlantic Fleet; Rear Admiral Arthur L. Bristol, Jr., raised his flag in Argentia, and organized a support force of three destroyer squadrons and some fifty aircraft. A de facto U.S. protectorate over Greenland, which had been loosely applied since Denmark had been overrun, was formally legalized on April 9, 1941, and U.S. survey expeditions started staging and other air bases; meteorological stations were gradually established; and intermittent operational patrols by sea, air, and land against Nazi activities on and around the vast icecapped island were undertaken.

On May 27, the day the German raider *Bismarck* was finally sunk, President Roosevelt said that the "war is approaching the brink of the Western Hemisphere," declared an "unlimited national emergency," and extended U.S. naval patrols and activities across much of the Atlantic. On July 8, the U.S. 1st Marine Brigade landed in Iceland to take over from the British defense of that key island; they were augmented in October and later by Army units. By mid-September, the U.S. Navy—its activities disguised in the semantics of "neutrality," but its guns loaded for bear—commenced convoy operations, escorting merchant ships of many nationalities to Iceland, or to a Mid-Ocean Meeting Point (MOMP), where British escorts took over responsibility for convoys bound to the United Kingdom.

Inevitably the camouflage wore thin; "all measures short of war" became shooting war. As early as April, U.S. destroyer *Niblack*, on reconnaissance patrol off Iceland, dropped depth charges, without result, on a sound contact; USS *Greer* dodged two torpedoes on September 4, and answered in kind, as geysers from her depth charges roiled the sea. On the black night of October 17, USS *Kearny*, with convoy, was torpedoed and the Germans had drawn first blood. *Kearny*, launched in 1940—"the latest thing on the sea"—did not sink; she struggled under her own power to Iceland, but 11 Americans were killed, the first of some 292,000 Americans to die in battle in World War II. And only two weeks later, on October 31, *Reuben James*, an old four-piper, was torpedoed and sank in furious explosion 600 miles west of Ireland, taking 115 Americans with her to death in the cruel sea—the first of more than 200 U.S. naval vessels and craft to be sunk in a world at war.

In the Atlantic Ocean, the U.S. Navy was at war—no matter that it was called by sweeter names—a full year before Pearl Harbor.[11]

The Surface Raiders

The grim statistics of the U-boat war, the sudden death in darkness, the slow strangling in the oil-coated sea, the epic of endurance —of men pitted against each other and men against the sea— represented by the submarine campaign was highlighted in 1941 by great sea chases. Despite the ever-keener eyes of the aircraft, despite the advent of radar, the era of surface raiders was not quite ended.

A few auxiliaries, or armed merchant raiders, that had put to sea in 1940, roamed over the wide wastes of water through the winter, spring, and summer of 1941. *Atlantis* and *Pinguin*, each armed with six 5.9-inch guns, torpedo tubes, and mines, and capable of 18 knots speed, were the most successful. *Atlantis* sank twenty-two ships— almost 146,000 tons—in the Atlantic, Pacific, and Indian oceans, until she was caught and sunk by HMS *Devonshire* on November 22, 1941. *Pinguin* cruised the Atlantic, Indian, and Arctic oceans and, in addition to sinking 136,551 tons of shipping, ravaged the whaling fleets and sent back to Germany as prizes of war three large whale ships with 22,000 tons of oil. She sank, guns flaming and drawing blood, under fire from HMS *Cornwall* on May 8.

Kormoran, which had roved the high seas since December 3, 1940, met her end in a blaze of glory off the Australian coast. In one of the most curious incidents of the sea, she sank—and was sunk by—the Australian cruiser *Sydney*, which incautiously approached the disguised raider to within point-blank range before identifying her. The

German gunnery was accurate, and a torpedo from one of *Kormoran*'s concealed tubes struck the *Sydney*. After an hour's action, both ships were doomed. *Sydney* drifted away over the dark horizon, blazing like a torch; *Kormoran*, with a lethal load of mines aboard, was afire, her engines useless. At about 10:00 P.M. the Germans saw a great flash in the darkness where *Sydney* had been; it was the Australian's Wagnerian end, with all aboard. *Kormoran*'s crew took to the boats. She blew up at midnight, and some 315 out of 400 German survivors were rescued by other ships or reached the Australian coast.

The German raiders that put to sea in 1941, in contrast to those that left home ports in 1940, were men-of-war—some of the most powerful vessels in the Kriegsmarine.

Once again battle cruisers *Scharnhorst* and *Gneisenau* (each armed with nine 11-inch guns) were the first, in the biting gales of January, with Vice Admiral Günther Lütjens commanding. They were sighted by, but eluded, British cruisers, were refueled and resupplied several times by some of the numerous supply ships that fueled both U-boats and surface raiders, sighted a number of battleship-protected convoys, and found that British men-of-war were as active on the deep-sea shipping routes as mosquitoes in New Jersey.

Twice, far at sea in the fog-shrouded waters of the high Atlantic west of Newfoundland, Lütjens had good pickings from dispersed convoys, sinking a total of twenty-two merchantmen, 115,000 tons, before breaking back to Brest, France. There *Scharnhorst* and *Gneisenau* joined the 8-inch gun cruiser *Admiral Hipper*, which had made a brief foray west of the Bay of Biscay in February (eight ships sunk) in a long-enforced "internment" under the bomb sights of the Royal Air Force.

The cruise of *Scharnhorst* and *Gneisenau* yielded far greater strategic results than the statistics of ships sunk indicated. In the words of the British official history, "for a time [they] completely disrupted our [the British] Atlantic convoy cycles, with serious consequences to our vital imports." But it was the high-water mark of World War II for German surface raiders. Throughout the rest of 1941, *Scharnhorst, Gneisenau,* and other German surface war vessels in French ports were bombed repeatedly and hemmed in by British mines, and spent more time repairing damage in drydock than afloat. The influence of airpower upon seapower was being felt increasingly, particularly in the Narrow Seas.

The Great Sea Chase

The short cruise of the *Bismarck* and her consort, the 8-inch gun cruiser *Prinz Eugen*, was the most dramatic sea chase of modern naval history. *Bismarck*, building when the war started, ready for sea in the spring of 1941, was in her time the stoutest warship afloat. A 41,700-ton (standard) mastodon of seapower, she was one of the last of the great armored leviathans. Her main battery was eight 15-inch guns—more powerful than any comparable British model—and she had a swift pair of heels (30 knots); but her great strength was her design: a honeycomb of cellular compartmentation to minimize and localize damage, strong and elastic torpedo inner skin, skillful placement of very heavy armor to protect vitals, and careful shielding of magazines and conning and engine spaces. She was more powerful than the ships that could catch her, faster than the ships that had roughly equivalent firepower. She was to need it all—and more—before her brief hour of glory had passed.

Grand Admiral Erich Raeder, Commander-in-Chief of the German Navy, believed in the aggressive use of Germany's heavy surface ships against the British sea lines of supply. Since the sortie of battle cruisers *Scharnhorst* and *Gneisenau*, the British had been escorting their important convoys with battleships as well as ASW craft. The *Bismarck*, stronger than any single British battleship, could challenge anything on the high seas.

Raeder had envisaged the *Bismarck* sortie as part of what he called "Operation *Rheinübung*" (Exercise Rhine)—a rendezvous in the Atlantic between *Bismarck* and *Prinz Eugen*, both breaking out from the Baltic, and *Scharnhorst* and *Gneisenau*, which were to sortie from Brest. Some seven to nine auxiliary supply and reconnaissance ships had been earmarked for support. But a protracted overhaul to the *Scharnhorst*, and bombs and torpedoes from the Royal Air Force which damaged *Gneisenau* extensively, eliminated the battle cruisers from one of the most dramatic sea battles of the war. The original D-Day in April was postponed, because of minor damage to the *Prinz Eugen* from a mine, until May, but Raeder was not willing to wait any longer. The invasion of Russia was imminent, and he believed the heavy ships of the German Navy had to justify their existence by aggressive operations against Britain's jugular.

Bismarck left Gdynia in Poland (then beyond effective range of British bombers) on May 18. Adolf Hitler personally bade *Bismarck*

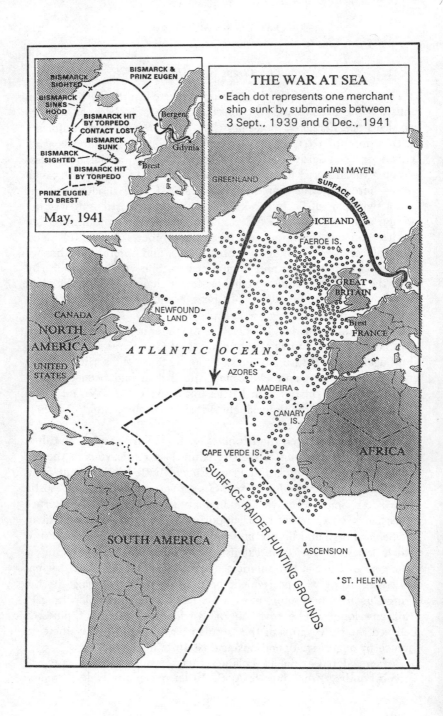

and *Prinz Eugen* goodbye. "You are," he said, "the pride of the Navy."

Admiral Günther Lütjens again commanded the most ambitious surface raiding force the Germans had sent to sea. Hopes were high; *Bismarck* with her great guns, fast speed, and power would get in among the transatlantic convoys like a wolf in the fold.

The sortie was no surprise to the British, nor was it taken lightly. Intelligence reports and air reconnaissance followed the enemy to the fjords of Norway. The British Home Fleet, based at Scapa Flow, Admiral John Tovey commanding, plugged the Iceland-Faeroes gap with a cruiser patrol line, and had cruisers *Suffolk* and *Norfolk* in the Denmark Strait, between the ice pack off the Greenland coast and the minefields off Iceland.

When *Bismarck* and her consort were photographed in Bergen Fjord by a "reccy" plane of the Coastal Command, Admiral Tovey sent the old battle cruiser *Hood*, the new battleship *Prince of Wales* (recently out of the shipbuilders' hands and still working up) with six destroyers to cover *Norfolk* and *Suffolk*.

Late on May 22, after a day of baffling fog, the British discovered the fjords were empty; Tovey, flying his flag in *King George* V, put to sea and the Admiralty alerted the big ships and the small, convoys and escorts, men-of-war and merchantmen across the North Atlantic.

Bismarck and Home Fleet headed into raider weather: snow squalls and fog patches, steep, rising seas and stiff westerlies flinging icy spray across forecastles and bridges. Lütjens laid a course for the Denmark Strait, his heart gladdened by the dour weather, and encouraged by his meteorological specialists, who predicted heavy fog and low visibility in the Strait.

But the weather predictions of World War II, particularly the localized forecasts of shipboard meteorologists, were not precise; weather is as volatile and variable as woman and to guess its sudden changes is always chancy. The weathermen were partially in error; near the ice banks, the Strait was intermittently clear—patches of fine visibility, checkered by fog and snow and hail—and, in the clear spots of the long Northern days, top hamper could be sighted miles away. *Suffolk* and *Norfolk* did their job; the antagonists made contact in the endless Arctic twilight late on May 23. The sighting reports reached *Hood* and *Prince of Wales* 300 miles away, and *King George* V, steaming hard 600 miles to the southeastward.

The chase was on, and Lütjens compounded error. He tried to shake off his cruiser shadowers by smoke screens and abrupt changes of speed and course, but they clung to his flanks "with what appeared to the Germans to be uncanny accuracy." The new search radar fitted in *Suffolk* was a rude surprise to the Nazis; they had thought the British used radar—as their own ships did—only for gunfire control.[12]

Throughout the short Arctic night, in snow squalls, ice floes, rain, and half-light, the deadly game went on. Now and again as the British cruisers sheered in too closely, Lütjens forced them to give him sea room by warning gunfire; contact was once lost but quickly regained. At 28 knots the chase continued through the night; out from the Strait into the steep Atlantic seas, the white smother of spume and spindrift beat aboard the racing ships.

The Death of HMS Hood

HMS *Hood* (eight 15-inch guns), twenty-two-year-old battle cruiser, fast but thin-skinned, now an obsolescent hybrid of naval architecture but still proudly wearing the glory of the Royal Navy and the flag of Vice Admiral L. E. Holland, C.B., sighted her quarry at 5:35 A.M., May 24.

With her, in company, steamed new *Prince of Wales*—ten 14-inch guns. The combined British broadside was thus far heavier than Lütjens could muster, with *Bismarck's* eight 15-inchers and *Prinz Eugen's* eight 8-inchers. By rights, the odds were strongly on the White Ensign, but in the short fight that was to come the British ships never brought their after turrets to bear; and *Prince of Wales*, with a green crew, was still working up, artificers and civilian technicians from the building yard still aboard. A strange and dramatic confrontation indeed, in those steep-running seas of the cold Northern waters between three of the world's last great armored ships.

It was a fitting day for naval battle, the sea a smother of white and the sky a dun and somber pall of leaden clouds. Holland did not wait to gather his cruisers and destroyers; the flag signal "Blue Pendant Four" was hoisted to *Hood's* yardarm, and the old ship and her consort, the *Prince of Wales*, turned toward the enemy.

The battle opened at 25,000 yards, with the great guns thundering over the lonely ocean. But, as it had been in another war a quarter century earlier, the German gunnery was more accurate than the British. The Germans opened on target; it took the *Prince of Wales* several salvos to find the range; by then, it was too late.

Hood was hit and flared within a minute or so; great flames leaped and spread amidships.[13] And then, at almost exactly 6:00 A.M. with a turn signal flying from her yardarm to bring the after turrets of *Hood* and *Prince of Wales* to bear, *Hood* was straddled again. As the signal was executed and the ships began to turn, flames, plating, bodies shot skyward in a cataclysmic roar of fire and thunder, and "the mighty" *Hood* was gone. Vice Admiral Holland, whose last fight was aggressive but unskilled, and all save 3 of that great company of "noble mariners"—95 officers and 1,324 men—were gone with a ship which epitomized British nautical tradition.

As Beatty had said when he lost three battle cruisers to German gunfire in the Battle of Jutland: "There's something wrong with our bloody ships today."

Prince of Wales, astern, shifted course rapidly to avoid wreckage, and was soon herself in grim case. The range had closed to 18,000 yards and both the Germans concentrated on the lone survivor. A heavy hit at 6:02 A.M. in the area of the bridge killed or wounded nearly all personnel there except the captain, and within eleven minutes she had taken three more hits from 15-inchers and three from *Prinz Eugen*'s 8-inchers. One gun in her forward turret was out of action due to mechanical trouble; another turret was now inoperative; several hundred tons of water had flooded into the hull, and the new ship had been having some engine problems. Discretion, under the circumstances, was by far the better part of valor, and at 6:13 A.M. Captain J. C. Leach turned away, making smoke.

It was the Germans' day, yet *Bismarck* did not escape unstung.

Prince of Wales pricked the leviathan's thick skin with three 14-inch projectiles, of which one, passing through a lightly armored portion of the hull, caused significant damage: it holed fuel oil tanks and *Bismarck* went down by the bow 1 degree, slowing to 28 knots.[14] To Lütjens the loss of precious fuel, the contamination, by salt water, of adjacent tanks, and the wide, telltale wake of spreading oil were decisive; within two hours he radioed Germany that he was detaching *Prinz Eugen* for independent commerce raiding and was shaping course in *Bismarck* south and eastward toward St. Nazaire in France.

Now the chase was on, and from all over the North Atlantic British men-of-war were mobilized for interception.

Off Greenland, Rear Admiral W. F. Wake-Walker in *Norfolk*, next in chain of command after Holland's death, broke off action and resumed the stubborn shadowing, while the Admiralty whistled up its ships.

Every large warship within thousands of square miles of ocean was vectored toward intercept. British pride had suffered a heavy blow with the demise of the *Hood*; *Bismarck* threatened the vital convoy lanes, and she must be destroyed.

From all over the Northern seas they steamed: Tovey, coming hard with the Home Fleet from Scapa (*King George V*, *Repulse*, carrier *Victorious*, and others); Force H—*Renown*, *Sheffield*, carrier *Ark Royal*—under Somerville, from Gibraltar; *Rodney* and four destroyers from mid-Atlantic 550 miles away; *Ramilies* from a mid-ocean convoy escort; *Revenge* from Halifax; cruiser *Edinburgh* from Atlantic patrol. In all there were some nineteen major ships, battleships, cruisers, aircraft carriers, and, in addition, the "small boys" of the fleet.

Through the long day of the 24th they steamed hard, pitching and rolling in the seaway, the bright spray sluicing high above forecastles —the might and power of the British Navy gathering to assert its dominion of the seas.

In turn Doenitz mustered his U-boats; in response to a request from Lütjens, seven Nazi submarines formed a patrol line off Cape Farewell as a trap—futile in the event—for the shadowing British cruisers, but throughout the 24th the latter clung doggedly to the heels of *Bismarck*.

Bismarck *at Bay*

About 6:00 P.M. on the 24th, *Bismarck*—a harried bear snapping at its pursuers—slowed, loosed some salvos against the British cruisers, and in the flame and thunder of the guns *Prinz Eugen* vanished in the ocean mists steaming hard to the southwest. (She escaped to Brest to survive the war, and to die, a target guinea pig in atomic tests, in a Pacific atoll named Bikini.)

Shortly after midnight the British again achieved a small hit. Carrier *Victorious*, newly commissioned, had been detached by Tovey to launch a torpedo-bomber attack on the fleeing German. The old Swordfish biplanes (speed about 85 knots) wallowed off a violently pitching flight deck in the gloom of Arctic twilight, and, coached by the shadowing cruisers, pressed home, gallantly but with beginners' skills, a torpedo attack against *Bismarck*. One fish struck home, with little apparent damage.

That night for the first time in hours, in the "treacherous twilight of a northern middle watch,"[15] *Bismarck* shook off her pursuers.

Throughout the 25th, *Bismarck* steamed hard undetected to the southeast. Tovey was within 100 miles, but did not know it; other ships were close by, but the meshes of the ocean net were still large. It was not until about 6:00 P.M. on May 25 that the Admiralty decided Lütjens was making for the French coast, their conclusion based on "Ultra" intercepts and on the radio bearings taken on messages that the Germans foolishly transmitted to home base. But it was not until 10:30 A.M. on May 26, 690 miles north and west of Brest, that *Bismarck* was sighted again by a Catalina of Coastal Command. (Unknown to the public until long after the war, the plane was American, "loaned" to Britain, with a U.S. naval officer as copilot.)

Now the British closed in for the kill. But the laws of logistics and the "fell clutch of circumstance" were still to play large roles in what was to come. Damaged *Prince of Wales* and *Repulse* and many destroyers, down in fuel, had been detached for resupply; *King George V* and *Rodney* were short, some British forces were still far away, and hour by hour *Bismarck* was steaming closer to the umbrella of air cover provided by the Luftwaffe, plus a patrol line of U-boats, waiting in baited trap some 450 miles off the French coast. But *Bismarck*'s fuel situation also was "urgent."

End of a Giant

In "heavy seas and a rising gale of wind,"[16] with the flight deck rising and falling more than 50 feet, the Fleet Air Arm launched a strike from carrier *Ark Royal* shortly before 3:00 P.M. But the "bludgeonings of chance" played them false, for the vessel they attacked was not *Bismarck* but one of the shadowing British cruisers, *Sheffield*. No hits. At 8:47 P.M. on May 26 fifteen Swordfish found the right target, and despite "low rain cloud, strong wind, stormy seas, fading daylight and intense and accurate enemy gunfire," they pressed home a thirty-eight-minute attack. Two torpedoes found *Bismarck*'s hull; one hit on the antitorpedo belt made little impression on the thick-hided monster, but the other sealed *Bismarck*'s fate. It struck under the turn of the bilge aft, jammed one of the battleship's two rudders in a hard-over position, and (apparently) slightly damaged one of her propellers and flooded the steering compartments. Immediately the great ship slowed to 8 knots and moved in erratic courses, turning in circles and heading up into the westerly gale.[17]

Lütjens apparently knew it was the end. At 2140, May 26, he reported by radio: "Ship unmaneuverable. We fight to the last shell. Long live the Fuehrer."[18]

Captain Philip Vian (of Norwegian fame) with five destroyers picked up the battle where *Ark Royal* left off. Vian had been steering for a rendezvous with Tovey's heavy ships but altered course when *Bismarck* was sighted, and he was now vectored toward the quarry in the dark by cruiser *Sheffield*—hanging, out of gun range, on *Bismarck*'s flanks. Polish destroyer *Piorun* engaged in a brief diversionary gun battle with *Bismarck*, like a gnat attacking an elephant, with no damage to either. The action covered continuous torpedo attacks—until dawn lightened the stormy sky—by *Cossack, Zulu, Maori, Sikh*. The result was a possible though unlikely two more hits,[19] which had no appreciable effect. *Bismarck*'s guns thundered in the night but the German gunnery had fallen off in accuracy; no hits.

In the dark of the mid-watch on May 27 Lütjens made his last recommendation, that the Knight's Cross be awarded *Bismarck*'s gunnery officer for the sinking of the *Hood*. Within an hour and a half Hitler had complied, but "Guns"—beset—had scant time for celebration.

With daylight, the British closed in for the kill. *Bismarck* was crabbing through the seas at slow speed, her skipper trying to conn her toward Brest despite the drag of her heavy immobilized rudder. In *Bismarck* a diver tried to free the jammed rudder but failed.

At 0710 Lütjens sent his last message: "Send U-boat to save war diary."[20]

At 8:47 A.M. Tovey (out of Scapa) came up after the long chase in *King George* V, with *Rodney* in consort, both vessels shipping it green over their forecastles. They opened fire at 16,000 yards in low visibility and heaving seas. *Ark Royal* was over the horizon, another strike ready but unable to fly because of weather; *Norfolk*, which had been in at the start, was nearby, and Vian's destroyers and other ships ringed the wounded giant in a large circle. It was the end and Lütjens knew it, but there was no thought of surrender.

Bismarck's 15-inchers could still wound mortally, and her first salvo nearly struck *Rodney*. British shells hit home on the third salvo and blew part of *Bismarck*'s foremast and fire control platform overboard. The speed and accuracy of the German fire diminished quickly.

By 9:00 A.M., as Admiral Tovey in *King George* V kept ordering: "Close the range; get closer; get closer—I can't see enough hits,"[21] *Bismarck*'s long immolation had started; her upper works were sieved with heavy-caliber projectiles.

There is a sort of crackling roar to port—the *Rodney* has opened fire with her 16-inch guns, and an instant later, the *King George V* lets fly with her 14-inch. . . . *Rodney* . . . just sat there like a great slab of rock . . . and suddenly belched a full salvo. I actually saw these projectiles flying through the air for some seconds after they left the guns, like little diminishing footballs curving up and into the sky. . . . There was only one great splash. . . . The others had bored their way through the Krupp armour-belt like cheese; and pray God I may never know what they did as they exploded inside the hull. . . . *Bismarck* . . . turned away, then back, writhing it seemed, under the most merciless hail of high-explosive armour-piercing shells that any ship has, I suppose, ever faced. . . .[22]

By 10:15, *Bismarck* was a blazing hulk, all her guns askew and silent; for much of the past hour the British heavy ships had pounded the German at almost point-blank range. She was a charnelhouse, wallowing—her propellers still slowly turning—in the heavy seas.

Tovey, low on fuel, warned of U-boats, broke off the action, and ordered a *coup de grâce* by torpedo. Cruiser *Dorsetshire* closed in, and put three more torpedoes into the tortured hulk.

In all *Bismarck* had sustained perhaps six torpedo hits and probably twenty or more rounds of 14-inch and 16-inch projectiles, plus numerous smaller-caliber hits. She was one of the toughest ships afloat, but no ship is unsinkable.

Now she was no longer a fighting vessel, barely a mobile one. Her forward turrets were out of action early on; her after turrets had ceased firing. The engine rooms filled with smoke. The turbines slowed. Power gradually died:

. . . red glow of fires illumined . . . darkened passages and thick smoke and fumes from bursting shells poisoned the atmosphere and poured from great holes six feet wide blasted in the upper deck. Listing to port and wallowing . . . the . . . pride of the German navy was now a black and burning hulk. . . .[23]

At 10:15, Lieutenant Commander Gerhard Junack, in the engine room, received a last order from the chief engineer: "Prepare the ship for sinking."[24]

Demolition charges were set and fuses lighted; sea cocks were opened; what was apparently the *coup de grâce* was to be given by *Bismarck*'s own crew.

At 10:36 A.M. on May 27, just nine days after her cruise had started, *Bismarck* heeled to port, turned over slowly some 400 miles off Brest, and sank stern first, her flag still flying:

Suddenly all over the hull we could see a number of black dots, hundreds of them it seemed. They were men making a last effort to avoid death. As the ship heeled over farther and farther, the dots crawled along the hull anywhere out of the reach of the water. The vessel took a last plunge and sank stern foremost and the dots for a while were seen on the face of the water. . . .[25]

British ships, working hurriedly to evade nearby U-boats and possible attacks by the Luftwaffe, picked up 114 survivors; a German submarine and a weather ship five more. Lütjens died along with most of the 2,400 men of what was then the most powerful battleship afloat. Almost, *Bismarck* had reached cover from the skies and succor from the land; a day after *Bismarck* died, German bombers sank destroyer *Mashona*, retiring slowly, short on fuel, after being in on the kill.

Bismarck's final cruise was the last hurrah for major German surface ships in World War II. Pocket battleship *Lützow* tried to break out to the high seas in June but was sighted and torpedoed by a Beaufort of Coastal Command off the Norwegian coast and limped back to Kiel out of action for months.

After *Bismarck*'s loss, Doenitz and his U-boats were the Navy's ace cards in Germany's bid for victory at sea.

13

East and West of Suez

The East African Campaign

It was in the peripheral theaters that the British, sometimes aided by their Free French allies, won short-lived successes in 1941.

In the first five months, the Italian empire and its conquests in East Africa crumbled as British and native forces, aided by Ethiopian Patriots based on Sudan and Kenya, and on Aden, overran Eritrea, British and Italian Somaliland, and the ancient kingdom of the Copts, Ethiopia. The highly successful campaign against the beleaguered Italians, cut off by British seapower from all hope of aid, was under the strategic direction of General Wavell, and represented, as he later wrote, "an improvisation after the British fashion of war."[26]

Wavell, something of a philosophical and literary stylist, understood strategy and what made men tick in war, but he could not be described as an overly aggressive commander. The campaign in East Africa jumped off early in the year chiefly because of continuous prodding from Churchill, and later from Jan Christiaan Smuts, Prime Minister of South Africa, a close compatriot and adviser of the British Prime Minister.

Lieutenant General W. Platt, with the 4th Indian Division (moved from Sidi Barrâni to the Sudan in December), the 5th Indian Division, Sudanese units, and a strengthening of British troops (a total of 35,000–40,000 men), mounted one prong of a pincer movement from the Sudan against Eritrea and Ethiopia. Lieutenant General Sir Alan G. Cunningham (succeeding Lieutenant General D. P. Dickinson), based in Kenya, commanded more than 75,000 men. He invaded Ethiopia and Italian Somaliland from the south, his principal units the 1st South African Division and two colonial formations, the 11th and 12th African divisions.

On January 18, the northern prong of the British pincer moved through Kassala, the important road junction on the Sudanese frontier which the Italians had captured and then evacuated, toward Agordat and the defile of Keren. Gallabat, another Sudanese frontier point, was abandoned by the Italians on January 31, who withdrew in good order, covered by minefields, toward Gondar, north of Lake Tana, source of the Blue Nile.

From the beginning the Italians in the north proved to be of sterner stuff than the defenders in the south, and the Duke of Aosta, aided by the competent leadership of General Luigi Frusci, conducted a very skillful and determined defense. The Italians, with a total force of 40,000 to 50,000 troops—some of them well equipped—first checked Platt at Keru, 40 miles inside the Eritrean frontier, then held again briefly at Barentu and Agordat, and finally pulled back into the barren mountainous plateau at Keren and established a stern defense aided by precipitous crags and stark rocky outcrops where British tanks were of little use. Keren was the key to Asmara and the Eritrean Red Sea port of Massaua, which the British wanted to safeguard their sea passage. Platt tried for it, starting on February 3. He got a bloody nose; Nicolangelo Carnimeo, the Italian general in immediate command, showed, as Liddell Hart puts it, "splendid fighting spirit and tactical skill."[27] After a week of fighting, the British drew off, nursed their wounds, and tried again in mid-March. Finally, on March 27, after a stout fifty-three-day defense, the pass was forced; the British reached Asmara on April 1, and Massaua on April 8.

It was easier going in the center and the south. The Italians held Gallabat, just inside the Sudanese border, until January 31 and then withdrew toward Gondar. The British were aided by the Ethiopian Patriots, an irregular force led by tribal chieftains in the Ethiopian province of Gojjam. Colonel D. E. Sandford, one of the first of World War II's guerrilla experts, had been a resident of Ethiopia, and he had made contact with the chiefs and prepared the way for the return of the exiled Emperor, whose personal leadership was regarded by them as essential to any widespread rising against the Italians: "When the *dagna* (judge) comes no one will be afraid. . . ," they told Sandford.[28]

The Emperor was ensconced by the British in Khartoum, and with British financing, training, and equipment, battalions of Ethiopian and Eritrean refugees were organized; irregular bands began to cut Italian communications in the interior and to isolated outposts. On January 20, 1941, the Emperor returned to Ethiopian soil for the first time since he had fled the Italian conquest in 1935. A man later to become world famous as an unorthodox military leader, Major General O. C. Wingate—a protégé of Wavell who had established a reputation of sorts in Palestine before the war—joined Sandford, and the Patriots flourished.

Under Platt's direction, Wingate established what he called "Gideon Force," and the advancing Indian brigades, aided by the Patriots and Gideon Force, moved steadily toward Addis Ababa, the ancient capital.

Soon, much of Ethiopia was in flames. The primitive tribesmen, with gun and spear and knife, hunted down weak or isolated Italian garrisons, the old tales of mutilation and emasculation passed by word of mouth through the Italian ranks, and even the stouthearted blanched.

Cunningham's drive into Italian Somaliland and Ethiopia from Kenya jumped off in February and, against weak defenses, made rapid progress. Kismayu was captured after a skirmish early in the month, and—250 miles later—Mogadishu fell on February 25, and with two ports under the British flag and the Royal Navy commanding the Indian Ocean, Cunningham's supply problems were resolved.

Now Cunningham split his forces. One prong marched overland toward Jijiga, where it met and merged with a small force from British Aden, which had captured, in an amphibious move, the conquered British port of Berbera. Another pushed up the Juba River toward Neghelli and Shashamanna, where it merged with a prong from Kenya, which had marched through the terrible heat and the lava rock of the Chalbi Desert, and had taken Mega and Moyale.

It was Cunningham's men—the units that reached Jijiga, and pushed through the precipitous defile of the Babile Pass toward Harar and Diredawa—who won the honor, on April 6, of recapturing Addis Ababa, 12,000 feet high in the mountainous plateau of Ethiopia. It had been a lightning advance; Harar was captured by a Nigerian brigade that had moved 1,000 miles under sweltering sun in some thirty-two days. The British paused but briefly. They pushed north as Platt's forces moved south to take Dessie on April 18 and to squeeze Frusci and the Duke of Aosta in the old nutcracker technique. It was the last stand; the Italians had no place to go.

The rest was anticlimax, with overtones of occasional horror, as the primitive tribesmen took intermittent vengeance on the wounded and on Italian men, women, and children, and looted and burned.

On May 19, the Duke of Aosta—Mussolini's viceroy and Supreme Commander in the ill-fated Italian East African empire—surrendered after a twenty-five-day battle in a wilderness of peaks, with 7,000 men and a few guns at Amba Alagi, between Asmara and Addis Ababa. For the rest of the year isolated Italian forces were rounded up piecemeal throughout the ancient kingdom. On May 5 Emperor Haile Selassie, the Lion of Judah, descendant of King Solomon, reentered his ancient capital in triumph to scenes of wild rejoicing and deep obeisance.

The East African campaign resulted in the capture or destruction of 350,000 Italian and colonial troops and of an immense amount of arms and equipment, much of it obsolescent. The Italians lost nearly all of their 400 planes; the British 138.

The British toll was not inconsequential, despite Cunningham's lightning advance and his slight casualties—some 500 men killed, wounded, and missing. In the north, Frusci's tactical skill and good eye for defensive terrain cost Platt dearly. At Keren alone, the British lost 536 killed and 3,229 wounded. But disease cost the victors far more heavily than the enemy's guns. The sick list during the campaign totaled about 75,000 men, with malaria and dysentery, the soldier's disease ever since Caesar's times, as major causes.

The most immediate effect of the East African campaign was upon the sea lanes. The British seaborne supply line through the Gulf of Aden into the Red Sea and the southern approaches to the Suez Canal was now secure, and Wavell was relieved of the threat—

real though static—to his southern flank. British men-of-war and aircraft, tied down by the presence of a small Italian "fleet in being" based in Massaua and other East African ports, were now freed for more important duties. Six Italian destroyers in Massaua were sunk or scuttled with nothing to show for their loss save a nasty sting against British cruiser *Capetown*, inflicted not by them but by an Italian motor torpedo boat.

But perhaps of greater long-term significance to the future of warfare was the revelation—new to those who had forgotten Lawrence of Arabia[29]—of the importance of guerrilla forces in suitable areas. Gideon Force and the Ethiopian Patriots had proved their worth, although their achievements have been exaggerated by some writers.

That strange ascetic, Wingate, commanded in Gideon Force some 50 officers, 20 British NCO's, 800 trained Sudanese, and 800 partially trained Ethiopians, with few mortars, no artillery, and no direct air support. Its commander, a Bible-toting, psalm-singing fanatic— "a prophet of the Lord"—insubordinate, egoistic, and contemptuous, but able, was a thorn in the flesh to most superiors; he was, in Leonard Mosley's words, "either a military genius or a mountebank, a Messiah or a fake, an idealist or a schemer, a man of dreams or a madman"[30]—or an amalgam of them all. History has probably given him some of the credit that should rightly accrue to Sandford, who prepared the ground for rebellion and proselytized the native chiefs. Nevertheless, the efforts and achievements of Gideon Force and the Ethiopian Patriots, although ancillary, were impressive indeed.

Gideon Force "operated in wild and often hostile country at the end of an immensely long line of communication along which nearly all the 15,000 camels died."[31]

With the help of the irregular Patriots it forced the Italians out of Gojjam Province, captured 1,100 Italians and some 14,500 colonial troops, killed or wounded 3,575 of the enemy, and captured 12 guns and much other booty.

It was a lesson that was to be repeated in World War II, and a primer textbook for the wars still to come. And Orde Wingate, architect of "penetration warfare," was to become one of its most famous —or infamous—practitioners.

Iraq, Syria, and Persia

The fall of France and the winds of war had disturbed the always volatile area of the Levant, dominated since World War I by the British Raj and the French. With the German victories, the stock of the Allies had fallen, and Nazi agents and Italian diplomats worked assiduously—helped by the anti-British activities of the Grand Mufti of Jerusalem—to undermine and to subvert. The situation came to a head first in Iraq, where the British maintained two air bases, important staging fields en route to India, supplemented by a few small naval vessels in the Persian Gulf.

In late March a pro-Axis former Premier, Rashid Ali, supported by four army and air force officers known as the "Golden Square," and stimulated by Axis gold and dreams of power, staged a coup, seizing power from the pro-British Regent, who fled to safety in a British gunboat. The movement of British Indian troops to Basra and Shaibah at the head of the Persian Gulf forced the issue in mid-April, and Rashid Ali determined to twist the lion's tail. British residents in Baghdad fled to sanctuary in the embassy and Iraqui ground forces threw a net around the British Habbaniya Airfield west of Baghdad. The Iraquis laid siege for about six days to about 11,500 British, Indians, Syrians, and Iraquis—most of them civilians, many of them women and children. The ensuing battle was chiefly a battle of bombs; the British had only about 350 riflemen and some armored cars to fight the ground battle. They attacked the investing Iraquis and their airfields with ancient Gladiators and Wellingtons based on Shaibah Airfield near the Gulf and old training planes modified for bombing and flown by fledgling pilots. The Iraquis quickly discovered that the lion might look mangy but he was not without fang and claw.

The close investment ended swiftly. The Iraquis had no stomach for the bombs, and then, despite some help from small detachments of the Luftwaffe (based on the Greek island of Rhodes, in Syria, and at Mosul), the Royal Air Force proceeded methodically to destroy most of Rashid Ali's air force (plus twenty-two German and Italian planes), while a hastily scratched-up little force from Palestine barreled across the desert under blazing sun to the rescue.

Despite opposition from Wavell (whose forces were spread thin in East Africa, the Western Desert, Egypt, the Middle East, and Greece), the small British units in Palestine, already "cadred to death" to provide reinforcements for other fronts, were milked dry to improvise a relief column for Habbaniya and Baghdad. It was a multi-mixed force, drawn chiefly from the 1st Cavalry Division, which was in transition from horses to motors, and including some RAF armored cars which had been in the Western Desert just a few days before. An advance party about 2,000 strong, with 500 vehicles, under Brigadier J. J. Kingstone—dubbed "Kingcol" (King Column)

—was given twelve days' rations and five days' water, and ordered to drive hard across 500 miles of blazing desert (roughly along the old Palestine-Damascus-Baghdad camel caravan route) to the relief of Habbaniya and the British Embassy in Baghdad.

It was an audacious move; there were something like 30,000 to 40,000 armed Iraquis around Baghdad and anti-British feeling was running high. Glubb Pasha, the famous commander of Transjordan's Arab Legion, came, along with his Bedouin desert patrol, picturesque "white-robed figures," with checkered pink *kaffiyehs* (headdresses), "cross belts of ammunition . . . the pointed bullets gleam[ing] like necklaces of shark's teeth [and] long silver-handled knives sparkl[ing] in their girdles."[32] Few of the units except the Bedouins were desert-trained; the trucks floundered in the sand; the heat reached 118 degrees in the shade and felled men like flies, and metal seemed "incandescent." Nevertheless, faced only by the lackadaisical Iraquis, whose hearts for the most part were not in it, the British muddled through.

Troops flown from Basra reinforced this mixed contingent, and Falluja, on the road to Baghdad, was secured, after a surprisingly scrappy fight, by May 21. Rashid Ali, a sadder but a wiser man, fled to Persia (Iran) on May 30; as the British reached the outskirts of the capital, the friendly Regent returned to Baghdad on June 1, and the short-lived rebellion in Iraq was virtually over. The threat to a British air-staging route to and from India, and to the land troop reinforcement and supply route from India by sea through the Persian Gulf to Basra and thence cross-country to the Mediterranean and Egypt, had been eliminated.

The Axis, with few plans and little action, had been too late in Iraq, but now one threat was succeeded by another. Syria and Lebanon became another cockpit of struggle. The British could not tolerate Syria as a German base, and they suspected that the pro-Vichy French forces there, 43,000 to 44,000 strong under the High Commissioner, General Henri Dentz, would permit, and indeed encourage, a German presence. But in the event, after their setback in Iraq the Germans had no intention of Syrian involvement. So the five-week Syrian campaign became a struggle of British and Frenchmen against Frenchmen, a diversion from the main effort that the British could ill afford.

Small Free French forces in Palestine, rallied by General Georges Catroux and, in a personal visit, by De Gaulle himself, were led in the invasion by General Le Gentilhomme. They consisted of only six battalions with a few tanks and one battery of guns.

The British units were a scratch force, as Wavell hastily shifted troops hither and yon. The King's men "suffered from the usual failing of being at the outset a collection of units and formations—handicapped by a shortage of tanks, signal equipment, transport and antiaircraft weapons."[33] Two brigades of the Australian 7th Division (recently arrived); the 5th Indian Infantry Brigade, shifted from conquered Eritrea; and two cavalry regiments of the 1st Cavalry Division—one still on horses—comprised the principal units. These were augmented by a medley of armored cars, RAF contingents, Glubb's Arab Legion, other Australians, and, in the later stages of the five-week campaign, by the units that had moved from Palestine to Baghdad and by the 10th Indian Division that had been transported to Iraq. The ground forces were supported by only fifty to seventy-five first-line RAF aircraft; they were outnumbered by about ninety Vichy planes, augmented later by almost an equal number flown in from French North Africa. The Royal Navy supplied a division of cruisers, eight destroyers, and a landing ship to contain Vichy war vessels based on Beirut. "Operation Exporter" was under the overall command of Lieutenant General Sir Henry ("Jumbo") Wilson, who had assumed command of troops in Palestine and Transjordan after prior battle experience in the Western Desert and Greece.

Lebanon and Syria are tumbled countries of desert and raw and rugged mountains, and communications follow the seacoast and the valleys. Wilson put in his main effort along the coast toward Beirut in Lebanon, headquarters of General Dentz and seat of the Vichy government for the Levant. Another thrust was directed up the Litani Valley toward Rayak; and a third, due north from Deraa to Damascus.

The leading units crossed the frontiers into Syria and Lebanon early on June 8 and soon had poked their heads into a hornet's nest; they found that Catroux's broadcasts and the Free French propaganda had irritated and inflamed, rather than tranquilized. As the official history put it, "The Vichy French not only fought well but showed great bitterness at the use of their own countrymen against them."[34]

A British Commando, landed from the sea to seize a principal bridge over the Litani River, failed in its objective and lost half the battalion including its commanding officer. The Australians later crossed on a pontoon bridge and reached Sidon on the coast, where they were stymied on the 13th by strong Vichy French positions.

The center column had also stalled near Merjayun; only in the desert had the invaders approached the environs of Damascus. The Vichy French also drew blood at sea; *Janus* and *Jackal* were damaged by shells from *Guépard* and *Valmy*, and German bombers scored heavily on destroyers *Isis* and *Ilex*. The recompense was *Chevalier-Paul*, a Vichy French destroyer steaming toward beleaguered Beirut, sunk by RAF torpedo bombers off Cyprus.

General Le Gentilhomme, tactical commander of the Free French forces, was wounded, but returned to his command in a few days.

From June 14 to 18, it was cut and thrust as the Vichy French counterattacked, threatened the invaders' lines of communications, and fought stubbornly. Casualties were heavy on both sides and at El Kuneitra, three companies of the Royal Fusiliers were overrun and most of them killed, wounded, or captured.

But gradually weight of metal began to tell. Fresh British troops were fed into the battle from Egypt and Iraq. After a tough fight at Mezze, near Damascus, where elements of the 5th Indian Infantry Brigade were cut off, the Vichy French weakened; on June 20, Australians and colorful Free French Circassians moved into Damascus and General Le Gentilhomme became military governor. The victory was primarily won by the blood and bodies of the 5th Indian Infantry Brigade, which lost 738 officers and men, and had been "fought to a standstill."

On the coastal road, Sidon fell, with the aid of naval gunfire late on June 14; but in the Litani River Valley at Merjayun the advance was still stalled.

By June 21 a new front had been opened in Syria. The British units that had roared across the desert to Baghdad streamed back across the sands from two directions, converging on the nodal junction of Palmyra. This ancient Roman ruin amid the sands, on the caravan routes to Asia Minor, was important to Vichy French communications from Damascus to the north and to Homs and Tripoli. It was garrisoned by only two Foreign Legion companies and a Light Desert company, but the British 4th Cavalry Brigade, which invested it, was weak in vehicles and understrength in men, seared by the desert and worn by long marches. Palmyra, described later by Winston Churchill as that "splendid affair amid the noble ruins,"[35] held out for more than twelve days, until on July 3, 187 men—all that were left—surrendered.

But the 4th Cavalry Brigade had been pounded repeatedly from the air; its casualties were sizable.

From June 23 to the end, it was all downhill for General Dentz and the Vichy French. Elements of the 10th Indian Division from Iraq joined the campaign in the north, driving toward the Turkish frontier, their lines of communication harassed by an Arab guerrilla leader with the euphonious name of Fawzi Qawukji. Elements of the 4th Cavalry Brigade moved toward Homs; and on the coastal road, after tough fighting near Damour, the French defense crumbled and the Australians had moved by July 10 to within 5 miles of Beirut. At about the same time Jebel Mazar, commanding the main road between Beirut and Damascus across the high massif, was nearly won by the invaders. Most of the Vichy French Air Force was out of action; harbors and ports were being constantly bombed, the British were approaching Homs and Aleppo; the morale of the Senegalese, colonial, and other defending troops was collapsing and several thousand had deserted. A troop ship sent from France with reinforcements, the *St. Didier*, had been sunk by the Fleet Air Arm from Cyprus, and two more French naval units had been put out of action: the *Vauquelin*, which had run the blockade with ammunition, was damaged by bombing at Beirut, and submarine *Souffleur* was sunk by British *Parthian* at sea.

General Dentz sued for peace. Hostilities ended at midnight July 11, and Vichy was forced to accept the British–Free French terms: Allied occupation and surrender of all remaining military matériel. Of some 37,736 French and colonial troops who surrendered, 5,668 later elected to join General de Gaulle.

The five-week sideshow was over, but it had been a costly diversion, and it reopened the old wounds.

The British casualties—killed, wounded, missing, and prisoners (the prisoners were later returned)—totaled some 3,300, and 27 aircraft, plus naval vessels damaged and out of action. The Free French casualties were 1,300. The defenders of the Vichy fief in the Middle East died hard. Their total casualties were 6,000, including 1,000 killed, and many who deserted to the Free French. Dentz had inflicted disproportionate losses on the superior Allied units.

Wavell, distracted by diversions, thin on resources, and lukewarm about the Syrian venture, had been more right than Churchill, but a soldier is not always helped on the way to promotion by disagreement with a politician.

There is little doubt in retrospect that the Iraqui revolt had to be crushed and was crushed with small effort. But the Syrian intervention represented the wrong war in the wrong place at the wrong time. Wrong because unnecessary. British intelligence had failed to realize that the Nazi goal was bigger than the Levant; if the Germans conquered Russia, the British position in the Middle East would be untenable, and in June and July London knew the German Panzers were moving eastward for the kill. After their failure to do much in Iraq, the Germans had no intention of intervening in Syria; after Mers-el-Kebir the British should have tried to suture wounds, not to open them.

Time might have healed; the Vichy French in Syria were static and no threat to the British. Far from strengthening the Free French, the Syrian imbroglio probably weakened them; it fostered civil war, increased bitterness, and strengthened the hold of Vichy on metropolitan France.

The British official history[36] puts the best possible face on the five weeks' war. Communications with Turkey, imperiled by the German conquest of the Balkans, were improved; positions in depth now guarded the overland supply and troop reinforcement route from India through the Persian Gulf to Basra, Baghdad, and Haifa; and the British acquired new bases and positions in the Levant of some importance in the struggle for the Eastern Mediterranean and to safeguard the Suez Canal.

But it was undeniably diversion. The British were fighting the wrong enemy, and the overthrow of General Dentz contributed nothing to the ultimate defeat of Germany. Nor was this the last round in the area.

The Axis "infection" in Iraq was also festering in Persia, where the British minister had been warning of the intrigues of 3,000 German nationals, many of them in key communications posts. The German invasion of Russia in June 1941 and the deep penetration of their armies toward the Caucasus bolstered London's alarm, and on August 25, Lieutenant General E. P. Quinan, commanding British forces in Iraq, was ordered into Persia to secure British communications from the Gulf, to open a supply line to Persia via the Caspian Sea and to "persuade" the Persian government of the error of its ways. German and Italian ships which had been harboring in Bandar Shahpur were seized, and in a few days—against very little opposition—the British were in effective control and a pro-British, pro-Russian government had assumed power. On September 17, British and Russian forces entered Teheran. It was the slow beginning of a defense against possible German attack from the north, and establishment of a Persian Gulf land supply route to Russia.

Italian Ebb Tide

To Wavell and his fellow commanders in the Middle East, North Africa was always the kingpiece on the chessboard, and control of the Mediterranean—particularly around its narrowest focal point, south of Malta and Sicily—a key to victory. The Suez Canal, shortest sea route to India, had long been regarded as a vital waterway. Around it and astride it the British had built up for decades bases, supply and maintenance facilities, camps and barracks which, collectively, formed the linchpin of their Middle East–African empire.

In this sense, the Egyptian position *was* of prime importance. But as the war progressed it became obvious that while the Suez Canal might well be an economic asset, it was not a military necessity. Indeed, most troop transports and important supply convoys had been "going the long way round" past the Cape of Good Hope since soon after war started. Only intermittent convoys, heavily protected, ran the gantlet of the Mediterranean, and these became more and more vulnerable as the Germans in 1941 extended their dominion to the Balkans and the island of Crete. As early as March 1941, German aircraft mined the Canal and closed it until the mines could be swept (causing major ship congestion in the port of Suez on the southern end of the Canal), and the Canal was periodically closed thereafter by heavy mining. In fact, it quickly became an unreliable military highway, and the British devised alternative routes: from Basra, from the Port of 'Aqaba, across Transjordan and Palestine; down the Nile, and by air across Africa from Nigeria.

Perhaps one of the major strategic deductions to be drawn from World War II was that the Suez Canal was virtually indefensible in the age of airpower, and that it was not indispensable—as the war and later postwar events proved—to either military victory or economic viability.

Wavell and the Allied forces in North Africa, so often described as defending the Suez Canal, were in reality fighting for larger stakes: the oil of the Middle East and the British positions in Africa and around the Eastern Mediterranean.

From January to March of 1941, Britain's triumphant surge across the Western Desert and along the coastal escarpment continued. Wavell and O'Connor—fox-hunting men—used the jargon of the hunt in reporting the desert victories to London. The commanding general had signaled, as Bardia was invested, that "it may be necessary to dig this fox."

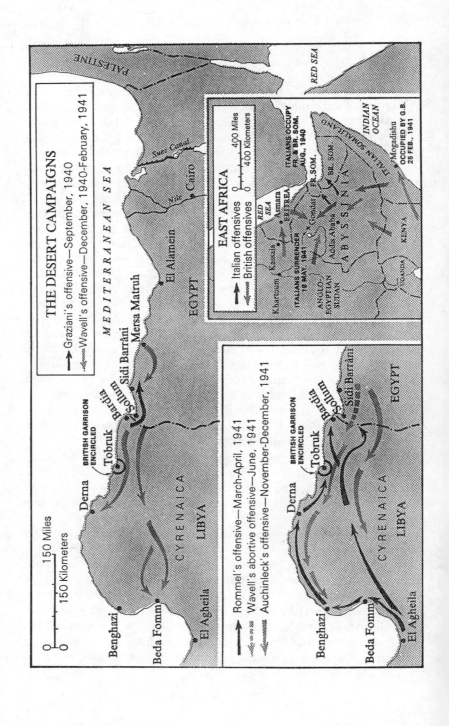

But not for long. On January 5, after air and naval bombardment engineers and infantry had cleared lanes in the antitank belts around Bardia, the tanks moved in. Quick collapse followed—the haul, some 40,000 prisoners, 462 guns, 127 tanks, and 700 trucks. Tobruk was next. It fell on January 22, cut off and isolated from the desert flank, yielding another 25,000 prisoners and 200 guns, and ancient Italian cruiser *San Giorgio*, used as a floating battery, aflame and awash behind her useless torpedo nets. The Italians changed commanders, but it did them no good.

The British had taken the measure of the Italians and found them soft as putty. Wavell had made up his mind by January 5. Despite East Africa, despite diversionary distractions elsewhere, pursuit of the beaten foe must be pushed to the limit: he wanted nothing less than annihilating victory.

In a great left hook, 7th Armored roared inland to the south of the Jebel Akhdar, the 2,500-foot range of hills (thickly settled by Italian colonists) that stretches across Cyrenaica. They pushed hard, from Tobruk and Gazala toward Beda Fomm and Agedabia, while the 6th Australian Division pursued along the coastal road to slice the Italians' principal line of communications and encircle and destroy all the enemy in the Cyrenaican bulge.

The British reached Beda Fomm first on February 5, only a few hours ahead of some 20,000 Italians, who had evacuated the important port of Benghazi and were retreating deeper into Libya. The British advance units had no tanks, and only 2,000 men, but they held the Italians until British tanks came up and charged into action in squalls and rain scud. On the 6th and 7th the Italians fought desperately but with scant skill to break through the British cordon.

It was that rare thing, a definitive battle. O'Connor, scrappy and tenacious, had hung on to the enemy like a terrier, and he jubilantly reported to Wavell on February 7: "Fox killed in the open." Some 15 miles of jumbled military wreckage, 25,000 prisoners—including the mortally wounded newest commander of the Tenth Army, General Giuseppe Tellera, and the XXIII Corps commander, General Bergonzoli—and thousands of guns, tanks, trucks, and other booty fell to the conquerors.

In some ten weeks of fire and maneuver in 1940–41, the British, with two divisions and corps troops, had destroyed the Italian Tenth Army of ten divisions, captured 130,000 prisoners, 380 tanks, and 845 field guns, and had pushed the shifting front 500 miles from Egypt deep into Libya to the borders of Tripolitania. Their own losses amounted to 500 KIA, 1,373 wounded, and 55 missing. In North Africa, the "Big Battalions" did not matter; the British had proven their superiority in nearly every aspect of combat effectiveness. Like the French before them, the Italians had had more tanks than the enemy, but, again like the French, they did not concentrate the armored monsters en masse. And some of the British tanks—the new Matildas—heavily armored for that day, were far superior technically to the Italian, so that most of the enemy's antitank projectiles bounced off their thick hides like Ping-Pong balls. The day of the shaped charge (a projectile which could defeat nearly any armor) had not yet come.

The RAF had completely mastered the Italians in the air, and had destroyed or captured more than half the enemy planes; and the Navy had controlled coastal logistics and stung and shattered the enemy's positions with its great guns. The Italian organizational, tactical, material, and morale weaknesses, and their appalling generalship, paved the way to one of the most complete defeats in the history of land warfare.

The British sent their forward patrols to El Agheila, where the Libyan coastline bends west and north around the Gulf of Sidra toward Tripoli. They consolidated their positions with a strong hold on Benghazi, set up a civil administration to rule conquered Cyrenaica, and savored strongly the sweet smell of victory.

It would not last long. The Wavell-O'Connor conquest was the second swing of the North African pendulum, and the handwriting spelling defeat and retreat was already on the wall.

Enter the Germans . . .

The approximately 50,000 men in uniform stationed in the Middle East at the start of war to guard British commitments had been strengthened by 1941 to approximately 336,000 in the Army alone. In the first six months of the year, troops and airmen from many parts of the empire were pouring into the theater at the rate of about 1,000 a day, capped in May by a convoy from Australia in which the two great old "Queens" (*Queen Elizabeth* and *Queen Mary*), now in war garb, stood up the Red Sea to deliver their men at Suez.[37] But this tremendous expansion was not enough; the British were dispersed across three continents—from Kenya, the Sudan, Eritrea, and Ethiopia, across North Africa and the countries of the Levant to Rhodes and Greece. Had the Italians been their sole enemy, Wavell

Blitzkrieg — the beginning. The Wehrmacht in the suburbs of Warsaw, September 1939.

The British "missed the bus" in Scandinavia. Troop ship *Orama* sinking on June 8, 1940, during evacuation of Narvik, Norway; German destroyer in foreground.

THE CONQUERORS

The days that shocked the world;
German troops advancing through a
Flanders village, May 29, 1940.

German infantry attacking in a Belgian village, May 1940.

THE CONQUERED

For them, the war is over in so brief a time. *Poilus* flushed in coveys from a French village, June 1940.

Paris, City of Light, beneath the Nazi heel. German troops near the Arc de Triomphe, June 1940.

The Grand Armada. A Lockheed Hudson flies above the "small boys" and the big, from all the ports of England, assembled off Dunkirk, France, May–June 1940.

THE HOME FRONT SUFFERS — FIRE AND FURY

A bombed building falls, Queen Victoria Street, London, 1940.

German firemen at the bombed Anhalter Railroad Station, Berlin, 1940.

RUSSIA—WAR OF NO QUARTER

Soviet peasants, in the thousands, dig tank traps and entrenchments as the Germans attack in the summer of 1941.

Ruin and devastation; the Germans were here.

The terror begins as the Germans pull back. Young Communists hung by the Nazis. The sign reads: "This will happen to all those who help the Bolsheviks and guerrilla fighters."

Winter adds its pall. The German attack stalls; Soviet sappers, covered by machine gunners, cut through defensive German wire.

EVERYWHERE THE DEAD

Australians burying Italian dead in the deep sand sea near Jarabub, Cyrenaica, November 1941.

EVERYWHERE THE WAR

British Bren gun carriers enter fabled Palmyra, in what Churchill called "that splendid affair amid th noble ruins." Syrian campaign, July 1941.

and his fellow commanders would have had strength enough. But now the Germans moved into the Mediterranean and North Africa, though reluctantly, compelled in large measure by circumstance, not design. All along, Hitler's grand obsession—the *Drang nach Osten*—had envisaged conquest of the Balkans by political and economic means, backed by the mailed fist; he had not wanted military campaigns. Neither he nor Halder, Chief of the Army General Staff, wished to become involved in North Africa even though Major General Wilhelm Ritter von Thoma, sent on a strategic reconnaissance to Cyrenaica in the fall of 1940, had reported that only four Panzer divisions would be required to overrun the keystone positions in Egypt.[38] Mussolini's pride—he would not ask for German aid as long as his Black Shirts were undefeated—played a part in the Axis decision; but it was Mussolini's vain search for glory in both Africa and Greece in 1941 that forced the Fuehrer's hand.

Hitler correctly believed that when he had defeated Russia, he could win the Mediterranean and North Africa. In November 1940, Directive No. 18 of the OKW tried to blueprint the broad lines of future German strategy. The directive contemplated, in the Mediterranean theater, the capture of Gibraltar by land attack with the permission and assistance (in the event never granted) of Generalissimo Francisco Franco, and—tentatively—air and ground assistance to the Italians in the Central Mediterranean and North Africa. Hitler was lukewarm in 1940 to the plan for Italian aid, as was Mussolini; *Der Fuehrer* wanted nothing to interfere with his grand design in Russia. Yet the British victories in the desert at the close of 1940 and the calamitous Italian adventure in Greece impeded his grandiose plans.[39]

Snide jokes about Germany's Fascist ally had begun to circulate widely in Berlin:

> . . . joke told . . . at the Berlin Kabarett der Komiker in January 1941: "Who wears a feather but isn't a cockerel? Who wears a steel helmet and isn't a soldier? Who keeps going backwards and isn't a crab?" Whereupon the audience replied in unison: "The Italians!"[40]

On December 27, 1940, Grand Admiral Erich Raeder told Hitler that:

> The naval staff views developments in the Mediterranean area with grave misgivings. . . . The threat to Egypt has been eliminated. . . . The Italian position has deteriorated decisively. . . . It is no longer possible to drive the British Fleet from the Mediterranean . . . decisive action in the Mediterranean . . . is . . . no longer possible.[41]

As early as Christmas 1940, Fliegerkorps X, from Norway, had been ordered to southern Italy and Sicily for "Operation *Mittelmeer*" (literally, Middle Sea), then regarded as a short campaign, to join the strained Italians in attacks against British shipping in the Sicilian Narrows. Almost 200 German aircraft were poised in Sicily by the middle of January.

Fear of a total Italian collapse in North Africa quickly led in Fuehrer Directive No. 22 (of January 11, 1941) to the formation of a new light motorized division for dispatch to Africa. On February 5, Hitler told Mussolini he would reinforce this division by sending one Panzer division—the 15th—to Africa, both divisions to be organized in the Deutsches Afrika Korps, under the command of a general soon to claim worldwide fame, Erwin Rommel.

14

The Western Desert

Characteristically, Rommel arrived in Tripoli on February 12, ahead of the advance elements of his combat troops. The hapless Marshal Rodolfo Graziani, at odds with what was, by courtesy, called the Italian General Staff and cloaked in the stigma of defeat, had left Tripoli the day before Rommel's arrival, to be succeeded by General Italo Gariboldi, who was left with four Italian infantry divisions, with little artillery and a so-called armored or light division (with few tanks), the Ariete Division. Gariboldi was the nominal commander, but the Ariete Division and, later, other Italian mobile units were placed under the German command, and there was no doubt that Rommel called the tune. From then on, North Africa was Rommel's war.

As the Italians built up a flimsy forward defense position at Sirte, Rommel pushed his antitank and reconnaissance units out toward British positions as fast as they were ferried to him from Italy. He covered his forces with dive bombers and fighters of Fliegerkorps X based in Africa, and long-range bombers flying from Sicily, and with the mobile 88 mm., an antiaircraft gun which was to achieve battlefield fame as a tank killer. The original Afrika Korps units, thrown hurriedly into action, contrary to contemporary reports had received no special hot-weather or desert training, and their equipment—air and oil filters, particularly—was in many ways deficient for the desert.

The German military adaptability to the sometimes frightful conditions of North Africa was remarkable. Rommel quickly experienced his first sandstorm and commented on the ferocious effects of the *Ghibli:*

> . . . Immense clouds of reddish dust obscured all visibility and forced the car's speed down to a crawl. . . . Sand streamed down the windscreen like water. . . . We gasped in breath painfully through handkerchiefs held over our faces and sweat poured off our bodies in the unbearable heat. . . .[42]

Later the heat of summer was to reach 107 degrees; the steel tanks baked to 160. Day and night the soldiers streamed with sweat and flies; fleas and bugs beat an incessant tattoo.

And the Germans were fighting with unreliable allies who had no stomach for the fight.

Rommel's aggressiveness coincided with British defensiveness. Far from offering a threat to Tripolitania, as the Duce and Fuehrer had feared, the victorious British rested on their laurels, held their forward positions in Cyrenaica thinly, and built up their base in Tobruk. The reason was essentially simple: another diversion, Greece.

For in February, just as the British completed their conquest of Cyrenaica, and Tripolitania seemed to lie within their grasp, the situation in the Balkans erupted. The Germans were obviously threatening Greece, an old ally, and London was worried, too, about Turkey. Anthony Eden, Foreign Minister, and the C.I.G.S., General Dill, were sent to the Middle East to determine what should be done next. After many doubts, they came to the conclusion that "the fullest measure of help ought to be offered to Greece at once," and that "the only chance of preventing the Balkans from being devoured piecemeal was to go to the help of Greece with everything we could."[43]

An Expeditionary Force was scraped together for Greece, and Cyrenaica suffered. Wavell garrisoned the vast bulge with minimum force—half an armored division, the 2nd (the "Desert Rats" of the 7th A.D. were refitting and repairing their tired tanks), and an Australian infantry division. Both units were green and understrength in men and equipment, and a new commander, Lieutenant General P. Neame, took over. It was a calculated risk on Wavell's part, although he did not realize how great until Rommel had shown his hand.

The "Desert Fox"

Rommel quickly decided the British forward positions were thinly held; he moved elements of the 5th Light Motorized Division, soon followed by the Ariete, toward Cyrenaica, and by mid-March the threat to Tripolitania had completely disappeared.

By the end of March, after a visit to Berlin to ask for reinforcements and to "sell" a daring offensive strategy, he had driven British patrols out of El Agheila and Mersa Brega, and the third reversal of the North African pendulum began.

Rommel was no book soldier. In his visit to Berlin caution was adjured. The High Command, its eyes on Russia, promised no reinforcements other than the 15th Panzer Division, scheduled to reach the front in May. When the Panzer division arrived, Agedabia (not far inside Cyrenaica) might be captured; then the great minds of OKW would decide on the next move. More Italian reinforcements might be necessary, and Rommel was urged to remember the difficulties of transport and supply—from Italy across the Mediterranean narrows, beset by the RAF and the Royal Navy, and thence across the desert.

But Rommel, like Nelson, at times turned a blind eye to higher authority. He was an opportunistic soldier—a superb, intuitive judge of his enemy's strengths and weaknesses, an aggressive commander with an ability to inspire his troops to almost superhuman exertion. He was a bold, front-line general, with an instinctive eye for terrain and tactical advantage; he reconnoitered in his Storch or led the action personally in his Mammoth (a captured British command car). To history he has become known as a great tactician and perhaps the war's greatest master of armored warfare, but he was much more than that; his strategic appreciations were sound, in many ways far sounder than those of his superiors. Like all generals, he had weaknesses. He was sometimes too impetuous and hasty. He paid too little attention to supply and expected his logistics to adjust, willy-nilly, to rapid tactical changes. And in the end it was supply which was to determine the outcome in North Africa.

The reputation which Rommel proceeded to build in those spring days of 1941 was made, it has often been said, by the British, who publicized his achievements globally. British correspondents and soldiers reflected first a grudging, then later an open, admiration for their foe's skill, and in time this developed into a British military inferiority complex. A more accurate description of Rommel's climb to fame, however, would be that he built his achievements solidly not because of, but despite and at the expense of, the British, who were outgeneraled, until the end, at nearly every turn.

Rommel now administered the first lesson. Despite the cautious caveats he had just received in Berlin and the protests of Gariboldi, the nominal commander, the 5th Light Division captured Agedabia on April 2, and with scant pause pushed deep into Cyrenaica. Task forces, with the German 5th Light Division as the spearhead, and Italian Ariete and Brescia divisions in train, drove fast across the desert toward Tobruk and followed up along the coastal road. The British lost the campaign piecemeal in a series of short, sharp battles, which quickly wore down their inadequate strength. They were dispersed and overextended, and the result was disaster. Benghazi was lost on April 4. The retreating British blew up 4,000 tons of captured Italian ammunition, and by April 5, the British armor—a jumble of old and captured tanks, many of them broken down or out of fuel—had been worn to the nub; the 3rd Armored Brigade, virtually all the tanks the British had in Cyrenaica, was "no longer of any use as a fighting formation."

Now, the German *Einheit* system of tactical organization (the capability of building up rapidly—from armor, infantry, engineer, and other disparate units—task forces designed for specific missions) proved its worth. Ranging far and wide across the front—and driving, always driving—Rommel formed a group of German-Italian task units, all under German command, and sent them plunging deep into Cyrenaica. Gariboldi, frightened, told Rommel to halt; Rommel ignored him. He was fully conscious of his insubordination; in a letter to his wife of April 3, he wrote: "I took the risk against all orders and instructions because the opportunity seemed favorable."[44] By April 7, after sharp fights and long furious marches, Derna was captured and El Mechili—a communications key which threatened all British positions north of the escarpment—was surrounded.

And, sometime in the night of April 6/7, the top British commanders in Cyrenaica, including two of the most successful and expert British desert specialists, disappeared, to surface later in German prison camps. The trio were the hapless Lieutenant General Neame, V.C., whose impression on the history of World War II was short-lived indeed; General O'Connor, the conqueror of Cyrenaica; and Brigadier General J. F. B. Combe, who had commanded a key unit of the "Desert Rats" and whose "knowledge of the desert was unexcelled." O'Connor and Combe had been sent from Egypt to

Cyrenaica by Wavell when Rommel had commenced to move—with the original intention, later changed, that O'Connor was to replace Neame. O'Connor remained, under Wavell's orders, as an adviser, an anomalous position in the midst of fast-moving battle, which did nobody any good. Wavell himself, who had visited Cyrenaica briefly in the early stages, had simply compounded confusion; it was clear that his touch, against Rommel, was far from sure. But then Rommel had a habit of making even the greatest generals look bad.

The Germans quickly reaped the fruits of boldness. A British major general and a brigadier, who had commanded British armor and an Indian brigade, respectively, were captured after a futile fight, along with the remnants of their units. By April 11, Tobruk was invested, and German reconnaissance units were soon operating against a small British mobile delaying force under Brigadier W. H. E. Gott in the Bardia-Sollum area on the Egyptian frontier. Rommel was talking, after only ten days of operations, about a drive to the Suez Canal.

Stalemate

But Tobruk and the inexorable demands of logistics imposed a halt. There were some 36,000 souls locked up in Tobruk; at least one-third were non-combatants, prisoners, or refugees. But Major General L. J. Morshead and his Australian garrison were stout fighters. The Germans made three attempts to penetrate the heavily defended fortress, circled by two lines of concrete and steel (built by the Italians), and supported by sea and air. They were repulsed by the Australians. The last attempt in late April and early May—in which the newly arrived 15th Panzer Division participated—cost the Axis about 1,150 casualties for a salient in the perimeter 2 miles deep and 3 miles long. So, for the moment, it was stalemate, with the sands of the desert and the science of supply and maintenance in charge. Tobruk was a thorn in the flank of any further German advance, and the Axis units were scattered, breathless, out of fuel, in need of maintenance. But so were the British.

A frantic period of regrouping, shifts of command, reinforcement, and supply began.

The rapid German reconquest of Cyrenaica—attributable alike to Rommel's leadership, German skills, and British weakness—emphasized some of the basic truths that were to dominate the desert fighting of the months and years to come. The rapid and ill-prepared attacks against the strong Tobruk defenses revealed (in addition to the weakness of the Italians) a chink in the Rommel armor, hasty impetuosity. But even more they demonstrated that the Axis now had a leader in North Africa who was a master of armored warfare and understood its principles well: ". . . In a mobile action, what counts is material, as the essential complement to the soldier. The finest fighting man has no value in mobile warfare without tanks, guns and vehicles. . . ."[45]

And what was perhaps more important, Rommel knew his own strengths: "A commander's drive and energy often count for more than his intellectual powers—a fact that is not generally understood by academic soldiers. . . ."[46]

For the top commands of all three belligerents it was time for stocktaking. General Halder and others of the High Command were jealously contemptuous of Rommel. He was unorthodox, often a military heresy; more important, he had not risen through channels and he owed Halder and his ilk nothing. Conventional wisdom suggested, as Halder noted in his diary, that the Afrika Korps halt and regroup. The forces were too small and scattered for further advances; supply was inadequate and Tobruk threatened the flank. General Friedrich Paulus, who was soon to preside over Germany's greatest defeat, was sent to North Africa to restrain Rommel and report on what Halder described as "this soldier gone stark mad."[47] It was essential in the High Command's view that North Africa should not divert strength required for greater tasks. And Rommel's somewhat cavalier treatment of his supply problems had now magnified them. It was 1,000 miles overland by tortuous and inadequate roads from the port of Tripoli to Tobruk; and from Italy to Tripoli, and along the African coast, Axis shipping was constantly vulnerable to air and sea attack. Rommel and his Italian allies needed continuous monthly supplies numbered in a large five figures and he had not—in the spring of 1941—been getting them.

To the British in their Egyptian cornerstone, supply was equally essential, equally desperate, and over even longer lines of communication. They had milked North Africa to aid Greece; in April they lost that battle, and in May Crete had been conquered with heavy British naval losses. On land, sea, and in the air, the British were spread thin—tied down in combat along the whole length and breadth of the Mediterranean. Malta was under siege and bombardment; British troops were fighting hard in East Africa; and Iraq and the Syrian campaign loomed as a dark cloud on future strategic prospects.

In North Africa, Wavell was reduced to a "weak unit of mixed tanks in Tobruk and one squadron of cruisers at Matruh."[48] Churchill was "spending the weekend at Daitchley and working in bed" when he received Wavell's alarming report on April 20. He immediately minuted orders for General H. L. Ismay for the British Chiefs of Staff, suggesting that a convoy—dubbed "Tiger"—run the gantlet of the Mediterranean, instead of passing around the Cape, as had been planned. It would save forty precious days, but the risk was great.

Churchill noted in one of his boldest conceptions:

The fate of the war in the Middle East, the loss of the Suez Canal, the frustration or confusion of the enormous forces we have built up in Egypt, the closing of all prospects of American co-operation through the Red Sea—all may turn on a few hundred armored vehicles. They must if possible be carried there at all costs.[49]

"Tiger" succeeded. It not only reinforced Malta's air strength but it landed about 238 tanks, most of them the heavily armored Matildas, and 43 much-needed Hurricane fighters at Alexandria on May 12.

Now it was the British turn to try. They started with a small operation, "Brevity," commanded by Brigadier Gott on May 15-16, its objective the important pass and communications junctions near the Libyan-Egyptian frontier. It was a quick failure; the British won Halfaya ("Hellfire") Pass through the 600-foot escarpment on the frontier, but of some fifty-three British tanks involved, five were lost, thirteen damaged, and six planes of the small Desert Air Force destroyed. The Germans lost three tanks, no planes, and in rapid counterattack on May 27 retook the strategic pass—gateway to Egypt.

"Battleaxe"

"Battleaxe" was next, an ambitious project to relieve Tobruk and move all the way to Derna and Mechili. Wavell, constantly prodded by Churchill, hoped to expel the Germans from most of Cyrenaica, but he understood now the difficulties. Despite the reinforcements provided by the "Tiger" convoy, and despite the continuous harassment of the Axis sea supply lines by the Royal Navy and the RAF, the 15th Panzer Division had reached North Africa in May and was now in action. The new British tanks required some modification and the crews to man them needed familiarity training. Wavell knew the British Matilda tanks were too slow for most of the desert fighting and were vulnerable to the German 88's; his cruiser tanks were undergunned, and his armored cars technically inferior to the Germans'. He had his doubts about success. But Churchill's impatient queries spurred him on, and D-Day was set for June 15 in the high hope that Rommel and his forces would be trapped and destroyed.

Lieutenant General Sir Noel Beresford-Peirse, who had had no experience in armored warfare and none in the desert, had been appointed to command the Western Desert Force. This he did, unlike Rommel, from a headquarters 60 miles from the scene of battle.

The 4th Indian Division and the reconstituted 7th Armored Division were the principal British combat units, supported by about 105 heavy and medium bombers, and some 98 fighters. Rommel had two tested German divisions, plus a number of understrength Italian units, and he was supported by fifty-nine German bombers and dive bombers and sixty fighters, and about one hundred Italian planes.

On paper, Wavell had a definite superiority. The RAF on June 15 established local air superiority near and over the frontier, but, as the war was to prove time and again, air superiority was not enough. The Germans showed, in "Battleaxe" that they could fight as stubbornly and skillfully on the defensive as on the offensive. They met the British armored assaults with hidden minefields, carefully sited concealed antitank guns in defilade, and with artillery and infantry strong points, disposed in depth. Their few 88 mm. guns were lethal—accurate at long range, and bravely manned.

The Indians, with armor, beat their heads in vain against the enemy positions around Halfaya Pass; fifteen of the eighteen British tanks were holed and destroyed. A wide sweeping envelopment above the escarpment and through the desert met stubborn resistance at Hafid Ridge (near Fort Capuzzo, south of Bardia), and by nightfall of the 15th, the 7th Armored Brigade had only forty-eight cruiser tanks in operation. "Battleaxe" was doomed, but the British, who had won transient successes at Capuzzo and south of it, persisted. On the 16th, German counterattacks with reinforcements precipitated ding-dong actions; the British held stubbornly to Capuzzo and the Scots Guards took Sollum barracks on the sea.

But Rommel had analyzed the intelligence reports and the radio traffic; he had anticipated the British offensive and pieced together the enemy intentions, and on June 17 he smashed the lingering British hopes. Two wide flanking movements reached out across the desert: the 5th Light Division sweeping through Sidi Suleiman toward Halfaya; the 15th Panzer from Hafid Ridge in an inner scythelike swing toward the strategic pass. By 8:00 A.M., tanks of the 5th Light Division had reached Sidi Suleiman. The British 22nd Guards Brigade, which had held stoutly at Capuzzo, was now threatened with encirclement and was short of ammunition. Rommel—the "Desert Fox," as he came to be known—had given ground in the center, but had enveloped the British on the desert flank; he was now positioned for a partial annihilation. But the British recognized checkmate when it stared them in the face. Wavell flew from Cairo to 7th Armored Division's headquarters at 11:45 to find that field commanders had already ordered 22nd Guards Brigade to withdraw to safety from Fort Capuzzo. Wavell confirmed the order, and added others: Break off all action; retreat and refit. As the night came to the desert on June 17, all surviving British troops were back where they had started, well inside the Egyptian frontier, and Wavell— heavy of heart—returned to Cairo and the pressing problems of the Syrian campaign.

The net result of two days of battle was a clear and definite check to the British and to British hopes. The Western Desert Force was back where it had started, and it had lost in some 2 days of battle 969 men killed, wounded, or missing, 4 guns, 91 tanks out of about 190 engaged, and 33 planes. The German losses (the Italians played a minor role) were 678 men killed, wounded, or missing, 12 tanks, and 10 planes.

The reasons for failure were several; most important, the British had no Rommel. The British attack was hastily mounted—too hastily, in part due to Churchill's insistence; the British were inadequately trained, and the German 88's proved to be a nasty surprise. Some thirteen of the 88 mm. caliber and considerably more of the powerful and more mobile 37 mm. and 50 mm. antitank guns were carefully sited, and the Germans utilized well the "luring" defensive tactics—which ironically the English military analyst Liddell Hart had suggested—of enticing the British armor within range. The German doctrine had envisaged the role of the tank as primarily a weapon of exploitation and annihilation, to be used chiefly against motor transport, infantry, and lightly armored vehicles; the enemy's armor, they believed, should be largely neutralized or destroyed by antitank guns. It was the first chapter of a worldwide military debate, then developing in the United States and elsewhere, about whether tanks or other specially designed antitank weapons and vehicles (they were to be called in the U.S. "tank-destroyers") were the best means of destroying enemy tanks.

The Fall of Wavell

The failure of "Battleaxe" was cumulative, following the British catastrophes in Greece and Crete. It was time for a change in the Middle East. On June 21, Churchill telegraphed Wavell that "the public interest will best be served by the appointment of General [Sir Claude] Auchinleck to succeed you . . ." Wavell's relief—he had already offered his resignation—had been preceded by a shift in command of Middle East Air Forces; Longmore had been relieved in May by his deputy, Air Marshal A. W. Tedder, a man of whom more was to be heard in history. At the same time various administrative and maintenance changes, long overdue, were made in the staff organization in the Middle East to keep more planes and tanks out of the workshops and on the battlefields. And, belatedly, a year after the initial suggestion had been made by Wavell, a Minister of State, to represent the War Cabinet on the spot in Cairo and to give political guidance to the military, was established in the person of Oliver Lyttelton.

Churchill had long been dissatisfied; he felt that the ground and air components in the Middle East had been led too cautiously and that neither Wavell nor Longmore had shown due deference for maintenance and administrative tidiness or for the old military principle of economy of force.

Churchill was, indeed, a difficult master to serve. He tried to run the war from Downing Street. His active mind and amazing fund of knowledge served as catalyst and resulted in a constant outpouring of detailed queries, suggestions, minutes, objections, criticisms, praise and blame. He was a goad—always pressing for action—and he believed in bold enterprises. He was sometimes fatuous and sometimes wrong, but always sought a way to close with the foe. And he had much reason for his queries, his objections, his admonitions. The British Army of that day still retained a Kipling complex, and in the Army list there were too many "Colonel Blimps" of World War I vintage. The ancient methodology of the War Office and the slow pace of progress infuriated a Prime Minister impatient for victory.

He was Minister of Defense as well as Prime Minister. Like the elder Pitt, with whom he was compared, Churchill felt that only he personally could save England from disaster. But the speed of modern communications and the sweeping horizons of the Churchillian mind often made the Prime Minister the bane of the generals. He not only dealt with what was to be done; he wanted to know, to the last bullet, how it was to be done.

Wavell was not Churchill's kind of general. As the British official history puts it, in an understatement: "the Prime Minister had never had full confidence" in him. Part of this breach was the marked difference in personality; Wavell, the classicist and intellectual, proceeded, if left to his own pace, carefully and methodically. He was shy and reserved in contrast to Churchill's pervasive public presence, and, in speech, inadequate or inarticulate. More important to Churchill, however, were Wavell's failures. He had been impressive against the Italians, adequate against the Vichy French; in Greece and in the desert he had looked bad against the Germans, and he had opposed the successful British shoestring expedition in Iraq and been exasperated by some of the Churchill telegrams about Syria. His estimates of the possibilities of success in Greece and of the forces required to hold Cyrenaica had been woefully wrong. True, he had been pushed by Churchill, in some cases, into precipitate adventures.

Nevertheless, Wavell—though quiet and dignified, a man who inspired personal loyalty, affection, and admiration among the few who knew him—appears more than a quarter century later to have been overcautious and overslow, and perhaps too indulgent with incompetent subordinates. He was probably miscast. Had he been dealing with global grand strategy instead of the day-to-day exigencies of a theater commander, his star might well have risen to the zenith. Like Ironside and Gort and so many British generals at the start of a major war, Wavell had the misfortune to be in key command of the armed forces of a democracy notoriously slothful in military preparation, stretched thin over vast areas of the world.

Kipling, in his immortal tribute to "Tommy Atkins," the British fighting man, delineated Wavell's principal problem better than any writer before or since:

> O it's Tommy this, an' Tommy that, an' "Tommy go away";
> But it's "Thank you, Mister Atkins," when the band begins to play— . . .
> For it's Tommy this, an' Tommy that, an' "Chuck him out, the brute!"
> But it's "Saviour of 'is country" when the guns begin to shoot. . . .[50]

So Wavell and Auchinleck exchanged places, by no means the last of a series of command changes in Africa and the Middle East as Churchill searched for the winning combination—a problem reminiscent of Lincoln's search for a Grant.

"The Auk" Takes Over

Auchinleck was moved to the hot seat with some reservations on Churchill's part, who had not forgotten the general's brief association with the ill-fated Narvik expedition the year before. But Churchill was perhaps a little less peremptory initially with the new commander than he had been with Wavell. "The Auk," as the general was inevitably known in many parts of the British Army, was a handsome six-footer. He had been commissioned in the Indian Army; most of his experience had been limited to tribal actions and he had little knowledge of armored warfare. (Wavell, who took "The Auk's" place in India, had never before served there. It was an inauspicious switch.)

Nevertheless, Auchinleck proceeded vigorously and with enthusiasm to reorganize and build up the British North African forces. Churchill's restraint did not last long, and the Prime Minister was soon pressing for an offensive to relieve Tobruk and the threat to Egypt and to sweep Rommel out of North Africa. "The Auk" refused to be hurried too much; he knew that both sides were struggling with supply, reinforcement, and build-up, and he understood —as the British official history later stated retrospectively—that ". . . in the Western Desert . . . the British were able to fight there at all, or indeed anywhere in the Mediterranean or Middle East, only because the sea communications with their sources of supply were kept open."

During the summer both sides prepared frantically, under constant harassment by opposing air and sea forces, for renewed offensives: Rommel to take Tobruk and clear his flank for an advance into Egypt, Auchinleck to relieve invested Tobruk and to regain Cyrenaica. The British formed the Eighth Army, for desert operations, with Lieutenant General Sir Alan Cunningham, brother of the British admiral commanding the Mediterranean Fleet, brought from East Africa, in command. The Army was built up to two corps—one of them armored (with the "Desert Rats" of the 7th Armored Division as its nucleus), one infantry corps composed of a New Zealand and an Indian division and a tank brigade, plus two South African divisions, a Guards brigade, and various bits and pieces. The Tobruk garrison—the 70th Infantry Division, a Polish infantry brigade, and a tank brigade—which had replaced the Australians, was also under Cunningham's command. (The relief of the besieged Australian garrison in Tobruk, which had cost the British heavily in time, effort, and shipping sunk or damaged, was necessitated more by empire politics stemming from heavy Australian losses in Greece and Crete than by the attrition of siege or bombardment.)

This tidying up of the British organization in the Middle East took time. Auchinleck found that the Army in particular was spread all over the landscape, with normal command channels broken down, and units widely separated from their parent organizations.

But by late October the Middle East had received some 770 tanks —300 of them, called "Stuarts," American-designed and -built light tanks—and hundreds of antitank, antiaircraft guns and field artillery. The Middle East Air Forces were also reorganized and heavily reinforced, via Malta, across Africa through Takoradi and round the Cape.

Despite the demands of the Russian front, Rommel and the Axis forces also received reinforcements and were reorganized, although even so all of the Axis African units were understrength. Marshal Ettore Bastico replaced Gariboldi in July as the nominal Axis commander in North Africa, and chiefly because of Italian sensibilities (Mussolini was insistent that the North African war should be much more than a German affair), an Armored Group Africa with Rommel commanding was organized under Bastico. It consisted initially of two corps, one entirely Italian, the other largely German. The German Afrika Korps of two armored divisions (the 5th Light had now become the 21st Panzer), with part of another German division, later to become the 90th Light, and the Italian Savona Division comprised one of Rommel's corps; the Italian corps, under Rommel, included four weak infantry divisions. The best of the Italian units, the Italian Ariete Armored Division and the Trieste Motorized Division, were excluded initially, because of Mussolini's proud jealousy, from Rommel's command and were directly under Bastico. But Rommel later succeeded in bringing them under his direct command.

In any case Hitler had the last word. He was determined to exert more influence in the Mediterranean war, and he insisted, despite Italian reluctance, upon the establishment at the end of October of a German Commander-in-Chief, South, subordinate only to Il Duce, whose mission it would be to win naval-air superiority in the Mediterranean narrows between Italy and North Africa and to cooperate with Axis forces in North Africa. Field Marshal Albert Kesselring was given the command, and the headquarters of Luftflotte 2 and Fliegerkorps II were diverted from the Russian front to Kesselring's new Mediterranean command. The change was to have some immediate effects by making things tough for the British and especially for Malta, but in the long view it was one of the first strategic dividends of the German involvement in North Africa; it represented a diversion (which it was later obvious could be ill afforded) from the main Russian front.

Aside from some frontier skirmishing, there was little action in the Western Desert in the searing summer of 1941; it was a struggle of the logisticians, which the British won. Rommel was building up his supplies and preparing his forces for an assault upon Tobruk. The British, conversely, extended the Egyptian railhead westward into the desert to a point just south of Sidi Barrâni, and built a 160-mile extension to Misheifa of a water pipeline from Alexandria. Together with reservoirs and pumping stations, this was to provide each British soldier with his strictly rationed, carefully hoarded three-fourths of an (imperial) gallon per man per day. The British in the battle of the build-up had some eventually decisive advantages: superior naval forces; a relatively secure supply route around the Cape of Good Hope and across Africa; greater ship replacement capability; the German concentration on the Russian front. The Axis fuel and supply losses at sea on the routes to North Africa from submarines, aircraft, mines, and surface ships increased dramatically during the summer and averaged from 20 to almost 30 percent of petroleum and military cargoes in September and October. In November, after a British cruiser-destroyer force had successfully intercepted an Axis convoy, cargo and fuel losses amounted to 62 percent of the total. Until November 1, an average of 72,000 tons each month had reached Africa (since July 1) despite the losses; but even this was insufficient for the build-up Rommel required for the assault on Tobruk and the invasion of Egypt. And in November—a crucial month of decision—only 30,000 tons were received.

"Crusader"

At dawn on November 18, when the bitter night of the winter desert began to warm slightly, the British struck first just as Rommel was about to start his long-prepared attack upon Tobruk. The British had a great superiority, not so much in numbers as in matériel. Including the forces in Tobruk, Cunningham had some 738 tanks of all types, compared to 244 German tanks and 146 Italian tanks—the latter not initially under Rommel's command. The British had reserves, behind the front, in the maintenance and modification shops, and in convoys at sea; the Germans had none. The British had some 650 planes of all combat types (550 of them "on the line" or immediately serviceable at start of battle), plus some 74 based on Malta. The Axis had almost 400 serviceable aircraft in Cyrenaica, of which a sizable number were obsolescent Italian planes. In numbers of military combatants, the odds were more even: 65,000 Germans, 54,000 Italians, making a total 119,000 as against 118,000 British.

"Operation Crusader"—the code name for the British offensive—was from the first a sprawling and confused battle in which nothing went according to plan for either side.

It was a battle at once of fixed positions and wide-ranging mobility; the German-Italian garrisons in the Bardia-Halfaya frontier strong points and the British garrison in Tobruk were the *points d'appui* around which the wheeled and tracked armies moved. But it was mobility which was to determine the outcome. Between Tobruk and Egypt some 30,000 vehicles—tanks, armored cars, tank transporters, fuel trucks, lorries, command cars, Bren gun carriers—left serpentine tracks across the sand and milled about in attack and retreat, offense and defense. The armies were dispersed and scattered, vehicles well apart to guard against attack from the air; at night, or at maintenance halts, they "laagered" (the Boer spelling), "leaguered" (British spelling), forming a protective circle against attack, like the old wagon trains of the American West.

The British XXX Corps drove wide across the desert, well south of the coastal strong points, in a roundhouse swing toward Tobruk; while the XIII Corps fixed and pinned down the enemy's positions in the Bardia-Sollum-Halfaya-Sidi Omar area. The XXX Corps included all the British armor, supported by infantry, with one glaring and well-nigh fatal omission; the I tanks—the strongest British vehicles—were assigned to the XIII Corps as "infantry-accompanying tanks," a tactical conception which the French campaign showed had outlived its time.

British air superiority and a driving storm over the German airfields which immobilized most of the Axis planes gave the British the advantage of surprise, and the initial air superiority once won was never lost. But Cunningham's battle plan depended, for its success, upon correctly reading the mind of Rommel.

And Cunningham was neither the first nor the last British commander to find this a difficult task. The British, by swinging south deep along the desert tracks toward Tobruk, had hoped to force the German Afrika Korps and the enemy's armored forces to disadvantageous battle. But Rommel, about to attack Tobruk, had expected a British diversion, and he did not react as Cunningham had hoped, waiting, instead, to ferret out British intentions.

By early afternoon of November 19, elements of the 7th Armored Division had reached the escarpment near Sidi-Rezegh, about 12 miles from the Tobruk defensive lines, and had overrun the enemy airfield, capturing some nineteen Italian planes. Other British armored columns—spread wide, too wide for mutual support—had attacked impetuously but not well the carefully prepared defensive positions held by the Italian Ariete Division at Bir el-Gubi, and had seized Gabr Saleh. Already tank casualties were heavy for both sides; at Gabr Saleh, the British lost twenty-three Stuarts, the Germans two tanks.

On the night of November 19, Rommel was still eying Tobruk. The great tank battle which Cunningham had hoped would spell the doom of the Germans had not yet been joined, and the German reaction was still to come. That evening Rommel ordered the Afrika Korps (15th and 21st Panzer divisions) to destroy the British intruders, while the Italians, stiffened by the 90th Light and other German elements, continued the Tobruk investment. The next day, the 20th, both armies were still thinking in terms of preconceived plans —the British anticipating with misplaced confidence a great armored battle, Rommel still intent on the capture of Tobruk.

The fog of war was obscuring the battlefield, and, for once, Rommel's sure touch seemed dulled.

But not for long. On the 20th the 4th Armored Brigade—an element of the British XXX (mobile) Corps—was mauled, for the second day, at Gabr Saleh by strong German armored forces. The 15th Panzer delivered a heavy blow, some twenty-six British tanks lost or damaged, and the 4th Brigade was probably saved from destruction by the restrictions of supply; the 21st Panzer Division ran out of fuel in the desert and was immobilized while it was resupplied.

By the night of the 20th, aided by a British broadcast from Cairo, the Germans had at length evaluated the serious proportions of the British offensive—no spoiling operation this, but an attempt at conquest. Rommel moved accordingly, and in a six-sentence letter to "Dearest Lu" (his wife) dated November 20, just two days after he returned to his African command from a visit to Italy, he correctly assessed the overall picture: "The battle has now reached its crisis. . . . Our position is certainly not easy. . . ."[51] From November 21 on, there was furious action around the Tobruk perimeter and on the escarpment near captured Sidi-Rezegh Airfield.

At dawn on the 21st, 70th Division drove southeastward through marked gaps in the defensive wire and minefields. The attempt of the "Rats" of Tobruk to break out of their invested fortress was marked, as Alexander G. Clifford described it, by a "touch of mad, incongruous pageantry. . . . The Black Watch advanced to the brave skirl of bag-pipes, a Major in kilts piping them into battle. . . ."[52]

The Tobruk garrison smashed a salient into the investing lines around the town, while simultaneously elements of the 7th Armored Division tried to push northwest from the escarpment at Sidi-Rezegh to join them. But just as the "Desert Rats" attacked, tanks of the Afrika Korps came barreling in from the east—followed later by British armor moving from Gabr Saleh—and a frenzied melee followed.

There had been nothing like it in the desert before, and rarely a precedent in the history of warfare. Over 20 miles from the Tobruk perimeter to the desert south of the escarpment, jumbled, mixed-up fighting raged, with the forces of both sides fronting in all directions, friend and foe wedged together in layered battle.

Around Sidi-Rezegh the battle swirled: "dust . . . smoke . . . flame . . . a crazy free-for-all . . . utter, indescribable confusion. . . ."[53]

Cunningham was now getting the tank battle he had sought, but the British had blundered into action piecemeal, thus losing the advantage of their great numerical superiority. The German tanks outgunned the British armored vehicles, and each night the Axis tank recovery system retrieved (far more efficiently than the British) the battle-damaged tanks, which workshops quickly repaired. Around the airfield and along the escarpment the guns—25-pounders and 88's—dueled, firing in all directions.

There was little real control on either side of this melee, and Cunningham fought from far away, way behind events. It was a struggle of small units, as battle so often is, and British indomitability saved them on the lip of disaster. Four Victoria Crosses were won at Sidi-Rezegh by a rifleman, a second lieutenant, a captain, and a brigadier general. Brigadier "Jock" Campbell, commanding the 7th Support Group of the "Desert Rats" and already famed for his daring, became a legend at Sidi-Rezegh.

... He led his tanks into action riding in an open unarmoured staff car, and as he stood there, hanging on to its windscreen, a huge well-built man with the English officer's stiff good looks, he shouted, "There they come. Let them have it." When the car began to fall behind, he leaped on to the side of a tank as it went forward and directed the battle from there. ...

The men loved this Elizabethan figure. He was the reality of all the pirate yarns and tales of high adventure, and in the extremes of fear and courage of the battle he had only courage. He went laughing into the fighting.[54]

By November 22, furious German concentric attacks had forced Major General Gott, commanding the 7th Armored Division, to withdraw his mauled elements from the Sidi-Rezegh Airfield. An armored brigade headquarters had been overrun and the division had only about fifty tanks in operation. Gott fell back into the desert toward a South African infantry brigade which had moved northward from Bir el-Gubi, with the Italian Ariete Division in pursuit. But the evening before Cunningham had unleashed Eighth Army's XIII Corps, which had been containing the German-Italian frontier strong points, and the New Zealanders, bypassing the strong points, started moving westward along the coastal road toward embattled Tobruk and the furious din of battle at Sidi-Rezegh.

November 23 was the German *Totensonntag*—Memorial Day for the dead of World War I. In the desert, too, it was a day of the dead. The Germans planned a concentric attack on the British XXX Corps. But Rommel, "unable for the first time to issue his orders verbally," had this day only incomplete control. Lieutenant General Ludwig Crüwell, commanding the Afrika Korps under Rommel, sent the 15th Panzer on a wide swinging movement into the desert to join the Ariete Division and attack the British positions along the escarpment from the rear. Early on, Crüwell's headquarters were overrun by the New Zealanders driving hard toward Tobruk from the east, and later Crüwell, in his captured British command car, found himself ringed by British tanks, only to escape in confusion. But the day was indubitably German. The mauled British armor of the XXX Corps was hurt again, and by nightfall, with "hundreds of burning vehicles, tanks and guns" scattered across the desert, the 5th South African Brigade had suffered 3,394 casualties, most of them prisoners, and no longer existed except on paper.

The German victories at Sidi-Rezegh on November 23 put Cunningham's wind up, and there was worse to come. Reports indicated that the overwhelming superiority the British enjoyed at the start of battle had been squandered. Cunningham believed the Germans now had more tanks available than the British; he feared that continuation of the offensive might mean total calamity and the invasion of Egypt.

"Crusader," indeed, hung on a thread; the ultimate decision could go to either side. At Cunningham's request, "The Auk" flew from Cairo to Eighth Army headquarters to decide whether to retreat or advance and attack. Auchinleck had a great attribute as a general; he never shirked the responsibility of command, and he got tougher when the going was tough. He directed Cunningham in writing:

> You will . . . continue to attack the enemy relentlessly using all your resources even to the last tank. Your main object will be as always to destroy the enemy tank forces. Your ultimate object remains the conquest of Cyrenaica and then to advance on Tripoli. . . .[55]
>
> . . . You have got your teeth into him. Hold on, bite deeper and deeper, and hang on until he is finished. . . . There is only one order, ATTACK AND PURSUE.[56]

So Cunningham issued new orders; XIII Corps, cooperating with the Tobruk garrison, was to capture Sidi-Rezegh "at all costs," link up and exploit to the west, while battered XXX Corps was to get a second wind and reorganize.

But at 6:00 A.M. on November 24, Rommel too issued fresh orders. General Crüwell reported that he had destroyed most of the 7th Armored and 1st South African divisions; he wanted to pursue and annihilate the remnants in the desert before they could regroup. Rommel, however, would have none of it. Always the advocate of the bold, he ordered a wide sweeping armored thrust along a desert track toward Sidi Omar and the Egyptian frontier, to threaten the entire British flank and rear, to sever their line of communications in Egypt, and to relieve the encircled German-Italian frontier garrison posts. It was a controversial decision. Crüwell was violently against it, and for once Rommel—the master of armored warfare—ignored the remaining British armored forces, determined to maintain the investment of Tobruk and to get the British wind up. Rommel was always a gambler, and this time his move almost came off.

The 21st Panzer Division, with Rommel in the van (but with only forty-five battle-worthy tanks), led the way, driving hard across the desert, followed by some sixty-one tanks of the 15th Panzer Division and, later, by the Italian Ariete and Trieste divisions. They brushed aside and overran scattered bits and pieces of the mauled XXX Corps, and the panic spread.

Rommel's dash eastwards toward the frontier took the German tanks straight across the British lines of communication:

A tank among unarmed lorries is like a shark among mackerel. . . .

British soft transports . . . scattered before them and confusion more deadly than shellfire spread everywhere . . . lost groups of men roamed about, passing and repassing through the enemy lines. Convoys of vehicles were scattered over 100 miles of desert. . . . Batteries of guns and tanks were left stranded. . . . Prisoners became gaolers. Men were captured and escaped three or four times. . . . Generals themselves were taking prisoners and corporals and brigadiers were manning machine-guns together. On the map the dispositions of the enemy and ourselves looked like an eight decker rainbow cake. . . .[57]

By 4:00 P.M., after a 60-mile dash punctuated by intermittent scuffles with scattered British forces on his flanks, Rommel reached the Egyptian frontier; and one hour later he issued his orders for operations the next day, November 25: all British forces on the Egyptian frontier were to be surrounded and destroyed.

The German units—like the British—were strung out and worn down after days of heavy combat. More important, they were operating at the end of a tenuous supply line, and the celerity essential to armored *Blitzkrieg* was frequently slowed by the requirements of resupply. The Germans were far superior to their foes in the battlefield recovery and repair of damaged tanks and vehicles; on the other hand, the British had a constant replenishment of reserve tanks, vehicles, and supplies from far behind the front; the Germans had none.

For the next two days, the movements of the opposing forces astride the Egyptian-Cyrenaican frontier resembled, as the British official historian puts it, "the scurrying of ants." Neither the British nor the Germans had much idea of where the enemy was, or how he was disposed; the Germans were inferior in the air, and the British air reconnaissance provided such a plethora of reports that the sightings merely confirmed confusion.

By the 26th, after some brief and indecisive but bloody tank versus artillery duels the previous day, came bad news from Tobruk for the Germans. The small German task force that had been left behind near the coast and along the Trigh Capuzzo had been squeezed and battered between the New Zealanders of XIII Corps advancing toward Tobruk and the Tobruk garrison, led by 70th Division, pushing south and east. The wild-swinging frontier battles had resulted in heavy losses to both sides, and the high-water mark of the Rommel thrust had overrun some British petrol and supply dumps and had reached (but not relieved) the beleaguered Axis frontier garrisons from Bardia southward. But the Italian units had lagged far behind; the Germans were strained and drained; tank carcasses littered the desert; and the panic that had started, like a forest fire, when Rommel's armor moved to the east had been checked by the Tobruk backfire and by "The Auk's" tough-minded decision to attack relentlessly, probably the high point of his career. Rommel had proved but human, after all. He had set his sights too high. His supply lines could not keep him going, and confusion of purpose, command, and countercommand seemed to reduce the usual smooth efficiency of the German war machine.

On the other hand, Cunningham, one of the first of a largely luckless succession of Eighth Army commanders, had been tried and found wanting. Auchinleck felt that Cunningham had faltered at the crux of battle; on the 26th, as the German tanks started to stream westward toward Tobruk, Cunningham was replaced by Major General N. M. Ritchie.

The German pullback from the frontier coincided with the British reinforcement of the New Zealanders south of Tobruk, and with the reorganization of the battered 7th Armored Division in the desert. The pell-mell rush of both sides toward the fortress resulted in heavy, sporadic battles with no flanks or rear, centered around the El Duda–Belhamed–Sidi-Rezegh key points.

It was bloody and tenacious fighting. The dressing stations and field hospitals of both sides were crammed with burned and wounded men; many lying on reddened stretchers on the sand were overrun but, knowing no flag, the medics of all nationalities continued to work with scalpel and hypos.

The German position became increasingly difficult, despite temporary recapture from the mauled New Zealanders of Sidi-Rezegh and Belhamed by the 15th Panzer Division on November 30. The bulge held by the 70th Division and the fortress troops in Tobruk reached almost to the Trigh Capuzzo, and the direct German line of communications was threatened.

The battle had become one of attrition, which the Germans, with no reserves and inferior strength, could not win. By the night of November 29, the 21st Panzers were reduced to twenty-one tanks.

As December opened and the weather cleared—aiding the hard-pressed British ground troops—Rommel achieved transient victory in the ebb and flow of battle. The 15th Panzers struck heavily at the

New Zealand positions on the escarpment and cut Major General B. C. Freyberg's troops in two. On the night of December 1, the decimated New Zealanders withdrew—save for a few detachments, which made their way into the Tobruk perimeter—to the Egyptian frontier. But they were speedily replaced by Indian troops, and the 1st Armored Division, fresh from England, had started to disembark at Suez in the last two weeks of November. Other fresh British units were converging on Egypt from Syria, Cyprus, and Palestine. This time the bulldog had his teeth in and would not let go.

December was harvest time for the British and the fruits of victory were sweet, but the strategic issue had been decided when Rommel's sweep toward the frontier had been halted. The Axis forces once again sent out weak strike-reconnaissance task forces toward their beleaguered frontier garrisons. They were quickly repulsed. The Germans failed to eliminate the El Duda bulge of the Tobruk perimeter, and by December 5, Germans and Italians had pulled out from their siege position to Tobruk's east, and were trying to eliminate what appeared to be a British southern flanking threat (by elements of the 7th Armored Division and Indian troops) near Bir el-Gubi in the desert. But the German blow was weak; the Italian units, as usual, were laggard, and for once the smooth German armored teamwork left much to be desired. That night Rommel got the answer to his warnings to Rome that all Cyrenaica might have to be abandoned and his appeals for reinforcements "of all kinds." He could expect virtually nothing, he was told, until the end of December; the Royal Navy and the RAF controlled the seas.

On December 7—as war became worldwide and history was written in smoke and flame in a place called Pearl Harbor—Rommel sounded retreat. He ordered his battered forces, weaker now by far in every classification than the enemy, to fall back upon El Gazala, where a fortified position had been partially prepared some 40 miles west of Tobruk.

The Relief of Tobruk

It was a skillful retirement, but the siege of Tobruk was lifted; by December 10, the eight-month ordeal of the garrison had ended. Only now, when defeat loomed large, was Rommel placed in command of all Italian, as well as German, forces in Cyrenaica.

The El Gazala position was rather quickly turned and overrun, although the Germans as always forced the British to pay a price and retreated in good order. But the two German Panzer divisions combined could muster only some 40-odd tanks; more important, the hemorrhages along the vital supply arteries were seeping the lifeblood of fuel from the Axis mobile forces.

Defeat fostered friction between the always uneasy Italian and German allies. On December 16, General Ugo Cavallero, Italian Chief of Staff, and Field Marshal Kesselring flew to North Africa from Rome to try to smooth things out. They brought bad news; events in other theaters (primarily Russia) meant reinforcements would be scarce; Tripolitania had to be held, but Cyrenaica might be traded for time. Rommel had already made his own decision. The El Gazala line, after a four-day delay, was abandoned, and a retreat to Derna on the coast and Mechili, inland, began.

By December 17, Rommel, blinded in the skies, threatened by continuous British flanking sweeps through the desert, had determined to pull back as fast as possible to Agedabia and El Agheila and the Tripolitanian frontier, thus reducing his own supply line and lengthening the enemy's. General Ritchie sent British armor barreling westward to cut off the enemy retreat from Benghazi, but the "Desert Fox" was as wily in retreat as in advance. The Germans actually unloaded twenty-two tanks on December 19 (remnants of a convoy from Italy) in Benghazi, despite heavy British air attacks. On Christmas Eve, after an Italian rearguard had pulled out, the British entered a town in shambles, a port cluttered with demolitions and filled with wrecks, only to find the enemy gone.

The retreat to Agedabia had been made good, and in the last days of the dying year, as Rommel drew his troops back to El Agheila, he exacted last blood. Near Agedabia, on December 28, General Crüwell, with his two Panzer divisions meshing smoothly, hit elements of the British 22nd Armored Brigade, knocked out thirty-seven British tanks, and lost only seven. On December 30—just to make the point—the hapless 22nd Armored Brigade lost twenty-three out of sixty-two tanks; the Germans seven.

And that, save for mop-up of the bypassed Axis garrisons on the Egyptian frontier 450 miles behind high water of the British advance, was it. The strong points fell, with some 14,000 Axis captives, early in the New Year, and hard-fought "Operation Crusader" had ended.

Ended in transient strategic victory for the British. Cyrenaica had been cleared of the enemy and reconquered, though briefly. Tobruk had been relieved, Rommel forced back into Tripolitania. The immediate threat to Egypt had been averted.

But not "according to plan." The battle had been much more protracted than the British had anticipated, their casualties far greater. Rommel's forces—despite British plans—had never been trapped and destroyed. The German general, disregarding some high-level second-guessing and frequent interference from both Italian General Bastico, the nominal commander in North Africa, and Field Marshal Kesselring in Rome, had conducted a masterful withdrawal; indeed, the braying hounds of the Allies never succeeded in forcing the "Desert Fox" to ground throughout the war. Wounded but still strong, the Afrika Korps and their Italian allies were soon to show their muscle.

Nor were the statistics of the campaign comforting to the British. They lost 2,900 killed in action, 600 more than the total Axis dead. Their total casualties—killed, wounded, missing, and prisoners for November and December 1941, and the first half of January 1942—were 17,700. The Axis total was 38,300 (including the 14,000 prisoners taken when the Axis garrisons in the Bardia-Halfaya areas, isolated by Rommel's retreat, surrendered in January). Of the total Axis casualties, more than 23,000 were Italian, chiefly prisoners.

The Germans lost at least 232 planes, the Italians about 100; the British 300.

By January 1, 1942, about 800 British tanks had been put out of action either by battle damage or breakdown (most of these were ultimately recovered and repaired); the Germans lost about 220, the Italians 120.

Tactically, the British had little to cheer about. Their men, rarely lacking in courage, lost engagement after engagement. Despite air superiority and the best air-ground support yet provided the British Army (not good), time after time the Germans exacted higher casualties, with weaker forces, than they received. The British generals—Cunningham and Ritchie—did not command as Rommel did, on the scene in person. They rarely controlled the battle; attrition and naval and air superiority won it for them. And the British expertise at armored warfare was sadly lacking. Their dispositions were too scattered, and only infrequently were they able to meld the kind of fighting team the Germans usually presented: tanks, antitank guns, artillery, and infantry. Some of the British tanks—particularly the mediums—were mechanically unreliable; the American Stuarts were fast and sound, but undergunned and vulnerable. The British artillery, however, distinguished itself; throughout the battle the Germans bestowed it ungrudging praise.

The Luftwaffe—its main strength on the Russian front, and its planes scattered across the entire Eastern Mediterranean—was not nearly as effective as it had been in France, even though the German Me-109F was far and away the best fighter in the Middle East.

Fundamentally the British tactical failures were due to adherence to an obsolete conception. Their own countrymen, Major General J. F. C. Fuller and Captain Liddell Hart, had long urged the principle of armored concentration. Instead, many of the British tanks were parceled out to accompany infantry units or to protect other formations which should have been able to protect themselves.

Nevertheless, "Crusader" represented a desert victory, and in North Africa the year 1941 ended for the British with the tonic of triumph, and the knowledge that Britain—with Russia and America now at war—no longer stood alone.

The campaign had indubitably shown that the British had something going for them which the enemy did not seem able to counter. Supply was the key to the desert battles, and control of the sea and air was the key to supply. Indeed, Rommel summed up the problem in a short letter to "Dearest Lu" on December 22: "Little ammunition and petrol, no air support."[58] In the arid wastes of Africa and the whirling sand of the *khamisen*, the influence of seapower upon history was now tangible. What happened at sea and in the air above it would ultimately determine what happened on land.

15

The Cockpit of the Mediterranean

The Significance of Malta

The war in the Mediterranean, and, once removed, in North Africa and the Balkans, came to a sharp focus around the Sicilian Narrows and Malta. Since the fall of France, the tiny island of Malta—in peacetime the headquarters of His Majesty's Mediterranean Fleet—had been the only British sea-air base available between Gibraltar and Alexandria. Its drydocks and repair facilities in the Grand Harbor at Valetta could handle virtually any ship on the Navy list; its limestone caverns offered excellent air-raid shelters and facilities for underground shops, and from its three airfields British planes could range in all directions over sea lines of communication.

As the Germans came to the aid of Rome in North Africa and as the fighting in Greece surged across the Balkans and Hitler turned to the East, the strategic importance of Malta increased. Both sides recognized it as a key to the sea lanes. No planner could miss its significance; its geographic situation south of Sicily highlighted the island. Winston Churchill was later to describe the defense of Malta as "a compulsive" requirement upon Britain, and its strategic importance as "never greater" than in World War II. The Germans, too, appreciated the importance of the island's possession, and in early 1941, the National Defense Section of the Supreme Command "voted unanimously for the capture of Malta—the only way to secure permanently the sea route to North Africa."[59]

The British strategy for Malta's defense and utilization was consistent and persistent throughout the war. Hitler, on the other hand, despite his lower-echelon advisers, followed an erratic policy; several times he planned to capture the island, only to be distracted by more distant horizons.

Throughout 1941 Malta epitomized the indivisibility of modern military power; over it, near it, and across most of the Central Mediterranean ebbed and flowed the tidal rips of battle. Troops and supplies were funneled across the Mediterranean by both sides, from Gibraltar to Malta to Alexandria, from Alexandria to Malta, from Egypt to Greece, from Greece to Crete, from Italy to Libya or Albania. Around the supply routes clustered the predators of sea and sky—planes, submarines, and ships and light craft—and occasionally the guerrilla depredations climaxed in the clash of major naval battle, and the sudden staccato eruption of duels in the skies.

The German intervention in the Mediterranean quickly changed the picture in the air and at sea, as it had on land. The British felt the sting early in 1941 as a series of convoys for Greece, Alexandria, and Malta (ammunition, reinforcements, seed potatoes, and Hurricanes) passed through the Narrows: Force H, under Admiral Somerville from Gibraltar, turning over the precious ships to Admiral Cunningham from Alexandria. At first, intermittent but unskilled air attacks by Italian planes kept the British sailors alert but did no damage. But early on January 10, destroyer *Gallant* struck a mine (sixty dead, twenty-five wounded, her bottom ripped open) just south of the Italian-held island of Pantelleria in the Narrows. She managed to struggle in tow into Valetta the next morning, but the Mediterranean Narrows had become a toll road, payment in blood.

On the afternoon of January 10, about 60 miles from Malta, with Cunningham flying his flag in battleship *Warspite*—battleship *Val-*

iant, aircraft carrier *Illustrious*, and five destroyers in company—the Luftwaffe struck with more than thirty dive bombers and Ju-88's. The British official history notes drily that "the attacks . . . were quite unlike anything the fleet had experienced at the hands of the Italians."[60] At the cost of some six German planes, the *Illustrious* was put out of action—her flight deck wrecked by six bombs, her plates buckled by three near-misses, half her guns out of action, fires raging fore and aft, 126 dead, 91 wounded. She had a grim odyssey. Her steering gear disabled, she steamed in circles; was bombed again (one hit) and finally, smoking, struggled into the narrow entrance of Valetta about 9:00 P.M. still in the center of the Malta bull's-eye.

Cruisers *Gloucester* and *Southampton*, covering one of the convoys, got theirs the next morning, January 11. Dive bombers swooped, undetected, out of the sun; a bomb whished through five steel decks of *Gloucester* but lay scorching to the touch, unexploded, deep in the ship's bowels. *Southampton* was more unlucky. She was hit several times; fires raged, steam dropped in her boilers. She slowed and stopped dead in the water, and that night, with most of her eighty dead aboard, her agonies ended with a mercy killing as three British torpedoes finished off a mortally wounded ship. All fourteen ships of the four convoys had gotten through undamaged, but at heavy cost, indeed, to the Royal Navy.

As for *Illustrious*, she was hit again while in dock in Malta, and other ships, the airfields, and the dockyard were all heavily knocked about by strong German raids throughout much of January. The carrier, still crippled but steaming strongly, crept away in the dark on January 23, and made it safely into Alexandria, to the cheers of British seamen, two days later.

For Malta, there was more—much more—to come. The heavy German attacks of January abated slightly after *Illustrious* left, but not for long. Throughout the first half of 1941 the island was violently attacked. It was bombed often by day and by night, sometimes by more than forty Ju-88's and Heinkels that roared—particularly on moonlit nights—high and low, bombed everywhere, and mined the harbor. The island's defense was pitifully weak when its Gethsemane started; twelve Hurricanes were its only fighters, and the heavy attacks quickly forced the transfer to Egypt of the island's few remaining Wellington bombers and Sunderland flying boats.

Neutralization of the island base was the German objective, and it was almost accomplished. But the demands on Fliegerkorps X increased faster than its strength; the needs of Rommel in North Africa and of the Axis in Greece (and later of the Russian campaign) siphoned away more and more units, and the stout British defense of Malta, reinforced by fly-ins and convoys to more than 100 fighters by June, had caused sizable German losses.

So Malta endured; the attacks waxed and waned. Toward year's end, as the Russian front congealed in bitter cold, the pitiless bombing of the dusty, sun-swept speck of land in mid-Mediterranean increased again.

Italy and Albania

In early February, Somerville, with Force H from Gibraltar, undertook to stir up the lethargic Italian Fleet, which ever since the Taranto raid had been sticking pretty close to the relative security of west coast ports.

With battleships *Renown* and *Malaya*, carrier *Ark Royal*, cruiser *Sheffield*, and ten destroyers, Somerville boldly steamed into the Gulf of Genoa, and on February 9 bombarded docks, oil refineries, and the waterfront, laid mines off Spezia, and bombed a refinery at Leghorn—all without British damage. It was a raid that had only minor military importance but was a boost to British morale. Not so to the already sagging spirits of the Italians, who had been run out of Cyrenaica, fought to a standstill by the Greeks, and were now bloodied in their own homeland.

In the land battles across the Adriatic Sea, the sour bile of defeat had already embittered the early taste of victory for the Italians. Mussolini's dreams of empire were turning into nightmares in the rugged mountains of Albania.

The year 1941 opened with about one-quarter to one-third of Italian-conquered Albania in Greek hands, and with the British already involved in Greece with air support and supply assistance.

By January 10, the Greeks, with some thirteen divisions in line, some of them transferred from the dangerous Bulgarian frontier, had captured Klisura, routing a hapless Italian unit, the Lupi di Tuscana (Wolves of Tuscany) Division, henceforth dubbed the Lepri di Tuscana (Hares of Tuscany).[61] British bombers were flying intermittently through cloud wrack and snow squalls to bomb Valona and Durazzo, and nodal Italian supply points. But the cruelty of the cold and the hard and barren land, torn into deep ravines and flung skyward into violent mountains, slowed and wearied both combatants. Winter congealed the hot blood of war.

In the harsh months of February and March, the exhausted Greeks still held the initiative; they inched toward Tepeleni (key to the important port of Valona), up the near-vertical hills and jagged rocks. But it could not be done. The ragged men were spent; the Italians had for long held air superiority; the tiny Greek Air Force was finished, and the British were flying from fields far away—too far and too few.

The Italians, too, tried very tentative initiatives in early March and planned for bigger ones; with some twenty-eight Italian divisions in Albania by mid-March, a spring offensive to restore the pride of Italian arms should be possible. But the toll of winter had been high; trench foot and the "white death" or "dry gangrene" of frostbite added a total of some 13,000 men to some 6,000 combat casualties: "Legs swelled above the ankle, all feeling disappeared from the foot, the flesh changed color, turned purple and then blackish. . . ."[62]

When the cold subsided, stalemate ensued.

Greece—The Preliminaries

Hitler had ordered tentative plans for the conquest of Greece in November 1940, just after the RAF had intervened in Greece. But the planning, which contemplated an attack through Bulgaria, was contingent and preliminary, and was to form part of a larger scheme for ousting the British from the Mediterranean. From November until the spring of 1941, the sails of Axis strategy backed and filled as the winds of war veered more and more toward the Balkans.

The British, too, planned and debated. In January, as the Germans moved troops into Rumania, through Hungary, London became convinced that an attack upon Greece via Bulgaria was imminent. General Metaxas, the carpet-slippered dictator who had tried to walk a tightrope in defending his country with British help while avoiding provocation to the Germans, died on January 29. With his death went some of the hardheaded Greek opposition to tentative British plans to land small forces at Salonika. The new Greek President, Alexander Koryzis, started his regime in early February by asking the British for specifics—how much, how many, when? Unlike Metaxas, who understood that British help against the Germans would not be adequate, Koryzis, faced with a gathering storm, tried to find a storm cellar. The result was Anthony Eden's visit to Athens, Turkey, and the Middle East, and the British were committed to land operations in defense of Greece, but with the details and the actions left vague.

The German plans, too, were subject to the whims of chance. Directive No. 20, "Operation Marita" of December 13, 1940, which was the move against Greece, contemplated an invasion through Bulgaria to eliminate actual or potential British air bases and to protect the Rumanian oil fields and the southern flank of the projected Nazi invasion of Russia. But the German military felt strongly that the use of the Yugoslav rail lines and road networks would considerably expedite the invasion, and Hitler agreed that at least a beneficent Yugoslav neutrality or collaboration was necessary. Worry, too, about the important Danube River supply line—particularly at the Iron Gate between Yugoslavia and Rumania, where the river is canalized—played a part in both political and military planning.

Thus both sides moved toward inevitable collision in the mountains of Greece. By late February, the German troop concentration and supply build-up in Hungary and Rumania had spilled over into Bulgaria; a heavy pontoon bridge across the Danube had been constructed by German engineers, and in early March German tanks and planes had flooded into the country in large numbers, just at the time when advance units of a British Expeditionary Force were landing at Piraeus and Volos.

In March, the German pressure on Belgrade to join the Tripartite Pact resulted in a short-lived triumph for the Hitlerian policy of cocked-fist persuasion. The Yugoslav government, pressured by the Regent, Prince Paul, and by the Germans, joined the Tripartite Pact on March 25 in a ceremonial signing in Vienna. Its reluctant surrender to Berlin's strong-arm methods was sugared by a Hitlerian promise of Greek Salonika.

At this juncture, a naval battle affected the fortunes of war.

The Battle of Cape Matapan

The clash of elements of the British and Italian fleets on March 28 was a direct result of an Italian effort, goaded by the Germans, to attack the British supply and transport convoys to Greece, and of a British effort to protect them. Since March 5, British troops had been landing in Greece. Berlin pressed Rome to undertake more aggressive naval operations against the Alexandria-Crete-Piraeus arteries. The reaction was intended to take the form of a raid, by eight fast Italian cruisers, covered and supported by thirteen destroyers and the new battleship *Vittorio Veneto*, to the north and south of Crete.

Vittorio Veneto, flying the flag of Admiral Angelo Iachino, and her consorts put to sea at dusk on March 26 from Naples and other

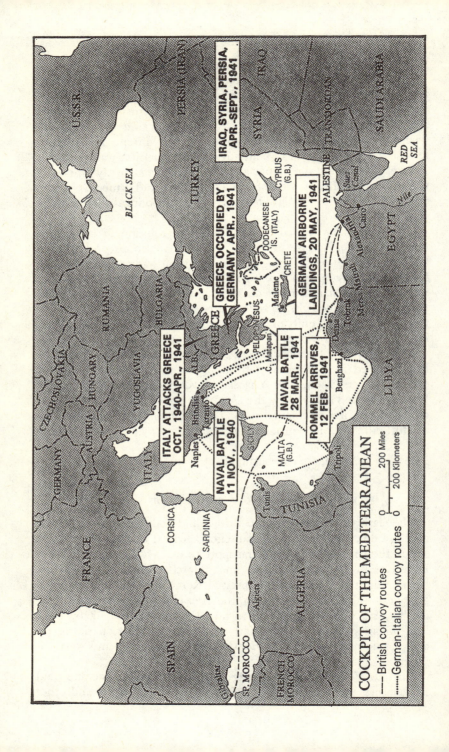

ports, and shaped a course, south and eastward, to round Cape Matapan—100 miles at sea—the southernmost point of Greece.

Admiral Cunningham, just back in Alexandria from covering a supply convoy to Malta, smelled a rat, received bad news.

Early in the morning of March 26, just before the Italian ships put to sea, six EMB's (explosive motor boats) sneaked in the dark into the harbor of Suda Bay in Crete, which the British had been using as an advanced base. The EMB's—a novel weapon keyed to daring, speed, and stealth—were one of several similar maverick systems developed by the special "Tenth Light Flotilla" of the Italian Navy, which devoted its time and energies to penetrating booms, nets, and other defenses in enemy harbors, and attacking anchored leviathans. At Suda Bay, the one-man EMB's, launched off the port from two Italian destroyers, pushed through a series of improvised booms, and crept to within close range of the moored ships. Then the "pilots" put the small craft on collision courses at high speed, locked their rudders, pulled levers to release rafts, bailed out of their skittering craft, climbed on the rafts, and watched the results. The explosive charges, timed to sink and detonate under the hulls, blasted in the vulnerable belly of the 8-inch cruiser *York*—Admiral Cunningham's only heavy cruiser—flooding boiler and engine rooms. Beached, she was never to sail again. Tanker *Pericles* was also hit and holed; the Italian crews were pulled from their ingenious rafts, exultant captives.

Suda Bay was the first of many Italian successes in this kind of unconventional naval war. Collectively the Italian Navy, as Cunningham said later, showed "little enterprise and initiative"; but ethnic traits and the Italian temperament produced in World War II, as in World War I, "men capable of the most gallant exploits," individuals who, in D'Annunzio's phrase, dared always to dare.

Cunningham had a light covering force patrolling to the west of Crete and in the Aegean, but intelligence information convinced him the enemy was up to something. He ordered the sole British convoy at sea to reverse its course toward Alexandria, canceled other convoys, and put to sea himself, covered by the darkness of the night of March 27. The admiral, in battleship *Warspite*, was accompanied by battleships *Barham* and *Valiant*, carrier *Formidable* with thirty-seven Fleet Air Arm Fulmars, Albacores, and Swordfish, and nine destroyers. Already at sea, steaming toward the southwestern coast of Crete, were cruisers *Orion*, *Ajax*, *Perth*, and *Gloucester* with four destroyers.

South of Gavdo Island, early on the 28th, air sightings sent the alarm bells ringing, and soon afterward, *Orion* and her sisters spotted the top hamper of the Italian heavy cruisers. The British cruisers turned and tried—as Beatty had done at the Battle of Jutland—to draw the enemy toward the main battle fleet. Outranged and outlegged, the lighter British might have had a hard time of it as Italian salvos spouted around them for more than forty minutes. But Admiral Iachino, who feared his ships were getting too far east, close to the British lair, recalled them at 8:55 A.M. With the morning dying and the British trying to keep contact, *Orion* sighted *Vittorio Veneto*. She almost lived to regret it; for fifteen minutes the British lights dodged 15-inch salvos as Iachino tried to trap the enemy force between his powerful guns and the Italian heavy cruisers.

The Fleet Air Arm came to the rescue: a strike force of torpedo planes launched from *Formidable* came skimming in, making no hits but causing considerable diversion. *Veneto* and the rest of the Italian Fleet in three separate groups hightailed it west and north at 25 knots, Cunningham in pursuit of the faster Italian ships.

Again in the afternoon watch, with the British "big boys" some 60 miles astern, Cunningham sent off a striking covey from *Formidable*. About 1510 (3:10 P.M.), the ungainly Albacores and Swordfish sent five torpedoes streaking toward the *Veneto*. There was only one hit, launched by Lieutenant Commander J. Dalyell-Stead, the squadron commander, who pressed in his attack so close to the great hull and her white wake that he could not miss. He paid with his life—he and two others of his crew the only British casualties of the entire battle. The explosion fractured the *Veneto*'s port outer shaft; some 4,000 tons of the Mediterranean poured into her hull and she slowed, listed, and settled by the stern. The great battleship—pride of the Italian Navy—stopped, then slowly worked up speed again, first to 10, then 16, then 19 knots. Damage control and the "technical skill . . . and the ability of the crew" had saved a wounded ship; thereafter, the British never laid a hand on her as she steamed toward Taranto, 420 miles away.

Hope flared for a time in the pursuing ships as RAF bombers from Greece and Fleet Air Arm planes based on Crete harried the Italians, but with near-misses, no hits. Just after dark, with the afterlight still glowing on the horizon, came the last chance. *Formidable* sent more of her peregrine falcons swooping in for a kill. They found the laboring battleship surrounded by most of her consorts, and the birds of prey met such a withering fire and found Italian smoke screens and searchlights so blinding that they scored only one hit, on Italian cruiser *Pola*. It was a lucky one; the cruiser's generators were knocked out with all power for her turrets. She was left dead in the water.

The sanctuary of the dark had seemingly saved the Italian ships, but Cunningham (the man with a touch of Nelson in him) still went on, determined, if he could, to bring the foe to bay. He ordered his small boys to the van for a night torpedo attack and steered toward crippled *Pola*.

About 2225, the dream of all admirals of all ages and all fleets came true for Cunningham on the bridge of *Warspite*. From out of the darkness directly across the bows of *Warspite*, *Valiant*, and *Barham* steamed several dark silhouettes, two of them unmistakably heavy cruisers of the *Zara* class. They were, in fact, *Zara, Fiume*, and four destroyers, ordered back to crippled *Pola*'s assistance. Cunningham turned his ships into column to bring their 15-inch broadsides to bear, and at 2228 the British battleships commenced the task of summary execution.

Surprise was absolute. The Italian guns were trained fore and aft:

Never, in the whole of my life [Cunningham was later to write] have I experienced a more thrilling moment than when I heard a calm voice from the director tower—"Director layer sees the target"; sure sign that the guns were ready and that his finger was itching on the trigger. The enemy was at a range of no more than 3,800 yards—point blank.

. . . One heard the "ting-ting-ting" of the firing gongs. Then came the great orange flash and the violent shudder as the six big guns bearing were fired simultaneously. . . . Our searchlights shone out with the first salvo, and provided full illumination for what was a ghastly sight. Full in the beam I saw our six great projectiles flying through the air. Five out of the six hit a few feet below the level of the cruiser's upper deck and burst with splashes of brilliant flame. The Italians were quite unprepared. . . . They were hopelessly shattered before they could put up any resistance. . . .

. . . One saw whole turrets and masses of other heavy debris whirling through the air and splashing into the sea, and in a short time the ships themselves were nothing but glowing torches and on fire from stem to stern.[63]

It ended in flame-lit darkness as quickly as it had begun. The British battleships, attacked futilely by the Italian destroyers, turned away; the melee of a night action between light craft followed. *Fiume* sank in flames, with its commander, at 2315; one of *Zara*'s boilers exploded; a "forward turret whirled overboard into the sea," and she blew up in a cascade of fire, half an hour after midnight. Destroyer *Alfieri*—holed and stopped and listing—sank; destroyer *Car-*

ducci, swept by a storm of fire, scuttling valves opened, died with her skipper; destroyer *Oriani*, one engine crippled by a shell hit, limped slowly back to port; only *Gioberti* escaped undamaged.

Hapless *Pola*, without power and crippled, unable to run or to sting, saw through the night the death of her sisters, and knew her time was come. The skipper ordered the sea cocks opened and directed his crew to abandon ship. As she was sinking slowly, her scuppers awash in the dark sea, British destroyers spat a few shells in her direction; then about 0300 on March 29, British destroyer leader *Jervis* pulled alongside. The sinking cruiser was "in a state of indescribable confusion. Panic-stricken men were leaping over the side. On the crowded quarter-deck, littered with clothing, personal belongings and bottles, many of the sailors were drunk. There was no order or discipline of any sort. . . ."[64] Officers' cabins had been looted and empty Chianti bottles lay about.[65]

A British boarding party armed with cutlasses leaped aboard *Pola*, itching for a scrap, but those of the cowed Italians who had not abandoned ship offered no resistance.

Jervis took aboard the 257 men of the crew still in the hulk, and sank the ship.

The Battle of Cape Matapan was over; the rest was mercy work. British ships picked up about 900 Italian survivors out of the oil-covered sea littered with bodies and debris or from life rafts, and Greek vessels another 110. About 160 more—half dead—were ultimately rescued by an Italian hospital ship sent to the scene after Cunningham, retiring from the threat of German bombers, had notified the Italian Admiralty of the position.

Even so, about 2,400 Italian sailors, three fast heavy cruisers, and two large destroyers died, and *Vittorio Veneto* and one destroyer were damaged. The cost to the British was one Albacore aircraft and its crew.

It was one of the most lopsided victories on record and one with traumatic strategic effects. To Cunningham and the British, Matapan was incomplete: *Vittorio Veneto* had escaped. But it was a "milestone along the path to British naval supremacy in the Eastern Mediterranean."[66] Capping Taranto, it neutralized and well-nigh eliminated the potential menace of the Italian heavy ships to British lines of communication.

Mussolini and Supermarina took the lesson hard. The Italian Navy had never envisaged night actions by battleships and heavy cruisers and their ships were not equipped with radar—a partial explanation for the devastating surprise of the night battle. But there was greater error. The German Luftwaffe and the Italian Air Force had failed to provide the air reconnaissance and support which Admiral Iachino had repeatedly requested before the battle. And the vanquished quickly noted that it was *Formidable*'s hornets which had tipped the scales of battle; the two torpedo hits on *Vittorio Veneto* and *Pola* determined the ultimate outcome.

At last, years too late, Mussolini ordered the conversion, first of the Italian liner *Roma*, then of the *Augustus*, to improvised aircraft carriers. They never served; more than two years later when Italy dropped from the war they still lay in dockyard, unfinished monuments to a massive misjudgment.

Matapan resulted in the imposition of even greater caution upon the Italian Navy. The Nelsonian tradition that no commander could go wrong if he laid his ship alongside an enemy's had been lacking in the Italian Fleet and particularly in the High Command since war's beginning, and the directives governing the employment of the Italian battleships had warned against "exposure . . . to undue risks." Now, after Matapan, the leading strings were shortened; the battleships, henceforth, would "not carry out any further missions 'beyond the range of fighter protection.'"[67] This meant very short leash indeed; the heavy ships had become, in effect, coast defense batteries. And their mobility, the major strategic asset of any navy, had been further restricted by fuel shortages. The inadequate Italian fuel reserves were almost expended by the spring of 1941; the monthly consumption for the Italian Navy had been rationed at 100,000 tons, and Italy received from Germany, which carefully restricted the amounts allowed Rome, only about 50,000 tons, or what Commander Marc'Antonio Bragadin describes in *The Italian Navy in World War II* as "one fourth of the operational amount desired."

"In the Summer of 1941," he continues, ". . . the Italian reserve was completely used up. From that moment on, the Italian Navy was forced *to conduct operations only as the arrival of fuel oil permitted.*"[68]

In essence, Matapan and the concomitant restrictions of logistics "were sufficiently shattering to remove a challenge" by the main body of the Italian Fleet to British sea communications in the Eastern Mediterranean. "The Italian Fleet was so roughly handled that it never again ventured into those waters. . . ."[69]

And Cunningham later pointed out that the "supine and inactive attitude of the Italian fleet" during the weeks of crisis now at hand (the Greek campaign) was "directly attributable" to Matapan.

But control of the sea in World War II meant more than ships-of-the-line, and the ultimate strategic consequences of the battle had limited effect on more immediate events. For the British Navy faced other, greater challenges: from the Luftwaffe, from enemy submarines, and from the light forces and sea guerrillas of the Italians.

The Flaming Sea

Throughout the Mediterranean in 1941 ships wearing the Union Jack or the Cross of St. George, vessels of Italy and Germany sank, flamed, or limped home, torpedoes in their bowels, joints racked by mine explosion. It was the hottest maritime battle area on earth. An enclosed sea, choked at both ends by the converging land masses of three continents, strangled at midpoint by the Sicilian Strait, and now in the age of airpower under surveillance throughout much of its length and breadth by the planes of both sides, it was at once watery battlefield and important supply route. Here unceasing vigilance, superior skill and firepower, and good luck were vital to survival. By day the menace from the air and from submarines and mines was constant; at night the hawks were generally blinded, but the threat of the submarine and mine was ubiquitous and persistent, and to them were added the ravages of surface naval forces—cruisers, torpedo boats, destroyers.

Within this flaming sea—the *Mare Nostrum* of neither side—men navigated at their peril. Death was catholic in its impartiality, long the list of ships and names of men removed forever from the rolls of the living. Nothing was spared; mines and bombs knew no differentiation. Italian liners such as *Conte Rossa*, sunk by HMS *Upholder* on May 2, long familiar to generations of travelers, and cruiser *Armando Diaz*, sunk February 25, joined in death British gunboat *Ladybird*, sloop *Auckland* (sunk respectively in May and June), and German U-boats. It was battle unending, with neither side in clearcut domination.

During the second half of the year, Malta was relieved of some of the pressure of the early months as the Germans turned toward Crete and then Russia. But it still remained the focus of mid-Mediterranean strategy, and upon the British supply and reinforcement efforts centered much of the intermittent action at sea.

The success of the German vertical envelopment of Crete forced the British garrison of Malta to turn apprehensive eyes skyward; in late July a reinforcement convoy—infantry, antiaircraft, artillery, and RAF personnel—reached Malta, escorted by Somerville's Force H, reinforced by battleship *Nelson* and three cruisers detached from the Home Fleet. The reinforcements made it in two installments, increasing Malta's garrison to 22,000 men, but the Italian Air Force, with their German allies largely withdrawn to Russia, made the British pay the price. In unusually effective attacks torpedo bombers sank destroyer *Fearless*, and damaged cruiser *Manchester*, destroyer *Firedrake*, and steamship *Sydney Star*.

Again in late September, with Force H reinforced by *Nelson*, *Prince of Wales*, and *Rodney*, another Malta convoy ran the gantlet. This time *Nelson* was damaged by an Italian torpedo (on September 27) and steamship *Imperial Star* was sunk.

But British submarines working out of Malta and Alex also exacted much Axis blood; on September 18, two 20,000-ton Italian liners used as troop and supply ships were sunk by HMS *Upholder* as they steamed hard toward Tripoli.

The British lost three submarines in July and August, and in September German U-boats started operating in the Mediterranean. German minesweepers and torpedo boats were to follow. These were interim measures; Hitler's Mediterranean plans, which had waxed and waned, still vaguely contemplated the capture of Gibraltar, the reduction of Malta, and the overrunning of the British imperial linchpin position astride the Suez Canal. These ambitious plans would have to be deferred, however; the conquest of Russia took priority. Meanwhile, with ancillary aid, the Italians would have to bear the brunt.

They did. For a short time late in the year, the British were able to base a surface striking force—Force K—on Malta. At 12:40 A.M. on November 9, 6-inch gun cruisers *Aurora* and *Penelope*, accompanied by two destroyers of Force K, intercepted an Italian convoy, sinking all seven merchant vessels and two escort destroyers (with assistance from a British submarine), despite an Italian covering force of two 8-inch gun cruisers and ten destroyers.

It was a portent of good hunting. Throughout the month as the British—with the Germans preoccupied deep in Russia—sent more surface ships to base on Malta, the island-based wasps stung again and again from the air, from beneath the sea, and on the surface. Merchant ships, tankers (one with 9,000 tons of fuel), destroyers died under the British onslaught; two Italian cruisers were torpedoed and damaged. Only in December, by using fast warships as transports and cargo ships, did the Italians succeed in ramming through to Africa some 82 percent of the cargo embarked in European ports.

On December 13, in the small hours of the morning off Cape Bon,

Tunisia, British destroyers *Sikh, Legion,* and *Maori* and Dutch destroyer *Isaac Sweers,* running the passage from west to east to join the Mediterranean Fleet, intercepted two Italian cruisers—*Barbiano* and *Giussano*—deep-loaded with gasoline in cans, Vice Admiral Antonino Toscano commanding.

Commander G. H. Stokes in *Sikh* conned his little force to hug the dark shape of the land, approached—with the aid of radar—undetected, and attacked at 1,000 yards with torpedoes and gunfire. In a two-minute action, both Italian cruisers were hit and immediately flared into huge funeral pyres. The sea was ablaze, the inferno dotted with a few survivors. Toscano wrote his name in a footnote to history as he, his entire staff, and 900 men died in water on fire.

But triumph was never final. At year's end, the bill for the Royal Navy was high indeed. The new menace of German submarines had soon been felt. On November 13, U-81, supported by U-205, put a torpedo into aircraft carrier *Ark Royal,* en route Gibraltar from an aircraft-ferrying trip to Malta. In half an hour "The Ark" was listing 18 degrees; in the deep dark of the early morning of the 14th a boiler room fire flared, and she sank at 6:00 A.M. just 25 miles from home with only one man lost. Misfortunes traditionally come in threes; two British merchant ships, trying to run the gantlet unescorted, were sunk off the Tunisian coast by Italian torpedo bombers on November 14 and 15; and on November 25 in the Eastern Mediterranean, U-331, penetrating undetected the destroyer screen of the Mediterranean Fleet, put three torpedoes into the venerable battleship *Barham*. *Barham* was on her beam's end in a few minutes, blew up, and was gone—taking with her her skipper and 806 men. Vice Admiral Pridham-Wippell was among 450 saved.

At midnight, December 14, cruiser *Galatea* was sunk just off Alexandria by U-557.

From December 16 to 18, there occurred what the British call the Battle of Sirte, a long-range, sporadic encounter between British cruisers and destroyers (under Sir Philip Vian, who had now been promoted to rear admiral) and an overwhelmingly superior Italian force of four battleships, five cruisers, and twenty-one destroyers (under Admiral Iachino, Italian Commander-in-Chief). The strength of the Italian force was symbolic of the desperate need for supplies in North Africa; it was covering a convoy of only four merchant ships. Vian, in turn, was escorting one ship to Malta. The paths of the two convoys crossed and the tangential battle—a kind of blindman's buff—drew sparks of long-range gunfire and intermittent air attacks with no real damage to either side. Both convoys got through and the Italian battleships withdrew unscathed, but in terrible aftermath Force K from Malta—the surface attack group which had done such summary execution—met its doom. Cruisers *Neptune* (Captain R. C. O'Connor in command of the squadron), *Penelope* and *Aurora* and four destroyers ran into an uncharted enemy minefield off Tripoli in the dark of December 19, and floundering about, like wounded great fish, the ships compounded their damages. *Neptune* died with all aboard save one man, who was picked from the sea five days later by the Italians; the two other cruisers limped back to Malta, water-logged and damaged; destroyer *Kandahar* was sunk.

There was worse to come. On the night of December 18/19, the Italians, with that peculiar combination of individual daring and ingenious technology which so distinguished their Navy's war effort, achieved a unique victory which they had tried—bravely but without marked success—to accomplish by similar means in Malta and Gibraltar earlier in the year. Six Italians, in rubber suits and astride "human" torpedoes, penetrated the heavily guarded harbor of Alexandria and put out of commission the only two battleships left to Admiral Cunningham.

The devices had been launched in the dark at sea, 5 miles from their targets, from submarine *Scire*. The daring raiders, their heads barely above water, manipulated three of the awkward, self-propelled two-man "pigs" into the harbor, penetrating an open boom gate, despite the shock of depth-charge explosions, and passing over ship torpedo baffles.

Two of the six Italians were fished from the water by battleship *Valiant* (the other four were subsequently captured on land), interrogated, threatened for a couple of hours, and imprisoned deep in the battleship's armored hulk near the keel. Not until 5:50 A.M. on December 19, ten to fifteen minutes before detonation, did the Italians warn *Valiant*'s skipper of the impending explosion.

The explosives—some placed on the bottom of the harbor, others attached, like limpets, to keels or plates—put out of action the remaining heavy ships of the Mediterranean Fleet. Tanker *Sagona* and destroyer *Jervis* alongside were seriously damaged; battleships *Valiant* and *Queen Elizabeth* were flooded and out of action for many months.

It was, for the British, a grim ending to a grim year. In addition, ten British submarines (plus one Greek and one Free French) had been sunk during the year by the Italians. Cunningham's strength was now less than it had been at low ebb after the fall of Crete.

But except for the Italian frogmen and intermittent surface luck at sea, Rome had accomplished little during the year. Ten Italian submarines had been lost in the Mediterranean in 1941, their only major prize a British cruiser, the *Bonaventure*, sunk on March 31.

For the Germans it was another matter. By the end of the year they had lost six boats, yet in two months of operation U-boats had sunk a battleship, an aircraft carrier, and a cruiser, and there were now twenty-one German submarines operating in "the most dangerous sea."

16

Blitzkrieg in the Balkans

Yugoslavia

In the Balkans, the fury of German *Blitzkrieg* was now, once again, to roll across new lands.

Hitler's power politics in Yugoslavia had only short-term success. The Serbs, a warlike mountain people, do not easily bend the knee; in comparison to cultured Croatia—which had once been a closely knit part of the Austro-Hungarian Empire—the Serbian part of Yugoslavia was primitive, independent, anti-German.

The violent anti-Axis sentiment was openly displayed; in the cafés of Belgrade the British song "Tipperary" elicited emotional acclaim; Mussolini's newsreel pictures provoked mocking jeers, laughter, and insults.[70]

Yugoslavia's adherence to the Tripartite Pact lasted just one day. Signed in Vienna on March 25, it was nullified in Belgrade by a *coup d'état* on the night of March 26/27. The collaborating government was thrown out; General Richard D. Simović, former commander of the tiny Yugoslav Air Force, headed a new one. Prince Regent Paul and his family fled to refuge in Greece, and a seventeen-year-old King—Peter II—ascended for a brief time a shaky throne. Anti-German demonstrations swept Belgrade and other Serbian (but not Croatian) cities. The Serbs stood tall; always they had believed it was better to fight and lose than never to have fought at all. On March 27, Belgrade was a bedlam of primitive emotion; a "surf-like roar" rose from the "shouting, chanting, singing . . . yelling, cheering, screaming mass of men, women, and students and schoolboys":

"Petra Drugy! (Peter Our Friend) *Petra Drugy! Petra Drugy!"*
... Huge Greek and American flags were held high overhead. There was a crash and the sound of splintering glass in the Spomenik off the Terazia as the crowds smashed the windows of the German Travel Bureau. ...

Up the street 30,000 voices rose in the war song of the beloved Chetniks:[71]

> Ready, now ready, Chetnik brothers!
> Mighty the coming battle,
> And on our glorious victory
> Will rise the sun of Liberty.[72]

But liberty was to be long delayed and tears of joy succeeded by tears of pain.

The Germans reacted with stunning swiftness. Hitler, angered by the failure of his carrot-and-stick diplomacy, piqued by Mussolini who had started all this unnecessary trouble in the Balkans, worried by the British air bases and troop movements to Greece, determined that nothing should delay his projected invasion of Russia, told his military leaders on March 27—even as Belgrade was celebrating—that he was determined to "destroy Yugoslavia as a military power and sovereign state."[73]

Directive No. 25 for a Yugoslav campaign was issued that evening, and with amazing efficiency and flexibility, the Army High Command within twenty-four hours had modified the plans for the Greek campaign, as well as the troop and logistic build-up for the approaching Russian invasion, to include Yugoslavia. Probably neither before nor since has so major a plan, involving so many terrain studies, strategic and political decisions, troop shifts and logistic arrangements, been produced in so short a time.

By Hitler's express orders, the destruction of Belgrade (by bombing) and the neutralization of all bases of the Yugoslav Air Force were to coincide with the initial invasion of Greece. The operational plan required the reallocation of troops of the Twelfth Army (under Field Marshal Sigmund Wilhelm List), already in Bulgaria and Rumania, and the rapid build-up of the Second Army (under General Maximilian von Weichs) in Austria and Hungary. Three divisions of the Second Army were moved from Germany, four from France, one from Czechoslovakia, and one from the Russian frontier by railroad and road. Although the size and rapidity of the concentration was probably unmatched until that time in the history of warfare, some of the units arrived only on D-Day or a few hours before, others well after the fighting had started, and some divisions went into action piecemeal—supply and support elements, delayed by icy roads and bad weather, straggling into the combat zone days after jump-off.

Despite the mountainous terrain, bad roads, numerous bridges to be crossed with rivers in spring spate—which many thought made the large-scale use of tanks impossible—General Ewald von Kleist's 1st Panzer Group (initially under Twelfth Army) and a Panzer corps in Rumania, as well as the armored divisions in the Twelfth and Second Armies, were earmarked for key roles in what Hitler and the Wehrmacht envisaged as lightning victories.

The German plans called for concentric and converging attacks from Austria, Hungary, Rumania and Bulgaria on Yugoslavia and Greece by some twenty-seven German divisions (seven of them armored). There was to be some ancillary help from the Italian Second Army (Ambrosio), with three corps pushing northeastward through the Ljubljana Gap and from Fiume, and from the Hungarian Third Army driving southward. In the event, a sizable number of these units, at least five or six of the German divisions, were not needed and never got into combat; some of them were just detraining as the campaign ended.

These Axis ground forces were supported by more than 1,000 German combat aircraft—bombers, dive bombers, fighters, and reconnaissance craft—some of them hastily concentrated at Austrian, Rumanian, and Bulgarian fields from as far away as France, Africa, and Sicily. The Fourth Air Force (under Colonel General Alexander Löhr) was the parent organization; but the subordinate operational unit was Fliegerkorps VIII, commanded by Lieutenant General Wolfram von Richthofen, who had established a reputation in the French campaign for effective support of rapidly moving armored forces.

The Yugoslav, Greek, and British forces opposed to this formidable concentration of military power were impressive on paper and in numbers but in nothing else. Both the Yugoslavs and the Greeks lived in countries slashed by mountains and swift-running rivers, with precipitous ridge lines and natural fortresses of stone and forest. Yet the vital parts of both countries were vulnerable to assault through the air and along natural invasion corridors, and the Greeks —winded by their long struggle with the Italians in Albania—had little left to face a far more formidable foe.

The Yugoslav Army on paper numbered at full mobilized strength more than a million men; seventeen regular and twelve reserve infantry divisions, three (horsed) cavalry divisions, a fortress division, and many smaller units. But it was never fully mobilized; indeed, it was smashed while uniforms were still being issued. Its equipment—much of it from the now German-operated Skoda armaments works in Czechoslovakia—was old, spare parts were lacking, and the Yugoslavs had no training in, or any real conception of, armored warfare or the means of countering it. The Yugoslav Air Force, some 700 obsolete planes of many types, was an expensive luxury rather than a combat force; like all second-best air forces it never had a chance.

The Greeks, in April 1941, had about shot their bolt against the numerically superior Italian field forces that had now been mobilized in Albania. Worry about their Bulgarian frontier and a possible invasion down the valleys of the Vardar and the Struma toward Salonika was counterproductive; unless the British could help, the Greeks simply had insufficient forces to face the Italians and the Germans at the same time. The bulk of the Greek Army—some fourteen divisions, the First Army—was concentrated in Albania; indefensible Thrace was held only by light border battalions, and the Greek Second Army along the Bulgarian frontier commanded three infantry divisions and one in reserve (some 70,000 men) manning the so-called Metaxas Line, astride the Strymon (Struma) River approach toward Salonika. In central Macedonia only three understrength divisions, organized in an improvised corps, were deployed near the Yugoslav frontier. These were placed under command of General "Jumbo" Wilson, the British commander of the Expeditionary Force to Greece. In all, Athens fielded the equivalent of only seven weak divisions to oppose the German war machine that had already brushed aside the greatest armies of Europe. The Greek Air Force, worn by months of combat against large numerical odds, was practically nonoperational at this time.

By early April 1941, the British had transported from Egypt to Greece about 58,000 soldiers (with more coming): the 6th Australian and 2nd New Zealand divisions, with corps troops and a brigade of the 2nd Armored Division. An additional Australian division and a Polish brigade were earmarked but never got there.

It was the best England could do. They had stripped the North African desert forces clean and had perforce abandoned their dreams (in retrospect vain in any case) of Tripolitanian conquest. British

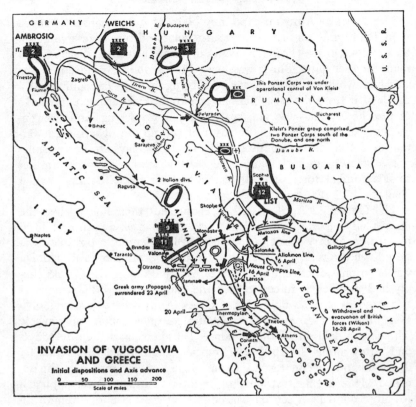

serviceable aircraft in Greece numbered only about eighty—a forlorn hope—but the British Navy, despite harassment and losses, moved almost at will about the Aegean and around Crete.

The result was foreordained.

Yugoslavia was defeated on the first day of war. About 7:00 A.M. on Palm Sunday, April 6, radio listeners in Belgrade homes heard a raucous voice proclaiming in German: *"Die Bomben fallen und jetzt in diesem Augenblick steht schon ganz Belgrad in Flammen."* (The bombs fall and now at this very instant all Belgrade is in flames.)[74]

The voice was Ribbentrop's, and the announcement, though slightly premature, would soon be accurate. Waves of German Stukas and Heinkels, flying in relays from Austrian and Rumanian fields, struck at the King's palace and government buildings in the heart of Belgrade. Accompanying German fighters shot down twenty

Yugoslav planes, losing only two themselves, and forty-four more aircraft were smashed on the ground. Flak defenses were riddled in the first assault; the pitiless vultures came down to roof level, and calmly, methodically, tore at the vitals of Belgrade. Streets were littered with inch-thick shattered glass, lamp posts tilted crazily, bodies were everywhere, the Drpski Kralj Hotel a heap of rubble, half the town in flames—"a corner of hell."[75]

> The scream of Stukas . . . like no sound ever heard in all the universe. . . . Bomb after bomb exploded . . . the effect almost inconceivable. . . . It was the perfectly appalling wind that was most terrifying. It drove like something solid through the house: every door that was latched simply burst off its hinges, every pane of glass flew into splinters, the curtains stood straight out into the room and fell back in ribbons. Everything that stood loose hit the opposite wall and was smashed. The ceilings fell with hardly a noticeable sound in the earth-shaking uproar.
>
> Then, with a weird, smooth sound like the tearing of heavy silk the neighboring houses began to collapse.[76]

About 17,000 people died in the flaming wreckage of Belgrade that Sunday, and the nerve center of all Yugoslav military operations was paralyzed. From then on, no real unified command and control was possible; the separate Yugoslav armies twitched spasmodically, but individually, with no coordination.

Two other great Yugoslav weaknesses contributed to the swift German conquest. The major fissure in the body politic between Serbs and Croats, still a blighting schism today to any kind of national unity, dated back to the days of Rome and Byzantium; the two peoples were long-time enemies. War revealed quickly the artificial nature of the Yugoslav state. Many Croats did not answer the call to the colors; others fought in a kind of minuscule civil war against Serbian soldiers, and even the Slovenes soon were talking of a new nation. Within a few days Croat leaders, supported probably by a great majority of their people, gladly formed a puppet government, and soon the Axis recognized a new "country," Croatia.

Belgrade's obsolete strategy contributed to the disaster. The Yugoslavs tried to defend everything and as a result lost everything. A cordon, linear defense of the entire 1,900-mile Yugoslav frontier had been planned in an age when the only possible answer to *Blitzkrieg* was defense in depth and concentrated mobile forces. Mobilization was never completed; the Yugoslavs were strong nowhere, and very soon straggling units were fighting hopeless little battles, with ox-drawn artillery and riflemen facing tanks and Stukas.

A three-pronged Axis drive on Belgrade from Bulgaria, Hungary, and Austria made rapid progress, after the initial jump-off of the 1st Panzer Group of the Twelfth Army (driving northwest up the Valley of the Morava against the Yugoslav Fifth Army) on April 8. By April 12, despite some sporadic stiff skirmishes, the German tanks had mauled the Yugoslav Sixth Army defending the capital, as well as the Fifth, and were within 40 miles of Belgrade. Simultaneously advanced elements of a motorized and armored thrust from Hungary had reached Pančevo, 10 miles from Belgrade, and was approaching the capital 45 miles away from the northeast. In the north, the Second Army, rumbling south and southwest toward Zagreb and Belgrade, met pockets of isolated resistance from elements of the Yugoslav Seventh Army (largely bypassed and tied down by the Italians along the Italian frontier), the Fourth Army between the Drava and Sava rivers, and the Second Army near the Danube. The German progress was aided by Croat mutinies, particularly in the Fourth Army; as early as April 10, "the disintegration of the . . . Yugoslav forces had reached an advanced stage."[77] Zagreb, center of Croatian culture, was captured on April 10, and the Nazi tanks were greeted by a "wildly-cheering, pro-German populace."

The three converging thrusts against Belgrade reached their objective about the same time. At 1700 on April 12, the Swastika was hoisted over the German Legation in the rubbled, ruined city by SS Obersturmfuehrer Klingenberg of the 2nd SS Motorized Infantry Division, who had ferried a patrol across the Danube in rubber rafts.

Some 30,000 Yugoslavs of the Seventh Army surrendered passively to the Italians, while the Hungarians brushed aside slight resistance from the Yugoslav First Army.

On April 15, Second Army elements captured Sarajevo (where World War I was conceived), center of what the Serbians had hoped would be a mountain redoubt fortress, and Serbs and Croats were at each other's throats in most of Dalmatia. The Yugoslav Fifth and Third Armies in the south near the Greek and Bulgarian frontiers, and the Coastal Defense Command along the Adriatic were hopelessly outflanked and split up.

An unconditional surrender was arranged on April 17, signed by Weichs of Second Army, and went into effect the next day.

In addition to the 20,000 or more civilians killed in Belgrade and elsewhere, the Yugoslavs lost their Army and their country. The Germans counted 254,000 prisoners, exclusive of thousands of Croats and other non-Serbian ethnic groupings serving in the Yugoslav Army. The 12-day *Blitzkrieg*—though hastily improvised at the last

THE UNDECLARED WAR

Atlantic convoy. U.S. aircraft carrier *Ranger (center foreground)*, November 1941.

Man against man. A torpedoed British tanker flames and dies.

Man against the sea. Convoy duty, fall 1941.

"Tora! Tora! Tora!" Japanese planes over Pearl Harbor, December 7, 1941. Ford Island and "Battleship Row" beyond it. A bomb geyser near USS *Oklahoma*.

End of an era. USS *Arizona*, awnings spread, flag still flying, explodes, burns, and sinks. Her mangled wreckage, with most of her entombed crew, still lies awash in the loch.

Requiem of flame and smoke. Destroyer *Shaw*, in floating dock, explodes.

Aftermath. The tangled wreckage of destroyers *Cassin* and *Downes* in flooded drydock, Pearl Harbor, after bomb hits, explosions, and fires. Battleship *Pennsylvania (in background)*, flagship of Pacific Fleet, sustained minor damage.

The Pearl Harbor of the Orient, December 10, 1941. Fire and holocaust, Cavite Navy Yard, Philippine Islands. Burning torpedoes in the barge *(right center)*; small arms ammunition exploding in the blaze *(left)*.

Aftermath. The Cavite Navy Yard, December 17, 1941. Wreckage of submarine *Sealion* alongside dock *(center)*.

INVASION OF THE PHILIPPINES

The conqueror lands. General Masaharu Homma, commanding, lands at Lingayen Gulf (Santiago) on December 24, 1941.

The conquerors move toward Bataan.

Twilight of the battleship. Death of the *Prince of Wales* off Malaya, December 10, 1941

minute—cost the Germans just 151 soldiers killed, 392 wounded, 15 missing.

The Western press and Allied leaders, with what had become a congenital overoptimism, had greatly overassessed the combat effectiveness and the unity of a country which was in fact divided by smoldering passions and wed to an ox-cart military syndrome.

Yet, as night descended on still another European nation, final peace was still incomplete. The new head of Croatia, Dr. Ante Pavelić, "Mussolini's hireling," proclaimed the German-supported independent state, "forever free" of Serbian domination. His Ustachi murder gangs started a campaign of liquidation and terror against Serbians in Croatia and Bosnia. In 1941 and 1942, scores of thousands died; another 600,000 Serbs and Jews were imprisoned or driven out.

Yet the Serbs' fighting spirit did not die. Gradually, as the tide of war receded from the Balkans to wash up on the Russian steppes thousands of miles away, little groups of armed men made their way to the mountain fastnesses and deep forest of Serbia. The first to pick up the fallen flag were the Chetniks—fierce, mustachioed guerrilla fighters who had won fame in other battles. They had long prepared for this day and they were men who would die before they surrendered. They were led by a proud nationalist patriot, General Draža Mihajlović. Later, other groups of different-thinking men, swayed by economic-ideological sympathies as well as love of country, followed them to hidden rendezvous: the Partisans led by one who was to be known to the world as Tito. Both groups were to be heard from again.

Greece

With Yugoslavia conquered, and only two British divisions in Greece, the position of Athens was hopeless.

A series of concrete pillboxes and fortified field positions exploited the steep Rhodope Mountains and deep defiles to guard the Greek-Bulgarian frontier. The Metaxas Line stretched 125 miles along this frontier to the Yugoslav frontier. But it was almost immediately outflanked by the Twelfth Army's push from Bulgaria into southern Yugoslavia. While the 1st Panzer Group drove toward Belgrade, XL Panzer Corps, jumping off on April 6, pushed in two prongs through the mountains of southern Yugoslavia against light opposition from the Fifth Yugoslav Army, to capture Skoplje and Veles, 60 miles from the Bulgarian frontier, on April 7. The quick conquest severed direct rail and highway communications from Yugoslavia into

Greece. Simultaneously, other German units drove west to capture Yugoslavian Strumica on the opening day of the offensive, April 6, and then turned south to follow the Vardar River Valley invasion route toward Salonika. Secondary thrusts through the Rupel gorge and the Metaxas Line encountered tough resistance; they also were aimed at Salonika as the first objective.

It was easy. By April 9, as Salonika fell and the Greek Second Army surrendered unconditionally, German tanks had reached Monastir in extreme southern Yugoslavia. By the 10th they were in Greek Florina in Macedonia and had outflanked a defensive line which the British had tried to establish along the Vermion Mountain range.

The land where Byron dreamed had always had an emotional appeal to English hearts, and the British still believed there was morality even in war. The Greeks had asked for aid; under the Anglo-Greek treaty the British were bound to give it or to renege upon their word. Wavell, who was loth to forgo a Tripolitanian venture and who understood the risks of a Greek expedition, nevertheless supported what was essentially a political decision. In February during the visit of the Anthony Eden mission to the Middle East, Wavell's staff had produced "a paper drawing attention to the great dangers of [the Greek] campaign in view of the German resources and methods." Wavell read it, and across the top of the paper added a quotation from the British general Wolfe (who had taken Quebec from the French in an earlier war): "War is an option of difficulties."[78]

But there were few options for the British Expeditionary Force to Greece in April 1941, only difficulties.

General Wilson, commander of "W Force," as the British, in the guise of secrecy, dubbed their expeditionary troops, arrived supposedly incognito in Athens in early March. From then until the early days of April thousands of tons of rations, ammo, petrol, medical, ordnance and engineer stores, and thousands of troops had been transported to Greece—all duly watched and reported by observers of the German Embassy who were still free to come and go, since, on the surface, "correct" relations were still maintained between Athens and Berlin.

The Britishers, as they landed, moved north from Piraeus and the port of Volos, through the important communications junction of Larissa, to take up positions already reconnoitered along the so-called

Olympus (or Aliakmon) River line, stretching some 70 miles from the forward slopes and coastal plain north of Mount Olympus northwestward along the crest of the Pieria and Vermion Mountains to the Yugoslav frontier.

It had all been done in a great hurry, and when the Germans struck, British units were incomplete and only partially positioned. Typical snafus beset the Expeditionary Force. Some of the troops, fresh from the heat of the desert, reached the cold snow-covered mountains of Greece with shorts, tropical shirts, and pith helmets, which the British called "Bowlers." They were, in the words of Brigadier George Clifton, "an unmitigated bloody nuisance"; many of the helmets were thrown away into the snowdrifts as the British retreated.

On the first night of the invasion—April 6/7—the greatly superior weight of German airpower started to tilt the already heavily unbalanced scales of conflict. Bombs and mines dropped on the port of Piraeus; SS *Clan Fraser*, carrying ammunition, was hit, flamed, and blew up, wreaking havoc. Other ships died with her in the gargantuan blast; lighters became matchwood and most of Greece's largest port was unusable.

From the first, retreat was inevitable. The Yugoslav collapse and the quick German capture of Monastir outflanked the Vermion Mountains barrier.

The Monastir Gap—a traditional invasion route of Greece—had been viewed by the Germans as a key to the swift conquest of Greece. A drive southward through the natural defile in the mountain ramparts and on across the Aliakmon River would put German tanks on the Plain of Thessaly, on the flank of and behind British-Greek positions in the mountains, and between the British and the Greek First Army in Albania; then it would all be over.

General Wilson had worried about this possibility, but there was not much he could do about it; he did not have enough troops. A scratch task force built around a tank regiment (the tracks of its tanks were so worn it had only limited mobility) was positioned on the left flank, but it was weak and the lines of supply were long, tortuous, and subject to air attack and extensive pilferage (the Greeks, after a long winter of war, were hungry).

As early as April 8, Wilson started to refuse his left flank—the first move in what was to become a constant series of withdrawals—and on April 10, General Papagos, the Greek commander of all Allied forces, ordered abandonment of the Vermion Mountain positions and a swing back to a new defensive line stretching from Mount Olympus to Servia on the Aliakmon River and thence northwestward to Lake Prespa on the Yugoslav-Albanian frontier. By April 12—too late—General Papagos, with heavy heart and doubtful whether the mercurial morale of the proud Greeks would stand the strain, ordered the fourteen Greek divisions in Albania to disengage, withdraw from the Italian armies facing them, and extend the Olympus-Servia Line across the Pindus Mountains to the Adriatic Sea to Santa Quaranta. There were mutterings. Some commanders vowed to ignore the order and to hold their hard-won gains.

Papagos hoped to plug the Monastir Gap and to keep the rampaging German tanks from the Plain of Thessaly and the heart of Greece.

But already the weary Greeks showed signs of collapse. German probes from Monastir and Florina were threatening the weak center, and two Greek divisions ordered to withdraw to mountain positions between Servia and Kastoria straggled and shambled in the disintegration of defeat. Withdrawal in the face of an active enemy—especially an enemy with air superiority—is one of the most difficult of military operations, and in Greece the rough mountain roads with many defiles were clogged with the discrepant vehicles and weapons of two vastly different armies: the foot soldiers and bullock carts of the Greeks, the Bren gun carriers and lorries of the Anzacs (Australian–New Zealand Army Corps).

For the defeated—the few men of the British Empire, and the ragged soldiers of Greece—the campaign of April 1941 was a nightmare of long, hard marches, bitter cold, little sleep, road jams, and occasional sharp fire fights.

Temperature . . . dropped to ten degrees below freezing. . . . Since the Germans began to invade Greece our men have been fighting in the snow, sleeping huddled together, wrapped in one or two blankets. . . .

Libya was like a billiard table compared with the terrifying ranges and yawning ravines. . . . The wind was cruel . . . blowing off the new snowfields formed on the mountain tops. . . . Truck drivers clung to their steering wheels with numb fingers. Their faces were blue with cold. . . .[79]

Despite misgivings, the Greek withdrawal from Albania began, as ordered, on April 13. The Italians offered no obstacles; in fact (feckless in the end as in the beginning), they were not even aware the Greeks had withdrawn until a day later.

But, as had been feared, the beginning of the withdrawal from these gloriously won positions was fatal to the staying power of the Greek armies. They had shown that they could resist and overcome an enemy offensive and maintain with spirit and enterprise an offensive of their own. They could cope with bitter weather and some of the most uninviting terrain of Europe. But to retreat from an enemy they had beaten, along a single road packed with transport vehicles of every kind and swarms of refugees, constantly dive-bombed and machine-gunned from the air, and to maintain their cohesion and fighting spirit through it all was not to be expected.[80]

By April 13, German advanced armored elements of the 9th Panzers had reached Ptolemaïs over roads and mountain tracks from Monastir and Veve—behind the Vermion Mountain positions—and a prong of the German offensive had swung westward toward Kastoria to cut off the retreat of the Greek armies from Albania. At Ptolemaïs a blown bridge, a cleverly sited antitank ditch, and difficult terrain facilitated a British rearguard delaying action and the Germans, in a day-long fight, were roughly handled. But the British hill positions were eventually outflanked by a German approach through a swamp, which mired down a number of Nazi tanks, and that night—at the cost of four tanks—the Germans opened the road to Kozánē. The British got away in the darkness but abandoned thirty-two tanks and antitank guns and some trucks in their hurried departure. The Battle of Ptolemaïs, fought—ironically—in what had been regarded as poor tank country, was the "first and last tank battle" in the Greek campaign.[81]

Quickly now the time of the British in Greece ran out.

By evening of April 14, the 9th Panzer had established a bridgehead across the Aliakmon, where for three days more the Panzers were stalled by the toughly defended British positions.

On April 15, General Wilson made the first moves in a withdrawal, approved by General Papagos on April 16, to a line hinged on the famous pass of Thermopylae, where a handful had died in glory 2,000 years before, across the narrowest neck of the Greek peninsula. But Papagos—a realist—knew his armies were done; he suggested that, to save Greece from devastation, the British armies should consider total withdrawal. From Athens to Egypt, to London and back again, the requests for instructions and answering directives flew back and forth.

The German Panzers moved almost as fast. By April 15, Kastoria Pass—a Greek retreat route from Albania—had been blocked; by April 20, the 1st SS Regiment had captured Janina in Epirus near the Adriatic after forcing the key Metsovon Pass through the Pindus Mountains in heavy fighting. The bulk of the Greek Army was trapped with the enemy in its rear.

W Force, harried and weary, made good its retreat—most of it, at least. By the evening of April 19, after running the gantlet of continuous German air attacks in the daylight across the Thessalian plain, most of the force (the dead and captured left behind and the flotsam of retreat lining its withdrawal route) was back at the Thermopylae position. On April 18, Alexander Koryzis, President of the Greek Council, committed suicide—a symbol of the stark defeat now at hand. The German tanks had driven a wedge between the Greek armies and the British, and German bombers and fighters had almost wiped out the small RAF contingents, still trying to fight against "almost fantastic odds." An entire squadron of six Blenheim bombers had been lost, together with the squadron commander and another senior officer, in futile attempts to slow the German penetration through the Monastir Gap. Ten Blenheims had been destroyed on the ground on April 15 near Larissa. Now on April 20, with the few remaining aircraft pulled back to Athens or Peloponnesian fields, and the handful of British bombers limited to night operations only, a heavy German strike eliminated most of the remaining British fighters. Of fifteen Hurricanes that rose to intercept, five were shot down, most of the others damaged, and from then on the planes with Nazi markings roamed the skies at will. In two days—April 21 and 22—some twenty-three Greek ships were sunk in coastal waters.

Wavell flew to Athens; for two days the King and Wavell, British and Greek leaders, thought about the unthinkable.

But the rampaging tanks and the roaring freshet of German might now pouring into Greece at every pass took the decision out of their hands. By April 21 a Greek corps retreating from Albania had surrendered to the German Twelfth Army; the Greek government, dignified in disaster, thanked the British for their help and urged immediate evacuation.

"Operation Demon"

Once again, as at Dunkirk, it was a question of improvisation. For almost two months, the Mediterranean Fleet had been transporting troops and supplies to Greece. Now, while continuing its unending tasks of supporting the British sea flank in Africa, sustaining Malta, and preying on Italo-German supply lines, it faced the problem of evacuating in a few days—under skies dominated by enemy airpower

—an Expeditionary Force it had taken weeks to build up. The task was obviously impossible without loss. Heavy weapons, much equipment and supplies had to be left behind, burned, or destroyed. Embarkation would be chiefly at night and from beaches; men and small arms would have priority. The reasoning was sound. Trucks and tanks can be built in hours; not so soldiers.

Vice Admiral H. D. Pridham-Wippell was in command afloat, with cruisers *Orion*, *Ajax*, *Phoebe*, and *Perth*, three antiaircraft cruisers, "every available destroyer" (about twenty), three sloops, and a miscellany of several dozen troop ships, landing craft, caiques, and motor boats. Egypt and Crete were the destination; the small ships would shuttle back and forth to Crete, some of the larger to "Alex."

From April 24 to May 1, the "miracle of Dunkirk" was repeated in Greece in small fashion. From points as far north as Athens and the Piraeus to the extreme southern Peloponnesus, a total of 50,732 men, including wounded and a smattering of Greeks, Yugoslavs, Palestinians, and Cypriots (serving with the British), were evacuated to Crete or Egypt. The King of the Hellenes, the Prime Minister, and British diplomatic personnel were flown to Crete on April 23, and hundreds of RAF personnel followed them in a flying boat air shuttle. Yacht *Hellas* was bombed and sunk—with a large toll of wounded soldiers and civilians—at Piraeus; *Ulster Prince* grounded, and later died at Nauplia, and at least three other transports and two destroyers and smaller craft were sunk. The Germans bypassed a British covering force, retiring from the last vain Thermopylae stand, and dropped parachute troops on both sides of the Corinth Canal early on April 26, just missing General Wilson, the British commander, who was en route to Myloi by car, thence by plane to Crete. The paratroopers cut the British line of retreat into the Peloponnesus and left scattered parties of the Expeditionary Force all the way from Olympus to Corinth.

"Operation Demon" had been highly successful in its primary objective—the saving of soldiers—but it had cost the British dearly during an era of what Cunningham was later to describe as "unrelieved gloom." A total of some 62,564 British service personnel (including the Air Force) had been in Greece when the Germans struck. The King and the government of Greece had escaped, and at Kalamata, a British destroyer had even safely embarked the Yugoslav crown jewels a few days before the Germans took the port and rounded up some 7,000 British prisoners. But dead, missing, captured, or left behind were a total of considerably more than 15,000 Englishmen,

Australians, New Zealanders, Palestinians, and Cypriots; hundreds who were evacuated were wounded.[82] Behind them, scattered across the mountains of Greece, W Force left all heavy arms and equipment, 8,000 trucks, burned-out tanks, and the smashed wreckage of 209 aircraft.

In twenty-four days the German war machine had driven across some of the best defensive terrain in Europe, captured some 270,000 Greeks (most of whom were released to return to civilian life), and engulfed another country. Their total losses were about 1,100 killed, 4,000 wounded and missing, plus worn tank tracks and tires.

Jackal-like, Mussolini cashed in on his ally's kill. The Greek First Army, which had already surrendered to the Germans, was forced to repeat the surrender ritual shortly afterward—this time to the Italians, who had had little part in bringing it about. Mussolini saved some face, but many Italians now understood the pomposity and fakery of their "sawdust Caesar." Hitler, looking toward Russia, left the occupation and government of conquered Greece to Italy, but not before including Italian troops in a victory parade in Athens. The victorious German troops—their *Blitzkrieg* tactics apparently still invincible on land—trained replacements, regrouped, and resupplied. Meanwhile, some of them turned their eyes toward the island of the Minotaur.

The Battle of Crete

Crete, which commands the approaches to the Aegean Sea and the Dardanelles, is strategically placed, but until May 1941 the island had played only a minor role in either Allied or German calculations. The campaign was not really planned; it simply happened.[83]

British high-level interest in Crete dated back to the fall of 1940, when Churchill in two memoranda (November 3, 1940) noted that Suda Bay—the island's fine harbor—and Crete itself ought to become a "second Scapa" (Scapa Flow, the Orkney Islands base for the British Home Fleet), and a "permanent war fortress." But not much was done about it; Wavell had too many other active fronts. Small numbers of troops were sent to the islands; shipping facilities in the primitive ports which were completely inadequate were slightly expanded, airstrips improved, antiaircraft guns emplaced. But it was neither an air base—it had few planes and virtually no aircraft support facilities —nor a naval base; its undeveloped ports were open to bombing, unprotected by nets. Seven different British commanders had rotated to the island command between November 1940 and April 30, 1941.

Clear-cut purpose and vigorous drive had been lacking, and even as late as April 18, when mainland Greece was already gone, the British Chiefs of Staff in a message to Wavell had assigned Crete the lowest priority.

For the Germans, Crete was an afterthought. Indeed, the decision to attack the island was not finally made until April 25. The decision itself was in considerable part a product of Göring's ambition and of interservice rivalry; he wanted to demonstrate the prowess of the Luftwaffe and sold the idea to a somewhat hesitant Hitler. An air assault against Malta, the proper objective, had been under study, but various objections had been raised, and the quick conquest of mainland Greece had facilitated the substitution of Crete for Malta. Hitler understood the geographic importance of Crete in the Eastern Mediterranean: in control of shipping, dominating the Aegean Sea, influencing the "Arab freedom movement," protecting the Ploesti oil fields, and ensuring Turkish neutrality, as a potential stepping stone to Cyprus and Suez. But he did not then envisage an onslaught against "the English position between the Mediterranean and the Persian Gulf," which he felt was "still in the lap of the Gods." For Göring and some of the Luftwaffe leaders, Crete was a stepping stone; for Hitler it was to be the definitive end of the Balkan campaign. Henceforth the onion-shaped domes of Moscow beckoned.

The injection of Nazi politics and interservice rivalries (Göring was air-minded, and he had a personal political stake in enhancing his role as Luftwaffe commander) affected the campaign. The planning for "Operation *Merkur*" (Mercury), difficult enough because of the last-minute decision to launch it and the rapid approach of the Russian invasion deadline, was inadequate on both sides. The German Army and its General Staff had nothing to do with the planning; it was the Luftwaffe's "baby," and, as in the Battle of Britain, Luftwaffe planning—dominated by Göring and political generals at the top of the hierarchy—showed some very rough edges. The German reconnaissance and intelligence was woefully inadequate; it grossly underestimated the British, Greek, and Allied strength on Crete.

Yet the Germans demonstrated once again the amazing energy, initiative, and flexibility which had characterized their prior battles. German airborne troops had been dropped over the Corinth Canal on April 26; the same Ju-52 transports which had dropped them had to be flown back to Austria for upkeep and overhaul and readied quickly for the new operation.

And it was to be an operation unprecedented in the history of warfare. An entire island, 100 miles at the nearest point from the Greek mainland, was to be conquered for the first time by air attack and vertical assault—troops dropped out of the skies. German airpower would be pitted against British seapower. Airfields in great numbers were needed for the swarms of planes required; they were improved or built in Greece, the Greek Islands, and Bulgaria within a few days to a few weeks by German engineers and construction troops, aided by swarms of conscripted Greek laborers.

In Crete, there was no comparable indefatigability. It was a potential battlefield in which a very thin and brittle crust of discipline and organization hid an island in chaos. Crete had been a dumping ground for refugees—the most prominent among them, King George II of Greece—of exhausted, wounded, and disorganized Allied units, of 16,000 Italian prisoners. For its defense, there were many bodies but little cohesion. There were about 8,700 fresh troops, but only three complete fresh infantry battalions; the rest were polyglot and disorganized—British, Australian, New Zealand units evacuated from the mainland incomplete, no heavy equipment—and Greek regulars and irregulars; Palestinians and Cypriots, men with high *élan* and boisterous spirits, men depressed by defeat, and stragglers resentful of discipline who looted and drank. Equipment shortages were ominous and stark. Many of the evacuated troops had no rifles or small arms; the Greeks had an average of less than thirty rounds of rifle ammunition per man. There was only a handful of tanks; a total of thirty-six planes, many of which were "beaten up" from the mainland operations; some units with no transportation and no tools; no plates, "knives, forks or spoons."

Over this conglomerate force and forlorn hope, General Bernard C. Freyberg, V.C., was placed in command on April 30, with orders to hold the Cretan air base against an imminent German air-sea attack, but with a dark reminder that because of Britain's shortage of fighters, he could not anticipate air reinforcements. Freyberg was a formidable figure from World War I, with twenty-seven "separate scars and gashes on his body." He was a favorite of Churchill's, with a "pipeline" directly to him. A New Zealander, he had commanded the New Zealand Division in the Greek mainland fighting, and at the last he relieved General Wilson in the rearguard of the evacuation. Freyberg had great courage and energy, but he had a makeshift, inexperienced staff and little support, and he blew hot and cold —alternatively confident and ominous—constantly dunning Wavell for more of everything while assuring Churchill that the island could be held.

Freyberg had under his tenuous command a total of more than 42,000 regulars (10,000–11,000 Greek regulars, the rest British, Australian, and New Zealanders), plus an unknown number, probably several thousand, of Greek cadets, home guards, gendarmes, and the wild Cretan irregulars, armed with fowling pieces, pitchforks, and anything that could shoot, cut, or slice.

Against this defense, the Germans earmarked a total assault force of some 22,750 men. Colonel General Alexander Löhr, who commanded the Fourth Air Fleet (which had supported the Army in the Greek and Yugoslav campaigns), was in overall command.

Army units were to participate, but this was not to be an Army show. General Kurt Student, who had conceived and enthusiastically supported the airborne invasion, was the pivotal operational commander. His XI Air Corps (subordinate to Löhr) was, for the Cretan operation, a tailored task force of assault troops, transport aircraft, and some mountain units which had already participated in the Balkan campaign. Fliegerkorps XI numbered some 500 Ju-52 transports, and 70 gliders, which were to carry in shuttles a special assault regiment (three battalions) of paratroops and a battalion of gliderborne infantry; also the 13,000 men of the 7th Air Division (three parachute rifle regiments), two regiments of the 5th Mountain Division, and one of the 6th. A Panzer battalion, a motorcyclist battalion, antiaircraft units, and the rest of the 6th Mountain Division were available, and an ancillary sea assault—troops and equipment to be transported in more than sixty Greek caiques, seven small steamers, seven Italian destroyers, and a dozen miscellaneous small naval craft—was organized under "Admiral Southest," a German admiral in command of the Aegean Sea area. The plan contemplated the landing of 10,000 troops by parachutes, 750 by gliders, 5,000 by transport aircraft, and some 7,000 by sea, including in the seaborne element, pro forma, a few Italian Marines.

Fliegerkorps VIII (with Richthofen commanding under Löhr) included about 680 combat aircraft of which some 500 were operational on May 16 when the air attacks reached crescendo, 280 Ju-88's, He-111's and Do-17 bombers, 150 Stukas, 200 Me-109 and Me-110 fighters, and reconnaissance aircraft.

Crete was to be the first (and, for the Germans, the last) major airborne assault of World War II. A few airborne troops had been used in The Netherlands campaign and in the capture of Fort Eben Emael and the Meuse bridges in Belgium, and German paratroops had been dropped—largely unopposed—across the Corinth Canal in the closing days of the Greek campaign. But Crete was far more ambitious; it was, indeed, the first real test of the technique of vertical envelopment: the conquest of an island 100 miles from the mainland, defended by superior enemy seapower and by large enemy ground forces. It was a retrospective to what might have been in the Battle of Britain, a forecast of what might come, a new kind of battle in a new kind of war.

The Germans, like the Russians, had experimented with the tactics and techniques of airborne warfare on a small scale, but in Crete they committed virtually all their specially trained airborne forces. Essential to the success of the concept was local air superiority, and in Crete, the Germans were able to achieve this and to turn it into air domination. Air domination was then used to saturate and destroy antiaircraft defenses, paralyze communications, and force many of the ground defenders to keep their heads down in the crucial seconds while gliders and parachutes were depositing the assault troops on the ground. Quick seizure or construction of a runway where transport aircraft could land with the bulk of the troops was a key to victory.

The glider and parachute assault forces were trained and timed to reach the ground almost simultaneously. The gliders carried not only troops but heavier arms, limited transport, and communications equipment to complement the lightly armed parachutists. There were two types of German gliders then in use, both purposely built with *Sollbruchstellen* (breaking points) near the wing roots or in parts of the fuselages, so that pieces of the gliders would break off, without necessarily fatal consequences to the passengers, when they collided with trees or walls in crash landings. The DFS 230 glider carried ten men with light equipment; the Gotha 242 could carry a 75 mm. antitank gun and crew, or twenty to twenty-five soldiers or other equivalent-weight equipment. They were towed to the landing area by He-111's or Ju-87's; when the tow was cut, the pilot tried to put his heavily loaded ship down as fast as possible to escape defending fire. Though landing speed was high, the skids or runners were sometimes wrapped with barbed wire to brake the landing run, or a strong barbed hook (faintly reminiscent of the landing hook used by naval planes aboard carriers) dug into the ground. The gliders also used trailing ribbon chutes to slow them. Landings could sometimes be made within a 35-yard space.

One of the techniques used to reduce those vulnerable seconds between the castoff of the tow rope (usually at 13,000 feet) and the touchdown of the glider was a gliding dive. At a speed of 125 miles an hour and an angle of 70 to 80 degrees, the powerless bird and its cargo swooped earthward, now and again checking its downward plunge by steps (*Treppensturz*) to throw off the ground gunners. Sometimes the glider even went into a spin briefly. At about 800 feet the pilot had to pull out, level off, and land quickly and precisely. That there were failures—often with catastrophic results—needs no emphasis.

The German paratroopers were also trained to get to earth quickly to escape the fate of all "sitting ducks," dangling in swaying harness, limned against the blue sky, vulnerable to ground fire. They jumped, therefore, from the open doors of the Ju-52's, or through jump hatches in the He-111's, at the extraordinarily low height of 300–400 feet, using static lines attached to the transport planes to jerk open their chutes and risking the increased injury rate always incident to low jumps. The *Fallschirmjaeger* (parachute troops) employed in Crete were picked men of high morale and great esprit, but some of the units and officers were not highly trained in airborne operations and, in both weaponry and techniques, the concept was still in its infancy.[84]

The technique of dropping heavy weights by parachute had not then been developed; the chutist himself was lightly armed. Most of them carried with them Schmeiser submachine guns or automatic rifles, with a few Mausers with telescopic sights. Each man also carried emergency rations: *Wittler* (dried) bread, chocolate, thirst quenchers, a type of Benzedrine energy tablet; some had hypodermic syringes with ampoules for the injection of a caffeine-sodium salicylate to neutralize fatigue.

The parachutists in Crete were, in effect, lightly armed infantry, and their lack of heavy supporting weapons was their greatest disadvantage. The Ju-52's carried a few 150 mm. rocket projectiles, which were dropped four at a time in wooden carrying crates by parachute. They were frightening but inaccurate weapons with great dispersion.

The rapidity or "improvisation," as Field Marshal Kesselring was later to describe it, with which the Crete operation was mounted led to some major incongruities in the parachutists' rations and uniforms. In one battalion at least, in the scorching heat of Crete the Germans still wore the same heavyweight uniforms tested north of the Arctic Circle, and the rations were also "northern," with much fat content which melted in the heat.

The British defenders, looking seaward as well as skyward, established four "insular," more or less independent commands, covering the three usable airstrips on the island, Heraklion, Retimo, and

Maleme, as well as the fine harbor of Suda Bay and the smaller harbors and landing beaches along the north coast. Because of the uncertainty of communications, poor roads, and scarcity of motor vehicles (there were few trucks and only six tanks, two guarding each airfield), the four main defensive sectors were more or less isolated, the defenders spread thin along 70 miles of north coast. In any case, Freyberg, his headquarters in dugouts near Canea, had available as "Creforce" reserve only one understrength New Zealand brigade and a British battalion, and most of his troops would have to get from here to there on foot. Thus, mobility was to be the key to the Battle of Crete, mobility through the air versus mobility on the ground.

Although neither side knew it, the die was really cast before the battle began; the 30-to-1 German numerical superiority in operational aircraft was far too great to be overcome.

It was, for Crete, unending punishment from the skies. The air attacks opened slowly in early May, gradually intensifying as new airstrips were completed and more bombers were overhauled and fed into the battle. From about May 14 the Germans began to bomb relentlessly day after shining day for a week. By week's end there were thirteen damaged or sunken ships in Suda Harbor; smoke and flames from roaring oil fires were beacons to the attackers, and the beached cruiser *York* was targeted again and again as the Germans tried to destroy her antiaircraft batteries. On May 19—two days after two downed German airmen, pulled from the sea, had told Freyberg that *Der Tag* was May 20—some four Hurricanes and three Gladiators (the remnants of British airpower) were flown to Egypt, leaving Crete to its fate. The rest of the British aircraft were either charred rubble or had been cannibalized for spare parts to keep a few planes flying. Prior to its evacuation of the island, the RAF claimed twenty-three enemy planes shot down in the Battle for Crete—nowhere near enough.

Der Tag was clearly forecast by both sides. Lord Haw-Haw, the British traitor who broadcast propaganda to Britain over the German radio during the war, predicted it and gloated.

May 20 blossomed like all the preceding days—clear air and a bright morning, with that luminous sheen peculiar at certain seasons to the Levant—with the hum of hundreds of aircraft engines and the crump of bombs. The British and the Greeks, the Australians and the New Zealanders, Palestinians and Cypriots, Caucasians and black-skinned men and tough little Maoris, all huddled, crunched up in foxholes and trenches, waiting.

The heavy AA guns—positions pinpointed by the enemy in prior raids—and roads and trails were the first targets. Then like fabled Icarus trying to reach the sun, "large silvery machines" with "long and tapering wings" passed "silently as ghosts" over the heads of the defenders. The sibilance of their passing was counterpoint to the racket of the bombs; they were the gliders—small ten-man ships and big Gothas—carrying the élite troops of the Assault Regiment. And behind and above them as the gliders whispered in to land, Ju-52 troop carriers—"huge black beasts with yellow noses"—disgorged at 300–400 feet strings of thirteen to fifteen paratroopers. Soon the air blossomed with black and white, yellow and violet and pink parachutes, among them the bursts of Bofors shells, the flash and fire as a plane was hit.

A large airborne landing, as Crete was to show, is in its first few hours an almost uncontrollable and unmanageable melee. Vertical envelopment means no front or flank or rear. Attackers and defenders are mixed in sometimes irreconcilable confusion, and the execution of larger plans and the seizure of important objectives is dependent, in the main, upon the skill, initiative, and leadership of small unit commanders, on the training and equipment of the combatants, and the intangibility of luck.

In the lemon and orange and olive groves of Crete, along the coast and on its slopes, amid the cacti and the Aleppo pines, the first hours were a wild free-for-all. Telephone wires were soon severed. Freyberg reverted to the Napoleonic era. He understood something of what he could actually see; beyond his line of vision he knew nothing.

Some forty-five to fifty gliders landed near Maleme airstrip, the great square-fuselaged birds—many with holes punched in their fuselages, or their wings ripped off by olive trees—disgorging heavily armed men with motorbikes, flame throwers, and mortars. Some met disaster. One was hit and swooped torching to earth. A shell from a Bofors gun (a Swedish-designed light 40 mm. antiaircraft) disintegrated another as it skidded to a halt; machine-gun bullets stitched the sides of other gliders as they whispered in to ground, and they landed—coffins for their men. The glider-borne elements of the Assault Regiment captured an AA battery and a key bridge, with positions near the western edge of the airstrip; but 22nd New Zealand Battalion, positioned on Hill 107 (about 580 feet high, dominating Maleme), beat back, with heavy casualties to the attackers, repeated German attempts to overrun it. The paratroopers suffered heavy casualties as many of them were landed in drop zones far out of planned positions. Inexperienced jump masters caused some losses;

some strings of parachutists who jumped too soon landed in the sea near Maleme. The Bofors gunners did heavy execution as the Ju-52's came in to the dropping pattern below the angle of fire of the heavy antiaircraft guns, flying in tight, disciplined formation through the puffs of flak.

"You could actually see the shot breaking up the aircraft and the bodies falling out like potato sacks."[85]

. . . each man dangling carried a death, his own, if not another's.

Even as they dropped they were within range and the crackle of rifle fire and Bren guns rose to a crescendo. Wildly waving their legs, some already firing their Schmeisers, the parachutists came down, in the terraced vineyards, crashing through the peaceful olive boughs, in the yards of houses, on roofs, in the open fields where the short barley hid them. Many found graves where they found earth.[86]

But still they came implacably out of the sun.

May 20 was a sanguinary day for both sides. Major General Wilhelm Süssmann, commander of the 7th Air Division and of the Center Group Task Force—its objectives the capture of Canea, Galatas, and Retimo and its airstrip—was killed, with some of his staff, in full view of Athens as the wings of the glider in which he was a passenger tore off in flight. Brigadier General Eugen Meindl, in command of the Maleme operation, was seriously wounded soon after landing; both of these key operations reverted to subordinates' control.

The Germans had planned on putting their troops down where the enemy wasn't; all three airfields, it was hoped, would be captured the first day. Maleme and Canea were to be attacked in the morning; Retimo and Heraklion in the afternoon. The clincher would be supplied by a seaborne assault force to be landed, as originally planned, on May 21.

None of this happened.

The Assault Regiment held the western edge of Maleme Airfield firmly in its grip at dusk, despite British attempts to dislodge it; but the German eastern pincer had been beaten back, with heavy casualties, and the attackers were isolated and split up, holed up in houses or ravines, gone to ground with little unit integrity.

The Maleme eastern assault force had dropped far out of position near the town of Modhion; the commanding officer of a New Zealand field punishment center armed his prisoners, and aided by savage Cretan natives—"women, children and even dogs," armed with "flintlock rifles . . . axes and even spades," he harried and hunted the scattered paratroopers.

Around Suda Bay and Canea, the action of May 20 was virtual stand-off. The British still solidly controlled both areas, but the Germans, at the cost of one parachute battalion destroyed or scattered and two others with heavy casualties, seized the high ground near Galatas. Similarly at Retimo the issue at nightfall was undecided; some of the paratroopers had landed on planned drop zones; others were widely scattered. They had died in droves; the Australians buried 400 Germans the next day. But by dusk at Retimo, too, the attackers held key terrain: a dominating hill and the east edge of the airstrip. In the Heraklion assault, for which four paratroop battalions were earmarked, timing was poor. The German troop transports lagged far behind schedule, some as much as three hours, but by night the attackers held the high ground near the airstrip and had reached the edge of the harbor, while Black Watch, Yorks and Lancs, Greeks and Aussies stalked Nazi troops in the streets of the old town.

Freyberg's report to Wavell was correct; the British defenses, as far as he knew, still held at the three airfields and two harbors, "though by a bare margin." But King George II of the Hellenes, his cousin Prince Peter, the Prime Minister, and the government of Greece were again in peripatetic flight—climbing the long slopes toward the stark south coast mountains of Crete, after evacuating the royal residence only a half mile from a German paratroop landing.

To Löhr and Student in their headquarters in the Grande-Bretagne Hotel in Athens, "the situation had not seemed encouraging" on the night of May 20. Like Freyberg—and like nearly all commanders in modern war in the early stages of battle—the German generals' knowledge of the exact situation on Crete was sketchy.

Student knew he had had some success at Maleme—that he held part of the airstrip there—and he decided, with Löhr's approval, to reinforce his success by throwing in the rest of his parachutists. About three and a half companies were to take Maleme and to land reinforcements (a battalion of the 5th Mountain Division) there in transport aircraft. And the next day—the 21st—the 1st Motor Sailing Flotilla, which was harbored at the island of Melos on the night of the 20th, would bring in more mountain troops and heavy equipment by sea.

It was a key decision, though even before the Ju-52's came roaring in in the early light of the 21st, the Assault Regiment—infiltrating during the night against a weakening British defense—had taken most of Maleme airstrip and the high ground south of it. About 8:00 A.M., as more paratroopers landed, this time in a safe drop zone well out of range of British guns, a Ju-52 put down daringly on the beach near the dry riverbed of the Tavronitis. And then, at 8:10—a definite harbinger of ultimate British defeat—a German transport landed on the strip itself. The strip and some of the beach nearby were still commanded by British artillery fire, but the Germans ran the gantlet, put their planes down on an 1800-foot strip with strong crosswinds, and despite the flaming wreckage of crashed aircraft kept on coming. By 5:00 P.M. a regimental headquarters of the 5th Mountain Division was landing, and an air shuttle to Greece was throwing in reserves far faster than the British could shift their scattered troops on foot. And, during all the long hours, British movement was hazardous, as German aircraft—unchallenged—swooped and bombed and strafed.

At Retimo and Heraklion, the other airstrips, the Germans gave their troops just sufficient air support and resupply on May 21 to keep them fighting.

It was enough. The 21st was, ultimately, the day of decision; with German transport aircraft landing on Crete the end was in sight unless the British could recapture Maleme and the beaches near it.

As the air shuttle to Greece was gradually overpowering the defenders, Freyberg was worried and alarmed by a developing threat to his sea flank—possibly near Canea. British reconnaissance aircraft from North Africa and Cyprus had been prowling high above the Aegean and had sighted German convoys at sea. The major elements of the Italian Fleet—shocked and battered by the Battle of Cape Matapan—were sticking close to port, despite German urgings. But the Nazis believed their Stukas and bombers could hold the Royal Navy at bay, at least long enough to put troops ashore in Crete.

It seemed logical, but they reckoned without the man the fleet called "A.B.C." Admiral Cunningham knew the odds; he had only one aircraft carrier, *Formidable*, her complement worn down by attrition to only four planes, with no spares or replacements, and even she could not be ready until May 25. Yet he signaled: ". . . Navy must not let Army down. No enemy forces must reach Crete by sea."[87]

It was a large order.

Cruising west of Crete as a covering force in case the Italian fleet should overcome its caution were battleships *Warspite* and *Valiant* and six destroyers. Light forces—five cruisers and eight destroyers, organized in two groups—roamed the north coast of Crete in the darkness and retired southward through Kaso and the Antikithera Straits at dawn.

About noon on May 21 the worst ordeal of any fleet until the advent of the kamikazes more than three years later started. High-level German bombers, approaching through the sun's glare and the cottony puffs of antiaircraft fire, laid down exceptionally accurate bombing patterns against the speeding, twisting British ships. Destroyer *Juno* took it twice; the second bomb detonated her magazines. She sank, a flaming torch, in seconds; six officers and ninety-one men were miraculously pulled from the sea. Cruiser *Ajax* took a damaging near-miss, and then the vultures came in droves on and on throughout the long daylight hours—Ju-87's and 88's, dive bombers, torpedo bombers, low-level attack planes. . . .

"There is no spot more naked under heaven than the deck of a destroyer as a stick of bombs falls slanting towards it." Near-misses "lift the ship as if a giant had kicked her, wrenching the steering gear, damaging frames and plates. . . ."[88]

Darkness brought interlude, a rest between the rounds; the British light forces, exhausted, turned north again into the Aegean to patrol the north coast of Crete. Here, when an Axis convoy had almost made safe haven some 18 to 20 miles north of Canea, damaged cruiser *Ajax*, *Dido* and *Orion* and their consort destroyers intercepted an enemy cockleshell fleet, the 1st Motor Sailing Flotilla. The caiques, with 2,331 troops aboard, crammed with men and equipment, were navigated and conned by lieutenants with pocket compasses and megaphones and escorted only by a single armed Italian torpedo boat, the tiny *Lupo* (commander Francisco Mimbelli). The slow, heavily laden caiques were easy prey to guns and ramming as searchlights silhouetted them against the dark waters. Some 320 German soldiers were killed or drowned. The convoy scattered and turned back, but many were saved by the audacity and effectiveness of little *Lupo*, which wove erratically—laying a smoke screen, firing guns, torpedoes, and machine guns—through the British formation. She was hit eighteen times but survived to fight again.

At first light on May 22, cruisers *Naiad* and *Perth* and antiaircraft cruisers *Calcutta* and *Carlisle*, their consorts, had their chance; they intercepted thirty small vessels bound for Crete, shepherded by Italian *Sagitarrio*. Like *Lupo*, *Sagitarrio* did her duty. Most of the convoy escaped.

But the seaborne landings had failed.

* * *

The British Navy paid that day; its seamen died in scores, its ships were shambles—the price of turning back the invasion of an island already lost.

Force C, steaming hard to clear Kithera Channel at the western end of Crete before the day was too long gone, never made it. For hour after hour the ordeal from the air continued. Cruiser *Naiad* was racked and damaged by huge bombs close aboard; *Carlisle* was hit, her skipper killed; destroyer *Greyhound* broke up and sank in minutes; destroyer *Gloucester* died afire, slowly, her upper decks a shambles. Cruiser *Fiji*, attacked by twenty separate waves of aircraft in four hours, took one hit late in the day, rolled over, and sank in the dusk. And Cunningham's two battleships did not escape; *Warspite*'s secondary batteries were put out of action; *Valiant* took two bombs.

To the British, May 22 was also fiasco on land. Freyberg's do-or-die counterattack to retake Maleme airstrip sputtered and stalled until daylight exposed it in horrible clarity to the hungry German planes. The Maoris tried with their old "ancestral fighting urge," using hand grenades and cold steel. They got to the lip of the airstrip —stacked with planes—but could go no further, and there were no reserves to help them.

Throughout the day the German troop carriers landed at Maleme and on the beaches near it, ferrying two infantry battalions of the 5th Mountain Division, an engineer battalion, and an artillery battery to Crete; and at nightfall Major General Julius Ringel, commanding the 5th Mountain Division, landed near Maleme and assumed command of all ground operations in Crete.

Elsewhere throughout the island vicious, swirling battles, each isolated from the others, continued with little centralized control by either side. But gradually the Germans were sorting out a pattern, reinforcing and resupplying by air, while for the British and the Greeks the problems of transport and communications proved insurmountable. More and more Freyberg—never really in control of the battle—became an isolated commander, issuing orders to cover imaginary situations. The British, with the indomitable courage and steadfastness which is always best exhibited in hopeless situations, did not flag; throughout the day small unit leaders and individuals added new luster to ancient history. Near Galatas Captain Michael Forrester, who was attached to the Greek military mission, led a charge the likes of which are rarely seen in war. He had assumed command of some Greek stragglers, and he went to battle in shorts and a long yellow jersey, looking like a "Wodehouse character." His soldiers included some fierce Cretan women, all with ancient weapons, and one man with a serrated bread knife tied on the end of a shotgun.[89]

In the midnight darkness of May 22/23, King George of the Hellenes said farewell to Grecian soil. For three days the King and his entourage, escorted by the British, had made their way up the 7,000-foot spiny mountains and through the snow-dusted outcroppings to the south coast. They had seen, from high above the northern coastal plain, the last battle for Crete, "the red earth and the fields of ripening corn—flecked and spattered with innumerable parachutes—white like patches of snow, sometimes red like patches of blood." They had roasted a tough mountain sheep and had pushed forward on donkeys and mules or bleeding blistered feet, to a rendezvous with boats from HMS *Decoy* at the little village of Ayla Roumeli on the south coast. Another government-in-exile had been established.

May 23 simply confirmed the German victory, although many of the British defenders, particularly at Retimo and Heraklion where attackers and defenders had contained each other in bloody stalemates far from the scene of decision, still did not know it. Many were yet to die; and the Royal Navy's ordeal from the skies was not over.

Fifth Destroyer Flotilla, commanded by Captain Lord Louis Mountbatten, that day was caught by daylight close to Crete's south coast, after destroying a couple of caiques bound for Crete during the night. Twenty-four Stukas took them on; *Kashmir* sank in two minutes, taking with her as she went a Ju-87, shot down by a burst from an Oerlikon. Mountbatten's flagship *Kelly* took a 1,000-pound bomb, turned bottom up in white water, her propellers still flailing; *Kipling* picked up the survivors—among them Mountbatten, a future C-in-C—and reached Alexandria. Out of oil, she was towed the last 70 miles after forty air attacks, eighty-three bombs.

A convoy with troop transport *Glenroy* and 900 reinforcements bound for the south coast of Crete was ordered by Cunningham, after consultation with Wavell, to return to Egypt; he considered it "sheer murder" to send her to Crete. It was clear to commanders on the spot that they were too late, even though two destroyers successfully landed some badly needed ammunition at Suda Bay on the night of May 23/24. But London thought differently. In one of the more amazing snarls of the war, the Admiralty in London sent a message direct to *Glenroy*, ordering her to turn north once more. The message was apparently inspired by Churchill, in one of his least brilliant exhibitions of "insight," who had just messaged Freyberg: "The whole world watches your splendid battle on which great things turn."

Cunningham, never one to take interference lightly, and unimpressed by rank, immediately countermanded the orders for *Glenroy* and told the Admiralty that if she had proceeded to Crete the troop ship would have arrived just in time for daylight air attacks. Later the admiral commented caustically, and with good reason, "The less said about this unjustifiable interference by those ignorant of the situation the better."[90]

London in these days was way behind events, still insisting that Crete must be held and that reinforcements be despatched. And some were; minelayer *Abdiel* actually succeeded in landing 200 Commandos in Suda, the night of May 24, even though Cunningham had told London that the Navy could no longer operate near Crete or in the Aegean by day. General Student, eager for confirmation of victory, flew to Crete on May 25. On May 26 all hope had ended, and Freyberg reported "the limit of endurance has been reached. . . . Our position . . . is hopeless."

The retreat started, hastened by German aircraft striking and clawing at the disorganized units on the ground. Long lines of men— many of them stragglers—started crawling up the steep slopes of the bitter mountains, discarding equipment, some of them throwing away their weapons, making their slow way toward Sphakia, a fishing village on the south coast. That night the Navy, running the gantlet again with *Abdiel* and two destroyers, landed more Commandos amidst the wrecks in Suda Bay, and the fresh troops formed the rearguard to the long and bitter trail across the mountains. But it was not until the next day—May 27—that Wavell, harried by Churchill and London, finally accepted the inevitable, and even then not until Churchill had cabled Wavell early in the morning one of his dated and totally unrealistic exhortatory messages that "victory was essential and that he must keep hurling in reinforcements."[91]

The reality, once again, was evacuation. It looked grim. The Royal Navy, its strength perilously reduced, its control of the Eastern Mediterranean threatened, nevertheless faced this newest task under a stout commander. "It takes the Navy three years to build a new ship," said Cunningham. "It will take three hundred years to build a new tradition."

The evacuation was to be mounted regardless of losses.

On May 27 the Germans captured battered Canea, killed or captured all save 150 of the 1,200-man "Creforce" reserve, landed the rest of the 5th Mountain Division and a battalion of the 6th at Maleme, and pressed hard on the heels of the long column of stragglers that had been an army. Over the steep trail—panting in the daylight heat, freezing in the cold night, over the snow-dusted mountains and slipping, sliding down the precipitous southern ravines and steep cliffs—the defeated from the Maleme–Suda Bay area made their way. One German mountain regiment followed hard, delayed briefly by disciplined British rearguards—the Commandos and New Zealanders and Australians leapfrogging each other in retreat. The main thrust of the German effort shifted to the east, with both ground troops and air effort concentrated now on Retimo and Heraklion.

Freyberg and his surviving staff, with one RAF radio, established headquarters in a cave; 2,000 men, with 3 guns and 3 light tanks fit to fight, reached the Sphakia area on the morning of the 28th. That evening the evacuation started, with four destroyers taking off 1,000 men, including some 230 walking wounded. They got away clean—but the luck could not continue.

That same night, May 28/29, the first seaborne landing in the Cretan campaign occurred, a distinct anticlimax which had no effect on the course of the battle. A small number of Italians from the Italian-held island of Rhodes landed close to Sitia on the northern coast near the eastern end of the island. They were unopposed.

As the Italians were landing farther east, the British at Heraklion, miles away, were leaving "one large stench of decomposing dead, debris . . . burst water pipes, hungry dogs scavenging among the ruins . . . stench of sulphur, smouldering fires and pollution. . . ."

Two cruisers—there had been three, but *Ajax* had again been damaged and had turned back—and six destroyers, one damaged, took off 4,000 men in three and a half hours of darkness, leaving behind a forlorn rearguard and the dead and the wounded. So far so good, but the gantlet still lay ahead. Damaged destroyer *Imperial*, with steering gear jammed, had to be abandoned and sunk; her crew and passengers were transferred to destroyer *Hotspur*, which crammed 900 passengers aboard. But it was almost full day when the force, with Rear Admiral H. B. Rawlings commanding, headed south through dreaded Kaso Strait an hour and a half behind schedule.

The Junkers dived pitilessly, talons raking, against the prey below. Destroyer *Hereward* was the first to go; she took a bomb and slowed.

Last seen, as the fleet left her, she was moving slowly toward the shores of Crete, her guns still firing. She never made it, but most of the men aboard were picked up by enemy small craft or struggled ashore into captivity. From 6:00 A.M. to 3:00 P.M.—hours of unending horror—the fleet took its punishment. Rendezvous with a few long-range fighters from Egypt was missed; the ships were naked to their enemies. *Decoy* was damaged by a near-miss; cruiser *Dido* was hit. *Orion*, cruiser flagship, was a charnelhouse: the flag captain killed (dying, he called on his crew to "Keep steady!"), and Rawlings, the admiral, wounded; three boiler rooms gone, dead, dying, and wounded littering her decks, steering gear inoperative, a heavy list to starboard and only one shaft turning. She made it, limping, to "Alex," but of the 4,000 troops evacuated from Heraklion, 800 had been lost after leaving Crete.

Yet the evacuation went on. Some 6,000 men, weary unto death, wounded, disorganized, most of them unarmed, were taken off from Sphakia the night of May 29/30 by *Glengyle, Perth, Calcutta, Coventry*, and six destroyers; only *Perth* took a bomb in a boiler room.

The garrison at Retimo had been fighting in a vacuum; orders for evacuation had never gotten through, and not until May 30, when the Germans moved eastward from Canea, did the defenders understand that Maleme, Suda Bay, and Canea had all been overrun. They surrendered and that same night Freyberg (in response to orders from Egypt) and some other key men were flown in Sunderland flying boats from Crete. A tattered rearguard under the Royal Marines remained for two more days, aided by the savage Cretans, who hacked and mutilated the German dead and showed no mercy to the German wounded. They held off the enemy as desperate men tried desperately to escape. On the night of May 30/31, almost 1,500 troops were taken off in two destroyers; a third destroyer was damaged by a near-miss. May 31, the twelfth day of the campaign, was the end of organized resistance in Crete; that night cruiser *Phoebe*, minelayer *Abdiel*, and 4 destroyers evacuated 4,000 men. But antiaircraft cruiser *Calcutta*, covering the evacuating force with her consort *Coventry*, died—blasted by two bombs from a Ju-88—just 85 miles from Alexandria. The Germans had exacted last blood and the first.

An Australian rearguard, under orders, surrendered on June 1; but hundreds of fugitives, many sheltered by the Cretan hill folk, roamed the countryside. Some evaded capture for weeks or months; 600 escaped by fishing boat or small craft to North Africa; many quickly surrendered; others—a few hard-bitten men—helped form the nucleus of a Cretan underground.

It had been a bloody campaign. The British Empire lost 11,835 prisoners, 1,742 killed or missing, 1,737 wounded. The Greek military and paramilitary units suffered 2,600 dead; the rest of their 10,000 to 15,000 troops were captured, wounded, or dispersed. Some 400 to 600 Cypriots and Palestinian laborers were captured; their picks and shovels henceforth served the German cause. The Royal Air Force lost 46 planes; the Royal Navy almost lost control of the Eastern Mediterranean. Three cruisers and six destroyers were sunk in the futile effort around Crete; one carrier, three battleships, six cruisers, and seven destroyers were damaged, some of them severely. The Navy counted 1,828 dead and 183 wounded, and at the end Cunningham's Mediterranean Fleet was reduced to two battleships, two cruisers, and thirteen destroyers ready for service, and was—on paper —inferior numerically to the harbor-hugging Italian Fleet.

But the German victory had been costly. The total German personnel losses (killed, wounded, and missing) were 6,116 men; the élite paratroops and Assault Regiment had been badly mauled; many senior and skilled commanders were killed or wounded, and the approximately 25 percent casualties (of the total of 25,000 Germans landed on Crete) was considerably higher than that of any preceding campaign. The Nazis lost 147 aircraft in combat, another 73 in operational accidents, and 64 damaged. They had made mistakes in intelligence estimates and their planning—due in part to interservice rivalry, the preemption of command by the Luftwaffe, and the political insistence upon speed—was creaky and inadequate. As so often occurred, the Germans—primarily because of the political astigmatism of Nazism—misjudged the strength of the anti-German feeling of the Cretans. And the initial concept of airborne operations fostered by General Student was faulty. He had dispersed the first German effort at too many airheads; a concentration of effort (achieved later at Maleme) might have won much sooner at less cost.

As it was, the tremendous logistical problems, great expense, command and communication difficulties, and the vulnerability—in the early hours—of airborne operations had been exposed. Hitler and Göring were both shocked and displeased; as far as large-scale airborne operations were concerned, Crete engraved a pattern of cautiousness on the German High Command throughout the rest of the war. Except for small specialized tasks, the paratroopers henceforth fought as élite infantry units.[92]

Nevertheless Crete, supposedly protected by the rampart of blue water and the guns of the British Fleet, was overrun in twelve days. Piled upon the defeat in Greece, Crete represented valiant catastrophe. The British senior leadership—political and military—had not distinguished itself; as Churchill later wrote, "there had been . . . neither plan nor drive." Wavell showed little prescience, strength, or aggressiveness; Freyberg blew hot and cold, and both he and his principal subordinate commanders demonstrated too much passivity, too little initiative, proving that scars of old wounds are not necessarily badges of present competence. Only Cunningham, with moral as well as physical courage, who tempered bulldog determination and the fighting spirit of the British past with judgment and a keen appreciation of what command of the sea meant, emerged from Crete with enhanced reputation. But neither London nor the British commanders in the Middle East ever put together a coherent Greek concept.

During this phase of the war in the North African, Greek, and Cretan campaigns—a period in which Churchill was constantly talking of "sacking" Wavell—the Prime Minister's greatest weakness was clearly revealed: a propensity for didactic meddling, often on the basis of inadequate or dated information. This tendency toward overcentralized control in London was abetted, not checked, by some of Churchill's subordinates, notably Admiral Sir Dudley Pound, the First Sea Lord. Pound was beloved by those who worked closely with him, but he was an ill man with a brain tumor which was eventually to kill him, a bad hip, and not really fit for duty. Like the Prime Minister, he too often second-guessed his seagoing subordinates, and some of them felt he did not back them up. But Churchill was clearly the dominant personality, a force which could simultaneously exhilarate and inspire the public and infuriate distant commanders. Frequently he sounded an exhortatory evangelical note; too often, the spate of messages contributed nothing. Churchill tried to run the war—sometimes in detail—from London, and despite Sir John Dill's (Chief of the Imperial General Staff) advice to the "P.M." about Wavell—"Back him or sack him"—he did neither but continued to criticize and interfere. It was about this time that "Someone . . . said, 'I don't see how we can win the war without Winston, but, on the other hand, I don't see how we can win it with him.' "[93]

* * *

There remained the larger questions, the lingering doubts.

Was Crete worth it, strategically? Was the Greek campaign justified?

Did Greece and Crete, along with the action in the Balkans, delay the subsequent German invasion of Russia?

Crete demonstrated the new three-dimensional nature of modern sea control. It dramatized—as the Pacific battles were to show—the influence of airpower upon seapower, and showed that the fleet which did not control the air above the sea faced either defeat or inordinate loss.

For the new technique of vertical envelopment, the Battle of Crete was both setback and boost. Setback in German development of the concept; the expense of airborne operations and the heavy casualties impressed Hitler and Göring more than the achievements. In any case the course of the war after Crete provided, for the Germans, few opportunities for large-scale airborne operations. The Allies, particularly Britain and the United States, were greatly—probably too greatly—influenced by Crete. For the United States, in particular, which was perhaps the only country with sufficient resources to afford the expense of great fleets of expendable gliders, transport planes, parachutes, and all the paraphernalia that went with vertical envelopment, Crete meant that the day of the paratrooper in the U.S. Army had arrived. From then on, thousands of zestful young men were leaping into the skies over Fort Benning, Georgia, and Fort Bragg, North Carolina, shouting "Geronimo" (the parachutists' battle cry) as the rip cords jerked open their chutes. But even the United States was to discover later in the war that airborne operations were extremely difficult to control and opportunistic in timing; that almost total local air domination was essential to success; and that against a stalwart enemy, a quick link-up between lightly equipped parachutists holding an insular airhead in enemy territory and friendly ground forces was essential to avert disaster.

Crete was a campaign that in a sense had never been planned by either side; both stumbled into it, the British in part because of their involvement in Greece, the Germans because of Mussolini's blunders in Albania and the jockeying for power in the Nazi political-military hierarchy.

Strategically Crete may not have been worth its cost to either side. Its capture did help reinforce the Axis hold on the Aegean Sea and gave Germany and Italy additional bases in the Eastern Mediterranean from which to threaten the British Middle Eastern foci of power. The German victory (and particularly their later deep drive into Russia) bolstered Turkish caution and helped to ensure Ankara's neutrality. But without plan for follow-up, the island campaign was scarcely worth it.

Malta, the fortress island in the Central Mediterranean which dominated the Axis sea and air supply lines to North Africa, was the proper objective, since the only Axis forces operating outside Europe and the only developed Axis strategy in the Mediterranean were focused on Rommel and his Italian allies. Had the units employed in Crete been concentrated, instead, against Malta, the island would probably have been overwhelmed, the supply of Rommel greatly eased, and the ultimate picture in North Africa vastly changed.

For the British the loss of Crete was a heavy blow—particularly to the scanty, hard-pressed forces of the Royal Navy and the RAF—but it was not a crippling one, it did not halt British operations in the Eastern Mediterranean or the resupply and reinforcement of Malta. And once Greece was gone, Crete—so close to enemy mainland bases, and too large to be a fortress—was strategically useless to the British.

The Greek Commitment

The Greek campaign itself, of which Crete was but an offshoot, was a walkover for the Germans, which scarcely interrupted their quick surge of conquest across Europe. For the Greeks, it was heroic tragedy; for the British, the only solace was a moral one. The British strategy was based on the concept that it was better to have fought and lost, and this is a position—involving those vague international concepts of honor, loyalty, treaties—that can well be defended. To many Britons the defense of Greece was obligatory, no matter how vain; not only a case of the good guys against the bad guys, but a moral imperative deriving from the Anglo-Greek treaty. Churchill—thinking of Salonika and Gallipoli in World War I, and always interested in peripheral strategy—obviously hoped that a flank position might be established in Europe. But he also saw the larger implications of Greek aid to the battle for men's minds, in winning and maintaining an unassailable position of moral advantage in both Allied and neutral countries. He felt (in a political and moral sense, though not on the military scales, quite correctly) that aid to Greece therefore outweighed the possibility of overrunning Italian Tripolitania before German reinforcements became too large. There was some bitter opposition on Wavell's staff to the Greek campaign (noted in Major General Sir Francis de Guingand's memoirs), and many of the veterans of the desert war still held thirty years later to the brief that, if it had not been for the Greek diversion—the milking away of the strength of the desert forces and the enforced defensive in Cyrenaica—a decisive victory might have been won in North Africa in 1941.

But these contentions are far from persuasive. The British supply line, which became longer and longer and more and more tenuous the farther west they drove into Africa, was not then capable of meeting the strain of a Tripolitanian campaign. They could scarcely maintain even small forces in Cyrenaica; German armor and armored tactics were much more effective in that year of combat and German generalship far superior.

One may well question the political necessity of the Greek campaign, however. It is true that if the Greeks wanted aid, the British were bound to give it, having "guaranteed" it in April 1939. While Metaxas lived, he was cautious in invoking the treaty. He did agree to, and accepted, the very limited aid of small RAF contingents after the first flush of the Italian attack, but it was not until the new Greek President—Koryzis—took power in late January 1941 that large-scale British help on the ground as well as in the air was requested. Even then, there is some evidence that a little arm-twisting was done by the British, that the Greek requests for aid were not entirely spontaneous, that both diplomatically and militarily the British—most specifically in the Eden mission and in the person of the British ambassador, Sir Michael Palairet—tried persuasion and manipulation to achieve Greek agreement to a British Expeditionary Force in Greece. Eden, indeed, appears to have been an enthusiastic messenger for Churchill, who repeatedly returned to the dream of a Balkan front; "Our aim [was] to animate and combine Yugoslavia, Greece and Turkey." Yet the Prime Minister himself was confused in purpose; he confessed later that there were many looming dangers in Greece, and that "the Greeks had departed in so many ways from the terms of the Athens agreement that we could, had we so wished, have asked for release from it."[94] Eden, determined if possible to bring Turkey into the war, did a salesman's job in Athens; in modern terminology it might be called, as De Guingand calls it in politer language, a "snow job."

De Guingand, in his book *Operation Victory*, records a visit to

Athens in February 1941 when Eden "stressed and enumerated the 'formidable' resources which we were prepared to send over":

> It sounded pretty good, but if a real expert had carried out a more detailed investigation I doubt whether those present [the Greek King, Prince Paul, the Prime Minister, and others] would have been so satisfied. Totals of men and guns are generally impressive. In the aircraft flying over I had been asked to produce a list showing totals of items we were proposing to send. My first manpower figures excluded such categories as pioneers [engineers] and in the gun totals I only produced artillery pieces. This was nothing like good enough for one of Mr. Eden's party who was preparing the brief. He asked that the figures should be swelled with what to my mind were doubtful values. I felt that this was hardly a fair do, and bordering upon dishonesty. . . .[95]

At the end, after the consultations had resulted in Greek acceptance of a BEF, De Guingand noted that:

> Eden came in looking buoyant. . . . [His staff] looked nearly as triumphant as he did and were positively oozing congratulations.
> Presumably he had done his job, and accomplished what he had set out to achieve. . . . But whether it was a job worth doing and in our best interests seemed to me very doubtful. . . .[96]

Major General Sir John Kennedy, who was on the Imperial General Staff in London, agreed with De Guingand that the Greek commitment was a "major error," that the military point of view was never given proper weight, that it was clear to all "except the wishfully-minded" (of whom there were then many) "that we could never have held the Germans for long in Greece," and that "the only sound basis for this adventure would have been to send only the minimum forces necessary to satisfy political requirements." To which he adds, in parenthesis: "When the Greeks were first approached they actually said they did not wish British forces to come to Greece, and we could have confined our effort to air operations on the mainland, and to the holding of Crete, without any loss of honor."[97]

In the event, the BEF went to Greece on the basis of prearranged plans, or assumptions, that were fallacious in concept and in execution, and contrary to the basic assumptions of London. The British and Greeks fought without help from Turkey or Yugoslavia. Their pre-planned defensive positions were outflanked, before they were manned, by the quick collapse of Yugoslavia.

Neither Greece nor Crete could really claim even the beneficence of delay in the Nazi march of conquest. The German legions scarcely paused in their goose-stepping stride across Europe. The Russian invasion, it is true, did not start until June 22; May 15 was the original date, set by Hitler, for operational readiness for "Barbarossa" (the Russian invasion).

Eden, who was a major architect of the Greek campaign, makes the strongest case for what he terms the decisive nature of the Greek and Crete campaigns. The delay in the invasion of Russia, he wrote later, justified all that occurred in Greece; in effect the delay (in the words of Karl Ritter, German Foreign Office liaison officer with the Nazi High Command, quoted by Eden) "cost the Germans the winter battle before Moscow and it was there the war was lost."[98] Some German generals support this conclusion in other terms; they attribute the delay to the Balkans campaign as a whole, but not primarily to Greece and Crete. Indeed, Army General Staff planners had agreed after the Yugoslav coup and the quick and unexpected concentration of German forces on the northern Yugoslav frontier that the Russian invasion would have to be postponed for four weeks.

Yet, in the event, even these tenuous evidences of delay are not conclusive. For May 15 was never a firm date for D-Day, merely a deadline for operational readiness—a deadline which was, in large part, met. And even so, the *Blitzkrieg* tactics Hitler planned in Russia depended—in the roadless steppes and vast distances—upon firm footing, which in turn depended upon the vagaries of weather. Rivers in spate and seas of mud would mean, in any case, enforced waiting. And the spring thaw of 1941 in western Russia and Eastern Europe was late indeed; in mid-May the ground was waterlogged, rivers in raging torrents. (As late as early June the Bug River, a major obstacle to the German advance, was well beyond its banks.) The unpredictable Serbs and British and Greek courage contributed to delay, but in the event, weather made the issue moot.

IV

THE GLOBAL WAR
1941

In the last half of 1941, the "little war" with Poland that Hitler had wanted became World War II.

Der Fuehrer turned to the East, and Nazi legions rumbled to the suburbs of Moscow. December 7 was a "day of infamy"—for the United States at Pearl Harbor, a moment of truth. Japan, still heavily engaged in China, moved over the oceans to new conquests in the Philippines, Hong Kong, Malaysia, and the Dutch East Indies.

In Berlin and Tokyo these were days of wine and roses, yet the bitter lees were still to be drained. Men did not perceive it then, but all over the world the old order was ending; the Axis conquests, though not to endure, would forever change the course of history.

The United States, which for a year had been engaged in undeclared war in the Atlantic, now faced an even greater threat in the Pacific. Unified by Pearl Harbor, it commenced history's greatest mobilization for history's greatest Total War. In the end, the guns and machines and ships and planes American industry produced in prodigious quantities were to be one of two decisive factors in the ultimate formula of victory.

The other was Russian manpower and Russian space.

17

Russia—The "Unknown War"

On June 22, 1941, the war washed new shores.

In scope, ruthlessness, and immensity, Hitler's invasion of Russia and the four years of relentless struggle that followed were unequaled in their consequences, unprecedented in the dimensions of fury. The "unknown war" of World War I, the war on the Eastern Front, though huge and sanguinary, was dwarfed a quarter century later as the combatants harnessed the tank and the plane, speed and mobility, to vast armies of struggling men.

The Russian campaigns of World War II were reminiscent of the far-ranging depredations of Genghis Khan and his successors, in reverse. The Mongols who swept across Central Europe in the thirteenth century have left, even to this day, the indelible mark of their conquests; but the dreaded horsemen from Asia penetrated a continent sparse in population as compared to twentieth-century Europe, and primitive in military technology.

In Western Europe *Blitzkrieg* filled the map; in Russia the map absorbed and diminished the great hordes of men. In Western Europe there were flanks—mountains, rivers, the sea; in Russia vast, open, empty spaces and flanks so distant that war was fluid; there was no continuous solid front.

Climate was implacable and extreme, the summers short, the winters long; temperatures varied from the subtropical warmth of the Black Sea–Caucasus valleys in summer to the subhuman cold of the steppes, from deep snow and fast-killing wind to hub-deep dust and morass of mud. Spring thaws and fall rains imposed *rasputitsy* (traffic halts) on nearly all military movement. There were few railroads, all of them of broader gauge than in Western Europe, and the land was largely roadless, ill-adapted to motorized wheeled vehicles. Animals and men, as in the days of Genghis Khan, played large roles in the Russian campaign. The German armies that invaded Russia in 1941 utilized 625,000 horses for transport, artillery, and supply, as compared to 600,000 motor vehicles; and the Russians initially counted about 32 cavalry divisions—most of them horsed—in their order of battle.

In one other characteristic—the inhumanity of man—the Russo-German fighting resembled the frightfulness of the conquests of Genghis Khan. The campaign started as an ideological struggle with no holds barred; it ended as a struggle for survival. Hitler considered the Russian *moujik* as *Untermensch* (inferior race) and he ordered, before the event, that the apparatus of communism in the person of party officials and political commissars must be liquidated. In turn the Communists had no mercy; Stalin was as implacable as Hitler. Both were completely amoral, power-hungry dictators with no scruples and great cunning.

It was indeed inevitable, this clash between Teuton and Slav, dictators of the right and the left. Karl Haushofer, the geopolitician, and many other Germans had often looked to the East, where the vast granaries of the Ukraine and the great land mass offered *Lebensraum*. In other days the last Kaiser and his generals had dreamed of the *Drang nach Osten*, and Hitler himself in *Mein Kampf* and in prewar conversations had made no secret of his Eastern ambitions. Communism and the Jews, in Hitler's mind, were virtually synonymous, and it was the destiny of the Greater Reich to spread its empire to the East and to harness the vast resources and the cheap labor of Russia to Germanic glory. The Russo-German Pact which sealed the fate of Poland and so astounded the world of 1939 was but a temporary marriage of convenience, which suited the needs and plans of both dictators.

Stalin, ideological head of a political faith that believed in world revolution and Communist domination, hoped to profit from a capitalist-versus-capitalist war. The Comintern (the international Communist organization) told the Communist parties abroad that "it is best to hold aloof from the conflict, while remaining ready to intervene when the powers engaged therein are weakened by war, in the hope of securing a social revolution."[1] Stalin in particular had a paranoid suspicion of the Western world, and of all foreigners, and an isolationist mentality. The Red Army, weakened from the bloody purges of 1937–38, its prestige diminished by the Finnish Winter War, needed time; Stalin feared the increasing might of Nazi Germany. Hitler, with the nightmare of World War I's two-front war still haunting his dreams, wanted a free hand against his Western enemies and a secure flank. He, too, feared the increasing might of the Soviet hordes—too big, he thought, for defense only—and he had no illusions of permanent peace on the eastern reaches of the Greater Reich. When he signed the prewar Berlin-Moscow Pact, he knew that the day of reckoning must come.

And so, in that brief period when Russia and Germany posed as allies, the "two great totalitarian empires, equally devoid of moral restraints, confronted each other [in Winston Churchill's words], polite but inexorable."

"Operation Barbarossa"

Events helped to force the issue; the chief battlefield was Hitler's ambivalent mind. He had signed the Soviet pact to secure his Eastern flank and to ensure, after the conquest of Poland, a free hand in the West. He got it, but after the fall of France, England persisted in her defiance, and gradually Hitler rationalized his strategy. The British stubbornly continued the war because, he thought, their hopes of victory were fixed on Russian intervention. Ergo, it would be necessary to eliminate Russia to bring England finally to her knees; invasion of England, temporarily delayed after the Luftwaffe's failure in the Battle of Britain, could be indefinitely postponed until the Russian hordes were exterminated. This rationalization was aided, in the interim, by the Soviet occupation of the Baltic republics and of Rumanian Bessarabia and by the Soviet victory in Finland.

Russia, it is true, had largely fulfilled the grain and raw material deliveries agreed to by the Berlin-Moscow Pact and, at the last, had made major efforts to placate Hitler and to avert or delay the inevitable. But the accommodation was, on both sides, superficial only; underneath was the dry rot of deep mistrust.

As early as July 29, 1940, while the Battle of Britain was still in the balance, General Jodl gathered a few trusted members of the OKW —Hitler's Supreme Command—around him in a car of the special command train *Atlas* in Bad Reichenhall Station. General Walter Warlimont, chief of the L (National Defense) Section of the OKW, tells what happened:

> . . . Jodl went round ensuring that all doors and windows were closed and then, without any preamble, disclosed to us that Hitler had decided to rid the world "once and for all" of the danger of Bolshevism by a surprise attack on Soviet Russia to be carried out at the earliest possible moment, i.e. in May 1941.[2]

And on July 31, Halder, Chief of Staff of the Army, recorded in his diary that Hitler, in a conference with his military chiefs in the Berghof, had said: "*Russia is the factor by which England sets the greatest store. . . . If Russia is beaten, England's last hope is gone. . . . Decision: As a result . . . Russia must be dealt with. Spring 1941.*"[3]

The decision, long germinating, was incorporated in Directive No. 21 on December 18, 1940—"Operation Barbarossa." In this top-secret preparatory alert Hitler ordered:

> The German Armed Forces must make preparations to crush *Soviet Russia in a lightning campaign,* even before the termination of hostilities with Great Britain. . . .
> . . . at least eight weeks before the intended start of the operation, I shall issue a directive for the strategic concentration against Soviet Russia.
> Any preparations which require more time . . . will be initiated immediately and brought to a conclusion before 15 May 1941. . . .

I. Overall Plan

During the initial phase the bulk of the Russian *Army* stationed in western Russia is to be destroyed in a series of daring operations spearheaded by armored thrusts. The organized withdrawal of intact units into the vastness of interior Russia must be prevented. . . .

. . . The ultimate objective of the operation is to screen European against Asiatic Russia along the course of the Volga and thence along a general line extending northward towards Archangel. . . .

The directive specified Moscow as *an* objective (italics mine), but stated that after the two Northern Army Groups had shattered the Soviet forces in White Russia, "strong motorized elements" of Army Group Center would drive northward on the flank of Army Group North to assist in the capture of Leningrad and Kronstadt.

"Only then will the offensive operations leading to the seizure of Moscow . . . be continued," the directive stated.[4]

The directive appeared to compromise, but did not totally obscure, some major differences between Hitler and his generals. Hitler understood Moscow's political and psychological symbolism, its locus as a communication hub, and its industrial concentrations. But he also emphasized, as of co-equal importance, the Donets Basin. He believed that he must capture Leningrad and Stalingrad, "the breeding grounds of Bolshevism," and that he must secure the granaries of the Ukraine and the principal industries and oil-producing areas of western Russia.

For the initial phase of operations, Directive No. 21 followed the sound principle that the proper objective of war is the destruction of the enemy's armies; but Hitler's views colored strongly—and later confused—the ultimate objectives of the German invasion.

And so the great dice of chance at length were cast. All the Balkan, Mediterranean, and North African operations were preliminary and ancillary, necessary as prelude but subordinate to the one great conquest in the East.

Between December 1940 and June 1941, the "Barbarossa" plans for conquest were molded and modified by the Yugoslav coup, the Greek invasion, and the vagaries of nature in the form of the late spring thaw.

As finally drawn, the plan—though it did not explicitly say so—contemplated a quick three-to-four-month victory. The bulk of the German Army and Air Force, supported by Rumanian and Finnish troops, and utilizing the railroads and roads of Europe (including the railroads of neutral Sweden), would "paralyze and eliminate" the Soviet Air Force, destroy the Russian ground forces in the West, isolate Murmansk, and capture Kronstadt, Leningrad, Kiev, Moscow, and the Donets Basin industrial area. The weight of the German attack was to be concentrated north of the Pripyat Marshes, that maze of virtually roadless swamp along the Russian-Polish frontier.

There was little or no preparation for a winter campaign. German industry was not mobilized for maximum production; the invasion was to be a war of *Blitzkrieg*, not attrition.

There were some misgivings in the German High Command, though few of them were voiced and none actively pressed. Hitler himself, intoxicated by the victories of yesterday and with a growing capacity for rationalization and delusion, had few doubts. Several times in the months before invasion he voiced the view that Russia would collapse in the summer of 1941, and that in the fall he could turn again to the Mediterranean and the war against England.

There was a greater mistake, its tap roots deep in the sour soil of the Nazi ideology. Undeniably dissidence and separatism existed in Russia, particularly in the Ukraine, sickened by the blood purges and communization of the land and the stern rule of the Bolsheviks. A skillful political and ideological plan might well have capitalized upon a real yearning for freedom. But, well before the event—in March 1941—the nature of the forthcoming campaign was clearly forecast. Early in March, General Jodl, reflecting Hitler's wishes, issued a general statement of special instructions to the OKW staff in which he stressed that the "forthcoming campaign is more than a mere armed conflict; it is a collision between two different ideologies." During the month, these instructions were elaborated into detailed plans; conquered areas would not be governed by the Army but would be administered by the Nazi Party, with Reich commissars and Gauleiters in control and the dreaded SS the ultimate authority. Conquered Russia was to serve as a granary for the Reich, even though "as a result many millions of people will be starved to death." On March 30, Hitler, in a far-ranging speech to his commanders, ordered that Soviet commissars and officials, civilian or military, were to be shot when captured, and that in Russia the German soldier was not to be bound by the ordinary rules of war.[5] At the same time, in a secret directive to Himmler, he ordered "immediately the campaign had begun the systematic mass murder of Jews in the rear areas of the Eastern Front." The Russian campaign was to be a "different" war, and its cruelties would become unending.

The Greatest Land Campaign in History

The Germans concentrated for the invasion three great Army Groups—about 162 divisions, including 14 Rumanian divisions. These 3 million ground troops were to be augmented later, after the German northern wing had approached Leningrad, by twenty additional Finnish divisions and about four and a half German divisions, transported to Finland via Norway or through Sweden. The order of battle included 3,400 tanks and more than 7,000 artillery pieces. The entire concentration was to be supported by about 2,800 to 3,000 German aircraft. Another 1,500 German planes—a sizable fraction of German air strength—were still employed, however, from Norway to the Mediterranean in operations against Britain and British shipping and in support of Rommel, and the German Navy was specifically ordered to continue to concentrate its main effort against Great Britain; the Russian campaign would be won or lost on land.

Indubitably, it was to be the greatest land campaign in history.

The order of battle of the German Army just before jump-off concentrated two Army Groups north of the Pripyat Marshes; one, south. From north to south these were:

Army Group North (East Prussia and the Baltic coastal area), Field Marshal Wilhelm von Leeb commanding (supported by First Air Force, under General Alfred Keller); Eighteenth Army; Fourth Panzer Group (or Army); and Sixteenth Army. A total of thirty divisions, three of them armored.

Army Group Center (from Suwalki and East Prussia to the Pripyat Marshes), Field Marshal Fedor von Bock commanding (supported by Second Air Force, under Field Marshal Albert Kesselring); Third Panzer Group (later redesignated an Army); Ninth Army; Fourth Army; and Second Panzer Group (later, Army). A total of fifty-one divisions, including nine Panzer divisions.

Army Group South (from south of the Pripyat Marshes to the Black Sea), Field Marshal Gerd von Rundstedt commanding (supported by Fourth Air Force, under General Alexander Löhr); First Panzer Group (later, Army); Sixth Army; Seventeenth Army; Eleventh Army; and Rumanian Army. A total of forty-three German and fourteen Rumanian divisions.

There were two armored, one motorized, and twenty-one infantry divisions in OKH reserve; and in Finland, in addition to twenty Finnish divisions, there were four and a half German divisions. Baron Mannerheim commanded in southern Finland; in the barren northern reaches, near the slob ice of the Arctic Ocean, some six German and Finnish divisions operated under the command of General Nikolaus von Falkenhorst, the German commander in Norway. Later, these immense forces were joined by Hungarian, Italian, Spanish, and Slovak units.

The campaign was envisaged as a grandiose battle of annihilation. Bock's Army Group Center (the strongest of the three major groupings) was to strike hard along the route Napoleon followed, toward Minsk, Smolensk, and Moscow, and in huge double envelopments by its two Panzer groups crush all Soviet forces to the west of the Dnieper. Army Group North was to sweep through southern Lithuania northeastward to trap all Russian forces in the Baltic states and south of Leningrad against the sea. Army Group South would send its armored elements surging southeastward toward Kiev and the Donets Basin and the Crimea, to secure the crossings of the Dnieper River and to trap all Russian forces west of the river. The Rumanian divisions and the German Eleventh Army, operating from Rumania, were to mount a limited holding offensive into Bessarabia to pin down the enemy.

The initial objectives were not territorial or economic but the destruction of the bulk of the enemy forces in western Russia. Once this was accomplished, specific geographic objectives were outlined for each of the Army Groups.

The Russian order of battle was not inferior in numbers to the German. More than 3 million men, supported by thousands of planes, were ranged in western Russia from Leningrad to the Black Sea—many of them close to the frontier. Another million or more were in Asiatic Russia, and there were potentially millions of reserves, most of them ill-trained.

In contrast to the Germans, the strongest Soviet concentrations were south of the Pripyat Marshes. When the invasion started, the Russian command system was based on military districts, which became, with hostilities, "fronts" or Army Groups. On June 22, there were five of these (soon merged to three, and expanded and altered again intermittently later in the war), commanding a total of some 12 armies, about 160–170 divisions. The defense lines in the west—still under construction—were mostly deep inside what had been, until the Soviet "grab" earlier in the war, foreign territory. The five fronts were Leningrad, Northwest, West, Southwest, and South; soon these became the Northwest, West, and Southwest.

The Soviet Air Forces, like the Soviet Army, were probably numerically the largest in the world in mid-1941. There were about 5,000 to 10,000 military planes at airstrips in European Russia (and another 1,500 to 3,000 east of the Urals). The Germans were faced by 3,000 to 5,000 fighters, some 2,000 to 4,000 bombers and ground support planes, several thousand reconnaissance aircraft, transport, and liaison planes.

The Russian armed forces of June 1941 were, man for man, division for division, grossly inferior in military effectiveness to their German foes. The Red Army was distinguished then for mass, not quality. It was, basically, an Army of foot soldiers, with a few excellent professionals and natural leaders (most of them in subordinate positions at war's start) and many hastily armed peasants—a mass of infantry that moved like locusts across the land, driving cattle, horses, and carts before them, living off the land, utilizing whole villages for labor and supply. Many of its units remained an "armed horde" throughout the war. Though its arms and equipment were spotty—the best and the worst, the most modern and the obsolete—it had a lot of everything, and the production rate of the Soviet factories and the recuperative power of the Russian system proved to be surprising.

Its soldiers were hardy and patient. General Reinhard Gehlen called them "tough and frugal." The Soviet supply system was not cluttered with the amenities of the West; even basic needs of the individual were largely ignored in the tables of organization. The medical service was small and primitive, grave registration units and casualty-reporting services conspicuous by their absence. Families—except those of high-ranking officers or Communist officials—were rarely informed, at least in the early stages of the war, of the death or capture of their men.

The Air Force, by modern standards, was obsolete. It was incapable of long-range strategic bombing and its antishipping, antisubmarine operations were primitive. But it had thousands of planes—most of them keyed to ground support, among them the heavy-gunned Il-2 Stormovik, specially suited for antiarmor use. There was no Soviet radar, and the backwardness in electronics extended to bombsights and navigation aids. There were no fighters even approximately comparable to the Me-109.

The best of the Red Army's ground equipment was, in many ways, equal to the German. The Red tanks had no creature comforts, but the fast diesel-propelled T-34, which surprised the Germans, was initially superior to the German tanks of 1941. The Red Army counted about 17,000 tanks (more than the combined tank strength of the rest of the world)—10,000 in European Russia—and production of the latest models was rapidly increasing. Many of the tanks were, however, obsolescent and only a few T-34's were available in the summer of 1941.

There were few divisions organized as tank units; most of the Soviet armored forces were grouped in smaller brigades or dispersed in even smaller units and were not—initially—organizationally or tactically concentrated.

Horsed cavalry was more numerous than in any other army, and was particularly useful during spring thaws or fall rains, in thick woods or deep cold:

. . . far from being an anachronism, [the cavalry] was of immense value. Recruited from Cossacks and Kalmuks—peoples who spent their lives in the saddle—it had an extraordinary mobility. Its men were trained to fight as infantry, but would use the horses to cover huge distances over bad ground, and to tow their light artillery and mortar limbers. . . . They were invaluable under conditions of fluid fighting, and their horses, shaggy little Kirkhil ponies from Siberia, could stand temperatures of 30 degrees below zero.[6]

The Katyusha rockets—known as "Stalin's pipe organs"—were inaccurate but fearsomely impressive in the delivery of area fire. The Soviet field artillery in World War II was distinguished, as in past eras of Russian history, by both quality and quantity; the Russians counted and used more guns than any army on earth, and their calibers compared favorably, in range and explosive charge, with foreign artillery pieces.

The initial Soviet strategy appears to have been a medley of ambivalent notions. Large concentrations—relatively immobile, as compared to the Germans—were ranged near the frontiers, apparently to discourage Nazi attack and to hold, if possible, should attack come. Soviet military doctrine believed then, as now, in the primacy of the offensive and in the holding of all Russian territory. The consequent Russian dispositions along the frontiers lent some slight substance to Hitler's charges that Moscow was planning an ultimate attack. Gehlen states:

. . . by the time we attacked Russia in June, 1941 . . . it was clear that Stalin had resolved to postpone his attack on his former ally [Germany] only so long as was necessary to see us bleeding to death and exhausted after a conflict with the Western Allies. . . . The advanced states of the Soviet Union's preparations for an offensive war support this conviction. For example, the echeloned, in-depth deployment of their divisions at the time of our attack indicated that they were putting together a powerful land force for an attack on us. The structure of their industrial economy led to similar conclusions as well. . . .[7]

Many of these units were disposed in only the most primitive of field fortifications; most of the frontier divisions were in barracks. A defensive system, based on detached strong points, sited well back of the frontiers, had been started in 1936 between the Baltic and the Pripyat Marshes. But it had been based on strategic plans developed by Marshal M. N. Tukhachevski, Deputy Commissar for Defense, and Tukhachevski and his plans had been liquidated, along with thousands of Red Army officers, in the great purges of 1937–38. The line, unfinished though still strong, was never fully occupied.

In the beginning, the concept of selling space for time was not followed; the inevitable result of trying to hold everything led to disaster.

On June 22 the Germans on large portions of the vast frontier achieved almost complete tactical surprise. Yet there had been many forewarnings.

To an alert army the German concentrations, so massive as to defy concealment (even though the Abwehr, the German military intelligence, tried many concealment and deception techniques), could not have been hidden, and indeed many Russian frontier commanders warned of the build-up. Allied intelligence, both British and American, had correctly assessed Berlin's aggressive intentions and had sounded the alarm. The efficient Communist espionage service, the largest in the world, had even learned of the date for D-Day.

The Warnings

The *Rote Kapelle* (a Communist spy network, the "Red Orchestra") had infiltrated every important German ministry and had some agents in many parts of Hitler-dominated Europe (alias "Gilbert," "Lucy," "Kent," etc.). It had funneled detailed information, much of it highly accurate, about German mobilization and concentration, Nazi military dispositions, and even Hitler's plans, to Moscow since the beginning of 1941. Early in the year, a commercial attaché of the U.S. Embassy in Berlin had learned details of "Barbarossa" and had sent the information on to Washington. British and U.S. diplomats had passed on warnings of increasing urgency; Sumner Welles, Under Secretary of State, had, for instance, advised the Soviet ambassador in Washington on March 20 that an attack by the Germans was impending.

The German naval attaché in Moscow cabled Berlin on April 25: "Rumors about impending German-Russian war greatly increasing in scope. British Ambassador gives 22nd. June as date of beginning of war."[8]

In Japan, Richard Sorge, perhaps the most famous and successful spy of World War II, had developed a Communist espionage cell which learned some of the most important secrets of both the German and Japanese governments. Sorge was a German Communist, who used a journalistic cover. He was completely trusted by the German ambassador and the military attaché, and he or his associates had access to important Japanese officials. As early as March 5, he sent to Moscow a microfilm of cables from Berlin to the German Tokyo Embassy fixing the date of the attack as mid-June. On May 15, he cabled the attack would come on June 22.

Later, in mid-June, an agent known as "Lucy"—part of the Red network in Europe—duplicated the Sorge warning, specifying the date of invasion and details of the German order of battle.

The warnings also came at the highest levels of government. As early as April 1941, two months before the invasion, Churchill had cabled Stalin of threatening German dispositions. About June 10, Foreign Minister Anthony Eden and a British intelligence official in London tried to convince the Soviet ambassador of the attack. On June 15, Churchill cabled Roosevelt that ". . . it looks as if a vast German onslaught on Russia is imminent."[9]

There were low-level tactical, as well as high-level strategic, warnings. Deserters, or prisoners, were picked up by Russian units near the frontier shortly before the attack, and in some instances revealed details that included actual dates, times, and units.

To all these rumblings the available record shows only a kind of lip-service reaction. There were general adjurations (by Timoshenko, among others) to maintain a state of readiness, and in April the Soviet War Council had issued a secret alert in the West. It was apparently more honored in the breach than in the observance.

In retrospect it seemed as if all the world except many of the Soviet frontier units knew about the German plans.[10]

The shock of surprise was Stalin's greatest failure, one which could be explained only in the context of the paranoia, suspicion, and fear that prevailed in Stalin's Russia and by the astigmatic distortion of facts as viewed through Communist lenses. In the Kremlin, the attitude which seemed to prevail at Pearl Harbor a few months later may have been dominant, but in Russia it was also the wishful thinking of a blind ideological faith which helped to lead to disaster, magnified by the centralization of power and the propensity of absolute dictators to believe what they want to believe.

Ever since the Russo-German agreement Stalin had been wed to a policy of appeasement; he had bent over backward—even to the point of obsequiousness—to avoid what he called "provocations" to Germany. His orders to his subordinates were strict: no "provocative" actions. German overflights were not to be fired on; Nazi reconnaissance patrols along the frontiers often evoked no Russian reaction. In part this Stalinist attitude was a product of a personalized policy; the dictator had staked everything on a German-Russian "rapprochement," and the Kremlin rejected warnings and did not believe what it did not want to believe. But the blindness was also produced by ideology; suspicions of the West and the belief that Britain and the United States were trying to embroil Russia in a "capitalist" war had become paranoid.

Wishful thinking fostered disaster. Across western Russia at dawn on June 22 a large fraction of the Soviet Air Force was destroyed on the ground. German reconnaissance planes—flying at the then extraordinary altitude of 30,000 to 40,000 feet—which had regularly overflown Russia in the months before invasion, had photographed the Soviet fields. The Communist planes were sitting targets, and falling bombs and cratered runways, the first warnings.

For some 200 miles behind Russia's western borders the Luftwaffe struck at some sixty-six airfields from the Arctic to the Black Sea, and in the first cold light—from 3:00 to 4:30 A.M.—on June 22 the bulk of the Soviet fighter forces in western Russia was destroyed in pyres of leaping flames, twisted metal, and sepulchral explosions.

Some authorities estimate that 2,000 Russian planes were destroyed in the first two days, a holocaust unsurpassed then or since. The Germans claimed almost 3,700 Soviet aircraft destroyed in the first week, more than 6,000 by July 12; and Hitler later boasted 17,000 for the entire Eastern Front from June to December. These figures, like all statistics dealing with the "unknown war," are surrounded by question marks posed by distortions of both antagonists, loss or destruction of German records, secrecy or falsification of Russian records. But no matter, the results were clear; the Luftwaffe won clear-cut air superiority in the first days of war. The Russians "not only had to bring in aircraft from schools, air transport divisions and

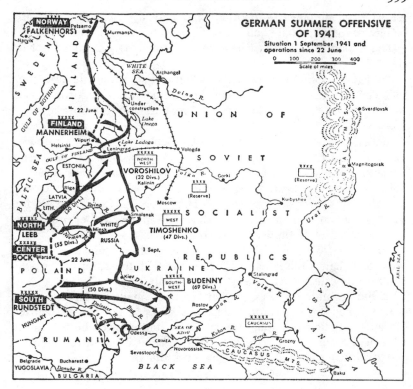

from the civil air fleet to replace bomber and fighter losses at the front, but also over 1,000 fighters and fighter bombers from the air divisions in the Far East."[11]

Battle of the Frontiers

From the Baltic to Bessarabia, the greatest land campaign in history opened with the roar of gunfire and the rumble of the tanks. Out of the night, the German legions came—the faint false dawn flickering on the horizon. Russian frontier guards, sleeping in their barracks, were gunned down as the tanks rumbled through border barriers and eastward—ever eastward—into the vast steppes. Consternation and disbelief were the initial reactions of the cumbrous, inert Soviet forces.

Front-line units—their commanders totally inhibited by the political dominance of the Communist Party and the fear of the dreaded

NKVD (secret police)—reported first, took action later: "We are being fired upon; what shall we do?"

The response: "You must be insane. And why is your signal not in code?"[12]

Confusion, sometimes panic, and then rapid wholesale surrender followed surprise, as the German Panzers cut deep into the Soviet concentrations and drew rings of steel around countless Russian *Kessels* (pockets).

In Berlin, that morning of June 22, Goebbels read Hitler's proclamation to the German people over the radio. The invasion of Russia, he said, was a preventive war to smash a "conspiracy between the Jewish–Anglo-Saxon warmongers and the equally Jewish rulers of the Moscow center of bolshevism." The campaign was a crusade for the "protection and salvation of Europe," and on it depended the "fate and future of the Reich and our people."

To which Goebbels added privately in a secret conference on the same day that, although the Fuehrer thought the campaign would last four months, "I tell you it will take only eight weeks."[13]

In the beginning, it seemed that Goebbels might be right.

In the key central sector, Guderian's tanks of the Second Panzer Group (actually the Group was an Army, but denied the title until later in the war, partly because of Wehrmacht intramural jealousies and rivalries) captured the bridges over the Bug, or forded it and moved on deep into the expanding chaos of the bewildered Russian Army.

At Przemyśl—the famous tongue-twisting site of battles in an earlier war—elements of Rundstedt's Army Group South, its flanks guarded by the Pripyat Marshes and by Hungarian troops along the Carpathian's crest, crossed the San quickly. Some units sliced easily into soft Soviet resistance, but with Russian mass concentrated in the south, and somewhat more alert than in other areas of the front, the going was slower—in some cases bitter and bloody.

In the fields of Stubienka the tall grain waved in the summer wind like the sea. Into this sea the troops now plunged. Both sides were lurking, invisible. Stalking each other. Hand-grenades, pistols and machine carbines. . . . Only with . . . dusk did this bloody fighting in the rye-fields . . . end. The [Russian] enemy withdrew. . . .[14]

In the north, against sporadic resistance—with some small units of defenders fighting fanatically—surprise was almost complete. There was little preparatory artillery fire, and the German attackers, moving like ghosts out of the morning mists, snipped barbed-wire defenses, captured or bayoneted terrified Russian sentries, and moved on. By the second day some units had burst out of East Prussia and were 40 miles deep in the Baltic states, on the Latvian-Lithuanian frontier.

In many instances in those first weeks retreat became rout. In the center and north the deep Panzer penetrations and the wide-sweeping envelopments caught whole armies in their net. In Lithuania and Latvia the Russians fought strong delaying actions, but the slicing armored hook by General Erich Hoepner's Fourth Panzer Group and the Sixteenth German Army promised to pin the defenders against the Baltic. By the end of June, the Dvina had been reached and an estimated twelve to fifteen Soviet divisions destroyed. Only in the south, where the bulk of the Soviet forces had been concentrated and fierce counterattacks delayed the attackers, was the going harder than anticipated.

By June 30, just eight days after D-Day, it looked as if Hitler had been right and the campaign would be short.

Encirclement

Particularly on the Central Front, where the Germans massed their major effort, the Soviet defeats in June and July were spectacular and massive. Despite the surprising tenacity of some Russian defenders, who held out, surrounded, for a week in the old fortress of Brest-Litovsk (a few holed up in the ruins were not mopped up until late July), the armored elements surged deep into Russia, followed by the infantry, marching and fighting an average of 20 miles a day.

On this front an encirclement within an encirclement was planned —two concentric *Kesselschlachts*—one deep sack by the converging pincers of the Third and Second Panzer Groups (Armies), another, within the outer sack, by the Fourth and Ninth Armies. The plan worked, but not completely. Many were captured or slaughtered; others escaped before the net could be tightly drawn. Again and again, with more and more success, the Germans penetrated the Russian front with armor, sealed the shoulders with infantry, drove hard to the east, turned inward, and in the cul-de-sac caught thousands of bewildered *moujiks*, struggling desperately, like floundering fish in a net, to escape annihilation. West of Minsk (its outskirts reached on June 26–27, captured on June 30), and around Bialystok, four Russian armies—some forty divisions—were trapped in the furious convulsions of death. Some escaped, but when the mop-up ended, 20 to 30 divisions had been wholly or partially destroyed, almost 300,000 taken prisoner, 2,500 tanks and 1,400 guns captured.

There was no halt. Army Group Center crossed the Berezina and the Dnieper, and by July 19, hundreds of miles deep in Russia, its tanks were closing another great sack around Smolensk, Vitebsk, and Orsha, with another 100,000 Russians, 2,000 tanks, and almost 2,000 guns entrapped.

Two weeks after the invasion started, Halder noted in his diary on July 3: "It is probably not an exaggeration when I contend that the campaign against Russia has been won in fourteen days."[15]

It seemed logical; on that day Guderian's advanced elements reached the Dnieper, 320 miles from the frontier, about halfway to Moscow.

On July 4, Hitler shared this optimism: ". . . For all practical purposes the enemy has lost this campaign. It is a good thing that we have destroyed the Russian armored and air forces right at the beginning. The Russians will be unable to replace them."[16]

In that hot and dusty summer of triumph, hundreds of thousands of Soviet soldiers surrendered, looking for the freedom they could not find under communism. In some units, the Russians shot their political commissars. In many villages deep in Russia German troops were greeted as liberators, particularly in the Ukraine, where nationalism had long burned bright and the yoke of the great Russians as well as the tyranny of communism were resented. Many peasants gladly helped the Germans, toasted the birth of a new nation in vodka, fashioned festive flower garlands, and worshiped with Te Deums the god that communism had so long denied. Little did they know they were exchanging one tyranny for another and that the implacable vengeance of opposing ideologies would crush them and their bright new dreams.

Yet even in these early days, there were signs. Not only did the Gauleiters and the Nazi bureaucrats follow hard on the heels of the Wehrmacht to turn the conquered peoples, first from willing alliance to sullen compliance, and then to active hate. But here in the East, the German military machine faced far more primitive peoples than those they had conquered so easily in the West. These were rugged peasants—hardy, fatalistic, accustomed to little. Properly led and properly inspired—and there were few who led them properly, fewer still who inspired them in the early months—they could stand and fight; they could be killed, but, like Antaeus, or the soldiers of the dragons' teeth, countless others sprang up in their place. Slowly the German casualties mounted, in men, and particularly in matériel. The huge mass of the Soviet Army, the immense numbers of men, guns, and tanks, exacted unending toll. But more important by far in the summer of 1941 were the tremendous distances, the serried rivers of the Russian steppes.

There was always one more river to cross; the endless horizon stretched on and on. The land, the people, the climate, and the environment were psychologically oppressive to men from Western Europe.

The space seemed endless, the horizons nebulous. We were depressed by the monotony of the landscape, and the immensity . . . of forest, marsh and plain. Good roads were . . . few, bad tracks . . . numerous . . . rain quickly turned the sand or loam into a morass. The villages looked wretched and melancholy. . . . Nature was hard, and in her midst were human beings just as hard and insensitive—indifferent to weather, hunger, and thirst, and almost as indifferent to life and losses, pestilence and famine. The Russian civilian was tough, and the Russian soldier still tougher. He seemed to have an illimitable capacity for . . . endurance. . . .[17]

Rains in July slowed and mired wheeled vehicles on the Central Front. The deeper the Germans moved into Russia, the greater the strain on their supply system; the thin links of railroad steel, the few rutted roads were grossly inadequate, and gradually the impossible strain on the service of supply slowed and weakened the far-ranging spearheads. Distance had, too, a tactical as well as strategic effect. The Germans had fashioned *Blitzkrieg* around the tank and the plane. But in sealing the *Kessels*, the final confirmation of defeat depended largely upon the infantry.

The German Army of 1941 numbered twenty-one Panzer divisions (two in North Africa), and about fourteen or fifteen motorized divisions; the rest were infantry. In part this ratio was due to shortage of fuel oil, in turn a product of the British blockade. Yet the infantry (except for the Panzer grenadiers, or the mechanized infantry that was part of or accompanied the tank units) depended for its mobility upon its own legs, some mechanized but chiefly horse-drawn artillery, and wheeled vehicles. In the circumscribed spaces of the West, this limited mobility was adequate; in the vast distances of the East, it was a different matter. The infantry found it, from the first, a difficult matter to keep close behind the Panzers. As a result, even in the first encirclements, many Russians escaped the tightening noose; the infantry had not arrived in time to plug the gaps. Years later, after the war, a general named Dwight D. Eisenhower was to estimate that one of the major lessons of the Russian campaign was the need for tracked cross-country vehicles, armored infantry personnel carriers that could bring the foot soldiers into action quickly and that could keep up with the tanks.[18]

In the first weeks of fighting a system of centralized command was developing on both sides, which left little initiative to Army or even Army Group commanders. In East Prussia in the pine forests near Rastenburg, the so-called *Wolfsschanze* (Wolf's Lair) was established, a formidable and heavily guarded series of bombproof concrete-and-steel bunkers, half underground, which Hitler was to use as his headquarters for much of the war. It was connected by special train and courier plane to Berlin and to Army headquarters nearby. Here Keitel and Jodl and Hitler's political sycophants held sway, and it was from here, increasingly, that the fate of Germany was to be decided.

In Moscow, Stalin—ever suspicious—reacted predictably to invasion. The rigid political controls which had helped to cost the Soviet Army so dearly in the Finnish Winter War had been slightly relaxed and some improvements in the structure of the Red Army made as a result of the lessons of that bitter conflict. But on June 23, Stalin, worried as Russian Communists have always been about the possible dangers of "Bonapartism" (a military revolt) and about German subversive and Fifth Column activities, strengthened the political commissar system in the armed services and in effect created in each unit a dual political-military command system. A five-man State Defense Committee under Stalin was established, which was replaced in July and August by the Stavka of the Supreme Command, with Stalin as both Defense Commissar and Commander-in-Chief. The Stavka (roughly comparable to Hitler's OKW) consisted, at various times, of twelve to twenty senior military officers of all services. Marshal Boris M. Shaposhnikov, Chief of the General Staff, who probably deserved his titular accolade "master of modern Soviet strategy," was the senior military officer in the Stavka until he retired as a result of illness in the fall of 1942. From the beginning, a general who in 1941 was virtually unknown in the West but who had beaten the Japanese in frontier battles in Siberia—Georgi Zhukov—was a member. He was to emerge as Russia's greatest general.

The centralization of control had, at first, strong political overtones. Lavrenti P. Beria, a member of the State Defense Committee, set up detachments of his dreaded militarized NKVD in various key communications junctions behind the front, with orders to shoot or arrest stragglers or soldiers who retreated without authorization. In early July, Stalin—trying to stem the freshet of the German advance —ordered the execution of the commanding generals and staffs of the shattered West and Northwest fronts, a mordant warning that any officer who permitted retreat without orders would henceforth suffer summary execution.

But it was clear by early July that all this was not enough. On July 3 in a nationwide radio address Stalin, the paranoiac dictator, invoked the image of Mother Russia. Communist ideology had not proved an adequate substitute for national patriotism; now he called upon the images of the past to rally the shattered forces of the present. Ironically, even the heroes of czarist days were cited to defend communism. Nationalism was enlisted for the duration to protect an alien ideology. Hereafter it was to be the "Great Patriotic" (or "Great Fatherland") War as a psychological carrot, with the firing squads of the NKVD as the whip. And it was to be Total War: scorched earth and partisan warfare.

Stalin, who appeared dazed, bewildered, vague, in the first days of invasion, emerged from his Kremlin seclusion to impose his iron will upon his shattered armies. In these early days he insisted upon centralized command; every detail was passed upon by the Kremlin. It was not until Zhukov had emerged as a trustworthy commander (and one who, apparently, stood up with brusqueness to Stalin's tyranny) that he relaxed, slightly, some of his comprehensive control.

The Russian discipline was brutal; the guns and firing squads of the NKVD slaughtered those who faltered. "Justice" to those who retreated without orders, or who simply failed, was swift and summary; in those months of summer and fall, with the Russian backs to the wall, thousands of Red Army officers and men were killed by their fellow countrymen. For the common soldier it was fight and die—at the hands either of the Germans or of his own countrymen; these were his only alternatives. Some officers, terrified by their fear of the NKVD, pistol-whipped or shot their men. The guns of the Russian Army were aimed at the enemy; the guns of the NKVD were aimed at the backs of the Russian *moujiks*.

The command system at high and low levels was revised. Incompetents who had escaped the German encirclements were removed or executed; the political prison camps were combed for able officers arrested in the 1937-38 purges and some of these, with the red welts of prison beatings still livid on their backs, were hurried to the front. Divisions and armies of all types were reduced in size to tailor maneuver and supply to the capabilities of command; Draconian measures in mobilization of both manpower and matériel were initiated.

On July 10, three great fronts were established: Northwest, under Marshal Klementi I. Voroshilov; West, under Marshal S. K. Timoshenko; and Southwest, under Marshal Semën M. Budënny, the walrus-mustached cavalryman "hero" of the civil wars (described by one of his contemporaries as a man "with an immense mustache but very small brain"). These fronts were intended to coordinate and accelerate the direction of the various armies; they compared roughly to Army Group commands in the West. The Russian commanders, however, were initially political reliables—not skilled professional soldiers—and events, particularly the continued advances of the Germans, made this new grouping obsolescent in a short time. Throughout the war the Russians created new "Fronts" as competent commanders were developed, and to meet the fluctuating tactical situation.

The Northwest Front (or Army Group), defending the Baltic states and Leningrad, was the weakest of the three great Russian groupings. It numbered less than thirty divisions—only two of them tank divisions—organized into the Eighth and Eleventh Armies, with reserves.

The West Front, defending the Niemen and the Berezina, and the direct Minsk-Smolensk-Moscow Corridor, numbered more than fifty divisions, organized in the Third, Tenth, Fourth, and Thirteenth Armies, with reserves.

The strongest Soviet grouping was the Southwest Front, south of the Pripyat Marshes and along the Rumanian frontier. These forces numbered almost seventy divisions—five of them armored units—organized into the Fifth, Sixth, Twelfth, and Second Armies, with reserves.

In these first weeks of war, there was little consistent pattern. Here and there the sanguinary thread of battle to the death, of unrelenting struggle, was exposed; more often the bewildered peasants of the Russian steppes, obeying a herdlike mentality, waited until too late for orders that never came, fought briefly and dispersed in confusion, each man for himself, or retreated and died. Outflanked, they were surrounded and scooped up in droves.

But early on, the Germans encountered technical surprise; the thick armor of some of the Russian tanks defied the invaders' tank and antitank guns; only artillery and the 88 mm. antiaircraft were strong enough to knock them out.

The 17th Panzer Division near Senno, between the Dvina and the

Dnieper, met their first T-34 medium on July 8, and those few who lived still remembered it years later:

> ... Two, three, and then four tanks of 9th. Company were weaving around the Russian at 800–1,000 yards distance, firing. Nothing happened. ... The Russian continued to advance along a farm track. A German 3.7 cm. anti-tank gun was in position there.
> "Fire!"
> But the giant just seemed to shrug the shells off. Its broad tracks were full of tufts of grass and crushed haulms of grain. Its engine note rose. The Russian driver was engaging his top gear. ... The gunners fired furiously. Only twenty yards to go. Then ten, and then five.
> Now it was on top of them. The men leaped out of its way scattering. Like some huge monster the tank went straight over the gun. It ... drove on, through the German lines, towards the heavy artillery positions in the rear. Its journey did not end until nine miles behind the main fighting line, when it got stuck in marshy ground a short way in front of the German gun positions. A 10 cm. long-barrel gun of the divisional artillery finished it off. ...
> There are two reasons why the T-34 did not become a decisive weapon in the Summer of 1941. One was the wrong Soviet tank tactics—their practice of using the T-34 in driblets ... instead of using them in bulk at selected points. ... The second mistake was in their combat technique ... [a crew of four in each tank but no tank commander, and only one radio in a whole company of tanks].[19]

The Great Mistake?

On July 19, with the sack around Smolensk still open at the neck and a spearhead of Third Panzer Group at Beloj just 200 miles west of Moscow, the way to the capital seemed almost open. True, the battle of the Smolensk pocket was still raging; German infantry was still coming up to aid the Panzers, and Russian reserves were being thrown hurriedly piecemeal into battle on the Smolensk-Moscow front. But the Dnieper had long been crossed and the German Panzers held the natural gateway to the Soviet capital between the headwaters of the Dnieper and the Dvina. Guderian (Second Panzer Group) and Hoth (Third Panzer Group) believed that time was vital; the armored spearheads must not halt, they thought, but must drive on rapidly toward Moscow, giving the enemy no chance to reorganize. Guderian thought Moscow was within his grasp and probably with it decisive victory in Russia. Bock, commander of Army Group Center, shared their views.

Hitler would have none of it. The architect of daring plans and grandiose dreams, his judgment faltered in the crux. Apparently he believed that he had destroyed the bulk of the strength of the Red Army, yet he appeared concerned about the relatively slow progress of Rundstedt's Army Group South—its northern flank raked by the Soviet Fifth Army, sheltered behind the vast bogs of the Pripyat Marshes. And in the north he saw Leningrad, where Bolshevism was born, as an objective which, if won, might result in the psychological collapse of the Communist resistance.

In Directive No. 33, issued on July 19, he ordered the diversion of the two Panzer Groups in Army Group Center to aid the flanks. Guderian's Second Panzers were to swing south to aid Rundstedt's Army Group South in a great roundup near Kiev; and Hoth's Third was to drive north to cut the Moscow-Leningrad railroad and road and help Leeb's Army Group North in the attack on Leningrad. An ominous supplement reiterated one of the great political errors of the war: in rear areas conquered by the Germans, greater security would be provided "by applying appropriate Draconian measures, not by requesting more security forces."

The result has been called a repetition of the "Marne miracle," in reference to the early battle of World War I which saved Paris from the German invaders. But in the hot summer of 1941 Moscow was saved not so much by its defenders as by its attackers, who—the prize almost within their grasp—turned away.

It took some time for the turning.

The *Kesselschlacht* around Smolensk was not cleaned up until August; there and elsewhere along the front, reorganization, consolidation, and resupply required several weeks, and discussion continued with various directives and conferences. In the meantime, Army Group South in early August achieved its first major encirclement around Uman, where Rundstedt's First Panzer Group and Seventeenth and Eleventh German Armies smashed ten to twenty Russian divisions, and moved on toward the Dnieper bend. This success seemed to serve as confirmation of the generals' well-nigh unanimous views that the bulk of the German power should be concentrated on the Central Front, not dispersed to the flanks.

Brauchitsch, Army commander, and Halder, Chief of Staff, agreed with their field commanders that the drive for Moscow should have first priority, but Hitler, contemptuous of the "ossified brains" of his generals, was obdurate.

In turn, Halder, as early as July 14, noted in his diary that "perpetual interference by the Fuehrer . . . is becoming a scourge which will eventually be intolerable."

In a conference at Army Group Center on August 4, Bock, Guderian, and Hoth all urged a continuation of the Moscow offensive. Hitler overrode their arguments, but for two weeks the debate continued.

The ultimate result, an order of August 21, 1941, showed what Warlimont calls "a classic instance of a basic fault in Hitler's leadership, the desire to command in detail, without having studied the background adequately."

Moscow, in Hitler's thinking, and in operational plans, remained in this crucial period a secondary objective. Directive No. 34 of August 21 stated that the principal objective

> that must be achieved . . . before the onset of Winter, is not the capture of Moscow, but rather, in the South, the occupation of the Crimea and the industrial and coal region of the Donets, together with isolation of the Russian oil region in the Caucasus and, in the north, the encirclement of Leningrad and junction with the Finns.[20]

Hitler's will prevailed, and the two Panzer Groups in Army Group Center were diverted to the south and north. Second Army from Army Group Center also turned south to help eliminate a large Russian pocket near Gomel and to aid Rundstedt in closing a gigantic pocket east of Kiev; and Army Group Center paused, on the defensive, giving a little ground to Russian counterattacks.

The results, at least in the Ukraine, appeared to justify Hitler's judgments.

Guderian's Panzers sliced southward—the left flank daringly exposed to Soviet attack; Kleist's First Panzers swung north across the Dnieper, and on September 15–16, despite rain and mud, the steel pincers met at Konotop and Romny.

But it was a loose sack, and for hundreds of miles behind the most advanced German units, Soviet soldiers were roaming—some in disciplined, organized units, others scattered, fleeing survivors. One unit, the 2nd Cavalry Division (horsed), using troikas (machine-gun armed carts drawn by three horses), harried some German units successfully and evaded both air surveillance and ground destruction. Off the main highway from Korosten to Kiev the Russians surprised a German bivouac:

> . . . there was the sound of horses, and . . . a dust cloud to the south. . . . Then they were upon us . . . like an American film of the Wild West . . . sturdy little horses riding at a gallop through our camp. Some of the Russians were using sub-machine guns, others were swinging sabres. I saw two men killed by the sword less than ten meters from

me. . . . The machine gunners started blasting us at very close ranges with enfilade fire . . . soon tents and lorries were ablaze and through it the screams of wounded men caught in the flames. . . .[21]

On September 19–20 Kiev, or what was left of it, was occupied by the German Sixth Army amidst sniper fire and street fighting and "wild chaos"; and by September 26 the greatest German roundup of the summer had been achieved.

It was wholesale slaughter and desperate battle. Some Russians—many units out of ammunition, fighting isolated actions—struggled to the death, advancing against German artillery firing over open sights that piled the corpses as high as grain. Soviet soldiers used teeth and nails in the last desperate struggles. For the surrounded units there was no surcease from exhortation and ideology; loudspeakers had been rigged to important defense positions and

During the fighting the words of Stalin, magnified to gigantic proportions by the loudspeakers, rain down upon the men kneeling in holes behind the tripods of their machine-guns, din in the ears of the soldiers lying amid the shrubs, of the wounded writhing in agony upon the ground. The loudspeaker imbues that voice with a harsh, brutal, metallic quality. There is something diabolical, and at the same time terribly naïve, about these soldiers who fight to the death, spurred on by Stalin's speech on the Soviet constitution. . . .[22]

It was as if the childlike soldiers of the steppes were listening in their death throes to the voice of God—or the Devil.

But it did them no good; Russian communications and control, Russian mobility, Russian generalship were grossly inferior to the Germans'.

Many Soviet generals were killed or taken prisoner; Budënny was relieved by Timoshenko. Thousands were killed around Kiev, almost 700,000 Russians (the Germans estimated) herded into prison camps; the booty included almost 900 tanks, 3,700 guns, 3,500 motor vehicles. It seemed as if the southern Russian fronts were forever smashed. Indeed, in the extreme south the Rumanians, by early October, were investing Odessa, and General Fritz Erich von Manstein's Eleventh Army had reached the Crimea.

Kiev was a tremendous tactical victory—perhaps the greatest of the summer—but, as events were to show, a strategic mistake.

As the cattle cars rumbled back from the Ukraine toward Germany carrying the bewildered Russian peasant-prisoners, some of whom would become the industrial fodder for German factories, the shape of the Northern Front was congealing as the dusk of the short days of winter and the cold of the Arctic settled over the battlefields.

While the Germans moved toward Leningrad, thousands of Russians were pinned against the Baltic Sea in small encirclements. In late August, an attempted seaborne evacuation of Tallinn resulted in disaster; the botched operation cost thousands drowned, and more than two dozen ships lost. In any other campaign Tallinn would have ranked alongside Dunkirk as an epic battle, but against the vast panorama of the Russian front, it was but a minor tragedy in a titanic struggle.

Leeb's Army Group North in late August and September completed the investment of Leningrad, the noble "Venice of the North." Leeb's progress had been helped, initially, by a narrower front and shorter distances than those of Army Groups South and Center, and the friendly peoples of the Baltic states had aided the advancing Germans. The German sea flank suffered little interruption from the Russian Baltic Fleet; in fact, throughout the war the Russian naval vessels in the Baltic were often conspicuous for their uselessness, except as floating batteries and occasionally as supply vessels. But, as Army Group North advanced, its front grew wider; that old factor, Russian space and distance, loomed large; the Germans were more dispersed and they faced not only north and northeastward but east. They moved through a region of many rivers and streams, swamps, bogs, and forest which slowed progress. And around Lake Ilmen and the Valdai Hills, the Sixteenth Army, with too few men for too vast a front, was running into a hornet's nest. Unlike the Southern and Central fronts there were no gigantic encirclements and battles of annihilation in the north; there were smaller *Kessels* and the Russians lost heavily, but usually some remnants escaped to fight another day.

As the German tanks rumbled closer and closer to Leningrad, the isolated metropolis, in extremis and virtually cut off from outside aid, rallied to save itself. A million civilians, working day and night, toiled on trench lines, antitank ditches, barricades, minefields, improvising field fortifications of any kind. Elements of the German 20th Panzer Division, pursuing the broken and fleeing remnants of the Forty-eighth Soviet Army, fought around Mga in late August and early September and severed the last rail and road connection between Leningrad and the rest of Russia. Desperately, using people's militia, short on training, lightly armed but led by Communist fanatics and prodded by the politically reliable workers' battalions, NKVD border guard and police troops, and scattered decimated units and bits of units rounded up from the straggling ruck of defeat, a defense line was built up along the Neva. This front, looping south of Leningrad from the Gulf of Finland along the Neva to Lake Ladoga, was held by a motley collection grouped under the Soviet Forty-second Army. Further west along the Gulf—isolated in a separate coastal enclave, its back to the sea—was the Russian Eighth Army, remnants battered and broken, but bolstered by sailors of the Baltic Fleet, militia from Leningrad, and armed civilians; its defenses covered the Communist island naval base and fortress at Kronstadt.

But now, at the end of summer, the Finns proved recalcitrant. Finland, hungry to regain the territories lost in the Winter War, officially joined the campaign against Russia on June 25, after "severe Soviet air attacks on the cities of Southern Finland." It was to be, in Baron Mannerheim's phrase, the "Continuation War," with Finland interested, above all, in regaining the "former Finnish territories, and secondly, in what might be called the Finnish Irredenta in Eastern Karelia."[23]

"Towards adventurous sallies into the wide-open spaces of Russia in support of the German strategy," Mannerheim was "cold."

The Finns, a nation of 4 million people, mobilized for the Continuation War half a million men in uniform, 30,000 military construction auxiliaries, and 80,000 women auxiliaries (*Lottas*).[24]

In accordance with concerted plans, Mannerheim struck first north of Lake Ladoga with three small corps, the equivalent of about six and a half divisions, reinforced by one below-strength German division. Initial progress in this area of glacial moraine—scooped-out lakes, boulders, pine forest—was rapid; some units advanced 65 miles in six days. Soviet defenses were riddled, units cut off, and in July, August, and September the Finns pushed on between Lake Ladoga and Lake Onega and retook the old Finnish city of Sortavala on August 16. They reached the Svir River east of Lake Ladoga—one of their objectives—on September 7–8. They had regained their lost territories and had cut the Murmansk-Belomorsk-Volkhov Railroad at several points (Svir Station on September 8; Petrozavodsk on October 1; and Medvezhegorsk on December 5–6). The encircled Russians, with their backs to Lake Ladoga, escaped by boat.

During the summer, the Finns broadened their offensive, throwing seven more divisions against the Russians with a main effort concentrated west of Lake Ladoga and southeastward down the narrow neck of the Karelian Isthmus directly toward Leningrad. In a four-week offensive ending in early September, the Finns overran Soviet defenses in the isthmus and returned the frontier to its former position. A Russian garrison in the old Finnish town of Viborg was cut off (August 29); much of it was ultimately mopped up, but a large group, leaving all heavy equipment behind, got away to islands off the coast, and eventually joined the defenders of Leningrad. Thus, by early September, the siege lines had ringed Leningrad; on the Karelian Isthmus, three Finnish corps faced the battered Russian Twenty-third Army.

It looked, as fall began, like the end of Leningrad; it was, in fact, the beginning of one of the grimmest sieges in history, the siege of the "900 Days."[25]

There was still a gap between Finns and Germans east and south of Lake Ladoga; and tenuous communication between Leningrad and the rest of Russia across the lake was still possible. The German High Command believed the gap must be closed around Lake Ladoga to reach the Svir, and along the eastern side of the isthmus itself to cut off the city of Leningrad from the shores of the lake. In August and September, there were numerous communications and high-level staff consultations between Germans and Finns; Jodl even flew to Finland to cajole Mannerheim with a fistful of Iron Crosses. But Mannerheim temporized; he would close up perhaps a mile or two to the Russian fortifications along the Karelian Isthmus, but no farther, nor would he move beyond the Svir.

The rest would be up to the Germans. And the Germans now believed that Leningrad—invested and besieged—would die on the vine; assault was neither necessary nor desirable.

In the extreme north, Dietl's XXXVI Corps and a mountain corps, under Falkenhorst, commanding in Norway, bolstered by some Finnish troops, had bogged down in a drive toward Murmansk, crippled more by terrain, weather, and logistics than by effective Soviet resistance. Murmansk and its nexus of Soviet bases, its ice-free port, its sea link to the West, was only 56 miles from the Finnish-Soviet frontier, but in the terrible wilderness of the North it might as well have been the moon.

> . . . East of Pechenga . . . the rock surface is gouged and molded into a wild jumble of rises and depressions; giant boulders, rocks and gravel . . . rocky tundra . . . hundreds of lakes . . . coniferous forests of the taiga . . . The Winter, which on this inhospitable coast, lasts from October to May [is] a succession of arctic storms and blizzards . . . patches of snow and ice often last through the Summer [when] . . . winds off the ocean drive in banks of fog which blanket the coast for periods ranging from a few hours to weeks. . . .[26]

As the birch leaves blazed with autumn gold in the Russian forests, Hitler turned again toward Moscow, pleased with his own successes. His strategic judgments, he thought, had been proven; he was becoming more and more intolerant and contemptuous of those who cautioned or opposed him. The tanks and infantry that had been diverted north and south from Army Group Center were ordered back to Bock's command, and the march on Moscow resumed. As late as August 21 Hitler had renounced Moscow as a principal objective before "the onset of Winter"; now, in a new directive, of September 6, he planned two great encirclements on the Central Front. He was confident that he could "break the enemy on the threshold of winter."

And so the new Napoleon turned again toward the city that to him symbolized the despised "*Untermensch*." But the change of objectives, the diversion from the inexorable theorem that a straight line is the shortest distance between two points, had cost the Germans the "unforgiving minute" and had bestowed upon the Russians on the Central Front the blessings of breathing space.

In September 1941 the German Army, after more than two months of lightning war, of the greatest land battles in history, of continuous operations and unending marching, was feeling the strain. Personnel casualties—although minimal compared with the huge Russian losses—had totaled 409,998 (87,489 killed in action, the rest wounded or missing) up to August 31, and only 217,000 replacements had been absorbed into the combat units. Some twenty-one out of the Army High Command's twenty-four reserve divisions had already been committed. And German intelligence was reporting more Soviet divisions in action than had been known to exist before the invasion started.

Even as early as August 15, Halder had noted in his diary: "We reckoned with 200 Russian divisions. Now we have already counted 360."

Even more mordant to the tactics of *Blitzkrieg* were the tank losses. Guderian's Panzers, which had been roaring across thousands of miles of roadless terrain, had been particularly stretched. About 47 percent of the total tank strength available in the Russian theater was ready for action; the rest was disabled or under repair. Trucks and other motor vehicles were also down, in huge quantities. Fuel was short. In fact, except for Army Group North, which had shorter lines of communication, supplemented by sea, the German Army hundreds of miles deep in Russia was already experiencing the exasperating restrictions of scarcity.[27]

Nevertheless, the first great blows of "Operation Typhoon" on the Central Front broke with ease through the thin and inadequate crust of the Russian defenses. On the road Napoleon trod, the Soviet generals had not used time well. The Germans concentrated under Bock three Panzer Armies (upgraded from Groups) and the Ninth, Fourth, and Second Armies on a 150-mile front against some fifteen disorganized and half-trained Soviet "armies" only loosely coordinated, and poorly commanded. Two great *Kesselschlachts* were planned—and quickly accomplished. The offensive jumped off on September 30. Guderian drove 85 miles in one day; by the fourth day, Orel was captured; by October 8, two great sacks had been drawn around the struggling Russian soldiers, enmeshed by the thousands in far-flung encirclements, around Vyazma and around Bryansk. By October 18, Mozhaisk, 65 miles from Moscow, was captured, and the thrashing, convulsive struggles of the armies in the net were weakening.

The brittle state of Communist morale was again, as at Kiev and Smolensk, exposed by the sharp blow of defeat. The will to fight—in many Soviet units never very strong in the summer and fall of 1941—was again fractured; many thousands of Russian soldiers and numerous officers deserted or easily surrendered. In the twin battles of Vyazma and Bryansk, the Germans claimed 663,000 prisoners, 1,242 tanks, and 5,412 guns.

Nothing like such bags of prisoners, such enormous booty, had ever before been recorded in war; there appeared to be sound reason for Hitler's confidence. Indeed, in Berlin Goebbels claimed that the great victories marked the end of the war against Russia.

Yet wars are not won by statistics. October presaged what was to come. On October 7, the first snow of the season fell, omen of the future. Then the rains came and "General Mud" aided the Russians. German movement was slowed and mired:

> Entire companies were pulling bogged-down lorries out of the mud. The motor cyclists made wooden skids for their machines from boards . . . and pulled them along behind them. . . . Motorized convoys were stuck in the mud [but] . . . light farmcarts [pulled] by . . . small tough horses, commandeered from local peasants got through. . . .[28]

The job of mopping up the giant pockets and an inching advance toward the spires of Moscow used up the rest of the days of fall.

The Gates of Moscow

In addition to nature, two men were to play key roles in the Battle of Moscow—one on the scene, the other a hemisphere away.

On October 7, the day the first snow fell, a general who had already earned a reputation against the Japanese in the Siberian border fighting and who had been, in September, in command of the encircled Leningrad defenses, reported to the Kremlin. Destined to become the Soviet Union's outstanding military leader in World War II, General of the Army (later Marshal) Georgi K. Zhukov was "tough, apparently nerveless, impassive, and often bitingly sarcastic."[29] He was ruthless and even implacable, but with a certain charm and childlike vanity,[30] and he was not afraid of Stalin, whose tight political rein on the Army he had in the past cautiously opposed.

After personally surveying the chaotic and confused Central Front, Zhukov reported to Stalin that "the routes to Moscow are virtually undefended."[31] He was appointed to command the newly merged Western Army (or "Front") and Moscow Reserve Army groups, upon whom victory or defeat in a decisive battle of World War II now rested.

With a terrible sleepless energy, a scourging tongue and will of iron, Zhukov set about his defense.

Early on, he clearly showed who was the boss. Marshal (then General) Konstantin Rokossovski, who commanded the Sixteenth Army on the Central Front, proposed to withdraw his troops to a better defense line. Zhukov, "having heard our proposal and request, categorically disagreed with us and ordered us to stand to the death without retreating a step."

Rokossovski went over Zhukov's head to Shaposhnikov, Chief of the General Staff, who authorized the withdrawal the Sixteenth Army commander proposed. The withdrawal "had undoubtedly been agreed upon with the Supreme Commander in Chief (Stalin), or . . . in any case, he knew of it."

But before the withdrawal could start a sharp telegram reversed it: "The troops of the Army Group are under *my* command. I revoke the order . . . and order that the defense be maintained on the present line without retreating a step backward. General of the Army Zhukov."[32]

Yet the Moscow defense might never have succeeded without the aid of a second man far from the scene of battle. In Japan, the Communist spy Richard Sorge, who had correctly reported to Moscow the date and the plans for the German invasion of Russia, had been reporting throughout the summer and early fall (even after a Japanese mobilization in August) that Japan would not attack Siberia, but would turn southward against Britain and the United States. His messages, which continued until shortly before his arrest and the breaking of one of the most successful spy rings of the war in October, were at last accepted by Stalin, and the dictator commenced to tap a reserve the Germans could not match, the thirty divisions of the Siberian armies in the Far East—tough, hardy, and well trained.

Near Borodino, 62 miles from Moscow, where Napoleon thought he had won a bloody victory, the Germans on October 14 first met these hard, fresh troops—the 32nd Siberian Rifle Division, transferred from Vladivostok. It was a grim battle, without quarter.

The Siberians were "tall, burly fellows in long greatcoats, with fur caps on their heads and high fur boots. . . . They fought impassively. There was never any panic. They stood fast and held on. They killed and let themselves be killed. . . ."[33]

To gain time—the precious minutes squandered in the summer when Hitler had turned south—the Siberians stood and died; the Russians used their new T-34 tanks en masse; their Katyushas laid down a barrage of rockets which saturated whole areas. But at the last the fighting was between man and man, armed with rifle butts, bayonets, spades, and picks. The Siberians "died on the hills of Borodino." They exacted tribute; a decimated regiment of the Reich Motorized SS Infantry Division had to be disbanded. And, allied with nature, they won some grudging minutes.

The German advance slowed, engulfed in mud. Some of Guderian's troops had to be supplied by air. In one short stretch of so-called motor highway, 2,000 to 3,000 vehicles were mired in mud morass and water-filled craters, and infantry divisions which had averaged a rate of advance in most of the summer months of 28 miles a day slowed to 1 to 3.[34]

But there was panic in Moscow. On the night of October 15/16 the flight began. It was rumored that the mummified body of Lenin had been removed from the Mausoleum in Red Square. Evacuation of part of the government, the diplomatic corps, and state records and valuables to Kuibyshev and other cities was ordered; with them thousands fled; eventually, perhaps 2 million people streamed to the east. Stalin and his principal advisers stayed in the Kremlin, but dissidents and panicmongers—as always in history—raised their heads as the enemy advanced.

Until October 19 there was an interregnum of terror. Factories closed down. Hoarding, particularly of sugar and flour, started. Rumors proliferated: German tanks were on the outskirts of the city; parachutists were "seen" everywhere; the war was lost. The anti-Communists were emboldened; Fifth Columnists dared to surface. Swastikas and death's heads were scrawled on posters or walls; handbills, lettered "Death to the Communists," appeared in mailboxes. There was looting and plundering, mysterious fires flared, and each night the city rang with rifle fire.

The disorders, threatening to flare into disaster, were not checked until October 19, when the Stavka (State Defense Committee) issued a state of siege order for Moscow and its environs, and NKVD troops were moved into the capital to shoot looters and panic-mongers on sight and restore order.

These late October and November days had an air of desperation, of catastrophe, about them. Not only the Germans but many Russians and most of the world thought Moscow was *kaput*. Stalin himself probably faltered. Zhukov—like Kutuzov a generation before—appears to have been the dominant force in the defense. There is some murky evidence that the Great Dictator sporadically lost in this year of crisis not only his iron confidence but his ability to command. (Earlier in the summer he had seemed to be on the verge of breakdown, and later, various callers found him "nervous . . . jittery . . . confused . . . eyes not steady. . . .")[35]

It was neither the ideology of communism nor the machinery of government that saved Moscow, but the slow burgeoning of nationalism—the invocation of long-forgotten pride and remembrance of things past, the call of the good earth, the primeval reaction of men fighting to survive against the depredations of their conquerors.

Moscow girded for siege. As new combat units were created out of hastily trained militia and thrown into the breach, as the Siberians were transferred from east to west, as the mud froze and the ground hardened, at least 100,000 Muscovites—most of them women, some of them from the thin upper crust of Communist society—organized in labor battalions dug miles of trenches and antitank ditches along the city's approaches, built more than 1,400 pillboxes, and strung barbed-wire fences. They worked with bleeding blistered hands and frostbitten toes day and night, strafed and killed and wounded by German planes.

Despite sporadic panic and wild confusion in Moscow and along the entire front, what had to be done was somehow accomplished.

The gaping holes in the front were plugged with new bodies—untrained, half-armed, badly led. Behind the fighting, sometimes just in advance of the approaching Germans, trains and trucks and manpower moved factories to the east. Almost 500 factories in the capital were emptied; the then Russian industrial heart in the Donbas was evacuated. The bulk of Soviet tank, plane, and munitions production was shifted gradually—and at the cost for many months of production quotas—to the Urals and Siberia, where displaced workers built new facilities, installed machine tools, and gradually resumed output.

On November 7, in a gesture intended to raise the morale of the defenders, units of the Home Guard and the Red Army paraded defiantly through Red Square, skidding on ice and snow, but fortunately protected from German bombs by low visibility.

The climactic battle now began.

By November 12, much of the ground on the Central and Northern fronts was frozen; Guderian, who had stalled within 2 miles of Tula in October, and the bogged German armies were now largely freed from the clutching mud.

And in north and south the sweet song of German triumph continued to ring in Hitler's ears. By mid-November, the siege ring around Leningrad had been tightened, islands in the Gulf of Riga captured; the town of Tikhvin, site of important bauxite deposits and a nodal communications point south and east of Lake Ladoga on the way to junction with the Finns, had been captured, and North and Central fronts were linked near the Valdai Hills. In the south Rundstedt, after his slow summer start, had easily penetrated the great flaring gaps in the enemy's broken front and had captured in a long procession of triumph Odessa—the key Black Sea naval base, seaport, and shipbuilding center—on October 16 and Perekop on October 29. By mid-November Kharkov and Belgorod had fallen. The German armies had reached and crossed the Donets, and were mopping up the Crimea; Sevastopol was ringed, the Kerch Peninsula being overrun, at least another 100,000 bedraggled prisoners captured, and German Panzers were nearing Rostov, gateway to the Caucasus and its oil and to the industrial locus of the Donets Basin.

When the drive for Moscow was resumed on November 16, it seemed all over save for the Iron Crosses, the laurel wreaths, the cheers. . . .

Yet the German leaders knew the hour was late, their armies worn and tired; that there would be, in normal seasons, just a brief interlude (perhaps a month at most) of light freeze before the onset of the bone-chilling temperatures of the Russian winter. The German armies were not properly equipped for winter fighting; the pre-planning had not contemplated it. Their lube oil was summer-grade. Batteries died, tank and truck engines were hard to start; fingers and toes froze and men suffered. General Günther von Kluge, who commanded the Fourth Army, a part of Army Group Center, sometimes brought to his daily map briefings in his headquarters a well-thumbed copy of Caulaincourt's famous account of the death of Napoleon's Grand Army during the retreat from Moscow.[36]

Combat effectiveness was down; high officer losses and tanks knocked out, disabled, or deadlined for lack of spare parts, and a tight supply situation—long lines, few roads, inadequate railroads, and the increasing harassment in rear areas of Soviet partisans—dictated a halt, resupply, replacement, and rest. Some of the German statisticians figured that in terms of real combat effectiveness there were now the equivalent of only eighty-three full-strength German divisions in Russia.[37]

Yet Moscow was so close, barely 40 miles away from the German vanguard; to take it might well be the knockout punch. The missed opportunity at the Battle of the Marne in 1914 was always in the German mind.

There were divided councils in the High Command—but not for long. Rundstedt in the south, Leeb in the north, wanted to call a halt; Bock, in the center, backed by Brauchitsch and Halder, wanted to attack. In a military conference at Orsha on November 13 the soldiers were divided; but the die had been cast. Halder told his colleagues that Hitler had already decided to attack in a great enveloping movement around Moscow. The rail junctions well beyond the city were to be taken to block the arrival of more Siberian reserves, and once Moscow was captured the Kremlin was "to be blown up, to signalize the overthrow of Bolshevism."[38]

These grandiose plans, somewhat tempered and modified by military realism, ultimately involved: a direct frontal attack by Kluge's Fourth Army, with thirty-six understrength divisions, and two Panzer pincers; Hoth, reinforced by Hoepner's Fourth Panzer Army (transferred from Army Group North), swinging around Moscow from the north and west; and Guderian's tanks coming in from the south, their flanks protected by Bock's other two armies.

The German soldiers were more confident—despite their hardships —than their generals. Moscow was so near; they had not read Caulaincourt. At times on clear, cold nights, they could see the flash of explosions on the distant horizon as German bombers wheeled above Moscow. Just one more push, and "the glorious conclusion of a hard campaign and the prospect of well-earned rest. . . . May the Lord of Hosts grant . . . success."[39]

On November 15, on lightly frozen ground and in snow-covered mud, the great offensive opened, both sides desperate for a victory that might change the course of history. Fourth Army, astride the Mozhaisk-Moscow road, which had been fighting off repeated Soviet counterattacks throughout November, immediately ran into problems. The Russian attacks were so vicious that in some parts of the front Kluge was hard put to hold, much less to advance. The wings made initial rapid progress; Guderian drove deep into the enemy's southern flank, and the Third and Fourth Panzer Armies looped close to Moscow in the north.

But weather and the Siberians, plus Zhukov's canny generalship, first slowed, then halted the high-water mark of German conquest. In the last two weeks of November and the early days of December 1941, the savage Russian winter with subzero temperatures, biting wind, and howling snow came early to the Russian land. Tank engines froze and died; immobile monsters dotted the landscape. Artillery recoil mechanisms jammed; rifles and submachine guns froze for lack of winter lubricants; the flesh of exposed fingers peeled off in strips on ice-cold triggers. The German soldiers had no winter boots, no adequate gloves. They cut strips from their overcoats for foot bindings or wrapped their feet in huge cumbrous "baskets" of straw; even as late as November 19, when some winter clothing started to trickle through to front-line units, certain detachments had only one greatcoat to a gun crew.[40]

The iron defense of winter was buttressed by the iron resolve of Zhukov and of Stalin; the battle cry of World War I, "They Shall Not Pass," was echoed by the Russians in the Battle of Moscow in World War II. The Soviet commanders expended blood like water. Again and again and again the sanguinary orders, to hold fast and die, were issued; again and again fresh troops or half-trained militia were fed piecemeal into battle to plug with their bodies—like sandbags atop a dike—the rising flood of German conquest. On November 17, near Klin, elements of Hoepner's Army were attacked by horsed cavalry, who swept out of a wood with drawn sabers and at full gallop in furious charge. They were greeted with antitank guns, field artillery, and machine guns at point-blank range. The result: "Two thousand horses and their riders—both regiments of the 44th

Mongolian Cavalry Division—lay in the bloodstained snow, torn to pieces, trampled to death, wounded. . . ."[41] Not a German hurt.

But the seemingly senseless sacrifice had won some fleeting minutes, and the Russians, rejecting a static defense, carried out unending insensate attacks and counterattacks which slowly wore the Germans down.

And on November 25 came another omen: two "strange-looking" Soviet tanks were destroyed; the Germans found they were British tanks shipped to Murmansk—the first installment of British aid to reach the front.

The cold forever deepened, but still the Germans moved closer to the glittering spires of Moscow. Elements of a Panzer Corps in the Third Panzer Army under a colonel to be known to fame, Hasso von Manteuffel, established a bridgehead across the last main Soviet line of defense along the Moscow-Volga Canal. Simultaneously they seized one of the capital's major electric power-generating stations, only to lose it in furious Russian counterattack. On November 30, Krasnaya Polyana fell; one battalion advanced to within 19 miles of the Kremlin, 12 miles from the city's outskirts. Another took Khimki, 5 miles from the city's boundaries; some small units actually penetrated the city's suburbs. . . .

In early December, with a deep freeze settled over the land and German soldiers suffering in tight summer hobnailed jackboots, Bock and Kluge made their final effort. It was against an enemy growing now in strength, some of them fresh troops, clad in winter greatcoats and camouflage capes to match the snow, in felt boots and warm mittens. Kluge's Fourth Army, in the center, pushed straight toward Moscow against fanatic opposition and in ever-deepening cold.

And in increasing darkness. The days were short. Twilight settled over the vast northern forests in midafternoon; the nights were long and cruel. Nowhere in these vast Russian spaces was the "front" continuous. Both sides seized and held in force key terrain features and communications points; in between, mobile forces—their mobility slowed now by the snow—roamed. There were open flanks and often open rear; the enemy could be anywhere and everywhere.

The Fourth Army pushed into the forests around Moscow. Later, when the war was won, the Russians admitted to "deep" penetrations.

But not deep enough, and the Germans were bleeding from a thousand cuts. Companies were down to twenty-eight men; regiments became battalions; divisions, regiments. Slowly in the first days of December, as the temperatures dropped to 20, 30, and 40 degrees below zero, the offensive congealed. Shelter in the appalling cold was vital; man could not long remain exposed and live. Many wounded froze to death, their anguish mercifully anesthetized by the cold. Some of the Russians—ill-prepared, hastily trained militia, inadequately clothed, warmed only by overdoses of vodka—suffered as much as the Germans. Little thatched-roof villages with log huts and storage sheds became the great prizes of battle; they offered shelter. Exposed sentries and pickets were reduced to a minimum number; most men crowded, with the frightened Russian peasants, into the houses and around the stoves. Bricks were warmed in the ovens, "wrapped in rags and placed on the locks of the [German] machine guns to prevent the oil from freezing."[42] The Russian counterattacks were implacable to their own as well as to the Germans. To deny the enemy shelter, Soviet guns fired at the farmhouses, flared the thatched roofs.

Fourth Army pushed within sight of Moscow, its forward units 27 miles from the Kremlin. Elements of the 258th Infantry Division actually infiltrated into the barricaded suburbs of the city; they were met by Soviet factory militia and a few hoarded tanks. But the German spearheads were heavily counterattacked in the darkness; Fourth Army was finished and Bock and Kluge knew it. Army Group Center should have halted days ago, retrenched, retired, and prepared defensive positions for winter. But Bock had originally favored the gamble, and Hitler had egged him on. On December 1, Bock had conceded the "dangerous" situation to OKH:

. . . large-scale movements of any kind are out of the question. . . . The attack will probably result in limited territorial gains . . . but any strategic results are very unlikely. The idea that the enemy forces opposing Army Group would "collapse" is an illusion, as the fighting during the past fourteen days has shown. . . . difficult to see what sense there is in continuing the operation . . . the moment is now very near when the strength of the troops will be utterly exhausted. . . . Army Group is holding a front approximately 600 miles long, with only one division, and a weak one at that, in reserve. . . . in view of its heavy losses in officers, and its greatly declining battle strength, it could not withstand a systematic and organized attack. . . .[43]

On the night of December 3, acting under "general permission [given by Hitler] to break off the attack at the point when it became quite clear there was no longer any hope of success,"[44] Bock and Kluge started to pull back the dangerously exposed forward elements of Fourth Army to their original jump-off positions.

In the next two days, the armored flanks of Army Group Center also broke off contact with the enemy and started withdrawals from exposed forward salients to shorter lines. The spires of Moscow receded into the distance, never again to loom—a mirage—upon the German mind.

A Fighting Retreat

The withdrawal was just in time, for catastrophe loomed for the Germans. Stalin and Zhukov, who had been throwing Siberians and militia and workers' battalions like cannon fodder into the breach, had been planning a switch to the offensive with fresh troops. The old adage—not always true—that the general who commits his reserves last wins the battle, was only part of the Russian strategy; its other allies were space for time and the onset of the curdling cold of the Russian winter. With an exquisite sense of timing, Zhukov judged that the Germans had reached the high tide of their effort. On the night of December 4/5, as the enemy pulled back all along the Moscow front, the continuous small-scale counterattacks that had distinguished the Russian defense blended into a single major counteroffensive, with three armies—the First Assault Army (strengthened by additional guns, mortars, and heavy weapons), and the Tenth and Twentieth Armies. At least eighteen fresh divisions, some of them Siberian, plus units scraped together by the Stavka and hoarded carefully by Stalin until the crucial moment, were committed. They were commanded by Russian generals, Rokossovski, Belov, Vlasov, whose names were to become famous, or infamous, in Soviet history.

The Russians had used their reserves last, and now their enemy was in perilous case indeed. At many points—particularly on the flanks of the Central Front—the Russians broke through, and isolated German units were soon fighting for their lives.

Throughout the rest of December 1941 the German legions backpedaled along much of the Russian front. In the center, Guderian abandoned his virtual encirclement of Tula, and the deep salient he had driven from the south toward Moscow; in the north, the armored spearheads pulled back from Klin and Kalinin (leaving behind many of their immobilized tanks) virtually to their starting point of mid-November.

Nor was retreat limited to the Central Front. The Tikhvin salient near Lake Ladoga was abandoned by the Germans on December 9, and, as the Nazis withdrew to a line from Novgorod to Leningrad, the strangling loop around Leningrad was loosened—though far from freed.

German troops and the Spanish Blue Division of volunteers raised in Spain by Franco to aid the Germans against Bolshevism (designated the German 250th Infantry Division) tried to hold along the Volkhov River. But the ice-congealed waters were no barrier; the Russians swarmed across in bitter fighting. By the middle of January, the Blue Division, which had originally numbered almost 18,000 men, had suffered about 3,000 casualties but had accomplished a political purpose—to preserve Spain's pro-Axis benevolent neutrality:

> The Blue Division enabled Franco and his foreign minister . . . to demonstrate their people's capacity for resistance to aggression, repaid a blood debt to the Germans and Italians for assistance in the Civil War, preserved their and Spain's anti-Bolshevik stance, and allowed certain ardent Falangists to work off their pro-Axis sympathies and political ambitions on the Russian front. . . .[45]

In the south, the Germans had seemingly scored their greatest success of the campaign, when on November 21, Rundstedt's spearhead —Kleist's First Panzer Army—had swept into Rostov on the Don, a great industrial city. But not for long. Army Group C was operating at the end of the longest supply lines of the war, tied to its home base of supplies in Germany by a slim thread—easily snapped—across the Dnieper. Mass, space, and time combined against the Panzers at the "gateway to the Caucasus." Timoshenko concentrated far superior forces against Rundstedt's extended spearhead, and the NKVD stationed riflemen in the rear of Soviet combat units, with orders to shoot any soldier who retreated or faltered.

On November 28, after a short-lived week of triumph, Kleist's Panzers were driven out of Rostov. Rundstedt sought permission to establish a defensive position along the Mius River, with Taganrog as a heavily fortified zone, or "hedgehog." Hitler refused; Rundstedt asked to be relieved. Reichenau took over, and the German spearheads were pushed back, in any case, to the line of the Mius, while in the Crimea, the German Eleventh Army was commencing at Christmastime to face fresh Soviet amphibious units, ferried by sea to the Kerch Peninsula.

Throughout December and on into the new year more and more Russian armies and divisions—some of them fresh, many of them still half-trained and half-equipped—were fed into what became a general counteroffensive. The fighting went on through lashing winds and waist-deep snow as Soviet ski patrols and the acclimated Siberians probed viciously at the beleaguered Germans. Stalin's purpose was grandiose, but his reach far exceeded his grasp. At this stage of the war he and many of his generals were still military novitiates with little understanding of the calculus of effort required for victory. He thought and apparently believed he could destroy the entire invading German Army in that first winter of fighting, even though the Russians enjoyed only slight—if any—superiority in numbers and none in guns or tanks. The Red Army was as tired, as broken, as bloodied as the Germans, and it did not have the discipline, the high level of leadership, and the superb organization and cohesiveness of its foe. Nevertheless from early December 1941 throughout much of that bitter winter the Germans were on the defensive, and the Russians held the initiative along most of the vast front.

The great gamble had failed. The granaries of the Ukraine had been overrun; much of the Soviet coal and iron production was in German hands. But the oil of the Caucasus was beyond the Nazi grasp; the line of the Volga had not been reached; Leningrad in the north had been almost encircled but not captured; and Moscow was receding in retreat. Neither the economic and political nor the military objectives of the lightning campaign of 1941 had been achieved. The Russian Army was still fighting, weakened but not annihilated. And (like the Battle of Britain, which transformed air *Blitzkrieg* into air attrition), lightning war had become a war of endurance, of attrition, a war against much of the world, a war which Hitler could not win.

Not all of these consequences could be clearly forecast in that frigid Christmas of 1941. The immediate dimensions of crisis forbade perspective, dwarfed in the minds of both sides the ultimate consequences. Throughout December crisis succeeded crisis. The Germans who had encircled were now, time after time, unit after unit, in danger of encirclement. The Russians, inexperienced in the handling of large units, too limited in mobility to seize breakthrough and outflanking opportunities quickly, nevertheless filtered through all gaps, pushing doggedly on.

Army Group Center still was in deep peril; Hitler, in what was perhaps his soundest decision of the war, stood firm against the near-panic of some of his generals and forbade any general retreat or major withdrawals.

They lead only to the irretrievable loss of heavy weapons and equipment. At the risk of their own lives, commanders and their officers must force their men to fanatical resistance, irrespective of whether the enemy may have broken through the flank or at the rear. Only by waging war in this way will it be possible to gain the necessary time to send reinforcements. . . .[46]

It was to be a fighting retirement, the shortening of the line by local retreats. But key supply and communications centers on railroads and main roads and the great dumps and support installations that had been built up around them were to be held as "hedgehogs," bristling with defenses against attacks in all directions. In areas where German units were caught in the open without houses or other shelter, explosives were used to blast deep craters in the frozen ground, and these were hastily roofed with logs and frozen dirt to provide dugouts and a modicum of warmth.[47] Thus the fabric of *Igelstellen*—a system of defended localities, where the soldiers could find shelter for the winter—was to be woven; the great spaces in between to be patrolled intermittently by small mobile units. The ultimate objective of victory was to be postponed, not abandoned.

Hitler's iron will averted what it had appeared might become another bloody, trampled trail of defeat, a second Napoleonic catastrophe. German units were encircled, but they fought their way out. Salients were being driven into the loose front, and as the year ended a key junction point, the town of Kaluga (an important "hedgehog" in the German defensive network), was recaptured by the Russians.

Yet, as 1942 dawned, the decimated German divisions on the Central Front—raddled by dysentery, eating the meat of dead horses—were still holding a serrated front line within 40 miles, at its closest point, to Moscow.

It was not the same Army as in the days of summer's bloom. By December 31, 1941, total German casualties in Russia—killed, wounded, prisoners, and missing—amounted to 830,903, about 25 percent of the average strength of 3.2 million men (exclusive of allies) employed in the Russian theater in this six-month period. There had been so many officer casualties that the reserve officer list was about exhausted; there could be no more replacements until the training schools turned out new officers in the spring. Rifles were scarce; production had to be increased. Tank and motor losses had been huge.[48]

The 6th Panzer Division, which had started the war with 260 tanks and had fought on both the Northern and Central fronts, consisted of a few soldiers and guns, but *no* tanks, by early January 1942.[49]

The Luftwaffe, a large part of its strength still tied down against the British (Luftflotte 2 was shifted to the Mediterranean during the campaign), at year's end numbered only about 1,700 aircraft on the Russian front.

The cold had been, perhaps, the greatest enemy of all, and the sudden onslaught of the terrible Russian winter was still costing the Germans heavily. The pre-campaign planning had estimated that winter clothing would be required only for some sixty divisions that would garrison conquered Russia after the fighting ceased; the shortfall became critical because of the early advent of the deep cold and major supply difficulties. Some German units, forced to fight without shelter, were hors de combat from frostbite. The cold cost the invaders more casualties in December than enemy bullets; the 12th Panzer Division in Army Group North reported in early December it had lost 63 men killed in action and 325 from frostbite. Some of the frostbite cases—more than 14,000—required amputations; at least 100,000 cases, with greater or lesser degrees of disability, were recorded.[50]

But the greatest blow of all was to German self-confidence and the knowledge that German mistakes, particularly a woeful underestimation of the enemy, had contributed to the severest German reversal of the war.

The Russians had gained grim determination and were settling down to learning the art of war from their invaders. Enough that they had survived; it had, indeed, been touch and go. Never before in history had a nation taken such losses; never before had an army been so badly beaten. In six months, the Germans had taken almost 3 million prisoners, an army almost as large as the original strength of the invaders; in six months the Germans had killed, by Russian admission, almost half a million Soviet troops and had wounded another million.[51] Never before had an army advanced so rapidly, so deeply, or overrun so much in so short a time; never before had the precision teamwork, the passionate attention to detail, the bravery— individually and collectively—and the superb morale of a military machine been so dramatically emphasized.

Never before had an army won such victories; never before had a nation suffered such defeats, yet without definitive end. And at the last, as the short days of winter brought the deep and awful cold, offense had turned into defense, advance into retreat. Victory had about it the taste of ashes.

But this was no time for doubt or recrimination. There was to be in that hard winter of 1941–42 short shrift indeed, on either side, for the fainthearted or the recalcitrant. In the German Army, heads rolled and reputations vanished in the first of many purges. Alan Clark states that "thirty-five corps and divisional commanders" were relieved.[52]

Commands of the Army Groups were changed. In addition to the Rundstedt-Reichenau shift in the south, Kluge relieved Bock in the center; and soon Leeb, Army Group North, who had shown little enterprise, was succeeded by General Georg von Küchler. The Ninth Army command was given to a junior general. But most important of all, Hitler, who was already Commander-in-Chief of all the German armed forces (OKW), accepted with alacrity the retirement of Field Marshal Walther von Brauchitsch, C-in-C of the Army, and assumed direct command of the Army (OKH, or Oberkommando Heeres), in addition to all his other duties. Brauchitsch, a weak man who had never been able to face Hitler's bluster or to influence him, had strongly favored the last abortive attempt against Moscow. But he had been ill; he had suffered a heart attack in November and he had to retire. Hitler welcomed the opportunity tacitly to pass the blame for failure to the Army generals, and to gain over them—his only potential rivals for power—that complete ascendancy which was to last throughout the war and was never successfully challenged.

Guderian, who so short a time before had been directing the southern pincer of the drive against Moscow from his headquarters at Yasnaya Polyana (where Tolstoy had fashioned his famous epic of the fate of another invader), lost his command, partly as a result of a dispute and personality clash with Kluge. Hoepner, whose Fourth Panzer Army had driven so close to the northern suburbs of Moscow, withdrew his forces—against Hitler's orders—to save them from encirclement. He was immediately cashiered and publicly disgraced, to die in a hangman's noose more than three years and millions of lives later, after his apparent participation in the abortive attempt to assassinate Hitler in July 1944.

And in the Soviet Army, the trial by fire had found wanting many of the old political reliables, sound of faith but militarily incompetent. Some were put out to pasture, or shifted to administrative tasks, like Budënny. A new generation of younger Soviet professionals began to take over; gradually generalship became more competent, in part as the tight reins of political control were somewhat relaxed. For the incompetent or the failures on either side there was little mercy, and for the enemy there was no quarter.

Retrospect

The Battle of Moscow undoubtedly was a turning point in World War II—more so than Stalingrad, which later was to mark the high tide of German effort. But it was not a turning point which can be defined only by the ebb and flow of battle around the Soviet capital, or in terms of military victories or tactical mistakes. In retrospect, it seems far clearer now than it did in 1941 that the fall of Moscow would not have ended Soviet resistance. It would have represented a great defeat, a powerful political and psychological as well as economic and logistical blow to the Russians. But, as in Napoleon's time, the Russian resistance would have continued; Stalin had everything to gain, nothing to lose by a fight to the death. And Hitler in a sense had defeated himself before the fall and winter battle started, not so much by diversion of his armored forces from center to south and north during the summer, nor by his emphasis on economic rather than military objectives, but by his own political policies.

Hitler was a perverted genius, but he was—or became—a megalomaniac whose desire for power knew no bounds. Even if Moscow had been captured and Russia defeated, Hitler's objectives would have been infinite, with only finite means of achieving them. As in the days of other conquerors, Persia and India already beckoned; instead of the spires of Moscow, the Taj Mahal. And it is clear that had Moscow fallen or had Russia sued for peace, sooner or later outright confrontation with the United States in a showdown for the world would have been inevitable. The fall of Moscow might have put a period to a chapter, but not the end to World War II.

Yet the attempt to achieve almost unlimited aims with finite or inadequate means which the invasion of Russia represented was only a part of Hitler's basic mistake, which was essentially political rather than military. Given the Europe of 1939–1941, a collision between communism and fascism at some point was inevitable. Hitler chose the time and the arena, and despite military mistakes he might, just possibly, have succeeded if his fundamental political and psychological policy toward the Russians had been conciliatory rather than ruthlessly abusive. (Which perhaps is to say that Hitler might have succeeded if he had not been Hitler.)

In the summer of 1941 Soviet Russia was restive, bitter under the

Great Dictator. Some 20 million people had died since the revolution that was to make men free, and freedom was further off than ever. The great famine and the great purges had left their unhealed scars, and the fear of the knock on the door at night and the specter of the Siberian slave labor camps were never far from the mind of any man. Ethnic minorities were chafing—the Balts, the Ukrainians, and the Cossacks particularly.

If Hitler had used his armies to form a shield deep in Russia, behind which a system of independent buffer states could be created; if he had treated the peoples of the conquered territories as equal collaborators, rather than as *Untermenschen*, just possibly Soviet communism might have been geographically and territorially fractionalized. That, in any case, was Hitler's only hope. And it seemed —in the beginning—that Communist Russia would fall apart.

Never before had there been such a huge number of desertions, or easy surrenders, as in the great battles of summer and fall. Rarely before had invading conquering armies been greeted on so massive a scale with so large a number of "laughing . . . waving" gift-bearing peoples as in the early months of the German invasion. Initially, the German armies were often helped in their invasion by the peoples they conquered. Never before had there been such a major opportunity to dissolve the strained ties that bound the ethnic minorities to Moscow.[53]

But Hitler's entire policy was one of conquest, not conciliation. The Russians were inferior folk to be ruled ruthlessly. The slightest sign of opposition was to be dealt with mercilessly, not as the act of an individual, but as the crime of a whole locality.

What Lieutenant General W. Anders, who commanded Polish forces in World War II, describes as the "barbarian methods of occupation and the treatment of prisoners of war"[54] was fundamentally responsible for cementing Russian nationalistic opposition to Hitler and for the build-up of the Soviet partisan movement.

The Nazi Party—not the Army—was put in charge of the conquered territories, and it was Himmler the Terrible, with his Sicherheitsdienst (Security Service) who ruled the Eastern territories with a scourge far worse than the knout of the czars. Erich Koch, who was appointed Reich Commissioner for the Ukraine, was later (in March 1943) to epitomize the policy: "We are a master race, which must remember that the lowliest German worker is racially and biologically a thousand times more valuable than the population here."[55]

Hitler had put the matter even more clearly as early as midsummer 1941; the best way to pacify the vast conquered territories, he said, was to shoot "everybody who shows a wry face."

From the Nietzschean concept of a German "Superman," four policies evolved:

1. Iron-handed rule and ruthless suppression of dissidence; a single act of sabotage or disobedience earned in retaliation the execution—and often the torture—of scores or hundreds. Jews, Communist officials, and "undesirable elements" were to be liquidated.
2. The occupied territories were to be exploited economically to the full for the benefit of Germany.
3. Some of the conquered peoples were to be transported to Germany, as needed, for slave labor; eventually, almost 2 million Russians were so utilized.
4. The deserters and the enthusiastic Ukrainian nationalists were not to be trusted; no non-German was to bear arms—a policy which was only altered, and then half-heartedly, when it was too late.

These policies played directly into the hands of Stalin and stoked mightily the blaze of partisan and guerrilla warfare that began (as an apparently spontaneous combustion) soon after the invasion. What the Germans might have made a war for liberation they turned into a fanatic defense of Mother Russia.

The Soviet partisan movement was not pre-planned, except sketchily in a few localities, and it produced in the early months only "meagre results."[56] It was at first composed chiefly of independent bands of Red Army men—bypassed by the swift German advance, isolated in the great forests. These were augmented, early on, by small, hastily trained, carelessly organized groups of parachutists, their objective sabotage, and by so-called annihilation battalions of about one hundred fanatic Communist Party members in a group—their mission not only sabotage but a terror campaign against the civilian population of the occupied areas to prevent political deviation and to show the conquered that the long arm of communism reached far.

The mass of the people had no part in the early months in this guerrilla campaign, which amounted—despite blown culverts and bridges—to very limited effectiveness in 1941, and remained strictly a secondary factor throughout the war. But Stalin in early July recognized it as an important contributing element to victory, and in September, with Germans deep in Russia, the direction and organization of partisan movements were centralized and placed under the direct control of the Communist Party in Moscow, with Voroshilov as the initial head.

From these small beginnings there emerged, during the years of Russo-German war, the "greatest irregular resistance movement in the history of warfare."[57] Part of the growth was due to the German expectation of quick victory; the German Army had done little planning for rear area security, and the Himmler security divisions and police were initially inadequate in both numbers and training. But fundamentally, it was the German reign of terror that nurtured and fertilized the wildfire growth of resistance. As in all guerrilla warfare, both sides made the peasant the man in the middle, and he found that under German occupation he had no place to go save back to the arms of the Bolsheviks. Dreams of liberation became a desperate struggle for survival; scorched earth and death to the invaders the battle cry.

* * *

The German invasion of Russia and the greatest land battles in the history of warfare that followed produced global political, psychological, and military results.

Britain, which had stood alone, found breathing space; the might of a conquered continent, marshaled by Hitler against the British Isles, had now turned eastward. The new dispensation required readjustment in British thinking from Churchill down. So short a time before England had projected an expedition to aid the gallant Finns against the Russians, and Churchill, stalwart anti-Communist, had always viewed the Soviet regime with great suspicion. In the democratic West communism was both feared and hated. But just a few hours before the German attack started, the Prime Minister clearly elucidated his policy on the croquet lawn at Chequers in a conversation with his private secretary:

". . . I have only one purpose, the destruction of Hitler, and my life is much simplified thereby. If Hitler invaded Hell I would make at least a favourable reference to the Devil in the House of Commons. . . ."

The next day, in a broadcast to the British people, Churchill promised to give "whatever help we can to Russia and the Russian people. . . .

We have but one aim and one single, irrevocable purpose. We are resolved to destroy Hitler and every vestige of the Nazi regime. From this nothing will turn us—nothing. We will never parley, we will never negotiate with Hitler or any of his gang. We shall fight him by land, we shall fight him by sea, we shall fight him in the air, until, with God's help, we have rid the earth of his shadow and liberated its peoples from his yoke. . . .[58]

But the Devil is never an easy ally. A British military mission was sent to Moscow in midsummer; an uneasy liaison was established, and aid began to flow over tenuous sea and land links to the beleaguered Russians. Stalin took everything, gave little, demanded ever more—most of all, a second front. Two Hurricane squadrons were sent, via HMS *Argus*, to Murmansk and, in early September, started three months of air defense operations around the important naval base and supply port. Some 200 American-built fighter aircraft in or earmarked for Britain were diverted to Russia; rubber, tin, wool, clothing, boots, mines, and weapons (the first small installments of millions of tons of supplies of all kinds) were shipped to Russia, chiefly via what was to become the most dangerous convoy route of the war: around the North Cape in the long Arctic darkness of winter through floating ice and stormy seas to Murmansk and Archangel.

The first of the PQ convoys to Russia sailed in late September. These convoys covered sea routes 1,400 to 2,000 miles long, mostly beyond British air cover, skirting the ice floes in those God-forsaken Northern seas. They initiated a bridge of ships from Scotland and Iceland to Murmansk and Archangel that would run the gantlet of ice and weather, fire, fury, and unequaled onslaught.

The Fleet Air Arm struck, with scant results, at the German-held ports of Kirkenes and Petsamo, and Rear Admiral Philip Vian of the *Altmark* led an expedition to the barren island of Spitzbergen in the Arctic, evacuated the Norwegian and Russian inhabitants, destroyed the coal colliery installations (which the Germans had been using), and captured a few prizes.

British submarines, led by *Tigris* and *Trident*, operating out of the Russian base along with Russian submarines at ice-free Polyarny, effectively harassed German coastal shipping, which had been used to help supply their Army in the north. The efforts had a bearing on the land campaign in northern Russia; the Germans diverted their supplies to roundabout overland routes, thus easing some of the pressure on the Soviet armies in the extreme north.

And in late December, as a decisive year of World War II ended, one of the first combined operations by the new "Commandos" was carried out against the Norwegian island of Vaagö near Stadlandet.

It was a minor though successfully executed raid; the British silenced enemy coastal batteries and sank some 16,000 tons of enemy merchant shipping. But it had an unexpected effect. It helped to create a fixation in Hitler's mind: that the British were about to invade Norway. From then on, throughout the war the German strategic dispositions would reflect this belief; and a disproportionate number of German troops, ships, and arms would be tied down in fixed defensive positions in the non-combat theater of Norway.[59]

The Vaagö raid did not create Hitler's fixation on Norway, but it helped to emphasize that, to *Der Fuehrer,* Norway was—as Warlimont puts it—"the OKW theatre of war Number One, even during the Russian campaign." The British did nothing to disabuse Hitler; throughout the war they employed various cover and deception techniques to focus German attention on Norway.

American Reaction

In the United States, still ostensibly at peace and not dependent upon the Devil for survival, the reaction to the German invasion of Russia was more mixed. Until the invasion, the small Communist Party in the United States and its more numerous allies, the fellow travelers and crypto-Communists, and some of the intellectuals of the big cities who thought it smart and chic to be radical, had been stridently opposed to American intervention. They were thus allied with the America First Movement and with that very large number of the American people who wanted to see Hitler defeated but did not want the United States to enter the war.

Overnight (with some embarrassment to those of the ideologically faithful who did not get the word promptly), the Communist Party line in the United States changed 180 degrees. But there was an obverse side to the coin of invasion; now that the world's two most brutal dictatorships were pitted in death struggle, there was considerable logic in the arguments of those who would keep the nation out of war, believing that now more than ever was the time for America to stay aloof. Many American Catholics, appalled by a godless Russia, strongly supported neutrality.

Actually, that time had long passed. As Bruce Catton, writing of another war, has commented: "American political leaders always respect the will of the majority, but in time of crisis they sometimes have even greater respect for the way an accomplished fact can force a majority to change its mind."[60]

And "accomplished facts," in the summer and fall of 1941, had already put the United States into the war against Germany, even though most of the American people did not really understand this. For the actions ordered by President Roosevelt, while advertised as "short of war," were war itself; a limited war, it is true, and one without a declaration, but still war.

The United States' position vis-à-vis Nazi Germany was officially about as "unneutral" as a nation can be, well before the invasion of Russia. As early as December 1939, Roosevelt had ordered U.S. naval vessels to trail the German liner *Colombus* out of Vera Cruz, Mexico, and to broadcast her position in order to aid British warships that were looking for her. From then on throughout 1940 and 1941, Washington—primarily in the person of Roosevelt and his close political associates—became progressively more belligerent and more inclined to bypass or fudge the niceties of international law. In accordance with the secret staff agreements with the British of January–March 1941, the newly formed Convoy and Routing Section of the Office of the Chief of Naval Operations "issued its first instructions for the naval control of merchant shipping" on June 17, prior to the assault upon Russia.[61] The occupation of Iceland by U.S. forces had been ordered in June, and President Roosevelt had declared "an unlimited national emergency" on May 27. Shots had been fired, American lives lost in the undeclared naval war in the Atlantic months before Pearl Harbor.

Nor was this all. The United States had become an arsenal for Britain; tremendous and increasing quantities of supplies were being shipped—much of the tonnage in U.S. vessels—to Britain. In late July, Harry Hopkins, the self-designated "Roosevelt's messenger boy," headed a U.S. mission to Moscow and was instructed by the President to tell Stalin that Washington wanted to know "how we can most expeditiously and effectively make available the assistance which the United States can render" to Russia. ". . . All possible aid will be given by the United States Government. . . ."[62]

This visit was followed by a second mission, headed for the British by Lord Beaverbrook and for the Americans by Averell Harriman, who saw Stalin on September 28, 29, and 30. As a result, Roosevelt cabled Stalin on October 30 that all the items of supply requested and agreed upon at the conference had been approved, and that he "had directed that shipments up to the value of one billion dollars be financed under Lend Lease."[63]

Roosevelt was a President capable of semantic twists and turns, of "devious procedure,"[64] and of subtly shading the meaning of events and even the facts themselves. Just a year before, on September 11,

1940, in his famous "I hate war" speech, he had emphatically reaffirmed the Democratic Party platform: "We will not participate in foreign wars. . . ." But that had been an election year. Now a few months later, the same President, reelected, had openly forsworn neutrality against Germany and ranged the moral and industrial power of the United States—and a sizable part of its naval power—firmly on the side of Britain and Russia.

Thus the "Imperial Presidency" of another era, in the person of Franklin Delano Roosevelt, who loved power and at the same time understood how to influence men's minds, had led America into an undeclared de facto war long before December 7, 1941. The general outlines of all these actions and events were known, at the time, to the American people—if sometimes after long delay. But the details and the planning were top secret, and few even of those who approved the general policies of the administration understood that they must inevitably lead to paths of glory—and of blood.

18

Pearl Harbor

Formal all-out war came to the United States in a different ocean and from a different enemy, but with history helped along in the Pacific as in the Atlantic.

In 1941 both the United States and Japan were led inexorably past the milestones on the road to war, a road that had had no turning since Japan's attempt to conquer and control China met head-on Washington's pro-China policy. The fundamental cause of conflict in the Pacific was, in Samuel Eliot Morison's phrase, Japan's "inability to make a competent synthesis between power and responsibility:

Japan was the only important nation in the world in the Twentieth Century which combined modern industrial power and a first-class military establishment with religious and social ideas inherited from the primitive ages of mankind, which exalted the military profession and regarded war and conquest as the highest good.[65]

By the spring of 1941, Japan and the United States were clearly committed to a collision course. The U.S. economic sanctions against Japan, initiated in attempts to persuade or force her to stop her march of conquest, had been progressively extended—first morally, then legally—since 1938. Strategic materials, aircraft engines and equipment, certain types of aviation lubricants and fuel, and all kinds of iron and steel scrap (the last particularly important to Japanese steel mills) had been embargoed. Yet Japan had concluded a self-serving "non-aggression" pact with Russia in April, had seized Hainan and other islands, had nibbled continuously at helpless French Indochina, and by late July 1941, had forced Vichy to agree to a "joint" Japanese-French protectorate. In July, Japan called to the colors more than a million reservists and recalled all her merchant ships from the Atlantic.

Just one day after the announcement of the Japanese protectorate in Indochina the United States, in collaboration with Britain and The Netherlands, froze all Japanese assets in the United States, thus eliminating Japan's major source of petroleum products.

For the next four months until the shadowboxing ended on that dramatic Sunday in December, both sides talked, negotiated, proposed, rejected, using the polite ambiguities of diplomacy to gain time—for military purposes. President Roosevelt appointed the Philippine Commonwealth's only Field Marshal, Douglas MacArthur (who had retired from the U.S. Army after serving as Chief of Staff), to command all U.S. Army Forces in the Far East, and nationalized all the Philippine forces under his command. Throughout the summer and with increasing urgency into the late fall, supplies and reinforcements were shipped or flown to those far Pacific outposts where the U.S. flag flew—Hawaii, Wake, the Philippines.

Not all the U.S. measures were positive, and it was late in the day, indeed, to try to strengthen outposts so far away, so long neglected. In late spring, to try to meet the increasing demands of the undeclared shooting war in the Atlantic, Admiral Harold R. Stark, Chief of Naval Operations, with misgivings transferred three battleships, one carrier, four cruisers, and two destroyer squadrons from Pacific to Atlantic. The transfer left the Pacific Fleet inferior in every major category of combat strength to the Japanese; in those days of imminent peril the U.S. "Two-Ocean Navy" was still a skeleton on the building ways. And, on February 1, 1941, Admiral James O. Richardson, who "was not the type of naval officer who simply does what he is told and asks no questions," was relieved somewhat abruptly as Commander-in-Chief by Admiral Husband E. Kimmel. Richardson thought the Navy's war plan was "obsolete" and useless, and he had told the Navy Department, the State Department, and the President (whom he did not trust) several times with emphasis that the fleet should be based on west coast ports, where (presumably) it would be more secure, it was better sited to do its job, the morale of the men would be improved, and it could be much more easily maintained and supplied. But Roosevelt, supported by Cordell Hull, insisted on Hawaii; the fleet's presence there, the reasoning went, "has had and is having a restraining influence on Japan."[66]

Kimmel, known for his tough efficiency, had as his opposite number and military peer in Hawaii General Walter Short, Army commander, who had established a reputation as commander of the 1st Division and had been specially selected by General George Marshall to pep up and strengthen the Army's Hawaiian defenses. In those days—as the American public was to discover—there was no unified command in the islands. On paper, the Army was responsible for defense, including the naval base and military installations there, but in practice each service more or less went its way and had complete operational autonomy.

Japan's agent of delay in the last months of semi-peace in 1941 was retired Japanese Admiral Kichisaburo Nomura, a former Foreign Minister, well acquainted with and well liked in the United States, and with a reputation among those who knew him for impeccable honesty. He was "known to be opposed to a breach" with Washington, but when he was sent there as Japanese ambassador, arriving in February, he was actually used (unknown to him) as "window-dressing" for the hidden ulterior purposes of the Japanese militarists. While he talked, the preliminary moves were being charted in Tokyo, and the few who feared to gamble all shunted aside. The Cabinet headed by Prince Fumimaro Konoye, who had tried to avert, or slow, the juggernaut of war, fell in October; and—sure portent of what was to come—General Hideki Tojo, militarist and symbol of the radical right, who believed Japan must stay in China and that she could lick the United States, became Prime Minister on October 18.

Time was running short. Japan's petroleum reserves, enough for about a year of war, were dwindling; she must eat crow or strike south for the oil wells of the Dutch East Indies.

About November 1, Japanese Army and Navy chiefs agreed upon what Morison rightly calls "a stupendous scheme of conquest,"[67] an amphibious seizure of the entire Western Pacific area from the Kurile Islands through the Marshalls and including the Bismarcks, the oil-rich Dutch East Indies, and Southeast Asia (Indochina, Malaya, Thailand, and Burma). Tojo set a deadline for agreement with Washington of November 25. He then sent Saburo Kurusu, a diplomat with an American wife, to the United States to help Nomura with what amounted to an impossible ultimatum: Japan must have a free hand in the Western Pacific and Eastern Asia or she would go to war. The day Kurusu left on his doomed mission the Japanese Navy, in great secrecy, completed its plans for a neutralizing attack on a place called Pearl Harbor. The project was the concept of a brilliant Japanese professional, Admiral Isoroku Yamamoto, Commander-in-Chief of the Japanese Combined Fleet, who had said more than a year before that he hoped Japan would avoid war with the United States and had warned he might "run wild" for a while; ". . . We can carry through for one year some way, but after that I don't know. . . ."[68]

In Washington on Sunday, December 7, Kurusu and Nomura had been instructed by Tojo to deliver a message in person to Secretary of State Hull at exactly 1:00 P.M. But the long message, radioed in sections from Japan, took time to decipher; the appointment at the State Department was postponed. It was 8:50 A.M. Hawaiian time (2:20 P.M. Washington time) before a stony-faced, cold-eyed, Secretary of State received the two Japanese—and by then in Pearl Harbor a fleet lay in smoking ruin.

About one hour before, at approximately 7:55 A.M., just as the "Prep" or Preparatory Flag for morning colors was to be hoisted on the Pearl Harbor signal tower, the bombs that were to end an era, shatter a national complacency, doom the past, and shape the future, began to fall on the naval air station on Ford Island, the Army's Hickam Field, and along crowded "Battleship Row" in Pearl Harbor.

"Air Raid, Pearl Harbor—this is no drill."

In plain English the alarum went out at two minutes before 8:00 A.M. from Ford Island in the center of the loch, followed almost immediately by a similar message from Admiral Kimmel: ". . . This is not a drill."

Appalled, disbelieving, the United States was shocked, first into numbness, then into rage. It could not happen here. . . .

"My God! This can't be true, this must mean the Philippines," was the instant reaction of Secretary of the Navy Frank Knox, and of most of the American people.

The surprise was overwhelming.

Yet there had been many warnings, numerous signals, buried in the chaff of large and small events, which should have cast a long shadow toward Pearl Harbor.

For two to three decades the Japanese and U.S. navies had considered each other as potential enemies; secret war plans had mapped the strategy of a Pacific war. As early as 1917, a Japanese plan, *Yohei-Koryo*, or "fundamental national strategy for the deployment of forces," declared that "in the outset of a war, the Navy will gain control over the United States fleet in the Orient."[69]

Since the Manchurian Incident, and increasingly as the militarists came to power in Japan, the blinders had come off in top U.S. government circles; increasingly since 1938, there was belief, indeed conviction, that the clashing policies of Japan and the United States could only end in war. As early as June 7, 1940, as France was dying, General Marshall had warned the Army in Hawaii to be on guard "against an overseas raid from the west by a hostile Nation."

The U.S. Navy's various "Orange" war plans (dealing with war between the United States and Japan) from 1923 to 1940 had contained two fundamental assumptions: that the war with Japan would start "without notice," and that it would be preceded by a period of "strained relations which will develop into actual hostilities before a formal declaration of war." These plans also contained assumptions of possible surprise raids on Pearl Harbor. From September 1940, when Japan joined the Tripartite Pact with Germany and Italy, until that fateful December day, the road to war became clearer and clearer.

But virtually all responsible officials, military and civilian, in Washington were preoccupied with the Orient, with Southeast Asia, where Japan's bid for conquest was already taking concrete form, and with the Dutch East Indies and the Philippines. The nation thought of war in those days of innocence in terms of tidy declarations; Stimson had once said that gentlemen didn't read each other's mail, so many Americans still believed that "gentlemen" didn't attack by surprise without diplomatic formalities. They had forgotten a formidable precedent, the Japanese surprise attack on Port Arthur a generation before.

The Warnings

Yet there had been specific clues that indicated a massive enemy blow against Pearl Harbor.

For months, Ambassador Joseph Grew in Tokyo had been reporting that Japan's public pronouncements were not bluster; that she was deeply committed to the realization of her "Greater East Asia Co-Prosperity Sphere," which in plain terms meant the expulsion of all Western interests and influence from the Orient and the economic, political, and military domination by Japan of Eastern Asia, the Western Pacific, and the South Seas.

The warnings were not confined to generalities. In late January, Grew told Washington that the Peruvian Minister in Tokyo had "heard . . . from many sources . . . that in the event of troubles breaking out between the United States and Japan, the Japanese intend to make a surprise attack against Pearl Harbor with all of their strength. . . ."[70]

Admiral Stark, the CNO, had discussed and written about the possibility of a Japanese attack on Hawaii; and Admiral Kimmel, the fleet commander, had told the CNO and twice warned the Pacific Fleet that a surprise attack on Pearl Harbor prior to the declaration of war was a "possibility." On March 31, the two senior officers directly in command of Army and Navy aircraft stationed in the Hawaiian Islands had stated, in a secret joint report, that "the most likely and dangerous form of attack on Oahu would be an air attack launched from carriers," and added that a dawn attack might probably achieve "complete surprise."[71]

On April 1, all Naval Districts, including the Hawaiian Islands, were urged by the CNO to take special precautions against sudden surprise attacks on weekends. And, ever since January 1941, after the Navy Department had absorbed some of the lessons of the British raid on Taranto and successful bombing attacks on ships in port, the eyes of both War and Navy Departments had been focused on improving and strengthening Pearl Harbor defenses. Secretary of the Navy Knox, in a letter to the Secretary of War, Henry Stimson, had written then: "If war eventuates with Japan, it is believed easily possible that hostilities would be initiated by a surprise attack upon the Fleet or the Naval Base at Pearl Harbor."[72]

There were good reasons for these warnings. The U.S. armed services had established, well before the war, an incomparable team of cryptographers, and before Pearl Harbor the U.S. Navy had broken or partially broken several—though not all—of the Japanese ciphers. William Friedman, a civilian employee of the Army Signal Corps, with the aid of a team of Army personnel and with Navy help, had broken the new Japanese "Purple" cipher in "the greatest feat of cryptanalysis the world had yet known." Friedman had solved the puzzle by August 1940, and in the next twelve months "Purple" machines perfected by Army, Navy, and civilian experts, which automatically "read" the complex cipher, were in the hands of the Navy and of Great Britain, and had been distributed to key points.[73]

Between July 1 and December 7, 1941, 294 Japanese messages had been intercepted, deciphered, translated into English, and distributed under the generic title "Magic" to a few top officials in Washington. The "Purple" cipher was the official top-security system used by the Japanese foreign office; some but not all of the Japanese military ciphers had been solved or were in process of solution. But the diplomatic messages left little to the imagination. These messages clearly warned the United States in advance of the attitudes and interpretations of Japanese diplomats around the world and of the "aggressive intentions" of the Tojo Cabinet, gave details of some of the preparations for the move into Southeast Asia, and provided forewarning of the Japanese deadline of November 29, when "things would automatically begin to happen."[74]

There was, indeed, as November ended a plethora of indications—too many of them; the significant ones were buried in a mass of the inconsequential or irrelevant. And by then, the emphasis given earlier in the year to the dangers of a possible Japanese attack on Pearl Harbor had been obscured, partially because the long debate in the intelligence community about when Japan would attack and whether Tokyo would move against Russia or to the south had been more or less resolved. Before the end of November, Cordell Hull, the Secretary of State, who had warned that the Japanese might strike anywhere at any time, had told the War and Navy Departments that negotiations had failed, that it was now up to them. Both Army and Navy intelligence experts in Washington believed that Tokyo would start an active campaign of conquest against British and Dutch possessions in the Southeastern Asia–Western Pacific area—including possibly the Philippines and Guam—on November 30 or December 7.

Coast watchers in China and elsewhere had reported Japanese convoys southward-bound; "Magic" messages had been decoded plainly referring to possible war; orders had been dispatched to most Japanese embassies about the destruction of codes; and Japanese citizens had been ordered home.

All of this and a good deal more was known to the U.S. government, but the sheer bulk of the data was confusing and much of it was tightly held in Washington to preserve security, so that it never reached the commanders in Oahu.

There had been, for instance, the dispatch from Tokyo in late September to the Japanese Consulate General in Honolulu (decrypted and available after some delay in Washington, but not in Honolulu) that asked for continuous and detailed berthing plans for the ships in Pearl Harbor. This had been intercepted by an Army monitoring station on Oahu, part of the communications intelligence network that picked up the raw material for "Magic." However, none of the new "Purple" decrypting machines had been furnished to Oahu; General Short, the Army commander, who like Admiral Kimmel was not included in the fall of 1941 in the distribution of "Magic," did not even know the intercept station was operating. The messages it intercepted were all bundled off to Washington for processing.

One of the more successful Japanese spies of the war, young Ensign Takeo Yoshikawa of the Imperial Japanese Navy, had been operating in Hawaii since March. He masqueraded, under an assumed name, as a kind of junior playboy vice consul, and, as such, wandered around Oahu. Always inconspicuous, he charted Pearl Harbor fully in answer to Tokyo's request, reported the ships in it, and—until the end—kept Tokyo fully informed in extravagant if sometimes erroneous detail. He was never suspected, and never apprehended; but long before Pearl Harbor, Washington knew of Tokyo's detailed interest in the harbor berthing plans and they also knew about some of the replies from the Honolulu consul general.[75]

And well before December 7, U.S. intelligence experts had been alerted to monitor all Japanese news and weather broadcasts for what appeared to be key "Wind" codes. Decrypted "Magic" messages had indicated that "in case of Japan-U.S. relations in danger," the phrase *"Higashi No Kaze Ame"* (East Wind Rain) would mean "Please destroy all code papers. . . ."[76]

Throughout the year there had been repeated alarms and many warnings urging alertness; these culminated on November 27, when Admiral Stark sent his famous "war warning" message to Kimmel and to Admiral Thomas C. Hart, in the Philippines, commanding the Asiatic Fleet.

Stark's message started bluntly:

"This is to be considered a war warning. Negotiations with Japan looking toward stabilization of conditions in the Pacific have ceased. An aggressive move by Japan is expected within the next few days. . . ."

But it ended partially off-target. The indications were, the dispatch said, that the Japanese were mounting an expedition against "either the Philippines, Thai or Kra peninsula or possibly Borneo."[77]

The Japanese *were* mounting expeditions against the Southeast Asian area, but they had other things in mind too.

On December 6, the first parts of a fourteen-part message from Tokyo to the Japanese Embassy in Washington were intercepted, decrypted, and translated. The first thirteen parts of what the Japanese—from their intercepted signal traffic—"obviously regarded . . . as extremely important,"[78] were in Washington in early afternoon (Washington time) Saturday, December 6. They proved to be a lengthy rehash of Japanese pejorative arguments about past policies and past events in the Pacific and Asia, filled with self-serving complaints about the "peace-obstruction" roles of the United States and Britain. This was nothing new, and Secretary of State Cordell Hull characterized it the next day, as the fleet lay burning in Pearl Harbor, as "crowded with infamous falsehoods and distortions."

But the key fourteenth part and the messages that followed—one of them directing delivery of the fourteen-part message to the U.S. government at 1:00 P.M. December 7, and the last ordering immediate destruction of "remaining cipher machine and all machine codes . . . [and] secret documents"—were not intercepted, decoded, and translated until early on Sunday, December 7.

Nevertheless, the final significant warnings (culmination of months and years of alarums) were in the hands of the decision-makers in Washington well before the first bomb burst. General George Marshall, Army Chief of Staff, saw the final messages about 11:30 A.M. after he had returned from his usual Sunday morning horseback ride. He suggested to Admiral Stark that a special war alert be sent to Pearl Harbor, Manila, San Francisco, and Panama; Stark demurred, pointing to his previous war warning, and arguing that Washington had already cried "Wolf!" too many times. Nevertheless Marshall sent his own message:

> The Japanese are presenting at 1 P.M. Eastern Standard Time today what amounts to an ultimatum. Also they are under orders to destroy their code machine immediately. Just what significance the hour set may have we do not know, but be on the alert accordingly.[79]

It was too late. The message left Washington at noon, but reached General Short in Hawaii after the attack had almost ended.

In Hawaii, where everyone expected the Japs to attack—but not the islands—there had been tactical as well as strategic warning.

More than a year after radar had helped win the Battle of Britain, the Army had installed six mobile search radars on the island of Oahu. But they were new gadgets and not operational; crews were untrained and officers did not really know how to interpret the little blips of light on the radar screen that indicated planes in the sky. One station, on the northern part of the island, was being operated on a training basis for three hours around dawn each morning. Normally the radar was shut down at 7:00 A.M., but on December 7, "because the breakfast truck was late," an Army private in training kept the power on until almost 7:40 A.M. At 0645 the radar picked up and tracked the trace of an unidentified plane some 60 miles away. A minute or so after 7:00 A.M. the private saw the blip traces of many planes about 132 miles to the north and tracked them, headed for Oahu. Both tracks were reported to a junior officer of the watch, who dismissed them as unimportant; a flight of B-17 bombers en route from the United States to the South Pacific was expected at about the same time and on approximately the same bearing.[80]

Actually the first hostile contact of the war had occurred hours before when USS *Condor*, a minesweeper patrolling the Pearl Harbor entrance, sighted at 0342 a midget submarine periscope about 2 miles from the entrance. Destroyer *Ward*, also on patrol, was notified, but was unable to make sonar contact. The midget escaped, passed through the open gate in the nets at the Pearl Harbor entrance, and there, undetected, settled to the bottom to await zero hour (only to be sunk later in futile attack). A little later, *Ward*, still on patrol off the harbor entrance, spotted the conning tower of a second midget. A Catalina flying boat dropped a smoke spot to mark the sighting, and *Ward* attacked and sank the submarine with gunfire and depth charges about 0645 near the harbor entrance in a "defensive sea area."[81] They were the first shots of the war; *Ward* reported her actions immediately. But the lethargy of peacetime and delays in communication and chain of command intervened; Admiral Kimmel, notified at his home on Makalapa, told the fleet duty officer he would "be right down," but the bombs began dropping as he was starting.

There were some seventy combat ships and twenty-four naval auxiliaries—a "major part of the Pacific Fleet"—in Pearl Harbor as the churchbells rang in Honolulu that Sunday morning. At Hickam Field near Pearl and three other Army fields in Oahu, the planes had been lined up in neat rows in the open, wingtip to wingtip, heavily guarded by M.P.'s, not against attack from the skies but against sabotage. Only a few days before, General Short had received several separate warning messages from the Army General Staff in Washington. One of them was a general alert, "Hostile action possible at any moment," but had added that any precautionary measures Short took should "not . . . alarm civil population. . . ." The other messages warned specifically against sabotage. Short, worried as were most of his contemporaries about the presence and possibly questionable loyalty of a large Nisei population in Hawaii, assembled and guarded his planes and reported—without response from his superiors in Washington—what he had done.[82]

A handful of the Navy's patrol planes were flying a 200-mile pie-wedge search sector to the west and south, but no long-range reconnaissance, and none at all to the north. It was weekend routine; a day of rest, church services, relaxation . . . and death.

Death came from the bellies of bombers and torpedo planes which had been launched in the overcast dawn from six Japanese carriers about 275 miles north of Pearl Harbor.

For Japan, the launching was the culmination of one man's dream and of months of planning. In January 1941, at about the same time that Ambassador Grew was reporting "rumors" of a Pearl Harbor attack, Admiral Yamamoto, Commander-in-Chief of the Japanese Combined Fleet, had ordered a top-secret study by his staff of a carrier air strike on the U.S. Pacific Fleet in the Hawaiian Islands. Through summer and fall, the Japanese planning and war games continued, and training of carrier and air crews started in September, with the aid of a miniature mock-up of Pearl Harbor, faithful in detail. With the infinite patience characteristic of their race, the Japanese spent much time in perfecting techniques and tactics to make "the impossible"—shallow-water torpedo attacks—possible. On November 1, Yamamoto issued the basic operation order for the attack (approved by the Japanese Chief of the Naval General Staff within two days); and on November 7, he set D-Day for the attack as Sunday, December 7 (Hawaiian time; December 8, Tokyo time) and assigned command of the Pearl Harbor Strike Force to Vice Admiral Chuichi Nagumo.

Within a week the task force had sortied, in complete radio silence, from Kure naval base, and had lost itself in the mists of the snow-covered Kurile Islands, where the ships rendezvoused in a desolate anchorage in the island of Etorofu. Here, all hands were told that the objective of the impending strike was to "crush" the U.S. Fleet in a naval "Waterloo,"[83] to cover and protect, and ensure "freedom of action" for, the Japanese seizure of Southeast Asia and the island archipelagoes near it.

To the crews of the task force that November day the news was exhilarating. Morison comments, with perhaps some slight exaggeration, that "No comparable armed expedition in history ever set forth better informed as to what it was about to do and why; or so full of black, bitter hatred against victims marked down for destruction."[84]

The Japanese Strike Force with 450 aircraft aboard 6 carriers sailed from the Kuriles on November 26, setting course north of the normal shipping lanes across the stormy seas amid the clouds and fog of the North Pacific toward Pearl Harbor. It was ostensibly a "Go" or "No-Go" mission; the date for the attack was to be finally fixed en route; if the United States yielded to the last-minute ultimatum, the fleet would reverse course.

On December 1, Tojo and his Cabinet formally confirmed what had already been decided: war, starting December 8, Tokyo time. The next day Yamamoto broadcast to the task force the three words: *"Niitaka Yama Nobore"* (Climb Mount Niitaka).

The attack opened—prematurely—from the seas beneath, rather than the skies above. Twenty-three of the big (1,955-ton) I-type long-range submarines, five of them carrying two-man midget submarines on their backs, preceded the carrier task force to scout, report, and attack opportunistically. They accomplished nothing. In addition to the two midgets sighted by *Condor* and *Ward* and subsequently sunk, a third midget ran on a reef; one other, along with one of the big I-boats, was sunk, and the fifth midget disappeared, fate unknown.

But the strike from the air was a different story.

The "Z" flag, which Japan's great hero Admiral Togo had flown on his flagship before the Battle of Tsushima in 1905, was flying from *Akagi*, flagship, as the first Japanese strike—forty torpedo planes, one hundred bombers, fifty fighters—took off from the decks of *Akagi, Kaga, Shokaku, Zuikaku, Hiryu,* and *Soryu*. The heavy cruisers *Tone* and *Chikuma* had launched float planes earlier to provide last-minute reconnaissance (it was one of these that was first picked up by the Oahu radar). The battleships *Hiei* and *Kirishima* were steaming nearby, the whole task force screened by nine destroyers. It was about 6:00 A.M. December 7, Hawaiian time, and above a heavy overcast, as the Japanese planes flew toward Pearl, the sky blazed in a magnificent sunrise.

The "Day of Infamy"

At 0740, under the overcast, the Japanese fliers picked up the coastline of Oahu—the greens and blues and whites of surf breaking on reefs and sun, filtered through clouds, reflected from sandy shoals.

"Pearl Harbor was still asleep in the morning mist . . . calm and serene inside the harbor . . . important ships of the Pacific Fleet, strung out and anchored two ships side by side in an orderly manner."[85]

Then, high in the heavens, Commander Mitsuo Fuchida, Air Group Commander of *Akagi*, radioed:

"*To-to-to!*" (Attack, attack, attack!)

Still, as the bombs started to drop and the Zero fighters wheeled in the sky, Pearl Harbor seemed to slumber. To Fuchida the surprise seemed complete, victory certain.

He did not wait; well before 8:00 A.M. he radioed the signal of triumph:

"*Tora! Tora! Tora!*" (Tiger! Tiger! Tiger!)[86]

As the enemy planes flew low toward Pearl Harbor, an old Marine sergeant in the Navy Yard "turned to the officer of the day and said: 'Sir, those are Japanese war planes.'

"The officer in charge took a hard look. He said, 'By God! you're right! Music, sound Call to Arms.' "[87]

The Japanese strikes on ships and airfields were virtually simultaneous. At 0755 the Army's Wheeler Field and Hickam Field (the latter near Pearl Harbor), where most of the Army's fighters and bombers were ranged in ordered rows, were strafed and bombed. Most of the planes at Wheeler were destroyed on the ground in the first attack; at Hickam eighteen aircraft, hangars and storage areas were exploding and flaming within a few minutes. The Army's P-40's at Bellows Field were almost eliminated and only Haleiwa was overlooked. The Army's antiaircraft batteries were either unmanned or had no ready ammunition; none opened fire until the attack was almost over. Only seven Navy patrol planes were in the air; most of the Army's planes were on three- or four-hour alert. In the first wave the Army's defenses on Oahu had been crippled.

The Navy's airfields were even harder hit. Ford Island got the first working over; about half the Navy's patrol planes were damaged or destroyed in the first few minutes. One combat aircraft and some non-combat utility planes got into the air between bomb bursts. At Kaneohe Bay, where only three of the Navy's thirty-three Catalina flying boats were in the air on patrol, the destruction was almost complete: twenty-seven PBY's destroyed, six damaged. The Marine Corps air station—similarly surprised—lost most of its fighters and more than half of its scout bombers in the first twenty minutes.

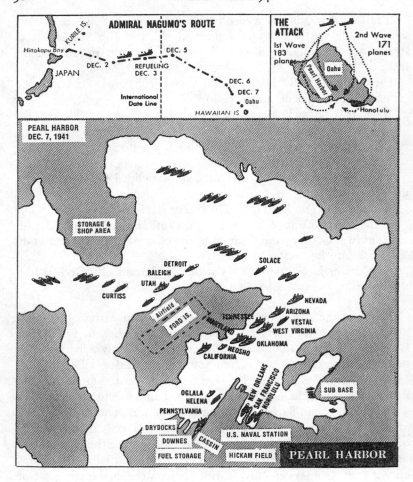

A chaplain, preparing for outdoor services, grabbed a machine gun and mounted it on an improvised altar. Sailors and soldiers and Marines, some of them dressed for Sunday church services or liberty, looked up in amazement as Japanese Val dive bombers whistled down from the skies. Some grasped immediately the significance of the red ball—the "meat ball" or rising sun—on the fuselages and started firing machine guns and rifles; others stared transfixed as the bullets skipped across the hardstands.

In the Navy Yard, Marines rushed out of the Marine barracks, some clad only in towels. Soon, as Colonel Cornelius C. Smith, Jr., recalled later, "We are shooting back like crazy. There are .30s and

.50s popping off everywhere. No coordination—just chaotic firing with tracers streaking up like Roman candles."[88]

In the calm waters of Pearl Harbor, *Pennsylvania*, flagship of the fleet, was in drydock, along with two destroyers, *Cassin* and *Downes*. Along "Battleship Row," moored to the great quays to the southeast of Ford Island, were seven more battleships: *California* at the seaward end, *Nevada* at the loch end, the rest nested in pairs, steam low, Sunday routine starting. The first bombers screamed down toward the white decks unopposed—but not for long. About one-fourth of the light antiaircraft guns[89] on all ships had been crewed on a stand-by alert, with ready ammunition nearby. Within some three minutes of the first attack, the Navy broadcast the first alarm, and almost simultaneously Rear Admiral W. R. Furlong, commander of the Mine Force of the Pacific Fleet and the senior officer present afloat (SOPA), had ordered "General Quarters" and had hoisted from his flagship, the *Oglala*, the signal: "All Ships in Harbor Sortie." A few minutes later aboard most of the ships the shrieking sound of the klaxons had called all those not already dead or dying to battle stations.

But it was too late. The Japanese high-level bombers laid heavy bombs—some of them 16-inch armor-piercing shells converted into bombs—accurately along "Battleship Row"; the bombs sliced through deck plates and burst, in many instances, in the ships' bowels, starting fires, wreaking havoc. Kate torpedo bombers swung low over the loch and dropped torpedoes, fitted with special fins to prevent them from porpoising into the bottom. There were no torpedo nets around the ships; adequate ones that were simple to handle had not yet been developed; and the harbor depth was considered too shallow for torpedoes.

In the first attack—a half hour of hell—every battleship afloat had been hit; they were flaming, flooding, sinking. *Oglala* capsized and sank at 1010 Pier; cruiser *Helena* took a torpedo in her guts, but stayed afloat; cruiser *Raleigh* settled to the bottom, astern of unarmed target ship *Utah* (an old battleship) which capsized.

Battleship *West Virginia* (the "WeeVee"), eighteen years old but the youngest of the fleet, was moored outboard of *Tennessee*. She was hit by the first of about six torpedoes within one minute of the opening of the attack. Her light and power were knocked out and the port-side AA guns would not bear; she listed to 28 degrees, was saved only by counterflooding, and settled flaming and smoking but fighting still into the mud. Her skipper, Captain Mervyn S. Bennion, gutted by steel shards from a bomb that hit *Tennessee* alongside, died slowly on his bridge, "His only thought ... for the ship and crew, and he kept asking what was going on until he died."[90]

Oklahoma, moored outboard of *Maryland,* took it quickly. Hit by torpedoes, she listed to 35 degrees and kept going; within twenty minutes she lay bottom up, her masts in the mud, the green slime on her keel marking the steel prison where some of her crew—trapped in pockets of air in absolute blackness—were living still.

Nevada sold her soul dearly; machine-gun fire brought down a Japanese torpedo plane close aboard. A bomb hit near the antiaircraft director, where young Ensign Joe Taussig, scion of a well-known Navy name, was at his station. Suddenly he found "his left leg tucked under his arm."

"That's a hell of a place for a foot to be."[91]

California, unlike some of the other BB's, was not buttoned up; she was preparing for inspection. Six manhole covers to the double bottoms were opened and she flooded rapidly.

Men react to sudden shock in sudden ways. Some sobbing furiously, fighting mad, wildly exhilarated, pumped ammunition from machine guns, rifles, .45's, shotguns blindly into the air; a few cowered in fear; aboard cruiser *New Orleans,* mess attendant Smith was singing "Swing Low, Sweet Chariot" as he dogged down the wardroom porthole covers.

Just aft of the paired *Tennessee* and *West Virginia* lay the *Arizona,* coupled—outboard—with the repair ship *Vestal,* which offered scant protection. About 0756, with Rear Admiral Isaac C. Kidd and her skipper on the bridge and her crew at general quarters, a heavy bomb sliced through number two turret and detonated the forward magazine—killing Kidd, the skipper, and nearly a thousand men, and wrecking the ship. Major Alan Shapley, Marine Corps, was blown out of the crumbling foremast into the water injured, and struggled ashore dazed in the trauma of shock. A second bomb went down or near a stack; at least six others struck her in the next few minutes and she settled to the bottom, twisted scrap (most of her crew trapped, burned, drowned) in the berth off Ford Island, where still she lies today. The smoke and flame of her going rose high into the soft Hawaiian air for 1,000 feet—a beacon for the attacks still to come.

The first wave of the Japanese strikes tailed off at about 8:25 A.M. Pearl Harbor was a pillar of flame, its waters slick with burning oil, dotted with the bobbing heads of seared or mangled men; small craft, tugs, garbage lighters hauling in the whole and the maimed; sirens shrieking ashore. . . .

* * *

About 8:40 A.M. the second wave came in: some 171 planes, horizontal bombers, dive bombers, and Zero fighters for strafing.

Airfields and ships were hit again, the lighter ships this time, and those that had so far escaped with little damage. *Pennsylvania* and destroyers *Cassin* and *Downes* in the same drydock were hit, and battleship *Nevada*, which had been damaged but had managed to get under way. *Nevada*, steaming proudly though badly wounded, was the focus of some of the second-wave attackers; bomb splashes towered around her, and hurt though not disabled, she was deliberately beached near the southern end of Ford Island. *Pennsylvania* took a hit about 9:06 and was damaged not too severely. Ahead of her in the same dock destroyers *Cassin* and *Downes* were ablaze, and ruptured oil tanks spread the flames. The drydock was flooded. *Cassin* rolled over against *Downes*; magazines and torpedo warheads were detonated. Just a short distance away, destroyer *Shaw* in a floating dock took a direct hit and exploded in cascading pyrotechnics of fire and flaming, blood-red smoke.

One damaged Japanese bomber crash-landed in the sea near Pearl City. The pilot survived the crash and a destroyer whaleboat tried to help him, but he fought off rescue and attempted to shoot his saviors.

Aboard capsized *Oklahoma*, the crew of a 14-inch turret were trapped in blackness underwater. The door was pried open; the air bubble in the turret briefly kept out much of the water. Ensign Charles Francis Flaherty, United States Naval Reserve, and Seaman 1/c James Richard Ward held flashlights outlining the way to safety, as one by one the turret crew dived through the door to swim to the surface. Flaherty and Ward died that others might live; they were awarded posthumous Medals of Honor.

For thirty-six hours after the *Oklahoma* capsized, a desperate battle for life on the slimy hull continued, as sailors and Navy Yard workmen, using acetylene torches and metal cutting machinery, painfully cut holes through the bottom plates to rescue some thirty-two men, imprisoned in darkness in gradually fouling bubbles of air. But the frantic tappings of others—here and on capsized *Utah* and flooded *West Virginia*—slowly died away . . .

It was all over before 10:00 A.M., this perhaps most successful surprise attack of all time. Pearl Harbor was a "battle" of such discrepant proportions that history offers few parallels. The Japanese used a total of about 360 planes in the two-wave attack; 9 in the first wave, 20 in the second were lost—most of them to antiaircraft fire, some claimed by the Army's P-40 and P-36 pursuit planes that took off from unattacked Haleiwa and other strips.[92] One large submarine and five midgets were lost, with all their crews save one man—Sub-Lieutenant Sakamaki of the class of 1940 at the Japanese Naval Academy, who swam ashore and surrendered after his damaged midget was beached.

In less than two hours the jubilant fliers of the Rising Sun had destroyed or neutralized the battle line of the Pacific Fleet. *Arizona* was forever gone; *Oklahoma* was capsized, bottom-side up, as was target ship *Utah*. *West Virginia* and *California* had settled to the bottom; *Nevada* was grounded to prevent sinking. *Pennsylvania*, *Maryland*, and *Tennessee* were damaged; cruisers *Helena*, *Honolulu*, *Raleigh*, seaplane tender *Curtiss*, repair ship *Vestal*, all were damaged—some with serious flooding. Minelayer *Oglala*, her bottom burst open, capsized, rested in the mud; *Shaw*'s bow was blown off, and *Cassin* and *Downes* were a pile of twisted metal. The Navy had lost some 80 planes; only 79 of the Army's 231 were immediately usable after the attack; 64 had been totally destroyed. Damage to air installations—including maintenance and administrative shops and buildings and storage, supply, and repair facilities—was heavy, particularly at Hickam Field.

But most of all the surprise was paid for in blood. Some 2,112 Navy and Marine officers and men were killed, almost another 1,000 wounded—some maimed for life. The Army lost 222 dead, 360 wounded.

Black was the scene, deep the despair as Oahu shuddered that Sunday morning. The flaming wrecks, the still-flaring fires, the speeding ambulances, the bodies laid out in serried rows, the oil-covered waters of the loch: defeat, crushing and complete, seemed at hand before war had even begun. And, in the hospitals, crammed to the eaves with wounded, the dying men—flesh seared with burns, smeared with tannic acid, eyes dulled with sedatives or bright with agony.

Yet the Navy's vital fuel storage tanks were untouched, the power plant, fleet repair, and machine shops and maintenance facilities undamaged. And—significant portent—none of the three aircraft carriers then available to the Pacific Fleet was in harbor on that day of devastation.

Enterprise, flying the flag of Vice Admiral William F. Halsey, Jr., whose name was to become a household word, had just transported a

Marine fighter squadron to Wake Island. With the Halsey task force was another admiral, in command of a cruiser division and flying his flag in *Northampton*. Raymond A. Spruance resisted fame but was to have it thrust upon him in the war years to come. Thomas Buell recalls that Spruance was at breakfast that Sunday morning when his flag lieutenant brought him a CINCPAC message: "Air raid on Pearl Harbor. This is not a drill."

"Spruance continued eating:

"'Thank you,' he said. 'You know what to do.' "[93]

On that Sunday, the 7th, the *Enterprise* task force was about 200 miles west of Oahu. Soon after dawn a squadron of eighteen SBD's (Dauntless dive bombers) was flown off to precede the ship to Pearl, and to conduct air search en route. The U.S. planes arrived over Pearl Harbor in the midst of the attack, and "there I was sitting in my cockpit fat dumb and happy and suddenly bullets started whizzing by." Thirteen of the planes, plus two others that had taken off earlier, landed safely—some of them pocked with bullet holes; five others were shot down during the attack, some of them in dogfights with Japanese, others by U.S. antiaircraft fire. Still other *Enterprise* planes were lost while returning to base later that day from futile scouting missions. The Japanese attack had disrupted communications and had produced symptoms familiar to any newly blooded Navy—that nervous reflex condition described as "trigger-happy"—and U.S. antiaircraft added a toll of about ten *Enterprise* planes to the losses inflicted by the Japanese.

The aircraft carrier *Lexington*, with another task force, was also well at sea on an air reinforcement mission to Midway Island. Carrier *Saratoga*, third of the flattops then available in the Pacific, was near San Diego.

The day after the attack the *Enterprise*, flying the flag of Vice Admiral "Bull" Halsey, returned to Pearl Harbor and its smoking, wrecked, and ruined ships. Halsey, a fighter, coined the first of the aphorisms which were to help make him famous. "Before we're through with them," he said, "the Japanese language will be spoken only in hell."

Thus the aircraft carriers which were to replace the battleship in the war to come as the capital ships of the new Navy escaped the ravages of Pearl Harbor, although more by good luck than good management.

Immune, too, was battleship *Colorado*, under overhaul in Bremerton, and most of the fleet's cruisers, destroyers, and submarines. And in Pearl Harbor the panorama of flaming desolation was deceptive.

The wreckage lay in shoal water—not sunk beyond trace in the ocean deeps; most of it was salvageable. Entirely intact was the tremendous industrial base of the United States, able to replace and to build faster than an enemy could destroy, and the fantastic know-how and Yankee energy which the Japanese surprise attack had unleashed. In the event, only two of the six battleships sunk in the Pearl Harbor attack never rejoined the fleet. *Arizona* and *Oklahoma* never sailed again; capsized *Oklahoma* was righted to clear the harbor but never restored. The *West Virginia*, with her underwater belly slashed by gashes more than 100 feet long, her decks distorted, her interior a shambles, was completely rebuilt and rearmed but did not join the fleet again until mid-1944. The others, damaged or sunk, came back from the drydocks and the shipfitters to blue water at varying intervals in the months to come. The old BB's rose, Phoenix-like, from the seeming crematorium of Pearl Harbor to take vengeance, in battles still to come, against the enemy who had wounded them. Even destroyer *Shaw*, fitted with a new bow, lived to fight again, and machinery and fittings from *Cassin* and *Downes* went into new hulls of the same names which carried the battle cry "Remember Pearl Harbor!" into the far reaches of the Pacific.

Thus things were not what they seemed that disastrous Sunday morning of 1941, and the "Banzais" and jubilation of the Japanese task force, retiring undetected and untouched from the most successful surprise attack in history, should have been tempered with the realization that this victory spelled its own defeat.

19

The War in the Pacific

The Pearl Harbor attack was only one strand of a vast web of aggression that spanned the Pacific.

In quick succession the high tide of Japanese conquest roared to the flood on distant shores far away where little groups of lonely Americans were suddenly overwhelmed in the spring tide of Japanese aggression. At Shanghai at 0300 on December 8, the 370-ton gunboat *Wake*, anchored off the Bund, was suddenly boarded and captured by Japanese crews of two destroyers—the only U.S. Navy vessel captured during the war. The British gunboat *Petrel* anchored nearby went down, colors flying, scuttled by her crew after firing a futile broadside. *Wake* had been wired for demolition charges, but her captain was ashore that dark night, and so *Wake* became His Imperial Japanese Majesty's ship *Tataru*—a propaganda talking point for the Sons of Heaven.

Other vestigial remnants of U.S. power in China were quickly swept from the boards. Gunboat *Tutuila* of the old Yangtze patrol retreated upriver and was turned over to the Chinese, to be renamed *Mei Yuan*. The small contingents of the Marine Guards at Tientsin and Peking were scooped up, and the ship that came to rescue them —the commercial liner *President Harrison*—was captured by the Japanese when she ran aground. No one knew it then, but it was virtually the end of an era of Western influence and power in China.

About the same time the bombs were exploding in Pearl Harbor, shells from two Japanese destroyers were exploding on Midway. Almost simultaneously, Japanese naval and air units—quickly followed by troops—struck at "Kota Bharu in British Malaya (0140 8 December–7 December, East Longitude); Singora, just across the border in Thailand (0305), Singapore (0610), Guam (0805), Hong Kong (0900), Wake and the Philippines."[94] And on December 9–10, small Japanese forces seized footholds on Tarawa and Makin, in the British Gilbert Islands.

The scope, speed, power, and precision of the coordinated Japanese offensive against objectives scattered across thousands of miles of the Western Pacific and Eastern Asia astounded the world. Few, indeed, in the Western world had believed Japanese capabilities were equal to such a task; few had thought that Tokyo would dare try to conquer all. A piecemeal approach, one step at a time, one campaign completed before another was begun, had been anticipated; not a typhoon of aggression that swept up all in its path.

The Japanese attack plans were enormously complex and required precise timing and careful coordination. In the first few hours of the war, Tokyo struck at some twenty-nine different targets, widely scattered across the Pacific and along the Asian coast. There had been nothing comparable, in modern memory, to such widespread geographic dispersion and boldness in execution.

Yet the Japanese strategic plan was based on the concept of a quick conquest of the vital "Southern areas": the oil, rubber, tin, and other raw materials of Southeast Asia and the Dutch East Indies, and the neutralization and conquest of all foreign-held positions along the vital shipping lanes between these areas and the Japanese home islands. Tokyo hoped to complete the first vast phase of

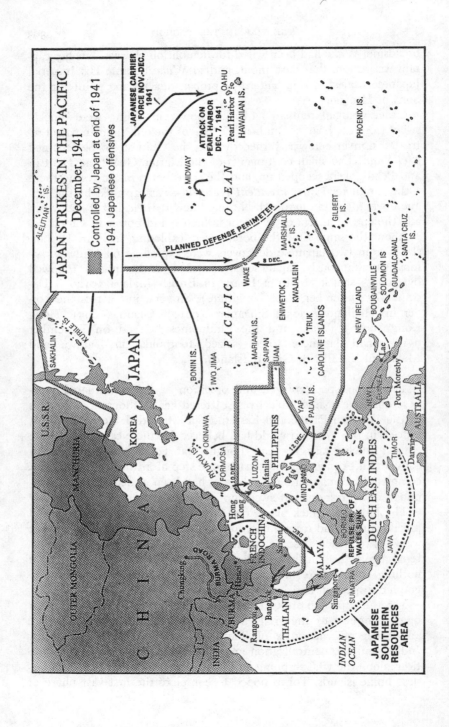

conquest in a few months and then—although the appetite for conquest subsequently expanded the original plan—to consolidate a vast defensive perimeter against which the West might batter in vain.

In November the separate war plans of the Japanese Army and Navy were lumped together, in overall terms, in a "Central Agreement between the Japanese Army and Navy." The objectives, as stated, were:

> The reduction of the primary foundations of American, British and Dutch power in Eastern Asia; the occupation of the Southern Areas.

Scope of Occupation.

> The Philippines, Guam, Hongkong, British Malaya, Burma, the Bismarcks, Java, Sumatra, Borneo, Celebes, Timor.[95]

Guam

The defenseless American island over which the Spanish flag once flew was the easiest. Guam lay within sight of Japanese-held Rota, and near the great Japanese Marianas base of Saipan. Its fortification had been prohibited by the naval arms treaties; it might have been a bastion, but when war came it was too late. Captain G. J. McMillin, the Naval Governor of Guam, had evacuated all American women and children (five naval nurses remained). He knew that his island, garrisoned by only 365 Marines and about 400 naval personnel (with an insular defense force of some 300 Guamanians), was indefensible. There were no coast defense or antiaircraft weapons, no guns larger than .30-caliber machine guns.

It did not take long. News of the attack on Pearl Harbor came before dawn on December 8 (West Longitude); soon after dawn, Japanese bombers from Saipan started two days of indiscriminate bombing against Marine installations, harbors, the little Navy Yard, small craft, and towns and villages. Before dawn on December 10, Rear Admiral A. Goto flying his flag in cruiser *Aoba* landed about 5,000 men at many beaches all over the island. Some 700 or 800 men of a Special Naval Landing Force (equivalent to U.S. Marines) came ashore on the shallow beaches around Agana, the island's principal town, and met, around the Plaza, a handful of defenders—Marines, sailors, Chamorros. The handful put up a brave fight; twice they beat back the enemy charges, losing seventeen dead out of their tiny number.

The final message from Captain McMillin reported: ". . . Civilians machine-gunned in streets. Two native wards of hospital and hospital-compound machine-gunned. . . ."

Sometime after 6:00 A.M. on December 10, with Japanese landing parties in overwhelming force everywhere closing in for the kill, the Governor surrendered the island. For the first time since the War with Spain, the Stars and Stripes came down over Agana, and the Japanese conquerors—arrogant, strutting—shouted a word that was to become familiar to Americans in the years to come: "Banzai!"

On December 13, 1941, in Communiqué No. 5, the dark shadow of defeat again cast a heavy cloud across the once complacent confidence of the United States:

"The Navy Department announced that it is unable to communicate with Guam either by radio or cable. The capture of the island is probable. . . ."[96]

Wake

Wake, that lonely sandy atoll in mid-Pacific more than 1,000 miles west of Midway, much closer to the Japanese bases in the Marshall Islands, was next, but it sold itself more dearly. Its strategic value as an outpost and patrol plane base had been recognized, and in the summer of 1941 frantic efforts to turn the atoll into a base and to strengthen it were begun. But Midway, closer to Hawaii, had higher priority, and Wake, along with Johnston, Palmyra, Canton, and American Samoa, was but one (perhaps the most remote) of the pinpoint dots in the vast Pacific which required garrisons, guns, airstrips.

By early December Wake had improvised a defense, strong in spirit, weak in detail. Some 1,200 civilian contract employees were hacking roads and building shops, utilities, and quarters in the sand and coral and dense jungle scrub; a 5,000-foot runway with ammunition magazines had been built, and a detachment of the 1st Marine Defense Battalion, and a Marine fighter air squadron—a total of 449 combat trained and equipped Marines—had established itself on the atoll. There was an embryo Naval Air Station, with a complement of sixty-eight officers and men (unarmed), and five men from the Army Air Corps, who were supposed to help with the refueling of B-17 bombers. These, like the commercial Pan American Clippers, were periodically using Wake as a staging stop en route to the Philippines. Twelve 3-inch antiaircraft guns had been emplaced on the three islands of the atoll, but only enough trained personnel were available to fully man half this number. Radar was programmed, but had not arrived. Six 5-inch seacoast defense guns had been emplaced, as well as .30- and .50-caliber machine guns, but shortages of personnel and equipment deficiencies restricted their effectiveness, and the guns had never been calibrated or fired.[97]

Until November 28, when Commander Winfield Scott Cunningham assumed duties as island commander, Major James P. S. Devereux had acted as both island commander and commander of the 1st Defense Battalion troops. As senior Marine officer, he was to be the coordinator of all the land and air defense of Wake.

VMF-211, the fighter squadron, numbered twelve new F4F-3 Grumman Wildcat fighters—potentially good aircraft, but so new that the maintenance men had no operating or instruction manuals; the planes had no armor, no self-sealing fuel tanks; the bomb racks "did not match the local supply of bombs";[98] and there were no spare parts. Fuel had to be pumped by hand. The runway permitted only a single plane takeoff; there was little dispersion and inadequate hardstands. And VMF-211, Major Paul A. Putnam commanding, flew to its first and only home from the deck of the *Enterprise* on December 4, just three days before the war started.

And so Wake, like America, was ill-prepared.

But not surprised. Devereux had ordered the "Call to Arms" sounded on the bugle about 7:00 A.M. after the first news of the Pearl Harbor attack reached the island. Pan American's great flying boat—Philippine Clipper—had just taken off for Guam and was recalled within ten minutes. Combat air patrols took to the air; guns were manned; revetments and foxholes frantically dug. Nothing happened until shortly before noon. Then, undetected until the last moment, some thirty-six Japanese bombers, based on Roi Atoll 720 miles to the south, glided down to about 2,000 feet, "masked in a drifting rain squall," the noise of their engines lost in the roar of pounding surf. They wreaked havoc. Fragmentation bombs and 20 mm. incendiaries destroyed seven and damaged one of the eight Wildcats on the ground (four were in the air but never made contact). Aviation gasoline and fuel drums roared into exploding flame and almost half of the Marine Squadron's personnel were killed. Pan American's hotel and its base facilities were fired, but the Clipper escaped with some machine-gun holes. The lack of radar and of ground control for the defending fighters proved decisive; the Japanese got away scot-free, with only a few bullet holes in their wings.

To add insult to injury, one of the four-plane Marine CAP (Combat Air Patrol) struck some bomb debris while landing after the raid's end, and bent its propeller. A bad beginning.

The Japanese bombers flew off in arrogant triumph, waggling their wings.

They came again the next day after the Clipper was sent off to Midway, breaking the midday monody of sun and surf and wind and sea. But the Marines had used their time well. The CAP was warned by radio from the ground, and the 3-inch AA guns started to weave a pattern of high-explosive bursts across the sky. The bombers—respectful of the bursts around them—stayed high at 13,000 feet, but they did not escape unscathed. CAP cut off a straggler and sent him into a flaming death spin; later, a second, hit by AA, exploded in fiery bits in mid-air; and at least four others disappeared toward Roi, smoking. Some fourteen of the Japanese planes received hits or damage during this raid; good shooting, indeed.

But the bombs again chewed up the tiny sea-girt fortress. Barracks, machine shops, and garage; storehouses; the contractors' hospital; air station facilities; and the radio station were all destroyed, four more Marines and fifty-five civilians killed. Two magazines—concrete-and-steel igloos—were emptied and turned into hospital wards with twenty-one beds each, and the island's two doctors (one Navy, one civilian) worked far into the night.

Again the Marines used their time well—and time, they knew, was running short. Improvised radio communications were reestablished and guns shifted. The Marines, aided by civilian volunteers,[99] worked all night to repair in hours damage done in seconds.

On December 10, twenty-six bombers struck again and detonated a contractor's dump of 125 tons of dynamite. The blast damaged an AA and seacoast battery, but the enemy paid again; CAP shot down two more bombers.

On December 11, with feckless confidence, Rear Admiral S. Kajioka, flying his flag in the light cruiser *Yubari*, led a task force of two other light cruisers (*Tatsuta* and *Tenryu*), six destroyers, two old destroyer transports, and two medium transports toward the surf-fringed waters of the atoll. The transports carried some 450 assault troops (Special Naval Landing Troops) and garrison soldiers who were to man Wake when it was captured. Kajioka came under the overall command of the Japanese Fourth Fleet in Truk, the same fleet that had provided the forces for the capture of Guam.

The seas were heavy, the wind high as the Japanese approached in the darkness; weather was, for the defenders, a strong ally. Boats and landing craft capsized and were lost in the darkness. But soon after dawn *Yubari* and the two old cruisers with her opened fire with their 6-inch guns, detonating a dump of diesel fuel and plowing up the scrub and coral. Devereux waited on orders from Cunningham until —in naval gunfire paraphrase—he "saw the whites of their eyes."

Then, at point-blank range with most of the Japanese armada 4,500 to 6,000 yards from gun muzzles, the Marines let them have it. *Yubari* took four or five hits and quickly opened the range, smoking and steaming. Her consort, an old destroyer, was hit once and turned at high speed to seaward. Another 5-inch battery without a rangefinder (it had been destroyed in the dynamite explosion) put two 5-inch shells into destroyer *Hayata*, which exploded, broke in two, and sank rapidly—the first of many Japanese ships to be sunk in the war in the Pacific. The Marine gunners, parched for victory, stopped to cheer; an old leatherneck, their platoon sergeant, thundered: "Knock it off, you bastards, and get back on the guns. What d'ya think this is, a ball game?"[100]

Another destroyer, close in to the beach, was hit, a transport was damaged, and a third destroyer, the *Yayoi*, took a 5-incher from another coast defense gun.

Shortly after 0700, it seemed all over. Admiral Kajioka had suffered the first Japanese reverse of the war, and he turned and headed back toward Kwajalein.

The four remaining Wildcats of VMF-211 lived up to their name. As the wounded Japanese pulled out of gun range, the Grummans swooped and dived, strafed and bombed. They had a circus; destroyer *Kisaragi*, with a deckload of depth charges, blew up and sank with all her crew; light cruisers *Tenryu* and *Tatsuta* were hit, transport *Kongo Maru* was bombed and fired, and one light transport was damaged. The Japanese probably lost about 700 dead; the Marines had 4 men wounded. But two of the precious Grummans which had crash-landed on Wake after damage from Japanese AA fire were out of action.

At dusk, the CAP bombed and damaged a surfaced Japanese submarine 25 miles off Wake.

The Japanese had lost face, but not determination, and Wake's long trial by fire continued. The bombers came in again on the 11th, only two planes now to oppose them. The Wildcats and the 3-inch AA claimed three downed, four more damaged. On the 12th, two great four-engined flying boats from Majuro attacked, for variation, at dawn; the one Grumman in the air shot down one of them. After dark that night Wake buried its dead in a mass grave near the magazines.

December 13 was a day of peace, but on the 14th the bombing came by night as well as day. Two more bombers were shot out of the skies, but Wake's air force was now reduced to one serviceable plane. And the dread routine continued: four-engined Kawanishi flying boats bombed by night; two-engined high-altitude bombers by day.

By December 17, VMF-211's maintenance crew—Marine, Navy, and civilians—working day and night, cannibalizing wrecked or damaged planes, shifting engines and parts from one fuselage to another, had gotten four aircraft into brief operation. But Wake's military assets were dwindling. By that same date Commander Cunningham reported half of the island's trucks and engineering equipment had been destroyed; most of its diesel fuel and commercial explosives, most of the above-ground structures, burned, destroyed, or damaged. December 18 was another quiet day, but they came again out of the skies on the 19th; it was becoming clearer and clearer that the end—without relief—was inevitable.

On December 20, with a heavy frontal area and low visibility all around Wake, the bombers did not fly, but a Navy PBY flying boat got through from Hawaii and Midway, brought news of reinforcements and aid on the way, plans and orders, and got off early the next day, December 21, just before a heavy raid of Japanese carrier-based bombers and fighters.

The end was now at hand. The Japanese, stung by their repulse, ordered carriers *Soryu* and *Hiryu*, which had participated in the attack on Pearl Harbor, to soften up Wake's defenses in two-day pre-invasion raids. The ships sunk in the first landing attempt were replaced; additional and more powerful ones added. Four heavy cruisers were assigned to screen the island against any attempted U.S. naval intervention, two others and another squadron of destroyers for support; and landings were to be made by surprise at night with the light transports deliberately beached on the atoll.

On the second day of the carrier raids, December 22, the last of the Marine Wildcats was lost in a wild melee in the skies. The Wildcats and their worn-down pilots died game; they shot down two or three Zeroes and dive bombers. The remaining air personnel of the fighter squadron took to the foxholes, manned rifles.

The final battle was joined in the dark at about 0235 December 23, two days before Christmas. The light Japanese destroyer-transports were deliberately grounded high and dry on the reef near the airstrip; landing barges touched down in various places as .50-caliber tracer bullets arced through the night sky and tore into the sides of the barges. Approximately 1,500 assault troops were available: 500 to 800 aboard the two light transports, 200 in medium landing craft, the rest in reserve.

The beached destroyer-transports were targeted and hit and fired almost immediately—but not before the landing parties had swarmed ashore with many of the ships' crews.

As Japanese cruisers shelled Wake in the darkness, the enemy landing force spread out across the island, infiltrated through the scrub protected by darkness, and closed in on the island's key defense strong points.

Devereux and Cunningham (their CP's in old ammunition igloos) knew little of what was going on except immediately around them; the land lines had been cut, the field radios failed. AA guns and 5-inch and dug-in machine-gun positions still had to be manned. Most of the Marines were pinned down; there was virtually no mobile infantry.

And despite heavy losses (more than 100 dead, an equal number wounded), the Japanese kept coming.

At 0500 Commander Cunningham sent his penultimate message: "Enemy on island—issue in doubt."

Wake died hard. The island was "ringed with ships," thirteen to seventeen around the low atoll. One of them, old destroyer *Mutsuki*, was hit and holed by a Marine 5-incher. About 0715 carrier strikes came roaring down out of the skies to add more travail to the besieged defenders. There was, at the last, no coordinated defense. The defenders of the three small islands that comprise Wake Atoll were cut off from each other; men in individual strong points knew little beyond their range of vision.

"The complete failure of communications . . . operated to isolate the defense detachment commander [Devereux] from most of his subordinate units. . . . As a result, he not only lost control over much of the battle, but also . . . he became unavoidably deceived . . . he surmised that all was lost" in areas where the Japanese had either been repulsed, or which the Marines still strongly held.[101]

As dawn came in cloudy glory, Captain Henry T. Elrod (U.S. Marine Corps, posthumous Medal of Honor), a fighter pilot who had shown great skill and courage in the skies above Wake, died in a clutter of bodies helping with what was left of VMF-211 to defend a gun emplacement. A Japanese who had feigned death in a heap of casualties shot him.

About 8:00 A.M. Commander Cunningham, the island commander, authorized Major Devereux to surrender and to make contact with the enemy. Stiffly, bearing a white flag, the Marine major marched out in the dust and rubble to meet his fate. But it was not until early afternoon that the last defenders—on Cunningham's and Devereux's orders—surrendered.

And so the U.S. flag came down over a hard-fought battlefield. Ironically, a relief expedition—the carrier *Saratoga*, with a task force—was about 425 miles away, and another carrier, the *Lexington*, 744 miles to the southeast. The relief expedition, conceived by Admiral Kimmel on December 9, initiated on December 14, was, from the first, doomed by delays, irresolute commanders, bad decisions, and the hesitations and anxieties spurred by the alarum of defeat. The Japs were reported everywhere and nowhere, and there was no firm hand at the helm of the Pacific Fleet; Kimmel, under fire, was relieved temporarily by Vice Admiral W. S. Pye, who took over as *Saratoga* steamed en route.

The defense of Wake was, indeed, a proud achievement, with glory enough for all. Plain Navy Department ineptitude and confusion (many key personnel did not even know Commander Cunningham was on the island, much less in command, until the battle was over), plus the tendency of the Marines to move into publicity vacuums, created the impression that Devereux, not Cunningham, commanded at Wake. And somehow a widely believed legend (entirely apocryphal) was created: that in the midst of battle, Devereux had messaged Hawaii: "Send us more Japs."

The aftermath of years of imprisonment, and the polite but pointed postwar exchanges between Marines and Navy, left a taste of aloes in the mouth of history. Cunningham wrote a bitter book,[102] and the Marines stood on their record.

Which no one could gainsay. For the defenders of Wake Island had suffered some 20 percent casualties, had lost a squadron of twelve aircraft, but had inflicted perhaps a thousand battle deaths, had destroyed four enemy ships and damaged eight, had shot down twenty-one aircraft and damaged fifty-one.

And the Philippines

The Philippines, vast archipelago of 7,000 islands, with a cultural melange of many tribes and races overlaid by Spanish and U.S. mores and institutions, influenced by Christian and Moslem orthodoxy, with peoples as primitive as in the age of stone and as sophisticated as the world of the 1940's, lay nearly 6,000 miles from the United States. It was a Commonwealth then, with its own President, Manuel Quezon, and increasing self-government, a proud gem in the tiara of American colonialism and manifest destiny. Washington had pledged complete independence to the Philippines by 1946, but when war came the islands—lying on the flank of the strategic Japanese lifelines to the riches of Southeast Asia—were ill-prepared for either war or independence.

The role of the Philippines in U.S. Orange (War with Japan) war plans had been something like the decisions of "off-again-on-again-Finnigan." In the 1920's and 1930's Manila Bay, with its beautiful harbor, had been the focus of U.S. Pacific planning; Corregidor, the other fortified islands, and the Bataan Peninsula would be strongly held by the United States when war came in order to deny Manila Bay to any enemy. It was believed the U.S. garrison could hold out for three to six months or more while the U.S. Fleet penetrated the screen of the Japanese-held Mandated Islands, forced the Combined Japanese Fleet to a Jutland-type showdown, and then—triumphant—fought its way into Far Eastern waters to relieve Manila.

In the light of Japanese strength, the increasing importance of airpower, and the realities of the Pacific situation in 1940–41, these plans were fanciful. And even though WPO-3 (War Plan-Orange-3) still paid lip service to the defense of Manila Bay, there was a tacit but clear understanding between the Army and Navy in Washington in 1940 and all the early part of 1941 that "the Philippines had been virtually written off as indefensible in a war with Japan."[103]

Staff talks with the British (U.S.-British Commonwealth Joint Basic War Plan) had led in March 1941 to "Rainbow Five." This plan envisaged the main enemy as Germany; until Hitler was defeated, the Pacific would be a secondary theater, and U.S. strategy in the Philippines and the Western Pacific would be defensive. It implicitly accepted the loss of the Philippines, Wake, and Guam.

However, General Douglas MacArthur, a man of strong character, persuasive personality, and political clout (particularly with the right or conservative wing in American politics) influenced the pre-arranged plans in the last half of 1941. As a field marshal military adviser to the Philippine Commonwealth, he had worn a "scrambled egg" hat of his own design (there was no such rank as Field Marshal in the U.S. Army), and he had devised plans—largely on paper when war came—for defense of the entire archipelago, instead of the Manila Bay area only. The Filipinos, as MacArthur saw it, were to be trained and equipped to provide their own defense—a task, however, that could not be completed, by prewar reckoning, until 1946. (Even so, some of the planning was fatuous. It put far too much reliance on a fleet of naval torpedo boats, too little on airpower, and did not recognize the inherent handicaps of inadequate Filipino leadership and the basic military weaknesses indigenous in the Philippine social structure.)

General MacArthur was a brilliant and enthusiastic man, who throughout his career identified himself with destiny. He communicated his optimism and dynamism to others, and many in the Army—including both General George Marshall, Chief of Staff in Washington, and General H. H. Arnold, Chief of the Army Air Forces—were carried along at least part way, sometimes despite their better judgment, by the flood tide of MacArthur's strongly stated beliefs that the islands could and would be held. These beliefs were increasingly buttressed in Washington by a mistaken prewar conception of the capabilities of airpower; as in Britain, it was then believed that a few bombers could accomplish much; there was far too little realism about the complex meaning of real airpower.

Thus the Army, which had agreed to a strategic defensive stance in the Pacific and had tended to believe a few months before that the Philippines were indefensible, enthusiastically started to reinforce the islands in the last half of 1941. And by mid-November, in a background secret press briefing in Washington, General Marshall, who knew war was imminent, regarded the American position in the islands as highly favorable. Marshall thought the United States could carry out an aerial offensive from the Philippines against the "paper" cities of Japan with the thirty-five B-17 Flying Fortresses then based in the islands, the greatest concentration (he said) of heavy-bomber strength anywhere in the world.[104] He was by no means alone in his mistaken, new-found optimism. General "Hap" Arnold, a persuasive air advocate, believed that a few bombers could accomplish much, and he and most of his fellow fliers were enthusiastic advocates of "Victory Through Air Power."[105] In October, Major General Leonard Gerow of the War Plans Division of the Army General Staff had said that scheduled Philippine reinforcements—air and ground—had "changed the entire picture in the Asiatic area" and could have "a vital bearing on the course of the war as a whole."

What Forrest Pogue describes as "the quickening flow of planes and equipment" and the contagion of exciting enthusiasm touched all War Department plans and calculations: ". . . Washington and Manila seemed to forget how quickly time was running out and how many months were still needed to prepare an adequate Philippine defense."[106]

The Navy Department did not share the Army's optimism, and on November 20 Admiral Thomas C. Hart, Commander-in-Chief of the small Asiatic Fleet, had been ordered, when war came, to shift the fleet southward away from Manila Bay and the Philippines.

Thus a strategic dichotomy between the Army and the Navy and the conflicting concepts of the Orange, Rainbow, and MacArthur–Philippine Commonwealth war plans ensured problems and cross purposes even before war began. Even so, it was the equation of power—lopsided in favor of Japan—rather than deficiencies in planning, that doomed the Philippines. The order of battle of the Japanese was overwhelmingly superior in 1941 to any strength the United States and its Allies could muster in, or around, the Philippines.

The Japanese Fleet, far superior in strength to the combined U.S. Pacific and Asiatic fleets and flush from the victory of Pearl Harbor, controlled the seas around the archipelago. The U.S. Asiatic Fleet, which was scattered from Manila Bay and the China coast to Borneo when war started, included one heavy and two light cruisers, thirteen destroyers (most of them old); eight old gunboats (six recently transferred, two left behind, from the Yangtze River patrol and Chinese coastal waters); some twenty-eight Catalina patrol planes (flying boats) with two tenders; five minesweepers; and twenty-nine submarines; with a clutch of tenders, tankers, tugs, and non-combatant auxiliaries.

The Catalina flying boats—the fleet's only aerial "eyes"—had long legs and great endurance, but little else. Heavily loaded and in quiet water they often found it difficult to break free from the surface; takeoffs often required miles of straining engines. The "Cats" were excellent for "negative" information (reporting where the enemy wasn't) but their slow speed, low altitude, and limited maneuverability made them extremely vulnerable to fighter aircraft or even well-aimed AA fire. Later in the war, a (probably) apocryphal report by a PBY pilot epitomized the hazard: "Have sighted enemy planes—please notify next of kin."

The submarines were impressively numerous. Much was expected of them, little realized. But the rest of the fleet, with no air cover except that which might be provided by the land-based planes of the Army Air Force, was completely outclassed by opposing Japanese forces.

The Japanese Third Fleet, Vice Admiral I. Takahashi commanding, was charged with the invasion of the archipelago, with the Second Fleet, Vice Admiral N. Kondo commanding, in general support. The Second Fleet was assigned two battleships and three heavy cruisers and destroyers. The Third Fleet, based on Formosa and Palau and the Ryukyus, organized in task forces, included one carrier, five heavy cruisers, four light cruisers, more than twenty destroyers, and several dozen transports, patrol craft, minelayers, minesweepers, and small craft. The Japanese air support assigned to the conquest of the Philippines was overwhelming; the bulk of it was based on Formosa until airstrips had been established in the archipelago. The Naval Eleventh Air Fleet, Vice Admiral Nishizo Tsukahara commanding, numbered about 360 planes, and the Japanese Army planes (the Fifth Air Army) another 144.

Lieutenant General Masaharu Homma, commander of the Philippine invasion forces, was initially assigned the Fourteenth Army (two divisions and a brigade reinforced) and counted upon a quick victory based on his tremendous superiority and on surprise and speed. Japanese plans envisaged conquest in about fifty days.

The Fourteenth Army, under General Homma, was one of four Japanese armies assigned to the so-called Southern Army, which was responsible for the conquest, not only of the Philippines, but also of Southeast Asia, Borneo, and the Dutch East Indies.

The U.S. order of battle was fatally weak in the elements that counted. In addition to the small Asiatic Fleet—most of its units already withdrawn, under orders, to the south—there was what had been bravely termed the "heaviest concentration of heavy bomber strength in the world": thirty-five bombers, and some sixty first-line operational fighters. There were only two operational radar sets in the islands. The number of fields for dispersion was inadequate, and they had only limited revetments or scattered hardstands. Most of the U.S. air strength was concentrated at Nichols Field and Clark Field near Manila, with sixteen B-17's at an inadequate new field at Del Monte, Mindanao. On paper, General MacArthur (who acted as Commander, U.S. Army Forces, Far East, and also as commander of the Commonwealth forces) could muster about 100,000 Filipinos in some kind of uniform, organized into nine reserve divisions and one regular division, plus militarized constabulary units. Most of these men, however, had had rudimentary training; arms and equipment, leadership, and the will to fight were all lacking save in a few units. The main defense of the islands rested on the small and motley U.S. Army forces, some 31,000 men, including Army Air Force and certain National Guard units recently mobilized, and 12,000 Philippine Scouts (Philippine enlisted men, officered chiefly by Americans), who then formed an élite, well-trained part of the U.S. Army.

The initial Japanese air strike against the Philippines was originally timed for dawn, December 8 (December 7, Pearl Harbor time), to coincide approximately with the attack on Pearl Harbor; but bad weather around Luzon intervened.

Not so, far to the south on the great island of Mindanao. The Navy's "Cats" had been loaded with bombs, had taken off on patrol, or had flown to dispersed operating bases in various parts of the archipelago before war started. Two planes were moored in a quiet bay in the Gulf of Davao, Mindanao, along with their seaplane tender the *Preston* as the dawn light brightened the sea that Monday. Japanese bombers, followed quickly by destroyers, attacked the "Cats" and destroyed them, missing *Preston*, which escaped to fight another day. Ensign Robert G. Tills of PatWing 10 (Patrol Wing Ten) was the first American killed in the Philippines; many others were to follow him to death.[107]

But the spearhead of the far-ranging Japanese attacks upon the Philippines was directed at Luzon, the principal island—site of the capital city Manila, with its beautiful, capacious harbor, and locus of major military installations. And it was not until shortly after noon that the first bombs, from some 192 long-range Japanese naval attack planes based on Formosa, burst at Clark Field.

News of the Japanese attack on Pearl Harbor was picked up by a commercial radio station in the Philippines at 3:00 A.M. December 8. Official confirmation came two hours later, when airfields were notified, and some U.S. pursuit planes took to the air. But the dawn hours were wasted.

There was, apparently, a shadow of hope in the minds of some in the Commonwealth government that a Japanese attack against Pearl Harbor did not necessarily mean an attack against the Philippines. This hope seemingly was the product of the strange semi-independent status of the Philippines; the United States had a High Commissioner there, Francis Sayre, but the Commonwealth had its own President, and its own system of self-government.

This political factor, a military tenderness toward the sensibilities of the semi-independent Filipinos, may also have helped to generate MacArthur's sweeping overoptimism about the feasibility of defending the islands. In particular, it may have persuaded him that it was politically and psychologically necessary to try to defend all of the islands, rather than to conform to the traditional Orange war plan and defend the Manila Bay area only. In some sense, the role of the Philippine government was akin to the roles of the occupied countries in Europe; the choice was clear: flight to exile or compromise with the conquerors. And, despite the postwar historical gilding of the lily, it is clear that there was major disagreement in the Philippines. When war came, there is little doubt that President Quezon was shaken by the rapid Japanese successes and there was considerable schism of purpose between Americans and Filipinos, which MacArthur, despite a bad beginning, later did much to heal.

The cautious attempts before the war to avoid provocation to Tokyo had prevented the United States from "casing" the Japanese bases on Formosa, and although Major General Louis H. Brereton, commanding the Army Air Forces in the Philippines, suggested a bombing mission against Formosa, the go-ahead was not given until late in the morning.[108]

The reasons and the responsibility for the delay are still the subject of military and historical controversy. Preliminary measures to prepare the B-17's for an offensive bombing mission were started before dawn, and General Brereton did discuss at about 5:00 A.M. "offensive action as soon as possible after daylight" with MacArthur's Chief of Staff. Sometime after 10:00 A.M. Brereton received permission to undertake a reconnaissance mission; then about 11:00 A.M. bombing missions were authorized.

It was too late. The virtually complete destruction of American airpower in the Philippines, a full nine to ten hours after first news of the Pearl Harbor attack, has been termed, quite correctly, less excusable than Pearl Harbor. Yet, in retrospect, the successful Japanese attacks in the Philippines had only a limited effect. There were some 25 Japanese airfields on Formosa, with more than 400 to 500 enemy planes, all fully ready for war. These fields had never been reconnoitered; there were no "calibrated bomb target maps or aerial photographs."[109] In these terms the thirty-five Flying Fortresses in the Philippines represented a minimal force against Japanese airpower; the B-17's might have died more gloriously in attempted offensive strikes, but they would have died quickly, and almost certainly (given the U.S. state of preparedness, and the inaccurate pattern of U.S. high-level bombardment) to little effect.

So an "ignominious" defeat came to the Philippines as it had to Pearl Harbor.

The B-17's and many pursuit planes had been on patrol in the early morning hours, but toward noon most U.S. aircraft in the islands were back on the ground, refueling, bombing up, preparing for attacks against Formosa later in the day.

Once again, the American forces were a sitting target.

Attacking Japanese formations were detected some distance away, but the alarm did not get through. The Japanese bombers high in the sky above Clark Field were "almost directly overhead at the time the air raid warning siren was sounded, and the bombs began exploding a few seconds thereafter."[110]

The field, "rimmed by a few trees and waist-high cogon" grass, had foxholes, trenches, and some revetments; they did little good. There was no air cover over Clark; it was time for the midday meal and most of the bomber and fighter crews and ground personnel were en route to and from the mess halls and flight line. Some eighteen P-40B pursuit planes were at the edge of the field, with the pilots resting in their cockpits or nearby. The big bombers clustered in a shining target close together, sunlight glittering from their wings.

A National Guard antiaircraft gun crew, grouped around their 3-inch and 37 mm. guns, looking up saw some black dots high in the sky . . . and some glittering silver objects falling beneath their bellies.

"Why are they dropping tinfoil?" someone asked. "That's not tinfoil, and those are goddamn Japs!" Then there was a roar like the sound of rushing freight trains.

At the other end of the field a crew chief of the 20th Pursuit Squadron shouted, "Good God Almighty, yonder they come!"[111]

Three P-40's got off in the midst of the falling bombs; four others were hit. The Japanese Zero fighters, accompanying the bombers, easily outmaneuvered them; the AA guns could not reach the bombing level and even so—plagued by corroded fuses—most shells were duds. Almost unopposed, the Japanese bombers, and particularly the strafing fighters, methodically demolished much of America's airpower in the Philippines.

Sakai Saburo, a Japanese Zero pilot who was to become an ace in the air war, later wrote of the "ludicrous" surprise: "The entire air base seemed to be rising into the air with the explosions. Pieces of airplanes, hangars, and other ground installations scattered wildly. Great fires erupted and smoke boiled upward."[112]

All but three of the Fortresses at Clark were destroyed in a few minutes, spiraling clouds of smoke and flame their pyre. And most of the fighter planes and miscellaneous aircraft were soon gone—in raids on Clark, on Iba, and on nearby Nichols early on the 9th, and on other fields in Luzon.

Colonel Carlos P. Romulo, who was to serve on MacArthur's staff and to become a symbol of U.S.-Philippine friendship, stood on a balcony in Manila observing the scene:

Unprotected and unprepared, Manila lay under the enemy planes—a city of ancient nunneries and chromium-fronted night clubs, of skyscrapers towering over nipa shacks, of antiquity and modernity, of East and West. . . .[113]

Again the broken bodies and the smashed debris were monuments to unpreparedness.

In less than 24 hours of hostilities, about one-half of all U.S. airpower in the Far East had been destroyed; 80 officers and men killed, 150 wounded. Hangars, shops, mess halls, supply buildings, the communications center, maintenance equipment, and radar installations were lost; runways cluttered with debris and bomb holes. All this at an insignificant cost to the Japanese, who had lost no bombers and only seven fighters.

In those shining hot days of December the Japanese aircraft bombed and strafed almost at will, ranging far and wide across Luzon and above the Visayans and Mindanao, completing the destruction. Nichols, Nielson, Del Carmen Field were hit; ships and small craft in Manila Bay were bombed, and on December 10 Cavite Navy Yard across the bay was virtually destroyed in a two-hour attack. At Canacao Hospital that day, the dock was red and slippery; the hospital attendants were splattered with the blood of hundreds of dead and wounded from the great raid at Cavite.

The Japanese bombers did their job with impunity; the 3-inch AA's protecting the naval base could not reach the 20,000-foot bombing altitude. The submarine *Sealion*, immobilized at the yard, was hit twice and settled in the mud; her crew blew up the tangled wreckage on Christmas Day, the first U.S. submarine lost in the war. *Seadragon* was pulled away, damaged but saved. The base itself was flaming chaos; air flasks and more than 200 torpedoes exploding in raging fires, many cremated, wounded, or dying in the flames: "The scene was one which brought to mind an old-time description of Hell. . . ."

Admiral Hart saw the holocaust from an office building in Manila; he was soon informed that most of the spare torpedoes for the Asiatic Fleet had been lost. He reported to Washington that Manila Bay was "untenable as a naval base," and ordered most of the surviving small surface craft southward. A few days later numerous commercial ships that had sought refuge in the supposedly safe harbor escaped before the tightening enemy blockade netted them.

Day after day the duck shoot went on. Baguio and Tarlac were hit, Cabanatuan and Batangas bombed; at Olongapo and Subic Bay, the patrol bombers of PatWing 10 were caught on the water, and within less than a week of war both the U.S. Army and Navy airpower in the Philippines "had been virtually destroyed." On the 14th, the remaining "Cats" of PatWing 10 were ordered south; all that remained in Luzon waters were some small craft—some of them damaged or under repair—and the submarines. A few days later the remaining B-17's, which had been based on the new field at Del Monte in Mindanao undiscovered by the Japanese, were ordered to Australia just in time; on December 19, Del Monte was raked and shattered by a carrier strike.

As far as U.S. airpower was concerned, the Philippine campaign had been a tale of almost total ineffectiveness, of calamity brightened only by many individual acts of bravery. It was in these first days that an American public, shocked and numbed by defeat, hungry for heroes, had been handed its first major myth of the war. Captain Colin P. Kelly, Jr., who was posthumously awarded the Distinguished Service Cross, piloted a surviving B-17 bomber over the sea off Luzon, and before he died in the wreckage of his bomber (shot down en route home to base) it was claimed he had sunk the Japanese battleship *Haruna*. Neither *Haruna* nor any other Japanese naval vessel was sunk; apparently a cruiser was attacked, but was undamaged. Then, as now, many pilots could not distinguish one type of warship from another, and in those days U.S. high-level bombing against moving targets was literally hit-or-miss—a matter of luck, not skill.

The Assault on Luzon

And so the defenders of the Philippines, isolated by sea and air, were caught in a closing net. The Japanese quickly followed their far-ranging air strikes with stepping-stone landings in many parts of the archipelago. Construction of advance air bases was started after landings on December 8 and 10 on little islands to the north of Luzon; then on December 10–11 about 4,000 to 5,000 Japanese troops landed, with little opposition, in extreme northern Luzon, near Aparri, a port of 26,000 people, and Vigan, to seize or establish airfields. From Palau 2,500 Japanese, with heavy sea and air cover, landed at Legaspi in South Luzon on December 12, again without opposition, and established a field. What was left of U.S. airpower tried to fend off these landings with futile results (two transports badly damaged by bombers and beached, a destroyer and light cruiser slightly damaged, two minesweepers beached or damaged).

WAR IN THE PHILIPPINES

About a week later, on December 20, another 5,000 men from Palau landed at Davao, principal city of the great southern island of Mindanao, with "the only opposition ... from a machine gun squad which inflicted numerous casualties ... before it was knocked out by a direct hit from a Japanese shell."[114] On the day before Christmas, a small Japanese force landed on the little island of Jolo, quickly routing the few defenders. The southern landings had put the enemy in position to hop, skip, and jump to Borneo and to command the important sea straits between the principal islands of the Philippine archipelago.

MacArthur's defense of the Philippines had concentrated its main strength on the most important island, Luzon. Under MacArthur, there were three separate commands in Luzon. Major General Jonathan Wainwright, an old cavalryman, commanded the North Luzon Force—virtually everything north of Manila. He had been assigned four Philippine Army divisions, one of which had strings on it and could be used only with headquarters' permission; the famous old 26th Cavalry Regiment, Philippine Scouts, and some supporting Scout artillery. The South Luzon Force under Brigadier General George M. Parker, who was responsible for the area east and south of Manila, consisted of two Philippine Army infantry divisions, with a small unit stiffening of U.S. and Philippine Scout and constabulary personnel. The Reserve Force, held around Manila, consisted of the U.S. Army Philippine Division and one Philippine Army division. The coast defenses of Manila and Subic Bay were manned by U.S. coast artillery regiments augmented by Philippine Scouts and by the 4th Marine Regiment (assigned to the fortified island of Corregidor), which had recently been transferred to the Philippines from China.

All the rest of the Philippine Islands south of Luzon—a vast stretch of sea, mountain, jungle, and accessible beaches—was assigned to the Visayan-Mindanao Force under Brigadier General William F. Sharp. His pitifully small defensive forces, scattered across many islands, consisted of three Philippine Army divisions, with a few Americans and Philippine Scouts in headquarters detachments.

General Sharp's primary mission was to defend U.S. airfields to be built in the Visayans; Del Monte, in Mindanao, was one of them. But in Luzon, Wainwright and Parker had been directed to hold the practical landing beaches "at all costs," especially those which gave onto the central Luzon Plain and the easy access terrain routes to Manila. The latest revision of the Orange war plans—WPO-3— specifically provided for a withdrawal to the Bataan Peninsula and a close defense of the Manila Bay position. MacArthur ignored this, however, and his plan for the defense of Luzon explicitly stated that there was to be "no withdrawal from beach positions"; they were to "be held at all costs."[115]

* * *

The main Japanese landing in Luzon came where it had long been expected, at Lingayen Gulf, with a secondary pincer landing in the south at Lamon Bay. Both were in a sense anticlimactic; the ultimate victory of the Rising Sun had already been assured. In two weeks American airpower in the islands had been wiped out; American naval power in the waters around the archipelago was negligible, and the Japanese had already established seaplane bases and land bases for short-range fighters in and around Luzon.

But Tokyo left nothing to chance. In the darkness before midnight on December 21, eighty-five Japanese transports, heavily protected by naval escort forces, dropped anchor in the shallow waters of the Gulf. At 0517, December 22, the first increments of the 43,000-man force—the bulk of General Homma's Fourteenth Army, spearheaded by the "best motorized division in the Japanese Army" (the 48th)—started landing on the shelving beaches of the Gulf. The Japanese planned to spread out along the good coastal highway, Route 3, which led through Damortis to the Luzon Plain and the gateway to Manila; to capture Baguio in the mountains, thus preventing an American flanking attack; and to make a junction near San Fernando with Japanese detachments, pushing southward from the earlier Aparri and Vigan landings.

High seas and bad weather aided the weak defenses. Some Japanese landing craft broached in the high surf; equipment was lost; radios were soaked, and the planned landing schedule disrupted. Most U.S. submarines, which had had little luck, found the shoal waters of the Gulf operationally impossible; S-38 managed to put a torpedo into the converted minelayer *Hayo Maru* and sink it. The next day the submarine *Seal* sank the small freighter *Hayataka Maru*, and a few Army planes and Navy PBY's strafed and bombed intermittently, "annoying" but not hurting the enemy. When the Japanese armada moved in closer to the beaches to escape the high seas, shore batteries bracketed some of the ships.

All this amounted to futility.

Two Philippine Army divisions, only one of them backed by artillery, were strung out along 120 miles of Gulf beaches, ill-sited and ill-prepared to meet assault. At just one point was there actual opposition to the landings at the beach; here one .50-caliber machine gun and several .30's caused some casualties among the attackers. But the .30's quickly jammed—defective ammunition that had been buried in the sand put them out of action—and the enemy moved swiftly inland.

By the night of the 22nd, the Japanese had pushed ahead against disorganized defenders to Rosario, a key junction town.

A wild melee in the night almost led to rout of the U.S. forces; Japanese tanks broke through a 26th Cavalry rearguard and "merged in the darkness with the struggling men and the terrified riderless horses." Major Thomas J. H. Trapnell blocked a bridge with a burning tank and saved his command.

By the 24th the Japanese had captured Baguio, the Philippine "summer capital" in the mountains, and the small American garrison had barely escaped after its commander radioed MacArthur: "My right hand in a vise, my nose in an inverted funnel, constipated my bowels, open my south paw."[116]

On the same day, despite a long, bitter delaying action by the 26th Cavalry, Philippine Scouts (now down to 450-man strength) along with some Stuart light tanks and small U.S. units, the Japanese were closing on the Agno River Line and facing a wide-open doorway to Manila.

The plain truth was evident. The much-vaunted Philippine Army units upon which General MacArthur had placed his principal reliance for defense of the islands had broken completely "at the first appearance of the enemy and then fled to the rear in a disorganized stream." It was not their fault; they were untrained, badly equipped, poorly led, with no will to fight. Close beside those who ran, there stood and fought and died their brother Filipinos of the 26th Cavalry, Philippine Scouts, an élite unit, well trained, well led, stiffened by U.S. professional officers—men who had long served in uniform and men who had pride in themselves and their outfit. Rather the fault lay higher up, with the fatuous notion that a mass of conscripts with little artillery, few tanks, no air support, "trained" after a fashion for five and a half months, could successfully oppose the best army in Asia. It was a bitter lesson in self-deception.

The second major Japanese landing on Luzon was made at Lamon Bay on Christmas Eve, just as the North Luzon Force was falling apart under the impact of the Lingayen Gulf landings. About 7,000 men (elements of the 16th Japanese Division) embarked at the Ryukyu Islands and streamed ashore to drive on Manila from the south in the classic hammer-and-anvil technique. The result in the south was much the same as in the north.

There was no defensive artillery within range of the landing beaches, and some of the defending infantry units were en route from one station to another. Some 51st Philippine Division troops had been ordered south to delay the advancing Japanese units that had landed at Legaspi. The new enemy landings took them in the rear; they were cut off and many were never heard from again. The invaders splayed out to either side of 7,100-foot Mount Banahao, their main effort to the west along Route 1. By nightfall the Japanese beachhead was completely secure, and despite the mountainous and difficult terrain the Japanese were well inland along Route 1—their casualties for this second pincer landing 84 dead, 184 wounded.

That day, General Homma landed at Lingayen, and advance Japanese elements were within 100 miles of Manila.

The Inevitable Defeat

It was a dismal Christmas season in the Philippines. On December 23–24, MacArthur, "viewing the broken, fleeing North Luzon force, realized that his cherished plan of defeating an enemy attempt to advance towards Manila from the north was not now possible"[117] and sent an order to all his commanders: "WPO-3 is now in effect."

Under brief but disastrous pressure, the bright dreams of holding all the Philippines had quickly shattered. U.S. forces reverted to the old plan of retirement into the Bataan Peninsula and Manila Bay's island fortresses.

But the sudden change of plans complicated and confused the supply situation, and came as a severe psychological blow to President Quezon and to many Filipinos who had been bemused by MacArthur's prewar optimism. Quezon and Francis Sayre (the U.S. High Commissioner to the Philippines) moved from Manila to Corregidor on December 24; MacArthur's headquarters shifted to the island Christmas morning. Behind them, Manila, which was publicly declared an "open" or undefended city on December 26, waited with apprehension. Flames and smoke rose from the Navy's million-gallon fuel tanks, deliberately fired with the evacuation. Enemy bombers wheeled above the city and bombed the waterfront. Supply trucks roared toward Bataan, where General Parker, shifted from the south, worked frantically with two Philippine divisions to prepare defensive lines and to stock the peninsula with supplies for a long siege. On December 26, at 2:00 in the morning, Admiral Hart, Commander-in-Chief of the Asiatic Fleet, boarded the submarine *Shark* and headed south to join his scattered fleet near the Malay barrier. The stiff-necked but plain-spoken and honest officer, respected by most who knew him, left in some dudgeon; staff work and cooperation between Army and Navy had been, in the Philippines as elsewhere, less than perfect, and Hart had not been informed by MacArthur of the intention to evacuate Manila. He "learned of it only by chance two days before."[118] The consequent loss of stores and shifting of facilities in the hurried evacuation reduced the period in which the submarines could continue to base on Manila, Hart had told General MacArthur.

In the event, they were gone by year's end. For much of December the submarines had been operating from a besieged base; when they returned from patrol for resupply or repairs and maintenance, Japanese bombers wheeling above Manila Bay had forced them to submerge during the daytime and lie on the Bay's bottom. Alongside *Canopus*, their only tender, they lay at night, working frantically under blackout lights and camouflage nets to prepare for the next patrol. The "secure" harbor of Manila Bay was no longer secure against the new third dimension of military power; the submarines, like the surface ships, had to retreat to the south.

They had been preceded in the last days of December by most of the Navy's few remaining surface ships: two damaged four-piper destroyers, *Pillsbury* and *Peary*, and seaplane tender *Heron*. Left behind for the trial of blood and endurance now beginning were the 4th Marines on Corregidor; the tender *Canopus*, which had been shifted to the Mariveles shore of the Bataan Peninsula (almost sunk on December 29 by an enemy armor-piercing bomb), and some small ships (three gunboats, three minesweepers, six motor torpedo boats, six small craft) which could not run the gantlet to the south or were held in Manila Bay to provide inshore patrol for the beleaguered Army.

The Asiatic Fleet—or large elements of it—had lived to fight another day, but it had accomplished little in defense of the Philippines. Navy men, shocked and frustrated by Pearl Harbor, were astounded that the enemy had made good all his landings in the Philippines with no serious losses, and that the Navy instead of selling itself dearly had lost no ships, save one or two to enemy bombs or grounding, around the islands. The failure of the submarines had been particularly depressing. The twenty-nine submarines in the Asiatic Fleet—probably the largest single submarine concentration in the world—had been assigned, even before war started, patrol stations, and they had not been frustrated by the niceties of international law. Ironically, as soon as World War II started, the United States employed almost the same unrestricted submarine warfare tactics as those used by the Germans—which had been instrumental in involving America in World War I. A directive was broadcast from Manila, soon after the first bombs dropped, to U.S. undersea craft already on patrol: "You will sink or destroy enemy shipping wherever encountered."[119]

But so far, as Manila cowered under enemy bombs, the submarines had sunk virtually nothing; only two unimportant little vessels near the Philippines.

There were a few sparse exceptions to the dismal tale of failure. *Swordfish*, on patrol off Hainan Island on December 16, sank the 8,663-ton *Atsutusan Maru*, the first enemy ship sunk by an American submarine in World War II.

The submarine failures were not due to lack of planning, or to political or military restrictions. In some considerable measure the most frustrating failure was technological. The magnetic and contact exploders in the new Mark 14 torpedoes were completely erratic. Some detonated the torpedoes on the way to the target; more frequently, hits were scored but the detonators failed to function; often the torpedoes ran too deep and passed under the targets. Time and again U.S. submarines in those early frustrating days scored hits, with no results.

"The history of the Asiatic submarines' attempt to check the Japanese invasion is a tale of torpedo misses too depressing to record in detail. . . ."[120]

There were other factors, too, which made for failure. As always in the transition from peace to war, many commanding officers with unblemished records in time of peace failed in war, ultimately ending up in desk jobs as censors or in administrative functions. Training and command and control were defective, and the submarines were too often "blind"; the air-submarine coordination essential to optimum achievements in maritime warfare was almost totally lacking. Nor was the "Magic" output—the product of intercepted, decrypted Japanese messages—available in systematized form in those early days. Later in the war, it would furnish valuable data about Japanese ship movements and convoy routings, which often helped U.S. submarines to find their targets, but in the defense of the Philippines it played little part.

For Admiral Hart—his headquarters in the Marsman Building bombed, his ships scattered—and for the Asiatic Fleet that he commanded, it was all over in the Philippines save for the missions of relief and rescue still to come.

But for the trapped forces on land the ordeal was just beginning. The retirement to Bataan was more easily ordered than accomplished. It involved the phased withdrawal of two widely separated forces in North and South Luzon, in the face of heavy enemy pressure and complete enemy air superiority.

And if it had not been for the discipline of the few and the brave leadership of a small cadre of American professionals, there would have been no retirement into Bataan. As it was, it was touch-and-go in those waning days of 1941.

Long lines of refugees fleeing a frightened city streamed north and south from Manila, as the disorganized defenders—fighting and falling back—tried to hold open a closing gateway from San Fernando along Route 7 into Bataan.

The withdrawal of the North Luzon Force had been preplanned as a series of brief delaying stands at five different positions, each selected for its defensive terrain. The limited success of the withdrawal—given the frightened, disorganized, and deserting Philippine Army forces—was dependent in very large measure upon engineers and their effectiveness in demolition and delay, upon several score light tanks (the survivors of the 108 tanks of a Provisional Tank Group), upon the exhausted 26th Cavalry, and upon some small infantry and artillery units (Americans and Philippine Scouts and Philippine Army) that had preserved their cohesion. The delaying positions covered the natural terrain gateway of the North Luzon Plain, commanding the main highways, with flanks anchored on the mountains to east and west.

The Japanese had reached and penetrated the Agno River Line, the second defensive position, by Christmas Day. By December 27, they had breached the third position; between the 28th and the 30th, they reached and penetrated the fourth between Tarlac and Cabanatuan; and by year's end, they were threatening the final position, which stretched in front of Mount Arayat and guarded Route 3 (up which the South Luzon Force must make good its retirement), and the junction at San Fernando of Routes 3 and 7 leading into Bataan.

The right flank of the American line was overrun and turned early on; the left flank was hard-pressed. At the battered city of Tarlac, one young American artillery instructor saved what was left of some Philippine infantry:

> . . . every man . . . who came out of Tarlac . . . alive should get down on his knees and thank God for that red-headed son of a bitch [First Lieutenant Carl J. Savoie]. He was everywhere he was needed at the right time. He kept the guns in almost three hours after he could have withdrawn to give us a chance to break off. We were all out and the enemy . . . into Tarlac before he pulled up a gun. . . .[121]

In about a week, the enemy had advanced some 50 miles; scarcely a position had been "really occupied and organized for defense"; many "stampeded . . . without firing a shot."

The small South Luzon Force pulled back across the peninsula from Lamon Bay to the west on two routes north and south of Mount Banahao. It was a retreat marked, like the one in the north, by the stout defense of a few men and the unreasoned reactions of the many untrained. On December 26, green Filipino troops were joined by some 300 retired, overage veterans of the Philippine Scouts, who had hurriedly been called back to the colors and rushed to the front in a fleet of taxicabs. But unlike Paris in World War I, when taxicabs helped to save the city at the Battle of the Marne, Manila was not to be saved. The veterans stiffened the "green 1st Infantry"; that was all.

Yet the withdrawal of the South Luzon Force (commanded now by Brigadier General Albert M. Jones, who had relieved Parker) across 140 miles of rugged terrain was far more successful than the retreat in the north. The Japanese, sluggish in advance, had been hampered—though never badly hurt—by skillful small unit actions and bridge destruction and demolitions. And in the end, Jones's force helped materially to save itself. Part of the 51st Infantry Regiment, rushed north past Manila, was in position by year's end, on Route 5, in front of Plaridel and Calumpit. Here the Japanese had turned the right flank of the North Luzon Force and were threatening the approaches along Routes 3 and 7 to the Bataan Peninsula.

At Baliuag, just to the north of Plaridel, one company of U.S. tanks fought a free-for-all battle with Japanese tanks and infantry in the nipa huts of the little town. In the fading twilight of the last day of 1941, the tanks "chased each other up and down the narrow streets" in wild action. Eight Japanese tanks were knocked out; the Americans had won brief time.

But the retreat continued pell-mell back toward Bataan, throughout the night and into the dawn of the New Year. At 6:15 A.M. on New Year's Day, the great bridge at Calumpit was blown. "In front of the defenders [the last of them the 51st Infantry from Jones's South Luzon Force] flowed the deep Pampanga [river]; to their rear lay San Fernando, where the road to Bataan began."

And so, as Manila—"pearl of the Orient"—lay awaiting the Japanese conquerors, the withdrawal to Bataan was made good.

In Manila, as the Old Year died, it was a strange end to an era. Cabarets and nightclubs were open, despite the bombed and blackened docks and flames among the nipa huts. Women in evening gowns thronged the Manila Hotel in last fiesta; toward midnight on the last day of the year some bartenders smashed their remaining bottles to keep them from the conquerors. Quartermaster stores and food stocks, left behind in the evacuation—soon to be sorely needed in Bataan—were distributed, gratis, to eager crowds. But along the Bay front, sunken ships, fire-blackened and bomb-blasted docks and buildings were "mute epitaph" to what had long been hailed as the great bastion of Manila Bay, nexus of American power in the Orient.

The withdrawal to Bataan had been a near thing but successful—"a complicated and difficult movement . . . with ill-equipped and inadequately trained Filipino troops . . . a tribute to the generalship of MacArthur, Wainwright and Jones and to American leadership. . . ."[122] But a limited "tribute"; not all the U.S. leadership was good. And retreat and defeat are always inglorious.

The North Luzon Force had lost some 12,000 of its original 28,000-man strength, most of them by desertion. Jones successfully brought some 14,000 of his original 15,000 men into Bataan. The Japanese had lost some 627 killed in action, plus double that number wounded.

Yet the Japanese themselves had accomplished much with little; their total strength on Luzon was considerably inferior, numerically, to the American-Philippine forces. And in the retreat many Philippine Army units had simply dissolved; recruits went home, never to return; thousands deserted. Others fled precipitously, leaving ammunition, supplies, heavy weapons behind. Units were disorganized. MacArthur's prewar assessments of the combat capabilities of the Philippine forces proved to be almost ridiculously optimistic.

The swift change in plans—from holding on the beaches to retreat to Bataan—had been almost catastrophic to supply. Tons of supplies had been left behind, or destroyed, in Manila and elsewhere. Instead of supplies for six months cached in the peninsula, much food and equipment had been shifted north and south to the invasion beaches. There were no mosquito nets, shelter halves, or blankets; clothing was in short supply, and there was very little quinine, even though the Philippines was a malarial area. Weapons, equipment, ammunition, all were in limited or short supply; no field fortifications had been built across the Bataan Peninsula. And into Bataan, with the tired soldiers, crowded some 26,000 civilian refugees to add to the mouths to feed. There was not nearly enough food, only sufficient for twenty to fifty days, some of it on short rations.

The retirement had been successful, after a fashion; it had spelled delay to the Japanese conquerors. But its manner forecast the inevitable end.

Thus 1941 closed in the Orient with American power everywhere in defeat or retreat. . . .

20

Asia for the Asiatics

In the ruck of great defeat, some slight solace for American emotions could be derived from two early air battles in China. In this great land—long tied by missionary associations and picturesque romanticism to American hearts—a prescient Army pilot named Claire L. Chennault, who had been retired for deafness since 1937, had been serving as special adviser to the Chinese Air Force. During 1941, while Japan was rampaging across China and Chiang Kai-shek was cut off from Western aid save by the tortuous Burma Road, Chennault "sold" to the White House (with some service reluctance) the idea of an American Volunteer Group of pilots and ground crew personnel to aid the Chinese in their struggle against Japanese imperialism.

In the summer before Pearl Harbor, volunteer American Army and Navy pilots on inactive status formed the first contingent of what history was to know as the "Flying Tigers." And by September 1941, some 100 P-40B pursuit planes (a model considered obsolescent in U.S. and British circles) had been transported to Rangoon, Burma, for initial training. In November, forty-three of the planes, eighty-four pilots were usable; after Pearl Harbor they were soon in action.

Two squadrons of "Flying Tigers" shifted to Kunming soon after Pearl Harbor and took a fliers' revenge for their comrades' losses in Hawaii and the Philippines. They caught attacking Japanese bombers by surprise and caused heavy losses (shooting down six). Three days later, at Mingaladon, Burma, another squadron, along with RAF fighters, took on a formation of bombers attacking Rangoon, with good results; these were the small beginnings of an increasing American involvement in China and with Chiang Kai-shek.

Save as a morale factor, they were of scant help to a China overrun by Japanese. In late 1941, China had been at intermittent war with Japan for almost a decade, and since 1937 the Japanese Army had overrun much of the country. In December the Japanese flag flew above Peking; Nanking, which had been Chiang Kai-shek's provisional capital; Canton; Tientsin; virtually all of the coastal littoral; and most of the principal cities. The Nationalist government had withdrawn to Chungking far up the Yangtze, and was cut off—save by air and an uncertain route through Burma—from the outside world.

The China fighting had been a costly war to both powers. In five years of struggle from 1937 through 1941, the Chinese had lost more than a million dead; the Japanese, perhaps 300,000. The "China Incident" had grown into the greatest land campaign of the war save only the struggle of the Titans in Russia. And it was still unended.

When Japan attacked Pearl Harbor, Tokyo had large forces tied down on the Asiatic mainland or adjacent islands: five or more divisions in the home islands; some thirteen divisions in the Kwantung Army in Manchuria, plus two in Korea; ten divisions in North China, eleven in Central China, four in South China, three in Formosa, one in Hainan Island, and two in French Indochina.

Chinese Nationalist troops—large in number, small in capability—were still fighting sporadically against the Japanese although Chiang viewed his remaining forces as political, as much as military, gambits; but they represented no threat to the Japanese southern ambitions.

But to Generalissimo Chiang, Hong Kong was important to Nationalist survival, and Chungking sent to the Crown colony a liaison mission under a one-legged Chinese admiral, Chan Chak, to try to coordinate Anglo-Chinese operations.

Hong Kong: The Eighteen Days

Implicit in the entire Japanese scheme of conquest in 1941 was the expulsion of the white man from the Orient; it was to be "Asia for the Asiatics," a not-unpopular rallying cry for the peoples of the East who had been so long ruled and patronized by white conquerors.

Hong Kong, one of the ancient symbols of British power and influence in the Orient, to the Japanese represented a secondary objective. Isolated behind the tide of Japanese conquests in China and in Asia's barrier islands, it had lost its usefulness as a military-naval base, and even London regarded Hong Kong as an outpost to be held as long as possible before it was overrun.

The Japanese saw in the conquest of Hong Kong an opportunity to humble the white man and to demonstrate to the stubborn Chinese Nationalist Government in Chungking that "Empire" in Hong Kong held no hope and that the way of the future lay with Japan.

Hong Kong, great entrepôt, trading and distributing center, wealthy and prosperous, was a gem in the British imperial diadem, home of the *Tuan* since the Opium Wars. It was, to Japan, only a military thorn, but its conquest promised a sharp blow to British pride and "face"—the all-important intangible of power in the Orient.

Lieutenant General T. Sakai, commanding the Twenty-third (or South China) Army, was assigned the task of overrunning Hong Kong, and the 38th Division, reinforced, was given the job.

Its opposition was far inferior, not in terms of numbers (the Japanese had only a slight margin of numerical superiority) but in combat effectiveness. The 38th Division was blooded in the China fighting and was well trained; it knew all of the British dispositions in Hong Kong, Kowloon, and the Leased Territories on the mainland, and had far more artillery and specialized engineering supplies. Sir Mark Young, Governor and Commander-in-Chief of the Crown Colony, and Major General C. M. Maltby, his Army commander, commanded six battalions—two of them Canadian, recently arrived, poorly trained, and inadequately equipped—augmented by 1,759 men (many of them over-age) of the Hong Kong Volunteer Defense Corps, and tiny Navy and Air Force contingents. There were some twenty-nine guns available in and around the main island, varying in caliber from 4-inch to 9.2-inch, most of which were intended for defense against seaborne attack.

The defense was greatly complicated and weakened by two factors: the water supply, and the large urban concentration (mostly Chinese). There were about 800,000 people on Hong Kong itself, chiefly in the main town, Victoria; another 154,000 afloat in junks and boats in the harbors, coves, and islets nearby; and another 775,000 in Kowloon, across the strait, and in the Leased Territories. Reservoirs and water catchment areas were barely adequate for the population, and the water mains (on the surface or lightly covered) were vulnerable to rupture by bombardment.

The greatest weaknesses were lack of air and naval power, Hong Kong's isolation, and the same complacent overconfidence that had helped to preface disaster at Pearl Harbor and in the Philippines. At Kai Tak Airfield near Kowloon, there were exactly five RAF planes— all of them obsolete—and little antiaircraft artillery. The naval contingent consisted of one destroyer, eight motor torpedo boats, four gunboats, and some armed patrol vessels, a boom across the narrowest part of the approach to the harbor and some minefields.

Hong Kong had, it is true, some natural defensive advantages—rugged terrain and, on the island itself, the spiny central massif crowned by The Peak, 1,800 feet high. This fact, its sea-girt shores, and some air-raid tunnels and depots dug into the hills, plus considerable stocks of food, seem to have helped persuade the British garrison that the island was "impregnable."

The British overconfidence and underestimation of the enemy was sublime. British intelligence about Japanese dispositions or strengths just across the border in China was grossly erroneous, and their estimation of Japanese combat effectiveness downright ludicrous:

> They were reported to be inexpert at night operations and addicted to stereotyped methods and plans and their automatic weapons were thought to be neither so numerous nor up to date as the British. . . . The Japanese air force . . . was believed to be inferior, its bombing poor and night flying little practiced . . . their aircraft for the most part obsolete, the pilots myopic and unable to carry out dive-bombing.[123]

But the myopic vision was a failure peculiar to the Westerner's view of the Oriental, and particularly to the limited vision of the white man in Asia. The white man—and particularly the British Raj—had had his way for so long that a racial superiority complex and a kind of contemptuous paternalism for what Kipling described as "lesser breeds without the law" had clouded military, as well as social and political, objectivity.

The rude awakening came to Hong Kong early in the morning of December 8. There was no surprise; the entire garrison stood to arms by 6:45 A.M., and by 7:30 all road and railroad bridges across the Sham Chun River—the frontier of the Leased Territories on the mainland—had been blown. It did scant good.

Thirty-six Japanese bombers and fighters bombed Kai Tak at 8:00 A.M., destroying all five British military aircraft and eight civilian planes, and chewing up the field. So much for British airpower in China.

The 38th Division crossed the Sham Chun River in force and pushed quickly—quicker than Maltby had expected—in two groups, the main effort with two regiments to the west, toward the British defensive positions on the mainland. British covering forces offered only slight delay. Maltby had committed three battalions to defense of the Kowloon–Leased Territory area, hoping to hold or delay the Japanese for a week or ten days on the mainland. He had too few troops to attempt to defend all of the British territory, so he put his main defensive position close in to thickly settled Kowloon, with a battalion of the Royal Scots holding the heights to the west and two Indian Army battalions (the Punjabis and Rajputs) in the center and right partially covered by Tide Cove. Aptly enough, for an era that was passing, this defensive position was called the "Gindrinkers' Line" (so-named from the bay of similar name on the western flank).

The British position had two faults: it could be dominated by terrain features in the Leased Territory; and it was so close to Kowloon, it was the last defensive position possible on the mainland. If the Gindrinkers' Line was breached, it was back to Hong Kong Island.

It was quickly breached.

By the afternoon of December 9, Japanese detachments had ferried Tide Cove on the right of the British position, and that night (December 9/10), a key redoubt—the Shing Mun Redoubt on Smuggler's Ridge, a vital terrain feature on the western end of the Gindrinkers' Line—was overwhelmed in a Japanese night attack. The attacking enemy, in "rubber-soled canvas shoes . . . cleared gaps in the wire . . . dropped down the ventilating shafts of the tunnels," and stormed their way in hand-to-hand fighting into the underground defenses. A platoon of the Royal Scots fought valiantly but futilely.

The loss of the redoubt compromised the whole line of defense; by 10:00 A.M. on December 10, Maltby was contemplating evacuation from the mainland.

The British worked frantically, hampered by a tremendous press of Chinese junks in the harbor. Naval and other supplies were evacuated from the mainland; Kai Tak was blocked and the runway obstructed; dockyards dismantled. Stonecutters Island, near Kowloon, site of gun emplacements, magazines, and radio station, which was under both dive-bombing and artillery attack, was prepared for demolition.

On December 11 the Japanese almost broke through on the western flank, but the Royal Scots, mauled, decimated, slowly refused their flank and fell back fighting.

At noon, December 11, the order to evacuate the mainland was issued—only three days after the start of war. It was a complex operation, made no easier by the desertion of the Chinese crews who manned the Kowloon-Victoria ferries. But the Kowloon dockyards and oil supplies were destroyed; Stonecutters Island batteries blown up; merchant ships trapped in harbor scuttled; power station in

Kowloon destroyed. As the British retired beneath clouds of oily smoke and blazing fires through the congested, blacked-out town, looting started.

Most of the mainland defenders got to Hong Kong Island across the narrow strip of water on the night of December 11/12; and by dawn of the 13th, the rest of the Rajput Battalion (leaving some of their stores and 120 mules behind) gave up their defense of Devil's Peak and were ferried by the Navy's small craft across the narrow neck of water—Lei U Mun—to the "impregnable" citadel of Hong Kong.

The island, with its steep peaks—not crowded then as now with high-rise apartment buildings and office skyscrapers—provided terrain and communications which both favored and hampered defense. The precipitous heights gave commanding observation points over all water areas around Hong Kong, and the narrow peninsulas of the coastline could be dominated and held at many natural constricting bottlenecks. But the size of the island and particularly the many miles of waterfront were too much for the capabilities of the few defenders, and a single coastal road around the island and one across it at Wong Nei Chong Gap greatly restricted mobility and hampered the rapid shifting of reserves.

Even more important, Hong Kong had no answer to the ceaseless pounding from the skies which ruptured water mains and destroyed communications, and the heavy artillery bombardment from the mainland. Japanese landings were made on Lamma Island off the south coast of Hong Kong, and guns commenced to pound the Aberdeen and Repulse Bay areas. In the congested slums of Victoria, some of the latent Chinese resentment against the British *Tuan* and against colonialism (encouraged, perhaps, by Japanese bribes and Fifth Column organization) surfaced in the form of looting, some violence, and alarmist reports.

On December 15, and for the next four days, the Japanese—their guns now in position ringing the island—commenced a deliberate and systematic pounding from artillery, mortars, and from the air. The shelling created havoc with both military and civilian objectives. It inhibited the distribution of ammunition to the defenders, tore up coast defenses and the Aberdeen Dockyard, and damaged three of the Navy's remaining small craft.

The Japanese made their first landing attempt, covered by the dominating Devil's Peak on the mainland, across the narrow gap of Lei U Mun channel, paddling rubber boats in broad daylight toward

Hong Kong. In the dry words of the British official history, they were "repulsed with considerable loss."

On December 17, after a heavy bombing of Victoria and other objectives, two launches with white flags bore Japanese emissaries to Hong Kong demanding, for the second time, surrender.

Sir Mark Young had received one of Winston Churchill's exhortatory messages on December 12:

> . . . You guard a link between the Far East and Europe long famous in world civilization. We are sure that the defense of Hong Kong against barbarous and unprovoked attack will add a glorious page to British annals. . .[124]

The Governor gave the Japanese envoys short shrift:

> The Governor and Commander-in-Chief Hong Kong . . . declines most absolutely to enter into any negotiations for the surrender of Hong Kong and he takes this opportunity of notifying Lt-Gen. Takaishi Sakai and Vice Admiral Masaichi Niimi that he is not prepared to receive any further communications from them on the subject.[125]

Brave words, but quickly answered with the unanswerable arguments of bombardment. On the 18th, Victoria was in panic after the center of the city had been mercilessly bombed and thousands of uncontrollable, panic-stricken Chinese streamed away from the narrow streets and flaming debris by every exit. More and more the attrition of high explosives wore down the defenders; observation points on the high hills were obliterated, batteries destroyed, pillboxes smashed, and communications broken.

On the night of December 18/19 the enemy came streaming across the mile or so of water from the mainland to the north shore in sampans, barges, small craft, ferries, junks. Most of the searchlights had been destroyed and the beach wire ripped up or cut—some by dissident Fifth Columnists. Although the Rajputs, who lost most of their officers, did some damage with machine-gun and mortar fire, six Japanese battalions (the first wave of the 38th Division) had made good their beachhead on the "impregnable" fortress island before midnight.

Thereafter, the issue was never in doubt. Broken communications, the lack of mobility of the defenders, and a brave but unskilled defense doomed Hong Kong quickly. By nightfall of the 19th, with Japanese streaming largely unhampered in "every type of craft" across the harbor from the mainland, the attackers were in the grounds of the Repulse Bay Hotel on the island's south coast—that citadel of British tradition and colonialism, where afternoon tea was still a daily ritual. The Japanese also pushed close to the vital cross-island road in the Wong Nei Chong Gap, and during the night occupied positions that dominated about half this crucial route.

The rest was a history of stubborn but largely uncoordinated small unit action. The fighting around the Gap and the Repulse Bay Hotel, a key to the southern approaches to the cross-island road, where some women and children had sheltered, with a Canadian company ordered to hold it "at all costs," was bitter; but the Japanese—despite losses—still came on, and the British strength weakened. The power station on North Point, held by a party of wounded men and a detachment of the Hong Kong Volunteer Defense Force called the "Hughesiliers" (for the name of their commanding officer), all over fifty-five, refused surrender, held out for twenty-four hours, and were all killed or captured in an effort to cut their way through the Japanese lines. Aberdeen Dockyard, defended by naval ratings and a military conglomerate, was heavily engaged and completely devastated; and the end of resistance at the Repulse Bay Hotel, and its helpless women and children, came on December 22.

By this date the Japanese had completely nullified British plans for long resistance. They had occupied key heights, cut main roads, won strategic positions, and had damaged, destroyed, or captured pumping stations and reservoirs which supplied precious water to the island. Mains were broken; Fifth Columnists were rampant, civilians fleeing, houses flaming; and the Japanese were slowly infiltrating the steep slopes and gulleys and the narrow streets.

About this time—December 21—came another of those now famous Churchillian exhortations, beautifully phrased, absurdly unrealistic, and chillingly irritating to men who were dying with their boots on.

Inspired, in part, by the disasters elsewhere in the Pacific, and alarmed by the quick collapse of British resistance on the mainland, Churchill adjured the Governor to "house to house" fighting: "Every day that you are able to maintain your resistance you help the Allied cause. . . ."[126]

Early on Christmas morning, time had run out. The Japanese were massed to push into Victoria itself; the defenders, exhausted, without food, low on water, most of their officers killed, organizations jumbled, were still fighting desperately but with little hope. One group of defenders consisted of the thirty-four surviving members of a Canadian company, fourteen RAF men, ten Royal Navy sailors, and some forty-three members of the Dockyard Defense Corps, a paramilitary organization.

Two British officials who had been captured by the Japanese were sent by General Sakai through the lines under a flag of truce to describe to Maltby and the Governor the immense Japanese superiority and to persuade the British that surrender was the only course. The Governor rejected the suggestion once again—but not for long. At 3:15 P.M. on Christmas Day, 1941, Maltby told the Governor "there was no possibility of further effective resistance," and that night in Kowloon, at a symbol of British tradition—the Peninsula Hotel—Sir Mark Young surrendered Hong Kong unconditionally to the Japanese conquerors, after a battle of eighteen days.

On the Stanley Peninsula, where a stout defense by a small isolated British force had cost the Japanese dearly, the surrender was viewed with incredulity; it was not warranted, Brigadier C. Wallis believed, "by the local situation." He demanded confirmation in writing of the surrender orders, and held out until he got them at 2:30 A.M. on December 26. But, enraged at their losses, and to help convince the defenders to surrender, Japanese soldiers celebrated the Christian Christmas by the same bestiality already displayed time and time again in China and to be repeated on other battlefields of World War II. In a captured field hospital they bayoneted sixty of the wounded patients, cornered Chinese and British nurses, doctors, orderlies, and aides, and engaged in mass and bloody sadism. A few at a time, the male prisoners were slowly dismembered, disemboweled, eyes gouged out, fingers chopped off. The nurses were gang-raped in a welter of blood, and seven were bayoneted to death.[127]

The Pacific's new battlefields were quickly showing that this was a different war, that life is cheap in the Orient, and that cruelty (horrible cruelty in Western eyes) was an inherent part of the nature of the new enemy. It would all be a profound shock to men of the West, bred in a very different culture.

Chiang Kai-shek's Chungking Mission, which had promised much in the form of Nationalist Army attacks against the Japanese rear, but had produced nothing, escaped. The British had told Chiang that Admiral Chan Chak and his officers would not be allowed to fall into Japanese hands. True to their promise, the British arranged evacuation by what remained of their motor torpedo boat flotilla on Christmas Eve. In a tragicomedy of errors, the Admiral and his party missed an initial rendezvous with the torpedo boats and procured a civilian launch which was sunk by Japanese gunfire. But indomitable Chan Chak, without his artificial leg and with a bullet through his wrist, swam ashore, found the MTB's, made it to the China mainland, and with the surviving British crews of the torpedo boats somehow eluded capture and stumped through Japanese lines, led by a guerrilla leader, to Chungking. It was his only impress upon history.

His mission, too, was premonitory. Chiang Kai-shek had been loud on promises, short on delivery, as indeed he was to prove again and again in the months to come.

Another stone in the imperial diadem had gone, taken by the might of Japan in a far shorter period than the Western world had expected. The fighting had been sanguinary indeed; there had been no lack of courage, only (on the part of the British) of means and skill. About 4,440 of the British defenders had been killed or wounded; the capitulation put the rest of the 11,848 men in uniform in Japanese prison camps, where death for many swiftly followed— the first large bag of Western prisoners since the Russo-Japanese War. The Japanese losses, heaviest in the fighting around the cross-island road and in the stout defense of the Stanley Peninsula, were about 675 killed in action, 2,079 wounded. The civilian toll in crowded Victoria, in Kowloon, and in the shacks and shanties of the smaller towns will never be fully known.

The Road to Singapore

But the sack of Hong Kong was incidental to the principal goals of Japan's "Strike South" plans.

The entire Japanese plan was keyed to the conquest of economic goals: oil, rubber, tin. It was timed, in part, to weather; in the north in Manchuria and along the Siberian frontier, the cold and snows of winter—and the Russian stand in front of Moscow—inhibited any major danger, Tokyo thought, from the Communists. On the other hand, the weather was favorable in the South Seas.

Only a fraction of the total Japanese land strength and part of its airpower could be used in the southern drive. In December 1941, forty or more of Japan's fifty-one divisions were tied down in Manchuria, China, and the home islands. Field Marshal Count Terauchi, who was designated Supreme Commander-in-Chief Japanese Forces, Southern Region, was assigned only 11 divisions and some 700 Army aircraft, aided by about 500 naval planes and major elements of the Japanese Fleet, to conquer the Philippines, Borneo, Malaya, the Dutch East Indies, Thailand (then generally known as Siam), and Burma. His headquarters were in Saigon, where some 40,000 Japanese troops had been stationed. Camranh Bay with its beautiful harbor, Saigon, then a sleepy French town deserving its self-appellation of "the little Paris of the Orient," and other areas in the helpless Vichy fief of French Indochina served as staging bases for the Japanese.

The plans for the southern advance contemplated the successive seizure of strategic stepping stones toward their major objectives. The conquest of Malaysia and the capture of Singapore, expected to require 100 days, was the linchpin of the first phase of southern expansion.

Four divisions of the Japanese Twenty-fifth Army (Lieutenant General Tomoyuki Yamashita commanding) were allocated for the Malaysian conquest; in the event, one was never used.

The first landings, timed to coincide roughly with the Pearl Harbor-Philippines-Hong Kong attacks, were made by troops phased through Hainan Island and Indochina before dawn, December 8, at Singora and Patani just north of the Malayan border and at Kota Bharu in northern Malaya. These landings were directed at a British group of airfields in northern Malaya, gave access to the main north-south roads leading toward Singapore, and ensured strategic domination of the narrow neck of the Kra Isthmus.

Almost simultaneously, the Fifteenth Japanese Army of two divisions,[128] charged with the conquest of Thailand and Burma, landed near Siamese airfields further north in the Kra Isthmus at Nakhorn, Bandon, and Jumbhorn, and at Prachuab. Units of the Imperial Guards Division, later shifted to Malaya, occupied and overawed Bangkok, the Thai capital, and subsequently, moving overland, occupied the railroad and airfields near it—all against little or no opposition.

While this three-ring military circus—a masterpiece of Japanese operational and logistic planning—was unfolding, Singapore itself was shocked into war by a Japanese air raid about 4:00 A.M. on the 8th by seventeen naval bombers, based on southern Indochina. The great city, blazing with lights, clearly outlined in the tropical moonlight, was psychologically and in other ways unready for war. The Japanese raiders were picked up some distance out and the AA guns were manned and ready but the Air Raid Precautions Headquarters was unmanned; the phone rang and no one answered. To the sleeping city, the raid was an "unpleasant shock," which had a "profound effect . . . complete surprise . . ." even though there was little military damage. Two hundred Oriental civilians were casualties.

On the eve of war Singapore, like Hong Kong, was fatuously self-confident. So many people had talked in terms of soothing reassurance, so many journalists and politicians had used confident platitudes and extravagant phrases to describe Singapore ("bastion of Empire," "Gibraltar of the Far East," "impregnable fortress")[129] that the British and their Allies, from Melbourne to Singapore to London, had sold themselves a bill of goods.

Singapore was viewed in 1941 as the pivot point of all British strategy in Southeast Asia. The city—in memory, in pride, in literature—had a proud place in British imperial tradition; the Raffles Hotel, the Singapore Club, citadel of the *Tuan* with its gin slings and pink gins, the *pukka-sahib* rubber planters—were familiar words in London, and there was a still lively romanticism, exotic with the strangeness of the East, in the opium dens, the Happy World Dance Hall, the scenes and settings popularized by Somerset Maugham and Joseph Conrad. Singapore was the ideological capital of British power in the East, a great shipping center, and a financial nexus.

It was also regarded as a fortress from which British sea- and air-power could dominate the adjacent areas. The great naval dockyard in Johore Strait had been planned to handle any ships of that day, and the harbor at the tip of the peninsula, protected by outlying islands, was a commercial haven. The island was heavily protected by fixed defenses—five great 15-inch guns, six 9.2-inch, and eighteen 6-inch commanded the seaward approaches. But these guns were sited to fire against ships, and most of their ammunition was armor-piercing, not designed for use against land targets. There were forty 3.7-inch antiaircraft guns for the defense of the island's three airfields, the harbor, and the naval base; the rest of the antiaircraft defense—3-inch and light automatic weapons—could not reach the ceiling of Japanese bombers.

But Singapore's defenses to the landward, or northern side, facing the Malaysian Peninsula, were negligible. It was a fortress with a natural moat, Johore Strait, but no towering ramparts, no portcullis, no crenellated towers to hold off an enemy, a fact which even Winston Churchill did not discover to his horrified surprise until too late.

Partly because of friction[130] which had distinguished the commands of prewar Army and Air Force commanders in Malaya, partly because it was obvious that air and ground strategy, plans, and operations had to be coordinated, and partly to pull together the far-flung and disparate British interests in the Far East, a unified command—

of a sort—had been created. Air Chief Marshal Sir Robert Brooke-Popham was recalled from retirement in the fall of 1940 and designated Commander-in-Chief Far East. The Royal Navy was exempt from his command. Nor was there any provision for coordination between the military and the civil authorities; Governor Sir Shenton Thomas, who had been directed to give top priority to rubber and tin production badly needed for the war (a directive which handicapped proper military preparations) had his own chain of communications to London and was in charge of civil defense and other vital elements of mobilization.

The command situation was so obviously defective and its failures so apparent in the first days of war that on December 10, Alfred Duff Cooper was appointed Resident Minister for Far Eastern Affairs and quickly established a war council of all the disparate commanders to try to make sense of an uncoordinated strategy and to harness individual efforts. Later in the month, December 27, Brooke-Popham, who had scarcely distinguished himself, was relieved by a younger man—Lieutenant General Sir Henry Pownall, British Army, whose command, however, was strictly limited to nonoperational matters. Almost it seemed that the hierarchical bureaucracy of the British government, particularly fractionalized and individualistic in the Far East with its numerous little satrapies and power centers, had doomed a defensive effort before it began.

Lieutenant General A. E. Percival was General Officer, Commanding, Malaya, responsible for the ground defense of all of Malaya and Singapore Island, and of the remote, thinly settled but rich British possessions in Sarawak and Brunei, Borneo, on the flank of the Japanese southward advance. One battalion was assigned around the oil-producing centers in Borneo; all the rest of Percival's 88,600 men were allocated to the defense of Malaya and Singapore. The British forces were organized in about three and a half divisions —the 8th Australian and the 9th and 11th Indian Divisions—polyglot forces of a few well-trained regulars and many amateur soldiers, including 19,600 British, 15,200 Australians, 37,000 Indians, and almost 17,000 Malaysian and Singapore local Asiatic volunteers. The numbers were considerably short of the total believed needed for adequate defense.

Air Vice Marshal C. W. H. Pulford, Air Command, Far East, had available at the outbreak of war about 180 operational planes in his entire command, 158 in Malaya—many of them obsolete. There were four day fighter squadrons, all flying the new but obsolescent American Brewster Buffalo which was no match for the Zero, and one night fighter squadron, two light bomber and two torpedo bomber squadrons, and three reconnaissance squadrons. The air strength was at least 400 planes short of the minimum considered necessary for adequate defense, and—more important—the planes available were grossly inferior to those of the enemy.

The deficiency in air strength was almost fatal, but it was to be coupled with other deficiencies—in, for instance, the techniques of jungle and night fighting—that brought calamitous defeat much sooner than anyone, save the enemy, had expected.

In truth, Singapore in December 1941 was a poor military relation.

Britain had muddled through the first three years of war, sore-pressed at home, on the verge of defeat in the skies, on the seas, and in the desert, with little to spare for that focus of British power far away in the East.

Furthermore, there had been muddled thinking as to Singapore's role.

Like Pearl Harbor, Singapore was of primary importance as a naval base, a nautical *point d'appui* upon which fleets could base and from which they could deploy to control the surrounding seas.

Prewar British planning about the Far East had been almost as unrealistic as had U.S. war plans. The original U.S. Orange war plan had contemplated the successful defense of the Manila Bay area for some sixty to ninety days, while the U.S. Pacific Fleet fought its way westward from Hawaii through the spiderweb of the Japanese Mandated Islands to defeat the Japanese Fleet in a setpiece battle and relieve the Philippines. (This concept, conceived before recognition of the importance of airpower, was gradually shelved in Washington before the war as Japanese superiority became manifest, and Pearl Harbor gave it the final *coup de grâce*.) Similarly, Britain had long planned in case of war against Japan to send the "main fleet to Singapore." As Captain Russell Grenfell, R.N., points out, "'the passage of the fleet to Singapore' became one of the standard exercises [between the wars] at the Staff College."[131] Under these plans Fortress Singapore was supposed to hold out for seventy days, with the fleet en route to relieve it. But by 1939, this time of passage had been stretched to 180 days, and when war actually came, it was soon apparent that the Royal Navy, hard-pressed in the Atlantic and the Mediterranean, would not be able to send the "main fleet" or even any very impressive fleet at all.

Throughout the war, there had been no fleets at Singapore, simply small, light local sea defense forces; Britain's fleet was stretched thin in other oceans. And seapower, as the Mediterranean battles had already shown, now needed wings in the skies above the waters to perform its traditional function. In 1941 there were nowhere near enough planes or ships. The priorities, as Winston Churchill saw them, were: first, Britain; second, the Mediterranean; third, Russia; and last, the war against Japan. As late as August 29, 1941, Churchill told the Admiralty, "I cannot feel that Japan will face the combination now forming against her of the United States, Great Britain, and Russia, while already preoccupied in China." But he added, with some prescience, that he thought Tokyo would "negotiate with the United States for at least three months" before making "any further aggressive moves."[132]

Nevertheless, Churchill tended to regard the presence of some major naval units in the Singapore-Indian Ocean area as a deterrent to Japanese aggression, just as Roosevelt thought the U.S. Fleet at Pearl Harbor (rather than on the Pacific coast) would discourage Tokyo. The Prime Minister, who never forgot he stood at the apex of empire, had also to consider the sensibilities of Australia and New Zealand, and their understandable desire for naval protection.[133]

"Main Fleet to Singapore"

Earlier in 1941, during the American-British staff conversations in Washington of January through March which led to the development of the U.S. Army-Navy Rainbow 5 war plan, the British had tried hard to persuade the United States to divide its Pacific Fleet between Hawaii and Singapore. There was no agreement except for a notation to disagree; "for Great Britain it was fundamental that Singapore be held; for the United States it was fundamental that the Pacific Fleet be held intact."

The divergence of view about the strategic importance of Singapore was only one difference, which emphasized the extremely tentative features of the planning and prevented any prewar arrangements for the joint use of available forces or for unified commands. The major conclusion of the staff talks and of Rainbow 5, which was to influence all Allied strategic planning and be a bone of contention throughout the war, was agreement on a "Germany-first" strategy, and an assumption of a "strategic defensive in the Far East, with the U.S. Fleet employed offensively 'in the manner best calculated to weaken Japanese economic power, and to support the defense of the Malay Barrier by directing Japanese strength away from Malaysia.' "[134]

Brave words indeed, but meaningless after Pearl Harbor and even before, given the discrepant Japanese strength in the Pacific.

In the debate about what should be based on Singapore and when, the purposes and capabilities of the base appear to have been overlooked. A naval base exists for the basing of a navy—its sustenance, maintenance, repair, and protection when it returns from the sea. Yet Singapore, which was not quite complete, lacked in 1941 the trained dockyard personnel, the spare parts, and the machine tools fully to carry out major repairs on large ships.[135]

Thus in December 1941, major units of British seapower had been assigned to Singapore to act as a deterrent to Japanese aggression and to defend a base that was not completed, rather than using Singapore as a springboard for control of the seas around it.

The force that was to perform this nautical conjuring trick consisted of the old battle cruiser *Repulse*, which had been assigned to the East Indies station in early October, and the new battleship *Prince of Wales*, detached from the Home Fleet (despite Admiralty objections) in late October. The new aircraft carrier *Indomitable*, which was to have accompanied her, was laid up for repairs after a grounding accident. This was the first irony; the second was that *Prince of Wales* flew the flag of Admiral Sir Tom ("Tom Thumb") Phillips, short of stature, quick of mind, who in the past had irritated some of the moguls of the Admiralty because of his rather clear-sighted emphasis on the capabilities and limitations of airpower.

Somewhat grandiloquently for the small force he commanded, he was designated Commander-in-Chief Eastern Fleet. But Phillips had had far more staff than command experience.

Prince of Wales touched at Capetown in mid-November; Jan Christiaan Smuts, the old Prime Minister, cabled Churchill that he did not think much of the Allied naval division in the Pacific: two fleets, one at Hawaii, another at Singapore, each inferior in strength to the Japanese; "If the Japanese are really nippy . . . there is . . . opening for first-class disaster."[136]

Prince of Wales rendezvoused with *Repulse* in Colombo, Ceylon, on November 28, and in early December the two ships were in Singapore, with the Admiralty already anxious about their fate, and suggesting withdrawal of the ships to less exposed positions.

Phillips left his command there and in the very last days of peace flew to Manila to confer with Admiral Hart and to try to coordinate ideas and defenses if war came. The conference was inconclusive, as it was bound to be, given the assumptions that had to be made and the political inhibitions which affected the actions of both men. What few tentative agreements it did achieve (for instance, to base Allied fleets at Manila, rather than Singapore, by April 1942) were highly unrealistic in light of the relative balance of power in the area and of what was to come.

Phillips got back to Singapore just before the Japanese struck.

In conference aboard the *Prince of Wales* at Singapore on December 8, Phillips and his staff agreed unanimously that "it was impossible for the Navy to remain inactive" while the Japanese landed in northern Malaysia. Their yen for offensive action was undoubtedly influenced by a signal from the Admiralty that had come in on December 6 and directed, "Report what action would be possible to take with naval forces," assuming Japanese invasion—a signal that had not been altered after war started.[137]

Some 26,000 enemy were streaming ashore, relatively unhindered except by a few hasty and largely abortive British air attacks at Singora and Kota Bharu; there were no reports of Japanese aircraft carriers in the vicinity and no surface units of the Japanese Navy that were superior in strength to *Prince of Wales* and *Repulse*. Phillips thought (and his officers agreed with him) that, given surprise and some air reconnaissance and fighter support from RAF land-based planes, he had a reasonable chance to raid the Japanese landings, destroy transports and supplies, and disrupt their line of communication.

He discussed his air requirements with Air Marshal Pulford, who made no promises. Nevertheless Force Z, Phillips's flag flying in *Prince of Wales* (Captain J. C. Leach, C.O.), with *Repulse* (Captain W. G. Tennant) and destroyers *Electra, Express, Vampire,* and *Tenedos,* stood out from Singapore at 5:35 P.M. December 8 just as the tropic dusk screened the seas. A moment before the ships got under way Pulford informed Phillips that the fighter protection he had requested off the coast near Singora at daylight on the 10th was doubtful; already the obsolete British fighters were having hard going in the skies and the airfields in the north near the Japanese landings becoming untenable.

"Although one of the two conditions [surprise and fighter support] postulated by Admiral Phillips . . . could not be fulfilled, he decided, nevertheless, to proceed with his plans provided he was not sighted by aircraft during the 9th. . . ."[138]

Phillips shaped course around the Anambas Islands and northward toward the north Malayan coast.

He was operating blind; although aware of the risks of his raid, he did not realize how great they were. A patrol of ten Japanese submarines was heading straight across his course. Battleships *Kongo* and *Haruna*, with heavy cruisers and destroyers—under Vice Admiral N. Kondo, Commander-in-Chief, Second Fleet—were moving off the coast of southern Indochina as distant support for the Japanese landings; also (a vital factor) enemy bombers were described to Phillips in a signal that night from Singapore as "in force and undisturbed" on fields in South Indochina.

On December 9 in London, in the Cabinet war room with the Pearl Harbor shock graven in the minds of the participants, there seemed to be agreement that the Far Eastern Fleet should "disappear" among the islands of the Malay barrier, to act as a kind of unseen "fleet in being."

Early on the 9th, Phillips was signaled from Singapore that no fighter protection for the Singora raid could be provided since Kota Bharu Airfield had had to be evacuated by the RAF after only one day of war.

Phillips persisted—hoping that rain squalls and low visibility would provide his force with the cloak of surprise, his second essential ingredient for success. It was not to be. Unknown to Phillips his force was sighted by a Japanese submarine, the I-56, early in the afternoon of the 9th. Late that evening, just as Force Z was coming into position for the high-speed run in toward the Malayan coast and the Japanese landings, three enemy aircraft were sighted.

Reluctantly, Phillips reversed course, heading south at high speed. But shortly after midnight on the 10th he changed course sharply and headed southwestward toward Kuantan—far south on the Malay Peninsula—still anxious to get to grips with the enemy and enticed by a signal he had received from Singapore: a report (fallacious at the time) of a Japanese landing at Kuantan.

The British force was sighted and attacked (without result) by I-58 early on the 10th; and before dawn, eighty-eight Japanese naval planes—Nells and Bettys, armed with 500-pound bombs and torpedoes, and escorted by Zeke fighters—had risen from Indochina fields and were swarming over the South China Sea.

At 10:00 A.M. elements of the 22nd Air Flotilla sighted the old destroyer *Tenedos*, which was low on fuel and had been detached from the main Force Z; she was then 140 miles away, south of the Anambas Islands, en route back to base. For thirty minutes *Tenedos* dodged and twisted, evading—save for one near-miss—high-level bombing. The bulk of the air flotilla had found nothing; the Japanese planes headed north back to base to refuel.

Just then Ensign Hoashi, flying a reconnaissance patrol high in the sky off the Malaysian coast, reported: "Have sighted two enemy battleships 70 miles SE Kuantan, course SE."[139]

And so Admiral Tom Phillips and Britain's Far Eastern Fleet made their rendezvous with the enemy off the coast of Malaya late in the morning watch on December 10, 1941.

There was an inevitability about this meeting, as if these men, these ships, these planes had lived their lives to focus in combat at this precise moment in history in the South China Sea.

Prince of Wales, with a lot of history already behind her in her brief career (engagement with the *Bismarck*; the Argentia Conference), was a braw ship, one of the most modern of the new battleships: 44,000 tons full load, 4 shafts, 29 knots, ten 14-inch main battery and a bristling secondary and AA armament of sixteen 5.25-inch, scores of 20 and 40 mm. light weapons, and 2-pounder pom-poms. *Repulse*, old battle cruiser (once lightly armored), displaced 32,000 tons full load, mounted six 15-inch guns, and could still make 29 knots. Her AA armament was less formidable than her consort's but not without consequence: eight 4-inch, and scores of lighter guns.

And the ships of the Far Eastern Fleet were not immobile as at Taranto and Pearl Harbor; they were in their element, capable of sharp turns and swift evasive action . . .

Far above them in the skies, the frail wings of the Mitsubishi torpedo bombers seemed no match for the stout armored decks below; their wings cast little shadow on the sea . . .

The high-level bombers came in first at about 10,000 to 12,000 feet, the sky "a robin's egg blue and the sun . . . bright yellow," the sea "pea-green."

Nine planes, flying steadily, pursued by the "black puffs" of bursting AA shells, stretched out "across the bright blue, cloudless sky like star sapphires . . ."

Cecil Brown, an American war correspondent for CBS aboard the *Repulse*, captured the moment in a classic report:

> . . . I see the bombs coming down, materializing suddenly out of nothingness, and streaming towards us like ever-enlarging tear-drops . . . a magnetic, hypnotic, limb-freezing fascination in that sight. . . .

It was about 11:16 A.M.

Open-mouthed and rooted I watch the bombs getting large and larger. Suddenly ten yards from me, out in the water, a huge geyser springs out of the sea, and over the side, showering water over me and my camera.[140]

The first salvo straddled all around *Repulse;* one bomb hit square; already at 11:17 *Repulse* loudspeakers sounded the alarm: "'Fire on the boat deck. Fire below!'"

Some fifty men were dead; catapult and scouting plane, Marine mess and hangar wrecked.

This was no Mediterranean high-level hit-or-miss. Against maneuvering ships, freely speeding in an open sea, the Japanese had straddled and hit in the first salvo. To those few who had time or logic to think of consequences, there could only be one prayer: "God help us."

It did not take long.

About 11:44 or 11:45 a flight of nine torpedo planes glided down against *Repulse* as bombs dropped from far above. The torpedo planes pressed home their attack to sea-level machine-gun range. Miraculously, Captain Tennant, maneuvering his ship, combed the torpedo tracks with exquisite skill; *Repulse* dodged each one with "elephantine grace."

Not so *Prince of Wales*. The flagship was crippled in the first torpedo plane attack. Two torpedoes exploding near her stern sheared off the outboard port propeller and jammed or wrecked her steering gear. The flailing propeller shaft, suddenly freed of its load, whipped around the shaft alley and opened gaping holes to the sea. She listed and slowed, turning erratically.

The crippled *Prince* now lay naked to her enemies. The flagship flew the "out of control" signal, but even though her decks were canting her guns still fired.

The decks of the *Repulse* are littered with empty shell-cases. Upon the faces of the sailors there's a mixture of incredulity and a sort of sensuous pleasure, but I don't detect fear. There's an ecstatic happiness, but strangely, I don't see anything approaching hate for the attackers. For the British this is a contest. This facial expression is interpreted by an officer. He turns to me and says "Plucky blokes, those Japs. That was as beautiful an attack as ever I expect to see."[141]

There was brief respite. Soon after noon *Repulse* closed *Prince of Wales*, her power dying, working some of her guns by hand. Destroyers ringed her round, and every gun spat defiance as the Japanese came on again.

Soon after noon, as Tennant closed the flagship, he signaled Singapore: "Enemy aircraft bombing." Too late, six Brewster Buffalo fighters—slow and awkward—took off for succor.

The score to date was fatal: two Japanese torpedo planes shot down; two capital ships damaged, one mortally, and the wasps still swarming to the hive.

About 12:20 nine more Bettys swooped down toward the big ships and the white-waked sea. *Repulse* took a hit on the starboard beam; her underwater bulges protected her; still she steamed at 25 knots. But *Prince*—helpless—took four more torpedo hits, and the great leviathan settled ever lower in the water, listing heavily to port.

The luck of old *Repulse* was over. Tennant, who had handled his ship with consummate skill, had avoided at least nineteen torpedoes, and had suffered no crippling damage, was overwhelmed. From all sides the torpedo bombers came; too many multiple targets for far too few guns.

Repulse took three torpedoes in quick succession on her port side, one to starboard:

> . . . I am thrown four feet across the deck. . . . Almost immediately . . . the ship lists . . . "Blow up your lifebelts. . . ." Captain Tennant's voice is coming over the ship's loudspeaker, a cool voice: "All hands on deck. Prepare to abandon ship." There is a pause for just an instant, then: "God be with you."[142]

Slowly the *Repulse* turns on her side and hangs at a 60- to 70-degree list; men leap off her canted decks into oil-soaked water. One, as the ship turns, dives from the top of the mainmast about 170 feet into the sea; some misjudge their leaps and crash into the slimy bilge. Tennant, quiet and calm to the last, is sucked from the side of his bridge into the sea. *Repulse* turns over, the red underwater plates of the bow reaching skyward as she sinks.

Cecil Brown, the "hot pokers" of oil in his eyes, sick from oil in his stomach, found himself fighting for his life in an oil-soaked sea with hundreds of heads bobbing beside him. His smashed watch had stopped at 12:35, one hour and twenty minutes after the first attack.

Phillips aboard *Prince of Wales*, which was settling lower in the water, still moving slowly, saw *Repulse* go down and knew his time had come. About 12:44 the *Prince* took another bomb hit. It was not needed; her quarterdeck was almost awash and she was doomed. *Express* came alongside and took off the flagship's wounded and excess personnel. About 1:15 the order "Abandon Ship" echoed through the wrecked vessel. At 1:19 she started to go; Admiral Tom Phillips and Captain J. C. Leach were last seen together on the bridge.

Captain Leach waved: "Goodbye. Thank you. Good luck. God bless you."[143]

At 1:20 she was gone and with her the Flag Officer, Commanding, and Britain's Far Eastern Fleet.

High in the skies above, Japanese pilots shouted "Banzai! Banzai!" and the Brewster fighters from Singapore flew over bobbing heads in the water amid largely empty skies.

The "battle," if it could be called one, had cost the Japanese four planes. The British lost 840 officers and men, 2 capital ships—one of them the proud adornment of a new Navy—and immeasurable face. Some 2,081 men, including Captain Tennant of *Repulse* (who literally went down with his ship but was spewed to the surface) were saved by destroyers *Express*, *Electra*, and *Vampire*.

Neither Phillips nor Leach was among the survivors.

For the first time in history capital ships with heavy firepower had been sunk by air attack alone, in the open sea, some 400 miles from the land bases of the planes that sank them.

The battleship's usefulness in World War II had not ended, but henceforth wings over water would cast by far the longest shadow across both the strategy and the tactics of maritime war.

The sinking of the *Prince of Wales* and *Repulse* was one of the heaviest blows of the war to Britain and her Allies. Coming on the heels of Pearl Harbor, it added to the aura of Japanese invincibility, forecasting an ominous succession of defeats. There was no excuse of surprise, no lack of prior hard experience.

Salvaged from it was only one intangible, the steady courage which has always characterized Britain at war; the factor that, more than any other, had helped Britain to "muddle through" crisis after crisis.

Tennant later reported he never "saw the slightest sign of panic or ill-discipline" as his crew prepared to die. A pilot of a Buffalo fighter, which arrived just too late but cruised above a sea bobbing with human heads for about an hour, paid highest tribute; he got, he said, the thumbs-up sign from the oil-choked survivors in the sea—"waving, cheering and joking as if they were holidaymakers at Brighton. . . . It shook me, for here was something above human nature"—the spirit which wins wars.[144]

But the immediate public reaction in Singapore, London, and New York was one of deep public depression, of chill foreboding, an end to the false sense of security nurtured by Western complacency and fallacious assumptions.

In England Winston Churchill was shocked by the "full horror of the news." Perhaps, as at Gallipoli in World War I, he felt himself partially responsible; it was he who had insisted against Admiralty objections upon sending the *Prince of Wales* to Singapore.

"There were no British or American capital ships in the Indian Ocean or the Pacific. . . . Over all this vast expanse of waters Japan was supreme, and we everywhere weak and naked. . . ."[145]

Flood Tide for Japan

After December 10, the operations in Malaya were anticlimactic.

By the time the *Prince of Wales* and *Repulse* were sunk, the Japanese had captured Kota Bharu; its airfield had been prematurely evacuated (its stores only partially destroyed) in a precipitous British withdrawal. The initial hours of the landings at Kota Bharu spawned a brief tornado of resistance. Hudson bombers and artillery and mortar fire from British troops defending the airfield damaged all three transports (one, *Awajisan Maru*, was fired and sank later), and destroyed a number of landing craft. But it was brief flurry; the successful Japanese landings in Siam had neutralized Kota Bharu.

By the evening of December 9 the RAF had abandoned all operations from five fields in northern Malaya, and the total serviceable British air strength in forward areas—concentrated now at Butterworth Airfield opposite Penang Island—was ten combat aircraft. Already, the Japanese were flying about 150 planes from the Singora and Patani area and the bases they had developed or seized in the Kra Isthmus.

The British command had foreseen the strategic dangers of a Japanese landing in the Thailand Isthmus near the northern borders of Malaya and the consequent neutralization of the northern Malaya air bases. A countermove, "Operation Matador," had been planned and discussed: a preemptive advance northward into the Isthmus and the seizure of key terrain features to dominate the lower part of the Isthmus. The III Indian Corps (under Lieutenant General Sir Lewis Heath, consisting of the 9th and 11th Indian divisions reinforced) was charged with the defense of northern Malaya—primarily the RAF forward airfields in Kelantan—and with "Matador." But reluctance to violate Siamese neutrality before actual Japanese landings and delay in approval from London until the "eleventh hour" made the plan academic.

The political situation in Siam, where there was a strong pro-Japanese clique in the Cabinet and warnings received from the British Minister in Bangkok that "irreparable harm would be done, if Britain were the first to violate Siamese territory,"[146] made the British hesitation understandable, and indeed necessary. But it proved fatal. The Japanese got there first.

The British, after the event, did send a task force into Siam to seize a key defensive terrain feature some 30 miles from the frontier, but not until the afternoon of the 8th. It was delayed by roadblocks manned by Siamese constabulary, and by the last-minute change in plans. The Japanese in sixty hours had landed men from the sea and covered some 75 miles of bad roads, and got there first.

In total numbers the Japanese invaders were far inferior to the British defenders. But that was their only inferiority. The Japanese commanded the sea and the air. Their troops were battle-hardened, jungle-trained; they had far more mobility than the road-bound British. And Percival, alert against possible landings in southern, as well as northern, Malaya, tried to provide defense everywhere. As a result, at points of actual combat contact the Japanese were sometimes (though rarely) superior in numbers, but nearly always greatly superior in combat effectiveness to their opponents.

Gurkhas and Punjabis delayed the advance, but not for long. Some of the Indian Army troops had never even seen a tank; a small Japanese mechanized force, with some of the armored clanking monsters, "caused utter consternation," in the words of the British official history.

Individual British units (a battalion of the Punjabis, another of the Gurkha Rifles) were cut up and cut off, virtually annihilated; the morale of the 11th Indian Division, trying to hold northern Malaya, fell lower than a snake's belly, and in a few days of war it looked as if the division was about to fall apart.

Before December 13 the Japanese had won their battle for the north. Around Jitra a "Japanese advanced guard of a strength equivalent to two battalions supported by a company of tanks (of the 5th Japanese Division) had, with comparatively few casualties, defeated 11th Division and driven it from its prepared defensive position in some thirty-six hours,"[147] with heavy losses to the British.

By December 14, most of Kedah State and Perlis—its Sultan angry at what he considered British betrayal by retreat—were in Japanese hands. By the 17th, the line of the Muda River had been breached, and on all available roads and trails southward along the coasts and on the railroad up the center of the peninsula and through the jungle, British forces were still backpedaling.

The retreat uncovered the rich prize of Penang Island, off Malay's west coast, a communications key with cable terminals and a good harbor. The Japanese raided George Town on the island early on, and met with brief defiance on December 13, when a squadron of Buffaloes, transferred to Butterworth Airfield on the mainland near Penang, shot down five Japanese bombers at a cost of one plane. But Butterworth was soon untenable, and on December 15–17 Penang, which the British had hoped to turn into a fortress, was evacuated. Its docks and buildings were devastated by bombs, dead and wounded Chinese and Malays cluttered the hospitals or lay in the streets, most of the police and civil servants had deserted or were in hiding, and cholera and typhoid were predicted. The British took their own people out to Singapore Island in four small coastal vessels; the Asiatics remained behind to meet the conquerors. The hasty evacuation was half-done. The broadcasting station was left intact, later to be a great prize in Japan's propaganda warfare; and the conquerors found many serviceable coastal junks and small craft, which they promptly put to use in amphibious outflanking movements.

By dawn of December 23 the mauled 11th Indian Division had withdrawn behind the Perak River. Two regiments of the Japanese 5th Division, reinforced now by elements of the Imperial Guards Division, crossed the river without opposition. The 12th Indian Infantry Brigade, which had been thrown into action to help the battered 11th, tried valiantly to hold Ipoh, important junction town and airfield, but three days after Christmas the town fell:

> The troops were very tired. Constant air attacks prevented them from obtaining any sleep by day. By night, they either had to move . . . or to work on preparing yet another defensive position. . . . Officers and men moved like automata and often could not grasp the simplest order. . . .[148]

It was not only the pitiful inexperience of the British troops that led to such rapid retreat. The Japanese had the habit of turning up in the most unexpected places; they slipped through supposedly impassable jungles with "the greatest of ease," evaded roadblocks and obstacles, and again and again turned flanks and cut off defending units.

Local Defense Corps units, many of them composed of middle-aged rubber planters and tin-mine managers, led lightly armed companies—one platoon of Europeans, three of Asiatics—to aid the regulars. Some of them fought valiantly, very few with skill; occasionally their delaying stands saved regular units from encirclement or destruction.

We had to hold the Japs. . . . I got them into trucks, Thompson and Fellowes and planters like them and tin-miners like Des Jardines and Blodgett, and the telephone man and the forester—all the people I'd been training for so many months. . . . Pretty soon we met the Japanese. They had brought bicycles and mortars through the jungle. . . .
They attacked us through the rubber. . . . We threw a barricade of logs across the road, and when they tried to rush it, we gave them all the fire we had. At first when they let off strings of firecrackers to draw our fire we were fooled. But we soon caught on. We had a few natives who knew their way round in the rubber. They could help us stop infiltrating parties before they got round us. . . . The Chinese, especially, were jolly good.
Well, we held them. One or two of our boys got their's, but we held them. We got word that some of the [regulars] . . . would be coming up in our rear if we could hold on a little longer. We stuck. . . .[149]

By the end of the year, in Singapore and in London, the British wind was up. The Australian Division, holding Johore State in southern Malaya, had not been in action; but the III Corps was hard-pressed, badly wounded, had never made an effective stand. The 11th Indian Division on the western flank, two of its brigades now merged in one, had little effectiveness as a fighting unit. The RAF had abandoned all its forward airfields (some in precipitous panic), which the Japanese promptly used, and its northernmost field at Kuala Lumpur was under such heavy attack, with only three Buffaloes left to defend it, that it was evacuated on December 23. On the east coast, the 9th Division still guarded the important Kuantan area and Singapore fortress. But nothing had stopped the Japanese; nowhere had they really been checked and Percival knew—as London was warned—that "Tiger" Yamashita still had major forces as yet uncommitted to battle. British airpower, despite some small reinforcements from the Dutch, had been largely neutralized or decimated; the Buffalo, it was clear, was no match for the Japanese Zero fighter, and the supposed astigmatic pilots of Japan came and went in the skies at will.

Through it all Singapore City pulsed with a frenetic fever, a result in part of the medley of peoples—Sikhs, Gurkhas, Tamils, Punjabis, "Aussies," Maoris, Englishmen and Scotsmen, Malays, and Chinese —and in part of the frantic lust for life that often distinguishes those who are living their last hours. The teeming vitality of life in Asia was blended with Oriental fatalism; life would go on regardless of death and of tomorrow's masters. The Happy World Cabaret, landmark of Singapore, had been hit and demolished in one of the first Japanese raids; but until the end the New World Cabaret—its dim lights blacked out to outside gaze, its atmosphere of a "sickish perfumed Turkish bath," its expressionless Chinese hostesses—continued to entertain those who were about to die.

And on Christmas Day Japanese aircraft fluttered down upon the teeming city thousands of crude propaganda leaflets attempting (unsuccessfully) to incite the polyglot population to burn "all foreign devils in a holy flame."[150]

Just before Christmas, Alfred Duff Cooper had chaired an Allied conference in Singapore, attended by British, U.S., Dutch, Australian, and New Zealand representatives. The members were aware of the rapid Japanese advance in Malaya and Hong Kong, and they also knew that the Malayan position had been flanked by small Japanese landings in British Borneo, where Japanese troops had started coming ashore early on December 16.

Borneo, a land of "primeval jungle" part Dutch part British, was indefensible, in the largest sense, save by sea and air. A single British Punjabi Battalion had been sent to British Borneo before the war started, to deny the oil at Miri and Seria to the Japanese, and to help defend an airfield at Kuching. The refinery at Lutong was demolished before the Japanese landings; Dutch aircraft, making sporadic raids, sank a destroyer, but the enemy, covered by a heavy Japanese air attack on a field in Dutch Borneo, which forced its evacuation, landed on Christmas Eve near Kuching. Dutch submarines claimed two enemy ships and one destroyer sunk (at a cost of one submarine) and Blenheims from Singapore bombed with little effectiveness. On Christmas Day, the lone Punjabi Battalion, after a brief but futile defense of Kuching Airfield, withdrew through thick jungle leaving behind the better part of two companies: 4 British officers, 230 Indian troops killed, captured, missing. The survivors, thirsty, hungry, tired but in good discipline, reached the evacuated Dutch airfield of Singkawang II on the last day of the year. The enemy had swiftly acquired their foothold and their airfields in Borneo, flanking the Malayan Peninsula. The approaches to the Dutch East Indies had been secured.

The Singapore Conference decided little. Urgent cables, some recommendations, went to London and other Allied capitals. It was obvious that Singapore could not be held without quick, heavy air and ground reinforcement of every sort; it was equally obvious that the

successful defense of the Malay barrier—the Dutch East Indies—
would depend upon control of the sea and the air. The conference
urged reinforcements for Malaya and suggested that an Allied naval
task force—to cover the Strait of Macassar and the Celebes Sea—
should be built up around the nucleus of Task Force 5 of the U.S.
Asiatic Fleet, commanded by Rear Admiral W. A. Glassford (heavy
cruiser *Houston*, light cruiser *Boise*, seaplane tender *Langley*, oilers
Trinity and *Pecos*; and later, light cruiser *Marblehead* and thirteen
destroyers).

Ominously, in a letter to Churchill, Duff Cooper mentioned that
he was worried about the restiveness in Singapore; he thought the
civil defense preparations were weak indeed, and that some "senior
civilian officials" (colonials by environment and colonials in mentality) "did not appear to be able to adjust themselves to war conditions."

It was, if anything, understatement. The psychology and the mentality of British officials—including many of the key leaders—the
poor training and discipline and inadequate equipment of the Army,
particularly the Indian components, and the obsolescence of British
aircraft had greatly aided rapid Japanese victories. Ultimate defeat in
Malaysia, Singapore, and Southeast Asia was probably inevitable in
December 1941, given the overwhelming Japanese superiority of sea-
and airpower. But that disaster came with such terrifying speed was
chiefly attributable to the defenders and their poor military quality,
rather than to the victors.

December 31 marked a bleak end for the Allies to a year of defeat
and retreat. In less than a month of war, Japan had achieved the first
objectives of her conquest in Southeast Asia: seizure of the rich
rubber plantations and tin mines of Malaysia, the oil of Borneo, the
rice of Thailand.

21

The Aftermath of Pearl Harbor

The effects of the Japanese tidal wave of aggression in the Pacific
were felt immediately around the world.

In Washington, on December 8, in a brief address to a joint session of Congress, Roosevelt characterized Sunday, December 7, as a
"day that will live in infamy," and asked for a formal recognition of

the existence of a state of war against Japan. Congress overwhelmingly approved the resolution in one hour, with only one negative vote—that of Representative Jeannette Rankin of Montana, who clung to her pacifist traditions to the last. Twenty-four years before, she had voted against participation in World War I.

Great Britain and the British Commonwealth of Nations added their pro forma declarations soon after Washington had acted. In fact, so anxious was Winston Churchill to enlist the United States as senior partner in World War II that he queried Roosevelt at 8:00 A.M. December 8 to inquire whether he should ask Parliament for an immediate declaration of war against Japan or wait until the U.S. Congress had put a de jure stamp of approval on a de facto war.

Roosevelt, always cognizant of the opposition to the war in the United States, was more cautious about Germany and Italy. He overruled his Secretary of the Army Henry L. Stimson, who wanted an immediate declaration of war against the two European Axis powers. The President reasoned that:

undeclared war already existed in the Atlantic and from the intercepted messages it was almost a foregone conclusion that Germany and Italy would fall in line with Japan . . . it would be far better from the standpoint of public reaction to have Hitler and Mussolini take the initiative. . . .[151]

Neither was slow to do so. Hitler had wanted Japan in the war to distract his two principal enemies—Russia and Great Britain—but though he professed profound scorn for the United States, "a decayed country . . . with everything built on the dollar,"[152] he had not wanted to add another enemy at a time when his armies were being beaten back before the approaches to Moscow. Pearl Harbor was a surprise to Hitler, as it was to Washington; unlike Rome, Tokyo was not manageable from Berlin, and the Japanese kept their own counsel.

But in 1941 Hitler had been more and more angered by Washington's attacks upon him and by the combat intervention of the U.S. Navy in the Atlantic battle; and in Berlin, Japan's widespread victories in the Pacific were welcomed as a psychological and political assist to the German fortunes of war, locked in winter's grip in Russia.

On December 11, in a violent diatribe directed primarily against Roosevelt, "the main culprit of this war," a "mad" man, Hitler demanded of his rubber-stamp Reichstag a declaration of war against the United States.

Mussolini, once again pompous on his balcony before a crowd that Ciano characterized as "not very enthusiastic," followed his master's lead on the same day. Then, in quick succession, the grim parade started; Cuba, Ecuador, other countries of the Western Hemisphere joined the lists against the Axis.

Roosevelt immediately took up the gantlet; Congress reacted almost instantly, on December 11, with the declaration of a "state of war" with Germany and Italy, and the deed was done.

But the recriminations and the imputations, the charges and the exonerations for Pearl Harbor had just started; three decades later, they still go on. To pinpoint the responsibility and to provide some answer to the increasingly clamorous question *Why?*, Secretary of the Navy Knox made a preliminary survey. And then, at his suggestion, the President appointed an ad hoc commission, headed by Supreme Court Justice Owen J. Roberts, to investigate and, in a nonlegal sense, adjudicate. It was a hasty and incomplete investigation, only the first of many culminating, after the war was over, in the most comprehensive and exhaustive investigation in U.S. history (but one which was inevitably politically partisan), that of a Joint Congressional Committee.

The American public was shocked, angry, and perturbed. Scapegoats had to be found, some sort of action taken. Yet at the same time the war must be fought, and no inquiry must damage the nation's combat capability. Given these parameters and the absolute necessity of secrecy, the Roberts Commission did, on the whole, a fast but fairly thorough job.

Commission or no commission, heads were bound to roll; Kimmel's and Short's were the first to go.

Whether responsible or not, they could scarcely remain in command of future operations during an investigation of their past actions.

Admiral Chester W. Nimitz was designated Commander-in-Chief Pacific Fleet on December 17, and on the last day of the year he assumed command from Admiral Pye, who had been interim commander after Kimmel's relief on the 17th. Nimitz was a quiet, calm leader, submarine-qualified; morale—sunk in gloom at Pearl Harbor —rose with his coming. General Short was relieved by Lieutenant General Delos C. Emmons, an Air Corps officer, and Major General Frederick L. Martin, the Army air commander in Hawaii, was succeeded by Brigadier General Clarence L. Tinker. Even more important than the new minds and new faces in High Command was the unification of command. By order of the President, the Navy (in the person of Admiral Nimitz) was designated the top command of all U.S. forces in Hawaii and much of the Pacific; the Army exercised that role in Panama. The nation was closing a lot of barn doors somewhat late in the day, but it was vital that what Louis Morton has called "the sharp crags of service jealousies and rivalries" be eliminated.

The opening of a new era extended to Washington. Admiral Harold R. Stark, the Chief of Naval Operations—known, alike to the President and to the Navy, as "Molly" Stark—was a gentle person, devoted, hardworking, with a good mind. For some time the star of Admiral Ernest J. King, a close-mouthed "sun-downer," tough and hard with none of the social graces, had been in the ascendant. He had been Commander-in-Chief of the Atlantic Fleet and had attended the Argentia Conference. He was able and impressive and far more forceful—some would later call him stubborn—than Stark; and Pearl Harbor was bound to weaken some of Roosevelt's confidence in "Molly" Stark. So, on December 20, Ernest J. King became Commander-in-Chief United States Fleet (the abbreviation CINCUS, pronounced "Sink us," seemed singularly inappropriate after Pearl Harbor and it was changed to COMINCH). As such, King was made responsible for all naval operations in all seas and all oceans, with the Chief of Naval Operations relegated to an administrative support role. CNO was now, in a sense, a fifth wheel, and in the New Year of 1942, the two jobs were to merge, with King in charge.

The shift caused, as all such changes do, many human regrets. Stark was liked and respected, though many in the Navy felt he had not kept Kimmel adequately informed. One of his own aides epitomized the reasoning: "Well, I guess when the going gets tough, they send for the S.O.B.'s."[153]

King issued one of his few statements as he took over; he was a terse man who believed that the Navy, particularly in wartime, must be a silent service:

> The way to victory is long.
> The going will be hard.
> We will do the best we can with what we've got.
> We must have more planes and ships—at once.
> Then it will be our turn to strike.
> We will win through—in time.[154]

No eloquence here, but a businesslike simplicity.

* * *

Ultimately in January 1942 the Roberts Commission report found Short and Kimmel guilty of some dereliction of duty, but noted Short's message to the War Department reporting that he had taken action only against sabotage. It added that a general, nationwide "sense of security" had resulted from the belief that if Japan attacked it would be in the Far East. (Yet, as long ago as 1928, planes from the converted collier *Langley*, first of the Navy's brood of "flattops," had made, in maneuvers, a successful Sunday morning surprise attack on Pearl Harbor.) There followed through the years about a dozen investigations and studies of the Pearl Harbor disaster, by an Army Board of Inquiry, a Naval Court of Inquiry, and various individuals, finally capped by the postwar congressional investigation.

Nearly all of them found loose ends of some sort, not only in Hawaii and the Philippines but in Washington. Revisionist historians and special pleaders of every description, Roosevelt-haters and military and naval friends of Kimmel and Short, have seized upon discrepancies or omissions in the testimony developed in these investigations to "prove" a particular point, to exculpate or to point the finger of blame. And the debate goes on.

Yet history has provided rather explicit answers to most, if not all, of the mysteries of Pearl Harbor.

The late Admiral William F. Halsey, in a postwar preface to a book by Rear Admiral Robert A. Theobald defending Admiral Kimmel (*The Final Secret of Pearl Harbor*), concluded simplistically: "I have always considered Admiral Kimmel and General Short to be splendid officers who were thrown to the wolves as scapegoats for something over which they had no control. . . . They are our outstanding military martyrs. . . ."[155]

At the other extreme Admiral Hart, who later conducted a naval inquiry directed by Secretary Knox, concluded that there was no "mystery" about Pearl Harbor. In 1966, with a simplicity similar to Halsey's, he emphasized the Navy Department War Warning message of November 27: "That is definite, cogent and as strong as words can be," and added that the directive to "effect an appropriate defensive deployment" was a "direct and definite order for all those addressed." He added that he did not know, "in all Naval history, a better command performance than was contained in the War Warning."[156]

But simplicity is rarely the handmaiden of history, and it is infrequently, indeed, that great disasters can be pinned to single individuals.

Kimmel and Short could plead some extenuating circumstances.

They did not have enough of anything. They were not "cut in" in the last months of peace on the "Magic" messages. They were not informed of all the nuances of the final negotiations with the Japanese. Short had reported his alert against sabotage only and could assume, since he received no reply, that Washington approved his preparations. And they were good officers, devoted, hardworking, professionally competent. There was no unified command and little real unified planning, but Short and Kimmel had cooperated and coordinated. Contrary to reports of the time, officers of the fleet were not in a bleary-eyed stupor that Sunday morning as a result of Saturday night bacchanalia.

Nevertheless Kimmel and Short were tried and tested in the furnace of war—and found wanting. Not so much by commission as omission. There was, in the last months of 1941, a complacent certainty in Hawaii that, while war might come, it would not happen there; as Admiral King was to put it later, "an unwarranted feeling of immunity from attack." Yet there had been ample warnings. The Sunday weekend routine—fleet in harbor, nested in neat targets and immobile—was still followed even after the war warning dispatch. Long-range reconnaissance patrols could have been flown, despite shortages. On the day of Pearl Harbor a tiny fraction of the Navy's patrol planes were in the air; it was Sunday, traditionally a day of rest. There might have been torpedo nets to protect ships in port. The fleet should have been warned before 7:00 A.M. by the midget submarine contacts; inefficient communications delayed this report with fatal consequences.

The Army too was guilty of omissions, the more serious since it was charged, by all prewar doctrine, with the local defense of the naval base. Its radars, though new, should have been continuously operating. The alert against sabotage should not have precluded provisions for a combat air patrol.

In short, the services in Hawaii were not as much on their toes—given the war warnings and continuous stream of information about Japanese aggressions—as they should have been. The basic responsibility, the primary responsibility, in any military organization for what happens in that organization, good or bad, is the commander's. Kimmel and Short, no matter how history is interpreted, share some of the onus for things left undone that should have been done, for things done that should not have been done.

But only some of the blame.

Admiral King's endorsement (November 6, 1944) of the report of the Naval Court of Inquiry into Pearl Harbor found some inefficiency in Admiral Stark's command in Washington, and scored Stark for failing to inform Hawaii that the Japanese were breaking off negotiations (determined in Washington by 8:00 A.M. on December 7 when the final part of the famous fourteen-part "Magic" intercepts was available). This latter criticism is not fully persuasive. Stark had sent all sorts of warnings in past weeks, and 8:00 A.M. in Washington on the day of infamy was almost certainly far too late to have saved Pearl Harbor.

There was, however, creaking bureaucracy in Washington, even more apparent in the Army than in the Navy Department. General Marshall did not escape some implied censure. But much of the public censure was focused on the scene of disaster, and those who presided over it. Kimmel and Short were good men, competent men, dedicated men—but they had been surprised; their commands were not prepared for what happened, and even within the limited means at their disposal they could have been better prepared.

Kimmel did not receive all the information from Washington he should have, though even if he had the outcome would almost certainly have been no different. And one must feel a particular sympathy for Short; he was, in part, a victim of the Army General Staff. His response within a few hours to the Army's urgent warning of November 27 specifically reported he had alerted his command against sabotage. He received no reply, and on November 27 and 28 two other messages—one from G-2 (intelligence) of the Army General Staff and one from the Army Air Force in Washington, both warning against sabotage—were sent to Short, thus further confirming his belief that in the opinion of Washington the only thing he had to fear was a Fifth Column.

Which was, indeed, probably Washington's belief. It is hard to understand in retrospect, but Washington's gaze and Washington's anxiety at the time had been largely focused on Europe, not Asia; and the handful of Far Eastern intelligence experts had little clout. There was increasing belief that war with Japan was almost certain, but there had been general agreement that, with Russia fighting for her life and Britain in extremis, the United States must delay the outbreak of hostilities in the Orient, if possible, to the spring of 1942, in order to gain time to reinforce the Philippines, Hawaii, and the Pacific island outposts. Diplomacy was to be the agent of time, and though in November it was late indeed, Secretary of State Cordell Hull, a "weary" old man, tried. In answer to a Japanese note of November 20 which the Japanese Foreign Minister regarded as their final proposal, an "ultimatum," Hull, on November 26, proposed a

Ten-Point plan, which the Japanese regarded—or deliberately chose to regard—as its own kind of ultimatum. It was not intended as such in Washington, but it was so starkly at variance with Japan's proposals that it could not possibly win delay. By then, with Japanese ships, planes, and men already en route to aggression, delay would have required some drastic concessions, or far more skillful diplomacy, or both.

From the flames and the many historical circumstantial bits and pieces of those days, revisionist historians have erected a "great conspiracy" theory of Pearl Harbor, a complete fabric of deception. President Roosevelt, it is alleged, deliberately planned Pearl Harbor as a means of ensuring U.S. entry into World War II. Roosevelt and his military commanders in Washington (Marshall and Stark) knew beforehand of the impending Japanese attack, the theory goes, and deliberately withheld the information from Kimmel and Short. The terse answer to such allegations is baloney. Roosevelt, it is true, was a political manipulator; he had flouted, circumvented, or with congressional approval revised the neutrality legislation of 1935–37 (which had, at the time, the overwhelming support of the American people). He often said one thing and did another; he did not hesitate to deceive the public. He believed strongly that the United States must for its own salvation enter World War II; he had ordered actions in the Atlantic, most of them ultimately approved by Congress but many after the event, which had already resulted in an undeclared limited war against Germany; and he had stressed that he wanted Japan to fire the first shot, strike the first blow. (Ironically, it was the United States that fired the first shot against a midget submarine outside Pearl Harbor early on December 7.)

At almost the eleventh hour in the Pacific (on December 1) Roosevelt had ordered Admiral Hart in Manila through Stark to "charter three small vessels for a 'defensive information patrol' " off the Indochina coast. They were to have an identity as "U.S. men-of-war" and were to be commanded by a naval officer. These "small vessels" may well have been intended as "tethered goats" to lure the tiger of Japanese aggression, on the theory—then widely believed in Washington—that Tokyo would bypass the Philippines and attack British and Dutch possessions only. The sinking by the Japanese of any one of the three little ships would serve, the theory held, as another *Panay* Incident, an excuse for U.S. hostilities. In the event, the "three small vessels" were never employed in their intended role; the

Japanese struck too soon, and the Philippine Islands were one of their first objectives.

In short, Roosevelt undoubtedly believed, like millions of Americans, that the United States' vital interests required the nation's entry into war, and in order to convince a large and reluctant portion of public opinion, he wanted the Japanese to strike first.

But all this proves no monstrous plot or heinous culpability. Neither Stark nor Marshall would have participated in such despicable connivings; nor—at a cost of 2,000 lives and a fleet destroyed—would Roosevelt. Every nation and every leader desires to make a record of rectitude for history, and Roosevelt was fully cognizant of American public opinion, which was overwhelmingly opposed to the aims of Germany, Italy, Japan, but also overwhelmingly opposed to entry into war. Roosevelt was a brilliant yet devious politician; like Churchill, he was inclined to meddle in military details. He had promised just about a year before that he would not send American sons to fight on foreign soil, and his highly controversial domestic policies amounting to social revolution exposed him, then and later, to the bitter hatred of many. This undoubtedly contributed to the myth of a great conspiracy. It remains a myth; nothing more.

Who, then, was to blame for Pearl Harbor?

Roosevelt certainly shares the blame, as the architect of U.S. policy. Roberta Wohlstetter, in her monumental examination of the "signals" that might have warned of the attack, takes a whole book to conclude that "the fact of surprise at Pearl Harbor has never been persuasively explained by accusing the participants, individually or in groups, of conspiracy or negligence or stupidity. . . .

"We have to accept the fact of uncertainty and learn to live with it."[157]

The leaders of 1941 lived amidst minute-to-minute alarms; they were inundated with "action signals" from all over the globe; there were clues in the Pacific, contrary indications from Europe. Amidst all this "noise," there was significance which, properly interpreted, might have prevented surprise. But there was then no such organization as there is today to evaluate and interpret the myriad reports from all over the world. And what seems so clear in retrospect was far from evident at the time.

Much of the preservation of surprise must be attributed to the rigorous security of the Japanese and to the detailed perfection of their planning. They kept their secret intact, and a major part of their effort was the meticulous care they exerted to solve each tiny technological and operational problem before the first bomb was dropped.

Above all, the Americans viewed the Japanese as a mirror image of themselves, at least in their reasoning processes. From this point of view a deliberate Japanese attack on the United States, a far stronger and industrially powerful nation, postulated a war against such great odds that no rational person would undertake it. However, as Ambassador Grew pointed out in the Pearl Harbor congressional hearings: "National sanity would dictate against such an event [as the attack on Pearl Harbor], but Japanese sanity cannot be measured by our own standards of logic."

Pearl Harbor reflected a national state of mind, a curious American psychological virginity, an innocence bred of naïveté. Even among many of our experts there was a vast overconfidence, and an abysmal ignorance of the Japanese character. Despite the achievement of "Magic" (or perhaps because of it), the collation and distribution of intelligence information was irrational and incomplete. G-2 of the Army and ONI (Office of Naval Intelligence) of the Navy were low in status. There were intense struggles for power and bureaucratic rivalries within the Navy (War Plans and ONI), and between Army and Navy (in Washington and, most particularly, in Manila). Each service tended to make its own plans, prepare for its own war; a frail connecting link, gradually strengthened by Marshall and Stark as war approached, was the Joint Army-Navy Board.

The Board dealt chiefly with matters of joint policy, and though it became in time a kind of forerunner of the Joint Chiefs of Staff, it included then none of the elaborate mechanisms, the large staff, or the statutory authority provided today in the organization of the JCS. The lack of such a body and of unified commands or staff planning in individual theaters such as Manila and Hawaii was compounded by the freewheeling methods of President Roosevelt, the Commander-in-Chief. All roads led to the White House in the Roosevelt administration; there was little effective decentralization, and the President played many of the cards of power close to his chest.

Indeed, as Field Marshal Sir John Dill, who had just been relieved by General Sir Alan Brooke as Chief of the British Imperial General Staff, reported at the time, the United States "has not—repeat not—the slightest conception of what the war means, and their armed forces are more unready for war than it is possible to imagine." This in retrospect somewhat harsh judgment was based on Dill's observation that there were no regular meetings between the service Chiefs of Staff, no joint secretariat, no system for regular consultation between the President and his military advisers, and such consultations as the President had with his military leaders were "haphazard."[158]

Roosevelt and most of his advisers—and in a different context Churchill in London—failed to see that what were intended as deterrents against aggression (the U.S. Fleet in Pearl Harbor, the B-17's in the Philippines; the *Prince of Wales* and *Repulse* in Singapore) were also inviting targets for attack. In each case the weakness and vulnerability of the supposed deterrent actually made it a magnet for deadly assault.

Pearl Harbor and the sweeping Japanese victories in the Pacific in December 1941 changed all this.

Out of Defeat—Alliance

From disparate efforts and individual weaknesses there had now to be knit together, somehow, collective strength; the great inferiority of the Allies in the Pacific had to be overcome, unless Japan was to run rampant.

Within a few hours after Pearl Harbor, Admiral Stark ordered back into the Pacific much of the naval strength he had transferred to the Atlantic a few months before: carrier *Yorktown*, battleships *New Mexico*, *Mississippi*, *Idaho*, patrol planes, and a destroyer squadron.

And within a few days the Allies were starting to resurrect and modify the very tentative agreements reached in various prewar staff conversations in order to establish some sort of coordinated command and planning. Admiral Hart had already discussed the dangerous tomorrows with British authorities at Singapore, and the Dutch and British had compared notes and allocated defense tasks; Dutch planes had tried futilely, in December, to aid in the defense of Singapore. In late December, Rear Admiral Glassford, commanding the surface striking force of the Asiatic Fleet—Task Force 5—established an advanced command post at Surabaya in Java (Dutch East Indies); his support and service base was far to the south at Port Darwin in Australia.

In Washington on December 22, Winston Churchill and his military commanders met President Roosevelt and his generals and admirals in the first of the great Anglo-American wartime conferences, which were to chart the Allied strategy of World War II, to determine joint policies and, indeed, to map the kind of peace to come.

The Arcadia Conference—idyllic name for a time of debate and confusion—was inspired by Churchill, who feared the transfer of the principal American effort from Atlantic to Pacific as a result of Pearl Harbor. After some stormy discussions and major disagreements, the conference achieved the beginnings of a system of unified Allied command. Field Marshal Wavell, in India, was appointed the Commander-in-Chief of ABDA: all American-British-Dutch-Australian forces in the Southwest Pacific-Southeast Asia area. This first pattern of what later came to be a recognized system of unified theater commands around the world was General Marshall's idea, achieved not without opposition. The Royal Navy had never before subordinated its ships to a landsman; Churchill, lying late a-bed in a White House guest room and chomping on a cigar, asked Marshall belligerently what "an Army officer could know about handling a ship. . . .

Marshall hotly retorted, "What the devil does a naval officer know about handling a tank?" . . .

"I told him," Marshall recalled later, "I was not interested in Drake and Frobisher, but I was interested in having a united front against Japan, an enemy which was fighting furiously. I said if we didn't do something right away we were finished in the war."[159]

Marshall prevailed.

Even more important than the ill-fated ABDA command, there grew out of the Arcadia Conference the establishment of a Combined (Anglo-American) Chiefs of Staff organization and the placement in Washington of a British Joint Staff mission, headed by Sir John Dill.

Arcadia was essentially a feeling-out process. It was the first conference during actual hostilities; both British and Americans were slightly suspicious of the other's motives and objectives; each had axes to grind. The Americans regarded their British counterparts, who had long been at war and had perfected mechanisms for coordinated planning and strategic direction, as military "city slickers"; depressed by the holocaust of Pearl Harbor, they felt a little like country cousins. Yet they were the representatives of the most powerful nation on earth; inevitably the balance of power must shift, in time, to Washington.

Arcadia conceived the corpus of combined effort—the skeletal outlines, fleshed out by time, of the high-level Anglo-American committees and organizations which were to plan and fight the greatest war in history. But it did not change in principle the prewar agreement that Germany was the major enemy; she must be defeated first. In fact, the overwhelming success of Japanese attacks in the Western Pacific had already forced diversion of U.S. strength to the Pacific, and as 1941 ended the Rising Sun of Japan—gleaming on ever-new conquests—was to force more and more.

* * *

In America, as the year died, the screaming headlines and the perpetual alarms drove from the thoughts of men the old and beautiful words of Christmas:

"Peace on earth; good will towards men."

There were long lines at the recruiting stations, far more men than the doctors could examine; hundreds were turned away. Pearl Harbor had unified a nation.

But it was a jittery nation, its sense of security behind two great oceans forever shattered. On the west coast, there were repeated air-raid alarms; San Francisco and Seattle were blacked out; sirens wailed, and even Lieutenant General John L. DeWitt, commanding the Fourth Army and the Western Defense Command, was unnerved. General DeWitt, normally a man of calm judgment, angrily told those who doubted there had been any Japanese planes anywhere near the west coast:

There are more damned fools in this locality than I have ever seen. Death and destruction are likely to come to this city [San Francisco] any moment. These planes were over our community for a definite period. They were enemy planes. I mean Japanese planes. They were tracked out to sea. Why bombs were not dropped, I do not know. It might have been better if some bombs had been dropped to awaken this city. . . .[160]

New York City waited a day; then on Tuesday, at the lunch hour, military authorities sounded an alert and solemnly affirmed enemy bombers were on their way. A million schoolchildren were evacuated from classrooms but strangely, as on the west coast, no planes were seen, no bombs were dropped. There was, indeed, no enemy within 2,000 miles of either coast.

The roundup of Japanese in the United States, both citizens and aliens, started early, and as always the super-patriots who emerge, like termites, from the solid woodwork of decency commenced their petty persecution of those who spoke with foreign accents or had Germanic names.

New personalities, some of them to become world-famous before the shooting stopped, started to emerge from the obscurity of their past. A little-known colonel, Dwight David Eisenhower, who had made his reputation in the largest maneuvers the United States Army had ever held (in Louisiana in the summer of 1941) was hurriedly called to Washington soon after Pearl Harbor. General Marshall promoted him to brigadier general and assigned him to the War Plans Division, the first rung on the ladder to Supreme command.

* * *

So war came to America in December 1941 . . .

Christmas and the New Year brought few glad tidings to the combatants in what was now a world at war.

On the Russian front, before the approaches to Moscow, some German soldiers, in the guttering light of candles, found brief relief from rigid cold and unending fighting in peasant sod huts. "*O Tannenbaum*" provided a retreat from reality—the reality of pain and suffering and death.

In Malaya and the Philippines the setting was different, the pitiful attempts at solace the same. The jungle heat, the sudden ambush, the bloody bodies, the crash of shells obscured—save for moments—the attempts of the few to salvage memories of the past from the bitterness of the present.

The day before Christmas Eve three men died at last, deep in the mangled wreckage of the battleship *West Virginia*, her bottom slit open, her guts torn out in the Pearl Harbor attack on December 7. They had been caught deep in the ship as she settled to the mud, imprisoned in a bubble of air in a watertight compartment, with the sea above and around them; there was no possible exit to the stars. The air slowly fouled, the emergency batteries failed. Weeks and weeks later when at length the ship was raised, three inert bodies on a low shelf in storeroom compartment A-111 and "a mute record chalked on a bulkhead" calendar (the days crossed off until the end) showed how slowly, for some sixteen days, three trapped Americans had died.[161]

Retrospect

The end of a European conflict, the beginning of a world at war . . .

The invasion of Russia, the Japanese attack upon Pearl Harbor, and Tokyo's triumphs in the Pacific and in Asia in 1941 changed forever the dimensions of the twentieth century, altering completely the outlook and the prospects of man.

In 1941, the war became the greatest armed conflict in history. Yet the year's events presaged much more than that; they were also the catalyst for permanent revolutionary change. This was the point in time which ended the bright complacencies and cherished concepts of millions and substituted a world in violent flux. It ushered in an era of troubles, forecasting the climax of a technological revolution which was to brush away the barriers of distance, time, and space and to culminate in the greatest challenge ever faced by man: the Atomic Age.

For two nations, the United States and Russia, after great suffering and almost four more years of war it was to mean a swift climb to global preeminence, the ascent to world power.

For two other nations, Japan and Germany, it was to mean, in time, utter and complete defeat in war, but in a strange blossoming from the carrion of the concentration camps and the dungheap of death, an economic triumph in peace. For others—Britain, France, The Netherlands—it was to mean the end of empire, and trials no less difficult than war.

The world was forever scarred by 1941, and many Americans who admired the past and basked in its reminiscent glow deplored the change.

Would it have been possible to have preserved the best of this past, to have avoided violent change, refrained from battle? Could the United States have remained neutral?

Not, of course, after Pearl Harbor. But earlier in the war and prewar years, different policies, different leadership just possibly might have altered history, although in retrospect this seems unlikely. Hitler's anti-Semitism and aggressive arrogance, the ultimate threat of a Hitler-dominated Europe to the Western Hemisphere, and the determination of the warlords of Tokyo to dominate China and all of "Greater East Asia" made compromise and aloofness almost psychologically and politically impossible. Most Americans wanted Hitler defeated and Japan ejected from China. To many, although not to a majority until Pearl Harbor, neutrality became a dirty word.

True, President Roosevelt expected war and led his nation toward involvement. True, his "imperial presidency" was high-handed, even, in terms of current history, undemocratic and authoritarian. Roosevelt and the Democratic Party were freed by war and its immense industrial, economic, and manpower demands from a morass of long standing, a Great Depression, the problems of continued unemployment and hunger that had been only slightly alleviated by all the measures of the New Deal.

Nevertheless, by 1941 the global battle lines were fully drawn. Vital interests, the interests of a free Europe and a free China, were more persuasive to American intervention than Roosevelt had ever been. And by then, with an oil embargo against Japan, a program of full aid to Russia starting, and a limited shooting war in the Atlantic, it was almost certainly too late for second guesses.

Nevertheless, the German invasion of Russia offered the United States alternatives short of all-out war which it did not even consider. The two most ruthless and authoritarian dictatorships in the world were locked in death-grip; it was certainly not—as the postwar decades have shown—in the American interest, or world interest, to help one menace replace another. The destruction of both systems and of both dictators, Hitler and Stalin, could only have benefited, not harmed. We might, by our policies, have encouraged this. And in the years of war still ahead, America compounded her errors. The unconditional surrender policies which governed her war strategy and actions were keyed to victory but to little else; Americans had developed no pragmatic conception of the kind of postwar world they wanted.

By the summer of 1941 men and events, that conglomerate of action and reaction, passion and counter-passion that is called history, were committed to an inexorable and tragic progression. Whether or not our non-neutral policy in the Atlantic would have led to open and declared war with Germany, it was certain, well before Pearl Harbor, that Japan and the United States were squarely on a collision course. And war in the Pacific would inevitably mean war in the Atlantic.

Langer and Gleason have probably summarized the American dilemma, and the inevitability of intervention, as well as possible:

Ever since the outbreak of the war in Europe, and indeed before it, most Americans had contemplated with resignation the day when the United States would join in hostilities against the Axis powers. In response to the logic of events, at least as much as to the leadership of the President, an ever increasing number had come to feel that it was not merely their country's hapless fate but its bounden duty to enter the great conflict. The dimensions of America's stake in the outcome had been measured by its Government and its citizens over a period of more than two years. The significance of each momentous step taken along the road which from the start so many believed destiny would compel the country to follow had been debated in Congress, over the air, in the press, and from the platform. Whatever, therefore, the final judgment on the wisdom of America's involvement in the global war, the indictment or the vindication must encompass the whole American people. It was not only the swift disaster of Pearl Harbor which explains the sobriety and even the grimness with which the United States now set its wartime course. The steadfastness and valor of all those warring peoples who were presently to become the United Nations had afforded the American democracy a unique opportunity, by democratic processes, to appraise and at long last to respond to the appeal for leadership in the struggle. Without the elation of 1917, but surely with profounder understanding of the values it sought to preserve, the New World again advanced to the rescue of the Old.[1]

Yet there remains the inevitable vein of uneasiness, and it is clear that in 1941 the great American mistakes were still to come. The moral issues could not be fully clear-cut; in December 1941, brave little Finland became tacitly one of our enemies, and suddenly, overnight, the bad guy became a good guy; we found ourselves allied with communism—an ideology alien to Americans, and with the absolutism of Stalin, as ruthless to the rights of man as Hitler's. It was an equation of uncertainty, a moral dilemma which the coming years of war were to show we did not solve with either deftness or acuity. Still, the manner of our entry, the violence to our blood and kin and to our ego at Pearl Harbor, dictated in many ways the nature of our reflexes; we set an angry course toward victory after 1941, grimly determined to win, willing to make an alliance with the Devil, if necessary, to assure triumph, determined upon unconditional surrender, rather vacuous about the political objectives of victory, blind to the nature of the ultimate peace.

Nineteen forty-one was a watershed of history; its rocky slopes directed—indeed, funneled—the course of future events.

In Russia, the great German invasion which had bogged down before Moscow not only changed the war from *Blitzkrieg* to attrition, but made it an ideological war. Until the invasion of Russia there had been some rules for the waging of war. Admittedly, great cities had been bombed in promiscuous attacks, and submarines were commencing to sink at sight. Nevertheless all belligerents had paid at least lip service to the Geneva Convention; prisoners of war in the West were generally regarded as prisoners and were treated as such by the Germans, harshly but legally, insofar as the tenuous terms of international law define "legality."

With the Russian invasion, all things changed. From the beginning, there were no rules on Hitler's part; this was a war without quarter. And soon, as the Russian peasant saw his hope of freedom vanish, it became an ideological war without mercy, a war to the death, certain to harvest—in after years—the bitter fruit of hatred. The invasion of Russia was to alter beyond belief the nature of Europe and of the world. In retrospect it was to ensure the defeat of Hitler; the triumph of communism, confined, until World War II, to Russia; and the expansion of the left wing of absolutism to a world force. Russia's ultimate emergence as a super-power, with consequences none yet can judge, was assured by the events of 1941.

So, too, in the Pacific and in Asia, the tidal wave of Japanese aggression washed away forever the colonial empires of the past. Ironically, in the war she started Japan was to fail, by force of arms, to eject the white man from the Orient; yet the powder train she laid at Pearl Harbor in December 1941 was ultimately to create an Asia for the Asiatics.

Americans could not know these things then, as 1941 ended; they did not understand the nature of this strange new enemy in the Pacific, the bitterness and the blood and the tears in the long years still to come.

Only later in retrospect, like adults looking back at adolescent extravagances, did they come to appreciate the ambivalence of the little brown men, with their samurai swords and their "Banzai" posturing. They were to learn that:

Both the sword and the chrysanthemum are a part of the picture. The Japanese are, to the highest degree, both aggressive and unaggressive, both militaristic and aesthetic, both insolent and polite, rigid and adaptable, submissive and resentful of being pushed around, loyal and treacherous, brave and timid, conservative and hospitable to new ways. . . . Their soldiers are disciplined to the hilt but are also insubordinate. . . .[2]

This was the bewildering new enemy that had attacked—so treacherously by our code, so gallantly by theirs—at Pearl Harbor, an enemy that refused to be captured, that fought to the death to pay his *chu* to the Emperor, that lopped off the heads of his prisoners, or with peculiar imperturbability condemned thousands of Occidental captives to slow death in a Bataan "death march" or by starvation, hard work, and disease in the jungles of Southeast Asia, an enemy capable of infinite cruelty and of tearful emotion.

This was an enemy almost impossible for Western minds, particularly those long fenced in by the provincialism of great parts of America, to understand. How, indeed, could Westerners comprehend the ambivalent actions of a people conditioned to ambivalence, a race which granted its younger children complete and absolute permissiveness and then rigidly enforced in adolescence and adulthood a whole code of complex hierarchical obligations which governed one's actions to the grave?

We did not understand the enemy before Pearl Harbor, or, for the most part, in the years of war to come. What our soldiers and Marines were to come to know was the special ferocity of the fighting, which became in its way, though without the ideological overtones of the Russian combat, a no-quarter conflict.

All this we did not comprehend in those early days of the nation's greatest war. Slowly we came to appreciate something of the battlefield nature of this new enemy, much later characterized by John Masters as

the bravest people I have ever met. In our armies, any of them, nearly every Japanese would have had a Congressional Medal or a Victoria Cross. It is the fashion to dismiss their courage as fanaticism, but this only begs the question. They believed in something and they were willing to die for it, for any smallest detail that would help achieve it. What else is bravery? They pressed home their attacks when no other troops in the world would have done so, when all hope of success was gone; except that it never really is, for who can know what the enemy has suffered, what is his state of mind? The Japanese simply came on, using all their skill and rage, until they were stopped, by death. In defense they held their ground with a furious tenacity that never faltered. They had to be killed, company by company, squad by squad, man by man, to the last. By 1944 many scores of thousands of Allied soldiers had fallen unwounded into enemy hands as prisoners, because our philosophy and our history have taught us to accept the idea of surrender. By 1944 the number of Japanese captured unwounded, in all theatres of war, probably did not total one hundred. . . . They wrote beautiful little poems in their diaries and practiced bayonet work on their prisoners. Frugal and bestial, barbarous and brave, artistic and brutal, they were the [enemy]. . . .[3]

This was the dim shape of the enemy that loomed above the flaming hulks at Pearl Harbor, the enemy that was to fight so tenaciously against overwhelming American power for almost four long years.

Ironically, although defeated in war, the Japanese did accomplish ultimately what they set out to do in December 1941—the virtual expulsion of the white man from the Orient. For World War II resulted in a global groundswell of anticolonialism, and the divestiture by the great Western powers of their overseas colonies.

Anticolonialism was already a latent factor at the time of Pearl Harbor; Chiang Kai-shek had harnessed Chinese nationalism to his purpose, and some of the peoples of India, Burma, the Dutch East Indies had already grown weary of the *Tuan* and the Raj, of the Dutch planter and the rich American. But the Japanese victories and the Japanese propaganda of "Asia for the Asiatics" gave a tremendous surge to the push for freedom. The Asiatics saw, at first hand, that the white god had feet of clay; yellow men and brown men could beat him, capture him, punish him.

In Malaysia, the Indian prisoners captured by the Japanese in their Malaysia-Singapore victory proved to be the nucleus of a subversive force of consequence in British India.

The Indian Army units employed in Malaya were poor to indifferent troops, a far cut, indeed, from some of the fine professionals of the old imperial Army. The units that fought in Malaya had been "cadred to death"—milked of experienced soldiers to form new units. Most had been enlisted since war started; they had received little training, virtually none above battalion level; they had inadequate equipment, few good officers and non-coms, and virtually no jungle training. As the British official history puts it:

. . . an almost unlimited expansion [of the Indian Army] had to be undertaken and . . . at a speed which had never been envisaged. There were not enough regular officers and men to leaven the whole. The flood of raw human material which had to be absorbed knew nothing of the old loyalties and consequently the mutual confidence and genuine deep-rooted friendship that had existed between officers and men, and between men of different creeds within the unit, were . . . lost.[4]

From the Indian prisoners captured in Malaya, the Japanese, led by a "passionately dedicated" intelligence officer, Colonel Iwaichi Fujiwara, built the beginnings of an Indian National League and Indian National Army, both dedicated to the proposition of freedom for India and the expulsion of the British Raj. The movement grew like wildfire, partly because of the leadership of a former President of the Congress Party, Subhas Chandra Bose, a fiery Bengali whose statues still dot the teeming streets of Calcutta. Bose, a fanatic Indian Nationalist, was regarded by the British as a renegade, by the Germans and the Japanese as a helpful puppet, by many Indians as a national hero, by himself as a scourge of nationalism, a sword of freedom. Out of the fertile soil of the undisciplined prisoners captured in Malaya, Bose and his Indian Nationalists—wed in a marriage of convenience to the Japanese concept of "Asia for the Asiatics"—were to erect an edifice of Indian opposition to Britain, inside and outside India, which was to cause much trouble for the Raj.

And in China, so long torn and divided, the seeds of 1941 were to burgeon in a strange blend of Oriental pride, Chinese dignity, and Communist cant that was to unify, for the first time in decades, the most populous country in the world.

All this was still to come to fruition at the end of 1941; men could not then see the end clearly.

But what was clear in the wreckage of defeat was twofold: there grew a short-term myth of Japanese invincibility, and with it a tacit acceptance of Tokyo's doctrine of "Asia for the Asiatics." Anticolonialism, though it was far from flowering then, was to be a major political result of the Japanese military victories of 1941.

* * *

Thus the seeds of today were sown in 1941. This was the year that marked the transformation of the small war Hitler had wanted into a world at war, the greatest in human history. This was the year that marked the dim beginnings of a Russian Communist superstate, and the slow flexing of American power, the year that was to doom the remaining empires of yesterday and to bestow all over the world the slippery gift of political freedom upon regions, countries, and colonies that knew little of the art of self-government.

It was the beginning of the end: of World War II, of the first half of the twentieth century, of the world-that-was, with its ordered security and accepted values; and the beginning of an uncertain future of rapid and violent change, whose end men still seek to divine.

Acknowledgment

I owe one overriding and preponderant acknowledgment—to my wife.

In addition to the authors and sources so liberally quoted in the text and cited in the notes I have drawn upon half a lifetime of living with World War II. I was thirty-six when the war started; I am seventy-two as I type these words. I knew during the war, or met later, a number of the wartime leaders—both political and military— cited in these pages, and I compiled, over the years, a fund of personal and background information, which has influenced the judgments expressed in this book. My thanks go to each of those who have helped me in the past with interviews, discussions, opinions and facts.

Roxbury, Connecticut, 1975

Notes and Sources

PART I. THE SWORD IS DRAWN

Chapter 1. The Road to War

1. Kenneth S. Davis, *Experience of War* (New York: Doubleday, 1965), pp. 3, 4.
2. *The New York Times*, May 5, 1940, p. 1; William Laurence, *Men and Atoms* (New York: Simon & Schuster, 1959).
3. The Gallup polls of the period illustrate this national ambivalence, and also national confusion. In 1939, before the war started, 57 percent of the American people thought the United States would be drawn in if there was a major war (and 44 percent thought there would be). If the war were between Russia and Germany alone, 83 percent wanted Russia to win. In November 1941, in answer to a question, "Which of these two things do you think is the more important—that this country keep out of war, or that Germany be defeated?", 32 percent favored keeping out of war; 68 percent thought defeating Germany was more important. On the other hand in March 1941, an overwhelming 83 percent of those polled said that if asked they would vote against the United States entering the war against Germany and Italy, and in a poll published on November 22 (with interviewing just a month before Pearl Harbor), 63 percent opposed, "at this time," the suggested passage of a state of war resolution between the United States and Germany, with 26 percent in favor, and 11 percent no opinion. Had it not been for Pearl Harbor, this division might well have continued for many months. President Roosevelt understood and catered to the anti-war sentiment, and stressed, privately, that all U.S. forces must be careful to avoid any aggressive acts—that the first shots must be, in effect, fired by the enemy. See the Gallup polls for 1939 to 1941.
4. In 1914, the German Chancellor Moritz von Bethmann-Hollweg described the joint German-British-Austrian-Hungarian-Russian treaty which guaranteed Belgian neutrality as a "scrap of paper." The invasion of Belgium by the Germans in 1914, which shocked the moral sensitivity of much of the world, was one of the direct causes of British entry into World War I.
5. Named for Frank B. Kellogg, Secretary of State (1925–29) under Calvin Coolidge (thirtieth President of the United States, 1923–29), and Aristide Briand, French Foreign Minister. The pact, which "renounced"

war, was signed in Paris by fifteen nations in 1928, subsequently joined by forty-five additional states.

6. Robert Conquest, *The Human Cost of Soviet Communism*, Senate Document #92–36, 1971. Conquest's comprehensive estimates of the human ravages of Soviet communism reach a minimum of 20 million people starved, executed, or otherwise liquidated.

7. The League endorsed limited sanctions against Italy, which were doomed to failure since oil (the most important commodity) was not embargoed, and Italian ships and troops continued to have passage through the Suez Canal.

8. These brigades were composed of some hard-core Communists, who inevitably dominated, and a number of idealistic, impressionistic young men who enlisted in what they thought was the defense of freedom. Many of them ultimately became disillusioned. The so-called Abraham Lincoln Brigade was recruited in the United States. Despite the U.S., British, and French policy of noninterference and no assistance to either side, the volunteers made their way to Spain, often with the help of false passports. There were five numbered international brigades, each composed of three or more battalions. At any one time the total strength of the international brigades (all of them fighting on the Republican or Loyalist side) never exceeded 18,000 men, but a total of some 40,000 foreigners served at one time or another—10,000 French, 5,000 Germans and Austrians, 3,350 Italians, 2,800 U.S., 2,000 Russians, and a medley of many other nationalities.

In addition to these volunteers fighting on the side of the republic, foreign intervention in the Spanish Civil War was considerable. About 40,000 to 60,000 troops of the Italian Army, and about 20,000 Germans, fought on the side of Franco. See Hugh Thomas, *The Spanish Civil War* (New York: Harper, 1961).

9. Barcelona, seat of the Loyalist government since October 28, 1937, was captured by Franco, aided by Italian troops, on January 26 (some 20,000 defeated troops were interned in France). Madrid and Valencia —last of the left-wing strongholds—surrendered on March 28, 1939. But the retribution and the killing did not quickly end; special tribunals condemned and executed hundreds of Loyalists. Repression settled again over Spain, and the nation remained for many years dissident and divided, its bitterness nurtured by bloodshed.

10. Thomas, *op. cit.*

11. George Orwell's famous novel, *1984*.

12. Henry L. Stimson and McGeorge Bundy, *On Active Service in Peace and War* (New York: Harper, 1947–48), p. 220.

13. December 12, 1937. The U.S. gunboat *Panay*, assigned to the U.S. Navy's Yangtze Patrol (a vestigial remnant of Western influence and extraterritoriality in the era of a weak China in chaos) was sunk in a deliberate attack, and a British gunboat damaged. U.S. casualties were two

dead, and forty-three wounded. A public uproar in the United States later helped to force a Japanese apology and the payment of an indemnity of $2,214,000.

14. Samuel Eliot Morison, *History of U.S. Naval Operations in World War II*, Vol. III, *The Rising Sun in the Pacific* (Boston: Little, Brown, 1948), p. 21.

15. *Ibid.*, p. 19.

16. Giulio Douhet, Italian general, was an imaginative—indeed, visionary—prophet of airpower; he foresaw wars won by aerial fleets of bombers, wreaking tremendous destruction on urban areas. Major General J. F. C. Fuller and Captain Basil H. Liddell Hart were British military theorists and historians, who stressed the importance of the tank and forecast, with the plane-tank team, the new mobility of World War II.

17. Alan Bullock, *Hitler—A Study in Tyranny* (London: Odhams, 1952), Chap. 7, pp. 340 ff.

18. *Ibid.*; also Emil Ludwig. *Three Portraits* (New York: Longmans Green, 1940), p. 24. See also Sir Nevile Henderson, *Failure of a Mission* (New York: Putnam, 1950), Otto Strasser, *Hitler and I* (Boston: Houghton Mifflin, 1940), and Albert Speer, *Inside the Third Reich* (New York: Macmillan, 1970). Portraits, characterizations, and reminiscences about Hitler all agree on his salient personality traits. He had a great capacity for self-dramatization, almost hypnotic charm (when he wanted to use it), and single-minded ruthlessness and megalomania. Alan Bullock's study, first published in 1952 and now dated in some details by more recent material, is probably the best-rounded in English.

19. Ludwig, *op. cit.*, p. 75.

20. New York Times staff, *Churchill in Memoriam* (New York: Bantam, 1965), p. 11.

21. The author's own experience. Regrettably, I heeded the advice and missed meeting one of the greatest men of my time until after World War II.

22. O'Donnell was the columnist of the *New York Daily News*, who bitterly opposed some of the Rooseveltian policies and U.S. entry into World War II.

23. Robert E. Sherwood, *Roosevelt and Hopkins* (New York: Harper, 1948), p. 9.

24. The fifty-eight nations include Australia, Canada, India, New Zealand, and the Union of South Africa (then dominions or otherwise associated with the British Empire), in addition to the United Kingdom. They also include a large number of Latin American countries that declared war on the Axis but had no combat role, or played only minor parts.

There were six so-called Axis powers: Greater Germany (including annexed Austria), Italy and Japan, Bulgaria, Hungary, and Rumania. Finland, though not a formal adherent of the Axis, fought as a German ally. These seven powers were allied against most of the rest of the world, although many of the smaller nations or dependencies which declared war on one or more of the Axis powers, or which found a state of war existed, were only nominal combatants, contributing little to military victory. The status of some of the nominal belligerents was hazy; Thailand, for instance, dominated by Japan, was in an ostensible state of war with the United Kingdom and the British Commonwealth nations, with Czechoslovakia (though absorbed and overrun by Germany), and with the United States. The nations that were in a "state of belligerency," or in a declared or de facto state of war with one or more of the eight Axis or Axis-associated powers (the six above, plus Finland and Thailand), were: U.S.A.; Argentina; Australia; Belgium; Bolivia; Brazil; Canada; Chile; China; Colombia; Costa Rica; Cuba; Czechoslovakia; Denmark; Dominican Republic; Ecuador; Egypt; El Salvador; Ethiopia; France; Greece; Guatemala; Haiti; Honduras; Iceland; India; Iran; Iraq; Lebanon; Liberia; Luxembourg; Mexico; The Netherlands; New Zealand; Nicaragua; Norway; Panama; Paraguay; Peru; Philippine Commonwealth; Poland; Saudi Arabia; Syria; Turkey; Union of South Africa; U.S.S.R.; United Kingdom; Uruguay; Venezuela; and Yugoslavia. (Washington, D.C.: Historical Office, Dept. of State). See also Department of State Bulletin, August 12, 1945, Katharine Elizabeth Crane, "Status of Countries in Relation to the War, Aug. 12, 1945."

25. Morison, *op. cit.*, pp. 19 ff.

26. Ed. W. F. Craven and J. L. Cate, *The Army Air Forces in World War II*, Vol. VI, *Men and Planes* (Chicago: University of Chicago Press, 1955), pp. 202 ff. From January 1940 to the end of August 1945, a total of 12,692 B-17's and 18,900 B-24's was delivered to the Army Air Forces, the Navy, and Allied countries. Peak inventory was 4,574 B-17's in the Army Air Forces in August 1944, and 6,043 B-24's in September 1944. The B-17 was a Boeing product, the B-24 a Consolidated (later Convair) design. The planes of that day were far simpler than the modern supersonic jets; they did not include the expensive and intricate "spaghetti"—miles of complex electronics and wiring—and the "lead time" between design and hardware was a fraction of today's. A prototype for the B-24, for instance, was contracted for in March 1939; its first test flight took place in December of the same year.

27. Craven and Cate, *op. cit.*, pp. 423, 173. Of the total 2,546 planes, only 39 were heavy bombers, and about 900 were non-combat types.

The Navy's planes included several hundred old biplanes and many were obsolescent. General Andrews, a quiet, proficient general with great leadership qualifications, characterized the Army Air Forces on the eve of war (January 1939) as a "fifth rate air force." Andrews, one of the nation's most capable military leaders, who probably would have been the Eisenhower of World War II, is little known to history. He died prematurely, probably on his way to high command and fame, in a plane crash in Iceland in 1943.

28. For a fascinating and comprehensive study of codes and ciphers, their role in military history and their particular importance in World War II, see David Kahn's *The Code Breakers—The Story of Secret Writing* (New York: Macmillan, 1968), particularly Chaps. 12 and 17; also Ladislas Farago, *The Broken Seal* (New York: Random House, 1967). For the British contribution to cryptanalysis, see F. W. Winterbotham, *The Ultra Secret* (New York: Harper, 1974), and for a broader treatment of "Ultra" deception and subterfuge, see Anthony Cave Brown, *Bodyguard of Lies* (New York: Harper, 1975).

29. Saul K. Padover, "France in Defeat," *World Politics*, Vol. II, No. 3 (April 1950), p. 311.

30. For a description of the Maginot Line, its concepts, origin, and fate, see Vivian Rowe's *The Great Wall of France* (New York: Putnam, 1961). The term "Maginot Line" came to be a symbol of futility—an attempt to achieve an impossible absolute security, an example of feckless expenditure for an impossible goal. But Rowe correctly exculpates André Maginot and states (p. 57) that "unkind fate has linked his name forever with a myth for which he was in no way responsible." He points out that the fortifications were "intended to protect the frontiers of Alsace and Lorraine for a limited period" only (in Maginot's conception), and that "they fulfilled that function perfectly."

31. The exact figures of French air strength in 1939, and during the Battle of France, are in dispute even now. French record-keeping left much to be desired, and many of the statistics produced since the war have been comparing apples and oranges. French aircraft strength was scattered all over metropolitan France and her colonies, and many of the planes listed in operating squadrons were either obsolescent or nonflyable for lack of equipment or spare parts. William L. Shirer in *The Collapse of the Third Republic* (New York: Simon & Schuster, 1969), pp. 616 ff. and elsewhere, tries to reconcile the irreconcilable. Suffice it to say that far more French aircraft were available, if anything that could fly was included, than were used in combat, that the production rate was fairly high on paper but low in actual completed flying squadrons, and that, as Shirer correctly notes (p. 179), the French Air Force "vegetated" after World War I (radios were not installed in fighter planes until 1937; the bombers did not have them) and was far behind Germany, Britain, and other countries in technology, tactics, concept, and organization. I disagree with Shirer about the effects of the nationalization of the French aircraft factories by the Léon Blum Popular Front government (1936–37) on the efficiency and productivity of the industry. To my mind, the industry had been poor before nationalization; it was worse afterwards. Even worse, the nationalization was another highly divisive factor in a France already torn apart by the strains and tensions of the Spanish Civil

War and the growing schism between left and right. I was in France at the time, and there is reason to believe that the aircraft production figures were inflated for political purposes.

32. Among the myths were: First, that the Japanese were copyists only and followed blueprints blindly. One story, widely believed but wholly without foundation, held that the British permitted Japanese espionage agents to steal the plan of a warship which had been deliberately designed to be top-heavy. The ship was supposed to have been duly built in Japan and launched, only to capsize immediately. This story made the rounds before World War II and was solemnly believed by many.

Second, that the Japanese, because of their slanted eyes (bad eyesight?) or other inherent physiological attributes, simply could not fly.

Third, perhaps the greatest, was that the Japanese would never dare attack the United States. Americans of that day were credulous; they knew relatively little of the world around them and tended to believe what they wanted to believe. Before the age of the long-range plane and the missile, they felt isolated and secure behind the barriers of oceans, and they still possessed some of the superiority complex of World War I —"One Yank can lick six Germans." Pearl Harbor eliminated much of this wishful thinking.

33. See Hanson W. Baldwin, "Moscow's Military Capabilities," a chapter in Harrison E. Salisbury, ed., *The Soviet Union—The Fifty Years* (New York: The New York Times, 1968), pp. 418, 419; also John Erickson, *The Soviet High Command* (London: Macmillan, 1962). Erickson's later work *The Road to Stalingrad*, the first volume of the most comprehensive history of the Russian-German fighting yet published (New York: Harper, 1975), cites many details of the effect of the purges on the Russian Army and clearly portrays the resultant trauma in the officer corps in 1941.

34. Hanson W. Baldwin, *Battles Lost and Won* (New York: Harper, 1966), p. 13 and n.

35. Samuel Eliot Morison, *History of U.S. Naval Operations in World War II*, Vol. I, *The Battle of the Atlantic* (Boston: Little, Brown, 1947), p. 5.

36. This figure varies slightly with various authorities. Admiral Doenitz puts the total at forty-six; Roskill agrees. Of the forty-six combat-ready "boats," some twenty-five were 250-ton, short-range coastal submarines with limited operating radius in the North Sea. The 500- to 750-ton U-boats which were later to wreak such havoc were then being produced at about two to four ships a month. Germany did not prepare for a U-boat war, traditionally the tactic of the inferior power at sea. "The war was in one sense lost before it began," Doenitz, commanding submarines in the German Navy, was later to write. The inadequacy of the German naval air arm, which initially hampered submarine operations, and throughout the war limited greatly the value of the German surface ships,

was an even greater weakness. Grand Admiral Erich Raeder, Commander-in-Chief of the German Navy at the start of the war, had three pocket battleships (ingenious ships, with 11-inch gun batteries and engines for 28 knots speed crammed into 10,000-ton hulls to exploit optimum technological advantage from the qualitative restrictions of the Versailles Treaty, which limited displacements to 10,000 tons); two battle cruisers *Scharnhorst* and *Gneisenau*; 6- and 8-inch gun cruisers; and some fifty destroyer types.

37. J. W. Wheeler-Bennett, *The Nemesis of Power* (London-New York: Macmillan, 1953), p. 360; William L. Shirer, *The Rise and Fall of the Third Reich* (New York: Simon & Schuster, 1959), pp. 304–308. Both authors derive their description of this conference—or more properly, Hitlerian monologue—from an account, written five days later from notes, by Colonel Hossbach, military adjutant to the Fuehrer (Nuremberg Record, ii, 262) who was present, along with Field Marshal von Blomberg, War Minister and Commander-in-Chief of the Armed Forces; General von Fritsch, Commander-in-Chief of the Army; Admiral Raeder, Commander-in-Chief of the Navy; General Göring, Commander-in-Chief of the Air Force; and Von Neurath, Foreign Minister. The Hossbach document, discovered after the war, was introduced as evidence at Nuremberg. Shirer—extravagantly, I think—characterizes this conference-monologue as "the decisive turning point in the life of the Third Reich." This is a definite exaggeration. Hitler's course toward expansion and aggression had been charted in *Mein Kampf* and in all his actions since he assumed power. His ambitions broadened as his power became more absolute and as he was met with appeasement rather than strength. The latent megalomania and the dreams of transcendent glory which had always characterized *Der Fuehrer* became more and more dominant factors as—in Lord Acton's famous phrase—absolute power corrupted absolutely. There were, moreover, many such rambling "conferences" as the one Hossbach describes during Hitler's regime as dictator. Each differed somewhat in detail and phraseology; all were lengthy; in all Hitler spoke with mixed venom and exaltation about the conquests and the glories to come.

38. These pacts, which played a relatively small part in the coming of the war, included the Anglo-Italian Mediterranean agreement in January 1937 to guarantee free passage through the Mediterranean and the integrity of Spain; an Italian-Yugoslav treaty guaranteeing existing frontiers in March 1937—a blow to French influence in the Balkans, and to the so-called Little Entente (an alliance directed primarily against Hungary, formed in 1920–21 between Czechoslovakia, Yugoslavia, and Rumania); a French-German pact in December 1938, guaranteeing French frontiers; a German guarantee of the integrity and inviolability of Belgium in October 1937; and Anglo-French non-aggression and mutual assistance pacts with Rumania, Greece, and, finally, Poland in 1939. The pacts had some psychological importance in the West in lulling fears

and contributing to appeasement, but war would have come with or without them.

39. Shirer, *The Rise and Fall of the Third Reich*, pp. 340 ff.
40. *Ibid.*, p. 365.
41. A. L. Rowse, *Appeasement* (New York: Norton, 1961), pp. 117–118.
42. P. K. Kemp, *Key to Victory* (Boston: Little, Brown, 1957), p. 26.
43. *Ibid.*
44. John W. Wheeler-Bennett, *Munich* (New York: Duell, Sloan & Pearce, 1948), p. 109.
45. *Ibid.*, p. 171.
46. *Ibid.*, pp. 178, 180–181.
47. *The Ciano Diaries, 1939–1943*, ed. by Hugh Gibson (New York: Doubleday, 1946), p. 110.
48. Baldwin, *Battles Lost and Won*, pp. 6, 17 n.

Chapter 2. The Beginnings: 1939

49. The Polish inventory totaled about 1,400 planes, but more than half of them were training, liaison, transport, and other non-combat types.
50. John Fricker and William Green, *Air Forces of the World* (London: McDonald, 1958), pp. 226, 227. Alfred B. Peszke, "The Bomber Brigade of the Polish Air Force in September, 1939," *The Polish Review*, Vol. XIII, No. 4 (August 1968), pp. 80–100.
51. F. B. Czarnomski, ed., *They Fight for Poland* (London: Allen & Unwin, 1941), pp. 33 ff.
52. Robert M. Kennedy, *The German Campaign in Poland* (Washington, D.C.: Department of the Army pamphlet #20–255, April 1956), pp. 127, 128.
53. Shirer, *The Rise and Fall of the Third Reich*, p. 660.
54. *History of the Second World War*, S. W. Roskill, *The War at Sea*, Vol. I (London: H.M. Stationery Office, 1954), comments, pp. 52–53, that Hitler's prewar assurances to his naval advisers that "no war would take place before 1944 or 1945" had greatly handicapped German naval planning, with the result that the German Navy in 1939 was actually below the strength permitted it (on paper) by the Anglo-German naval agreement of 1935. ". . . It was not until 1939 that full-scale naval preparations for war with Britain were started . . . when war actually broke out the German Navy was far less well prepared for it than the German Air Force. . . ." Had war actually started as Hitler originally forecast in 1944–45, the German Navy would "indeed have been of formidable strength . . . 13 battleships, 33 cruisers, four aircraft carriers . . . 250 U-boats. . . ."
55. Julian S. Corbett, *England in the Seven Years War* (New York: Longmans Green, 1907), Vol. I, p. 5.

56. Vice Admiral Friedrich Ruge, *Der Seekrieg—The German Navy's Story, 1939–1945* (Annapolis, Md.: U.S. Naval Institute, 1957), pp. 43 ff.
57. Roskill, *op. cit.*, pp. 99 ff. See also Ruge, *op. cit.*, pp. 60 ff.; George W. Gray, *Science at War* (New York: Harper, 1943), pp. 12 ff.; and A. M. Low, *Mine and Countermine* (New York: Sheridan House, 1940), pp. 114 ff.
58. Roskill, *op. cit.*, pp. 118–121; Ruge, *op. cit.*, p. 71; Kemp, *op. cit.*, pp. 41 ff.; Lord Strabolgi, *The Battle of the River Plate* (London: Hutchinson, 1940); Trevor N. Dupuy, *The Military History of World War II*, Vol. IV, *The Naval War in the West—The Raiders* (New York: Franklin Watts, 1963); Dudley Pope, *The Battle of the River Plate* (Philadelphia: Lippincott, 1957); Geoffrey Bennett, *Battle of the River Plate* (Shepperton, Middx.: Allen, 1972).
59. Albin T. Anderson, "Origins of the Winter War," *World Politics*, Vol. VI, No. 2 (January 1954), pp. 169 ff. The Stalin quotes are translations. Väinö Tanner, *Finlands Väg, 1939–40* (Helsingfors: 1950).
60. Baron Marshal Mannerheim, *The Memoirs of Marshal Mannerheim* (New York: Dutton, 1954), pp. 367, 368.
61. *Ibid.*
62. John Langdon-Davies, *Invasion in the Snow* (Boston: Houghton Mifflin, 1941), p. 17.

PART II. THE YEAR OF PERIL—1940

Chapter 3. *War in the North—Scandinavia*

1. Laurence Thompson, *1940* (New York: Morrow, 1966), p. 27 and Chap. 1.
2. William L. Shirer, *Berlin Diary* (New York: Knopf, 1941), pp. 271–272.
3. Langdon-Davies, *op. cit.*, p. 64.
4. Churchill, January 20, 1940.
5. For the off-again, on-again Allied aid programs and the political and diplomatic nuances and repercussions of the Winter War, see John H. Wuorinen, *Finland and World War II* (New York: The Ronald Press, 1948).
6. Thomas Babington Macaulay, "Horatius at the Bridge," in *Lays of Ancient Rome*.
7. Seweryn Bialer, *Stalin and His Generals* (New York: Pegasus, 1969), p. 130.
8. Robert Murphy, *Diplomat Among Warriors* (New York: Pyramid Books, 1965), p. 66.
9. Donald Macintyre, *Narvik* (New York: Norton, 1960), p. 28.
10. Christopher Buckley, *Norway, The Commandos Dieppe* (London: H.M. Stationery Office, 1951), p. 16.

11. The German ships sunk in the second battle of Narvik were U-64 and destroyers *Georg Thiele, Hans Lüdemann, Hermann Künne, Diether von Röder, Wolfgang Zenker, Erich Giese, Erich Koellner,* and *Bernd von Arnim.*

12. Buckley, *op. cit.*, p. 52.

13. Leland Stowe, *Chicago Daily News*, April 25, 1940.

14. *History of the Second World War*, T. K. Derry, *The Campaign in Norway* (London: H.M. Stationery Office, 1952), pp. 142–143.

15. Macintyre, *op. cit.*, p. 212.

16. Ruge, *op. cit.*, p. 91.

17. J. L. Moulton, *A Study of Warfare in Three Dimensions* (Athens, Ohio: Ohio University Press, 1967), p. 297.

18. ". . . while it is obvious that the cutting off of vital imports would have had a fatal effect on both the quality and quantity of iron and steel production [in Germany] if the war had continued only a little longer, it is unlikely that these shortages played a major part in Germany's defeat." (W. N. Medlicott, *The Economic Blockade*, Vol. II [London: H.M. Stationery Office, 1959], p. 658.) Medlicott's authoritative official history points out that both the import of iron ore and steel production in Germany fell sharply as the war drew to a close, but only then (Greater Germany and the occupied countries produced 31,819,000 tons of steel in 1941; 34,644,000 in 1943; and 28,501,000 in 1944). However, shortages of alloys, and eventually of magnesium and aluminum, became severe.

19. Thompson, *op. cit.*, p. 96.

20. Winston S. Churchill, *The Second World War*, Vol. I, *The Gathering Storm* (Boston: Houghton Mifflin, 1948), pp. 666–667.

Chapter 4. Blitzkrieg in the West

21. Various authorities generally agree, within narrow limits, as to the strength statistics and order of battle of the German forces in the French campaign, but there are widely discrepant estimates about the French forces. Some of the French leaders—writing after the event—juggled figures in their own defense or to prove their particular points; others used statistics without definition. The figures given in the text are believed to be the best available approximation. For a detailed discussion see Colonel A. Goutard, *The Battle of France, 1940* (New York: Ives Washburn, 1959), Chap. 2; Guy Chapman, *Why France Fell*, a comprehensive and excellent study (New York: Holt, Rinehart, 1968), particularly Appendices A and B; and the more general and less expert discussion of Shirer, *The Collapse of the Third Republic*, particularly Chap. 29. See also the detailed British account in *History of the Second World War*, Major L. F. Ellis, *The War in France and Flanders—1939–1940* (London: H.M. Stationery Office, 1953).

22. The British 1st Armored Division, just formed, never fought in France as a division; it was incomplete at the time of the battle. The French were just forming a fourth armored division, which did not join the battle, piecemeal, until about May 16. In addition to the Allied armored forces available on the northeastern front, there were probably another 1,000 to 1,500 tanks (chiefly French) in the interior, overseas in the colonies, and newly produced but not yet operational. The "scratch" nature of the French armored effort is evidenced by the fact that none of the French armored divisions was in existence until January 1940, and the 4th Armored Division—so called—was hastily scooped together from bits and pieces in the latter half of May, *after* the battle was decided.

23. J. Benoist-Méchin, *Sixty Days that Shook the West* (London: Cape, 1963), p. 58.

24. The casualties resulting from the bombing of Rotterdam were vastly exaggerated at the time, and until Dutch official figures were furnished after the war to the International Military Tribunal (814 dead). The Nazi terror bombing was roundly condemned, as it was in the case of Warsaw. A mistake, blamed by the Germans on poor communications, appears to have forestalled the complete cancellation of the bombing, after negotiations for the surrender of Rotterdam started. In the larger sense the bombing of Rotterdam and the earlier strafing of streets in The Hague by German fighters were all part of the ruthless policy of conquest of Adolf Hitler. But within the narrower parameters of the rules of war, no unilateral blame can be so easily assessed, and at Nuremberg no person "was convicted of criminal guilt in connection with the Rotterdam bombing." (Telford Taylor, *The March of Conquest* [New York: Simon & Schuster, 1958], p. 202 n.) Dutch strong points and artillery within the city of Rotterdam commanded the German bridgehead across the river; the city had *not* been declared an open one; like Warsaw it was defended, and hence subject to attack by air, artillery, and infantry assault. Rotterdam, like so many other cities during and since World War II, was the victim of twentieth-century Total War.

25. Taylor, *op. cit.*, p. 214. See also the personal account of the German commanding officer, then Lt. Rudolf Witzig (commanding the sapper detachment of a parachute infantry battalion), in Purnell and Sons, *History of the Second World War*, Vol. I, No. 7, Bristol: May 10, 1940.

26. Ellis, *op. cit.*, pp. 38 ff.

27. *Ibid.*, p. 42.

28. Quoted from Chapman, *Why France Fell*, p. 152.

29. Benoist-Méchin, *op. cit.*, p. 98.

30. Hans Habe, *A Thousand Shall Fall* (New York: Lancer Books paperback, 1969), pp. 172–173.

31. Pertinax, *The Grave Diggers of France* (New York: Doubleday, Doran, 1944), p. 196.

32. Commander Pierre Lyet, quoted in Ellis, *op. cit.*, p. 76.

33. Winston Churchill, *The Second World War*, Vol. II, *Their Finest Hour* (Boston: Houghton Mifflin, 1949), pp. 56–57.

34. Some of the details of Leopold's reasoning, and a defense of the King, are embodied in a pamphlet by Joseph P. Kennedy and James M. Landis, published privately by the Joseph P. Kennedy Memorial Foundation in 1950: "The Surrender of King Leopold." This pamphlet includes the correspondence between Admiral Keyes and Lord Gort and many of the messages between Keyes and the King and the British and French governments and commanders. Leopold's rationale for remaining in his conquered country is capsuled in a despatch of May 21 from Keyes to Churchill, and in a letter from Leopold to King George VI of May 25. In the former Keyes wrote: "His [Leopold's] government is pressing him to flee with them to Le Havre before the Army is forced to capitulate. Needless to say, he has no intention of deserting his army and believes that he can better serve his country by remaining here [in Belgium] than by fleeing with a Government which represents no one the moment it crosses the frontiers." In the letter to King George VI, Leopold states: "In spite of all the contrary advice which I have received, I feel that my duty compels me to share the fate of my army and to stay with my people; to act otherwise would be a desertion. I am convinced that I can better aid my people by remaining with them than by trying to act from outside the country, especially against the rigors of a foreign occupation, the threat of forced labor or of deportation and food shortages. In remaining in my country I fully realize that my position will be very difficult but my main thought will be to prevent my compatriots from being obliged to associate themselves in action against the countries which have aided Belgium in her struggle."

Who, viewing history in retrospect, is to say Leopold was wrong? Ironically, Queen Wilhelmina of The Netherlands, who at British urging fled to England, was criticized by some of her subjects for "abandoning" her people. She also abdicated, in favor of her daughter, in 1948.

(See also "The Belgian Campaign and the Surrender of the Belgian Army," a pamphlet, with foreword by Herbert Hoover, published in New York by the Belgian American Educational Foundation in 1940; and "Belgium—The Official Account of What Happened, 1939–1940," published for the Belgian Ministry of Foreign Affairs by Didier Publishers, New York, 1942.)

35. B. H. Liddell Hart, *The Other Side of the Hill* (London: Cassell, 1951), p. 201. Hart presents an extensive discussion of this controversial halt order in Chap. XII of his book. But see also Ellis, *op. cit.*, pp. 138, 139. There is not much doubt that Rundstedt, who was already looking beyond the encirclement at Dunkirk toward the impending Battle of France, initiated the halt; Hitler fully approved it, and may indeed have anticipated it. Rundstedt's reasoning at the time, as shown in the War

Diaries of his Army Group (quoted in Ellis, p. 138), was as follows on the evening of May 23:

"(a) The possibility of concerted action by Allied forces in the north and French forces south of the Somme had to be reckoned with.

"(b) It was of vital importance to close up the mobile formations as well as to consolidate the German northern flank. British and French attacks about Arras and Cambrai had underlined this need.

"(c) The XIX Corps having so far failed to take Boulogne and Calais, and the defense of the Somme flank not yet being secure, the advanced units of Kleist and Hoth Groups should deny the [Aa] Canal Line to the enemy but should not cross it."

Ellis, who pins the responsibility for the halt order almost entirely on Rundstedt, adds that "Rundstedt saw that if he was to get his own way when it differed from the intentions of O.K.H. he must make it appear that what he did was 'by the Führer's orders.'" There is every indication, however, that Hitler not only fully shared Rundstedt's judgment in this case but, for reasons of his own, may even have come to the same conclusion before he confirmed Rundstedt's order. In my judgment the verdict of history must be that Rundstedt and Hitler share the responsibility for one of the great mistakes of the war, for it is very probable that most of the BEF and their French compatriots would have been trapped had the advance been allowed to continue on May 24. Guy Chapman (*Why France Fell*, p. 228) provides a cautionary note, much needed, of course, when one discusses the "might-have-beens" of history. "It may be," he says, "that the port [Dunkirk] would have been captured and some 300,000 or so put in the bag. But it is not certain. . . . The whole of the area around Dunkirk is a maze of drains and banks. It is possible that the final battle . . . might have done so much damage to the Panzer divisions as to postpone the assault [along the Somme] that began on 5 June, with what consequences it is idle to speculate. The Germans preferred to make sure."

36. Rundstedt was authorized by OKH to resume the attack on the Aa Canal front early on May 25, but he disregarded it and held his forces in leash—and essentially on the defensive—until May 26, noting that "the principal thing now is to husband the armored formations for later and more important tasks."

37. Gun Buster, *Return via Dunkirk* (London: Hodder, 1940), quoted in Desmond Flower and James Reeves, *The Taste of Courage* (New York: Harper, 1960), pp. 83–84.

38. More than 300,000 of these were lifted by British ships; French vessels took off most of the remainder, with the help of some Belgian and Dutch small craft, tugs, and coastal vessels. Chapman points out the truism that war is by no means all heroics. The evacuation of the French ports was "not . . . all as well-mannered, as coolly classical, as comradely as some writers would have us believe. There were many groups, espe-

cially at Malo, who considered they had been deserted. There were unpleasant incidents . . . 'the horrifying mob at Malo . . . to produce order successfully machine guns were needed.'" (Chapman, *op. cit.*, p. 228.)

39. The British official history concludes that "Fighter Command's contribution to the success of the evacuation was substantial. . . ."

Chapter 5. The Death of the Third Republic

40. Benoist-Méchin, *op. cit.*, p. 262.
41. Ellis, *op. cit.*, p. 270.
42. *Ibid.*, pp. 272–273.
43. Colonel de Bardies, quoted in Benoist-Méchin, *op. cit.*, p. 261.
44. *Ibid.*, p. 284.
45. De Gaulle, quoted in *ibid.*, p. 287.
46. Major General Sir Edward Spears, *Assignment to Catastrophe*, Vol. II (New York: Wyn, 1955), p. 161.
47. Raoul de Roussy de Sales, *The Making of Yesterday* (New York: Reynal & Hitchcock, 1947), p. 141.
48. Charles de Gaulle, *The Call to Honor* (New York: Viking, 1955), pp. 72 and 73.
49. *Ibid.*, p. 51.
50. Churchill himself wrote in *Their Finest Hour* (p. 229) that "Darlan . . . had repeatedly assured that whatever happened the French fleet should never fall into German hands." He added (p. 231) that Darlan had "certainly built up in the minds of the officers and men of the French Navy that at all costs their ships should be destroyed before being seized by the Germans, whom he disliked as much as the English."
51. Cordell Hull, *Memoirs*, Vol. I, p. 799. For full accounts of Mers-el-Kebir, Oran, and the other Anglo-British naval encounters, see Churchill, *Their Finest Hour*; Roskill, *The War at Sea*; and *History of the Second World War*, Major General I. S. O. Playfair, *et al.*, *The Mediterranean and Middle East*, Vol. I (London: H.M. Stationery Office). See also Admiral of the Fleet, Viscount Cunningham, *A Sailor's Odyssey* (New York: Dutton, 1951) and Warren Tute, *The Deadly Stroke* (New York: Coward-McCann, 1973).
52. Murphy, *op. cit.*, p. 77.

Chapter 6. The Battle of Britain

53. Churchill, *Their Finest Hour*, pp. 225–226.
54. *History of the Second World War*, Basil Collier, *Defense of the United Kingdom* (London: H.M. Stationery Office), p. 143.
55. To set "a sea of flame" was not easily done; in fact the scheme had more psychological than practical value. An inordinate amount of oil,

carefully mixed with gasoline, was required even for small areas; even so, ignition was a problem. The Germans got wind of the scheme, and devised fire-fighting tugs and towed log chains to contain or neutralize the burning area. As Walter Ansel points out in his thorough study of the abortive invasion—*Hitler Confronts England* (Durham, N.C.: Duke University Press, 1960)—the flaming sea defense was one of many schemes and ideas, most launched only on paper, some physically tested.

56. Churchill, *Their Finest Hour*, pp. 161 ff., 263 ff., 398 ff.; Morison, *Battle of the Atlantic*, pp. 33 ff.; Langer, *The Challenge to Isolation*; and Mark S. Watson, Chief of Staff, *Prewar Plans and Preparations* (*U.S. Army in World War II*) (Washington, D.C.: U.S. Government Printing Office), pp. 309 ff. See also Jim Dan Hill, *The Minuteman in Peace and War* (Harrisburg, Pa.: Stackpole, 1964).

57. Ansel, *op. cit.*, pp. 43 ff. Ansel thoroughly discusses the genesis of abortive invasion plans. See also Collier, *Defense of the United Kingdom*, and Ronald Wheatley, *Operation Sea Lion* (London: Oxford University Press, 1958).

58. Baldwin, *Battles Lost and Won*, Chap. 2; pp. 31 ff.

59. Ansel, *op. cit.*, p. 153.

60. Collier, *Defense of the United Kingdom*, p. 430.

61. *Ibid.*, p. 162.

62. Some authorities regard August 15, when Luftflotte 5 from Scandinavia joined the battle, as "Eagle Day."

63. Shirer, *The Rise and Fall of the Third Reich*, pp. 779, 780, and Denis Richards, *Royal Air Force 1939–1945* (London: H.M. Stationery Office, 1953–54), Vol. I, *The Fight at Odds*, p. 183.

64. Shirer, *The Rise and Fall of the Third Reich*, p. 770.

65. Group Captain J. E. Johnson, *Wing Leader* (New York: Ballantine Books, 1957), pp. 171–174.

Chapter 7. The War at Sea

66. Cunningham, *op. cit.*, pp. 239, 270 ff.

67. There is not much doubt that Malta could have been eliminated by capture, or neutralized by saturation bombing, in 1940 and 1941. It *was* heavily and repeatedly attacked, but the attack patterns rose and fell like a sine curve, and the decision to capture it, though discussed, was never taken.

68. Commander Marc'Antonio Bragadin, *The Italian Navy in World War II* (Annapolis, Md.: U.S. Naval Institute, 1957), p. 20. Italics in the original text.

69. Cunningham, *op. cit.*, p. 269.

70. *Ibid.*, pp. 258, 259.

71. *Ibid.*, p. 286.

72. Second Officer Nancy Spain, WRNS, *Thank You—Nelson*. Quoted in Captain Eric Bush, RN, editor, *The Flowers of the Sea* (London: Allen & Unwin, 1962), pp. 269, 270.

73. Some Irishmen throughout the war carried on a frank flirtation with the Nazis, German agents smuggled arms, and U-boat contacts off the Irish coast fueled their activities. The paranoid suspicion and hatred of Britain on the part of some Irishmen led to the utilization of extremist policies and methods which have too often—as the history of the Irish Republican Army illustrates—disgraced the name of Ireland.

Chapter 8. Keystone of Empire

74. Playfair, *The Mediterranean and Middle East*, Vol. I, p. 33.

75. John Strawson, *The Battle for North Africa* (New York: Scribner's, 1969), p. 32.

76. *Ibid.*, p. 33.

77. *Ibid.*

78. Playfair, *op. cit.*, Vol. I, pp. 181, 182.

79. Alexander G. Clifford, *The Conquest of North Africa* (Boston: Little, Brown, 1943), pp. 7, 8.

80. Playfair, *op. cit.*, Vol. I, p. 116.

81. Strawson, *op. cit.*, pp. 22 ff.

Chapter 9. The Italian Invasion of Greece

82. The Italians never acknowledged responsibility for the sinking until long after World War II had ended.

83. John A. Lukacs, *The Great Powers and Eastern Europe* (New York: American Book Co.), pp. 310 ff.

84. Mario Cervi, *The Hollow Legions* (New York: Doubleday, 1971).

85. *Ibid.*, pp. 136, 137.

Chapter 10. The Blitz

86. Churchill, *Their Finest Hour*, p. 362.

87. See Collier, *Defense of the United Kingdom*, for details; also, Winterbotham, *The Ultra Secret, op. cit.*; Brown, *Bodyguard of Lies, op. cit.* There are some differences as to the amount of pre-warning.

88. Richards, *op. cit.*, p. 206.

89. Constantine FitzGibbon, *The Winter of the Bombs* (New York: Norton, 1958), pp. 200, 201.

90. Collier, *Defense of the United Kingdom*, p. 273.

91. FitzGibbon, *op. cit.*, p. 132.

92. Collier, *Defense of the United Kingdom*, pp. 258–259.

PART III. MARCH OF CONQUEST—1941

1. The Atlantic Charter outlined eight points which were intended to be the Anglo-American moral blueprint for the postwar world. Most of these were too general or too vague to serve as war objectives; they were more a statement of ethical principles, applied to international politics. They were described at the time by the isolationist and anti-British *Chicago Tribune* as "pretentious and meaningless." In fact, most of the points have never been realized, and they in no way served as actual guideposts after World War II. The Atlantic Charter cannot be described as a pragmatic substitute for fundamental war objectives. The greater importance of the Churchill-Roosevelt meeting, which was held aboard the U.S. cruiser *Augusta* and the British battleship *Prince of Wales* off Argentia, Newfoundland, from August 9 to 12, was its immediate military and political impact. It was the first of many similar summit meetings held during the war. Both tacitly and explicitly, it ranged the United States definitely against the Axis, and as a de facto, if not de jure, ally of Britain. It arrived at no agreed-upon joint Anglo-American statement of strategy, but did illuminate many of the questions and problems confronting both High Commands and, even more important, made possible face-to-face meetings and assessments of the British and American Chiefs of Staff. To most Americans, whose sympathies lay with Britain, the meeting and the principles enunciated by the Atlantic Charter seemed unexceptionable; but the partisan and non-neutral position adopted by the U.S. administration was violently attacked by many, including Senator Robert A. Taft, who wished to keep the United States out of war. No matter what its achievements, or lack of them, there is no doubt that the Argentia meeting was another milestone on the U.S. road to war. For details, see Churchill's account, *The Second World War*, Vol. III, *The Grand Alliance*, pp. 433 ff.; William L. Langer and S. Everett Gleason, *The Undeclared War* (New York: Harper, 1953), pp. 663 ff.; and Sherwood, *op. cit.*, pp. 349 ff.

2. The Hess flight, cloaked with all kinds of rumors, turned out in retrospect to be the aberration of one man. Hess was a most loyal Nazi and, as with many of the leaders of the party, his emotional instability led to erratic actions. Late on Saturday, May 10, 1941, Hess—dressed in a Luftwaffe uniform, and flying solo—navigated with considerable precision from Augsburg, Germany, to an area near the Duke of Hamilton's estate in Scotland, where he bailed out by parachute. He had met the Duke before the war, and Hess, who was a "Deputy Fuehrer" and high in party councils, had conceived a strange notion that he could persuade the British to quit fighting (as Churchill puts it in *The Grand Alliance*, p. 54, "if only England knew how kind Hitler really was, surely she would meet his wishes") and negotiate an end to the war on Hitler's terms. Hess was

treated as a prisoner of war; after the war he was tried as a war criminal and sentenced to Spandau Prison in Berlin, where he remained in 1975—the last of the famous "war criminals" behind bars.

Chapter 11. "Victory Through Air Power"

3. Collier, *Defense of the United Kingdom*, p. 276.
4. C. F. Rawnsley and Robert Wright, *Night Fighter* (New York: Henry Holt, 1957), pp. 115–116.
5. Collier, *Defense of the United Kingdom*, p. 280.
6. Average daily availability. Sir C. Webster and N. Frankland, *The Strategic Air Offensive Against Germany*, Vol. IV, Appendix 39, p. 428.
7. Webster and Frankland, *op. cit.*, Vol. I, p. 168.
8. The transition to area bombing was greatly affected by the doubts of Lord Cherwell, Churchill's influential scientific adviser, about bombing accuracy and the results of a so-called Butts report (Mr. Butts was a member of the British War Cabinet Secretariat) in the summer of 1941. The report concluded that only one-third of all aircraft that reported attacking their targets had actually got within 5 miles of them; two-fifths of all aircraft that reported attacking Ruhr targets in full moonlight actually got within 5 miles of them; on moonless nights, only one-fifteenth got within a 5-mile circle. "If the total number of aircraft despatched was considered, the proportions would have to be reduced by another third . . . even these proportions were only established to have dropped their bombs within the seventy-five square miles which surrounded the actual target. Thus, many . . . aircraft . . . would in fact have dropped their bombs in open country." This report plus Churchill's advocacy of tit-for-tat was influential in the formation of Britain's subsequent bombing policies. Like all great war leaders Churchill had a quality of ruthlessness. See Webster and Frankland, *op. cit.*, Vol. IV, Appendix 13, p. 205, and *ibid.*, Vol. I, p. 178.

Chapter 12. The Battle of the Atlantic

9. Herbert A. Werner, *Iron Coffins* (New York: Holt, Rinehart, 1969), pp. 102, 31.
10. Morison, *Battle of the Atlantic*, p. 56.
11. See *ibid.* for details of the road to war; also Langer and Gleason, *op. cit.*
12. Kemp, *Key to Victory*, p. 167. For details, see Chap. 7, "The Bismarck Operation." The definitive and most accurate and dramatic account of the *Bismarck*'s last cruise is Ludovic Kennedy, *Pursuit* (New York: Viking, 1974).
13. The fire was apparently caused by almost 10 tons of antiaircraft ammunition stowed on the open deck in unprotected lockers. This am-

munition was to be used for the so-called Naval Wire Barrage, or U.P. (Unrotated Projectile), a Rube Goldberg device of rockets and trailing wires, designed to foil low-flying attack planes. The device was never effective and the Admiralty learned the hard way. The loss of the *Hood* caused the removal of all U.P.'s from His Majesty's ships.

14. *Fuehrer Conferences on Naval Affairs, 1941* (London: The Admiralty, 1947), p. 65.
15. Roskill, *War at Sea*, p. 410.
16. *Ibid.*, p. 412.
17. Ruge, *op. cit.*, p. 172.
18. *Fuehrer Conferences*, p. 70.
19. These two "hits" are in dispute. Survivors of the *Bismarck* said there were no hits at this time; on the other hand, they also claimed, incorrectly, that *Bismarck* had sunk one attacking destroyer and damaged another.
20. *Fuehrer Conferences*, p. 80.
21. Francis McMurtrie, *The Cruise of the Bismarck* (London: Hutchinson), quoted, p. 33.
22. *Ibid.*, pp. 32–33.
23. Vice Admiral B. B. Schofield, *Loss of the Bismarck* (Shepperton, Surrey: Allen, 1972), pp. 66–67.
24. Lt. Comdr. Gerhard Junack, *The Last Hours of the Bismarck* (London: Purnell, *History of the Second World War*, Vol. II, No. 5).
25. McMurtrie, *op. cit.*, quoted, p. 29.

Chapter 13. East and West of Suez

26. Playfair, *The Mediterranean and Middle East*, Vol. I, p. 392.
27. B. H. Liddell Hart, *History of the Second World War* (New York: Putnam, 1970), p. 126.
28. Playfair, *The Mediterranean and Middle East*, Vol. I, p. 403.
29. Curiously—or perhaps not so curiously for one of his ego—Orde Wingate looked down his nose at the methods of his relative T. E. Lawrence. He considered them, in Leonard Mosley's words, "wasteful and ineffectual, psychologically wrong. . . ." For a character study of this strange leader, see Mosley's fascinating book, *Gideon Goes to War* (New York: Scribner's, 1955), specifically p. 127.
30. *Ibid.*, p. 6; see also John Masters, *The Road Past Mandalay* (New York: Harper, 1961), pp. 148–152.
31. Playfair, *The Mediterranean and Middle East*, Vol. I, p. 427.
32. Somerset de Chair, *The Golden Carpet* (New York: Harcourt, Brace, 1945), p. 71.
33. Playfair, *The Mediterranean and Middle East*, Vol. II, p. 205.
34. *Ibid.*
35. De Chair, *op. cit.*, p. ix.

36. Playfair, *The Mediterranean and Middle East*, Vol. II, p. 222.
37. *Ibid.*, p. 223.
38. Von Thoma was, however, distinctly unenthusiastic about an African adventure.
39. Walter Warlimont, *Inside Hitler's Headquarters* (New York: Praeger, 1964), pp. 104 ff.
40. *The Secret Conferences of Dr. Goebbels*, ed. by Willi A. Boelcke (New York: Dutton, 1970), p. 117.
41. *Fuehrer Conferences on Matters Dealing with the German Navy* (Washington, D.C.: Navy Department Office of Naval Intelligence, 1947), Vol. II, pp. 68 ff.

Chapter 14. The Western Desert

42. *The Rommel Papers*, ed. by B. H. Liddell Hart (New York: Harcourt, Brace, 1953), p. 105.
43. Playfair, *The Mediterranean and Middle East*, Vol. I, p. 375.
44. Rommel, *op. cit.*, p. 111.
45. *Ibid.*, p. 133.
46. *Ibid.*, p. 119.
47. Playfair, *The Mediterranean and Middle East*, Vol. II, p. 153.
48. *Ibid.*, p. 159.
49. Churchill, *The Grand Alliance*, p. 246.
50. *Rudyard Kipling's Verse, Inclusive Edition* (New York: Doubleday, 1925), "Tommy," p. 453.
51. Rommel, *op. cit.*, p. 160.
52. Alexander G. Clifford, *The Conquest of North Africa* (Boston: Little, Brown, 1943), p. 190.
53. *Ibid.*, pp. 145, 146.
54. Alan Moorehead, *The March to Tunis* (New York: Harper, 1965), p. 225. Clifford, *op. cit.*, p. 153, describes Campbell "like one possessed . . . he took the . . . [Brigade] into battle, yelling, shouting, literally hurling rocks at people to make them go faster. . . . He was everywhere all the time, running from tank to tank, banging on steel doors, encouraging, helping, giving orders, directing fire. . . ." Soldiers, fatalistically, say that it is the best who die. "Jock" Campbell, one of the most promising armored leaders of World War II, was promoted to major general and given command of the 7th Armored Division in February 1942, only to die a few days later "in the senseless, trivial way V.C.'s so often die—a car smash in the desert, only a few miles from where he led his tank charges. . . ."
55. Playfair, *The Mediterranean and Middle East*, Vol. III, p. 52.
56. Clifford, *op. cit.*, p. 176.
57. Moorehead, *op. cit.*, pp. 228–229.
58. Rommel, *op. cit.*, p. 175.

Chapter 15. The Cockpit of the Mediterranean

59. Warlimont, *op. cit.*, p. 131.
60. Playfair, *The Mediterranean and Middle East*, Vol. I, p. 319.
61. Cervi, *op. cit.*, p. 201.
62. *Ibid.*, p. 194.
63. Cunningham, *op. cit.*, p. 332.
64. *The Flowers of the Sea*, ed. Bush, p. 277.
65. S. W. C. Pack, *Night Action off Cape Matapan* (Shepperton, Surrey: Ian Allan, 1972), p. 98.
66. Kemp, *op. cit.*, p. 124.
67. Bragadin, *op. cit.*, p. 99.
68. *Ibid.*, p. 82. Italics in the original text.
69. Kemp, *op. cit.*, p. 125.

Chapter 16. Blitzkrieg in the Balkans

70. Lukacs, *op. cit.*, p. 364.
71. Ray Brock, *The New York Times*, March 28, 1941.
72. Ruth Mitchell, *The Serbs Choose War* (Garden City, N.Y.: Doubleday, 1943), p. 6.
73. *The German Campaign in the Balkans* (Washington, D.C.: Dept. of the Army Pamphlet #20–260, 1953), p. 22.
74. Mitchell, *op. cit.*, p. 86.
75. Sam Pope Brewer, *Chicago Tribune* Press Service, April 27, 1941.
76. Mitchell, *op. cit.*, pp. 87–88.
77. *German Campaign in the Balkans*, p. 53.
78. Major General Sir Francis de Guingand, *Operation Victory* (New York: Scribner's, 1947), p. 55.
79. Christopher Buckley, *Greece and Crete, 1941* (London: H.M. Stationery Office, 1952), quoted, p. 54.
80. *Ibid.*, p. 62.
81. *German Campaign in the Balkans*, p. 94.
82. The somewhat discrepant figures about the British losses in the Greek campaign represent the differences between the British Commonwealth Army, Navy, and Air Force units in Greece, and the ancillary labor personnel—Cypriots and Palestinians.
83. For a detailed account of the Crete campaign, see Chap. 3 of Baldwin, *Battles Lost and Won*.
84. *Airborne Operations—A German Appraisal* (Washington, D.C.: Dept. of the Army Pamphlet #20–232, 1951), pp. 49 ff.
85. Alan Clark, *The Fall of Crete* (New York: Morrow, 1962), p. 59.
86. D. M. Davin, *Crete (Official History of New Zealand in the Sec-*

ond World War, 1939–45) (Wellington, N.Z.: Dept. of Internal Affairs, War History Branch, 1953), p. 89.
87. Cunningham, *op. cit.*, p. 373.
88. Bartimeus, *East of Malta, West of Suez* (Boston: Little, Brown, 1944), p. 118.
89. Davin, *op. cit.*, pp. 234–235.
90. Cunningham, *op. cit.*, p. 375.
91. Davin, *op. cit.*, p. 367.
92. The Germans mounted two battalion-size airborne operations later in the war—one against the island of Leros in the Aegean, another in the Ardennes during the Battle of the Bulge. Otherwise, the use of paratroopers was confined to small task force or Commando-type units, tailored to specific small and specialized missions.
93. Major General Sir John Kennedy, *The Business of War* (New York: Morrow, 1958), p. 123.
94. Churchill, *The Grand Alliance*, pp. 94–95.
95. De Guingand, *op. cit.*, p. 57.
96. *Ibid.*, p. 59.
97. Kennedy, *op. cit.*, p. 139.
98. Anthony Eden, *The Reckoning* (London: Cassell, 1965), p. 230.

PART IV. THE GLOBAL WAR—1941

Chapter 17. *Russia—The "Unknown War"*

1. *The War in Eastern Europe, June 1941 to May 1945* (West Point, N.Y.: U.S. Military Academy, 1949), p. 2. The most detailed and thorough study of the campaign in Russia—particularly as seen by Russian eyes—is John Erickson's *The Road to Stalingrad*, Vol. I of a projected two-volume history (New York: Harper, 1975). I have drawn heavily upon it for this chapter.
2. Warlimont, *op. cit.*, p. 111.
3. Halder, *op. cit.*, July 31, 1940. Italics in the original text.
4. *The German Campaign in Russia—Planning and Operations (1940–42)* (Washington, D.C.: Dept. of the Army Pamphlet #20-261a, March 1955), pp. 22 ff.
5. Warlimont, *op. cit.*, p. 161.
6. Alan Clark, *Barbarossa* (New York: Morrow, 1965), p. 41.
7. General Reinhard Gehlen, *The Service* (New York: Popular Library paperback, 1972), p. 26.
8. Paul Carell, *Hitler Moves East, 1941–43* (Boston: Little, Brown, 1963), p. 56.
9. Churchill, *The Grand Alliance*, p. 369.
10. See Lyman B. Kirkpatrick, *Captains Without Eyes* (New York: Macmillan, 1969), Chap. 2.

11. Asher Lee, *The Soviet Air and Rocket Forces* (London: Weidenfeld & Nicolson, 1959), p. 52.
12. Clark, *Barbarossa*, p. 44.
13. *The Secret Conferences of Dr. Goebbels*, pp. 175–176; also Clark, *Barbarossa*, p. 44.
14. Carell, *op. cit.*, p. 27.
15. Halder, *op. cit.*, July 3, 1941.
16. *The German Campaign in Russia*, p. 45.
17. Liddell Hart, *History of the Second World War*, p. 162, quoted from an anonymous German general.
18. Dwight D. Eisenhower. An interview with the author when General Eisenhower was president of Columbia University.
19. Carell, *op. cit.*, pp. 78–79.
20. Halder Diaries, August 22, 1941, quoted in Fuller, *op. cit.*, p. 431.
21. Clark, *Barbarossa*, pp. 138–139, quoted from narrative of Corporal Täsch.
22. *Ibid.*, pp. 142–143, quoted from C. Malaparte, *The Volga Rises in Europe*.
23. Ziemke, *The German Northern Theatre of Operations*, p. 193.
24. *Ibid.*, p. 188.
25. Harrison Salisbury, *The 900 Days—The Siege of Leningrad* (New York: Avon Books paperback, 1969).
26. Ziemke, *op. cit.*, pp. 140–141.
27. *The German Campaign in Russia*, pp. 71–73.
28. Carell, *op. cit.*, p. 139.
29. Malcolm Mackintosh, *Juggernaut* (New York: Macmillan, 1967), p. 165.
30. Personal impressions of the author after meeting Zhukov, Konev, and other Soviet World War II leaders in Moscow in 1956.
31. Zhukov, quoted in *Stalin and His Generals*, ed. Bialer, p. 280.
32. Rokossovski, quoted in *Stalin and His Generals*, pp. 296–298. Bialer's fascinating compilation of Soviet military memoirs not only reveals factual background on the Russian campaigns unavailable in the Soviet official histories, but illuminates the character of many of the Russian leaders, the roles they played, and the personality clashes between them. As in all political systems—especially in dictatorships—jealousies, intrigue, and egoism were of some importance in shaping the course of history. As late as 1956 when the author was in Moscow, it was evident from personal meetings with both men that there was—and had been—considerable rivalry between Zhukov and Konev. The latter, like Rokossovski, served under Zhukov in the Battle of Moscow.
33. Carell, *op. cit.*, p. 140. Stalin actually transferred about ten divisions and hundreds of tanks and aircraft from the Far East to the European front in October and November. These were replaced by hastily mobilized and largely untrained units.

34. *Ibid.*, p. 149.

35. Salisbury, *op. cit.*, pp. 251–253. The evidence about Stalin's exact role in the defense of Moscow and in the Soviet operations in the summer and fall of 1941 is conflicting and murky and is likely to remain so. There is no doubt that the Great Dictator passed through an initial period of great doubt and uncertainty—almost withdrawal. Later, as both Erickson and Salisbury have noted, Zhukov appeared to have assumed almost full authority over operational matters on the Central Front, and a number of memoirs speak of the authoritative brusqueness of Zhukov's manner with Stalin, with others present. Yet, in the last analysis the ruthless policies that destroyed millions but helped to save Moscow were almost certainly dictated by Stalin; he it was who mobilized, shifted, and hoarded reserves, and his political grip grew stronger and stronger as the war progressed. Erickson (*The Road to Stalingrad, op. cit.*, p. 142) describes him as "overlord of the battlefronts, overseer of the drastic mobilizations, scrutineer of details, manipulator of vast bodies of men . . . vindictive against failure, impatient for success, unyielding . . . to reality . . . unlearned as yet in how to fight. . . ."

36. Liddell Hart, *The Other Side of the Hill*, p. 284.

37. *The German Campaign in Russia*, p. 83.

38. Liddell Hart, *The Other Side of the Hill*, pp. 284–285.

39. Carell, *op. cit.*, p. 169, quoted from Hoepner's Order of the Day, November 17, 1941.

40. *Ibid.*, p. 173.

41. *Ibid.*, p. 171.

42. *Ibid.*, p. 185.

43. H. A. Jacobsen and J. Rohwer, *Decisive Battles of World War II* (New York: Putnam, 1965), pp. 158, 159.

44. *Ibid.*

45. Gerald R. Kleinfeld and Lewis A. Tambs, *Military Affairs* (February 1973).

46. Jacobsen and Rohwer, *op. cit.*, p. 166.

47. *Military Improvisations During the Russian Campaign* (Washington, D.C.: Dept. of the Army Pamphlet #20–201, 1951), p. 24.

48. *The German Campaign in Russia*, p. 101.

49. *Military Improvisations, op. cit.*, p. 24.

50. Clark, *Barbarossa*, pp. 181, 182; and Mark Arnold-Foster, *The World at War* (New York: Stein and Day, 1973), pp. 131, 132.

51. Casualty figures in the Russian campaign are approximations only, derived from all the works cited in this chapter and from Baldwin, *Battles Lost and Won, op. cit.* The Russians dispute the German prisoner-of-war claims for the summer and fall campaigns—particularly those for the Kiev encirclement. Before the snows began, the Soviet demographic, agricultural, and industrial losses were staggering. Already overrun by the Germans, subjected to "scorched earth" policies or immediately threatened were: almost one-half of the population, three-fifths of its coal and alumi-

num production, more than two-thirds of its pig iron and steel production, and about half of its grain areas and railroad network. More than 300 ammunition plants had been captured or evacuated; the rich Donbas, then the industrial heart of Russia, was being overrun, or threatened. See Erickson, *Road to Stalingrad*, *op. cit.*, p. 223; also, Baldwin, *op. cit.*, p. 433, quoted from Yu. P. Petrov, ed., *The History of the Great Patriotic War of the Soviet Union, 1941–45*, Vol. III.

52. Clark, *Barbarossa*, p. 182.

53. Fuller makes a strong case (*The Decisive Battles*, Vol. III, pp. 434 ff.) for the view espoused by Walter Goerlitz in his book, *The German General Staff*, that "The fact that the destruction of Bolshevism began soon to mean simply an effort to decimate and enslave the Slav people was the most fatal of all the flaws in the whole campaign."

54. Lt. Gen. W. Anders, *An Army in Exile* (London: Macmillan, 1949), p. 310.

55. Bullock, *op. cit.*, quoted (from Nuremberg documents), p. 633.

56. Edgar M. Howell, *The Soviet Partisan Movement, 1941–44* (Washington, D.C.: Dept. of the Army Pamphlet #20–244, 1956), p. 49.

57. *Ibid.*, p. 203. In the Army Group Center area, the partisans grew in number before the war ended to between 80,000 to 100,000 men, "who tied down a security force conservatively estimated at 100,000 men." *Rear Area Security in Russia* (Washington, D.C.: Dept. of the Army German Report Series MS T19, 1950), p. 74.

58. Churchill, *The Grand Alliance*, pp. 370–372.

59. Roskill, *The War at Sea*, Vol. I, pp. 513–514; see also Joseph H. Devins, Jr., *The Vaagso Raid* (Philadelphia: Chilton, 1967); and Warlimont, *op. cit.*, p. 196. There were some 372,000 German troops in Norway as late as June 1944.

60. Bruce Catton, *The Coming Fury* (Garden City, N.Y.: Doubleday, 1961), p. 371.

61. Morison, *The Battle of the Atlantic*, p. 50.

62. Sherwood, *Roosevelt and Hopkins*, *op. cit.*, p. 321.

63. *Ibid.*, p. 396.

64. Langer, *The Undeclared War*, p. 748.

Chapter 18. Pearl Harbor

65. Morison, *The Rising Sun*, p. 5.

66. *Ibid.*, pp. 46, 47. See also Richardson's own memoirs, *On the Treadmill to Pearl Harbor*; James O. Richardson and Vice Admiral George C. Dyer (Washington, D.C.: Navy Dept., 1973).

67. *Ibid.*, p. 71.

68. There are several versions of this now famous Yamamoto prediction. See U.S. Strategic Bombing Survey, *Interrogations of Japanese Offi-*

cials, Vol. II, p. 325; interrogation of Admiral Soemu Toyoda; also Morison, *The Rising Sun*, p. 45; quoted from Prince Konoye's memoirs.

69. Commander Sadao Seno, "A Chess Game with No Checkmate (Admiral Inoue and the Pacific War)", *Naval War College Review* (January–February 1974), pp. 26–39.

70. Kirkpatrick, *op. cit.*, p. 142 quoted. See also Walter Millis, *This Is Pearl* (New York: Morrow, 1947), p. 33.

71. Morison, *The Rising Sun*, p. 128 quoted.

72. Kirkpatrick, *op. cit.*, quoted, pp. 140–141.

73. For a fascinating description of Friedman's work, and an account of the role played by broken codes and ciphers during World War II and throughout history, see David Kahn's *The Code Breakers*; for Pearl Harbor, see pp. 1–67.

74. Roberta Wohlstetter, *Pearl Harbor, Warning and Decision* (Stanford, Calif.: Stanford University Press, 1962), pp. 382–386.

75. See Kahn, *op. cit.* Also Farago, *The Broken Seal*, pp. 234 ff.

76. Kahn, *op. cit.*, p. 32. The other "Winds" were Russia: *Kita No Kaze Kumori* (North Wind Cloudy); Britain: *Nishi No Kaze Hare* (West Wind Clear). After the event, one of the U.S. experts later testified that the "East" and "West" wind messages—signifying hostilities with the United States and Britain—had been broadcast about December 4 or December 5. This statement was never verified; apparently an authentic Wind Codes message was not broadcast until after Pearl Harbor.

77. Morison, *The Rising Sun*, p. 77.

78. Wohlstetter, *op. cit.*, p. 222.

79. Morison, *The Rising Sun*, p. 140.

80. Twelve B-17's, so heavily loaded with gasoline for the ferrying flight from the mainland they carried no ammunition, arrived during the Japanese attack, and landed wherever they could—one of them on a golf course. Some were shot up, one was a total loss, and three were badly damaged.

The same radar station that (unknowingly) picked up the track of the Japanese attacking planes later tracked them to the north as they flew back to the carriers, but the information was never evaluated or acted upon.

81. U.S. forces had been alerted repeatedly and authorized to fire in self-defense or to attack Japanese units found in prohibited areas, but they also had been warned against provocative incidents and had been told that it was desired that Japan strike the first blow.

82. Forrest C. Pogue, *George C. Marshall* (New York: Viking, 1966), Vol. II, pp. 209 ff.

83. Morison, *The Rising Sun*, pp. 86 ff. See also U.S. Strategic Bombing Survey, *The Campaigns of the Pacific War*, pp. 13 ff.

84. Morison, *The Rising Sun*, p. 90.

85. Commander Nakaya, quoted in *ibid.*, pp. 94–95.

86. *Ibid.;* and David Bergamini, *Japan's Imperial Conspiracy* (New York: Morrow, 1971), Vol. II, pp. 843–844.
87. Brig. Gen. Samuel R. Shaw, *Shipmate* (December 1973).
88. Col. Cornelius C. Smith, Jr., *Naval Institute Proceedings* (December 1973).
89. Despite prewar criticism, many of the fleet's light AA guns at this time were the rather ineffective 1.1-inch "hose guns," developed by the Navy's Bureau of Ordnance, which were inaccurate and subject to jamming. They were subsequently replaced by the Swiss Oerlikon 23 mm. and the Swedish Bofors 40 mm., supplemented by machine guns.
90. Morison, *The Rising Sun*, p. 106.
91. Walter Lord, *Day of Infamy* (New York: Holt, Rinehart, 1957). See also for eyewitness accounts of Pearl Harbor, John Toland's *But Not in Shame* (New York: Random House, 1961) and Howell M. Forgy, *And Pass the Ammunition* (New York: Appleton-Century-Crofts, 1944).
92. The Japanese losses cited are combat losses only. In addition, landing crashes or accidents (some of them perhaps due to damage sustained in combat, most of them to pitching carrier decks caused by freshening winds and heavier seas when the returning planes landed aboard) added another twenty planes, with perhaps thirty others damaged. The exact number of Japanese planes shot down by U.S. interceptors will probably never be known; neither the P-40 nor the P-36 was a match for the Japanese Zero fighter; nevertheless, these two types probably flew a total of about twenty-five sorties between 8:30 and 9:30 A.M. on December 7 and shot down Japanese planes numbered in less than two figures. See *Army Air Forces in World War II*, Vol. I, pp. 197 ff.
93. Thomas Buell, *The Quiet Warrior* (New York: Little, Brown, 1974), p. 90.

Chapter 19. The War in the Pacific

94. Louis Morton, *The Fall of the Philippines, U.S. Army in World War II* (Washington, D.C.: U.S. Government Printing Office, 1953), p. 77.
95. U.S. Strategic Bombing Survey, *Campaigns*, p. 43.
96. Morison, *The Rising Sun*, pp. 184–186; Walter Karig and Welbourn Kelley, *Battle Report* (New York: Farrar & Rinehart, 1944), Vol. I, pp. 107–111.
97. Lt. Col. Robert D. Heinl, Jr., *The Defense of Wake* (Historical Section, U.S. Marine Corps, 1947), p. 11. This monograph provides by far the most complete and accurate account of the Wake battle, an account which was used by Morison, *The Rising Sun* (pp. 223 ff.) as the basis of his narrative. See also Walter Karig and Welbourn Kelley, *Battle Report*, pp. 101 ff.; W. Scott Cunningham, *Wake Island Command* (Boston: Little, Brown, 1961); and Frank O. Hough, Verle E. Ludwig,

and Henry I. Shaw, *Pearl Harbor to Guadalcanal, History of U.S. Marine Corps Operations in World War II* (Washington, D.C.: Historical Section, U.S. Marine Corps, undated), Vol. I, pp. 95 ff.

98. *Ibid.*

99. About 10 percent of the 1,200 civilian personnel who had been working for Pacific Naval Air Bases contractor volunteered as soon as war started to help the combatants in any way possible. Some of them tried to enlist, and the general superintendent on the island, the civilian doctor, the Navy's construction representative, and others worked and fought (some of them died) along with the uniformed personnel. But civilians never were under full military control, and the great majority of them refused to do any labor or take any part in the defense; they scattered through the scrub, dug foxholes, and cowered; some numbed their fear with drunkenness. It was largely as a result of the lessons of Wake that the "Sea-Bees" (the Naval Construction Battalions, trained to build and to fight) were organized.

100. Morison, *The Rising Sun*, p. 232.

101. Heinl, *op. cit.*, p. 61.

102. Scott Cunningham, *op. cit.*

103. Kent Roberts Greenfield, Gen. Ed., *Command Decisions*, p. 33 (Louis Morton, "Germany First").

104. Baldwin, *Battles Lost and Won*, p. 117 and n.

105. Alexander P. de Seversky's controversial and mistaken but highly popular book, *Victory Through Air Power*, did a great deal to persuade the public that "cheap" victory was possible, and that airpower—acting independently—could defeat Germany and Japan.

106. Pogue, *op. cit.*, p. 187.

107. Karig and Kelley, *Battle Report*, p. 138.

108. *Army Air Forces in World War II*, pp. 203 ff.

109. *Ibid.*

110. *Ibid.*, p. 210, quoted.

111. John Toland, *The Rising Sun* (New York: Random House, 1970), Vol. I, p. 293.

112. Bergamini, *Japan's Imperial Conspiracy*, quoted, p. 856.

113. Carlos P. Romulo, *I Saw the Fall of the Philippines* (New York: Doubleday, 1942), p. 30.

114. Morton, *op. cit.*, p. 113.

115. *Ibid.*, p. 69.

116. *Ibid.*, pp. 135–136.

117. *Ibid.*, p. 163.

118. Morison, *The Rising Sun*, p. 195.

119. Theodore Roscoe, *Submarine Operations in World War II* (Annapolis, Md.: U.S. Naval Institute, 1949), p. 26. It should be emphasized that this directive specified "enemy" ships; the German unrestricted submarine warfare ultimately applied to any ships within certain sea

areas. But practically speaking there was often little difference. The difficulty of identification through a submarine periscope compounded the problem of separating the few neutrals from the many enemy.

120. W. J. Holmes, *Undersea Victory* (Garden City, N.Y.: Doubleday, 1966), p. 66. Clay Blair, Jr., in *Silent Victory* (Philadelphia: Lippincott, 1975) describes in detail the torpedo, command, and other problems that reduced U.S. submarine effectiveness to a negligible factor at the start of the war. *Silent Victory* is probably the most comprehensive book about U.S. submarines in the Pacific in World War II yet published and it reveals many hitherto neglected details. But some of its judgments and its wide-ranging generalizations must be faulted.

121. Morton, *op. cit.*, p. 188, quoted from Colonel Richard C. Mallonee, *Bataan Diary*.

122. Morton, *op. cit.*, p. 230.

Chapter 20. Asia for the Asiatics

123. *History of the Second World War*, Major General S. Woodburn Kirby, *et al.*, *The War Against Japan*, Vol. I (London: H.M. Stationery Office, 1957), pp. 116–117. This section on Hong Kong is heavily dependent upon this official history.

124. Churchill, *The Grand Alliance*, p. 633.

125. Woodburn Kirby, *The War Against Japan*, pp. 128–129.

126. Churchill, *The Grand Alliance*, p. 634.

127. Bergamini, *op. cit.*, pp. 876–877.

128. Woodburn Kirby, *The War Against Japan*, p. 183.

129. Ken Attiwill, *The Singapore Story* (London: Muller, 1959), p. 13. In part—but only in part—the published exaggerations of Singapore's strength were the result of a kind of governmental public relations campaign to "sell" to the Japanese the idea that Singapore was too tough a nut to crack. The campaign backfired; the Japanese were never fooled, and the British were hoist on their own petard.

130. The RAF had planned and constructed airfields in northern Malaya without any consultation with the Army. The result, in the opinion of the Army, was that the fields were indefensible because they were sited too close to nearby landing beaches—as indeed they were.

131. Russell Grenfell, *Main Fleet to Singapore* (New York: Macmillan, 1952), pp. 47 ff.

132. Churchill, *The Grand Alliance*, p. 589.

133. *Ibid.*, pp. 588 ff.

134. Louis Morton, *The War in the Pacific—Strategy and Command, The First Two Years* (Washington, D.C.: U.S. Government Printing Office, 1961), p. 88.

135. Morison, *The Rising Sun*, pp. 49–51. For a detailed examination of war planning see, particularly, Morton, *Strategy and Command*, **pp.**

86 ff. Rainbow Five was a statement of general objectives and overall missions for both countries; from it detailed war plans were produced.

136. Roskill, *The War at Sea*, Vol. I, p. 558.
137. Geoffrey Bennett, *The Loss of the Prince of Wales and Repulse* (Annapolis, Md.: Naval Institute Press, 1973), p. 41.
138. Woodburn Kirby, *The War Against Japan*, p. 194.
139. Bennett, *op. cit.*, p. 49.
140. Cecil Brown, *Suez to Singapore* (New York: Random House, 1942), p. 315.
141. *Ibid.*, p. 319.
142. *Ibid.*, pp. 321–322.
143. *Ibid.*, p. 336.
144. Woodburn Kirby, *The War Against Japan*, quoted, p. 198.
145. Churchill, *The Grand Alliance*, p. 620.
146. Woodburn Kirby, *The War Against Japan*, p. 189.
147. *Ibid.*, p. 210.
148. *Ibid.*, p. 243.
149. George Weller, *Singapore Is Silent* (New York: Harcourt Brace, 1943), p. 102.
150. *Ibid.*, pp. 66, 74 ff.

Chapter 21. The Aftermath of Pearl Harbor

151. Langer and Gleason, *The Undeclared War*, p. 940.
152. Shirer, *The Rise and Fall of the Third Reich*, p. 895 n.
153. A remark made by then Lt. W. R. Smedberg to the author in December 1941.
154. Morison, *The Rising Sun*, p. 255.
155. Rear Admiral Robert A. Theobald, *The Final Secret of Pearl Harbor* (New York: Devin-Adair, 1954).
156. Kemp Tolley, *Cruise of the Lanikai* (Annapolis, Md.: Naval Institute Press, 1973), p. 89.
157. Wohlstetter, *op. cit.*, pp. 392, 401.
158. Pogue, *op. cit.*, p. 262.
159. *Ibid.*, p. 280.
160. Richard R. Lingeman, *Don't You Know There's a War On?* (New York: Putnam, 1970), quoted, p. 26.
161. Karig and Kelley, *Battle Report*, Vol. I, p. 74.

Retrospect

1. Langer and Gleason, *op. cit.*, p. 941.
2. Ruth Benedict, *The Chrysanthemum and the Sword* (New York: World, 1967), pp. 2, 3.
3. Masters, *The Road Past Mandalay*, pp. 147–155.
4. Woodburn Kirby, *The War Against Japan*, p. 515.

Index

Abdiel, 310, 312
Acasta, 109
Achilles, 79–80
Aden: British forces, 178, 179, 180, 185, 226, 228
Admiral Hipper, 97–98, 109, 177, 204, 216
Admiral Scheer, 177
Afridi, 106
airpower, theories of, 28, 39–40, 44, 52, 88, 166, 174, 191–93, 200–06, 209, 315, 404, 435, 443
Ajax, 80–81, 273, 295, 307, 311
Akagi, 384, 385
Albania: Greek forces, 189, 191, 269, 284, 285, 292, 293, 294
  Italian forces, 61, 187, 188, 189, 190–91, 269–70, 292, 315
  RAF, 191, 269
  see also Balkans
Albanian forces: Greece, 188, 189–90
Albert, King, 132, 133
Alexander, Gen. Sir Harold, 43, 139
Alexandria: Royal Navy, 149, 169–70, 248, 281; see also Egypt, British and British forces
Alfieri, 275
Alfonso XIII, King, 19
Algeria, 150–51, 169, 178
Allied Expeditionary Force (Norway), 104–10
Alsace-Lorraine, 17, 41
Altmark, 78, 95, 96, 370
Altmayer, Gen., 142
Amery, Leopold, 111
Anders, Lt. Gen. W., 367
Andrews, Gen. Frank M., 39
Anti-Comintern Pact, 54
Antigua, 155
Anton Schmidt, 102
Antonescu, Gen. Ion, 187
Aoba, 395
Aosta, Amedeo Umberto, Duke of, 180, 227, 229
"Arab freedom movement," 297
Arab Legion, 232, 233

Arcadia Conference, 460
Arctic Ocean and region: shipping and naval action, 82, 94, 207, 215, 327, 349, 358, 370–71
Ardent, 109
Argentia Conference, 200, 440, 452
Argentina: naval action off coast, 64, 78–81
  U.S. naval base, 155
Argus, 173, 370
Arizona, 388, 390, 392
Ark Royal, 77, 174, 222, 223, 224, 269, 280
Armando Diaz, 278
Arnold, Gen. H. H. ("Hap"), 40, 404
Astor, Lord, 56
Athenia, 75
Atlantic Charter, 200
Atlantic Ocean: shipping and naval action, 64, 74–81, 98, 111, 160, 161, 168, 175–78, 193, 200, 201, 203, 317, 371–73, 374, 435, 450, 456; Battle of the Atlantic, 200, 206–16, 219–26
Atlantis, 177, 214, 215
atomic energy and research, 14, 15, 44, 222, 463
  bomb, 167, 206
Atsutusan Maru, 418
Auchinleck, Gen. Sir Claude J. E., 108, 253
  Middle East, 251, 253, 254, 260, 262
Auckland, 278
Augustus, 277
Aurora, 279, 281
Australia: Bismarcks, 375, 395
  defense, 436, 448, 449, 459
Australian forces, 43, 153
  Crete, 254, 297–99, 302–03, 304–05, 311, 313
  cruiser Sydney, 172, 173, 215
  Greece, 254, 285–86, 292, 295–96
  Lebanon and Syria, 232–33, 235
  Libya (and Western Desert), 185, 239, 243, 246, 254

Australian forces (cont'd)
  Palestine, 179
  Southeast Asia, 434, 448, 449, 459
Austria: German invasion and occupation, 54, 55; as Balkan campaign base, 283, 284, 286, 288, 297
Austro-Hungarian Empire, 17, 282
Awajisan Maru, 444
Axis, 54, 89, 191, 377–78

Badoglio, Marshal Pietro, 189, 190
Bahamas, 155
Balbo, Marshal Italo, 180
Baldwin, Stanley, 56
Balkans, interest in, 54
  Germany, 187, 191, 200, 202, 236, 237, 241, 297, 319
  Great Britain, 191, 243, 316–17
  Italy, 187, 191, 283
  U.S.S.R., 187, 326, 367
  see also Albania; Bulgaria; Greece; Rumania; Turkey
Baltic Sea: shipping and naval action, 63, 66, 70–71, 94, 96, 217, 219, 347, 348
Baltic states: Soviet occupation, 64, 86; and German campaign, 329, 337, 342, 347, 355
  see also Estonia; Latvia; Lithuania
Baltimore, 39
Barbiano, 280
Barham, 169, 273, 275, 280
Bartolomeo Colleoni, 173
Baruch, Bernard, 37
Bastico, Marshal Ettore, 254, 265
Bataan, 403, 413, 416–22 *passim*, 467
Battle of Britain, 89, 153–57, 159–67, 196, 297, 300, 325, 327, 362, 381
Battle of the Atlantic, 200, 206–16, 219–26
Baudouin, King, 133
Beatty, Adm. Sir David, 221, 274
Beaverbrook, Lord, 159, 372
Beck, Gen. Ludwig, 59, 114
Belfast, 76
Belgian forces, 50, 118–19
  in France, 130–31, 135, 140
Belgium: and France, 119, 132, 133
  and Germany, 24, 54
  and Great Britain, 119, 132, 133–34
  invasion and occupation, 89, 109, 112, 113, 115, 116, 118–19, 122–26 *passim*, 130–34, 299
  neutrality, 113, 119, 133
Belgrade, 282, 283, 286–88
Beneš, Eduard, 55, 58

Bennion, Capt. Mervyn S., 387
Beresford-Peirse, Lt. Gen. Sir Noel, 249
Bergonzoli, Gen. Annibale, 183, 239
Beria, Lavrenti P., 340
Berlin, bombing of, 163, 167, 193, 195, 203
Bermuda, 155
Bernd von Arnim, 97
Berwick, 177
Besson, Gen. A. M. B., 116
Best, Capt. S. Payne, 114, 115
Bethouart, Gen. M. E., 108
Beveridge, Sir Malcolm, 23
Bickford, Lt. Comm. E. O. B., 77
Billotte, Gen. Gaston H., 117, 129, 130
Birmingham, bombing of, 194, 201, 202–03
Bismarck, 74, 200, 214, 217, 219–26 *passim*, 440
Bismarcks (island group), 375, 395
Bison, 107
Blanchard, J. G. M., 117
Blomberg, Field Marshal Werner von, 60
Blücher, 100
Bluecher, Marshal Vasili K., 47
Blum, Léon, 29
Bock, Field Marshal Fedor von, 66, 116, 120, 123, 142
  Russian campaign, 329, 343, 345, 350, 351, 356–60 *passim*, 365
Bohr, Niels, 14
Boise, 449
Bolzano, 172
Bonaventure, 282
Bonnet, Georges, 57
Borneo: British Borneo (Sarawak and Brunei), 434, 448
  Dutch Borneo, 448
  Japanese conquest, 380, 395, 406, 413, 432, 448, 449
Bose, Subhas Chandra, 469
Bradley, Gen. Omar N., 37
Bragadin, Comm. Marc'Antonio, 170, 277
Brauchitsch, Gen. Walther von, 114, 344, 356, 365
Brereton, Maj. Gen. Louis H., 408
Brétagne, 150
Bristol, Rear Adm. Arthur L., 214
British air force *see* Royal Air Force
British Army and military forces, 40–41, 43–44, 59, 251
  Commandos, 310, 311, 370

INDEX

British Army (cont'd)
  Crete, 191, 251, 254, 274, 295–300 passim, 301–16 passim, 318, 319
  Cyprus, 235, 263, 306
  East Africa (British Somaliland, Kenya, Sudan), 178, 179–80, 181, 226, 227, 240
  Egypt, 179, 184–85, 231, 255
  Far East, 433–34, 444; Hong Kong, 423–29 passim; see also Burma; Malaya; Singapore
  France, 141–45 passim, 147; see also British Expeditionary Force (France)
  Greece: before invasion, 191, 269–70, 316–17; see also British Expeditionary Force (Greece)
  Iraq, 178, 230–36 passim, 247, 252
  Italian East Africa, 182, 200, 226–30, 240
  Lebanon and Syria, 232–33, 234, 240, 247, 248, 263
  Libya (and Western Desert), 182–85, 231, 237, 239, 240, 241, 244–50 passim, 252, 253, 256–66 passim, 285, 290, 317
  Mediterranean and Middle East, 178, 179, 180, 181, 231, 237, 240, 248
  Norwegian campaign and Allied Expeditionary Force, 104–10
  Palestine, 178, 179, 232, 263
British Borneo see Borneo
British combined armed forces:
  Allied command cooperation: ABCD (alphabet) plans, 213; Arcadia Conference, 460; Singapore Conference, 448; "Rainbow" war plans, 213, 372, 403, 405, 436, 437
  Churchill's meddling, 251, 309, 310, 314, 444, 457
  inadequate defense preparation, 45, 251, 252, 425, 432–33, 435, 449
  interservice rivalry and command cooperation, 77, 105, 112–13, 117–18, 130, 137, 138, 143, 151, 176, 179, 186, 254, 433–34
  British Expeditionary Force (France), 64, 73, 116, 117, 129, 130, 131, 134–40, 151, 152, 153, 155
  British Expeditionary Force (Greece), 240, 243, 247, 251, 252, 254, 270, 271, 283, 285, 289–91, 293, 295, 299, 314–19 passim
British Guiana, 155

British intelligence, 44, 45, 114–15, 236, 332, 333, 425
  "Ultra," 45, 195, 211, 223
British Malaya see Malaya
British navy see Royal Navy and sea-power
British Somaliland, 178, 179, 181, 226
British Sudan see Sudan
Broch, Thedor, 107
Brooke, Gen. Sir Alan, 139, 146, 458
Brooke-Popham, Air Chief Marshal Sir Robert, 434
Brown, Cecil, 440, 442
Brunei see Borneo
Budënny, Marshal Semën M., 342, 346, 365
Buell, Thomas, 391
Bulgarian forces, 50
Bulgaria: German use of, as base for Balkan campaign, 270, 271, 283, 284, 288, 289, 298
  and Greece, 188, 269, 285, 289
  Rumanian territory ceded to, 187
  and U.S.S.R., 187
  see also Balkans
Bullitt, William, 126
Burma: anticolonialism, 468
  Japanese conquest, 375, 395, 422, 432

Calabria: naval battle off coast, 89, 172
Calcutta, 307, 312
California, 387, 388, 390
Campbell, Brig. "Jock," 258
Campioni, Adm. Angelo, 174
Canada, 212; see also Newfoundland
Canadian forces: convoy escort, 211, 212
  overseas, 146, 159, 424, 429–30
Canopus, 417
Cape Matapan, Battle of, 200, 273, 274–77, 306
Capetown, 230
Carducci, 275–76
Carlisle, 307
Carnimeo, Gen. Nicolangelo, 227
Carol, King, 50, 89, 187
Carolines (Caroline Islands), 27; see also Mandated Islands
Carton de Wiart, Maj. Gen. Sir Adrian, 105, 106
"Case Green," 55, 58, 61
Cassin, 387, 389, 390, 392
casualties: Albania, 270
  Battle of Britain and blitz, 162–66, 193, 196, 201, 203, 205

Casualties (cont'd)
  Battle of the Atlantic, 210, 212, 214, 215, 226
  China/Japan (1937-41), 423
  Crete, 312
  Finnish "Winter War," 47, 93
  Germany/U.S.S.R., 334, 337, 350, 363, 364
  Greece, 296
  Hong Kong, 431
  Italian East Africa, 229, 230
  Libya (and Western Desert), 183, 185, 239, 247, 250, 260, 265
  Low Countries and France, 122, 140, 152
  Norwegian campaign, 109, 110-11
  Pearl Harbor, 389-91
  Philippines, 421
  Poland, 71
  Syria and Lebanon, 235-36
  U.S., in World War II, 215
  Wake Island, 401-02
  Yugoslavia, 288
Catroux, Gen. Georges, 232, 233
Catton, Bruce, 371
Cavagnari, Adm. Domenico, 168
Cavallero, Marshal Ugo, 190, 264
Cavour, 174
Celebes, 395; see also Dutch East Indies
Cervi, Mario, 188, 190
Cesare, 172
Chamberlain, Neville, 56, 57, 58, 61, 75, 111, 112
Chan Chak, Adm., 423, 430-31
Chennault, Lt. Col. Claire L., 40, 422
Cherwell, Frederick A. Lindemann, Lord, 206
Chevalier-Paul, 234
Chiang Kai-shek, 21, 23, 33, 422-23, 430, 431, 468
Chiang Kai-shek, Mme., 33
Chikuma, 384
China, 15, 21, 422, 423, 430, 468
  Communists, 23, 33, 469
  Hong Kong, lack of aid to, 423, 430, 431
  Japanese aggression, 15, 20-21, 23, 45, 46, 322, 373, 422, 423, 424, 430, 431, 464; Formosa bases used, 406, 407, 408, 423
  and U.S., 15, 33, 373, 393, 422, 464
Christian, King, 99
Churchill, Winston S.: and the Balkans, 191, 316-17
  Battle of Britain and blitz, 153, 157, 165, 167, 198
  bombing raids on Germany, 204, 205-06
  and Crete, 296, 298, 309, 310, 314
  and Dunkirk, 134, 140
  and the Far East, 428, 429, 433, 436, 444, 449, 459
  on Finland's plight, 92
  as First Lord of the Admiralty, 75, 94, 95, 112; see also World War I *below*
  and French invasion by Germany, 128, 145, 146; concern for French Navy, 146, 150-51
  Hitler on, 156
  on Hitler, 369
  on Leopold's surrender, 132, 133
  Mediterranean and Middle East, importance of, 178-79, 227, 234, 236, 248, 249, 251-52, 253, 267
  military strategy, 206, 251, 316, 436; meddling, 250, 309-10, 314, 444, 457; unified command, 113, 176, 459-60; see also Balkans; Far East; Mediterranean and Middle East *above*
  personal characteristics, 33-34, 112, 251-52
  Roosevelt and the U.S., 129, 146, 154-55, 165, 333, 450; conferences, 200, 459-60
  Stalin and the U.S.S.R., 324, 333, 369
  World War I, 34, 75, 112, 316, 444
Chu Teh, 23
Ciano, Count Galeazzo, 62, 190, 451
City of Flint, 81
Clan Fraser, 291
Clark, Alan, 365
Clement, 78
Cleveland, 39
Clifford, Alexander G., 258
Clifton, Brig. George, 291
Clyde, 110
Colbert, Adm. Richard G., 38
Colombus, 372
Colorado, 391
Combe, Brig. Gen. J. F. B., 245
Comintern, 324
  Anti-Comintern Act, 54
Commandant Teste, 150
communism: China, 23, 33, 469
  Finland, 82
  France, 41, 53, 56
  Germany, 14, 17, 18, 51

Communism (cont'd)
  Hitler's hatred of, 323–27 passim, 336, 344, 366–68, 466
  Hungary, 17
  Poland, 16
  Spain, 19–20; see also Spain, Civil War
  U.S., 28, 371
  Western fear and hatred, 369
  after World War II, 466
  see also Comintern; U.S.S.R.
Condor, 382
Conte Rossa, 278
Cooper, Alfred Duff, 434, 448, 449
Corap, Gen. André G., 117, 125, 126, 128
Corbett, J. S., 74–75
Cork and Orrery, Adm. Lord, 108
Cornwall, 215
Cossack, 95, 104, 224
Courageous, 75
Coventry, bombing of, 194
Coventry, 312
Crete, 296, 297
  British and Allied forces, 191, 251, 254, 274, 295–300 passim, 301–16 passim, 318, 319
  Churchill on, 296, 298, 309, 310, 314
  German invasion and occupation, 237, 278, 297–316, 318
  Italian plan to capture, 188
  native forces and underground, 299, 304–05, 308–09, 312, 313
  naval action off coast, 89, 173, 247, 271, 273, 286, 297, 298, 300, 302, 305–14 passim, 316
Cripps, Sir Stafford, 34
"Croatia" (country), 287, 289
Croats, 16, 282, 287, 288
Crook, Pilot Officer D. M., 161
Crüwell, Lt. Gen. Ludwig, 259, 260, 264
Cuba, 451
Cumberland, 80, 186
Cunningham, Lt. Gen. Sir Alan G., 227, 228–29, 254, 255–60 passim
Cunningham, Adm. Sir Andrew, 43, 169–74 passim, 179, 267, 281, 295
  Cape Matapan, Battle of, 273, 274–77 passim
  Crete, 306, 308, 310, 313, 314
Cunningham, Adm. J. H. D., 186
Cunningham, Comm. Winfield Scott, 397, 398, 400, 401, 402

Curlew, 110
Curtiss, 390
Cypriot forces: Crete, 298, 302
  Greece, 295, 296
Cyprus, 297
  British forces, 235, 263, 306
Cyrenaica, 183, 239, 240, 244–48 passim, 253–64 passim, 269; see also Libya (and Western Desert)
Czech forces, 59
  in RAF, 159
Czechoslovakia, 16, 54–55
  and France, 55, 57, 61
  and Germany, 54, 55, 57; invasion and occupation, 55, 58, 61
  and Great Britain, 55, 57, 58, 61
  and Hungary, 58
  and Poland, 58, 65
  and Rumania, 58
  Sudetenland, 16, 55, 58, 59
  and U.S.S.R., treaty, 58

Dakar, 146, 150, 186
Daladier, Édouard, 57–58, 126, 128
D'Albiac, Air Comm. J. H., 191
Dalyell-Stead, Lt. Comm. J., 274
d'Annunzio, Gabriele, 18, 273
Danzig, 17, 62, 66, 67
Darlan, Adm. Jean, 149, 151
Decoy, 309, 312
de Gaulle, Gen. Charles, 36, 42, 71, 118
  Free French forces, 148, 151, 186, 232; see also Free French forces
  German invasion of France, 127, 138, 144
  on Pétain, 147
Denmark, 93, 94
  Army, 97
  German invasion and occupation, 89, 97, 99
Dentz, Gen. Henri, 232–36 passim
depression (Great Depression), 15, 19, 23, 24, 25–26, 464
Derry, T. K., 107
de Seversky, Alexander, 192
Deutschland (Lützow), 27, 74, 78, 81, 100, 226
Devereux, Maj. James P. S., 397, 398, 401–02
Devonshire, 110, 215
DeWitt, Lt. Gen. John L., 461
Dickinson, Lt. Gen. D. P., 227
Dido, 307, 312
Dietl, Maj. Gen. Eduard, 101, 107, 108, 109, 349

INDEX

Dill, Field Marshal Sir John, 153, 243, 458, 460
Dodecanese Islands: Italian forces, 168, 172, 180
Doenitz, Adm. Karl, 73, 209–10, 212, 222, 226
Dollfuss, Engelbert, 54
Dorsetshire, 225
Douglas, Air Marshal W. S., 202
Douhet, Gen. Giulio: on airpower, 28, 40, 44, 52, 88, 166, 192, 204
Dowding, Air Chief Marshal Sir Hugh, 44, 159, 163, 167, 202
Downes, 387, 389, 390, 392
Dresden, bombing of, 206
Duilio, 174
Dunkerque, 74, 78, 150
Dunkirk, 129, 130, 131, 134–40, 151, 153, 278
Dutch air forces, 50, 120
   Far East, 448, 459
Dutch Army and military forces, 50, 118
   Far East, 448, 459
   German invasion, 120, 121, 122
Dutch Borneo see Borneo
Dutch East Indies, 122, 377, 468
   defense, 448–49, 459
   Japanese conquest, 322, 375, 393, 406
Dutch intelligence, 115
Dutch Navy and seapower, 136–37, 280
   Far East, 448

Eagle, 172
"Eagle Attack" see Battle of Britain
East Africa (British territory) see British Somaliland; Kenya; Sudan
East Africa (French territory) see French Somaliland
East Africa, Italian see Italian East Africa
Ecuador, 451
Eden, Anthony, 333
   Middle East mission, 243, 270, 290, 317, 318, 319
Edinburgh, 222
Egypt: British and British forces, 149, 168, 169–70, 178, 179, 180, 184–85, 214, 231, 237, 247, 248, 250, 255, 261, 295
   French Navy, 149
   Italians and Italian forces, 89, 183–84, 185
   neutrality, 184, 214

   see also Sudan; Suez Canal
Eisenhower, Gen. Dwight D., 37, 339, 461
Electra, 438, 443
electronics, development in, 28, 45, 159, 201, 211–12; see also radar
Elrod, Capt. Henry T., 401
Elser, Georg, 115
Emmons, Lt. Gen. Delos C., 451
Empress of Britain, 175
Enterprise, 38, 391, 397
Eritrea, 18, 180, 226, 227–28, 233, 240
Eskimo, 104
Espero, 172
Essex, 39
Estonia: Soviet occupation, 62, 81, 89; see also Baltic states
Ethiopia: British and native forces, 182, 200, 226–30, 240
   Italian and native forces, 18, 54, 180, 181, 227, 228, 229, 230
Ethiopian Patriots, 226, 228, 230
Exeter, 79, 80
Express, 438, 442, 443

Faeroes, 81, 111
Falkenhorst, Gen. Nikolaus von, 97, 329, 349
Farouk, King, 184, 214
Fawzi Qawukji, 235
Fearless, 279
Fegen, Capt. E. S. F., 177
Fermi, Enrico, 14
Fifth Column: Czechoslovakia, 55
   Finland, 82
   Hong Kong, 427, 428, 429
   Netherlands, 120, 123
   Norway, 94, 99, 102
   Poland, 68
   U.S.S.R., possibility of, 340, 354
Fiji, 308
Finland, 81, 85
   Communists, 82
   and France, 91, 92, 95, 104
   and Germany, 91; Finnish troops aid in Russian campaign, 326–27, 328–29, 345, 348–49
   and Great Britain, 92, 95, 104, 369
   and Sweden, 92
   and U.S.S.R., 62, 81; "Winter War," 47, 48–49, 64, 81, 82, 83–85, 86, 89–93, 324, 325, 340
   and U.S., 92, 465
Firedrake, 279
FitzGibbon, Constantine, 192

INDEX

Fiume, 275
Flaherty, Ens. Charles Francis, 389
Fletcher, 39
"Flying Tigers," 422-23
Formidable, 273, 274, 277, 306
Formosa, 406, 407, 408, 423
Forrester, Capt. Michael, 308
"Four Freedoms," 200
France, 23, 26, 29, 59, 61
  and Belgium, 119, 132, 133
  Communists, 41, 53-54, 56
  and Czechoslovakia, 55, 57, 61
  and Finland, 91, 92, 95, 104
  Franco-Prussian War, 17
  and Germany, 24, 53-54, 72-73;
    invasion and occupation, 89, 118, 122, 124-50 passim, 152, 154, 155, 157, 265, 284 (see also "Plan Gelb"); war declared, 63
  and Germany—Vichy regime, 148-52 passim, 186, 236; Algeria, 150, 178; French Indochina, "joint protectorate" with Japan, 89, 149, 374, 423, 432, 439; Lebanon and Syria, 178, 232-36 passim; Tunisia, 178
  and Great Britain see Great Britain, and France
  and Italy, war declared, 89, 144, 145, 148, 154, 168
  Poland and German invasion, 62, 63, 72-73
  and Scandinavia, 95, 102
  and U.S.S.R., alliance, 53-54, 62
  and U.S., aid appeals, 145, 146
  World War I, 41, 113, 344, 356, 420
  see also entries under French
Franco, Gen. Francisco: Civil War, 19, 20
  Hitler seeks aid for Gibraltar attack, 191, 241
  volunteers aid Germany in Russian campaign, 361
Franco-Prussian War, 17
Frank, Dr. Hans, 71
Free French forces: birth of, 148, 151
  and British forces: Dakar, 186; Lebanon and Syria, 226, 232-36 passim
  French Navy, 281
French Air Force, 42, 50
  German invasion and occupation, 118, 125; Vichy regime, 233-34, 235

French Army and military forces, 41-42, 118, 148
  colonial forces, 41, 117, 142-43, 152, 235; see also Lebanon; Syria
  German invasion, 126-46 passim, 150, 152; of Low Countries, 116, 118, 119, 120, 125
  Italian invasion, 145, 149
  Maginot Line, 41, 73, 116, 119, 141, 142, 146; "Little Maginot Line," 59, 119
  Norwegian campaign, 105, 106, 108, 109
  at outbreak of hostilities, 41, 64, 72-73
French Army (Free French) see Free French forces
French Indochina: "joint" protectorate with Japan, 89, 149, 374, 423, 431-32, 439
French intelligence, 45
French Navy and seapower, 42, 74, 78
  German invasion and occupation, 118, 136, 140, 145, 146, 148, 149; Vichy regime and British seizure of vessels, 149-51, 186, 233, 235
  naval disarmament conferences, 16, 26, 27
  Norwegian campaign, 107, 110-11
French Navy (Free French), 281
French Somaliland, 180
Frère, Gen., 142
Freyberg, Gen. Bernard C., 263, 298, 302-06 passim, 308-12 passim, 314
Freydenberg, Gen., 143
Friedman, William Frederick, 40, 378
Fritsch, Gen. Werner von, 59, 60
Frusci, Gen. Luigi, 227, 229
Fuchida, Comm. Mitsuo, 385
Fujiwara, Col. Iwaichi, 469
Fuller, Maj. Gen. J. F. C., 28, 43, 71, 166, 266
Furious, 104
Furlong, Rear Adm. W. R., 387

Galatea, 280
Gallant, 267
Gallilea, 171
Gallipoli, 34, 75, 112, 316, 444
Gamelin, Gen. Maurice, 36, 41, 72, 118, 124, 126, 128
Gariboldi, Gen. Italo, 242, 245, 254
Gehlen, Gen. Reinhard, 330, 331

508   INDEX

Geneva Disarmament Conference, 16
Gensoul, Adm. Marcel, 150, 151
George II, King, 294, 295, 298, 305, 309
George VI, King, 64, 88, 112, 198
Georges, Gen. A. J., 117–18, 124
German airborne troops, 156–57, 299–301, 313, 315
  Crete, 297–306 *passim*, 308, 313, 315
  Greece, 295, 297, 299
  Low Countries, 120, 122, 123, 299
  Norway, 96, 99, 101, 106
German Air Force *see* Luftwaffe
German Army, 41, 51, 52, 61, 62–63
  Austria, 54
  Belgium, 116, 120, 122–27 *passim*, 130–32, 299
  Crete, 298–308 *passim*, 310–15 *passim*
  Denmark, 97, 99
  France, 72–73, 116, 122, 125–31 *passim*, 133–46 *passim*, 148, 152, 154
  Great Britain, invasion plans, 156, 157, 163, 164–65, 166–67
  Greece, 270–71, 283, 284, 285, 286, 289–90, 293–98, 299
  Libya (and Western Desert), 180, 183, 200, 242–50 *passim*, 253–66 *passim*, 268, 280, 316, 317, 339
  Netherlands, 116, 119–21, 122, 299
  Norway, 96–102 *passim*, 105–09 *passim*
  officers and leadership, 50–51, 59, 60, 135–36, 336, 362, 365
  Poland, 63, 64, 66–67, 70, 71
  U.S.S.R., 283, 319, 323, 325–30 *passim*, 331, 332, 334–39, 342–53 *passim*, 355–69 *passim*, 370, 462
  Yugoslavia, 283–85, 287–88, 289
  see also German military forces
German intelligence and espionage, 44–45, 63, 68, 71, 114–15, 179, 231, 297, 313, 332, 350
  and "Ultra," 45, 195, 211, 223
  see also Fifth Column
German military forces, 50, 51, 77, 297–98, 362, 364
  Blitzkrieg tactics, 28, 52, 53, 54, 71, 116, 339
  conscription and rearmament, 27, 50–51, 53
  Einheit system, 245
  Great Britain and invasion plans, 155, 156, 157, 167
  Nazi politics and interservice rivalries, 135, 156, 157, 167, 297, 313, 316, 336
  OKW (Oberkommando Wehrmacht) established, 60
  see also Hitler, Adolf, and the military
German Navy and seapower, 27, 52, 62, 73, 74, 100, 193, 215–16, 299, 328
  Atlantic, 64, 75–81 *passim*, 98, 175–78, 200, 203, 207–16, 217–26
  Baltic Sea, 63, 66, 70, 96, 111, 216, 217
  Crete, 299, 305–08 *passim*
  France, 73, 74, 138; bases in, 176, 177, 204, 209, 216
  Great Britain: blockade, 64, 73–78 *passim*, 119, 175, 176, 178, 203, 211; invasion plans, 155–56, 157, 165, 167
  Indian Ocean, 177, 215
  and Luftwaffe, cooperation, 52–53, 74, 176, 209, 210, 211, 223, 226
  Mediterranean, 278, 279, 280, 281
  Norway and Norwegian campaign, 94–101 *passim*, 104, 107–10 *passim*
  Pacific, 177, 215
  submarines (U-boats), 27, 53, 64, 73–77 *passim*, 110, 171, 175, 177, 203, 204, 207–13 *passim*, 215, 222, 223, 226, 278, 279, 280, 282
  supply ships and problems, 74, 77, 216
Germany: appeasement, 54–61
  and Austria, invasion and occupation, 54, 55; as Balkan campaign base, 283, 284, 286, 288, 297
  Axis, 54, 89, 191, 377
  Balkans, interest in, 187, 191, 200, 202, 236, 237, 241, 297, 319
  and Belgium, 24, 54; invasion and occupation, 89, 109, 112, 114, 115, 116, 119, 123–26 *passim*, 130–33 *passim*, 299
  and Bulgaria, as Balkan campaign base, 270, 271, 283, 284, 288, 289, 298
  Communists, 14, 17, 19, 51
  conscript labor, 71, 72, 133, 298, 313, 346, 368
  and Crete, invasion and occupation, 237, 298, 296–316, 318
  and Czechoslovakia, 54, 55, 57; invasion and occupation, 55, 58, 61

Germany (cont'd)
  and Denmark, invasion and occupation, 89, 96, 99
  economy and industrial production, 24–25, 26, 51, 53, 59, 74, 205–08 *passim*, 363; British naval blockade, 74–75, 76–77, 94, 95, 97, 178; iron ore imported, 74, 92, 94, 95, 101, 111; *see also* oil *below*
  and Finland, 91; Finnish troops aid in Russian campaign, 326–27, 328, 345, 348–49
  and France *see* France, and Germany
  Gestapo, 60, 72, 149
  and Great Britain: bombing raids by Luftwaffe, 192–98 *passim*, 201, 206, 207, 328; bombing raids by RAF, 163–64, 166, 167, 191–95 *passim*, 202–06 *passim*; invasion plans and Battle of Britain, 89, 153–56, 157–67, 196, 297, 300, 325, 328, 362, 381; naval blockade by, 74–75, 76–77, 94, 95, 97, 178; naval blockade of, 64, 73–78 *passim*, 119, 175, 176, 178, 203, 211; Naval Treaty (1935), 27; war declared, 64; *see also* individual areas of war
  and Greece *see* Greece, German invasion
  and Hungary, 191; as Balkan campaign base, 270, 271, 283, 284, 288
  and Iraq, 179, 231, 232, 236
  Jews, 19, 26, 61; *see also* Jews
  League of Nations, withdrawal from, 19
  and Libya *see* Libya (and Western Desert)
  and Lithuania, 61, 329, 337
  Malta, attacks on, 170, 247, 267–69, 279, 297
  Mediterranean and the Middle East, 191, 237, 240, 241, 254, 266–69, 297, 316, 327
  Nazi Party, 28; Austria, 55; *Kristalnacht*, 61; and military, rivalries, 135–36, 156, 157, 167, 297, 313, 315, 336; Munich Beer Hall explosion (1939), 114, 115; Netherlands, 120, 122–23; Norway, 94, 99, 102; Reichstag fire (1933), 14; and SA, 14, 19, 60; *see also* SS and SD *below*
  and The Netherlands, invasion and occupation, 89, 108, 111, 114, 115, 116, 118–22, 157, 299
  and Norway, invasion and occupation, 89, 94–101 *passim*, 104–11, 157, 371
  oil, importance and shortage of, 187, 191, 197, 204, 207, 271, 277, 297, 339, 345, 355, 362
  Organization Todt, 53
  and Poland, invasion and occupation, 61–68 *passim*, 70–72, 86
  Ruhr occupied by France and Belgium, 24
  and Rumania, 89, 187, 191, 270, 297; as Balkan and Russian campaign base, 270, 271, 283, 284, 286, 328, 329
  SA (Sturmabteilung), 14, 19, 60
  "Siegfried Line" (West Wall), 53, 72, 116
  and Spain, 19, 20, 52, 191, 241, 329, 361
  SS (Schutzstaffel) and SD (Sicherheitsdienst), 60, 71; Poland, 63, 66, 71, 72; U.S.S.R., 327, 338, 367; Venlo Incident, 114–15
  and Sweden, 327, 328; iron ore, 74, 92, 94, 95, 101, 111
  and Syria, 231, 232, 233, 236
  and Turkey, 297, 316
  and U.S.S.R., 51, 62, 91, 324, 334; invasion, 155, 198, 202, 236, 241, 244, 254, 255, 264, 265, 266, 268, 269, 271, 279, 283, 296, 315, 316, 319, 322–70, 431, 462, 464, 466; invasion, foreign troops, 326, 327, 328, 329, 336, 345, 348–49, 361; Non-Aggression Pact, 62, 64, 65, 81, 324, 325, 334; Rapallo agreements, 16
  and U.S., 61, 450–51
  World War I, 16–17, 24, 27, 50, 54, 113, 171, 192, 221, 273, 417
  and Yugoslavia, 271, 282, 284–90, 299
  see also Hitler, Adolf; merchant shipping, German
Gerow, Maj. Gen. Leonard, 404
Gibraltar, 211
  German plan to capture, 191, 241, 279
  Royal Navy, 77–78, 169, 174, 281
Gilbert Islands, 393
Gioberti, 276
Giraud, Gen. Henri H., 117, 120, 128
Giussano, 280
Glassford, Rear Adm. W. A., 449, 459

Gleason, S. Everett, 465
Glengyle, 312
Glenroy, 310
Glorious, 109
Gloucester, 172, 268, 273, 308
Glowworm, 98
Glubb Pasha: and Arab Legion, 232, 233
Gneisenau, 74, 99, 109–10, 204, 216, 217
Godwin-Austen, Maj. Gen. A. R., 181
Goebbels, Dr. Joseph, 336, 351
Göring, Reich Marshal Hermann, 60, 135–36
 and Luftwaffe, 136, 206, 209, 297; Battle of Britain, 160, 162, 163, 167; Crete, 297, 313, 315
Gort, Gen. Lord, 73, 129, 131, 132, 134, 139, 252
Goto, Rear Adm. A., 395
Gott, Maj. Gen. W. H. E., 246, 248, 259
Graf Spee, 27, 74, 79, 80, 95
Grand Mufti of Jerusalem, 231
Graph, 211
Graziani, Marshal Rodolfo, 180, 183, 184, 185, 242
Great Britain, 23, 25–26
 Balkans, interest in, 191, 243, 316–17
 and Belgium, 119, 132, 133–34
 and China, lack of aid to Hong Kong, 423, 430, 431
 and Crete see Crete, British and Allied forces
 and Czechoslovakia, 55, 57, 58, 61
 defense preparations, 27, 59, 129, 153–54, 157, 159, 160, 162, 163, 164–65, 166, 197, 201, 212; evacuation of civilians, 88, 154; see also radar
 and Egypt see Egypt, British and British forces
 Fascists, 56
 and Finland, 92, 95, 104, 369
 and France, German invasion, 141–47 passim; see also British Expeditionary Force (France)
 and France (Vichy), French Navy seized, 149–51, 186, 235; see also Lebanon; Syria, British forces
 and Free French, 186, 226, 232–36 passim
 and Germany: bombing raids by Luftwaffe, 192–98 passim, 201, 206, 207, 328; bombing raids by RAF, 163–64, 166, 167, 191–95 passim, 202–06 passim; Hitler fears British invasion of Norway, 371; Hitler's attitude toward Britain and peace hopes, 54, 72, 73–74, 136, 155, 156, 324–25; invasion plans and Battle of Britain, 89, 153–57, 159–67, 196, 297, 300, 325, 327, 362, 381; naval blockade by, 64, 73–78 passim, 119, 175, 176, 178, 203, 211; naval blockade of, 74–75, 76–77, 94, 95, 97, 178; Naval Treaty (1935), 27; war declared, 64; see also individual areas of war
 and Greece: British forces before invasion, 185, 191, 269, 317; treaty, 191, 290, 316–17; see also British Expeditionary Force (Greece)
 industrial production, 59, 160, 162, 163, 167, 175, 194–95, 201, 212
 and Iraq see Iraq, British and British forces
 Italy enters war against, 89, 144, 154, 168
 and Japan, 21, 374, 379, 392, 395, 436, 450; see also individual areas of war
 and Lebanon see Lebanon
 and Libya see Libya (and Western Desert)
 Locarno Pact, 16, 54
 and Norway, 94, 95, 97, 99, 101, 102, 371; Allied forces, 94–98 passim, 101, 102, 104–12 passim
 at outbreak of hostilities, 55–58, 61
 pacificism, 29, 56, 74
 and Persia, 236
 and Poland, 61
 and Russia, civil war, 17
 and Scandinavia, 94–95, 102
 and Syria see Syria, British forces
 and Turkey, 236, 243, 270, 317, 318
 and U.S.S.R., 62, 325, 332, 333, 369; aid to, 358, 370
 and U.S.: aid, 15, 154–55, 213, 214, 372; Arcadia Conference, 460; Argentia Conference, 200, 440, 452; and British seizure of French Navy, 151; see also British combined armed forces, Allied command cooperation
World War I, 34, 75, 112, 141, 171, 192, 206, 221, 273, 316, 417, 444
see also Churchill, Winston S.;

INDEX 511

Great Britain (cont'd)
  merchant shipping, British; individual possessions and territories; entries under British
Greece: Albania invaded, 189, 190, 269, 284, 285, 291, 292, 293, 294
  and Bulgaria, 187, 269, 285, 289
  German invasion and occupation, 191, 200, 240, 243, 247, 251, 252, 254, 267, 268, 269, 270–71, 274, 283, 284, 285, 289–90, 292–300, 314–19 *passim*
  government-in-exile, 295, 305, 309
  and Great Britain: British forces before invasion, 185, 191, 269, 317; treaty, 191, 290, 316–17; see also British Expeditionary Force (Greece)
  and Italy: invasion attempt, 89, 184, 187–91 *passim*, 240–41, 269, 317; occupation and government after German invasion, 296, 298
  see also Balkans; Crete
Greek Air Force, 189, 270, 285
Greek Army, 50, 189, 285
  Albania, 189, 190, 269, 284, 285, 291, 292, 293, 294
  Bulgarian frontier, 269, 285, 289
  Crete, 298–99, 302, 305, 308, 314
  German invasion, 285, 289–90, 292, 294, 296
  Italian invasion attempt, 189, 190, 292, 296
Greek Navy and seapower, 276, 281
  Crete, 299–300, 307, 308
Greenland, 212, 214
Greer, 215
Grenfell, Capt. Russell, 435
Grew, Joseph, 377, 458
Greyhound, 308
Guam, 27, 379, 393, 395–96
Guderian, Gen. Heinz, 52, 71, 120, 125, 128, 130
  Russian campaign, 336, 343, 345, 350, 353, 355, 357, 360, 365
Guépard, 234
guerrilla warfare: Crete, 312–13
  Italian East Africa, 226, 228, 230
  Spanish Civil War, 20
  U.S.S.R., 368
  Yugoslavia, 50, 282, 288–89
Guingand, Maj. Gen. Sir Francis de, 317–18
Haakon VII, King, 101, 110

Habe, Hans, 127
Haile Selassie I, Emp., 18, 200, 228, 229
Halder, Gen. Franz, 67, 71, 127, 161, 241, 247
  Russian campaign, 325, 338, 344, 350, 356
Halifax, Lord, 58, 112
Halsey, Vice Adm. William F., Jr. ("Bull"), 390–91, 453
Hamburg, bombing of, 195, 206
Hardy, 102
Harriman, Averell, 372
Harris, Air Marshal Sir Arthur Travers ("Bomber"), 44, 192, 205
Hart, Adm. Thomas C., 380, 404, 410, 416, 418, 437, 453, 456, 459
Haruna, 411, 439
Harwood, Comm. Sir Henry, 79, 80
Haushofer, Karl, 323
Havoc, 102
Hawaii (Hawaiian Islands): U.S. forces, 27, 37, 374–75, 377, 435, 458; command and coordination, 375, 451, 454, 458; see also Pearl Harbor
Haw-Haw, Lord (William Joyce), 302
Hayata, 399
Hayataka Maru, 414
Hayo Maru, 414
Heath, Lt. Gen. Sir Lewis, 444
Helena, 387, 390
Hellas, 295
Helle, 187
Henderson, Sir Nevile, 58
Hereward, 311
Hermes, 150
Heron, 417
Hertz, Heinrich, 44
Hess, Rudolf, 200, 203
Hiei, 384
Himmler, Heinrich, 60, 114, 327, 367, 369
Hindenburg, Field Marshal Paul von, 60
Hipper see *Admiral Hipper*
Hirohito, Emp., 20, 28, 32, 46
Hiroshima, bombing of, 167, 206
Hiryu, 384, 400
Hitler, Adolf: and the Balkans, 191, 241, 297
  Churchill on, 369
  on Churchill, 156
  communism, hatred of, 324–27 *passim*, 336, 343–44, 367, 466

Hitler (cont'd)
  conquest, plans for, and strategy, 50–55, 59, 60, 62, 71, 114, 324, 366; hopes for peace with Britain and France, 54, 72, 73–74, 136, 156
  and Crete, 297, 313, 315
  and Czechoslovakia, 55, 58, 61
  Denmark and Norway, 94, 96, 371
  and France, invasion and peace hopes, 54, 72, 73–74, 114, 115, 116, 124–25, 127, 131, 148
  and Franco, 191, 241
  and Great Britain, attitude toward and peace hopes, 54, 72, 73–74, 135–36, 155, 156, 324–25; blockade ordered, 75, 176; British invasion of Norway feared, 371; invasion plans, 155, 156, 163–64, 165, 167, 187, 324–25, 327; see also Mediterranean below
  and Greece, 191, 270–71, 283
  and Jews, 324, 327, 336, 368, 464
  on Locarno Pact, 54
  and Low Countries, 118, 122; see also France above
  and the Mediterranean, 191, 241, 254, 267, 279, 297, 327
  Mein Kampf, 19, 72, 324
  and the military: conscription and rearmament, 27, 50–51, 52, 53; loyalty and opposition, 51, 60, 114–15, 319, 325, 326, 327, 365; Navy, 74, 75, 78, 219, 224
  Munich Beer Hall explosion (1939), 114, 115
  Munich Beer Hall "Putsch" (1923), 19
  and Mussolini, 55, 184, 187, 188, 241, 254, 283
  Pearl Harbor, surprise at, 450
  personal characteristics, 30, 31, 136, 323, 368
  and Poland, 61, 63
  rise to power, 14, 24, 25, 26, 59
  on Roosevelt, 450
  Rumanian oil, interest in, 187, 297
  and U.S.S.R.: invasion, 155, 198, 241, 266, 283, 296, 319, 322–27 *passim*, 331, 334, 336, 338, 339, 344, 350, 356, 359–66 *passim*, 466; Non-Aggression Pact, 324, 325; see also communism *above*
  World War I, 18, 324
  and Yugoslavia, 271, 283
Hoepner, Gen. Erich, 337, 356, 357, 365
Holland, Vice Adm. L. E., 220–21
Homma, Lt. Gen. Masaharu, 406, 414, 416
Hong Kong (Kowloon and Leased Territories), 423, 424
  Japanese attack, 322, 393, 395, 423–31, 448
Honolulu, 390
Hood, 219, 220–21, 222
Hoover, Herbert, 25
Hopkins, Harry, 372
Hostile, 102
Hoth, Gen. Hermann, 343, 345, 356
Hotspur, 102, 312
Houston, 449
Howard, Michael, 179
Hull, Cordell, 151, 375, 376, 379, 381, 455
Hungarian forces (with Axis troops), 284, 288, 329, 336
Hungary, 17
  and Czechoslovakia, 58
  and Germany, 191; as Balkan campaign base, 270, 271, 283, 284, 288
  Rumanian territory ceded to, 187
Hunter, 102
Huntziger, Gen. C. L. C., 117, 125, 126, 148

Iachino, Adm. Angelo, 271, 274, 277, 280
Iceland, 81, 111, 211, 212, 215, 372
Idaho, 459
Ilex, 234
Illustrious, 173, 268
Imperial, 311
Imperial Star, 279
India, 231, 232, 237
  Nationalist movement, 469
  Indian Army, 43, 468
    Africa and Middle East, 179, 185, 227, 228, 231, 233, 234; Libya (and Western Desert), 246, 249, 253, 263
    Far East, 437, 448; Hong Kong, 426, 427, 428; Malaya, 434, 444, 445, 446, 447, 468; Singapore, 434, 447, 468
Indian Ocean, 168, 177, 215, 228, 436
Indochina see French Indochina
Indomitable, 437
Indonesia see Dutch East Indies
Iran (Persia), 236

INDEX

Iraq: British and British forces, 178, 231–36 *passim*, 247, 252
  Germans and German forces, 179, 230, 231, 232, 236
Ireland, Northern, 195, 202
Ireland, Republic of, 176
Ironside, Gen. Sir Edmund, 153, 252
Isaac Sweers, 280
Isis, 234
Ismay, Gen. H. L., 248
Italian Air Force, 42, 168, 169, 194, 231, 267, 269
  Dodecanese Islands and Greece, 172, 180, 189
  Italian East Africa, 180, 229
  Libya (and Western Desert), 180, 184, 239–40, 249, 256, 257, 265
  Malta, 170, 171, 278
  Navy's dependence on, 42, 169, 172–73, 276–77, 280
Italian Army and military forces, 42, 178, 180, 188, 189, 329
  British East Africa, 181, 227
  characteristics of, 31, 42, 169, 183–84, 185, 188, 190, 240, 273, 280
  Crete, 299, 301
  France, 145, 148
  with German troops in Russia, 329
  Italian East Africa, 18, 54, 180, 181, 182, 226–30
  Libya (and Western Desert), 89, 168, 170, 172, 178, 180, 182–85, 239–50 *passim*, 254, 256, 259–65 *passim*, 270, 316, 317
  Yugoslavia, 284, 288
  see also Albania; Greece
Italian East Africa, 18, 180, 226–30
  native forces, 180, 184, 185, 228
  see also Eritrea; Ethiopia; Italian Somaliland
Italian Navy and seapower, 42, 168–69, 170, 273, 276–77, 280–81
  Air Force, dependence on, 42, 169, 172–73, 277, 278, 280
  guerrilla raids, 271–73, 277, 281
  Mediterranean, 42, 80, 168–74 *passim*, 188, 269, 273–82 *passim*, 313; Cape Matapan, 200, 271, 273–77, 306; Crete, 89, 173, 271, 273, 299, 307, 308; Taranto, 89, 173–74, 269, 276, 378, 440
  naval disarmament conferences, 16, 26, 27
  Red Sea, 168, 171, 227, 229–30
  submarines, 168, 171, 186, 211, 281
Italian Somaliland, 18, 168, 180, 226, 227, 228
Italy, 18, 55
  and Albania, 61, 187, 188, 189, 190, 269–70, 293, 315
  Axis, 54, 89, 191, 377–78
  and the Balkans, 187, 191, 283
  Crete, plan to capture, 188
  and France, war against, 89, 144, 145, 148, 154, 168
  and Great Britain, war declared, 89, 144, 154, 168
  and Greece: invasion attempt, 89, 184, 187–91 *passim*, 240–41, 269, 317; occupation and government after German invasion, 296, 297
  League of Nations: and Ethiopian invasion, 18; withdrawal from, 54
  Locarno Pact, 16, 54
  and Spanish Civil War, 20, 361
  and U.S., 144, 451
  World War I, 273
  Yugoslavia and Axis invasion, 187, 282, 284, 288
  see also merchant shipping, Italian; Mussolini, Benito; individual possessions and territories

Jackal, 234
Jamaica, 155
Janus, 234
Japan: Axis, 54, 89, 191, 377–78
  and Borneo, 380, 395, 406, 413, 432, 448, 449
  China, aggression against, 15, 20–21, 23, 45, 46, 322, 373, 422, 423, 424, 431, 464; Formosa bases, 406, 407, 408, 423
  and French Indochina, "joint" protectorate, 89, 149, 374, 423, 431–32, 439
  and Great Britain, 21, 374, 379, 392, 395, 436, 450; Burma, 375, 395, 422, 432; Hong Kong, 322, 395, 423–31, 448; Malaya, 375, 393, 395, 432, 438, 440, 444–47 *passim*, 462; Singapore, 393, 433, 448, 449, 468; *see also* Borneo *above*
  League of Nations and Manchurian conquest, 21
  militarism, 21, 27, 32–33, 45, 375, 377, 432, 467; *see also* war/war plans *below*
  nationalism, 21, 28, 32, 47, 467–68
  and The Netherlands, 374, 379, 393; Dutch East Indies, 322, 375, 393,

Japan (cont'd)
406; see also Borneo above
Russo-Japanese War, 46, 378, 384, 431
and Thailand see Thailand, Japanese conquest
and U.S.S.R., 431; border incidents, 46, 340, 352–53; "non-aggression" pact, 374; Soviet espionage, 333, 352–53
and U.S., 21, 373, 376, 379, 395, 432, 465–68; Allied "Rainbow" war plans, 213, 372, 403, 405, 436, 437; diplomatic negotiations, 373–74, 375, 380, 384, 454, 455–56; exclusion acts, 28–29; Guam, 379, 393, 395, 396; Japanese intelligence and espionage, 47, 378, 379–81; Midway Island, 393; U.S. bombing of mainland, 167, 204, 206, 404; U.S. intelligence see "Magic"; U.S. "Orange" war plans, 377, 403, 405, 407, 413, 416, 435; Wake Island, 393, 397–402; war declared, 450; war warnings, 377–83 passim, 453, 454; see also Pearl Harbor; Philippines
war/war plans, 21, 322, 373, 376–81 passim, 384, 393, 395, 431, 432, 438, 448–49, 464, 466, 467, 468; anticolonialism stemming from, 469; need for food and raw materials, 45, 47, 373–74, 375, 393, 406, 431, 449
see also Mandated Islands
Japanese air forces (Army and Navy), 43, 45, 47, 393, 425, 448, 449
Borneo, 432, 448
Burma, 422, 432
Dutch East Indies, 432
Formosa, bases, 406, 407, 408
French Indochina, bases, 432, 439
Guam, 396
Hong Kong, 425–29 passim
Malaya, 432, 438–44 passim, 448
Pearl Harbor see Pearl Harbor, Japanese attack
Philippines, 406–11 passim, 413, 415, 417, 418, 419, 432
Singapore, 432, 447
Thailand, 432, 444
Wake Island, 397–98, 399, 401
Japanese Army and military services, 21, 40, 45, 46, 373, 393, 406, 423, 425, 431, 432, 445
Borneo, 406, 432, 448
Burma, 432
characteristics of men, 430, 466–67
China, 15, 20–21, 23, 45, 46, 322, 373, 423, 424, 430, 431, 464
Dutch East Indies, 406, 432
French Indochina, 89, 423
Hong Kong, 424–30 passim
Korea, 46, 423
Malaya, 432, 438, 440, 444–47 passim
Nanking and Peking, 21, 423
Philippines, 406, 411, 413, 415, 416, 419–21, 422, 432
Shanghai, 21, 22
Thailand, 432, 444
Wake Island, 398
see also Japan, militarism; Japan, war/war plans; Japanese air forces
Japanese intelligence and espionage, 47, 378, 379–81
Japanese Navy and seapower, 26–27, 38, 45–47, 374, 377, 393, 403, 405, 406, 448
Borneo, 432, 448
Burma and Dutch East Indies, 432
Guam, 396, 398
Malaya, 432, 439–44 passim
naval disarmament conferences, 16, 26, 27
Pearl Harbor, 376, 382–83, 384, 385, 389, 391, 454, 458
Peking and Shanghai, 392–93
Philippines, 405, 406, 407, 411, 413, 418, 432, 435
submarines, 46, 382, 384, 390, 439, 454
Thailand, 432, 444
Wake Island, 399–400, 401
see also Japan, militarism; Japan, war/war plans; Japanese air forces
Java, 395, 459; see also Dutch East Indies
Jervis, 276, 281
Jervis Bay, 177
Jews, persecution of, 19, 26, 61, 70, 71, 72, 289, 324, 327, 336, 368, 464
Jodl, Gen. Alfred, 96, 209, 325, 327, 340, 349
Joffre, Marshal Joseph, 41
Johnson, Group Capt. J. E., 167
Jones, Brig. Gen. Albert N., 420, 421
Jones, Dr. R. V., 159
Junack, Lt. Comm. Gerhard, 225
Juno, 307
Jutland, Battle of, 171, 221, 274, 417

INDEX

Kaga, 384
Kajioka, Rear Adm. S., 398–99
Karlsruhe, 101
Kashmir, 309
Kearny, 215
Keitel, Field Marshal Wilhelm, 60, 135, 340
Keller, Gen. Alfred, 328
Kellogg-Briand Pact, 16
Kelly, Capt. Colin P., Jr., 411
Kelly, 309
Kemp, Lt. Comm. P. K., 57
Kennedy, Maj. Gen. Sir John, 318
Kent, 170
Kenya: British forces, 178, 179, 180, 181, 226, 227, 240
Kesselring, Field Marshal Albert, 157, 255, 264, 265, 301, 328
Keyes, Adm. Sir Roger, 131, 132
Khartoum, 171
Kidd, Rear Adm. Isaac C., 388
Kido, Marquis, 32
Kimmel, Adm. Husband E., 374, 380, 402
  and Pearl Harbor, 376, 378, 380, 382, 451–55 *passim*
King, Adm. Ernest J., 38, 200, 214, 452, 454
King George V, 219, 222, 223, 224, 225
Kingstone, Brig. J. J., 231
Kipling, Rudyard, 252
Kipling, 309
Kirishima, 384
Kisaragi, 399
Kleist, Gen. Ewald von, 284, 345, 361
Kluge, Gen. Günther von, 356–60 *passim*, 365
Knox, Frank, 376, 378, 451, 453
Koch, Erich, 367
Komet, 177
Kondo, Vice Adm. N., 405, 439
Kongo, 439
Kongo Maru, 399
Königsberg, 101
Konoye, Prince Fumimaro, 32, 375
Korea, 46, 423
Kormoran, 215–16
Koryzis, Alexander, 270, 294, 317
Kowloon *see* Hong Kong
Kretschmer, Otto, 176
Küchler, Gen. Georg von, 120, 145, 365
Kun, Béla, 17
Künna, 102
Kurile Islands, 375, 384

Kurusu, Saburo, 375

Ladybird, 278
Lafore, Laurence, 56
Langer, William L., 465
Langley, 449, 453
Langsdorff, Capt. Hans, 80
Latvia: Soviet occupation, 62, 81, 89; German attack; *see also* Baltic states
Laurence, William, 14
Laurentic, 176
Laval, Pierre, 148, 151
Leach, Capt. J. C., 221, 438, 443
League of Nations: German withdrawal, 19
  Italian invasion of Ethiopia, 18
  Italian withdrawal, 54
  Japanese conquest of Manchuria, 21
  U.S. abandonment of, 16
  U.S.S.R. expelled, 86
Leased Territories *see* Hong Kong
Lebanon: British and French (Vichy) forces, 232–33, 234, 235, 240
Leeb, Field Marshal Wilhelm Ritter von, 72, 116, 142, 146
  Russian campaign, 328, 344, 347, 356, 365
Le Gentilhomme, Gen. Paul L., 180, 232, 234
Legion, 280
Leipsig, 76
Lemp, Lt. Comm. Fritz-Ludwig, 75
Leningrad: defense and German attack, 326, 328, 342, 344, 347, 348, 349, 352, 355, 361, 362
  defense and "Winter War," 82
Leopold III, King, 118, 126, 131–32, 133
Lewin, Ronald, 34
Lexington, 38, 391, 402
Libya (and Western Desert), 18, 182
  battles and defense, 89, 168, 170, 172, 178, 180, 182–85, 237, 239–50, 253–66, 268, 269, 280, 285, 291, 316, 317, 328, 340
Libyan forces, 180, 184, 185
Liddell Hart, Capt. Basil H., 28, 43, 71, 136, 227, 250, 266
Lindbergh, Col. Charles, 164
List, Field Marshal Sigmund Wilhelm, 283
Lithuania: and Germany, 61
  Soviet occupation, 81, 89; German attack, 329, 337; *see also* Baltic states

Littorio, 168, 174
Litvinov, Maxim, 62
Liverpool, bombing of, 193, 194, 196
Lloyd, Lord, 147
Lloyd George, David, 132
Locarno Pact, 16, 54
Lofoten Islands, 94, 98
Löhr, Col. Gen. Alexander, 284, 299, 305, 328
London: bombing of, 160, 163, 164, 192–97 *passim*, 201, 203
　evacuation of, 88
　Port mined by Germans, 64, 76
London Naval Disarmament Conference, 16, 26, 27
Longmore, Air Chief Marshal Sir Arthur, 179, 185, 251
Lubbe, Marinus van der, 14
Ludendorff, Gen. Erich, 19
Lüdermann, 102
Ludwig, Emil, 31
Luftwaffe, 27, 52, 59, 71, 159, 166, 187, 193, 206, 209, 340
　Crete, 297–313 *passim*
　France, 116, 125, 126, 127, 129, 130, 135, 137, 138, 140, 265, 284; bases, 157, 161–62
　Great Britain, 192–98 *passim*, 200–03, 205, 206, 328; *see also* Battle of Britain
　Greece, 268, 290, 292, 293, 294, 295, 298, 299
　Libya (and Western Desert), 242, 249, 250, 256, 257, 261, 265, 328
　Low Countries, 116, 119–20, 121, 122, 123, 131; bases, 122, 156, 157
　Malta, 170, 247, 268, 297
　Mediterranean and Middle East, 241, 254, 265, 267–68, 276, 277, 328, 364; bases, 231, 233, 241, 242
　and Navy, cooperation, 52–53, 74, 176, 210, 211–12, 223, 226
　Norway, 96–97, 99, 100, 101, 105–06, 107, 108, 111; bases, 104, 157, 161–62
　Poland, 63, 64, 66, 67, 68, 70, 71
　Spanish Civil War, 20, 52
　U.S.S.R., 202, 255, 265, 268, 269, 279, 327–28, 334, 353, 355, 357, 363
　Yugoslavia, 284, 286–87, 299
　see also German military forces; Göring, Reich Marshal Hermann
Lupescu, Magda, 89
Lupo, 307

Lütjens, Vice Adm. Günther, 98, 216, 219–24 *passim*, 226
Lützow see Deutschland
Lyttelton, Oliver, 251

MacArthur, Gen. Douglas, 25, 37, 404
　Philippines and Japanese attack, 374, 404–08 *passim*, 409, 413–17 *passim*, 421
MacDonald, Ramsay, 56
Mackesy, Maj. Gen. P. J., 108
McMillin, Capt. G. J., 395
"Magic," 40, 45, 379, 380, 418, 454, 455, 458
Malaya (British Malaya): British and native forces, 432, 433, 434, 438, 440, 444–48 *passim*, 468
　Japanese conquest, 375, 393, 395, 432, 438, 440, 444–47 *passim*, 462
　naval action off coast, 431–32, 438–46 *passim*
Malaya, 169, 170, 269
Malta: British base and defense, 169–74 *passim*, 247, 254, 255, 256, 266–69, 273, 278, 280, 281, 294, 297, 316
Maltby, Maj. Gen. C. M., 424, 425, 426, 430
Manchester, 279
Manchuria (Manchukuo), 21, 377
Mandated Islands, 27, 403, 435; *see also* Marianas; Marshalls
Manila, 403, 404, 406, 435
　Japanese attack, 407, 409–10, 413–21 *passim*
Mannerheim, Baron Carl Gustaf von, 82, 83, 85, 90, 91, 93, 328, 348–49
Manstein, Gen. Fritz Erich von, 115, 346
Manteuffel, Col. Hasso von, 358
Maori, 224, 280
Maori forces, 302, 308, 447
Mao Tse-tung, 23, 33
Marblehead, 449
Marianas (Mariana Islands), 27, 395; *see also* Mandated Islands
Marne, Battle of the, 113, 344, 346, 420
Marshall, Gen. George, 37, 200, 457, 462
　and Pacific theater, 375, 377, 381, 404, 455
　unified theater command urged, 458, 460

Marshalls (Marshall Islands), 27, 375, 396; *see also* Mandated Islands
Martin, Maj. Gen. Frederick L., 451
Maryland, 388, 390
Masaryk, Jan, 55, 58
Masaryk, Tomáš G., 55
Mashona, 226
Masters, John, 467
Matapan *see* Cape Matapan
Mediterranean Sea *see* merchant shipping; individual navies
Meindl, Brig. Gen. Eugen, 304
merchant shipping: Allied and neutral, 74, 76, 79, 81, 176, 210, 372
  British, 177, 229, 232, 237, 358, 370; Atlantic and coastal, 75, 76, 77, 78, 160, 175, 176, 177, 178, 193, 201, 203, 207–12 *passim*, 328; Mediterranean, 168, 169, 170, 172, 174, 181, 237, 241, 247, 248, 253–54, 267, 268, 271, 276, 278, 280, 281, 328
  German, 53, 74, 94, 96, 99, 104, 156, 164, 165, 178, 207, 371; Mediterranean, 247, 248, 255, 267, 278–79
  Italian, 168, 170, 172, 174, 244, 247, 248, 255, 267, 279, 280
  see also Battle of the Atlantic
Metaxas, Gen. Ioannis, 188, 270, 317
Michael I, King, 187
Midway Island, 391, 393, 396
Mihajlović, Gen. Draža, 289
Mimbelli, Comm. Francisco, 307
Mindanao, 406
  Japanese attack, 407, 410, 411, 412, 413
Mississippi, 459
Mitchell, Gen. William ("Billy"), 39, 192
Mitford, Unity, 56
Mogador, 150
Molotov, Vyacheslav, 62
Montgomery, Gen. Sir Bernard, 43
Morgenthau, Henry, Jr., 35
Morison, Samuel Eliot, 373, 375, 383
Morrison, Herbert, 197
Morshead, Maj. Gen. L. J., 246
Morton, Louis, 452
Mościcki, Ignacy, 70
Moscow, Battle of, 319, 327, 329, 343, 345, 350–51, 366, 431, 466
Mosley, Leonard, 230
Mosley, Sir Oswald, 56
Mountbatten, Capt. Lord Louis, 43, 309

Munich: Beer Hall explosion (1939), 114, 115
  Beer Hall "Putsch" (1923), 19
  bombing of, 195
Munich crisis, 56, 57, 58–59
Murmansk, 82, 94, 327, 349, 358, 370
Murphy, Robert, 152
Murrow, Edward R., 198
Musashi, 27
Mussert, Anton, 123
Mussolini, Benito, 17, 18, 31
  and Albania, 187, 189, 190, 315
  and the Balkans, 187, 191, 283
  and Czechoslovakia, 58
  France, war declared, 89, 144, 148, 168
  German invasion of Austria, 55
  German invasion of Poland, 63
  Great Britain, war declared, 89, 144, 168
  Greece: attempted invasion, 89, 187, 188, 189, 190, 241; surrender to Axis, 296
  and Hitler, 55, 184, 187, 188, 241, 254, 283
  Mediterranean and Africa, 18, 89, 184, 241, 254; and Navy, 42, 168, 276
  U.S., war declared, 451
Mutsuki, 401

Nagasaki, bombing of, 206
Nagumo, Vice Adm. Chuichi, 383
Naiad, 307
Nanking, 21, 423
Narvik: attack and naval action, 94, 97, 98, 99, 101, 104, 105, 107–09, 253
Naujocks, Alfred Helmut, 63, 114
Neame, Lt. Gen. P., 243, 246
Nelson, 76, 279
Neptune, 172, 281
The Netherlands: German invasion and occupation, 89, 108, 112, 114, 115, 116, 118–22, 157, 299;
  Fifth Column, 120, 123
  government-in-exile, 122
  and Japan, 374, 379, 393; *see also* Borneo; Dutch East Indies
  neutrality, 113, 118, 122
  see also entries under Dutch
Nevada, 387, 388, 389, 390
Newfoundland, 155, 214
  Argentia conference, 200, 440, 452
New Mexico, 459
New Orleans, 388

Newton Beech, 78
New Zealand: defense, 436, 448
New Zealand forces: Crete, 298–99, 302, 303, 304, 308, 311
　cruiser *Achilles*, 79–80
　Greece, 285, 292, 296, 298
　Libya and Egypt, 179, 253, 259, 261, 263
　Maori, 302, 308, 447
Niblack, 214
Nicolson, Harold, 56
Nigeria and Nigerian forces, 229, 237
Nimitz, Adm. Chester W., 38, 451
Nomura, Adm. Kichisaburo, 375–76
Norfolk, 219, 224
Northampton, 391
North Sea, 74, 76, 78, 94, 104
Norway, 92, 93–94, 95
　German invasion and occupation, 89, 96–102 *passim*, 104–11, 157, 371; Nazis and Fifth Column, 94, 99, 101
　government-in-exile, 100–01, 110
　and Great Britain, 94, 95, 97, 99, 101, 102, 371; Allied Expeditionary Force and naval support, 94–98 *passim*, 101, 102, 104–09 *passim*
　naval action off coast, 74, 93–101 *passim*, 104, 105, 107–11 *passim*
Norwegian forces, 97, 99, 105, 107
Norwegian Navy, 95, 100, 101
Nürnberg, 76

O'Connor, Capt. R. C., 281
O'Connor, Gen. Richard, 183, 184–85, 237, 239, 240, 245
Oglala, 387, 390
Oklahoma, 388, 389–90, 392
"Operation Barbarossa" *see* Germany, and U.S.S.R., invasion
"Operation Battleaxe," 248–51
"Operation Brevity," 248
"Operation Catapult," 149–51
"Operation Compass," 185
"Operation Crusader," 255–66
"Operation Demon," 294–96
"Operation Dynamo," 129, 131, 134–41
"Operation Exporter," 233–35
"Operation Marita" *see* Greece, German invasion and occupation
"Operation Matador," 444
"Operation Menace," 186
"Operation *Merkur*" see Crete, German invasion and occupation

"Operation *Mittelmeer*," 242
"Operation *Rheinübung*," 217–18
"Operation Lion (Sea Lion)" *see* Battle of Britain
"Operation Typhoon" *see* Moscow, Battle of
"Operation *Weser*" see Norway, German invasion and occupation
Orama, 109
Oran, 150–51, 169
Oriani, 276
Orion, 177, 273–74, 295, 307, 312
Orzel, 98
Ouvry, Lt. Comm. J. G. D., 76

Padover, Saul K., 41
Paget, Maj. Gen. B. C. T., 105
Palairet, Sir Michael, 317
Palestine, 228
　British and British forces, 178, 179, 180, 231, 237, 263
　Free French forces, 232
Palestinian forces: in Greece and Crete, 295, 296, 298, 302
Panama Canal Zone, 37, 452
Panay Incident, 22, 456
Pantelleria, 168, 170
Papagos, Gen. Alexandros, 188, 292, 293
Parker, Brig. Gen. George M., 413, 416, 420
Parthian, 235
Patroclus, 176
Patton, Gen. George S., 37
Paul, Prince, 271, 282, 318
Paulus, Gen. Friedrich, 247
Pavelić, Dr. Ante, 289
Pearl Harbor, 38, 374, 435, 453, 459
　Japanese attack, 15, 322, 334, 376, 377, 379–80, 382, 383–84, 387–92, 417, 436, 440, 450, 454, 456, 458, 462; inquiries and investigations, 451–58 *passim*; warnings, 377–82 *passim*, 453–54
Peary, 417
Pecos, 449
Peking, 21, 393, 423
Penelope, 279, 281
Pennsylvania, 387, 389, 390
Percival, Lt. Gen. A. E., 434, 445, 447
Pericles, 273
Persia (Iran), 236
Persian Gulf: British interests, 178, 179, 231, 232, 236
Perth, 273, 295, 307, 312
Pertinax, 128, 152

INDEX

Pétain, Marshal Henri, 36, 41, 126, 128, 147–48
French armistice and Vichy regime, 143, 147, 148, 149, 151
Peter, Prince, 305
Peter II, King, 283
Petrel, 392
Philippine Army, 374, 403, 406
  Japanese attack, 413, 415, 416, 419, 420, 421
Philippines (Philippine Commonwealth), 402–03, 407–08
  Japanese attack, 322, 379, 380, 393, 395, 406–11 *passim*, 413–22 *passim*, 432, 435, 456, 462, 467–68
  U.S. responsibility for defense, 27, 37, 374, 377, 403, 404, 458, 459
Philippine Scouts, 406, 413, 415, 419, 420
Phillips, Adm. Sir Tom ("Tom Thumb"), 437, 438–39, 442, 443
Phoebe, 295, 312
Pierlot, Hubert, 132
Pile, Gen. Sir Frederick A., 196
Pillsbury, 417
Pilsudski, Józef, 17, 50
Pinguin, 215
Piorun, 224
"Plan *Gelb*," 114, 115, 116, 119–26; see also German invasion and occupation under Belgium; France; The Netherlands
"Plan *Weiss*" see Poland, German invasion and occupation
Platt, Lt. Gen. W., 227, 228, 229
Ploesti, 187, 191, 271, 297
Pogue, Forrest, 404
Pola, 275, 276–77
Poland, 16–17, 49, 64
  and Czechoslovakia, 58, 65
  and France, 62, 63, 72–73
  German invasion and occupation, 61–68 *passim*, 70–72, 86
  and Great Britain, 61
  and U.S.S.R., 62, 65; occupation of eastern region, 64, 70, 85
"Polish Corridor," 17, 62, 66, 67
Polish Air Force, 50, 66, 67, 71
  in RAF, 70, 159
Polish Army and military forces, 50
  German invasion, 64–67 *passim*, 70
  join with Allied forces, 105, 109, 146, 254, 285
Polish intelligence, 45
Polish Navy, 50, 71, 98, 224

Portal, Air Chief Marshal Sir Charles, 203
Portes, Comtesse Hélène des, 146, 149, 152
Pound, Adm. Sir Dudley, 314
Pownall, Lt. Gen. Sir Henry, 434
Prasca, Gen. Count Sebastiano, Visconti, 188, 190
President Harrison, 393
Preston, 407
Prétilat, Gen. A. G., 116
Pridham-Wippell, Vice Adm. H. D., 280, 295
Prien, Lt. Comm. Günther, 75–76
Prince of Wales, 219, 220, 221, 223, 279, 437, 438, 440, 441, 442, 443, 459
Prinz Eugen, 217, 219, 221, 222
Provence, 150
Pulford, Air Vice Marshal C. W. H., 434, 438
Putnam, Maj. Paul A., 397
Pye, Vice Adm. W. S., 402, 451

Queen Elizabeth (battleship), 281
Queen Elizabeth (troopship), 240
Queen Mary, 240
Quezon, Manuel, 402, 408, 416
Quinan, Lt. Gen. E. P., 236
Quisling, Vidkun, 94, 99

radar, 28, 44, 196
  American, 39, 44, 382, 406, 454
  British, 43, 44, 45, 59, 159–63 *passim*, 196, 201, 202, 206, 212, 219, 381–82
  German, 44, 122, 217
Raedel, 102
Raeder, Grand Adm. Erich, 74, 96, 99, 155, 217, 241
Raleigh, 387, 390
Ramilies, 170, 222
Ramsay, Vice Adm. Sir Bertram H., 134, 136, 137, 138
Ranger, 38
Rankin, Jeannette, 450
Rashid Ali, 231, 232
Rauenfels, 102
Rawalpindi, 81
Rawlings, Rear Adm. H. B., 311
Red Army *see* Soviet Army
Red Sea, 168, 171, 179, 227, 229–30
Reichenau, Field Marshal Walter von, 123, 361, 365
Reinberger, Maj. Helmut, 115
Renown, 80, 96, 97, 98, 222, 269

Repulse, 222, 223, 437, 438, 440–41, 443, 444
Requin, Gen., 143
Resolution, 186
Reuben James, 215
Revenge, 222
Reynaud, Paul, 36, 95, 126, 128, 132, 133, 143, 144, 145–47, 149, 152
Reynaud, Mme. Paul, 95, 152
Rhodes, 231, 240
Ribbentrop, Joachim von, 62, 286
Richardson, Adm. James O., 374
Richelieu, 150, 186
Richthofen, Lt. Gen. Wolfram von, 284, 299
Ringel, Maj. Gen. Julius, 308
Rio de Janeiro, 98
Ritchie, Maj. Gen. N. M., 262, 264, 265
Ritter, Karl, 319
Roberts, Owen J. (and Roberts Commission), 451, 453
Robin Moor, 214
Rodney, 222, 223, 224, 225, 279
Röhm, Ernst, 60
Rokossovski, Marshal Konstantin, 352, 360
Roma, 277
Rommel, Gen. Erwin, 183, 244, 245
 France, 125, 127, 129–30, 137, 181
 Libya (and Western Desert), 181, 183, 242–50 *passim*, 253–65 *passim*, 316, 317; supply problems, 244, 247, 249, 254, 255–56, 261, 262, 263, 264, 266, 268, 316, 328
Rommel, Gen. Juliuscz, 70
Romulo, Col. Carlos P., 409
Roope, Lt. Comm. G. Broadmead, 98
Roosevelt, Franklin Delano, 23, 25, 89, 144, 457, 464
 and Churchill, 129, 146, 154, 165, 333, 450; conferences, 200, 459–60
 "fireside chats," 23, 35, 198
 Hitler on, 450
 military decisions, 214, 372, 373, 375, 436, 452, 456, 457, 459
 "neutrality" and Allied aid, 154, 214, 372
 Pearl Harbor, "conspiracy" theory, 453, 456, 457
 personal characteristics, 35–36, 456
 and Stalin, 35, 372
 war declared against Axis, 450, 456–57
Rotterdam, 122, 193

Rowse, A. L., 56
Royal Air Force, 40, 44, 56, 59, 166, 192, 203, 216, 217
 Albania, 191, 269
 Battle of Britain, 89, 157, 159 *passim*
 blitz, 195–96, 201, 203
 coastal patrols, 175, 205, 210; see also naval air arm *below*
 Crete, 299, 302, 313, 316
 Far East, 422, 424, 425, 429–30, 432, 434, 438–48 *passim*
 foreign and volunteer pilots, 70, 159
 Germany, 163–64, 166, 167, 192–95 *passim*, 202–06 *passim*
 Greece: bases, 185, 191, 269; German invasion, 269, 274, 283, 285, 294, 295, 317, 318
 Libya (and Western Desert), 240–41, 249, 250, 254, 255, 257, 261, 264, 265
 Low Countries and France, 116–18 126, 140, 159
 Malta, base, 170, 171, 248, 256, 266, 268, 278, 279; see also Malta
 Mediterranean and Middle East, 179, 180, 185, 229, 231, 233–34, 236, 237, 240, 244, 247, 248, 254, 255, 263, 266, 306
 naval air arm, 43, 77, 176, 210
 U.S.S.R., 370
 see also British combined armed forces
Royal Marines, 105, 312
Royal Navy and seapower, 43, 58, 75, 104, 129, 168, 211, 223, 316, 370
 Atlantic, 64, 74–81 *passim*, 98, 111, 176–77, 200, 206–16, 219–26
 Battle of Britain, defense, 157, 161, 164, 166
 Dunkirk evacuation, 130, 134, 136–40, 155
 Eastern Fleet, 179, 392, 424–30 *passim*, 433–34, 435–43 *passim*, 445, 446
 Fleet Air Arm, 43, 101, 172, 173–74, 222, 223, 235, 269, 273, 276, 370; Coastal Command, 43, 176, 207–12 *passim*, 219, 223, 226
 Germany, blockade, 74–75, 76–77, 95, 97, 178
 Mediterranean and Middle East, 77, 89, 150, 168–74 *passim*, 179, 181, 184, 186, 226–31 *passim*, 233,

INDEX

Mediterranean (cont'd)
  235, 237, 240, 241, 244, 247,
  248–49, 255, 263, 266, 267–68,
  269, 271, 273–74 passim, 294–95,
  306, 309–10, 316, 435; bases see
  Alexandria; Gibraltar; Malta;
  Taranto, 89, 173–74, 269, 276,
  378, 440; see also Crete
  naval disarmament conferences, 16,
  26, 27
  Norway and Norwegian campaign,
  95–98 passim, 101, 102, 104, 106–
  12 passim
  Scapa Flow, base, 76, 77, 99, 193,
  219, 296
  submarines, 76, 101, 170, 171–72,
  279, 281, 370
  U.S. "destroyers-for-bases" deal, 155,
  213
  see also British combined armed
  forces
Royal Oak, 76
Royal Sovereign, 170
Rumania, 70, 187
  Bulgaria and Hungary, territory
  ceded to, 187
  and Czechoslovakia, 58
  and Germany, 89, 187, 191, 270,
  296; as Balkan campaign base,
  271, 283, 284, 286; as Russian
  campaign base, 328, 329
  and U.S.S.R., 326, 328, 329; territory annexed by, 62–63, 187, 325,
  329
  see also Balkans
Rumanian Army, 50
  with German troops in Russia, 326,
  328, 329
Rundstedt, Gen. Karl Gerd von, 66,
  135
  Low Countries and France, 116, 119,
  125, 128, 135, 142, 145
  Russian campaign, 328, 336, 344,
  355, 356, 361, 365
Russia, 16, 17, 47
Russo-Japanese War, 46, 378, 383, 431
Rydz-Śmigly, Marshal Edward, 65, 70

Saburo, Sakai, 409
Safford, Laurence F., 40
Sagitarrio, 307
Sagona, 281
St. Didier, 235
St. Lucia, 155
Sakai, Lt. Gen. T., 424, 430

Salmon, 77
Salonika, 188, 285, 290, 316
Sandford, Col. D. C., 228
San Giorgio, 239
Saratoga, 38, 391, 402
Sarawak see Borneo
Savoie, Lt. Carl J., 419
Sayre, Francis, 407, 416
Scapa Flow, 76, 77, 99, 193, 219, 296
Schacht, Dr. Hjalmar, 26
Scharnhorst, 74, 81, 98, 109–10, 204,
  216, 217
Schellenberg, Gen. Walter, 114
Schleswig-Holstein, 63, 70
Schlieffen, Count Alfred von, 113,
  115–16
Schuhart, Lt. Comm. Otto, 75
Schuschnigg, Kurt von, 55
Scire, 281
Seadragon, 410
Seal, 414
Sealion, 410
Seeckt, Col. Gen. Hans von, 50
Serbs, 16, 282, 287, 288–89, 319
Seyss-Inquart, Arthur von, 55
Shanghai, 21, 22, 392
Shapley, Maj. Alan, 388
Shaposhnikov, Marshal Boris M., 340,
  352
Shark, 416
Sharp, Brig. Gen. William F., 413
Shaw, 389, 390, 392
Sheffield, 222, 223, 224, 269
Sherwood, Robert, 36
shipping see merchant shipping
Shirer, William L., 88
Shokaku, 384
Shoreham, 171
Short, Gen. Walter, 375, 380
  and Pearl Harbor, 380, 381, 382,
  451–55 passim
Sicily, 168, 170, 242
Sikh, 224, 280
Simović, Gen. Richard D., 282
Sims, Adm. W. S., 210
Singapore, 432–33, 448
  British base and defense, 27, 433–38
  passim, 442, 447, 449, 459, 468
  Japanese attack, 393, 432, 447, 449,
  468
Singapore Conference, 448
Slavs, 16, 187
Slovak forces, 329
Smith, Col. Cornelius C., Jr., 386
Smuts, Jan Christiaan, 227, 437
Soddu, Gen. Ubaldo, 190

INDEX

Somaliland *see* British Somaliland; French Somaliland; Italian Somaliland
Somerville, Vice Adm. Sir James, 150, 169, 174, 222, 267, 269, 278
Sorge, Richard, 333, 353
Soryu, 284, 400
Souffleur, 235
South African forces, 182, 227, 253, 259–60
Southampton, 268
Soviet Air Force, 49, 333
  Finland, "Winter War," 81, 82, 90, 93
  German invasion, 326, 330, 334, 337
Soviet Army (Red Army), 47–48, 51, 70, 93
  characteristics of men, 48, 83, 330, 338, 342, 351, 353, 355
  Finland, "Winter War," 47, 49, 64, 82, 83–85, 89–91, 93, 324, 340
  Japan, border incidents, 45, 340, 352
  German invasion, 323, 325, 326, 329–31, 333–69 *passim*, 370
  guerrilla warfare, 368
  military leadership, 49, 93, 330, 335–36, 338, 340, 341, 343, 346, 357, 362, 365; dual command with Party and NKVD, 47, 49, 335–36, 338, 340, 341, 348, 352, 354, 357, 360, 361, 362, 365, 366; purges (1937–38), 47, 324, 332
Soviet intelligence and espionage, 45, 333, 353
Soviet Navy, 47, 48, 82, 347, 348, 355, 370
Spain: Civil War, 15, 19–20, 52, 361
  and Germany, 19, 20, 52, 191, 241, 329, 361
  Tangier seized by, 186
Spears, Maj. Gen. Sir Edward, 143, 146
Sperrle, Field Marshal Hugo, 157
Spruance, Adm. Raymond A., 391
Stalin, Joseph, 17, 31, 49, 82
  and Churchill, 333, 369–70
  and Germany, 324, 334; invasion and dual political-military command, 47, 335–36, 338, 340, 341, 348, 352, 354, 357, 360, 361, 362, 365, 366; Non-Aggression Pact, 62, 81, 324, 334
  personal characteristics, 32, 323, 324
  and Roosevelt, 35, 372
Stalingrad, Battle of, 326, 366

Stark, Adm. Harold R. ("Molly"), 210, 374, 452, 457, 458–59
  war warnings, 378, 380–81, 452, 453, 455
Stevens, Maj. R. H., 114, 115
Stimson, Henry L., 21, 40, 377, 378, 450
Stokes, Comm. G. H., 280
Stowe, Leland, 106
Strasbourg, 74, 78, 150
Student, Gen. Kurt, 122, 299, 305, 310, 313
Stumpff, Col. Gen. Hans-Jürgen, 157, 162
Sudan (Anglo-Egyptian Sudan): British and native forces, 178, 179, 180, 181, 185, 226, 227, 229, 230, 240
  Italian forces, 181, 227
Sudetenland, 16, 55, 58, 59
Suez Canal, 77, 168, 170, 178, 229, 237, 246, 248, 279, 297
Suffolk, 110, 219, 220
Sumatra, 395; *see also* Dutch East Indies
Surcouf, 150
Süssmann, Maj. Gen. Wilhelm, 304
Sweden: and Finland, "Winter War," 92
  German plan to use railroads, 327, 328
  iron ore, importance of: to Allies, 74, 92, 94, 104; to Germany, 74, 92, 94, 95, 101, 111
Swordfish, 418
Sydney, 172, 173, 215
Sydney Star, 279
Syria, 233
  British forces, 233, 234, 240, 247, 248, 263
  Free French forces, 226, 232–36 *passim*
  French forces (Vichy), 178, 232–36 *passim*
  Germany and German forces, 231, 232, 233, 236

Takahashi, Vice Adm. I., 405
Tangier, 186
Taranto, 89, 173–74, 269, 276, 378, 440
Tataru (*Wake*), 393
Tatsuta, 398
Taussig, Ens. Joseph, 388
Taylor, Telford, 130

INDEX

Tedder, Air Marshal A. W., 251
Tellera, Gen. Giuseppe, 239
Tenedos, 438, 439
Tennant, Capt. W. G., 137, 438, 442–43
Tennessee, 387, 390
Tenryu, 398
Terauchi, Field Marshal Count, 431–32
Thailand: Japanese attack, 375, 380, 393, 432, 444, 449
Theobald, Rear Adm. Robert A., 453
Thoma, Maj. Gen. Wilhelm Ritter von, 241
Thomas, Sir Shenton, 434
Thomme, Gen. Wiktor, 70
Thor, 177
Tigris, 370
Tills, Ens. Robert G., 407
Timor, 395
Timoshenko, Marshal S. K., 90, 333, 342, 346, 361
Tinker, Brig. Gen. Clarence L., 451
Tirpitz, 74
Tito, Marshal, 389
Tizard, Sir Henry, 206
Tobruk, 239, 243, 246, 247, 248, 253–64 *passim*
Togo, Adm. Heichichiro, 46, 384
Tojo, Gen. Hideki, 375, 379, 384
Tokyo, bombing of, 206
Tone, 384
Torricelli, 171
Toscano, Vice Adm. Antonino, 280
Touchon, Gen., 142
Tovey, Adm. John, 219, 222, 224, 225
Transjordan, 178, 232, 233, 237
Trapnell, Maj. Thomas J. H., 415
Trenchard, Lord, 40, 44, 192, 204
Trident, 370
Trinidad, 155
Trinity, 449
Tripolitania, 243, 264, 285, 290, 316–17; *see also* Libya (and Western Desert)
Truant, 101
Tsushima, Battle of, 46, 384
Tsukahara, Vice Adm. Nishizo, 406
Tukhachevski, Marshal M. N., 47, 332
Tunisia, 178
Turkey: and Germany, 297, 316
and Great Britain, 236, 243, 270, 317, 318
World War I, 34, 75, 112, 316, 444
see also Balkans
Tutuila (Mei Yuan), 393

Ukraine, 327, 367
German invasion, 324, 326, 329, 338, 345–46, 362, 367, 368
Ulster Prince, 295
"Ultra," 45, 195, 211, 223
Union of Soviet Socialist Republics, 17
and the Balkans, 187, 325, 366–67
and Baltic states *see* Baltic states
and Bulgaria, 187
Communist Party, 32, 47, 49, 323, 324, 330, 338, 340, 354, 466; guerrilla warfare, 369; Hitler's hatred of, 324–27 *passim*, 336, 345, 367, 466; Soviet Army and dual command, 47, 49, 335–36, 338, 340, 341, 348, 352, 354, 357, 360, 361, 362, 365, 366
and Czechoslovakia, treaty, 58
and Finland, 62, 81; Finnish troops in German campaign, 327, 328, 344, 347–49; "Winter War," 47, 49, 64, 81, 82, 83–85, 86, 88, 89–93, 324, 325, 340
and France, alliance, 53–54, 62
and Germany *see* Germany, and U.S.S.R.
and Great Britain, 62, 325, 332, 333, 369; aid, 358, 369–70
and Hungary, 187
industrial production, 49, 330, 331, 355
and Japan, 431; border incidents, 45–46, 340, 352; "non-aggression" pact, 374; Soviet espionage, 333, 352–53
League of Nations, expelled from, 86
NKVD (secret police): intelligence and espionage, 45, 333, 352–53; Soviet Army and dual command, 47, 49, 335–36, 338, 340, 341, 348, 352, 354, 357, 360, 361, 362, 365, 366
and Persia, 236
and Poland, 62, 65; eastern region occupied, 64, 70, 85
and Rumania, 326–27, 329; territory annexed, 62, 187, 325, 329
slave labor camps, 367
Spanish Civil War, 20
and U.S., 35, 332, 372, 465
West, paranoia of, 59, 324, 333, 334
see also Russia; Stalin, Joseph; entries under Soviet
United States: and China, 21, 33, 373, 393, 422, 464

INDEX

United States (cont'd)
  Communists, 28, 371
  depression, 15, 23, 25, 464
  and Finland, 92, 465
  and France, 145, 146, 151
  and Germany, 61, 450
  and Great Britain: aid, 15, 154–55, 213, 214, 372; Arcadia Conference, 460; Argentia Conference, 200, 440, 452; on British seizure of French Navy, 151; *see also* U.S. armed forces, Allied command cooperation
  industrial production, 37, 40, 47, 86, 322, 392
  and Italy, 144, 450
  and Japan, 21, 373, 377, 379–80, 395, 431, 465–68; Allied "Rainbow" war plans, 213, 372, 403, 405, 436, 437; diplomatic negotiations, 374, 375–76, 381, 384, 454, 455; exclusion acts, 28; Japanese intelligence and espionage, 47, 379, 380; U.S. bombing of mainland, 167, 204, 206, 404; U.S. intelligence *see* "Magic"; U.S. "Orange" war plans, 377, 403, 405, 407, 413, 416, 435; war declared, 449–50; war warnings, 377–82, 453, 454, 455; *see also* Japan, war/war plans
  and League of Nations, 16
  National Guard, 37, 154
  neutrality, 15, 29, 86, 146, 213, 372, 456, 464; aid to Allies, 15, 92, 154, 213, 214, 215, 371–73, 455, 464
  and Russia, civil war, 17
  and U.S.S.R., 35, 332–33, 372, 465
  war declared, 450–51, 456, 461–62
  World War I, 15, 29, 450
U.S. armed forces, 154
  Allied command cooperation: ABCD (alphabet) plans, 213; Arcadia Conference, 460; "Rainbow" war plans, 213, 372, 403, 405, 436, 437; Singapore Conference, 448–49
  interservice rivalry and command cooperation, 40, 373, 403, 404, 405, 416–17, 451, 453, 458–59
  "Orange" war plans, 377, 403, 405, 407, 413, 416, 435
U.S. Army, 36, 37, 315, 393
  Iceland, 215, 372
  Philippines, 37, 402–09 *passim*, 413–16, 419, 420, 421
U.S. Army Air Corps, 37, 39
U.S. Army Air Forces, 40, 406
  Hawaii (and Pearl Harbor), 376, 382, 385, 389, 390
  Japanese mainland bombed, 167, 204, 206, 404
  Philippines, 403–10 *passim*, 413–14, 459
U.S. fliers: "Flying Tigers," 422
U.S. intelligence, 40, 332, 378, 380–81, 455, 457
  "Magic," 40, 45, 379, 380, 418, 454, 455, 458
U.S. Marine Corps, 38, 39, 386, 393
  Guam, 395, 396
  Iceland, 215, 372
  Philippines, 413, 416
  Wake Island, 387, 391, 397–402
U.S. Navy and seapower, 27, 36, 37–38, 39, 374, 405, 452–53, 458
  airpower, 40, 43, 376, 383, 385, 390, 391, 397, 406, 407, 411, 413
  Asiatic Fleet, 21, 380, 393, 405, 417, 418, 437, 449, 460; Philippines, 403, 405, 406, 407, 410–11, 413, 414, 416, 418, 419, 421, 435
  Atlantic, 212, 214–15, 372, 374, 450, 456; Caribbean bases, 155, 213
  Australia, base, 459
  Guam, 395, 396
  Java, base, 459
  naval disarmament conferences, 16, 26, 27
  Pacific Fleet, 27, 374, 391, 393, 402, 403, 435, 436, 437, 452, 459; command and coordination, 374, 402, 451, 453, 459; *see also* Hawaii; Pearl Harbor
  submarines, 405, 410, 411, 414, 416–18
  see also U.S. armed forces
Upholder, 279
Uruguay: naval action off coast, 64, 78–80
Utah, 387, 390

Valiant, 267–68, 273, 275, 281, 306, 308
Valmy, 234
Vampire, 438, 443
Vauquelin, 235
Venlo Incident, 114–15

Versailles Treaty, 16–17, 27, 50, 53, 56, 61
Vestal, 390
Vian, Rear Adm. Sir Philip, 95, 224, 280, 370
Victor Emmanuel, King, 18
Victorious, 222
Vittorio Veneto, 168–69, 174, 271, 274, 276
Voroshilov, Marshal Kliment E., 90, 342, 369

Wainwright, Maj. Gen. Jonathan, 413, 421
Wake Island: Japanese attack, 393, 398–402
 U.S. forces and defense, 374, 387, 390–91, 396, 402
Wake (Tataru), 392–93
Wake-Walker, Rear Adm. W. F., 221
Wallis, Brig. C., 430
Warburton-Lee, Capt. B. A. W., 102
Ward, James Richard, 389
Ward, 382, 384
Warlimont, Gen. Walter, 325, 345, 371
Warsaw, 64, 66, 67, 68, 70, 193
Warspite, 169, 172, 267, 273, 275, 306, 308
Washington Naval Disarmament Conference, 16, 26, 27
Watson-Watt, Robert Alexander, 44
Wavell, Field Marshal Sir Archibald, 226, 252, 460
 Mediterranean and Middle East, 89, 178, 179, 180–81, 185, 200, 227, 228, 229, 231, 237, 239, 240, 243, 246, 248, 249, 250, 251, 252, 290; Churchill, disagreements with, 235, 248–49, 251, 252–53, 314; Greece and Crete, 229, 243, 252, 290, 294, 297, 298, 305, 309, 310, 314, 317; Lebanon and Syria, 231, 233, 235, 250, 252
Weichs, Gen. Maximilian von, 283, 288
Welles, Sumner, 332
Western Desert see Libya (and Western Desert)
Westerwald, 78
West Virginia, 388, 389–90, 392, 462
Weygand, Gen. Maxime, 41, 128, 147, 148

Whalen, Grover C., 28
Wheeler-Bennett, John W., 54
Wilhelm II, Kaiser, 121
Wilhelm Heidekamp, 102
Wilhelmina, Queen, 118, 122
Wilson, Lt. Gen. Sir Henry ("Jumbo"), 233, 285, 290, 291, 293, 295, 298
Wilson, Woodrow, 16, 24, 55
Wingate, Maj. Gen. Orde C., 228, 230
Winkelman, Gen. Henri G., 118, 121
"Winter War," 47, 49, 64, 81, 82, 83–85, 86, 88, 89–93, 324, 325, 340
Wohlstetter, Roberta, 457
Wood, "P.," 37
World War I, 16, 17, 322
 Gallipoli, 34, 75, 112, 316, 444
 Jutland, 171, 221, 274, 418
 Marne, 113, 344, 356, 420
 see also Versailles Treaty; individual countries

Yamamoto, Adm. Isoroku, 46, 376, 383–84
Yamashita, Lt. Gen. Tomoyuki, 432, 447
Yamato, 27
Yayoi, 399
York, 273, 302
Yorktown, 38, 459
Yoshikawa, Ens. Takeo, 380
Young, Sir Mark, 424, 428, 430
Yubari, 398–99
Yugoslav Air Force, 283, 285
Yugoslav Army and military forces, 285, 287–88, 289, 295
Yugoslavia, 287
 Axis invasion and occupation, 200, 283–89, 295, 299, 319, 326
 Croats, 16, 282, 287, 288
 and Germany, 271, 282
 guerrilla warfare, 50, 282, 288–89
 Serbs, 16, 282, 287, 288–89, 319

ZamZam, 214
Zara, 275
Zhukov, Marshal Georgi G., 340, 341, 352, 354, 357, 360
Zog, King, 187
Zuikaku, 384
Zulu, 224

DATE DUE

NOV 19 1999
041408

DEMCO 38-297

Tennessee Tech. Library
Cookeville. Tenn.

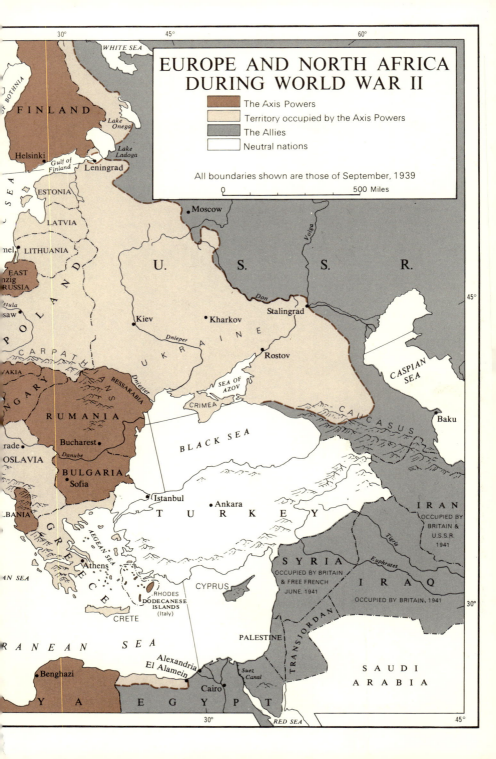